SPORT FINANCE

SECOND EDITION

GIL FRIED, JD
STEVEN J. SHAPIRO, PhD
UNIVERSITY OF NEW HAVEN

TIMOTHY D. DeSCHRIVER, EdD
UNIVERSITY OF DELAWARE

Human Kinetics

Library of Congress Cataloging-in-Publication Data

Fried, Gil, 1965-
   Sport finance / Gil Fried, Steven J. Shapiro, Timothy DeSchriver. --
2nd ed.
      p. cm. --
   Includes bibliographical references and index.
      ISBN-13: 978-0-7360-6770-6 (hard cover)
      ISBN-10: 0-7360-6770-1 (hard cover)
1. Sports--Finance. 2. Sports administration. I. Shapiro, Steven
J., 1955- II. DeSchriver, Timothy D., 1968- III. Title.
   GV716.F75 2007
   796.0691--dc22

                              2007038770

ISBN-10: 0-7360-6770-1
ISBN-13: 978-0-7360-6770-6

The Web addresses cited in this text were current as of June 2007, unless otherwise noted.

Acquisitions Editor: Myles Schrag; **Developmental Editor:** Amanda S. Ewing; **Assistant Editors:** Melissa Zavala and Kyle Fritz; **Copyeditor:** Patricia L. MacDonald; **Proofreader:** Pam Johnson; **Indexer:** Joan K. Griffitts; **Permission Manager:** Carly Breeding; **Graphic Designer:** Joe Buck; **Graphic Artist:** Carol Smallwood; **Cover Designer:** Keith Blomberg; **Photographer (cover):** © Human Kinetics; **Photo Asset Manager:** Laura Fitch; **Photo Office Assistant:** Jason Allen; **Art Manager:** Kelly Hendren; **Associate Art Manager:** Alan L. Wilborn; **Illustrator:** Brian McElwain; **Printer:** Sheridan Books

Printed in the United States of America   10   9   8

The paper in this book is certified under a sustainable forestry program.

Human Kinetics
Web site: www.HumanKinetics.com

United States: Human Kinetics
P.O. Box 5076
Champaign, IL 61825-5076
800-747-4457
e-mail: humank@hkusa.com

Canada: Human Kinetics
475 Devonshire Road, Unit 100
Windsor, ON N8Y 2L5
800-465-7301 (in Canada only)
e-mail: info@hkcanada.com

Europe: Human Kinetics
107 Bradford Road
Stanningley
Leeds LS28 6AT, United Kingdom
+44 (0)113 255 5665
e-mail: hk@hkeurope.com

Australia: Human Kinetics
57A Price Avenue
Lower Mitcham, South Australia 5062
08 8372 0999
e-mail: info@hkaustralia.com

New Zealand: Human Kinetics
P.O. Box 80
Torrens Park, South Australia 5062
0800 222 062
e-mail: info@hknewzealand.com

To my parents, Louis and Haya Fried, who continue to encourage and inspire me. I love you.

Gil Fried

To my parents of blessed memory, Philip and Charlotte Shapiro, who taught me that success comes to those who are not afraid to ask the right questions; and to my wife, Phyliss, and my children, Stuart and Lauren, who are there through thick and thin and keep me grounded.

Steven Shapiro

To my parents, Richard and Jean, who have inspired me to be an educator.

Tim DeSchriver

CONTENTS

              Red Flags   304
              Informal Reorganization   305
              Informal Liquidation   306
              Bankruptcy Protection   306
              Removal of Business Assets   310
              Selling a Business   311

              Appendix A Time Value of Money   317

              Appendix B Formulas   325

              Appendix C Suggested Resources   329

              Glossary   333

              References   363

              Index   373

              About the Authors   381

If you saw the movie *Jerry Maguire*, you might have thought about studying sport law or becoming a players' agent. Similarly, if you have been tracking Tiger Woods' phenomenal success in endorsing various products from Nike to Buick, you might want to study sport marketing. If you enjoy watching Super Bowl advertisements more than the games themselves, you might want to enter the exciting field of sport advertising. Sport finance can be more exciting than all these disciplines. Marketing, sponsorship, facility construction, sport law, and all the other sport management disciplines cannot be undertaken without knowledge of the financial position of the team, business, or organization. Thus, sport finance is the linchpin for all decisions and actions in sport business.

Students who think that sport accounting and finance are not as exciting as sport law, marketing, or advertising are wrong. Some of the most interesting jobs in sport focus on finance-related issues. For example, National Football League and National Basketball Association teams normally have "capologists" who are directly responsible for ensuring that the team does not violate the salary cap for its players. Financial numbers can tell us many important facts about a business. So, even though sport finance has never been considered an exciting component within any sport and fitness administration curriculum, it might be one of the most important topics that you study.

No business, organization, or government entity can survive without money. The saying "Money makes the world go 'round" accurately reflects the sport industry, with some professional sports organizations now worth more than a billion dollars and with television networks spending billions to air premiere events. Sport finance analyzes where the money comes from, where the money goes, and how to effectively utilize any remaining money to help foster future growth. Thus, sport finance is the key for the decision-making process in any sport business, and a thorough knowledge of sport finance is the key to making it into high-level managerial positions where the decisions are made.

The stock market skyrocketed several hundred percent in the 1980s and 1990s. Thereafter it fell significantly, costing people millions of dollars in paper losses. However, if you held on and kept investing in the market when it declined, you would have been rewarded as stocks increased from 2003 through 2007, when the stock markets hit all-time highs once again. The stock market is one of the diverse examples of how financial conditions can grow and shrink over time and why some companies can be strong one day and file for bankruptcy the next. Sport businesses were not immune to this financial carnage. Some sport companies have had ups and downs during the past 20 years. If you had invested a small amount in 1980 in Nike stocks, you could have made a fortune. However, you could also have made a significant amount of money if you had invested in Nike shares in early 2006 when the price was as low as $75.52 per share and sold those shares at the peak when they were selling for $101.20 in late 2006.

Stocks have a tendency to increase and decrease based on multiple factors, from increased profits to the loss of a major account or the retirement of a major endorser. What factors drive the stock price down? Does such a decline represent market conditions alone, or can the company's board of directors develop policies that can reduce the stock's value? Would any resulting turnaround in the company's performance significantly enhance the company's value? What can the company do to increase its stock value? Would a high stock value indicate corporate financial strength? If the company reduced overall salaries by $100 million per year, would the stock value increase as a result of the increased savings? If all shoe production was moved from Asia to America, would profits change and why? A thorough financial analysis can help answer these questions. This book is designed to help you understand the numerous financial issues faced by any sport or fitness business or entity.

PURPOSE OF THE TEXT

The need for a strict sport finance text has come to the fore over the past several years with the push to build new sports facilities and the financial projections made by the facilities' opponents and proponents. Similarly, fitness facilities have fueled significant career opportunities, and managers in this industry encounter numerous unique financial issues. Sport entrepreneurs have to deal with financial issues such as how to develop a business plan with a pro forma budget, what finance vehicle is most effective for raising start-up capital, and how to control inventory. With professional football teams selling for $800 million, a team owner or general manager will not trust financial decisions to anyone who does not have a strong background in finance. Last, with Title IX affecting many high school and college athletic programs, schools need to know how to work with the dollars they have in order to comply with the law. These represent just some of the issues you might face in your future career, and an aim of this text is to give you a framework to help you deal with these issues.

To date, no single text has covered critical sport finance topics such as balance sheets, income statements, industry ratios, banking policy, venture capital, stock markets, inventory systems, accounting strategies to maximize financial returns, and related topics deemed critical for a sound knowledge in sport finance. This text aligns itself with the requirements set forth by the National Association for Sport and Physical Education and the North American Society for Sport Management for a sport finance course (2000, pp. 7-8). While guidelines can change, the fundamental principles for studying sport finance remain the same.

Required Content (All Topics Must Be Addressed)

- Basic accounting principles—types of accounting
- Financial statements
- Sources of revenue for financing—public sector versus private sector, governments, membership, fees, personal seat licenses (PSLs), taxes, bonds, and so on
- Principles of budgeting—types (capital, master, departmental, line item, zero based, PPBES)
- Budgeting as a method of control, organization, and reallocation
- Budget development
- Spreadsheet utilization (Lotus, Excel, Quicken, or QuickBooks)—basic laboratory experiences
- Financial aspects of facilities management

Recommended Content (Minimum of 50% Must Be Addressed)

- Present financial status of the sport industry—collegiate, professional, private, manufacturers
- Concessions and merchandising—trademark licensing, inventory, cost control, cash management
- For-profit and not-for-profit budgeting
- Development and fund-raising principles and methodology (campaigns, alumni, auctions)
- Financing facilities

Sport Finance is designed to walk the reader through the finance process. It provides you with the basic skills needed to help raise, manage, and spend money in sport settings. It covers a number of key financial concepts such as the following:

- What a business needs to succeed
- What makes businesses operate
- Where businesses obtain necessary start-up capital
- How to determine how much money is available
- How to read newspaper business pages for meaning
- What typical expenses sports organizations incur
- Why sport businesses succeed
- Why sport businesses fail
- How sports organizations can grow

The purpose of this text is to give a broad overview so the reader can understand what drives the financial success or failure of any entity in the sport industry.

INTENDED AUDIENCE

Our goal is to create an intermediate finance text that is ideal for business school–based sport and fitness administration programs, sport finance classes, and graduate programs in various other disciplines. The point of the designation is to emphasize that the book is comprehensive, but we believe it is also important to develop the text for people who have never read a finance or accounting text. With this book you will be able to grasp fundamental finance and accounting concepts regardless of your knowledge level. If you have some finance or accounting skills, this text will help expand your knowledge and provide some real-world application of that knowledge. The real-world situations in the case studies provide a strong framework within which you will be able to apply financial principles in your future career.

If you are already an industry professional, you could rely on the text to help you understand financial markets, develop money-saving strategies, learn how to properly invest for future growth, and develop business finance strategies. With a significant discussion on budgeting, executives can refresh their knowledge and skills on a daily basis.

ORGANIZATION

Sport Finance is organized into six parts that help the reader understand the impact of sport finance on a business. The chapters are arranged so the reader can understand the elements that influence the financial world and then apply specific issues to the sport business world.

Part I deals with the importance of finance in the sport industry, including a thorough analysis of the various issues that compose sport finance. Since financial planning is impossible without an understanding of accounting basics, part I gives special attention to fundamental finance and accounting issues. Part I also stresses the various environments that affect finance, ranging from business structures and financial markets to government entities that control taxes and interest rates.

Part II addresses the information needed to answer questions or solve problems posed by the case studies. Through analyzing data contained in income statements and balance sheets, students will learn how to analyze a business' strengths and weaknesses. Industry ratios, financial statements, the time value of money, and the financial planning process are highlighted in this section of the book.

Part III examines where the money is located. These chapters look at how businesses find the capital they need to operate. Discussions focus on funding options for various types of entities, ranging from a government entity that needs to raise more taxes to a business that is searching for venture capital, pursuing a public offering, or selling corporate bonds.

Part IV discusses where the money goes. What are the typical expenses, and how do businesses budget for them? This part of the book also highlights short-term planning and how to document monetary needs. These discussions are especially appropriate for those interested in developing business plans and the accompanying pro forma budgets. An additional focus is on ways to manage the money you obtain or owe as a sports manager. Finally, this part of the book provides a comprehensive overview of the inventory management and production control processes, which are critical for concession and sporting goods businesses.

Part V centers on the profit distribution process, including retained earnings, dividends, and company growth through acquisition of additional businesses.

This part of the book also analyzes several financial issues, including taxation and fiscal risk management.

Part VI covers the tracking of money and details accounting techniques you can implement to make sure that financial auditing is successful. A final topic in part VI is how to close a business through bankruptcy or other techniques.

Each chapter ends with various pertinent class discussion questions. These suggestions are designed to channel dialogue among students and to give instructors ideas for helping students engage with the material over and above just reading the text. Boldfaced words in the text are found in the glossary at the back of the book. Key points are highlighted throughout each chapter. In addition, an instructor guide is available that provides more discussion topics and material.

SPECIAL FEATURES

This text contains several special features designed to enhance the reader's knowledge of the subject area. Although professional sport presents some very useful examples, *Sport Finance* focuses on the following five case studies that are discussed throughout. As concepts come up in the text, we highlight how the concepts apply to one of the case studies. Icons will alert you to the application of the case study. Read the introduction to the case studies (pp. xv-xviii) for complete background information on each example.

1. **The Smiths** just graduated from New Haven State University and want to open their own fitness center with a little gift shop and juice bar. You will proceed step by step with Bob and Cheryl as they explore how they might raise the necessary capital, what possible business structure will fit their needs, whether they should grow by issuing stocks or bonds, if they can raise capital by pre-selling memberships, how to avoid financial identity theft, and how best to purchase necessary supplies and handle related concerns.

2. **Sport Manufacturing Company (SMC)** manufactures golf clubs and tennis rackets. The company, which acquires raw materials and processes them into high-end equipment, has been in business for more than 20 years and is publicly traded on the NASDAQ exchange. SMC's seasonal business requires careful financial planning so that the company

can maximize revenue during the peak months and borrow as little cash as possible during the winter.

3. **The University of Milford** is a large urban university serving more than 20,000 students. The athletic department has a rich tradition, having produced such stars as Bob "the Nose" Smith, Sara Smart, Fred "Hacksaw" Jones, and a host of others. Unfortunately, in the mid-2000s the athletic department fell on hard times and was losing about $5 million a year. You have been retained as an outside consultant to help determine what fiscal steps need to be taken to obtain government assistance, develop internally generated funds, borrow from a bank, develop capital investment options, and grow donations.

4. **The Stars of David** have given you the dream job you wanted with a professional team. You are  now the chief financial officer for a professional basketball team based in David, Connecticut. You have been hired to examine the team's financial statements and to reinterpret the numbers and explain them in "plain English" for the shareholders. You will analyze such issues as insider trading scandals, amortization of intangible assets, and asset depreciation.

5. **West Hartford Badminton Club** is a nonprofit organization that raises money through three primary means: donations, nightly playing fees, and  tournament fees. Primary expenses include gym rentals, equipment, and mailing expenses. The club has had a difficult time raising additional funds and thus has basically just made it every year for the past 5 years. One major disaster such as an increase in rental fees or a poorly attended tournament could spell financial ruin for the club.

Whenever possible, the case studies are analyzed with the use of financial data obtained from real businesses or government entities to provide information that is as authentic as possible.

INSTRUCTOR RESOURCES

As an added benefit to instructors, this new edition features several ancillaries to aid in your teaching of classes that use this text. The authors appreciate that some sport finance instructors have training in other disciplines and might need some additional assistance. Thus, these new resources make it easier to develop and teach basic through advanced concepts.

- The instructor's guide includes a student syllabus as well as chapter outlines for the instructor. The chapter outlines contain a summary, lecture aides, in- and out-of-class activities, additional readings, and teaching tips.

- The test package includes more than 300 multiple choice questions that the instructor can use to build tests.

- The PowerPoint presentation includes more than 300 slides that present the text information in an easy-to-follow format. Several tables from the book are included in the presentation package to help further student understanding.

ACKNOWLEDGMENTS

I could not have asked for two better coauthors. They diligently wrote their chapters and assisted with the instructor guide, making this one of the best texts I have had the pleasure to work on. Tim was helpful throughout the entire process, and his patience and understanding during some of our unexpected delays were greatly appreciated. Steven was a significant boost to the project as an economics and finance department chair helping write a finance book. His participation provided significant credibility and knowledge unmatched by any other author we could have used. My two coauthors went beyond the call for this text, and I thank them for their effort.

I would like to extend a special thanks to Dr. Allen Sack, Dr. Jim Murdy, Dean Jess Boronico, and the entire College of Business faculty and staff at the University of New Haven for all their assistance. I would also like to thank my graduate research assistant Robyn Lubisco for her help in researching changes for this revised edition.

A special thanks also goes out to my wife and children (Gavriella, Arieh, and Rebecca) for all their patience during the writing and revising of this text. It was a multiyear process with several major snafus that created delays. However, the final product shows that the wait was worth every second, and the final combination of authors was outstanding. Each coauthor brought significant value and helped shape the text into one of the strongest in the sport management area.

The folks at Human Kinetics were wonderful in helping us make this second edition that much stronger. Many second editions just contain minor updates. However, the gang at HK including Myles Schrag and Amanda Ewing challenged us to make the book fresh and improved.

Gil Fried

It has been a pleasure to continue to work with my talented coauthors on the new edition of this book. Their patience and support continue to be appreciated. As always, the extensive sport management backgrounds of both Gil and Tim were especially helpful as they suggested industry-specific pedagogical examples. The anonymous reviewers of the text provided critical insight that makes this a better book. I am sure my coauthors would agree with the standard statement that although the reviewers were important in finding pedagogical and other errors and making this a more readable book for the sport finance community, we take the blame for any shortcomings that remain.

I want to extend special thanks to Dean Jess Boronico of the College of Business at the University of New Haven for providing an academic atmosphere that made it possible to work on this book. The encouragement and feedback of my sport management colleagues at the University of New Haven, including Allen Sack, Jim Murdy, and of course Gil Fried, have made it easier to complete the latest edition of the book. I also want to acknowledge the work of Myles Schrag, Amanda Ewing, and other staff at Human Kinetics who have made it a pleasure to work on this text.

I especially want to acknowledge my wife, Phyliss, for her continued support and understanding as I worked on this time-consuming project while continuing to juggle the time demands of teaching, research, writing, consulting, and above all family time. I also appreciate the mentoring concerning the mind-set of today's students that I have received from my children, Lauren and Stuart, one who is a recent college graduate and the other a current undergraduate student. However, Stuart and Lauren are not responsible when their father does not always get it.

Steven Shapiro

I would like to extend a special thanks to my two coauthors. Gil Fried has been the driving force behind this project since its inception. His guidance and persistence were critical for ensuring the successful completion of this book. Steve Shapiro did a marvelous job of stepping into a project that was already in progress. The addition has been invaluable, and his background in financial management was very helpful. I would also like to thank Myles Schrag, Amanda Ewing, and the staff at Human Kinetics. Their patience and willingness to see the project through to completion have been greatly appreciated.

I would also like to thank my colleagues in the sport management field whom I have worked with over the past years. Their encouragement and kind words have not gone unnoticed. It is people such as

Dave Stotlar, Bill Sutton, Jay Gladden, Dan Mahony, Dennis Howard, Carol Barr, Lisa Masteralexis, and Matt Robinson (just to name a few) who make me proud to be an academician in sport management. Last, I would like to thank my parents, Richard and Jean DeSchriver, for loving and supporting me for all these years. I may be getting older, but they are still the two most important people in my life. They instilled within me a passion for education and teaching that will last forever.

Tim DeSchriver

INTRODUCTION TO THE CASE STUDIES

As mentioned in the preface, the following case studies are discussed throughout the book. In this section, we provide the background information you'll need in order to understand the case studies when they are applied in the main text. The icons shown here are used to identify the case studies in the chapters to follow. You will also want to refer to this section to answer discussion questions and do assignments.

THE SMITHS

Bob and Cheryl Smith are recent graduates of the sport and fitness administration program at New Haven State University. Both have loved being certified fitness instructors, and they thought that after they earned their degrees they would have all the skills necessary to open their own fitness center in the Hartford, Connecticut, area. Neither had ever owned a business before, but they believed their combined five years' experience with the YMCA qualified them to understand and operate their own business.

Bob and Cheryl start planning for their future facility. They want to include the following options:

- A 5,000-square-foot wood-floored aerobics area, with mirrors on the wall, that can be used for aerobics and various dance classes
- A 5,000-square-foot free-weight and exercise machine room for those interested in weight training and cardiovascular workouts
- Two 1,000-square-foot locker rooms for male and female patrons
- A 1,000-square-foot office and reception area
- A gift shop and juice bar where fitness apparel and food and beverages can be sold

Although the Smiths have big ambitions, they are also realistic. They know they are not going to get rich. However, they want to control their own destiny and make it or break it by themselves. They do not come from wealthy families, but they think they can work hard and put in as many hours as necessary to make their dream come true. Bob and Cheryl have $5,000 saved to help pay their start-up expenses. They have 50 friends who are willing to sign five-year contracts at $600 per year for using the fitness center. Each friend would pay the first year's dues up front when the plans are finalized. The $30,000 will help pay for equipment or help secure a bank loan. There are 20 other clubs in the metro area, but there's only one other club in a 2-square-mile area with 30,000 residents.

SPORT MANUFACTURING COMPANY

Sport Manufacturing Company (SMC) is a seasonal business that requires constant financial analysis to optimize its profits. The business is publicly traded on the NASDAQ exchange. SMC was formed to manufacture golf clubs; however, over the years it has added tennis rackets to its product inventory. SMC manufactures all the clubs and rackets around the same schedule so the manufacturing side of the business can stop production in December and January, reducing operating costs. However, the company maintains its trained employees on the payroll, otherwise it would lose its valuable employees and would have to spend much more to train new hires. Thus, even when the machines are down, the company is incurring expenses. Similarly, sales expenses increase during the springtime as commission-sales staff members start turning in their sales orders. Thus, the other side of the business (besides manufacturing) is the sales department, which works all year long to secure orders from various retailers. The secret for the company is to balance its financial obligations through obtaining funds from the bank for its financial needs during the winter and to properly invest its income in the spring and summer to maximize revenue. This cyclical pattern has been successful for 20 years. The company's production and sales volumes in 2007 are shown in table I.1.

Sport Manufacturing Company incurs $15 million in fixed costs each year. Variable costs, such as the raw materials used for making the equipment, are $7 per piece. The company also incurs $1.25 per piece

Table I.1   SMC's Production and Sales Volumes

Month	Manufacture (units)	Sales (units)
January	0	10,000
February	400,000	30,000
March	400,000	60,000
April	400,000	300,000
May	400,000	600,000
June	400,000	700,000
July	400,000	600,000
August	400,000	500,000
September	400,000	400,000
October	400,000	500,000
November	400,000	50,000
December	0	250,000
Total	**4,000,000**	**4,000,000**

in administrative and selling expenses. The total cost per piece, excluding fixed costs, is $8.25. If SMC manufactures four million units, then the total production costs are as follows:

$15,000,000 fixed costs
+ $33,000,000 per piece cost
($8.25 × 4,000,000)

$48,000,000 total production costs

Dividing the $48 million by four million pieces yields a per piece total cost of $12.

UNIVERSITY OF MILFORD ATHLETIC DEPARTMENT

 The University of Milford (U of M) has a proud history of athletic success. However, the financial picture has not been marvelous over the past several years. Dwindling attendance, no basketball games played on campus, low student interest, low season-ticket base, and a host of other concerns led to threats from the university's president that the entire athletic program could be canceled by the year 2010, or the school might become a National Association of Intercollegiate Athletics (NAIA) member school.

The revenue and expenditures from 2002 through 2006 for the University of Milford athletic department are highlighted in table I.2.

Although the deficit numbers seem large, they are not unusual in the world of big-time athletics. In fact, most National Collegiate Athletic Association (NCAA)

Division I-A athletic programs lose money. In 2006, the University of Milford offered seven men's and seven women's sports, with 226 athletes on full or partial scholarships and a total of 295 student athletes. The 2007-2010 projected revenues and expenses are shown in tables I.3 and I.4. These projections are based on a number of assumptions, including moving home basketball games back to the main campus, adding women's lacrosse, moving concession operations to a new company, strengthening the caliber of opposing teams, and building luxury boxes at the football stadium and basketball arena.

Table I.2   University of Milford Athletic Department's Revenues and Expenditures

Year	Revenues $	Expenditures $
2002	5,200,000	$7,000,000
2003	6,000,000	7,700,000
2004	8,500,000	8,600,000
2005	9,700,000	11,100,000
2006	11,104,450	13,046,710

THE STARS OF DAVID

 The Stars of David are a publicly traded company, with its stocks (symbol: SOD) traded on the famous Newark Stock Exchange. The team went public in 2001 after its original owner, Jane Doe, decided to make a killing and have the company become publicly traded. The players are locked into long-term contracts so it is easy to plan for future expenses. The gym is leased over a long term as well so the primary fixed costs are very stable. The only other major fixed costs are front-office salaries, and those expenses are kept down by hiring a number of interns each year.

Figure I.1 shows the stock's performance over the past five years.

WEST HARTFORD BADMINTON CLUB

 The city of West Hartford has a very active badminton club that holds weekly practices and regular tournaments. The club is a nonprofit organization that raises money through three primary means: donations, nightly playing fees, and tournament fees. The club's

Table I.3 University of Milford's Projected Revenues

Income category	Actual 2006 ($)	Projected 2007 ($)	Projected 2008 ($)	Projected 2009 ($)	Projected 2010 ($)
Ticket sales	1,000,600	1,400,000	1,600,000	1,750,000	1,900,000
Premium seating					
Concessions	70,000	100,000	110,000	115,000	120,000
Parking fees	6,000	6,600	6,600	6,700	7,000
Advertising	17,000	20,000	25,000	50,000	75,000
Sponsorship	75,000	100,000	125,000	150,000	200,000
Program and novelty sales	15,000	18,000	20,000	22,000	24,000
Guarantees received	725,000	860,000	885,000	925,000	980,000
Guarantees paid	(725,000)	(845,000)	(870,000)	(885,000)	(900,000)
Miscellaneous revenues					
Conference distribution	450,000	500,000	550,000	600,000	650,000
Subtotal	**$1,633,600**	**$2,159,600**	**$2,451,500**	**$2,733,700**	**$3,056,000**
Student service fees	2,330,000	2,330,000	2,330,000	2,350,000	2,350,000
Endowment revenue	2,435,150	2,440,000	2,445,000	2,450,000	2,455,000
Gifts		—	—	—	—
Milford Athletics Foundation:	100,000	100,000	125,000	150,000	200,000
Premium seating	80,000	100,000	140,000	140,000	150,000
Annual fund	500,000	700,000	800,000	900,000	950,000
Net nonathletic special events revenue	25,000	100,000	125,000	150,000	175,000
Total athletic revenue	**$7,103,750**	**$7,929,600**	**$8,416,500**	**$8,873,700**	**$9,336,000**
Plus university support	4,000,700	5,000,000	6,000,000	6,500,000	6,600,000
Total revenue	**$11,104,450**	**$12,929,600**	**$14,416,500**	**$15,373,700**	**$15,936,000**

From University of Houston Athletic Department, Schedule of Revenues and Expenses, 1995.

Table I.4 University of Milford's Projected Expenditures

Expenditure category	Actual 2006 ($)	Projected 2007 ($)	Projected 2008 ($)	Projected 2009 ($)	Projected 2010 ($)
Salaries, wages, and benefits	4,340,240	4,584,215	4,584,215	4,584,215	4,584,215
Printing	139,050	146,000	153,300	160,900	169,000
Utilities	600,000	590,000	607,700	625,900	644,700
Postage and telephone	239,375	241,700	244,100	246,600	249,000
Advertising and fund-raising	10,000	100,000	125,000	127,000	129,000
Rentals, leases, and maintenance	357,810	360,000	362,000	365,000	368,000
Insurance	285,000	290,700	296,500	302,400	308,400
Uniforms and equipment	202,400	206,000	210,000	214,000	218,000
Administrative fees	631,059	662,629	700,733	738,027	755,039
Game expenses	387,150	390,000	409,500	429,975	451,474
Scholarships	1,917,766	2,000,000	2,100,000	2,200,000	2,300,000
Travel	1,163,200	1,395,800	1,465,600	1,538,900	1,615,800
Other marketing and operations	875,660	963,200	1,060,000	1,166,000	1,282,000
Addition of women's sports (Title IX)	0	0	300,000	650,000	650,000
Total athletics expenditures	**$11,148,710**	**$11,930,244**	**$12,618,648**	**$13,348,917**	**$13,724,628**
Debt service	1,898,000	1,898,000	1,898,000	1,898,000	1,898,000
Total expenditures	**$13,046,710**	**$13,828,244**	**$14,516,648**	**$15,246,917**	**$15,622,628**

From University of Houston Athletic Department, Schedule of Revenues and Expenses, 1995.

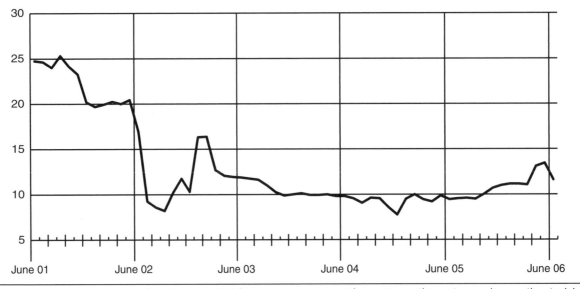

Figure I.1 Although The Stars of David have not had the greatest success on the court over the past several years, the stock has performed steadily.

primary expenses include gym rentals, equipment, and mailing expenses. The club has been around for more than 60 years and has a nice following. However, as a nonprofit organization it has had a difficult time raising additional funds and thus has basically just made it every year for the past 5 years. That means they have raised just enough money to cover their expenses. In other words, revenue equals expenses. This could lead to a major disaster because if there is an increase in rental fees or a poorly attended tournament, the club could face financial ruin.

There are 150 people who pay a yearly fee of $100 to be an official club member. This fee entitles the member to attend the practices. Since it is a closed club, a person cannot just walk in without being a member or being sponsored by a member. Club members still need to pay each time they attend a practice, but they get free shuttlecocks. Someone who is a member can invite a guest to play as well, but guests must pay a higher fee each time they play and also must buy the shuttlecocks, which are sold for $20 a tube. The club breaks even on selling the tubes. The club's tournament attracts several hundred people who pay a small fee to help cover the approximately $3,000 in expenses to market and produce the tournament.

The badminton club rents a gym from a local high school. There is a contract with the school board to pay $25,000 a year to use the gym two nights a week through the school year. In addition to its lease obligations, the club is required to pay the custodian for overtime, which costs $7,000 a year.

The club's income statement and balance sheet for the year 2007 are shown in tables I.5 and I.6.

Table I.5 WHBC Income Statement 2007

Dues (150 members @ $100 per year)	$15,000
Daily playing fees	$32,000
Tournament revenue	$4,000
Tournament advertising revenue	$500
Total income	**$51,500**
Facility rental	$25,000
Custodian	$7,000
Rackets and shuttlecocks	$12,000
Tournament preparation and marketing	$2,000
Tournament trophies and prizes	$1,000
Total expenses	**$47,000**
Total gross income	**$4,500**
Taxes	$0 (nonprofit)

Table I.6 WHBC Balance Sheet 2007

Liquid assets		**Liabilities**	
Cash	$12,000	Accounts payable	$3,000
T-bills	$3,000		
Accounts receivable	$1,500		
Equipment	$3,000	Member's equity	$16,500
Total assets	**$19,500**	**Total liabilities & ME**	**$19,500**

PART I

THE BASICS OF SPORT FINANCE

It is impossible to fully grasp sport finance without knowing the fundamentals. The information in part I will help you understand and apply financial concepts in later chapters.

Chapter 1, Financial Issues in Sport, highlights the basics of sport finance with an introduction to various issues such as how sports teams have increased in value over the years, how sport businesses have merged in order to grow, and how the sports apparel market has been changing for more than 20 years. The chapter then covers two of the key issues facing sports today: the high cost of sports sponsorship and whether government funding of sports facilities produces a benefit to the local community or team.

Chapter 2, Basic Financial Concepts, covers the most basic and critical financial terms and issues. Sport businesses cannot survive without generating revenue, but at the same time they generate significant expenses. From ticket sales to broadcasting revenue, sports teams can generate millions of dollars, but they also need to pay millions for big-name athletes. The chapter then covers the importance of financial objectives, which are documented in organizational budgets. The chapter ends with an analysis of some accounting principles that help you understand how the revenue, expense, and budgetary numbers are calculated.

Chapter 3, Financial Systems and How They Operate, covers the basic systems that allow finance to occur. For example, if there were no standard currency, how would people buy and sell items? For the economy to function, we need stable markets that everyone accepts. The financial world includes markets (such as stock exchanges) and financial institutions (such as banks), and it requires government oversight to make sure there is honesty and accountability. The chapter ends with a review of some environmental conditions that influence the various markets.

Chapter 4, Business Structure, highlights the various types of businesses that exist in the sport industry. Business structure is important because it determines how government rules can affect a company and influences the financial strategies a business can undertake. For example, a sole proprietorship cannot issue stocks and become a publicly traded company without changing its structure. Furthermore, recent rules such as the Sarbanes-Oxley reporting requirements affect C corporations, but not many other businesses at this time. Business structures covered include sole proprietorships, general and limited partnerships, subchapter S corporations, C corporations, limited liability corporations and partnerships, and nonprofit organizations.

FINANCIAL ISSUES IN SPORT

CHAPTER OBJECTIVES

After studying this chapter, you should be able to do the following:

- Understand how money affects every facet of the sport industry.
- Understand how industry trends and economic conditions affect every aspect of sport.
- Analyze why the sports apparel industry faces financial hardships.
- Appreciate that some sport businesses are owned by individuals and some by the public.
- Understand major developments in stadium construction trends.
- Describe some of the concerns associated with economic impact analysis for planned stadiums and arenas.

Imagine a world without money. How would we obtain the items we need? How could businesses grow? How could we save for the future? These are typical questions that could arise if our society did not utilize money. More practically, what would happen to us if our checking accounts did not balance? What would happen to us if our cars broke down and we needed to buy new ones? Would we have a favorable credit history for obtaining a loan? Would we need someone to **cosign** a loan, agreeing to pay the balance if we defaulted on the loan? How would we balance our financial obligations with another obligation added to the mix? Would the new car increase our insurance costs to the point that we might not be able to afford the monthly payments? These are questions that typically arise when we make personal financial decisions.

Businesses raise similar questions with every decision they make. Should a new franchise join a league? Should an athlete be signed at $5 million or $6 million a year? How much should ticket prices rise in any given year? If someone wants to start her own sport business, where can she obtain the funds? These questions are asked and answered every day by means of financial analysis. Monetary issues come up throughout the business day, and each business needs individuals who are trained to analyze where the money is or where to obtain additional funds if necessary.

Sport finance entails numerous unique issues, but these nevertheless mirror the finance issues faced by all other businesses. This chapter highlights those similarities. The chapter focuses on current sport finance issues, beginning with the valuation of sports teams and the borrowing of money or issuance of stock by pro sports teams. We then consider mergers of larger sport businesses, changes in the sports apparel area, some of the changes that are affecting sports sponsorship, and the financing of new stadiums and arenas. The background material in this chapter should give you a strong foundation in some of the basic concepts you must understand in order to appreciate the complexities of sport finance. This chapter focuses on financial planning, financial skills, and various industry trends and issues such as billion-dollar teams, broadcasting contracts, publicly traded stocks, industry mergers, sports apparel, sports sponsorship, and financing new arenas and stadiums.

MANAGING MONEY

Although **money** is important for everyday decisions, money is not an end in itself for most people. We strive for personal financial independence, but we also normally realize that money only helps us enjoy our lives to the fullest. What good is a million dollars if we cannot enjoy spending the money? Individuals traditionally work hard to earn money to enjoy the finer things in life (e.g., traveling, retiring, or spoiling family members). However, businesses traditionally do not have the same vision about the role money plays in their existence. Businesses exist solely to make money for their owners and stockholders. If a company has other goals besides earning profits, it still needs to focus on the bottom line in order to pay **bills** and meet its payroll. For example, even if a company's primary goal is to make ecologically friendly products to save the rain forest, the company will not be in business if it is unable to sell these products at a price sufficient to cover the costs of running the business. Nonprofit organizations also exist to make money in order to further their primary goals. The Special Olympics needs to engage in selling products, sponsorship, and advertising to raise the funds necessary to offer programs for its athletes.

Besides paying the bills, making and managing money provide the framework for future growth. Finding, managing, tracking, and spending money refer to specific finance-related functions within a company or business. Failure to properly manage funds will cause a business to fail. Successful financial management results in business growth. The best product in the world would not survive if sound financial planning did not support the sales effort. Economic forecasts help determine potential sales patterns or the times when raw goods need to be purchased. If sales are expected to be phenomenal, then it might be necessary to borrow money from a lending institution or the public to finance new manufacturing facilities.

Sound financial planning is especially critical when the development process for a product is expected to be long. For example, new nutritional supplements typically require several years of development and testing on humans before they are approved by the Food and Drug Administration (FDA) for consumer distribution. Sport nutrition products such as Gatorade are a good example. Gatorade had to go through the entire FDA review process (which is cumbersome and involves multiple hurdles that can take years to overcome) before it could be sold, and then it had to meet government guidelines concerning the health information on the label. Most pharmaceuticals do not make it through the review process and do not get FDA approval to be sold. During the FDA review process, a company might not have any income but still needs to pay bills, wages, and operating expenses. By managing money wisely and working with potential investors such as venture capitalists, the company could generate the needed finances without jeopardizing product development. The key to financial success, as highlighted by this simple example, is financial planning.

All managerial decisions require a comprehensive review of internal and external constraints. Environmental factors such as the cost of borrowing money also involve both types of constraints. Internal constraints can include a company's past credit history, sales volume, product lines, accounts receivable, inventory balances, and management structure. External constraints can include inflationary conditions, significant competition, high interest rates, weak **economic indicators**, shrinking of the money supply by the government, and the political environment. Although it takes money to make money, you cannot make money unless you understand all the internal and external variables that affect your ability to properly manage your finances. Thus, a team owner cannot start budgeting for future growth based on a new stadium if the voters have not yet approved public funding for the stadium. Internal constraints, such as ticket prices, are moot issues until the external constraints—the votes—are finalized.

Financial principles apply to every business, nonprofit organization, and government entity. In the United States, people are concerned about the financial health of the Social Security system and whether it might go bankrupt in the future. Some nonprofit organizations have suffered from scandals involving key executives who abused financial control to live a lavish lifestyle. Countless businesses have filed for bankruptcy protection because they failed to make required payments in a timely manner. All these scenarios are examples of poor financial planning. The sports world is not immune to such problems. From the building of a public stadium that sits almost dormant for years to the folding of a new league because of a stronger rival league's aggressive marketing efforts, problems in the sports world often result from the lack of critical financial planning. The main common denominator in most professional sports strikes is financial planning. For example, some owners have raised the salary bar for other owners, and once the bar has been raised it becomes almost impossible, without violating antitrust laws, to lower the salaries. That has led to an environment of haves and have-nots. Some teams are able to survive and generate enough revenue to constantly put forth a strong product, while other teams flounder with low salaries. Other teams use strategic financial planning to help their bottom line.

One of the most famous examples of leveraging a team to reach financial success involves the San Diego

Padres. They spent a significant amount of money on top-level talent during the 1998 season to help win the National League championship. They also won a vote to utilize public funds to help build a new ballpark. The team spent $53 million in 1998 compared with only $32.8 million in 1997 (Truex, 1999). Thereafter, the team was dismantled, and some of the top talent was traded, was not signed, or signed with other clubs as free agents, thus significantly reducing the payroll (Truex, 1999). However, their increased spending and winning record helped garner public support for building a facility. The team's $20 million investment was returned many times over by the increased revenue the team received from the new stadium.

Other teams in various leagues have undertaken similar spending sprees. The Florida Marlins went on a spending spree before the 1997 World Series and then dismantled their high-salaried team. After winning the World Series, the owner cut the team payroll by 70% the next year to $16 million. In the San Diego case, analysts

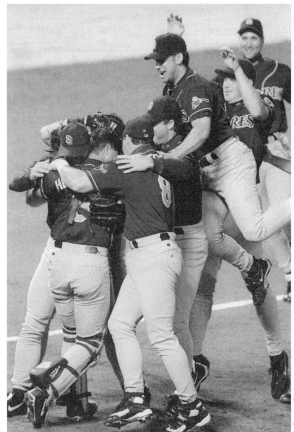

© Getty Images

By spending a lot of money on player salaries some teams, such as the San Diego Padres, have won major titles. However, as the large payroll of the New York Yankees demonstrates, money will not always buy you a title.

conjectured that the owners spent lavishly to produce a great product and a winning team. Voters would have a harder time voting against a new stadium for a winning team. In contrast, voters would probably not feel bad about turning down a stadium bond vote for a team that had never won. Once the team had received the positive vote, the need for a winning and expensive team ended, and the Padres could return to a lower payroll level. Team payrolls do not occur by chance. Financial planning sets the stage for team success.

FINANCIAL SKILLS

Executives do not just make decisions. The most successful executives use financial skills to carefully plan their decisions. To document and plan for future financial success, a sports organization needs someone trained in developing, analyzing, projecting, and interpreting financial information. The need for strong financial skills keeps growing as the sport industry evolves and more money is at stake. When budgets were small, it was often a coach who was asked to run the athletic program. However, now with huge budgets and demands for financial accountability, more specific training is needed to succeed. For example, in 2006 the budget for Ohio State University's athletic department became the first college athletic department in the United States to surpass $100 million to run 36 sports. To manage such a large operation, trained professionals are needed. The job description in the box below is typical for a high-level financial job.

As highlighted by this job description, a senior executive with solid financial skills can have a significant number of opportunities available to him in the future. However, it should be clear that different jobs and tasks require different financial skills. The terms *finance*, *accounting*, and *economics* often cause confusion for students. **Accounting** is the process of calculating revenue and expenses through receipts and other facts to determine the numbers for a company or entity. Finance is the process of examining the numbers and determining what they mean and what the past was and future will be for a company or entity. **Economics** in contrast takes the numbers and financial projections from numerous companies or entities to explore future trends. If numerous sporting good companies are projecting very strong returns because of a new fitness craze, for example, the economists could take that information and hypothesize about new economic changes or trends that affect the sporting goods segment of the industry. Thus, some careers involving sport finance can be described as accounting, finance, or economic positions rather than all being lumped in the category of sport finance.

No matter what skills are developed or what specific job an executive might pursue, the newspapers throughout the world are replete with sport finance articles. Whether such articles are on the front pages or in the business or sports sections, many people meticulously follow sport finance stories because of their fan interest or the thrill associated with seeing multimillion-dollar deals. It would be impossible to highlight a year's worth of such headlines in a single text. However, the following are some key sport finance issues raised over the past several years that indicate the breadth of the field. Because of numerous internal and external constraints posed by teams, athletes, facilities, communities, and other variables, no two stories or issues are the same.

BILLION-DOLLAR TEAMS

The 21st century witnessed the first sale of a professional team for more than $1 billion when Malcolm Glazer, owner of the Tampa Bay Buccaneers, purchased a controlling interest in vaunted soccer powerhouse Manchester United. The $1.47 billion

A Typical Job Description
for a High-Level Sport Finance Position

XYZ is a sport management company seeking a highly motivated chief financial officer. This person will serve as a strategic partner and internal consultant by providing guidance to all individuals associated with our various financial systems. Responsibilities will include, but are not limited to, company-wide budgeting, financial forecasting, statistical reporting, audits, new business development, payroll preparation, state and federal tax compliance, and information systems. Qualified candidates should hold a certificate such as a CPA or CMA or possess an MBA in conjunction with an accounting bachelor's degree. Five to eight years of senior-level financial experience is necessary in order to gain a full understanding of projections, techniques, systems, and methodology. The ideal candidate will also possess strong leadership and managerial skills to help lead a group of 20 employees in various areas such as ticket processing, accounts receivable, accounts payable, and outside contracts administration.

takeover bid included Glazer's using $503 million of his own money, taking out loans for $490 million, and issuing preferred securities in the amount of $509 million. In essence only one-third of the money came from Glazer, while the rest came from lenders and other investors. Since he did not put that much of his own money forward, the team was going to be saddled with significant loan obligations, with interest estimated at more than $55 million a year just to pay for borrowing the money to finance the deal. A $55 million obligation is significant for the team. The year of the transaction, Manchester United had revenues of only $300 million and $90 million in profits (Cohen & Holmes, 2005). Glazer purchased the club by buying 97.3% of the team's shares that were trading on the London Stock Exchange. Before his takeover attempt, the shares were selling for between 250 and 280 pence a share. Glazer offered 300 pence per share in cash to buy his majority share, which allowed him to make the team private. Mr. Glazer is now the sole owner, as opposed to when the team was publicly listed and owned by numerous investors (Sharecast, 2005).

In the United States, teams were also being sold for record amounts. For example the Washington Redskins and their stadium were sold for $805 million, surpassing the previous record of $530 million paid for the Cleveland Browns just several months earlier (Hiestand, 1999). The Redskins appeared to be a strong investment vehicle because the new stadium, with over 200 luxury suites, was capable of generating more than $20 million a year from just those suites and an estimated $5 million a year in stadium naming rights. These figures, added to shared ticket, broadcasting, and licensing revenue, made even $800 million seem like a wise investment

(Hiestand, 1999). With huge television revenues locked in for years, the NFL appeared to be a great investment for team owners.

Even with such large sums offered for a team, team values can be affected by numerous variables, such as what is included in the deal, whether a new or existing franchise is being sold, and the league's financial strength. In fact, the $800 million offer for the Redskins from New York Islanders owner Howard Milstein was rejected by the other National Football League (NFL) owners ("Owners Unlikely to OK," 1999). The Redskins deal included both the team and a stadium, but several months after that sale a new NFL franchise was awarded. The NFL sold a franchise to Houston for $700 million (Zimbalist, 1999). National Football League teams have shown more **appreciation** than baseball teams because of the hard salary cap limiting the amounts teams can pay their players, a loyal fan base interested in attending the limited number of games played, and huge television broadcast contracts. However, every sport business has to face the ups and downs of economic conditions, and team values can fluctuate as well. For example, Major League Soccer (MLS) considered eliminating teams troubled by financial hardships. The league had lost $250 million from 1996 through 2001; and one owner, billionaire Phil Anschutz, in essence controlled the destiny of the league by owning 5 of the league's 10 teams (Wahl, 2001). By 2005, MLS seemed to be much stronger, with new soccer-only facilities already built in Ohio, California, and Texas and several more planned to help solidify the league. As another example, Major League Baseball (MLB) decided not to eliminate the Montreal Expos franchise. Instead, MLB took over the team (bought for $120 million) and moved

The Most Valuable Teams in the World

According to a book titled *Keeping Score: The Economics of Big Time Sports*, in 1996 the Dallas Cowboys were the most valuable sports team in the world, valued at $428 million. Three college teams—Michigan, Florida, and Notre Dame—were also listed among the 25 most valuable sports franchises, even though the college teams could not be sold (Sheehan, 1996). Only three years later, $428 million would appear to be a steal compared with the selling prices for the Houston Texans and the Redskins. Six years after that, the value of franchises had exploded again. The 2005 *Forbes* magazine listing of the most valuable sports franchises in the United States showed that for six straight years the Washington Redskins were the most valuable team, with a 2005 value of $1.26 billion according to the magazine's analysis. The Cowboys were in second place at $1.06 billion, and the New England Patriots were valued at $1.04 billion ("Big-Bucks Redskins Top 'Forbes' List," 2005). Manchester United was also cited as the most valuable team internationally. In 2005, Forbes estimated the team's value to be at $1.251 billion.

With NFL franchises valued at around a half-billion dollars, it is hard to believe the teams' values when the original franchises were issued. Curly Lambeau paid $50 in 1922 for the Green Bay franchise. In 1925, Tim Mara paid $500 for the New York Giants franchise. Art Rooney acquired the Pittsburgh Steelers franchise in 1933 through an unconventional method—he won the rights in a card game ("From $50 in 1922," 1999).

it to Washington, D.C., where it is now called the Washington Nationals. By 2006 the Washington Nationals were valued by *Forbes* magazine as the sixth most valuable MLB franchise at $440 million. Thus, a financially strong team can still attract buyers, as evidenced by the Nationals' increased value and the $755 million sale of the Boston Red Sox along with storied Fenway Park and the New England Sports Network (Farhi, 2001).

Why would a team's **value** fluctuate so much in such a short time period? The simple answer could be the team's profit margin or total **assets**, as discussed later in this text. Another reason could be an arbitrary value based on fan and investor speculation rather than true financial value. Some wealthy individuals are interested in owning an expensive toy and could throw all logic out the window if they are in a bidding war with a rival and want more than anything to own a professional team. As Dallas Mavericks owner Marc Cuban said, "It's every little kid's dream . . . to own their favorite team. I think it's a tremendous opportunity" ("Web Billionaire," 2000).

BILLION-DOLLAR BROADCASTING DEALS

The financial growth of sports in North America has been fueled by the phenomenal growth of broadcasting rights deals. There are several jewels in the sports broadcasting empire. The top jewels are the NFL, the NCAA basketball championships, the Olympics, and college football's Bowl Championship Series. Although events such as NASCAR races, golf tournaments, and the Kentucky Derby are popular, the broadcast rights fees are not in the same stratosphere as those of the crown jewels. For example, the NCAA received $2.8 billion from CBS for a seven-year contract. The NFL, while seeing its ratings decline almost 10% since 1998, has seen its rights fees soar. DirecTV is paying $3.5 billion over five years for its exclusive NFL Sunday Ticket package, which is a 75% increase from their prior rights deal (Lowry & Grover, 2004). In total, the previous NFL contract generated $3.735 billion a year for the NFL, which was more than all the national rights fees for the NBA, MLB, NASCAR, the PGA, and the NCAA basketball tournament combined (Hiestand, 2004).

ESPN's first broadcast was on September 7, 1979, and the network aired its first NCAA basketball championship in 1980. ESPN started with 1.4 million viewer homes and by 2004 rose to more than 88.3 million households. An average of 94 million Americans consumed ESPN's diverse array of media (TV, radio, magazine) each week for an average of about one hour each day (Martzke & Cherner, 2004). The growth of aired events has also spawned a growth in competition

between broadcasters. ESPN was the first specialized sports broadcaster, but others have emerged on the scene and have helped foster a bidding war. A number of professional teams who used to air their games on Fox Sports switched in 2004 to Comcast. The battle between the two powerful regional sports networks (RSNs) is fueled in part by their popularity. As they acquired additional sport properties, their ratings increased, and with the increased demand for their programs they were able to increase the price per subscriber. Although a channel such as CNN charges a cable company $0.40 per subscriber, ESPN charged $2.25 per subscriber in 2004, with the RSNs not far behind at $2 per subscriber (Grover & Lowry, 2004).

As highlighted already, broadcast networks are dishing out huge sums to air sports events. Cable providers (from regional networks to sports packages such as "all-access" football, hockey, basketball, and baseball games), ABC, CBS, NBC, and ESPN are all competing to win sports fans. The economic reality is that sports broadcasts draw viewers, which means they draw advertisers. Advertisers are willing to pay more for advertisements on the top broadcast, which has fueled the bidding war for the best shows and has led to low bids for less popular broadcasting events.

The biggest moneymaker by far is football. The National Football League's contracts are a multibillion-dollar enterprise. Fox extended its National Conference deal by agreeing to a $4.4 billion contract ($550 million per season), which included rights to half the Super Bowl games during that time. Both FOX and CBS have renewed their Sunday-afternoon broadcast packages through 2011, in both cases with modest increases. *Monday Night Football*, on the other hand, will move to ESPN, with the Disney-owned network paying $1.1 billion per year from 2006 to 2014 for the rights to the lucrative broadcasts. Meanwhile, NBC, after losing their AFC package to CBS in 1997, has reclaimed its share of the NFL broadcast rights with a deal worth an average of $650 million per year from 2006 to 2012 that will give them the Sunday-night package as well as the Super Bowl and Pro Bowl in 2009 and 2012 ("Univision," 2005).

One of the best broadcasting properties after the NFL is NASCAR. According to Nielsen ratings, NASCAR is second only to the NFL in sports viewership. In 2005, NASCAR's 5.8 average rating beat the NBA's regular season and playoffs; the NCAA tournament; PGA golf; and the NHL's regular season, playoffs, and Stanley Cup finals (Patsuris, 2003).

NASCAR also follows the NFL in the money race. NASCAR is now in the third year of its $2.4 billion six-year contract with General Electric–owned NBC and AOL Time Warner's TNT, which together air half the season. News Corporation's Fox and F/X networks air the rest. NBC and TNT highlight that NASCAR's ratings jumped 59% from 2000 to 2002, and those numbers continue to grow on a yearly basis (Patsuris, 2003).

A sport that is huge in Europe and on the rise in the United States is soccer. Univision Communications and the ABC and ESPN television networks have paid a record $425 million to air World Cup soccer and other events from 2007 to 2014 ("Univision," 2005). Univision also paid $325 million for exclusive Spanish-language rights to air the events throughout the United States and Puerto Rico. ABC and ESPN, both owned by the Walt Disney Company, paid $100 million for English-language rights ("Univision," 2005).

While the big networks continue to offer big money for broadcasting rights, new networks are popping up hoping to get a foot in the door. When ESPN offered the NHL less than $60 million to broadcast the league's games, negotiations broke off. Comcast's Outdoor Life Network (OLN) offered $135 million over two years for the rights to National Hockey League telecasts. If your cable provider does not offer OLN, you can catch your favorite hockey team on XM Satellite Radio. XM currently has 4.4 million subscribers and announced a 10-year $100 million agreement to become the exclusive satellite radio network of the NHL in 2007 (NHL Press, 2005). Besides new broadcasting entrants, new technology is also changing the way sports broadcasting attracts fans.

Sporting events are also moving into the digital, wireless age. ESPN started to sell a wireless service for sports fans called Mobile ESPN. Mobile ESPN delivers sports scores, breaking news, and commentary as well as some audio and video clip services to ESPN mobile phones ("Univision," 2005). However, after several months ESPN stopped selling the phones because they were not successful. The content is still being provided, but to other phone companies as an additional service. High-technology companies are also cashing in on broadcasting rights. BSkyB, or Sky television, features sports, entertainment, and breaking news via mobile phones, personal digital assistants, and portals including Sky.com and Skysports.com (Sky Media, 2005). World Championship Sports Network (WCSN) is the first programming network dedicated to capturing athletes and international sports federation competitions from around the world. WCSN showcases a wide variety of global sports including track and field, gymnastics, skiing, and volleyball (World Championship Sports Network, 2005).

STOCKS FOR SALE

Individuals now have greater opportunities than in the past to invest in their favorite teams. People can invest in public stock offerings for teams such as the Green Bay Packers, even though the recently issued shares are more of a collectable than a valuable investment. Fans could have owned parts of other teams that once were publicly traded, such as the Boston Celtics and Orlando Predators. Individuals can also purchase stock in sport-related businesses such as International Speedway Corporation (which owns 12 NASCAR racetracks), internationally recognized companies such as Nike or Disney, and even sport-specific stock funds. Some sport-specific investment funds have attempted to focus on such areas as auto racing, golf, sports sponsors, and sporting goods manufacturing companies ("Investing's Fast Track?" 1999). An investment fund called the Sportsfund was launched in 1996 but never succeeded. The company's brochure included the following warning:

> Since the fund focuses its investment on a set of industries related to a single theme, it may be more volatile than a fund that does not focus its investments in this manner. Because sports activities are not a necessity, companies focused on sports may be more affected by economic downturns than other companies. (Sportsfund, 1996)

Another sport fund is the StockCar Stock Index, which had assets of about $5 million in 1999 and was down while the rest of the market was up. In 2002 shares in the fund were valued at $20, then the price dropped to $14 in 2003. With a growing stock market, the index fund increased in value to $22 in 2007, with still around $5.8 million in assets (stocks the index owned). The Value Trend Links Fund had trouble finding golf-oriented stocks, so it started acquiring stocks in companies that sponsor golf events. By October 1999, the fund's value had increased 8.8% (O'Brian & Tam, 1999). By 2007, the fund could no longer be found.

Focusing on sport- and entertainment-related funds serves as a vehicle to invest in an industry but minimize the potential for losing money. When a person purchases shares in Nike, the price can fluctuate from day to day and year to year. If someone bought shares at $100 each and then the stock declines in value five months later, the investor could lose a significant amount of money. Similarly, if the stock increases in value the investor can make a proverbial "killing." However, most investors fall within these two extremes and hope for a modest return with as little risk as possible. That is where sport funds come in. A sport fund invests in several to hundreds of companies. By investing in so many companies, the fund increases the chance of having a nice return on investment with limited risk. One stock may decline, but 10 might increase to help offset the losses. This attractive feature explains why numerous people invest their retirement money in funds.

MERGER MANIA

The sporting goods industry sustained significant growth in the 1990s through the success of shoe brands such as Air Jordans. However, the industry experienced a major downturn in the late 1990s, with several manufacturers losing significant earnings. These losses led to a consolidation within the retail sales side of the industry. For example, in 1998 the Woolworth Corporation (now Venator) agreed to buy Sports Authority for stock valued at $579.6 million and the **assumption** of $179 million worth of Sports Authority debt ("Woolworth Corp.," 1998). Sports Authority was expected to report losses of $0.12 a share before the acquisition was announced. The acquisition allowed its shareholders to receive 0.8 shares in Woolworth stock for each Sports Authority share. Woolworth already owned more than 3,000 athletic shoe stores, including Foot Locker, Lady Foot Locker, and Champs Sports stores, and would add the 202 Sports Authority stores to its family of sporting goods sales units, which generated over $5.5 billion in annual worldwide sales ("Woolworth Corp.," 1998).

Investors did not view the merger positively when it was first announced. In May 1998, the Venator Group and Sports Authority announced the planned merger when both companies' shares were trading at approximately $20 per share. Six months later, their shares were valued at around $10, with Sports Authority's stock dropping to as little as $4.06—signaling lack of investor interest in the merger (Bernstein, 1998). However, Venator was able to successfully complete the merger and start producing strong returns. For the quarter ending January 2000, Venator's net income rose to $73 million on sales of $1.33 billion. For the year, Venator's 4,529 stores produced a $48 million profit, or $0.35 per share. The prior year (1998), the company had recorded losses of $136 million, or a $1 loss per share. On the basis of the reported goods news, Venator's stock rose $0.25 to $7 per share ("Venator Net Surges," 2000). This example shows that even when significant planning goes into a financial decision such as a merger, numerous problems can arise. One major problem can be investor response. In this case the investors were proven wrong, and the merger was a success.

We have also seen a recent wave of mergers in the sporting goods industry. In 2003 Nike purchased the Converse Company, and in 2005 adidas-Salomon acquired Reebok. The adidas–Reebok merger brought together the second and third largest companies in the industry. It will be interesting to see if the resulting new company can surpass Nike for supremacy in the athletic shoe industry. Nike currently owns about 40% of the market share for sports shoes.

Major industry consolidations also occurred in the sports agency arena (e.g., SFX Entertainment purchased Falk Associates Management Enterprises for $100 million). Super agent David Falk is most famous as Michael Jordan's agent. That acquisition occurred less than one year after Interpublic Group, an ad agency, purchased Advantage International, which represents more than 200 athletes (Fatsis, 1998, May 8). However, not long after SFX started its acquisition spree (see chapter 15), it was acquired by another company. Clear Channel, which owns 867 radio stations, 19 TV stations, and more than 500,000 outdoor billboards, offered to acquire SFX for $2.99 billion. Ironically, SFX obtained a significant amount of the cash it needed to purchase other companies by selling its radio stations.

SFX's class A shareholders were to receive about $40.125 for each share. However, class B shareholders were given one share of Clear Channel (valued at more than $66.00) for each class B share. This deal structure caused some concern, since the only holders of class B shares were SFX's chairman and CEO (Tejada, 2000). Individuals could be concerned about this purchase structure since the class B shareholder would be compensated at a higher level than other stockholders. Although class A and class B stocks are technically different, if investors paid the same amount for their interest and had the same risks, they would be concerned if they did not receive similar compensation, and in this case the difference was over $25 per share. The potential exists for class A stockholders to believe their compensation for selling their interest in SFX was inadequate given the higher amount paid to class B stockholders for their shares. SFX used its live entertainment assets as a key component for the 2002 merger with Clear Channel, the nation's largest radio station owner. This synergy allowed SFX/Clear Channel to dominate the music and events industry through radio stations, billboards, and entertainment venues.

Additional consolidation occurred in the broadcasting industry. Disney's acquisition of ABC and ESPN appeared to be a natural fit for the entertainment giants, which positioned themselves to bid for large packages such as the National Basketball Association (NBA) broadcast contract in 2001 (Fendrich, 2001). Another major merger that occurred in 2000 involved America Online (AOL), which in essence purchased Time Warner to form the media, entertainment, and sports giant AOL Time Warner. Because of poor financial performance, the AOL title of the new company was dropped in 2002 even though the two companies were still together. In 2003 the combined companies sold some of their premiere sport holdings, the Atlanta Thrashers and Atlanta Hawks. In 2006 Time Warner sold its Turner South regional sports broadcasting network. Time Warner has several divisions besides AOL, including Warner Brothers, CNN, and HBO. Mergers such as these are covered in greater detail in chapter 15.

SPORTS APPAREL BLUES

Product repositioning represents one of the major transitions facing the sports, or athletic, shoe industry. In the 1980s, almost every player in the NBA had a shoe deal. However, by 1998, only about half of the 400 players in the league had shoe contracts, and that number was dwindling rapidly (Fatsis, 1998, May 14). Reebok alone dropped more than 110 NBA players who had previously been under contract. Reebok also slashed its baseball sponsorship lineup from 280 to 140 athletes and its football players from 550 to around 100 (Fatsis, 1998, May 14). Several years later the focus had shifted to sponsoring and having exclusive long-term licensing agreements with leagues such as the NFL, NBA, WNBA, NBDL (National Basketball Development League), and IRL (Indy Racing League) and stars such as Allen Iverson. Other shoe and apparel companies reduced their sponsorship commitments as well. Major stars such as Shaquille O'Neal had their contracts terminated or bought out. Larry Johnson had earned around $800,000 a year from Converse in the early 1990s, but in 1998 he received only $7,500 in free merchandise (Fatsis, 1998, May 14).

The sponsorship downturn was the result of a significant downturn in the $8 billion U.S. athletic shoe market. Reebok sales in the United States slumped 12% in early 1998. Converse sales plummeted 50%, and Nike sales fell 18%, resulting in Nike's laying off 7% of its workforce (1,600 employees) (Fatsis, 1998, May 14). Analysts thought the primary reason Nike was experiencing slower gains than expected was the numerous shoe stores that had closed or filed for bankruptcy. For example, Just For Feet filed for bankruptcy in 1999, depriving Nike of numerous outlets for selling its products (Gomes, 2000). Nike sales have rebounded and fluctuated since 1998, with third-quarter sales ending in February 2000 hitting $2.16 billion and the company beating analyst projections with earnings per share of $0.52 ("Nike Net Rose," 2000). By the second quarter ending November 30, 2001, Nike sales had hit $2.3 billion, but the earnings per share had declined to $0.48 (Pritchard, 2001). By 2004 Nike was on a financial tear. The company made the cover of *Business Week* with its strong showing in the now $35 billion annual athletic footwear industry. In 2004 Nike's revenue exceeded $12 billion and earnings of $1 billion, which represented a 15.3% rise in sales and a 27% increase in profits.

Nike's profits were driven in part by strong global sales that rose 10.7% in 2004. Global apparel sales have risen 30% alone in three years to $3.5 billion. U.S. sales also rose 10%, but that was the first quarter in two years. Nike's market share in the United States for basketball sales is 60%. Flush with over $1 billion in unencumbered cash, Nike has been strengthening itself by buying back $1 billion in its own stocks, and it intends to repurchase more shares. Such aggressive steps shot its stocks to the $80 range in 2005 and are expected to propel the company to almost $20 billion in value by 2010. Part of this growth has included acquiring companies such as Hurley International (a skateboarding equipment company); Cole Haan (dress and casual shoes); Bauer (skates and hockey gear); and Converse (athletic shoes), which Nike acquired for $305 million in 2003 (Holmes, 2004).

In the past decade, athletic shoe companies have sought out athletes with the greatest marketing power. The Air Jordan series has been the best-selling line since the 1980s, helping build Nike's popular global brand image (Tang, 2003). The athletic shoe industry is a $25 billion business worldwide, with Nike leading the way; adidas and Reebok are second and third respectively. Nike's position was solidified with the signing of LeBron James over archrival Reebok to a $90 million deal.

© NBAE/Getty Images

The on-court success of LeBron James helped generate significant revenue for Nike. Is this a good investment for Nike, which had strong success with Michael Jordan but not as significant as with Tiger Woods?

Nike was founded as a company that made shoes for track and field athletes. It currently has deals with 20 sports federations worldwide and is outfitting more than 2,000 athletes (Walker, 2004). In 2005, Nike signed an apparel and equipment deal with 15-year-old golf sensation Michelle Wie, reportedly worth $5 million per year. Before Wie, Nike signed a deal worth $40 million over five years with Tiger Woods when he turned pro in 1996. Because Woods had not yet accomplished anything on the Professional Golfers' Association (PGA) Tour, some critics viewed the deal as risky. But Nike got its investment back and much more. Before signing Woods, Nike's golf revenue was negligible; today, it is estimated to be $500 million per year. Woods' latest Nike deal pays him $25 million per year (Badenhausen, 2005). Nike's golf business could be contributed in part to Tiger Woods, but the company did not sell golf shoes before Tiger. Therefore, some of the growth is attributable to just developing a new product line.

Reebok's United Kingdom–based ancestor company was founded for one of the best reasons possible: Athletes wanted to run faster, and Reebok wanted to help them along ("Reebok," 2005). In June 2005, Reebok hired hip-hop rapper 50 Cent to promote the new GXT II trainer. The TV advertisements also featured Boston Red Sox slugger Manny Ramirez, Philadelphia Eagles quarterback Donovan McNabb, and WBC junior middleweight world boxing champion Ronald "Winky" Wright to showcase the new cross-trainer as a shoe that performs across many sports ("Reebok," 2005).

German-based adidas has its roots in soccer and track and field, while Reebok's line of sneakers and athletic gear is visible across North American sports such as football, baseball, and basketball (Moore, 2005). Nike's annual sales are approximately $14 billion worldwide; adidas generated about $8 billion in annual sales, while Reebok had nearly $4 billion (Moore, 2005).

In 2005 adidas-Salomon agreed to buy Reebok International for $59 a share, combining two major brands with links to both athletics and lifestyle (Moore, 2005). With the number two and three athletic shoe companies merging, Nike will face a fierce challenge to stay at the top.

Because the shoe industry is so competitive, companies are reaching out to the collegiate, high school, and Amateur Athletic Union (AAU) ranks to increase their product awareness. March Madness is one of the most anticipated sporting events of the year. Sneaker companies try to lure college coaches, especially coaches representing the final four, to their products (see table 1.1). Nike, Reebok,

and adidas are just a few of the shoe companies that benefit from the NCAA playoffs. Of the 65 schools participating in the 2002 NCAA playoffs, 49 sported the Nike swoosh or the Brand Jordan logo, including all of the top 8 seeds. The other 16 entrants included adidas (9), Reebok (4), and AND 1 (3) (Douchant, 2002). Recently, the major shoe companies have expanded their marketing to the high school and AAU levels. Elite high school and AAU teams may receive funding or product from companies such as Nike, adidas, and Reebok. The major requirement of these teams is that they must wear the companies' shoes and apparel. The companies are using these deals with high schools and AAU teams to reach potential endorsers at the youngest age possible. In 2004, Nike signed soccer phenom Freddy Adu to a multimillion-dollar endorsement deal. This may

Table 1.1 Major College Shoe Endorsement Contracts

School	Company
Southeastern Conference	
Alabama	Nike
Arkansas	adidas
Auburn	Nike
Florida	Nike
Georgia	Nike
Kentucky	Nike
LSU	Nike
Mississippi	adidas
Miss. State	adidas
South Carolina	Nike
Tennessee	adidas
Vanderbilt	Nike
Atlantic Coast Conference	
Clemson	Nike
Duke	Nike
Florida State	Nike
Georgia Tech	Nike
Maryland	Nike
N.C. State	adidas
North Carolina	Nike
Virginia	AND 1
Wake Forest	Nike

Data from M. Knobler, "The shoe wars: Sneaky pressure—shoe companies' investment in players might also influence their choice of college" (Atlanta Journal-Constitution, March 7, 2004) [Online]. Available: http://ajc.com/highschool/content/sports/highschool/0304/07shoeimpact.html [October 18, 2005].

not seem strange except for the fact that Adu was 13 years old when the deal was signed.

Another athletic shoe company making strides in the industry is New Balance. New Balance focuses on advertising in *Runner's World* magazine and promoting its products to retailers (Pope, 2004). Bought for $100,000 in 1972, New Balance has grown into a company worth $1.3 billion. Although the company wants to hook younger athletes to the brand, it does not believe its marketing campaign needs large endorsements deals. The New Balance slogan is "function over fashion" (Pope, 2004). New Balance's only endorsement deal within the big-four professional sports leagues was with NBA star James Worthy in the early 1980s for $1 million.

With the pressure of finding the next great athlete, companies realize they need to reach out and develop relationships with young talent. By establishing rapport early on, companies hope these athletes will remain loyal to them after entering the pro ranks. At the tender age of three and a half, Mark Walker can sink 18 basketball shots in a row. With an eye to the future, Reebok International has signed the talented toddler to an advertising deal (Tang, 2003).

These companies show us that volatility exists with any business from year to year or even month to month. Sales can be flat in the winter, except for a spike in Christmas-related purchases, and they often heat up when spring arrives and people are once again participating in sports.

The season can also affect sports apparel sales, which are often best right before schools are back in session. However, sales in the industry had declined to such an extent in the late 1990s that Starter, one of the premiere sports clothing manufacturers, filed for Chapter 11 bankruptcy in 1999 and was liquidated shortly thereafter ("Starter Seeks Chapter 11," 1999). Creditors pushed the company into bankruptcy even though Starter had a significant number of orders to fill for the preschool buying cycle (Sack & Nadim, 2002). A similar fate befell Pro Player, which went bankrupt in 1999 (although there is still a stadium in Miami named after the now defunct brand) (Sack & Nadim, 2002). Furthermore, licensed sports apparel company Logo Athletic filed for Chapter 11 bankruptcy protection in 2000 ("Logo Athletic," 2000).

Financial hardships in the sports shoe and apparel industries were not the result of decreased sales alone. Converse suffered from decreased sales, but its bankruptcy was not entirely related to falling sales. According to Converse's spokesperson Mark Shuster, "It's not a lack of business, but our debt structure that made it difficult for the company to thrive" (Byrt, 2001).

SPORTS SPONSORSHIP

The sports shoe and apparel industries were not alone in experiencing financial turmoil in the early 21st century. Sports sponsorship in general was facing some hard times. Sponsors sometimes have difficulty placing a value on a sponsorship property, so any sponsorship decision is subject to significant fiscal scrutiny. Coca-Cola had a 12-year relationship with the NFL through 1998. The subsequent deal paid the NFL only $6 million a year as compared with $15 million in prior years ("Coke Signs," 1998). The new and greatly reduced sponsorship package allowed teams for the first time in many years to negotiate their own local sponsorship deals.

The reduced value associated with the new contract (a decline from $15 to $6 million) was possibly the result of Dallas Cowboys owner Jerry Jones striking his own deals with competing sponsors. Jones sold sponsorship rights for Texas Stadium to Pepsi. Since it was the stadium that was sponsored by the competing soft drink manufacturer, not the team, Jones was technically not violating the old NFL and Coca-Cola contract. However, because the Cowboys were the only team that played in Texas Stadium, the sponsorship agreement implied indirect sponsorship of the Cowboys by Pepsi. The resulting confusion reduced the sponsorship value for Coca-Cola, leading to the subsequently smaller sponsorship agreement. After losing their NFL sponsorship exclusivity, Coca-Cola focused on other leagues such as FIFA (4-year $500 million sponsorship agreement) and the NBA, which has a "100-year" agreement with the company, signed in 1993 and renewed every 4 years.

However, the entry of PepsiCo (parent company of Pepsi) into the NFL mix helped the newcomer grow its relationship with the entire NFL, which led to a full-fledged league contract. In 2004, PepsiCo and the NFL extended their partnership agreement through February 2011 in an estimated $560 million deal. PepsiCo contracted to acquire the rights to all NFL trademarks, including use of the NFL shield logo, Super Bowl, and Pro Bowl as well as collective use of the 32 NFL team marks for the Pepsi, Tropicana, and Frito-Lay brands. This was in addition to PepsiCo's Gatorade division's announcement of a similar partnership extension with the league through 2011. In total, PepsiCo is projected to spend more than $1 billion for both deals (Parry, 2004).

Sponsorship can come in various forms. For example, a professional league can sponsor a farm team. The NBA in fact had a partnership arrangement with the Continental Basketball Association (CBA) through 2001. The NBA then decided to move away from the CBA and start its own developmental league. The loss of the NBA as a sponsor doomed the CBA, which filed for bankruptcy in 2001 ("CBA Ceases Operations," 2001). Losing sponsors also hurts smaller events, community events such as run-a-thons, and even larger events such as collegiate football bowl games. However, sponsorship is a fickle beast, and trends can change quickly. This was seen in the early part of this century with the phenomenal growth of NASCAR and golf sponsorship. Will corporate interest in sponsoring NASCAR continue? The key is in the numbers. If the broadcast ratings and attendance stay strong, the sponsors will keep coming back. For any sponsorship effort, the key is proving value through strong numbers.

FINANCING NEW STADIUMS AND ARENAS

The most dynamic sport finance topic in the past 20 years is stadium construction deals. Through 2001, 111 major professional sports franchises were operating in North America, and 91.9% (102) moved into new or significantly renovated stadiums (Smith, 2001). Several additional teams, such as the Arizona Cardinals, moved to new facilities as the 21st century was starting. Bond issues, economic factors, taxing issues, financial guarantees, legal wrangling, and political shenanigans can all be explored when examining stadium construction deals. Venerable Yankee Stadium was built in 1923 for $2 million. In 1973, New York City refurbished the stadium for $100 million. In 1996, New York City proposed a new stadium on the west side of Manhattan with an estimated cost of $1.06 billion (Sportsfund, 1996). In 2001, New York recommended two new $800 million stadiums for both MLB teams, which would require the teams and cities to split $50 million a year in **debt service** (to repay the money borrowed to build the stadiums) ("Double Play for New York," 2001).

Although the push for these two new facilities took various forms, the drive to land the 2012 Olympics in New York helped fuel the rapid planning for the stadiums. The Yankees unveiled plans to build an $800 million stadium next door to the existing Yankee Stadium, built with private funds (Smith, 2005). The Mets were also hoping for support and funds for a new stadium that could have been used for the opening ceremonies and other competitions. However, when New York lost the bid to host the 2012 Olympic Games, the plans were put on the back burner, even though the Mets still wanted to build a new stadium. As of 2007, both the Yankees and the Mets were pursuing building their own facilities, with minimal public funding, next to their existing facilities.

In addition to baseball stadiums, New York is currently pursuing various facility options such as moving the New Jersey Nets to a new home in Brooklyn. The total taxpayers' cost for stadiums or arenas built from 1995 through 2000 has been estimated at more than $9 billion (Kraker, 1998). Another estimate capped the building boom at $7 billion from 1998 through 2006, and the number keeps increasing when new stadiums and arenas are approved by voters (Noll & Zimbalist, 1998). The building boom has slowed after the hot run in the 1990s, but facilities are still being built at both the professional and collegiate level, such as new soccer stadiums for Major League Soccer teams.

The Rockies' Stadium Deal

The Colorado Rockies built their stadium with a six-county-area 1% sales tax, with the team contributing $53 million and Coors Brewing making **scheduled payments** of $1.5 million a year for naming rights. Under the 17-year lease, the city receives 20% of parking revenue on game days and 3% of the revenue from a brew pub. The team receives 100% of net concession revenue (Rogus, 1997). In the old facility, Mile High Stadium, the team averaged 55,350 spectators each game, and around 4.5 million fans came through the turnstiles in 1993. The Rockies opened Coors Field in 1995 and during their honeymoon years were averaging around 48,000 fans per game and 3.8 million fans for the first three seasons. These numbers were lower than Mile High's attendance totals, but Coors Field was built with a smaller seating capacity. By 2006, the team was drawing only around 25,000 fans per game and totaled only 2.1 million over the season ("Colorado Rockies Attendance Records," 2007). Even with lower attendance totals, the team was able to make more money through luxury seating and increased broadcasting revenues. The high attendance average for the first couple of years in a new stadium is commonly called the honeymoon effect since fans will want to come out to see what is new at the facility. But similar to many marriages, over time the passion decreases, and that is when attendance starts to decline.

Although numerous facilities were being built to keep or attract professional sports teams, such investments might not always make economic sense or stand on sound financial analysis.

In a 1990 study, the Heartland Institute examined 14 stadiums from 1954 through 1986; these facilities had a net accumulated value of negative $139.3 million ("Sports Stadiums," 1990). The city that had lost the least was Buffalo, New York; the War Memorial Stadium had lost taxpayers only $836,021. In contrast, the New Orleans Superdome lost Louisiana taxpayers $70,356,950 ("Sports Stadiums," 1990). After the construction boom in the 1990s, additional research showed that stadiums and arenas were not a wise financial investment if examined strictly from an economic perspective (Smith, 2001). Although stadium proponents claim significant benefit to building a new stadium, one researcher studied per capita income growth in 48 metropolitan areas. In the 30 cities that had facility changes in the preceding 10 years, 27 showed no significant relationship between income growth and building a facility, and 3 experienced reduced income (Baade, 1994). Another study by researchers from the University of Dayton concluded that public subsidies for constructing MLB stadiums were not necessary since teams recovered all or almost all of their construction costs, typically within 12 years of completing a facility ("Study: No Taxes for Stadiums," 2004).

Municipalities interested in luring a new team or keeping an existing one argue that tax dollars should help finance facility construction because entertainment dollars are brought from outside the community, thus infusing "new" moneys into the local economy (Howard & Crompton, 2004). The municipalities are urging voters to approve the allocation of funds to build the facilities, and the teams are also supporting these efforts. However, the average level of team contribution to new NFL stadiums built through 2001 was only 29%, or $82 million, of the typical construction cost for a football stadium ("NFL Stadium Financing," 2001). Even without any team contributions, some municipalities are willing to foot the entire price of a facility to become a "big-league" city. Besides the increased economic activity and the increased sales, income, and employment tax revenues from those attending games and working at the facilities, proponents argue that the facilities help promote community image (Baim, 1994).

Although significant benefits can be derived from new sports facilities, projections highlighting potential increased tax revenue or other benefits are often significantly inflated to help support the case for building a new facility (Howard & Crompton,

2004). In fact, the combined revenue of the five major professional sports teams in Chicago accounts for only 0.08% of the personal income throughout the city of Chicago (Kraker, 1998). One recent study concluded that the departure of an NBA team from a city results in no measurable impact on a region's per capita income, and thus building a new arena does not make sense as a cornerstone for economic development ("Football Strike?" 2001). One of the reasons projected economic impacts may conflict is that the individuals who determine them may not be reliable sources. Consultants who prepare economic impact reports can utilize incorrect multipliers, or assume that everyone who attends the facility would not have spent money elsewhere in the city, or build in a host of other incorrect assumptions (Baim, 1994). Thus, as is the case for all issues associated with financial analysis, the numbers are only as good as their source and need to be verified, more or less the same way financial statements should be **audited** by a neutral third party.

Although numerous consulting reports show potential profits attributable to a facility, many studies have shown that very few facilities are able to cover their costs (Baim, 1994; Noll & Zimbalist, 1998; Smith, 2001). One major study concluded that older arenas with little debt and numerous scheduled events (NBA, NHL, Ice Capades, family shows, circuses, and so on) tended to make the highest profit, while new stadiums for outdoor sports were least profitable (Baim, 1994). The disparity among economic impact studies is highlighted by two studies conducted in 1992 when the San Francisco Giants were considering a move to San Jose, California. A study conducted in San Francisco estimated economic losses of $3.1 million per year if the team moved. A study conducted for San Jose produced different results. The San Jose study concluded that if the team moved the approximately 45 miles from San Francisco to San Jose, the yearly economic impact for San Jose would be between $50 and $150 million annually (Howard & Crompton, 2004).

The potential hypocrisy associated with stating the financial need to build a stadium or arena was highlighted in a suit by former Tampa mayor William Poe, who tried to stop a referendum to build a new stadium for the Tampa Bay Buccaneers. The Buccaneers were claiming significant financial hardship and the need for a new stadium in order to be economically competitive with other NFL teams. Poe was able to show that at no time did any city official ever ask to see the Buccaneers' financial statements to ensure that the team owner was telling the truth (Henderson, 1996).

Projects such as the Louisiana Superdome, Arrowhead Pond, United Center, the Rose Garden,

Texas Motor Speedway, and the new Busch Stadium rely on various funding techniques ranging from private contributions to **municipal bonds**. Municipal notes and bonds are publicly traded securities with the benefit of not having to comply with all of the registration requirements that other publicly traded securities do (Greenberg & Gray, 1996). Chapter 10 covers several different types of municipal bonds including general obligation, special tax, revenue, and lease-backed financing bonds, as well as certificates of participation. Municipal bonds utilize public funds to help build new facilities. For example, by negotiating a strong agreement requiring the municipality to pay the bulk of the costs, the team interested in playing in the facility can preserve its capital and increase its revenue stream.

In addition to considering municipal bonds, facilities and various government entities can examine other critical financing issues such as the tax status of the bond interest income (taxable or tax exempt), the credit strength of the bond-issuing entity, and the collateral or security that would be utilized to secure the bonds. All these concerns come into play when the final financing package for the facility is being negotiated. Negotiations are an opportunity to creatively design a comprehensive financing package containing any necessary bells and whistles to encourage all parties to commit to the project. The following examples point to the economic and financing backdrop behind several stadium or arena deals.

LOUISIANA SUPERDOME

In *The Sports Stadium as a Municipal Investment* (1994), Dean Baim highlighted several unique stadium deals, including the Louisiana Superdome deal. In 1966, Louisiana voters approved the state constitutional amendment that formed the Louisiana Superdome Authority and allowed the state to borrow $35 million for the project. The facility was completed at a cost of $125 million. The original bond issue was to be backed by a 4% hotel and motel occupancy tax. The full faith and credit of the state of Louisiana were to be *excluded* from backing the bond offering. Since the costs far exceeded the initial $35 million price tag, the state agreed to lease the stadium at an annual rent equal to the shortfall experienced by the authority for servicing the facility's debt obligation. Thus, the state's credit was not utilized to secure the debt obligation (Baim, 1994).

Chase Manhattan Bank led a syndicate prepared to underwrite the Superdome's bonds, but the syndicate collapsed when a gubernatorial candidate threatened to derail the project if he was elected. This led to collaboration between a local banker and an Arkansas bank to sell the $113 million in bonds needed to start construction (Baim, 1994).

To become economically successful (self-sufficient), the Superdome needed to earn between $26,000 and $35,000 in daily rental income (Baim, 1994). This number was projected even before any tenants were being considered for the facility. Thus, Louisiana was hoping for a dream to come true—"If you build it, they will come." Louisiana is not alone. Stadium and arena projects are routinely passed even if no host tenants exist or the facility cannot cover its own debt obligations once it has been completed (Andelman, 1993). Opponents of a San Diego facility referendum explicitly projected that the stadium could not pay for itself, yet the measure passed with 72% of the votes (Baim, 1994). Such possibly foolish investments in a losing venture are made not strictly for financial reasons but for the prospect of economic growth, urban revitalization, or possibly improved quality of life in the area. The value of the investment in Louisiana was called into question after Hurricane Katrina caused significant damage to the dome. Through hard work and a significant investment of time and money, the Superdome was fixed and was used by the New Orleans Saints for the 2006 football season.

ARROWHEAD POND OF ANAHEIM

Located in the heart of southern California, Arrowhead Pond of Anaheim (now the Honda Center) is a 650,000-square-foot arena that serves as home to the NHL Ducks. Arrowhead Pond was constructed through a comprehensive financing package involving several parties. The city of Anaheim issued $103 million in a certificate of participation bond. This bond was guaranteed by a **letter of credit** from Ogden Facility Management. Because the city of Anaheim was *not* forced to underwrite the bond with its own security, it repaid Ogden by giving the company the exclusive right to manage the arena for 30 years. Ogden also receives a management fee and can earn between 75% and 85% of all yearly profits from the facility (Greenberg & Gray, 1996).

UNITED CENTER

The Chicago Bulls and Blackhawks play in the United Center, built in 1994 at a cost of $175 million; 80% of the financing was from private bank loans, and 20% was from the building owners. The entire project was privately funded by the United Center Joint Venture, which is headed by William Wirtz (owner of the Blackhawks) and Jerry Reinsdorf (majority owner and team chairman of the Bulls) ("Building Information," 2001). United Airlines pays $1.8 million a year for naming rights (Rogus, 1997). The original Chicago Stadium, which housed the Bulls and Blackhawks for years, was built for $7 million in 1926. The new center is almost four times the size of the first stadium, and its average electric bill is $155,000 each month ("Building Information," 2001).

ROSE GARDEN

The Rose Garden in Portland is a 785,000-square-foot facility that hosts a range of events from NBA and WNBA games, college basketball, and professional hockey to concerts, rodeos, ice shows, and monster truck rallies. In a complex blend of private and public funding, the Rose Garden was built with the help of Portland Trailblazers owner Paul Allen, who contributed $46 million in cash. Three major banks loaned a total of $16 million to the pot. Last, nine insurance companies purchased $155 million in privately placed bonds, paying 8.99% interest over 27 years (Greenberg & Gray, 1996). The city of Portland paid $34.5 million for street, parking, and other improvements. These city-funded projects will be paid for by a ticket tax of 6.5%, which will pay off the city's contribution in six years and thereafter provide Portland with a perpetual return on its investment (Greenberg & Gray, 1996).

TEXAS MOTOR SPEEDWAY

Stadiums and arenas for professional sports teams are not the only facilities currently being built. Several companies with nationally traded stock are developing and building racetracks throughout the United States. The largest such track to date is the Texas Motor Speedway. The Speedway was paid for by Speedway Motorsports but received significant government assistance (e.g., the city of Fort Worth spent $7 million on road improvements and $4 million for water and sewer improvements, with the county throwing in $5 million for road improvements). The facility can hold more than 250,000 spectators for a race.

Before the Speedway was built, economists pegged the potential economic spending impact at between $11 and $200 million annually for only several events each year (Moffeit, 1999). The potential economic impact to the region was greatly reduced by a "sweetheart deal" in which the owners would not have to pay any city or county property taxes for 30 years—a

benefit valued at over $100 million. Thus, while the city and county would generate some economic benefits from events, the city and county also lost a significant amount of tax revenue from the sweetheart deal. Each year the city captures approximately $700,000 in Speedway-related tax revenue. Because the Speedway opened only in 1997, the figures are fairly new. However, the initial numbers indicate that the $700,000 in added tax revenue represented 10% of the city's sales tax revenue in 1998. Furthermore, the Speedway helped increase motel and hotel tax revenue by 20% in 1997. A unique aspect of the racetrack is that condominiums and Speedway Club towers have been built on the property, and all the condominiums are already sold. The facilities and track contribute 400 full-time jobs to the local economy year round and 5,000 part-time jobs during race week (Moffeit, 1999).

BUSCH STADIUM

The St. Louis Cardinals played in the old Busch Stadium through the 2005 season and ended the facility's remarkable history in the playoffs. In January 2004, groundbreaking began for the new Busch Stadium. It was completed in two years and held its first game in April 2006. The Stadium was financed through private bonds, bank loans, a long-term loan from St. Louis County, and money from the team owners. The development, including Ballpark Village, was estimated to cost $646 million, with the stadium alone costing $346 million. In 2006 every game sold out, giving a total attendance of 3,407,104 for the season, the second largest in team history ("A New Ballpark for Missouri," 2007). As part of the negotiation process with the city and state, the Cardinals agreed to donate more than 100,000 tickets each season to community groups, and the team capped the price of 6,000 seats to a 2002-adjusted $12.00 per ticket to make sure affordable seats would be available.

The new Busch Stadium was designed by HOK Sports and built by Hunt Construction, both internationally known for their work with stadiums and arenas. The facility was constructed in three stages, with part of the stadium built and then the old structure demolished before the new stadium was completed. Because the facilities were so close to one another, implosion (using explosives to make the building cave in on itself) of the old stadium was not an option; the crew had to spend a month tearing it down with a wrecking ball. Directly north of the stadium, the team plans to build Ballpark Village, which will contain residential space, commercial space, a hall of fame, and an aquarium.

CONCLUSION

The examples presented in this chapter demonstrate the breadth of financial issues that can affect a sports administrator. Other issues not yet touched on include Title IX compliance for high school and college athletic programs, fund-raising for youth sports, ways a sporting goods company might issue stock to gain critical expansion funds, and countless others. These topics indicate the wide range of issues that intertwine sport and finance.

Financial concerns permeate every decision made in the sport industry. Even a decision that might seem innocuous from a financial standpoint, such as whether to play a given athlete, presents critical financial considerations. Any time a player participates, he may draw additional fans, may foul a significant number of pitches and so give rise to more commercial break opportunities, or may get a hit that qualifies him for a financial benefit. If the player is injured, the team can lose revenue, face higher workers' compensation premiums, and incur higher rehabilitation-related costs.

CLASS DISCUSSION TOPICS

1. How many pairs of sports or athletic shoes do you own? What are the brands? Did you buy the shoes? How much did you pay? What is your most expensive model?

2. Did you attend a professional sports event within the last year? Where did you go? Did you buy the tickets? How much did you pay? Did you buy any concession items? What items did you buy? How much did you pay? Is price a factor in your purchase decisions as they relate to sport?

3. Have you ever developed a budget? What have you developed a budget for, and did you follow it? If you were able to follow the budget, did you meet your financial goal(s)? If you did not follow the budget, what influenced your ability to stick to your plan?

4. What problems might affect a student's ability to balance a checkbook?

5. Have you ever set up a bank account? What steps were involved?

6. Have you ever borrowed money? What was that experience like? Were you able to pay everything back that you owed?

7. If you had lots of money and wanted to invest in a sport, which sports team or event would you buy or sponsor? Why? If you did not have much money, would you make a sport-related investment or take a more traditional approach, such as banks or the stocks of large corporations?

8. Do you think it is a wise investment to build new stadiums or arenas? Back your answer with some analysis of the economic justification as well as the financial justification.

9. Do you think the AOL Time Warner merger was a good idea? Why would they have wanted to merge? Should they split up?

10. Do you think there are too many sports teams or events? Does a high number of teams and events hurt the industry by diluting the market?

2

BASIC FINANCIAL CONCEPTS

CHAPTER OBJECTIVES

After studying this chapter, you should be able to do the following:

- Analyze the problems or failures that might result from inaccurate financial and economic analysis.
- Understand the basics of how a business uses a budget.
- Distinguish between revenue and expenses.
- Understand basic financial goals and how to maximize shareholders' wealth.
- Describe the difference between finance and accounting.
- Understand the objectives of an accounting system.
- Understand the basics of T-accounts and general data-entry techniques.
- Understand the difference between cash and accrual accounting systems.
- Explain the need for accuracy in accounting and financial data.
- Explain the importance of audited financial statements.

Chapter 2 deals with financial terms and principles. The chapter begins with an analysis of revenue and expenses. We then examine the principles of budgeting and the importance of proper documentation. Next we discuss the issues that managers must consider when determining financial objectives. The final section of the chapter presents an overview of accounting concepts.

REVENUES AND EXPENSES

We all have bills to pay. We also normally have a source of funds, whether from a job, loans, or family. This section highlights how we make and spend money in the sport business. **Revenues** represent money coming into a sport business. Revenue can come from ticket sales, broadcast contracts, concession sales, sponsorship agreements, and a host of other opportunities. The opposite of revenues is expenses. **Expenses** are costs that are incurred. Typical expenses for a professional team include player salaries, equipment, travel, executive salaries, and other expenses ranging from rent to insurance premiums. Each business has different revenues and expenses, and they are constantly changing. A health club might have revenues of $1 million one year, but if 100 members do not renew their membership, the revenues can plunge. Similarly, if you have ever spent more than you could afford on a credit card, your expenses might spiral out of control and create debt. **Debt** is the owing of money to others. If you pay all your expenses as they arise, you can avoid debt.

The following example presents the revenues and expenses of a typical public high school athletic program:

Revenues	Expenses
Local and city school taxes	Facility repair and maintenance costs
Federal tax subsidies for education	Uniform and equipment costs
State taxes	Travel and lodging costs
Participation fees	Insurance costs
Donations	Umpire costs
Booster clubs	Utility costs
Concession revenue	Salaries and benefits
Attendance revenue	Advertising costs
Broadcasting revenue	Promotional costs
Advertising revenue	Office supplies
Fund-raising efforts	
Licensing revenue	
Sponsorship revenue	

For a multitude of reasons, many revenue-generating techniques do not work in a given community. Parents may not want to support a program. Possibly no local advertisers are willing to spend their advertising dollars on the school. City regulations may prohibit utilizing certain fund-raising techniques. Although the revenue-generating options may be limited, the expenses normally do not share the same fate. Expenses were outpacing revenues by such a large amount in the 1990s that some schools started charging students for each sport they played; canceling busing to road games; and eliminating sports such as golf, water polo, and junior varsity sports (Chi, 1992). This trend continued into the next century, with more schools charging athletes or eliminating sports altogether. The sport most affected by rising expenses is ice hockey, where the cost for high school athletes and their parents can be in the thousands of dollars.

Budget cuts are also being felt by colleges. Given various concerns such as compliance with Title IX and the Americans with Disabilities Act, numerous collegiate athletic programs are facing difficult financial times. The problems are compounded by the fact that most Division I athletic programs operate at a deficit. At one point in the 1990s, the Illinois state legislature was even considering eliminating all state funds for intercollegiate athletics (Hiestand, 1992). But the revenue and expense problems in intercollegiate and interscholastic sports are not unique—the same concerns can affect any business.

Revenues and expenses are often very similar for almost all industries. For example, all businesses, nonprofit organizations, and government entities have salary expenses and need to pay rent in some manner. The following lists the typical revenues and expenses of a health club (or possibly West Hartford Badminton Club).

Revenues	Expenses
Membership fees	Employee salaries and benefits
Health food sales	Rent
Equipment sales	Equipment (purchases and leases)
Interest from investments	Insurance
	Advertising
	Professionals (accounting, legal)
	Maintenance and repair expenses
	Utility expenses
	General expenses

In professional or collegiate sports, revenues are primarily derived from ticket sales, broadcasting rights, or both, while the primary expenses are salaries and benefits (Howard & Crompton, 2004). Regardless of the team or league, every sports organization has the same basic revenue streams from the sale of goods or services and the same basic expenses of salaries, rent or mortgage, maintenance, advertising, raw goods, and various supplies. Any of these numbers can be large and may appear impressive. However, after critically examining such numbers, anyone trained in financial analysis can see that many businesses with substantial revenue streams are not profitable. Many professional sports teams earn significant revenue from attendance and broadcast rights but fail to cover their fixed operating costs (Howard & Crompton, 2004). No business can survive a constant monetary wound that keeps bleeding. That is why so many Canadian hockey teams have packed their bags or are considering packing their bags to move to greener pastures in the United States

(Harper, 1999). By the 1996-1997 National Hockey League (NHL) season, only six clubs remained in Canada after teams left Winnipeg and Quebec City for the United States (Kowall, 2001). Teams were leaving Canada because of such economic hardships as high taxes (expenses), payment of players in American dollars (expenses), and the lower value of the Canadian dollar (revenues) (Harper, 1999).

In order to have revenue, a team needs to play. With the NHL lockout in 2004-2005, teams were not able to generate revenue from games but could generate revenue from licensed goods. To reduce expenses, many NHL teams laid off most of their staffs, but this does not change other fixed expenses such as interest on loans or accountant and attorney fees.

Professional sport has changed drastically since the 1930s (see the sidebar on p. 22). Contractually obligated revenues such as broadcasting contracts and luxury box revenue have made the prospects for significant one-day losses highly unlikely. However, sport has a way of producing strange results,

© Getty Images for NASCAR

Revenues (money coming in) and expenses (money going out) are fundamental to sport organizations and businesses. What revenues and expenses can you identify here?

A Costly Rain Delay

An example of a team's revenue and expenses gives an idea of the potential monetary gains and losses that may be present in professional sport.

Although it does not appear that the team's economic condition is all that bad, the revenue, expenses, and pretax profits can swing sharply at any given moment. In fact, the numbers shown are not hypothetical; rather, they are the actual revenue and expense numbers for a professional team in 1935. The numbers appeared in an article by a professional team owner who was highlighting the potential perils associated with a team's bottom line. The writer also recounted how in 1934 another team, the New York Giants, had been within a game of first place and had been scheduled to play a doubleheader against the Philadelphia Phillies. A capacity crowd of 50,000 was expected for the games. But a drizzle began to fall, resulting in postponement. When the games were later replayed, the Giants were already out of the pennant picture, and a crowd of only 2,000 attended the doubleheader. Because of the rain delay, the Giants lost more than $55,000 (Lewis, 1936).

Professional Baseball Team X Income Statement

Revenues ($)	
Baseball attendance revenue	650,000
Revenue from facility rental	60,000
Revenue from concessions	35,000
Total revenue	**$745,000**
Expenses ($)	
Players' salaries (35 players)	235,000
Price for new players	90,000
Transportation bills	15,000
Hotel bills	15,000
Rental expenses and salaries	85,000
Maintenance costs	20,000
Spring training costs	25,000
Players' supplies	11,000
Insurance costs	12,000
Salaries and expenses for 3 scouts	20,000
Expenses for 12 newspapermen	38,400
Sundries	11,600
Total expenses	**$578,000**
Profit before taxes	**$167,000**

Data from J. Lewis, 1936, "Basehits, incorporated," *Liberty*: 48-49.

and rain delays, freak injuries, and unexpected economic conditions can all affect a team's bottom line. The following paragraph appeared in the same 1936 article we saw in the sidebar:

> *Last year the New York Yankees sent Ruth to the Boston Braves. It was soon apparent that they had made a big mistake, for their attendance fell off even though the team was leading the league. Ruth, despite the fact that he had slowed to a walk, was still a terrific drawing card in New York. When the Braves made their first 1935 appearance in Tammany Town, 42,000 fans turned out to cheer him. Ruth, with the Braves for less than half the season, made enough money for them in that short space of time to allow them to break even on the season despite the fact that they finished in last place. (Lewis, 1936)*

The Babe Ruth case is not an isolated example of a financial blunder involving trading or releasing an athlete. In any given year, a player might be a low-level performer for one team but blossom for another. Conversely, a player can be a star one day

and "washed up" the next. Thus, the business of managing sports teams, organizations, or facilities is fraught with potential profit centers or with traps that can lead to financial ruin. The convergence of numerous variables that can increase or decrease revenue in a moment makes sport management traditionally more complex than financing in other business sectors. However, by analyzing a company's financial objectives, sport finance students can often determine that a short-term loss might be beneficial for generating larger profits in the long run. Financial objectives are often found in financial **disclosure** documents required by federal regulators. For example, Nike's financial objectives are included in its **Form 10-K** annual report. The company's annual 10-K and quarterly **Form 10-Q** reports are filed with the Securities and Exchange Commission (SEC) as required by law. The reports can be accessed from numerous financial Web sites, including the SEC's own Web site at www.sec.gov.

By seeing how revenues and expenses change over time, students can learn much about an industry. For example, in the 1930s, professional sport was not as popular as it is today, and the teams had to promote themselves constantly. That is why the team income statement highlighted in the previous sidebar shows $38,400 to pay the travel expenses of 12 newspaper reporters. Since the team was paying the way for the reporters, they were less likely to write negative stories. The resulting positive publicity was designed to help sell more tickets. Teams no longer have to pay reporters to travel to cover them. However, teams still need to include a line item in their budgets to pay for food that is given to reporters in the pressroom.

BUDGETS

Revenues and expenses are included in various types of **financial statements**, such as budgets, income statements, and balance sheets. A **budget** is a road map that shows where the sport business intends to spend its money. All members of the business can use the budget to help make decisions. If the budget allocates a certain amount of money for marketing and the marketing department reaches that limit halfway through the year, then it may be difficult for the department to receive additional funds for the rest of the year. The only way this is likely to happen is if sales are exceeding the sales forecast or if another area in the budget, such as customer service, is reduced to free money for the marketing department.

Budgets, as will be discussed in chapter 7, are often developed by examining existing business successes or failures. These business stories are found in income statements and balance sheets. An income statement highlights a company's **income** and expenses over the past year. A balance sheet shows the worth of a company at a specific time. These are just two of the types of financial statements discussed in greater detail in chapter 5. Investors, stakeholders, analysts, and government officials are the primary readers of most financial statements. The two examples in the sidebar on pages 24-25 illustrate the stories that can unfold when one critically analyzes income statements, as well as show how budgets influence sport businesses. By examining past income statements, a business can help plan for its future budget and also determine whether or not its prior budget was accurate.

PROPER DOCUMENTATION

Finance affects all business decisions, from acquiring funds to allocating various resources and tracking performance (Spiro, 1996). The documentation of these funds and their **expenditures** and returns forms the basis for stockholders' decisions concerning a company. However, although record keeping is stressed throughout this text as an integral component of financial success, record keeping should not be seen as an end in itself. It is simply a tool. If too much emphasis is placed on just developing the right documents, managers will not be able to see the forest for the trees and may make decisions that look great on paper but become major disasters. Nevertheless, the documentation process is critical and is highlighted throughout this text. At the same time, documentation is only one of the many functions required by law or contract for obtaining necessary funds. That is why analyzing revenues and expenses is so critical. Finance necessitates analyzing the financial feasibility of various projects based on the projected revenues to be gained, the expenses that will be incurred, and the availability of moneys to fund the project through to completion. When potential income from a project is properly documented, a potential investor is more inclined to back that project.

The ability to make appropriate financial decisions is predicated on proper documentation. The Atlantic Olympic Organizing Committee had to pay an accounting firm to develop an audited financial statement that could be shown to the government and other stakeholders. When a sport business finds itself in a financial plight, the only way it can analyze the situation accurately is through proper documentation. Did someone fudge the sales numbers? Is someone embezzling money? Is the company carrying too much inventory? Are the costs of employee benefits out of control? Is extra cash just lying around in unknown accounts? Proper documentation enables you to find the answers to these types of questions. Thus, when examining a balance sheet or income statement, people need to ask themselves if they can trust the numbers. If the financial statements are not audited or otherwise certified by an independent party as accurate, the reader should be cautious.

DETERMINING FINANCIAL OBJECTIVES

For many managers, making the highest profit possible is a financial objective. However, profit is not the only criterion for financial success. Most managers of corporations are interested in one primary overall objective—keeping stockholders happy. If a manager is interested in keeping stockholders happy, then she should focus more on earnings per share than on total corporate profits (Brigham & Gapenski, 1994). A company that earned $10 million and had over 100 million outstanding shares would generate earnings of $0.10 per share. In contrast, a company that earned only $1 million with only 100,000 outstanding shares would generate earnings of $10 per share. The shareholders of the second company would have higher earnings per share and would probably feel they had a better investment. This assumes that the criterion for analysis used by the shareholders was earnings per share rather than stock price appreciation or total earnings.

Earnings can also be reflected in increased stock value. Especially for stocks that do not pay dividends, the increase in share value will be the hallmark for determining financial success. Thus, if two companies (company A and company B) have earnings of $50 million each, the hallmark of yearly success could be the companies' stock values. If company A's stock rose $2 per share from $28 to $30 and company B's shares rose $1 from $4 to $5 per share, most analysts would consider company B more successful. Since the earnings were identi-

cal, the focus turns to increased stock value, and company A's 7.125% increase in stock value pales in comparison with company B's 25% rise.

Earnings per share is just one of the factors that influence the health of a corporation. A corporation is a business entity that is incorporated under state law and is entitled to issue ownership interests in the form of stock certificates (see chapter 4 for a thorough analysis of business structures). Individuals interested in investing in stocks, also called **shares** in a corporation, are interested in determining if their investment will generate a return, such as **dividend** payments or an increased stock price. Besides whether or not the stock will pay a dividend, a potential investor might want to know the following:

- How often the dividends are paid
- How risky future earnings might be
- How much debt the company carries
- What the corporate policies are (e.g., whether they are going to try to purchase a competitor or what dividend rate they pay)

Two Budgets

Similar to other major universities, the U of M has its own nonprofit [501(c)(3)] foundation in charge of raising money through hosting various events and fund-raising drives. The U of M Athletic Foundation reported $7.1 million in income and expenses in its 2005 annual report. The table below shows how the numbers broke down in amounts and percentage of total funds for various categories.

Among the stories these numbers tell are the following:

- More than 50% of all moneys raised helped pay for program services.
- Investment income will increase on an annual basis if the U of M Athletic Foundation continues increasing its net assets, because the primary assets are investment securities that will generate future income.
- Only 6.6% of expenses were dedicated to managerial tasks, while 26.5% of expenses helped raise operating funds.
- Although direct mail and telemarketing costs were $634,965, this investment was very successful in helping to raise almost $2 million.
- The greatest revenue source came from fund-raising efforts and donations by individuals to the annual campaign.

2005 U of M Athletic Foundation Income Statement

Income ($)	
Fund-raising and annual campaign (45.4%)	3,220,266
Direct mail and telemarketing (27.2%)	1,936,589
Investment income (11.8%)	838,773
Program services (5.6%)	395,540
Game sponsors (5.2%)	366,930
Foundations and grants (3.0%)	215,007
Souvenir sales (1.8%)	126,895
Total income	**$7,100,000**
Expenses ($)	
Program services (52.8%)	3,742,385
Revenue development (17.6%)	1,252,106
Net asset increase (14.1%)	1,001,196
Direct mail and telemarketing (8.9%)	634,965
Management and general (6.6%)	469,348
Total expenses	**$7,100,000**

Data from "Texas Special Olympics," 1996.

The income statement from the 1996 Olympic Games in Atlanta (table at right) tells a completely different story. The sheer magnitude of million-dollar budgets presents a sharp contrast to relatively small budgets like the fictitious U of M Athletic Foundation budget. Most sport-related budgets are for midsized companies and range from $2 million to $8 million.

These Olympic numbers indicate that revenue is derived primarily from broadcasting rights, ticket sales, and national sponsorship programs. Construction and venue operating expenses dominate the Atlanta Olympic Organizing Committee's (AOOC) expenses. However, the human resource expenses are fairly large and compose a significantly higher percentage than the human resource expenses generated by the U of M Athletic Foundation. The budget also highlights that although the AOOC earns interest income from excess cash reserves invested in various interest-earning **accounts**, it also has to pay interest on various loans. The interest earned ($19.4 million) and the interest paid ($19 million) are almost equal, but the strategy did generate an additional $400,000 in revenue. Any budget utilizing such large numbers would be impossible to follow without proper documentation to track all the funds.

1996 Atlanta Olympic Organizing Committee's Income Statement

Revenue and support ($ Millions)	
Broadcast rights	568.3
Ticket sales	427.2
Joint marketing: USOC	426.7
Top III sponsorship	81.1
Rate card rentals	63.2
Merchandising margin	34.6
Interest	19.4
Local sponsors	14.8
Housing	14.2
Ticket fees	12.6
Contributions	10.2
License plate sales	9.5
Parking and transportation	9.3
Disposal of assets	8.0
Other	30.0
Total revenue	**$1,729.14**
Less royalties	6.4
Net revenue	**$1,727.0**
Expenses ($ Millions)	
Salaries and wages	315.7
Benefits	21.1
Professional services	209.7
Construction and venues	541.2
Contracted services	94.5
Rent and occupancy	147.2
Equipment	197.1
Materials and supplies	68.5
Insurance	25.2
Conference, travel, hospitality	55.0
Interest and other financing	19.0
Other	10.3
Reserve: liabilities	10.3
Reserve: operations	7.9
Total expenses	**$1,723.0**

Data from R. Glier, "With expectations unfulfilled, Atlantans still searching for legacy from games" (*Houston Chronicle*, July 20, 1997, p. 18B).

All these questions become critical for financial analysis because corporate policies concerning stocks and bonds help dictate stockholder and analyst interest in the stock.

Stars of David

The Stars of David feel a deep amount of gratitude to the city's citizens for supporting the team over the years. The Stars are looking into building a new practice facility and are considering several funding options. The team can borrow money from various institutions, from bond lenders to banks, or can use their own dividends (profits that are normally distributed to shareholders). Each option has benefits and detriments. What should the team do? The following paragraph illustrates some of the issues that can influence the team's financial objectives and decisions.

If the Stars need to build a new practice facility, they could possibly lower their dividend rate to current stockholders and retain the extra funds to help finance the new building. However, if the Stars do not want to

© Getty Images

Proper documentation is crucial to one's ability to analyze and evaluate performance. A sport business can't make sound financial decisions if it can't trust the numbers.

upset the investors, they might attempt to borrow the funds instead. But increasing the team's total debt could also have negative ramifications, such as lowering their creditworthiness. Because both positive benefits and negative repercussions are associated with each decision, the Stars would have to thoroughly analyze each potential financing option before deciding which one to pursue. Furthermore, stock analysts critically examine any decision a major corporation makes. If the Stars make a decision that the analysts think is wrong, the analysts could send the stock into a nosedive by publishing a negative opinion.

The Stars example demonstrates the numerous concerns an entity faces when financing any business decision. Furthermore, it demonstrates that business decisions must be made in light of the fact that numerous external individuals and entities will critically analyze those decisions. The organization needs to examine all these variables when determining the financial objectives. Are the Stars going to build the practice facility to increase revenue? Will any increased revenue benefit the individual

stockholders? Is the facility being built to appease creditors or analysts?

Chapter 7 looks at the planning process in greater detail. However, it is worth mentioning here that whether one is examining a stadium construction project or a team's revenue stream, any analysis is futile if it does not address where the team stood financially last year, what it projects this year, what its financial goals are, and how success or failure will be measured. Critically analyzing financial objectives can hold the key to business success or failure. But it is also impossible to analyze any financial decision without understanding the underlying objectives. Just as a corporate executive might sponsor a golf tournament because of love of the game rather than business sense, financial decisions can also be made on grounds other than business sense. Unless one knows the true underlying objective for any financial decision, it becomes a matter of guesswork to determine what a team or business is trying to accomplish. Chapter 7 covers long-term planning and the tools needed to help develop more informed financial objectives.

OVERVIEW OF ACCOUNTING CONCEPTS

Finance and financial management cannot be understood without knowing basic accounting concepts. Accounting is the art of processing the revenue and expense numbers to develop appropriate reporting procedures upon which financial decisions are made. Accounting issues we touch on in this chapter are basic T-accounts, how cash is received and processed within a business, and methods by which businesses make sure the numbers managers rely on are correct. It is impossible to understand a balance sheet or income statement without knowing how the numbers were obtained. This section presents some of the basic accounting concepts you will need to know once you start analyzing comprehensive financial records.

Accounting requires the identification, measurement, recording, and communication of financial information associated with various critical events. A high school might be required to engage in statistical accounting to track students or supplies and might have to engage in financial accounting to track revenues and expenses (Horine, 1999). This text overviews financial accounting and the methods a sport business manager might use to track revenues coming into the business and expenses flowing out of the business. Although keeping track of the number of towels used at a health club might seem a simple task, financial accounting can be very difficult and complex, as the following case study example shows.

Suppose the Smiths' fitness center has 2,000 members who pay at different times during the month, or possibly not at all. Some members may have the funds electronically removed from their bank accounts. Others may pay with their credit cards, in which case the health club has to process and track all the credit card transactions and then pay the credit card companies a small percentage of the amount charged. Other members may pay with cash or checks, or pay late and need to pay a late fee, or demand a refund.

With all the cash, checks, and credit card transactions, money can be quickly lost or stolen. To avoid such a problem, the owners can develop policies and procedures to monitor revenues and minimize losses. The Smiths could develop a policy that one person receives the payments, another needs to enter the material into the accounting software system, and a third person deposits the payments at the bank. With three people handling the revenue, it is harder for one to steal money without the others finding out. However, such a system increases overhead since more employees are involved in the process. The flip side is that hopefully the cost will be offset by the benefit of avoiding significant employee theft. Bob and Cheryl could also hire an accountant to review all the financial records at the end of the year to verify their accuracy.

On top of all the issues the Smiths need to consider in the preceding case study example, accountants must track all the money that is owed to countless vendors, employees, or even the government. All in all, financial accounting is a complex art and science that tracks revenues and expenses from numerous areas to provide an accurate record of a business' financial position.

The objective of accounting for any organization is to provide information for the following purposes (Freeman, Shoulders, & Lynn, 1988, p. 6):

- Making decisions about the use of limited resources, including the identification of crucial decision areas and determination of objectives and goals
- Effectively directing and controlling an organization's human and material resources
- Maintaining and reporting on the custodianship of resources
- Contributing to the overall effectiveness of the organization

Finance emphasizes recording, monitoring, and controlling the financial consequences of various activities and analyzing the need for additional funds to meet current and future demands (Spiro, 1996). These tasks cannot be completed without economic analysis and the data system that has been developed through accounting. Accounting is often performed by a **controller** who is responsible for documenting what happened, not what should have happened. Thus, the focus is on accuracy as dictated by industry-defined rules. **Managerial accounting** is the process utilized to develop financial forecasts and monitor various budgets and costing models (Spiro, 1996). The output produced by the controller provides the opportunity for a company to open the lines of communication among different divisions or echelons to help achieve the company's goals and objectives. Through managerial accounting, the controller can produce data designed to facilitate internal success, but the same data can be utilized for external needs, such as shareholder relations.

In contrast to the responsibilities of a controller and the managerial accounting process, a **treasurer** has distinct responsibilities that focus mostly on external factors. Thus, while the controller manages internal financial and accounting-based concerns, the treasurer deals with banks, stockholders, institutional investors, bondholders, and other stakeholders or potential stakeholders. The information developed through the accounting process assists the treasurer in obtaining additional funds to help achieve business goals and objectives.

The accounting objectives just identified are highlighted in detail by Larry Horine of Appalachian State University in his book *Administration of Physical Education and Sport Programs*. Horine (1999) highlights 12 important objectives for a sports organization's accounting system:

1. The data should be collected to help plan for the program's future.

2. The financial records must be kept in an orderly manner.

3. An orderly and professional accounting method must be implemented to track authorized expenditures.

4. Appropriate forms must be prepared to help standardize and create a definite paper trail for receipts and expenditures.

5. A system or process needs to be developed and implemented to coordinate the receipt of goods and services and to ensure that all such goods and services meet required standards before any final payments on the goods or services are made.

6. Transactions need to be documented in such a way that an independent auditor can examine the transactions and determine to whom money was paid and for what purpose.

7. Revenue must be tracked to determine if fiscal obligations can be paid. Tracking should determine what funds were obtained, from whom, and for what purpose.

8. Special funds need to be accounted for in a separate accounting manner to track such items as planned giving and major gifts, which are nontraditional revenue sources.

9. All information documented through the accounting process needs to be prepared in such a way that an external reviewer can adequately audit all accounts.

10. Any accounting system must be adequate to meet the organization's needs, with special consideration for size and complexity.

11. Any accounting system must meet all state, federal, regional, and association standards and guidelines.

12. Any accounting system must provide the opportunity to critically analyze management decisions and produce appropriate reports to evaluate past managerial decisions and pave the way for future decisions.

When we are analyzing accounting issues, it is imperative to understand the difference between the concepts of stock and flow. **Stock** refers to wealth, in a variety of forms such as cash, assets, real estate, and accounts receivable, that is available at any specific point in time. In contrast, **flow** refers to expenditures or receipts between two specific points in time. These two concepts are associated with two of the most important types of documents produced through the accounting process. Stock is shown on a balance sheet that documents the value of a company at a specific time. An income statement, on the other hand, portrays the flow that has been occurring in a company throughout a specified business year. Every company needs to utilize both the stock and flow concepts to analyze its financial position.

To track revenues and expenses between balance sheet dates, accountants utilize their own unique systems. Accountants have developed the **T-system** to document monetary transactions. This text includes a brief discussion of T-accounts; students who take a course in accounting can spend several weeks on this topic. The discussion here is intended to overview the process through which the final total numbers used in financial statements are determined. For additional information on T-accounts, please refer to a basic accounting textbook.

Accountants refer to entries made on the right side of the "T" as **credits** and to entries on the left side of the "T" as **debits** (see figure 2.1a). Whereas people who are not accountants might interpret the terms *debit* and *credit* to mean specific activities, such as paying a bill or buying on credit, for the purpose of accounting these terms just refer to sides of the "T" where various transactions are recorded (Spiro, 1996). A company's balance sheet may provide the best example of the application of the T-system (see figure 2.1b). Corporate assets are listed on the left side (debits), and liabilities and **owners' equity** are listed on the right side (credits). In conventional usage of the terms, something that is owned by the business would be thought of as a credit to the bottom line, not a debit or reduction in the company's value. But in the T-system, when assets are added to the company's bottom line, the process is referred to as debiting that asset. Similarly, if liabilities are increased, then the specific liability account is credited. The confusion associated with accounting terms can be easily set aside if the terms are not the focal point of analysis; rather, the reader should just know that certain entries are placed on the right and others on the left side of the "T."

T-account		Balance sheet	
Debits	Credits	Assets	Liabilities
			Owners' equity
a		b	

Figure 2.1   (a) A T-account and (b) the T-system applied to a company's balance sheet.

Although the terminology might be confusing, the process is important and is universally utilized to properly document financial transactions.

Assume that Bob and Cheryl Smith have two customers who owe money on their monthly dues. The T-accounts for customer A and customer B would show the monthly $100 fee added to accounts receivable for the business (see figure 2.2).

Customer A		Customer B	
$100		$100	

Figure 2.2   T-accounts for two of the Smiths' customers who owe money on their monthly dues.

If these customers are the only two individuals who owe money, then the Smiths would have $200 debited to their accounts receivable account. Assume that the Smiths also have $10,000 in their cash account. Figure 2.3 shows how these two accounts would look.

Accounts receivable		Cash	
$200		$10,000	

Figure 2.3   T-accounts showing the Smiths' accounts receivable and cash accounts.

If customer B pays $50 toward his overdue **balance**, the following changes would need to be made to the T-accounts (see figure 2.4). Customer B's prior obligation of $100 has been reduced by the $50; the Smiths are now owed only $150 through accounts receivable and have gained $50 for their cash account.

Customer B		Accounts receivable		Cash	
$100	$50	$200	$50	$10,000	
				50	

When these entries are synthesized, they will appear as follows:

Customer B		Accounts receivable		Cash	
$50		$150		$10,050	

Figure 2.4   T-accounts reflecting customer B's $50 payment.

Because multiple accounts are being changed, the process is often referred to as **double-entry bookkeeping**. Use of this technique, along with other accounting practices, must comply with generally accepted accounting practices in order to be accepted by the greatest number of potential readers, such as government officials, shareholders, and financial analysts. If troublesome questions arise regarding the documentation of more complex transactions, an accountant might refer to guidelines called **generally accepted accounting principles (GAAP)**, as interpreted by the Financial Accounting Standards Board (FASB) and the American Institute of Certified Public Accountants. FASB is mostly relevant to public companies.

CASH VERSUS ACCRUAL BASIS

It is beyond the scope of this text to analyze many accounting-related issues, but a key topic that requires discussion here is the method for reporting income. Although most business owners charged with keeping their own business records would record a cash receipt the day it is received and would record a payment the day the bill is paid, this technique might not be correct. According to GAAP, revenues and expenses can be recorded either on a cash basis or on an **accrual** basis. The accrual basis is the preferred technique, but the cash method is allowed by GAAP under specific limited circumstances, such as when a business conducts all transactions with cash. In **cash basis**

budgeting, income and expenses are recorded when cash is received or paid; sales made on credit or bills that are owed are not recorded until they are actually paid. This process is also referred to as the **cash system of accounting**. The accrual method recognizes revenues when they are earned and recognizes expenses when they are incurred. In other words, accrual-based reporting does not consider when money is received or paid, only when the act occurred that resulted in the revenue or expense. Normally GAAP requires the use of accrual accounting regardless of the size of the business. Only in rare circumstances when all transactions are in cash will the GAAP allow a company to use the cash system of accounting. Thus, the Smiths would have to record income when lessons are given or memberships are due regardless of whether or not the customer has paid.

ART OF ACCOUNTING

Many refer to accounting as an art rather than a science (Griffin, 1991). Although financial analysis cannot exist unless accounting systems have developed the appropriate numbers for analyzing past performance, there is never any guarantee that the numbers relied on are actually correct. Accounting produces financial statements consisting of numbers. However, the numbers refer only to those components of a business that are quantifiable.

 The Stars' balance sheet might show an income decrease, but that number would not explain why the decrease occurred. If the decrease occurred because another team was having a banner season, then nothing internal to the Stars resulted in the decreased revenue. The financial statements would not indicate the objective reason for the decline but only present the quantifiable results. That is why one needs to analyze the financial objectives for the business in order to learn the entire story that the numbers might not disclose.

Accounting systems also utilize professional judgments and estimates when absolute objective evidence does not exist (Griffin, 1991). Although such judgments are typically very accurate, anyone reading financial statements has to assume there is some risk that the information includes inaccuracies. There is never a sure bet in finance, and the best you can hope for from financial statements is a very accurate portrait of a business based on data analyzed by an accountant—a human being who can also make errors.

AUDITED FINANCIAL STATEMENTS

Accountants can make errors; an auditor is often the last individual who can possibly discover any discrepancies. This concern was highlighted in the multiple accounting scandals at companies such as Enron, WorldCom, Tyco, and Adelphia. The ease with which companies, executives, and accountants could manipulate company records encouraged Congress to pass the Sarbanes-Oxley Act of 2002, forcing executives of publicly traded companies to certify that all their financial data were accurate or else they could face significant fines and even incarceration. Executives still need accountants to audit the numbers to make sure they are accurate. Most companies attempt to obtain an independent audit of the work performed by their accountants. Such an audit is often undertaken even if an external accounting firm was used to prepare the initial financial statements. An auditor utilizes the Statements on Auditing Standards issued by the Auditing Standards Board of the American Institute of Certified Public Accountants. These standards were developed to help ensure that audits are conducted in a systematic manner. After thoroughly analyzing all the financial statements, the auditor prepares a report that includes the following statements (Griffin, 1991):

- The auditor is independent from the company's management.
- The financial statements were audited.
- The financial statements are management's responsibility, and the auditor's role is to express an opinion on the financial statements.

Once the audit is completed, the auditor prepares an opinion that addresses the fairness of the financial statements, the degree to which the financial statements comply with GAAP guidelines, and any noticeable changes in accounting principles from industry norms (Griffin, 1991). The final opinion reached by the auditor can be

- an unqualified opinion that the statements are accurate,
- a qualified opinion,

- an adverse opinion indicating that the statements do not conform with required principles, or

- a **disclaimer** indicating that the auditor was unable to complete the report because the company failed to provide certain data.

A typical unqualified opinion might include a statement such as the following: "In our opinion, the financial statements above present fairly, in all material respects, the financial position of the Stars of David as of June 31, 2005, and the results of its operations and its cash flows for the year then ended in conformity with generally accepted accounting principles." Auditing is covered in greater detail in chapter 16.

The accounting system objectives discussed in this section relate to what has already happened. Accounting statements are reviewed to determine what occurred during the designated time period. However, accounting does not indicate what should occur in the future. Budgeting is the process that can indicate what steps should be taken in the future. The budget sets the company's road map for the future and is based on the company's goals and objectives. Budgeting, which is covered in chapter 7, is the first step in the financial process after the accountants analyze past performance.

CONCLUSION

This chapter provides an initial glimpse into sport accounting and finance. Sport finance is a numbers game. Numerous revenues and expenses constitute the game pieces. Profits and losses are highlighted in the game's final outcome. Through adherence to basic accounting protocol, the finance game is played with a host of additional rules such as tax considerations and stock regulations that affect a sport entity's movements in the game. By understanding all the necessary moves and the various strategies available to the contestants, a sports organization can win the game.

Although this game metaphor may appear contrived, it represents a reality in sport finance. Sport finance is as much a game as the games played on athletic fields or courts. Sport finance professionals need to play a heads-up game to take advantage of various laws, economic conditions, or other variables to maximize their value. Through intelligent financial manipulations, a skilled player can turn a loss into a profit. As Paul Beeston, former president of the Toronto Blue Jays, said, "Under generally accepted accounting principles, I can turn a $4 million profit into a $2 million loss, and I can get every national accounting firm to agree with me" (Howard & Crompton, 2004, p. 12). This text does not analyze the ethical issues associated with such conduct, but it raises the red flag so you will understand that financial data can be manipulated. Thus, care should be exercised in reviewing all financial statements, and whenever a question arises you have the ultimate responsibility to ask questions and not just assume that others have done the analysis work for you.

The free enterprise system centers on finance. Any business dealings need to entail significant financial analysis. Finance involves three primary areas of analysis: money and the capital markets, investments, and financial management (Brigham & Ehrhardt, 2005). These three skills are critical for anyone interested in working in the sport industry and, more specifically, for anyone responsible for fiscal oversight in a sport-related program. An individual charged with financial-related duties will need to assume the following responsibilities (Brigham & Ehrhardt, 2005):

- Forecasting and planning to help lay the foundation for future success

- Investing in major assets such as plants and equipment

- Coordinating other employees and managers to ensure that individuals are working in the most effective manner

- Managing the business' interaction with financial markets (e.g., determining how much money to raise and in what manner)

This text provides a general overview, but it cannot fully prepare any student to assume complete responsibilities in managing a finance department or performing a similar job. Financial managers need to obtain more specific knowledge in areas such as which assets a firm should purchase and why, how to finance those assets, how to forecast future revenue streams, and how to effectively manage existing resources. Although the skills discussed in this chapter are important, financial managers are judged primarily on whether or not they have been successful in maximizing a corporation's stock value. Accomplishing increased stock valuation is an immense task that requires every unit within the business to operate together (Brigham & Ehrhardt, 2005).

CLASS DISCUSSION TOPICS

1. What is the difference between accounting and finance?

2. Why is accounting important for financial analysis?

3. What is the value of budgeting?

4. Analyze the revenue and expense projections for the University of Milford Athletic Foundation (see p. 24), and try to determine some of its potential financial objectives.

5. Compare the team expenses for a baseball team in the 1930s versus today, and identify the greatest differences.

6. What key items need to be documented in order for a business to accurately analyze its financial performance?

7. Develop a list of revenue and expense streams for a professional baseball team.

8. Develop a list of revenue and expense streams for a nonprofit health club.

9. Develop a list of revenue and expense streams for a publicly traded sportswear company.

10. Develop a list of revenue and expense streams for a NASCAR racing team.

3

FINANCIAL SYSTEMS AND HOW THEY OPERATE

CHAPTER OBJECTIVES

After studying this chapter, you should be able to do the following:

- Describe what a financial market is.
- Compare the different types of financial markets and how they affect sport.
- Understand the differences among marketable securities such as stocks and bonds.
- Explain how sport businesses can acquire needed capital through institutions such as banks and savings and loans.
- Comprehend government's role in influencing financial systems and sport industries.
- Understand the forces that propel the stock market and the various publicly traded sport-related stocks.

This chapter deals with the key elements in various financial systems and institutions and how they interact to help sport businesses. The primary focus is on what constitutes value and how value can be exchanged to help facilitate business transactions. Financial systems are affected by financial markets, financial institutions, government influences, and environmental factors. Financial **markets**, such as stock markets, are the arenas in which value is transferred. Financial institutions, such as banks, are entities that help transfer value. **Interest rates** are controlled by a combination of economic factors and government regulations. Two final sections of this chapter address government's greater role in regulating businesses, through such strategies as taxes, and the effect of environmental conditions on a sport investment.

Financial systems are mechanisms that allow anything of value to be exchanged between different parties. Financial systems are involved when individuals receive their paychecks from an employer. The employer draws the check from a bank, credit union, savings and loan, or other type of financial holding entity. The money that is drawn might have been received from the employer's customers or from other sources such as borrowed funds or extra cash in the employer's accounts. If the bank does not have enough cash to cover the check, the bank may need to borrow money from the Federal Reserve System. The paycheck will have some taxes withdrawn, reflecting participation by various government units in the financial exchange. Various financial institutions are also utilized when the employee deposits the check and starts paying bills, such as credit card bills and the **mortgage** on a home loan.

This is an oversimplified example of some financial systems and institutions at work. The financial systems work in a cyclical manner, with the same types of transactions occurring on a regular basis. Businesses face the same cyclical patterns in their financial dealings. Each month new orders are received, meaning new funds. However, some debts are paid immediately, while others might not be paid for several months. Money will be trickling in from accounts receivable while the business attempts to pay its own **obligations**, which are **accounts payable**. If there is not enough money to pay outstanding debts, the business may need to turn to financial institutions such as banks, the bond market, the **stock market (stock exchange)**, or possibly venture capitalists to obtain money.

FINANCIAL MARKETS

Businesses and individuals needing funds are brought together in financial markets. Funds can be obtained from numerous financial markets, and every business will have several markets from which to choose. The following are the primary types of markets (Brigham & Ehrhardt, 2005):

- Tangible or physical markets involve items of value such as products or property. Examples of items in these markets are golf clubs, tennis rackets, golf courses, race cars, and manufacturing machinery.

- **Financial asset** markets involve evidence of value or ownership such as stocks, bonds, loans, and mortgages.

- Spot markets involve assets that are bought, sold, and delivered within several days. Precious metals are an example of such assets.

- Futures markets involve assets that are bought, sold, and delivered at a later date, which could be six months or several years later. A sport drink company might buy ingredients for its drinks, such as sugar or salt, on the futures market if the company anticipates that certain ingredients might increase in cost and wants to lock in a lower price.

- Money markets are for **debt securities**, such as loans with a very low risk of default, that mature in a shorter time period—usually less than one year.

- In **capital markets**, long-term debt (e.g., bonds) or ownership rights (e.g., stocks) are traded.

- In the mortgage market, residential loans or business loans backed by real estate are traded.

- International markets allow individuals in one country to tap financial resources in another country. As an example, Canadian professional teams that have to pay players in U.S. dollars may wish to exchange currency on the international market to obtain good exchange rates.

- **Primary markets** are markets in which businesses raise new capital by offering securities for sale. A primary market exists for a particular security only the first time the security is issued and sold.

- Secondary markets exist after a security has been sold in the primary market. Thus, the first time the Boston Celtics issued their stock, it was offered in the primary market. After the initial issues were sold, someone who wanted to buy shares from other owners could acquire the shares only in the secondary market.

This listing indicates the numerous arenas in which businesses can obtain or sell assets. Businesses are not required to use only one market exclusively. There are numerous overlaps in the various financial markets because some financial assets are also capital assets and are part of both markets. Businesses can use several markets, and most businesses utilize several markets concurrently. Furthermore, most businesses utilize several different markets when raising capital.

 The West Hartford Badminton Club accepts cash payments and checks to pay for dues, equipment, tournaments, and daily play. The money is deposited into the company bank account, and from this same account WHBC writes all the checks to pay for the facility, equipment, and tournament. In contrast, a large corporation such as SMC might have multiple bank accounts throughout the world to speed up the collection process from buyers. SMC might also have multiple accounts for automatically writing payroll checks, as well as investment accounts containing cash and other accounts for stocks and bonds. The key is that the financial market allows for significant customization so that any business can create the investment and borrowing climate most ideal for the company's needs.

A sport business could raise money on the capital market, or possibly from foreign markets. The mar-kets listed earlier are primarily based in the United States; however, a business can also raise money from markets anywhere in the world, such as the London Stock Exchange or the European currency market. A financial manager's job could include con-stantly tracking these markets to minimize borrowing expenses or to raise additional funds. No matter what market is utilized, the key to funding business growth and facilitating movement within all financial markets is money.

MONEY

Money is the means by which commerce can occur. A bill or coin has no value in and of itself without agreement on the part of the government and people that it has value. We are accustomed to taking a dollar out of our wallets and buying a candy bar. We prob-ably do not think twice about such a transaction. But the situation is different if we are buying something for $1 million. No one would expect us to bring in $1 million in small bills. Over time, the growth of com-merce necessitated the creation of instruments that functioned similarly to money but were easier to use for conducting business. Checks are an everyday example. Although money is the backbone of most financial transactions, numerous individuals and busi-nesses are starting to use alternative payment options, such as automatic withdrawals and bill payments through electronic funds transfers (EFTs).

Money, credit, and checks are not the only instru-ments of commerce. Wealth can be transferred and

History of Financial Institutions

Date	Activity
600 BC	Lydia, a Greek state in Asia Minor, uses coins for the first time.
600-200 BC	The Athenian drachma and Roman denarius are first used.
54 AD	Roman emperor Nero is the first official to start reducing the amount of gold and silver in coins.
1409	The first stock exchange is established in Brussels.
1587	One of the first public banks is established in Venice, Italy.
1661	The first paper money is printed by the Swedish National Bank.
1816	England introduces gold as an official currency.
1918	The international gold standard ends.
1925	England returns to the gold standard.
1929	All major international currencies are once again linked to gold, and that link continues until the Great Depression ends gold's influence.
1945	After World War II, the world's monetary systems start operating on a standard linked to the U.S. dollar.
1978	The European monetary system is introduced.
1999	Euro coinage is phased in for all nations in the European Union, although the currency has not yet been adopted by all EU members.

Data from "From coins to credit cards," 1999.

documented through other instruments as well. A deed to a piece of land demonstrates that you own the land and have certain rights that might include the right to transfer the land. Similar rights are conferred by marketable securities, which represent documentation of ownership or indebtedness that can be transferred to others under the right circumstances. Stocks and bonds are typical examples of marketable securities and are discussed in the sections to follow.

MARKETABLE SECURITIES

Marketable securities are instruments so widely accepted and purchased by others that they are very similar to cash (Brigham & Ehrhardt, 2005). Any asset that is easy to convert to cash is called a **liquid asset**. For example, common stock in a publicly traded company can be sold through a broker and the resulting cash deposited into the seller's account within a day. In contrast, **hard assets** are assets that a company might not be able to convert to cash as quickly but that can still have significant value. A factory building that has significant value but might take a year to sell is an example of a hard asset.

Accounts receivable (A/R) and **inventories** are between these two extremes. An A/R is an owed obligation. If you have a yearly membership to the Smiths' new fitness center that requires a payment of $50 a month, a missed payment becomes a receivable owed to the club. The Smiths may develop a group of similar obligations that are past due; these obligations are categorized as accounts receivable. Although significant value exists in A/R and inventories, it may take a business several months to collect these funds, and some funds will be lost because of spoilage or because they are uncollectible. However, factoring (discussed in chapter 8) makes it possible to sell A/R and inventories within several days and to use the proceeds to pay other expenses. Thus, through factoring, some assets are more **liquid** than they were in the past and might be classified as marketable securities.

Marketable securities are the most liquid assets available for investment because of their shorter **maturity** periods (T-bills), their ability to sell on a daily basis (stocks), or their status as relatively risk free (certain bonds and government securities). Relatively risk free means the chances of the borrower's not paying are negligible. The U.S. government is considered one of the most risk-free investments because of the very low risk that the government will collapse. Examples of marketable securities include the following:

- Treasury bills: **Treasury bills**, or **T-bills**, are direct obligations of the U.S. government that mature in 3 to 12 months. Direct obligation means the U.S. government must repay the debt itself when the loan comes due, which is called the maturity date. The U.S. government regularly borrows and repays money—which is often how a national deficit is created.

- Treasury notes: Similar to T-bills, **Treasury notes** are obligations of the U.S. government, but they mature in 1 to 5 years.

- Government agency securities: The maturity on these obligations can be up to 30 years. These securities differ from Treasury notes, however, in that although individual government agencies can issue them, the taxing authority of the U.S. government does not directly back them.

- Certificates of deposit: **Certificates of deposit**, or **CDs** as they are commonly called, represent cash deposited in commercial banks, savings and loans, and credit unions. CDs normally mature in 1 month to 5 years. **Jumbo CDs** are for deposits of more than $100,000. These investments have very low risk, especially if they are maintained in a federally insured savings institution.

- Commercial paper: **Commercial paper (CP)** is a **short-term debt** obligation issued by a large corporation for an amount over $25,000. These debt obligations can have maturity dates ranging from one day to a year. Most of these promissory notes mature in 90 days and carry an interest rate around the prime rate based on the company's credit rating. A promissory note is a simple contract in which the borrower agrees to repay the **lender** for money borrowed. The **prime interest rate** is the interest rate charged by banks on loans to their best customers (those with minimal credit risk).

Table 3.1 lists liquid securities as well as investments or securities that are not as liquid. Riskiness represents the potential of a borrower's defaulting on an obligation. A default-free investment is basically guaranteed, so the lender is certain to be repaid. A low default risk is the next best protection; with this level of risk there is potential for the borrower to default. When a risk is identified as based on the insurer, the risk of default is contingent on the entity that borrowed the money. Some companies are so strong that the risk of default is minimal, while other companies have a high default risk. See chapter 8 for a discussion of the role of credit ratings in assessing credit risk.

Table 3.1 Securities from Risk Free to High Risk

Security	Typical maturity	Riskiness
Liquid investments for near-cash reserves		
U.S. Treasury bills—sold by the U.S. Treasury	91 days to 1 year	Default free
Banker's acceptance—promise to pay backed by a bank	Up to 180 days	Low risk if backed by a strong bank
Commercial paper—issued by large firms	Up to 270 days	Low default risk
Negotiable certificates of deposits (CDs)	Up to 1 year	Low default risk
Money market mutual funds—investment in T-bills, CDs, commercial paper, and so on	Various maturity dates	Low degree of risk
Euro market time deposits	Up to 1 year	Based on issuing bank
Consumer credit loans—banks, credit unions, finance companies	Variable	Based on issuing bank
Floating rate and market auction preferred stocks	Variable	Based on issuer
Liquid investments not suitable for near-cash reserves		
U.S. Treasury notes—price can change based on interest rate changes	3 to 10 years	Default free
U.S. Treasury bonds	Up to 10 years	Default free
Corporate bonds (rated AAA)	Up to 40 years	Based on issuer
State and local government bonds (rated AAA)	Up to 30 years	Based on issuer
Preferred stocks (rated AAA)	30 years to perpetual	Based on company
Common stocks in corporations	Unlimited	Variable

Most CP is very liquid; only the top corporations with strong credit histories can effectively issue this type of security. Commercial paper is an effective funding source in that it can be issued very inexpensively compared with bonds and stocks, which take considerable time and money to issue. Commercial paper also entails less governmental regulation, can help raise significant cash, and does not require the issuer to maintain any compensating balances with a bank. (A **compensating balance** is a required amount of cash kept with the lending institution that serves as a type of security. Since the corporation itself issues the CP, there is no need for any compensating balance to protect the lender.) A final benefit associated with CP is the prestige a company can generate from being financially strong enough to issue this type of instrument (Griffin, 1991). Thus, as with government-issued securities that can be treated much like **cash**, a corporation's CP can inspire a high level of investor confidence.

This section has covered the most liquid types of investment vehicles, which are almost like cash. However, other assets are also considered liquid assets but are not as liquid as cash or cash-equivalent assets. Thus, ownership of a business can also be considered a liquid asset if the ownership is evidenced through publicly traded stock. However, in contrast to the situation with cash, T-bills, or CDs, which all have a definite value, if you have ever owned stock and sold it, you might have obtained less than the stated value of the stock. Stock redemption refers to the process of selling stocks back to the open market or to the original issuing company. A stock may be hard to sell if investors are not interested in it. Furthermore, market volatility can affect the value of the investment. When times are good and a bull market keeps driving up the value of stocks, more companies put excess cash into acquiring shares in various other companies. If a balance sheet indicates $1 million in investment assets such as stocks, that value will drop $100,000 in one day if the stock price declines 10%. When investors redeem their shares of stock, they might receive less than they originally paid for the shares. Thus, the **liquidity** of stocks is lower than cash or cash equivalents because of the volatility of the stock market.

At the start of 2002, the World Wrestling Federation (which soon after changed its name to World Wrestling Entertainment, or WWE) had a market capitalization of $949 million; shares were selling at $13 each, and the 52-week range for the stock price was $10 to $22. As of October 26, 2001 (a couple of months earlier), the company had had total current assets of more than $332 million. The company also had over $90 million invested in property, plant, and equipment. The WWF's net tangible assets, combined with the total shareholders' equity, totaled more than $361 million and included $68 million in retained earnings and $296 million in capital surplus (Yahoo! Finance—WWF, 2002). By 2007, WWE shares were selling above $15 per share. The company had more than $465 million in assets, generated $189 million (over the prior six months ending October 2006), earned $27 million before taxes, and earned $0.31 per share during that six-month period (Form 10-Q, 2006).

On the same day in 2002, the Boston Celtics had a market capitalization of $29.2 million. Shares were trading at $10.80, and the 52-week range was $8.80 to $12.11. The team had $32 million in current assets, with $2 million in cash and $30 million in short-term investments. The Celtics had more than $87 million in total liabilities as of their last reported quarter at that time (September 30, 2001). With liability so much higher than total assets, the team had a negative stockholders' equity of over $53 million (Yahoo! Finance—BOS, 2002). Since then the Celtics were purchased by Lake Carnegie LLC for $360 million and became a privately held company, and they do not need to disclose their financial position.

These examples highlight the fact that two stocks can be trading at very similar price ranges but represent completely different pictures, with the WWF having significant assets and shareholders' equity and the Celtics having significant debt. The financial positions of companies can change based on numerous factors, from investor sentiment to ownership changes to legal changes. A perfect example of a legal change is the new U.S. law passed in 2006 prohibiting banks from interacting with online gambling establishments. Within hours of the law's passing, the stock value of numerous offshore companies (i.e., companies based in other countries) dropped significantly because of investor perception that the companies were going to lose a significant amount of their customers.

STOCKS

Obviously, value can be demonstrated in other vehicles besides money. One of the strongest value indicators is stocks. A stock certificate is a document demonstrating ownership interest in a company. This ownership interest is often referred to as equity value. The equity value in companies in general increases over time. The **Dow Jones Industrial Average** (Dow), one of the major **market indexes (market averages)**, had reached 11,000 in 1999 and in 2000 was flirting with 12,000 before declining to around 7,000 in 2002 (Lamiell, 1999). The average rose more

than 1,000 points ($1,000) in only a 24-day period in 1999. The previous record for the length of time it took the Dow to rise 1,000 points (from 6,000 to 7,000) had been 89 trading days in late 1996 into 1997. From 2002 through 2005, the average stayed around the 10,000 range until a bull market (optimistic market) drove the average up to 14,000 in 2007.

Charles Dow established the Dow in 1896 as an index to be used in the *Wall Street Journal*. The Dow closed its first day at 40.94, and it was almost 10 years before the index passed 100. The stock market went through some tumultuous times in the early 1900s; there were large drops in 1901 and 1907, and the famous Black Thursday occurred on October 24, 1929. The Dow started to rise in the World War II period and soared through the 1950s, reaching 500 in 1956. In 1970, the Dow ended the year at 838.92 (Dunphy, 1998). In 1972, the Dow surpassed 1,000 points. In 1979, the index ended at 838.74; and in 1987, it passed the 2,000-point mark, having entered the bull market leading to the 1999 level. By mid-1999, the Dow had surpassed 10,000.

However, even during the "good" times of a bull market, when prices advance at an aggressive pace, a bear market, or even a day of large losses, can significantly alter such a run. In 1987, Black Monday occurred on October 19 when the index collapsed 508.32 points, which represented a 22.6% drop in one day. This drop was approximately twice as large, in percentage terms, as the drop in 1929. However, the prospect of war pushed the Dow up again in 1991, with the Persian Gulf War fueling a rise past 3,000 (Yip, 1999). These highlights suggest the volatility of the Dow in relation to financial, political, and global concerns. For example, right after the attacks in New York and Virginia on September 11, 2001, the Dow dropped to 8,235, but it rose 20% within four months ("Dow Jones Continues," 2002). As highlighted already, by 2007 the Dow had passed its all-time high.

The Dow has undertaken a number of renovations to more effectively reflect the change in the economy from smokestacks to high-tech. Several major corporations were removed from the Dow in 1999, including such household giants as Chevron, Goodyear, Sears Roebuck, and Union Carbide. These businesses were replaced by Intel, Microsoft, Home Depot, and SBC Communications to complete the 30-stock list. The change represents the first time the Dow has included two stocks (Intel and Microsoft) from the NASDAQ rather than just New York Stock Exchange–listed shares ("High-Tech Injection," 1999). By 2004 the Dow had changed again, with AT&T, Eastman Kodak, and International Paper leaving the Dow and being replaced with Verizon Communication, American International Group, and Pfizer (Isidore, 2004).

The Dow does not value stocks. It is just one tool to measure investor confidence in the stock market. During strong economic times, individuals are willing to invest in companies by acquiring stocks. Investors hope the company will do well enough that the stock will increase in value, and any profits will be split with the stockholders through dividend payments or increased share values. The value of the Dow increases as the values of the businesses that compose the Dow increase. Conversely, if the stocks of companies on the Dow decline, so will the Dow. This very visible volatility helps dictate whether analysts consider the market to be a bull or bear market. A **bear market** is a stock market in which investors are scared and prices drop approximately 20%. A **bull market**, on the other hand, occurs when investors are optimistic and the stock market increases more than 20%. Instead of analyzing all stocks, analysts can look to the Dow and other market indexes to develop a quick barometer of market conditions.

Similar to what happened with the Dow, the NASDAQ index also showed significant strength in 1999. The index was so strong because of Internet stocks that it increased more than 84% in 1999 and closed at over 4,000 for the year ("Up, Up and Away," 1999). However, just two years later the NASDAQ was down more than 50%, at around 1,990 ("Dow Jones Continues," 2002). Similar to the Dow average, the NASDAQ was also hit with weak growth through 2005, but its recovery increased in 2006 and 2007.

BONDS

Bonds represent another measure of value. Unlike stocks, which denote ownership interest in a company, bonds represent an obligation owed by a company or institution. The entity issuing the bond is the **debtor**, and the purchaser of the bond is the **creditor**. Creditors are interested in investing their money in bonds that provide a reasonable **yield (rate of return)** with the lowest possible risk level. Similar to the situation with CP, the greater a company's financial strength, the easier it is for that company to issue bonds. A company that has a poor financial picture has to pay investors a premium to interest them in buying their bonds. Bonds issued by established companies normally pay lower interest but present a significantly lower default risk.

Bonds are not as frequently seen in the sport industry as in the consumer goods or manufacturing industries. However, the recent strong increase in professional team values may create more opportunities for issuing bonds. For example, the New York Yankees and the New Jersey Nets merged and undertook a bond offering through YankeeNets LLC that raised $250 million. Proceeds were used to help purchase the New Jersey Devils. Analysts thought that the YankeeNets offering was unusual and that most bond offerings would still come from stadium and arena construction projects because facilities have a more predictable revenue stream than teams, whose revenues can be volatile based on their win–loss record ("Corporate Debt," 2000). The YankeeNets merger ended in 2004, with the Nets being sold to an investor who wanted to move the team to New York.

Marketable securities, stocks, bonds, and other methods utilized to finance a business are discussed in greater detail in chapters 8, 9, 10, and 11. They are relevant in this chapter as vehicles that help facilitate financial transactions. An issuing company can use these instruments to raise money, or companies can purchase these instruments in an effort to acquire another business or as an investment vehicle to earn a return. The only limits regarding which corporations can issue stocks and bonds are internal or external variables such as a corporation's articles of incorporation or its credit rating. If a corporation's bylaws allow the corporation to issue only one million shares, then after that number is reached no more shares can be issued without amending the bylaws. No matter who issues or acquires value, institutions need to facilitate the flow of value through these documents.

FINANCIAL INSTITUTIONS

Several major types of financial institutions facilitate the transfer of capital. These institutions are involved in the process either to obtain an interest in the transaction or to be paid a fee for their services. For example, seats on the New York Stock Exchange (NYSE) are sold to companies wishing to engage in buying and selling listed stocks. A seat gives the seat owner the right to trade stocks on the NYSE. A seat is similar to a personal seat license (PSL) for a sports team. Once you buy a PSL you can use it, sell a game-day ticket to someone else, or leave the seat empty. Similarly, a seat on the NYSE allows the owner to personally buy and sell shares or allows others to do the buying and selling on his behalf. Thus, a seat is the right to be able to do business. Other institutions such as banks charge various fees for services and also obtain revenue by acquiring money at a low interest rate and then turning around and loaning the same money to others at a higher rate.

BANKS

The Babylonians are often credited with developing the first true banks sometime around 2000 BC. These banks were run by the Babylonian temples and were involved both in lending and in safekeeping of valuables. The temples charged as much as one-sixth of the deposits for the safekeeping of gold, silver, and other valuables entrusted to them. A temple then charged people who borrowed deposits around 20% interest, compounded monthly (Rodgers, 1966). Fifteen hundred years later, the Greeks also turned their temples into safes for the wealthy. Athens developed a specific body of law covering banking transactions, as well as a court system, which required repayment of debts within 30 days (Rodgers, 1966).

The Roman *argentarii* (silver dealers) began offering additional services such as lending money, selling mortgages, and providing letters of credit. However, they often made loans to individuals such as politicians who were unable to pay them back. These high-risk loans caused significant losses that forced the Roman bankers to seek higher interest payments from other borrowers. Through stringent control, the Roman Empire was able to eventually rein in interest rates to 2.5% per year (Rodgers, 1966). However, by that time the damage had been done, and the bankers had developed a poor image. Banking was not as commonly utilized in the Dark Ages because of edicts of the Christian Church, which did not distinguish between interest and **usury** and thus forbade any payments for using money. This edict did not affect other religions, whose adherents were still able to loan money and collect interest (Rodgers, 1966).

The first publicly owned bank was the Bank of Venice, founded in 1171 AD. The success of the Bank of Venice in its limited lending role spawned future banks such as the Bank of Barcelona in the 14th century, the Bank of Amsterdam in 1602, and the Bank of England in 1694 (Rodgers, 1966).

Banking in the American colonies experienced numerous failures in the early years. In 1791 Alexander Hamilton convinced Congress to charter a national bank called the Bank of the United States, which failed shortly thereafter (FDIC, 2002).

Banking history has had numerous success stories, such as the Bank of England, which started as a 1,200,000-pound loan to the English government in 1694 and is still around today. However, many disasters befell the French banking system, which collapsed numerous times from unbridled spending and abuses. Banks as we know them today have learned many lessons from the past, but greed has crept into the system at various times and led to problems such as the Great Depression and the savings and loan scandal of the 1980s.

Even with all the faults one can see in the commercial banking system, the system is essential for economic and financial survival. For example, if bankers start reducing the credit offered to businesses, then economic growth is slowed and the standard of living for all citizens decreases. Conversely, if too much credit is extended to the business community, the rate of growth and the standard of living will rise significantly, but they will also reach a pace that is not economically sustainable. It may happen, for example, that the demand for money is great, but there is not enough money to meet the demand; this can cause significant competition for funds and higher interest rates. These two examples of banks' influencing the economy in the direction of success or failure are commonly referred to as "boom and bust" (Rodgers, 1966).

Clearly, our everyday bankers wield significant power and help run the monetary system for the entire economy by helping to establish—either directly or

Banks and other financial institutions, such as JP Morgan, are a vital part of all sport businesses.

© AFP/Getty Images

indirectly—prices, interest rates, economic growth, and capital creation (Rodgers, 1966). The power of bankers can be diminished to some extent in markets where there is competition from nonbank lenders or when the government significantly manipulates the banking system by changing interest rates. To obtain funds to help foster economic development, banks need to acquire money from other sources. The primary sources include invested capital, borrowing from other banks or the Federal Reserve and primary deposits.

CAPITAL

A bank's capital can come from money initially used to start the bank. Several major investors might each contribute $20 million to create a bank. Publicly traded banks might issue stock to raise more capital. Capital can also take the form of retained earnings accumulated from income generated by the bank. A bank may choose not to pay dividends and instead use the accumulated earnings as capital. Banks need extra capital to pay daily bills and to extend credit to a broad base of individuals and businesses that need to utilize that capital. The amount of capital required by any bank for its own reserves is set by law. Capital reserves are also analyzed by the **Federal Deposit Insurance Corporation (FDIC)** when a bank makes a request to reduce its capital stock, establish a new branch, merge or consolidate, or move its main office ("Who Is the FDIC?" 2006).

The amount of capital available for issuing loans is affected by the risks associated with other loans, the liquidity of other assets, whether deposits are increasing, and whether enough profit is being made to sustain shareholder confidence. If a bank loaned a significant amount of money to a real estate company and the real estate market collapsed, the bank would lose significant money if it was unable to recover its investment. This loss would deplete the bank's available capital since money would be spent covering losses and paying for attorneys to help recover as much of the investment as possible. Thus, banks need to critically analyze every loan decision to make sure the investment will not jeopardize their loan portfolios or their available credit reserves.

One of the primary reasons banks are required by law to maintain adequate capital reserves is to prevent a run on the bank. If depositors think their money is at risk, they can pull out their deposits, and the bank must have enough capital to repay all such demands. Before depositing funds, people need to feel comfortable that the bank's management will take care of their money. Although there

is no guarantee that any bank or savings and loan will not face financial hardships, investors have federal protections that have been designed to help safeguard their deposits. This protection includes reserve requirements, which are funds that cannot be loaned out, and can include account insurance offered by the federal government, which is discussed later in the chapter.

BORROWING

Banks sometimes run out of money, just as everyday citizens do, and need to borrow money in order to continue their operations. Banks can turn to other banks for short-term loans or, if they are a member, can approach the Federal Reserve Bank for additional funds. To obtain these funds, a bank might conduct a temporary sale of assets or a temporary deposit of primary funds (short-term funds deposited by other banks), or it might just borrow money and pay the prevailing market rate for loans to banks.

A bank most often borrows when it has to fund a special deal or when a client needs a large sum for several days. At other times a bank might borrow to build new offices or to fund other ventures without creating any reserve-related concerns. If the bank uses its own funds, it may not have the amount of money in reserve that is required by federal banking regulations. But if the bank borrows money from the Federal Reserve, it does not dip into funds of its own that are fulfilling the reserve requirements.

FEDERAL RESERVE SYSTEM

The **Federal Reserve System**, established by Congress after 1913, comprises 12 Federal Reserve district banks, 25 branches, and more than 5,800 national and state banks (see figure 3.1) (Federal Reserve System, 2006). The Fed, as it is commonly called, was established to provide central banking facilities for the entire United States. The system operates to manage the nation's money supply by raising or lowering the reserve amount banks need to keep on hand, changing the discount rate (which is the rate charged to commercial banks for borrowing money), and purchasing and selling government securities (Siegel, Shim, & Hartman, 1992). The Fed has jurisdiction over the following activities (Spiro, 1996):

- Commercial bank regulatory function
- Reserve requirements and bank discounts
- Selective credit control
- Open market operations
- International operations

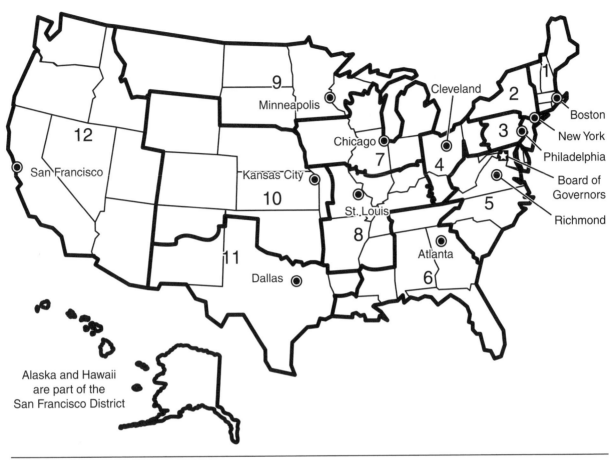

Figure 3.1 The 12 Federal Reserve districts.

The Fed is responsible for conducting field audits of member banks but typically conducts such audits only for state-chartered banks. Nationally chartered banks are under the statutory domain of the Comptroller of the Currency and can be examined by that office rather than the Fed. The Comptroller of the Currency also audits banks under its charge and works with the Fed in controlling the practices and procedures of nationally chartered banks. The Fed is responsible for administering the Bank Holding Act of 1956, which was enacted to prevent bank monopolies while permitting banks to expand into some nonbank endeavors such as the credit card business or investment management (Spiro, 1996). Another federal law the Fed is responsible for promulgating and enforcing is the **Consumer Credit Protection Act (CCPA)** of 1968 (also called the **Truth in Lending Act**), which requires lenders to provide user-friendly information about the true terms and interest rates on loans.

The Fed is responsible for some regulations concerning credit-related borrowing and lending. For example, the Fed can specify which securities can be purchased on credit and the amount or percentage of credit that lenders are able to extend to purchase the securities. Although the Fed engages in significant policy making, its decisions and actions do not require any governmental approval from either the executive or the legislative branch. The Fed is run by a board of governors who are appointed by the president of the United States with the Senate's consent. After being appointed, the governors and the Fed chairperson work autonomously but report on a yearly basis to Congress. The current Fed chairman is Ben Bernanke. The six other members of the board of governors serve staggered terms, and no member can be reappointed.

The Fed operates similarly to a bank in that member banks can deposit funds with and borrow funds from the Fed. Member banks are required to keep a specific fraction of their deposits as a cash reserve. The money can be kept by the banks in their vaults or can be deposited with the Fed. The Fed determines what percentage needs to be kept on reserve and varies this amount to help stimulate the economy. The Fed can also influence the economy through its discount window. A discount window is the range of interest rates at which a bank can borrow money from the Federal Reserve. The discount window allows banks to borrow against their loan portfolio to raise additional money for offering more loans. By changing the discount rate that it charges commercial banks, the Fed can either encourage more loans (by offering a lower rate) or discourage more loans (by increasing the rate banks need to pay to borrow the funds) (Spiro, 1996).

PRIMARY DEPOSITS

Primary deposits are deposits in a bank that come from other banks. Banks that have excess cash, but not enough borrowers, may deposit the extra cash in another bank in order to obtain some interest. If the funds just sit in a bank, that bank is forced to pay interest to the depositors, but the funds do not generate any revenue. Depositing the funds in another bank makes it possible to obtain some interest, but the funds can also be quickly withdrawn if other borrowers need the money.

These funds can be utilized to increase reserves with the Fed, which frees more capital for investing. The Fed can also affect bank reserves. The Fed is responsible for maintaining the nation's money supply, and one technique entails purchasing securities. When the Fed buys securities, the funds used to pay for the securities end up as increased deposits in the banking system, which ultimately translates into higher reserves. Thus Fed member banks can increase their reserves without having to deposit any more cash into their reserves. During World War II, the Fed purchased more than $22 billion in securities to help create reserves to finance the war. The banks throughout the nation had more capital they could loan, but they did not need to do anything to acquire the extra capital.

BANK DEREGULATION

After the 1930s, banks were heavily regulated to prevent them from engaging in other business enterprises such as selling insurance or providing investment advice. However, new laws passed in the late 1990s resulted in bank deregulation. Commercial banks are now allowed to establish or acquire investment banking and merchant banking subsidiaries that can engage in extending loans, purchasing ownership interests, or underwriting bond offerings. Banks can now invest in as much as 5% of a company outright or purchase up to 49% of a company through bank-owned subsidiaries. This

opportunity to own other businesses has fueled significant investment by banks in high-tech start-ups. Banks can derive significant profit from venture capital investment, which is one of the first stages of investing in a new business. Chase Manhattan's venture capital arm had $2.5 billion in revenue in 1999 and generated $1.4 billion of Chase's profits (Mclean, 2000).

Deregulation created an environment with significant banking investments in potentially riskier businesses, which resulted in the threat that banks could lose a large amount of their deposits. The Fed was called in to analyze this concern, and it developed policies in 2000 to address the situation. Banks are now required to set aside more capital to cover riskier equity investments. An **equity investment** is not a loan but a purchase of an ownership interest in a business. Since a business can increase or decrease in value, it is a riskier investment compared with most bank portfolios, which contain a large number of commercial and personal loans (Sapsford, 2000).

BANK LENDING RULES

The various rules and regulations enforced by the Fed can also interact with a bank's own written or unwritten rules. All banks utilize a loan-to-deposit ratio: They will not loan money as freely once their loans reach more than a certain percentage—often 70 to 75%—of all deposits. The remaining percentage is kept in reserves or invested in short-term or other liquid investments such as **Treasury bonds**. If the loan-to-deposit ratio is reaching the tip of a bank's comfort zone, a borrower could be caught in a credit squeeze. A credit squeeze occurs when a business borrows too much money and a bank or other lending institution will not loan the business any more money unless it repays previously incurred obligations. This is similar to when a bartender sees a person has had too much to drink and refuses to serve that person any more alcohol. A bank will put a credit squeeze on a company if it feels the company is overextended or cannot repay debts as they become due. A credit squeeze could be caused by a bank, lender, borrower, the economy, or any other external conditions. To avoid such a problem, most financially astute managers develop multiple banking relationships so they can approach several different banks for the same loan.

Banks may also establish specific rules about the types of loans they might entertain. Banks typically do not want to issue capital loans because the repayment period for loans to help start a business is much longer than repayment for typical commercial loans. Thus, it would be much more difficult for the Smiths to obtain initial financing from a bank than it would for Sport Manufacturing Company to get a loan. Banks can demand a security pledge from someone who wants to obtain a loan. These **secured loans** can utilize anything of value as a pledge from which repayment can be extracted if a borrower defaults. Sport loans are often secured by the item purchased. If a golf course borrows money to purchase a golf cart, the cart can become the collateral securing the loan repayment. Each bank has specific rules about each facet of a loan, from the application process through repayment requirements. These rules are designed not to waste valuable paper but rather to reduce the risks associated with collecting the loan.

BANK SERVICES

Besides providing loans and facilitating economic growth by making money available to borrowers, banks perform various additional services. These services include

- allowing individuals to deposit their money in a bank account for safekeeping,
- allowing checking account holders to write checks demanding that the bank pay another party a specific amount,
- providing clients with cashier's checks or certified checks when necessary,
- providing numerous specialty savings accounts for customers, and
- acting as general depositaries for U.S. Treasury funds.

These services are provided at different costs, depending on the bank and the special programs offered by each bank. Many banks charge a fee for every check written; other banks provide interest payments to customers who write fewer checks. The costs or interest rates available are based on supply and demand factors as well as competition from other banks. When rates are fairly equal among banks, the banks often engage in sales promotion strategies to encourage business and may offer potential customers various prizes, from stuffed animals and piggy banks to toasters or other kitchen appliances. All sport businesses utilize checking accounts; and if a business has enough money in an account, that business can negotiate how much it will pay for the services it receives.

Banks handle more than just money; they also handle sensitive personal information and numerous financial instruments, from ATM cards to credit cards. The Smiths' credit card information was stolen from XYZ Bank's data room, and the thieves used this information to open several new accounts and charge several thousand dollars on the new credit cards. This case of identity theft infuriated Bob and Cheryl, who were upset that their bank did not protect their identities and personal information in a safer manner.

PROTECTING DEPOSITS

Banks can use numerous gimmicks to win clients, but the depositors' primary concern is probably whether their money will be safe. Through the 1930s, banking's history made depositors skeptical about their ability to remove funds. There were several early attempts to protect deposits, but they all failed. In fact, the Depression was further flamed by the failure of approximately 15,000 banks from the 1920s through the 1930s. The federal government was asked to step in to help protect depositors' money. The government, though, was skeptical about taking on this role because guaranteed accounts would provide a disincentive for bankers to be vigilant with depositors' money.

In 1933 the first form of federal **deposit insurance** was developed as an attempt to facilitate better banking (Rodgers, 1966). The Banking Act of 1933 helped establish the FDIC as a government unit charged with insuring bank deposits. In 1950, the law was superseded by the Federal Deposit Insurance Act. The FDIC is now privately owned by the banks rather than the government. Similar to the Fed, the FDIC is run by a board of directors that includes the Comptroller of the Currency and two other individuals appointed by the president with the Senate's consent. The FDIC reviews reports from insured banks, including insured banks that are not members of the Fed. The FDIC has a strong weapon to help ensure compliance with safe banking practices. If a bank engages in and is found guilty of unsafe, unsound, or illegal banking activities, the FDIC can terminate that bank's insurance. Part of the insurance termination process involves contacting all depositors to let them know that insurance coverage will be terminated.

If a bank cannot cover withdrawals, the FDIC can pay all claims and liquidate the bank's assets. This is an extreme measure and one that produces negative publicity. If at all possible, the FDIC tries to find another bank willing to assume the defaulting bank's deposit liabilities. Furthermore, under the 1950 act, the FDIC can purchase assets from, extend a loan to, and make deposits in any insured bank facing financial hardships.

The insurance covers funds not on the basis of the depositor but on the basis of the account, covering the first $100,000 in any account. Thus, if a depositor has $400,000 in an account, only the first $100,000 is insured. In contrast, if a depositor has four different accounts each of which contains $100,000, each is fully insured.

Account protection through insurance is critical to ensure the availability of funds. For example, suppose a sports team kept all moneys from ticket and broadcasting sales in one bank account, and the bank faced financial problems and closed. Even if the team had $40 million in the account, only $100,000 would be insured. Thus the team could face significant financial trouble and be unable to cover bills because of the bank's closing. To avoid this problem, the team would probably keep only smaller amounts in each bank (a maximum of $100,000 per account), possibly only bank with the largest and strongest banks, or possibly keep a smaller amount in the bank and invest more of the money in marketable securities. Such exercises in distributing money—constantly juggling money to provide the greatest return and protection—are among the key duties of financial managers.

QUASI BANKERS

The discussion so far has focused on commercial banks. However, many other banking-related businesses also provide needed capital for corporations and individuals. These entities can range from savings and loans, which are very similar to banks, to mortgage companies, which are discussed further on.

Investment bankers specialize in raising long-term funds for both corporate expansions and capital needs. Insurance companies, on the basis of their large cash reserves, can also provide significant capital for corporations seeking additional funds. **Pension funds** and retirement accounts are often utilized as borrowing sources. The largest teacher pension and retirement fund in the world, TIAA/CREF, has provided significant financial support to several major stadium construction projects ("Top Holders," 1997). Credit unions can also provide substantial capital based on their large membership numbers. Since credit unions receive money from members and loan money only to members, they are often the cheapest source for borrowing funds. However, it is sometimes impossible to join a credit union without being affiliated with a specified employer or social group. For example, if the Smiths currently work for a company that is affiliated with a credit union, it might be easier for them to secure a loan and obtain more favorable terms.

Other sources of funds include **consumer finance companies**, sales finance companies, pawnbrokers, and even unlicensed lenders such as loan sharks. An example of consumer financing is a car purchase agreement in which the car serves as the collateral for the amount financed by the purchaser. If the purchase price of the car was $20,000 and the down payment was $5,000, then $15,000 is the financed amount. The $15,000 note could be sold to large finance companies that purchase millions in loans to consumers for numerous products. A sales finance company sells items such as photocopiers, or even zambonis, and instead of accepting cash can also finance the items through loans secured by the equipment.

Mortgage companies loan money to individuals willing to pledge their homes as collateral. Mortgage companies rarely receive deposits except for initial capital infusions by investors. Since mortgage companies are very specialized, they can offer additional services and can often provide comprehensive benefits.

If the Smiths are willing to mortgage their house to start their business, they might approach both a bank and a mortgage company to determine which would offer the best value. The mortgage company might have a lower initial interest rate but also might charge a special handling fee (often called **points**) for writing the loan. The mortgage company might also allow repayment without any penalties. The bank might impose an early-payment penalty if Bob and Cheryl pay early. The Smiths would need to analyze each option carefully to determine which would give them the greatest value.

Sport Manufacturing Company

Sport Manufacturing Company wants to purchase some new equipment but does not want to use any of its cash. One equipment manufacturer has a program where SMC could purchase the equipment for $10,000 down and then assume a lease for $2,000 a month. This arrangement allows SMC to save some money for other needs and write off the monthly expense payments from their taxes as a business expense (rather than depreciating the purchase over several years). It also allows the equipment manufacturer to sell more equipment and earn a nice interest rate from the lease payments.

STOCK EXCHANGES

There are very specific requirements for admission to established stock exchanges, as well as regulations concerning who can **trade** the shares. Only firms that are members of a particular exchange can trade stocks on that exchange. This policy was established when the **securities exchanges** were chartered. Since the exchanges are owned and operated by their members, they can establish rules for future members. One rule is that any company wishing to buy a seat (place) on a particular exchange must purchase the seat from a departing member and must pay the prevailing market rate for the seat, which can exceed $2 million on the New York Stock Exchange. Having a seat makes the company a member of the exchange. Someone who wants to purchase shares of a stock listed on an exchange contacts a member to purchase the shares. Nonmembers cannot purchase the shares.

Three major stock exchanges exist in the United States. The most prestigious is the **New York Stock Exchange** (NYSE), which was founded in 1792 and recently became publicly traded. Approximately 3,000 companies meet the stringent requirements for size and profitability that a company must fulfill in order to be listed on the NYSE (Dunphy, 1998). To be listed, a company typically must have at least 2,000 shareholders; must have a market value of at least $100 million; and must have been profitable for the last three years, with earnings of at least $6.5 million per year during those years ("U.S. Standards," 2002). Normally, only the most prestigious companies can be listed on the NYSE.

The **National Association of Securities Dealers Automated Quotations** (NASDAQ) system is a computerized national trading system for more than 3,300 publicly traded companies. The NASDAQ began operating on February 8, 1971, with several larger companies such as American Express and Anheuser-Busch (Ip, 2000, March 10). Both companies are now listed on the NYSE. Some companies listed on the NASDAQ, such as MCI, Microsoft, Intel, Compaq, Starbucks, Apple Computer, Coors Brewing, and Ben and Jerry's, have become big and profitable enough to be listed on the NYSE but for various reasons have not moved their stock from the NASDAQ. One reason may be that many start-up and high-tech companies are launched on the NASDAQ, and there is an image that NASDAQ companies are more cutting edge than some of their more established counterparts trading on the NYSE. The NASDAQ is also the primary U.S. market for trading securities in overseas companies such as Toyota, Volvo, Canon, Fuji Photo, and Cadbury Schweppes.

Besides listing major national and international companies, NASDAQ also has several ancillary services that help people trade securities in smaller companies. The OTC (over-the-counter) Bulletin Board is an electronic market for securities not listed on NASDAQ or any other U.S. exchange. Bid and ask quotations are captured and displayed in real time so that trades can be accomplished almost instantaneously. The **ask**, or **offer**, **price** is the price a seller would like to receive for the item he wishes to sell. The **bid price** is the amount a potential buyer might want to spend to acquire the item. Somewhere between these two amounts a compromise might be reached. However, numerous deals are based on firm asking prices or bid prices where the party making the firm offer refuses to budge. Similar to what occurs with bidding on eBay or other Internet auctions, the

Major International Exchanges

Market or exchange	Year founded	Avg. daily no. shares traded	Avg. daily trading volume	Market capitalization	Largest stocks
NYSE	1792	1.08 billion	$35 billion	$12 trillion	GE, Exxon, Wal-Mart
NASDAQ	1971	1.76 billion	$41.5 billion	$5.02 trillion	Intel, Cisco, Microsoft
Deutsche	1585	N/A	$4.5 billion	$1.5 trillion	Siemens, Allianz
London	1801	2.1 million	$13.5 billion	$2.8 trillion	British Telecom, BP Amoco
Tokyo	1878	0.6 billion	$6.8 billion	$4.1 trillion	Toyota, Nippon Tel. & Tel.
Australian	1837	1.02 billion	$0.78 billion	$370 billion	News Corp., Aust. Bank
Toronto	1878	197.5 million	$2.85 billion	$1.7 trillion	Nortel, Seagram, BCE

Data from S. Calian and A. Latour, "Stockholm, once a David, is a high-tech Goliath" (*The Wall Street Journal*, May 15, 2000, p. C1).

highest price offered at the designated time wins, and the item is automatically shipped or transferred once the payment is verified.

The **National Association of Securities Dealers** (NASD) regulates the NASDAQ and other **over-the-counter exchanges**. Regulation is accomplished through education programs, on-site examination of member firms, automated market surveillance, registration and testing of security professionals, review of members' sales and advertising practices, an arbitration program to resolve disputes, and review of underwriting arrangements associated with new offerings (*An Introduction*, 1992). Automated market surveillance and reviewing of underwriting arrangements are undertaken through close examination of the launching and selling of stocks to ensure that no improprieties are occurring. For example, the system can track whether weird spikes in stock prices are due to manipulation or insider trading. These powers are derived through federal legislation such as the 1938 Maloney Act amendments to the Securities Exchange Act of 1934, which established the NASD. The NASD was organized through the joint effort of Congress and the Securities and Exchange Commission. Although the NASD was given significant power by federal legislation, it is a privately financed and managed company, with its members and listed companies contributing to its approximately $500 million annual budget ("NASD," 2006). The NASD is responsible for regulating more than 5,200 brokers and dealers and 657,690 registered sales representatives ("NASD," 2006).

Another exchange is the American Stock Exchange (AMEX), which lists 700 small to midsized businesses, with a large number of these companies servicing the oil industry. AMEX merged with the NASD at the start of the 21st century which shows that the exchange was evolving based on technological demands. However, several years after the merger the AMEX spun off on its own again in 2004. Technology can have an impact on various exchanges that might not be necessary in the future. Smaller regional exchanges exist throughout the United States, such as the Boston, Cincinnati, Chicago, Pacific, and Philadelphia stock exchanges and specialty exchanges such as the Chicago Board Options Exchange and the Chicago Mercantile Exchange. There are also international exchanges; the most prominent are those based in Tokyo, London, Madrid, Paris, Tel Aviv, and Hong Kong.

Exchanges list their shares' prices on a daily basis in major financial papers such as the *Wall Street Journal*. Typical daily newspaper business sections list only the most active shares from the biggest exchanges. Typical stock listings show the bid and ask prices, the difference from the prior day if any, the 52-week high and low prices for the shares, and possibly the price–earnings ratio (PE ratios are covered in chapter 5).

The major stock exchanges operate differently from one another. The NYSE and the AMEX utilize an auction style, with investors sending orders through their brokers to the stock exchange floor. The floor is the trading area where buyers and sellers have a chance to swap stocks or other commodities. Brokers on the floor gather together in groups to buy and sell a particular company's stock. The brokers utilize the time-honored negotiation tool of supply and demand to develop a fair market price for the stock. If someone asks too much for her shares, they will go unsold. If someone offers to sell a stock at a low price, numerous brokers may try to buy. Through negotiations the parties reach a mutually acceptable price. If a block of shares is offered for sale or purchase and no one steps forward to make a deal, an exchange specialist can sell or purchase from his company's own account (Dunphy, 1998). An exchange specialist typically sells shares from a range of stocks sold on a specific exchange. If someone wishes to purchase the shares, a deal is concluded and the shares exchange hands. Actual stock certificates are not exchanged on the floor; instead, slips of paper evidencing the deal are exchanged, and ownership changes are recorded at a different time.

The NASDAQ and OTC markets operate differently from the NYSE in that there is no trading floor. Brokers do not gather in any specific location but negotiate with others through computers. Thus, NASDAQ is a computer-driven dealing system in which orders are bought and sold based on prices posted by various buyers and sellers (Dunphy, 1998). An OTC brokerage operates as a normal securities retailer and wholesaler and also trades in select securities from its own accounts (Spiro, 1996). Securities retailers and wholesalers buy and sell whatever stocks are being demanded in either small or large lots. Brokers are often called market makers; they advise other brokers and the investment community at large of the price at which they are willing to buy or sell shares. With the speed of today's top computers, buying and selling stocks can occur in just seconds.

Electronic trading is the current rage among investors, who can now utilize Internet-based trading companies to purchase and sell stocks at the touch of a button. Commissions on these trades are often lower than traditional commissions, which run approximately $50 and up depending on the volume traded; electronic commissions are often less than $20 per trade. For example, if you purchase 100 shares of Nike for $50 a share, you are buying an entire lot, or **even lot** (100 shares). In addition to the $5,000 paid for the stock, you might have to pay an extra $20 to possibly $200 dollars to compensate the broker who purchased the stock for you. You would also need to pay a commission when you sell the stock. If you were to purchase an **odd lot**, which is anything but an even lot (1-99 shares), you might have to pay a higher commission since it might be harder for a broker to find a buyer for the shares. Commissions can be negotiated with the brokerage house based on the number of stocks traded, the number of trades each month, or the dollar value of your account.

On the basis of the changing dynamics presented by online trading and the potential for new online stock exchanges, in 2000 the NYSE considered a merger with NASDAQ. The announcement came after both exchanges had announced plans to convert to for-profit companies to compete with newer computerized trading systems ("Markets Consider Merger," 2000). New exchanges have already emerged; the first major new exchange, Archipelago, created a trading alliance through the Pacific Stock Exchange in 2000 (Ip, 2000, March 15). In the Pacific Stock Exchange, founded in 1882, the 552 seat owners traded 23 million shares on a daily basis. Archipelago was started in December 1996, its ownership including Merrill Lynch, Goldman Sachs, ETrade Group, J. P. Morgan, CNBC TV, and Instinet. The young screen-based trading service had a daily volume of 50 million shares and generated enough revenue to buy the Pacific Stock Exchange to launch its effort to deal in NYSE-listed shares (Ip, 2000, March 15). By 2005, Archipelago was doing so well that the NYSE merged with the exchange to help switch the NYSE to an electronic format. The merged companies are estimated to be worth $6 billion, with the merger valuing each chair on the NYSE at $3.5 million (Farrell, 2005).

Various techniques are used to assess market conditions and track stock movement. As discussed earlier in this chapter, the most famous barometer of the stock market is the Dow, which includes 30 large U.S. companies. The representative mix of companies ranges from computer giant IBM to Disney. The primary benefit of the Dow is that it has an established track record. The primary disadvantage is that the average represents only a small spectrum of all available stocks.

Another indicator is Standard & Poor's 500 Composite Index, which tracks the 500 largest companies based on market capitalization. Since the Standard & Poor's index has more stocks than the Dow, it is considered a more reliable indicator of market movement. The only indexes that provide more in-depth coverage are the Russell Indexes, which cover 1,000, 2,000, or 3,000 different stocks. The NASDAQ also has a composite to track its shares. The NASDAQ Composite Index first closed above 1,000 on July 17, 1995. Because of skyrocketing Internet offerings, the index had shot up to over 5,000 by the year 2000 (Ip, 2000, March 10). The opening months of the 21st century saw a rapid decrease in the technology-heavy NASDAQ. The collapse of the "dot-com" economy from overspeculation caused the NASDAQ to lose more than 3,000 points ("Dow Jones Continues," 2002). This downturn represents one of the major concerns associated with exchanges that specialize in a given industry segment. If that industry segment experiences a downturn, the exchange will also suffer significantly.

Examples of sport-related stocks available on the NYSE include Comcast, Disney, Time Warner, Tribune, and many companies in the golf, shoe, fitness, and auto and horse racing industries. The NASDAQ system also includes similar prestigious companies. Table 3.2 highlights some of the major sport-related companies that are publicly traded on various exchanges.

The securities industry is regulated by its own rules, but also needs to comply with federal regulations. In the following section we consider how the government also affects financial systems.

GOVERNMENT'S INFLUENCE ON FINANCIAL MARKETS

In addition to the Fed, discussed earlier in connection with banking, numerous federal and state government units can exert considerable influence over financial systems. Various regulatory bodies at the state or federal level make laws in many areas, from how to incorporate to what taxes are to be paid. One such federal regulatory agency is the **Securities and Exchange Commission** (SEC), which was formed after the 1929 stock market crash and started operating in 1934. The SEC's initial primary emphasis was ensuring accuracy in the underwriting of stock offerings and proper disclosure (Spiro, 1996). The goal was to ensure equal access among investors to information from companies. Activities of the SEC have evolved into analyzing practices at the private exchanges and monitoring the accounting practices used by companies in their initial security offerings and subsequent annual reports.

Table 3.2 Major Publicly Traded Sport-Related Companies

Company symbol	Company name	Primary sport product	Exchange
AASP.OB	All-American SportPark	Sport parks	OTC
ADGO	Adams Golf	Golf clubs	OTC
ALDA	Aldila	Golf clubs	NASDAQ
AGPDY.PK	Amer Sports Oyj	Sporting goods (Wilson, Salomon)	OTC
ASHW	Ashworth	Golf equipment	NASDAQ
BFT	Bally Total Fitness Holding	Fitness centers	NYSE
BIKEQ.PK	Cannondale	Bicycles	NASDAQ
BOLL.PK	Bollinger Industries	Fitness equipment	OTC
BOOT	LaCrosse Footwear	Sports shoes	NASDAQ
CCU	Clear Channel Communications	Event management and agents	NYSE
CHDN	Churchill Downs	Thoroughbred racing	NASDAQ
CMCSK	Comcast	Media and team	NASDAQ
CVC	Cablevision	Knicks, Rangers, and media	NYSE
DIS	Walt Disney	Anaheim teams, ESPN, ABC	NYSE
DVD	Dover Downs Entertainment	Motor sport	NYSE
ELY	Callaway Golf	Golf	NYSE
ERTS	Electronic Arts	Video games	NASDAQ
EGLF	Element 21 Golf	Golf accessories	OTC
FINL	Finish Line	Apparel	NASDAQ
FTSTQ.PK	Footstar	Shoes	NYSE
GET	Gaylord Entertainment	Media and resorts	NYSE
GTA	Golf Trust of America	Golf course owner	AMEX
HED	Head N.V.	Manufacturing and marketing	NYSE
HIBB	Hibbett	Apparel retail	NASDAQ
HSPO.OB	Healthsports	Manufacturing	OTC
ISCA	International Speedway	Motor sport	NASDAQ
KSWS	K-Swiss	Athletic footwear	NASDAQ
KTO	K2	Skis	NYSE
MECA	Magna Entertainment	Horse racing tracks	NASDAQ
MTN	Vail Resorts	Skiing	NYSE
NICH	Nitches	Sports apparel	NASDAQ
NKE	Nike	Shoes	NYSE
NUCO	NUCO2	Services	NASDAQ
NWS	News Corp.	Dodgers and media	NYSE
OO	Oakley	Sunglasses	NYSE
PERY	Perry Ellis	Sports apparel	NASDAQ
PKS	Six Flags	Amusement parks	NYSE
PMMAY.PK	Puma	Footwear, apparel	OTC
RADA	Radican Games	Game manufacturer	NASDAQ
RBK	Reebok	Shoes	NYSE
RML	Russell	Shoes	NYSE
SGDE	The Sportsman's Guide	Catalog retailer	NASDAQ
SGMS	Scientific Games	Technology	NASDAQ
SPCHB	Sport Chalet	Sporting goods retail	NASDAQ
SPOR	Sport-Haley	Golf apparel	NASDAQ
SRR	Stride Rite	Shoes	NYSE
SSPY.PK	Sports Supply Group	Sporting goods	OTC
SSTR	Silverstar Holdings	Fantasy sports	NASDAQ
TRB	Tribune	Cubs and media	NYSE
TRK	Speedway Motorsports	Motor sports	NYSE
WWE	World Wrestling Entertainment	Wrestling	NYSE

AMEX = American Exchange; NASDAQ = regular NASDAQ; NYSE = New York Stock Exchange; OTC = NASDAQ's Over-the-Counter Bulletin Board.

The U of M is a private university, which means it normally does not receive any government assistance. However, the university can receive benefits such as tax abatements and government-backed bonds, and the government can even pay for buildings if there is a potential for public benefit. It is not that difficult for a mayor or governor to put pressure on local financial institutions to come to the aid of various entities such as local businesses or even a university.

The SEC's current primary focus is proper disclosure. The scandals affecting publicly traded companies such as Enron, WorldCom, and Global Crossing highlight the importance of following the SEC's disclosure rules. Proper disclosure often centers on **annual reports**; proxy statements; audited financial statements, including management's analysis of operating and financial conditions (Form 10-K); and quarterly reports, including unaudited financial statements (Form 10-Q) prepared by the corporation but not verified by an independent auditor (*Securities Regulation*, 1994). With the passage of the Sarbanes-Oxley Act of 2002, corporate executives now need to certify these filings to attest to their truthfulness.

Certain decisions made by a corporation's board of directors, such as election of new board members or a change in the bylaws, are subject to shareholder voting. At a corporation's annual meeting, stockholders who cannot attend are allowed to vote by proxy. A **proxy** enables someone else to vote in the shareholder's place. The proper disclosure of proxy-related issues is designed to ensure that all stockholders have the opportunity to air their ideas or concerns. A proxy statement needs to disclose the date, time, and location of the meeting; which types of stockholders (those holding class A or class B stock) are allowed to vote on certain issues; information about directors, including their compensation; and any significant decisions to be made such as changing the charter, issuing new securities, or discussing mergers and acquisitions (*Securities Regulation*, 1994). Although most annual meetings are

By closely analyzing and monitoring performance, government agencies ensure accuracy of financial practices.

not contentious, companies going through tough times or internal strife may need to discuss critical issues at the annual meeting. The government steps in to ensure that the competing groups provide appropriate and accurate information to all shareholders.

INSIDER TRADING

One key concern addressed by the SEC is **insider trading**. Pursuant to Section 1b of the Securities Exchange Act of 1934, insider trading is illegal. The definition of an insider has expanded over the years. Initially only the top corporate officials had confidential information that could guide their buying or selling practices associated with the company's securities. Over the years, the definition of an **insider** has come to cover other investors, even those not associated with the company, who acquire confidential information and utilize that information for their own or another's financial gain.

A good example of an insider trading case was publicized in 2000. A former temporary employee with several securities trading firms used his position to find information in garbage cans, in desks, and on computer printers (McMorris, Smith, & Schroeder, 2000). This was the first case of an insider trading ring on the Internet, in which information on 23 corporate deals was discussed with friends who met in chat rooms. In all, 19 people were charged with insider trading for their activities, which generated $8.4 million in profits. Some of those charged were fairly distant from the initial illegal tip. The case showed that the government was serious about all individuals involved in insider trading. The government was willing to go so far as to prosecute individuals who had heard the news from others who had heard the news from another source who could be traced to the original insider. Thus, the government does not care where people might have heard the inside information; the fact that they used inside information makes them liable (McMorris et al., 2000). It should be noted that one of the most prominent insider trading cases did not involve a conviction on that charge. The Martha Stewart case involved actions associated with using inside information to sell stocks, but Stewart was convicted of obstructing justice and lying to investigators about her alleged insider trading activity.

Bob Jones is one of the directors of the Stars of David. At one of the meetings, he hears that a major sponsor is leaving. He knows the sponsor represents more than 15% of the team's revenue, and the loss will significantly affect the company. With this information in mind, he sells all his shares before anyone else knows about the lost account. Mr. Jones would be liable for insider trading.

The sports world is not immune to insider trading. Reebok stocks rose 30% on the news that adidas was going to make an all-cash purchase of Reebok. Nine people were accused by the SEC of making more than $6 million in profit after placing suspicious stock and option trades based on inside information (Shell, 2005).

POWER OF THE SECURITIES AND EXCHANGE COMMISSION

Congress tracks the securities industry through the Committee on Banking, Housing, and Urban Affairs in the Senate and the Committee on Energy and Commerce in the House of Representatives. The Securities Exchange Act of 1934, mentioned earlier, concerns the sale and trading of existing securities and created the Securities and Exchange Commission (SEC). In contrast, the Securities Act of 1933 primarily concerns the issuing of new securities. The 1934 act provides the primary underpinning for rules governing brokers and dealers, financial responsibility requirements, regulations restricting borrowing to purchase securities, and rules for manipulation of security prices. The numerous regulatory requirements are beyond the SEC's scope. Thus, the SEC has delegated significant regulatory authority to several self-regulatory organizations that oversee their respective markets. The NYSE, NASDAQ, and AMEX are examples of self-regulatory organizations. However, as already mentioned, the NYSE and NASDAQ are both considering a change to for-profit status, which could possibly change the manner in which the government might try to regulate them.

STATE REGULATIONS

In addition to federal regulations, state regulations apply to any company issuing securities. A company issuing securities needs to ensure first that it follows all corporate laws in the state in which it is issuing stocks. Next, the certificate of incorporation needs to comply with all applicable state laws. The certificate of incorporation is the formal application and approval form from the state, authorizing the corporation's formation and ability to operate. Last, the corporation's bylaws must not conflict with either state laws or the certificate of incorporation (*Securities Regulation*, 1994).

State laws can cover such diverse areas as classes of stocks that can be issued, limitations on dividend policies, restrictions on transferring stocks, the rights and obligations of officers and directors, amending corporate charters to change capital structure, mergers and consolidations, selling corporate assets, and final corporate dissolution. Some laws are similar in the federal and state systems but provide for different legal conclusions. For example, state laws can cover mergers or consolidations, but many mergers require federal approval to avoid antitrust violations. Similarly, although state laws cover corporate dissolution, most dissolutions revolve around bankruptcy proceedings, which are covered by federal laws.

Government regulations affecting financial systems abound. Chapters 14 and 17 of this text cover additional issues such as laws affecting business structures, tax considerations, and bankruptcy protection. Government units can also work to shore up failing financial systems. After the stock market crash in 1929, states as well as the federal government tried to protect the banking industry. In late 1932 and early 1933, several governors called banking holidays, which prohibited depositors from removing their funds. Congress followed the lead and passed the Emergency Banking Act (Klise, 1972). The strategy could not save all banks, but it saved a large number of banks that were able to use the holiday closure to reorganize and strengthen. Although the government is supposed to protect the public, the sport finance examples in the following section might point to the scenario of the wolf guarding the sheep.

IN GOD WE TRUST

Government entities are elected to represent the interests of citizens within their jurisdiction. However, government interaction with sport can produce mixed results that affect the bottom line. A good example of such a connection is the Olympic bribery scandal that unfolded in 1998 and 1999. Officials within the Salt Lake Olympic Committee were accused of misappropriating funds to bribe International Olympic Committee members involved in the host-city bidding process ("Briefly," 2000). Some officials might consider such payments justified to help secure an event that could bring tremendous growth and income to Utah. Others would consider such actions an affront to the notion of amateurism and fair play. Moreover, such conduct can also be illegal as a violation of federal or state laws, or both, against corruption and bribery.

Financial wrongdoing was also alleged in a case involving the Tampa Bay Lightning. Former city and Lightning officials were cleared of criminal charges after team officials allegedly altered their balance sheets before city officials reviewed them (Gilpin, 1998). Charges were dropped by the prosecutor, possibly because of perceived difficulty in prosecuting the case. City officials backed a $160 million arena deal and agreed to guarantee $1 million a year in the package. Former Lightning executive David LeFevre allegedly ordered the removal of $1.1 million in short-term liabilities from the balance sheet and transferred the funds to another building project that did not become active until nine months later (Gilpin, 1998). Thus, the balance sheet did not accurately reflect all the team's debt. The criminal probe failed because there was no proof that the city had relied on the altered documents to make the decision (Gilpin, 1998).

As highlighted earlier in the text, there have been a number of recent scandals. One of the bigger scandals involved Adelphia, one of the nation's biggest cable operators and owner of the Buffalo Sabres. Adelphia and Sabres owner John Rigas was convicted of embezzling billions of dollars and using the Sabres to secure millions of dollars in loans. During the bankruptcy proceedings in 2002, the team was taken over by the NHL, which eventually found a buyer in 2003.

In a lawsuit against the city of San Francisco, plaintiffs alleged that city officials failed to comply with voting secrecy requirements and allowed early voting at four public housing projects during the elections that would decide on the proposed San Francisco 49ers' new stadium (Chiang & Wilson, 1998). The two propositions authorized $100 million in lease revenue bonds for the proposed stadium and changed some land zoning restrictions. A state court of appeals dismissed the suit (Chiang & Wilson, 1998).

But not all government interaction with sport entities results in litigation or fiascoes. The relations between government entities and sports organizations are often very amicable and frequently produce positive results for both sides. A good example is the action the Canadian government was considering in order to protect Canada's professional teams. Canadian teams have fared poorly over the years because of a weak Canadian dollar (compared with the stronger U.S. dollar) and heavy tax burdens. The Vancouver Canucks, for example, had $54.8 million in 1998 revenue but anticipated losing between $20 and $25 million. A portion of these losses was attributed to the players' salaries, which increased more than 30% in one year to $55.4 million (Canadian) (Schreiner & Damsell, 1998).

The Canucks are not alone. Combined, the Ottawa Senators and Montreal Canadiens pay more property tax than all 21 U.S.-based NHL teams combined (Harper, 1999). Some of the taxing shortfalls that affect the Senators follow:

- $17 million in provincial and federal income taxes for employees, including players
- $4.5 million in property taxes for the Corel Centre
- $5.6 million in amusement taxes on ticket sales
- $5 million in general sales taxes
- $2.1 million surcharge for a highway overpass built for the arena
- $1.1 million in corporate and capital taxes
- $450,000 in withholding taxes for nonresident employees on the team

In total, the Senators and the Corel Centre paid $36.6 million in taxes—not including the arts tax on broadcast rights, which forces the Senators to pay 5% of their television revenue to help fund the making of Canadian films (Harper, 1999). Interestingly enough, the Ontario government levies the amusement tax because under provincial law an NHL game is not considered "Canadian entertainment" (Harper, 1999). The taxes listed are often avoided by U.S. teams, which might pay only sales, income, and a ticket tax to help repay facility construction costs. Teams in the United States can also negotiate away some of these tax obligations when they move to a new facility and obtain significant incentives to relocate.

On the basis of such losses, the Canadian legislature was examining an annual government subsidy of $5 million Canadian ($3.3 million U.S. dollars at the time) to each of the 10 professional teams in Canada (only NBA, NHL, and MLB teams). The government was also examining a 150% tax **deduction** for corporate sports sponsorship, including the purchase of luxury boxes ("Canada Eyes," 1998). However, after a significant public outcry, the Canadian government backed out of the pledged aid for professional teams (Beltrame, 2000). As of 2007, only eight professional teams remain in Canada (one NBA, one MLB, and six NHL teams).

ENVIRONMENTAL CONDITIONS

The fact that the Canadian economy does not help professional teams in Canada is a critical environmental condition. Professional teams might seem like a very solid investment if one considers how some franchises increased in value in the 1990s. However, there is no such thing as a guaranteed financial winner. Numerous environmental concerns can affect any sport investment. The following quote from a Baltimore Orioles annual report highlights the various threats.

Escalating player salaries have become our most serious problem; baseball is experiencing a rapidly changing environment. We have entered a period of financial extravagance and, while it lasts, salaries will continue to escalate wildly and the stability of our game will be put to a severe test. (Much, 1997, December 1, p.1)

The rapidly escalating salaries for professional athletes have fostered the tremendous boom in new arena and stadium construction—new revenue streams are needed to fund salary increases. The previous quote might have appeared in a press release from MLB concerning the aftermath of the 1994-1995 player strike and the continuing increase in player salaries through the beginning of the 21st century. However, the quote appeared in the 1977 Baltimore baseball club's annual report. Baseball salaries in 1977 averaged $76,066 (Ruxin, 1989). By 1998, the average baseball salary was $1.4 million, with 750 players expecting to earn over $1 million (Singer, 1998). By 2001, the average salary in baseball was $2.138 million, with four teams (New York Yankees, Los Angeles Dodgers, Boston Red Sox, and Cleveland Indians) averaging more than $3 million per player on their rosters ("Average Salary," 2001). The average MLB player's salary in 2006 was $2,699,292 (Blum, 2006).

The team with the lowest average payroll in 2001 was the Montreal Expos (now the Washington Nationals), which averaged $926,333 per player and was being considered for elimination through contraction ("Average Salary," 2001). By 2006 there was one team at the very bottom of the salary pole, and that was the Florida Marlins with a team payroll of just under $15 million. The next closest team was the Tampa Bay Devil Rays at just over $35 million. The team with the highest player salaries was the New York Yankees, with a payroll of more than $194 million. There were 10 teams in 2006 with payrolls over $90 million and 5 with payrolls over $100 million (*USA Today* Salaries Databases, 2007). Player salaries represent just one internal constraint that affects a professional team's financial bottom line.

Internal constraints are factors within a business that can be controlled. Player personnel issues can involve both internal and external constraints. A baseball team may have a farm system to help train young players, as well as gifted scouts who can help sign top talent. The team can also carefully plan the payroll to optimize bonuses and planned player retirement or free agency. These internal variables must be contrasted with external variables such as whether baseball is losing popularity, whether fewer high school teams are being formed, whether other sports are drawing greater fan support, whether other teams are paying their players more, and whether a municipality taxes the team or athletes in an unreasonable manner.

CONCLUSION

Every business has to balance the internal and external constraints in its financial environment. The Smiths need to deal with their own banks, their customers' banks, and possibly the financial institutions of their suppliers or landlord. The Smiths can face a multitude of other financial systems and concerns, from having to manage their accounts to ensure that they are protected from a bank default to understanding the SEC's authority if they wish to sell shares in their business. Although the number of entities involved is limited, the interactions can be highly complex. The interactions are that much more complex for the Stars of David. Imagine the millions of interactions each season that relate to attendance alone, with fans buying their tickets with bank **drafts** or credit cards; remember that each transaction requires the involvement of at least two financial institutions. In addition, when the Stars need funds, they will need to go beyond the banks if they wish to issue additional stocks or bonds.

Every successful business at one point or another handles money, stocks, bonds, and other assets, ranging from liquid to hard assets. Similarly, every business needs to be concerned about the inner workings of all the financial institutions. It is impossible to know where you might need to obtain your next round of capital infusion. One year a business might obtain necessary funds from a bank or a public offering. The next year the business might have to borrow from an insurance company or pension fund. The options are limited only by the various internal and external constraints. These constraints can include such elements as the corporation's own bylaws or articles of incorporation (discussed in chapter 4) or its credit rating (discussed in chapter 8). Government regulations can dramatically affect the options if interest rates rise or if borrowing regulations are tightened. No matter what capital criteria might arise, businesses need to be proactive in their capital funding operations to help reduce borrowing or capital acquisition expenses and to increase their ability to raise any necessary funds.

CLASS DISCUSSION TOPICS

1. What is the difference between the NYSE and the NASDAQ?
2. What determines value?
3. Why would the price of a stock increase or decrease?
4. What is the difference between stocks and bonds?
5. Should governments control banks?
6. Should governments control monetary policies?
7. Why would a bank want or need to borrow money?
8. Should banks be allowed to sell insurance, securities, and related products or services?
9. Discuss some of your positive and negative banking experiences, such as bouncing a check.
10. What is the difference between a bank and a savings and loan?
11. If you were going to take a minor league baseball team public, what stock exchange would you try to get it on and why?

4

BUSINESS STRUCTURE

CHAPTER OBJECTIVES

After studying this chapter, you should be able to do the following:

- Understand why a business structure can affect a company financially.

- Understand when each type of business structure should be used.

- Define the requirements for each type of business structure utilized in sport.

- Compare the advantages and disadvantages of sole proprietorships, partnerships, corporations, and limited liability corporations or limited liability partnerships.

The previous chapter highlights the financial systems that come into play when we examine financial issues, but the structure of a sport business can also generate particular financial benefits or hardships. Thus, it is just as important to understand business structures as it is to understand financial systems. The Smiths could form their business as a sole proprietorship, a partnership, an S corporation, a C corporation, or a limited liability corporation; and each business type would have different tax and legal concerns or benefits. A company such as Nike needs funds to expand and grow, and corporations have the ability to issue stocks and bonds as a vehicle for acquiring additional funds. Thus, one of the most important decisions for any sport business is what form the business entity should take.

The various options for raising funds highlighted in chapters 8 through 10 are often contingent on the type of business structure that is seeking funds. This chapter covers the various types of business structures that exist and considers the advantages and disadvantages associated with each structure type.

Most businesses start as small single-owner companies and expand from that point if they are successful. The owner of a sporting goods store could invest his life savings in a business and own the entire business with no obligations to any lenders. However, if the business is not structured properly, it could be lost through litigation.

 Assume that Mr. Smith owns a supplement business himself that he never incorporated. He keeps the business separate from the fitness center he owns in partnership with his wife, Cheryl. Bob operates the business himself, within the most popular type of business structure in the United States, the sole proprietorship. As discussed in more detail later, a sole proprietor is completely liable for any business debts. Thus, if Bob sells a defective product and is sued, he could lose his life savings and possibly any other money or property he might have. However, if he had utilized a different business structure, such as a limited liability corporation (LLC), his financial picture could have been significantly brighter.

The various types of business entities that exist include governments, nonprofits, sole proprietorships, partnerships, limited partnerships, limited liability corporations (LLCs) or limited liability partnerships (LLPs), subchapter S corporations, and C corporations. This text does not focus on government structures, even though they can be found throughout the sport industry, but they are highlighted here. Government entities can run numerous sport entities such as park and recreation departments, high school athletic departments, community centers, public college athletic programs, and numerous other programs sponsored in whole or in part by the public. In fact, most sports organizations throughout the world are owned or operated by government entities. Since such programs are government entities, their liability and financial status are significantly different from those of traditional private businesses. For example, a business that exceeds its budget may need to borrow funds to survive but will still owe the funds even if it goes out of business. In contrast, an institution such as a public university can exceed its budget by millions and traditionally the state will assume the obligation and pay the bills, even if the expenses were not authorized, since the state government is ultimately responsible for the debts of its own agencies.

NONPROFIT ORGANIZATIONS

In most countries the Olympic programs are run by the government. However, in the United States, the federal government passed a law (the Amateur Sports Act of 1978) that allowed for the creation of the United States Olympic Committee (USOC), which is supposed to be a nonprofit organization. The USOC can utilize its nonprofit status to receive gifts from donors who would possibly give money only if they were able to write off the donation from their tax obligations. Nonprofits can own and operate sport businesses. It is easy to find examples of nonprofit organizations that operate sporting events; some examples are the New York City Marathon, Special Olympics, Pop Warner Little Scholars, Little League Baseball, and health clubs associated with YMCAs and hospitals.

Nonprofits can also own professional sports teams. For example, the Massachusetts attorney general investigated the sale of the Boston Red Sox in 2002 to ensure that charities received the largest amount possible under the proposed sale. The Yawkey Trust, which was the majority owner of the team, benefits numerous charities, and the state examined the sale to make sure the highest price was received so the **trust** would be able to give the greatest amount back to these charities ("Attorney General," 2001). The sale proceeds were used for various purposes, including a multimillion-dollar donation by the Yawkey Trust to Boston College for construction of a football building attached to the football field.

Nonprofits face different financial concerns, primarily in relation to raising funds. Although some nonprofits can use traditional bank lending, the primary fund-raising options for nonprofits are donations and the selling of various items, from memberships and registration fees for special events to television and sponsorship rights.

 The West Hartford Badminton Club (WHBC) was started by a group of badminton enthusiasts. After they started earning some money and growing, however, they ran into a problem. The city rents their buildings only to nonprofit organizations. Thus, to be able to use the city's gym, the initial members decided to incorporate as a nonprofit organization. Their first step was to complete all the necessary paperwork from state and federal agencies to obtain appropriate recognition. The most important recognition is the 501(c) designation of a nonprofit for tax purposes. Without this designation, donations would not be tax deductible. It should be noted that regular playing fees are not deductible, but membership fees paid without receiving any significant benefits would probably be tax deductible for members. Once the tax-exempt status is obtained, WHBC cannot rest on its laurels. The club has to comply with numerous regulations such as government filings and maintain its nonprofit status. A nonprofit status is given if the organization has a cultural, artistic, educational, or other public benefit. Thus, the club often goes to local schools and performs free badminton demonstrations to educate kids about the sport.

Although it might seem that only large entities can be nonprofits, any group of people can form a nonprofit (usually you need at least two people to form a nonprofit organization as there needs to be at least two different officers such as a president and vice-president). Chapter 14 includes additional discussion of the tax consequences of raising funds for nonprofits.

SOLE PROPRIETORSHIPS

A sole proprietorship is a business entity owned by a single person. If the Smiths decided not to form a partnership but to have one person as the sole owner, then the business would be classified as a sole proprietorship. The primary benefits of this business structure are that no formal paperwork is needed to start the business, the cost of organizing the business is not significant, and profits and organizational control do not need to be shared with anyone else (Cheeseman, 2001). The primary disadvantages are that a single individual has limited ability to raise significant capital, the owner can face unlimited personal liability, and the business ends when the owner dies (Siegel, Shim, & Hartman, 1992). Another disadvantage is that a sole proprietorship is normally a single-person operation without access to support from partners. This lack of support can render decision making more difficult.

Other advantages and disadvantages associated with a sole proprietorship are listed here:

Advantages

- Total control over decision making
- Revenues taxed only once
- Great flexibility
- Easy to form
- All profits retained by owner
- Less concern about confidentiality
- Easy to sell
- Fewer government restrictions

Disadvantages

- Limited managerial experience
- Unlimited personal liability
- Lasts only as long as owner lives
- Limited access to capital funds

Most businesses in the world are sole proprietorships (Cheeseman, 2001). In the sports world, many entities fall under this classification. In thinking about sole proprietorships in sport, you may envision small mom-and-pop businesses such as a specialized sporting goods store, a bowling alley, or a martial arts studio; but this leaves out another whole classification of sole proprietorships. Independent contractors are often sole proprietors and are prevalent in many sports (e.g., professional bowlers, skiers, figure skaters, or race car drivers). These individuals have a minimum of expenses apart from travel and entry expenses and are often living on meager purses won at events.

Once they become more successful and have larger income streams and expenses, they can become incorporated (incorporation is discussed later in this chapter).

GENERAL AND LIMITED PARTNERSHIPS

If the Smiths decide to run the business equally and if each owns 50% (or any other division of ownership) of the business, they are considered partners. A partnership's primary benefits are minimal formation costs and few government regulations. The primary disadvantages are difficulty in raising capital, unlimited personal and business liability for all partners, and immediate termination of the partnership once one partner dies or withdraws from the partnership (Cheeseman, 2001). The advantages and disadvantages associated with a partnership are highlighted here:

Advantages

- Some control over decision making
- Revenues taxed only once
- Great flexibility
- Easy to form
- All profits retained by owners
- Easy to sell
- Fewer government restrictions

Disadvantages

- Limited managerial experience
- Joint personal liability
- Limited access to capital funds
- Lasts only as long as partnership survives

There are two primary types of partnerships. In a general partnership, individuals or groups combine their resources to share in operating, managing, and controlling a business and also share in all profits and liabilities. This type of partnership has several advantages. General partnerships have greater access to capital than sole proprietorships do; profits are taxed only once when distributed to the partners; and the combination of at least two parties helps enhance managerial decision making. The primary disadvantages are that this type of partnership has a limited longevity based on each partner (e.g., a human partner may die, or a partner that is a corporation or other business

structure may be terminated by dissolution or by court order); partners are jointly and severally liable for partnership debt or liability; capital acquisition is limited compared with that of corporations; and the managerial talent pool is often limited to only those individuals who are partners, while corporations may have many more voices from which to harness expertise.

A general partnership can be created in one of two ways. An express partnership is developed through a written contract. An implied partnership is created through the actions of the parties.

 If the Smiths did not formalize any agreement, but their conduct of the business was similar to that of a partnership, their business would be considered a partnership. If the Smiths shared profits, managed the facility together, and were each able to sign the company's checks, the business would be an implied partnership.

In contrast to a general partnership, a limited partnership involves a general partner who is responsible for managing the company and one or more "limited" partners who provide only financial input (Cheeseman, 2001). A **limited partner** is entitled to share profits but is not engaged in day-to-day management. Because the limited partner's stake in the company is purely financial, her liability is limited to her financial contribution. Limited liability provides a strong incentive for people to invest in a partnership. Other benefits associated with a limited partnership include the ability to generate more capital than sole proprietorships, maintenance of a pass-through benefit for the profits paid to a limited partner (i.e., limited partners are paid their profits without the partnership being taxed first), and the fact that limited partners can invest in several different businesses without exposing themselves to significant liability. The two biggest disadvantages of a limited partnership are the lack of managerial involvement by the limited partner and the fact that the general partner is still subject to unlimited liability.

Both general and limited partnerships can be ended through express language in the partnership agreement or through addition or subtraction of a partner. By law, a partnership ends when a partner dies, a partner goes bankrupt, or the partnership engages in any illegal activity. A partnership can also end if a partner is adjudicated insane by the

To have a strong partnership you need more than a handshake; you need a strong contract to protect all parties. Would you be willing to become a partner with anyone?

courts, if a partner can no longer perform his duties, if a partner engages in improper conduct, or if the partnership can never make money (Cheeseman, 2001). Some businesses, no matter how hard they try, might not make any money. If a partnership has entered this trap and cannot make any money, a partner can ask the court to dissolve the partnership. This is a last alternative if the other partners refuse to close the business and one partner does not want to invest any more money because of the business' inability to make a profit. The partner that wants to exit the partnership will need to prove that there is no likelihood that the partnership will ever make money.

SUBCHAPTER S CORPORATIONS

Subchapter S corporations (often called S corporations) represent almost half of all corporations

(Marullo, 1997, February). S corporations can have up to 35 shareholders and can own subsidiaries, and S corporations that are tax-exempt organizations such as charities can own shares. The primary advantage of S corporations is that their income flows through the corporation to the shareholders, who pay taxes as personal income. This avoids the double taxation situation inherent in C corporations, in which the corporation is taxed and dividend income to the shareholders is also taxed. The option of owning subsidiaries allows S corporations to insulate themselves further from liability (Marullo, 1997, February).

Assume that the Smiths incorporate their fitness center as an S corporation and become very successful. They decide to branch out into manufacturing exercise equipment. They can start a separate subsidiary company under the S corporation to manufacture the equipment. Someone who was injured on the equipment could sue the manufacturer, but because the manufacturer is a subsidiary, the fitness center could not be touched, nor could any other subsidiary of the Smiths' S corporation.

A major disadvantage for an S corporation is that the corporation can issue only one form of stock. A traditional corporation can issue various types of shares that entitle shareholders to different **voting rights**, or it can issue preferred stock that entitles stockholders to better dividends. An S corporation must be based in the United States, and no more than 20% of its income can be derived from passive investments (providing financial resources without any other assistance). Furthermore, corporations, partnerships, and international investors cannot invest in an S corporation. Last, an S corporation cannot own 80% or more of another corporation's stock (Cheeseman, 2001).

The S corporation fell somewhat out of favor through advancements in LLCs in the 1990s. Limited liability corporations, as discussed later on, are simpler to form and manage than S corporations. Thus S corporations are not as popular, and numerous S corporations are being converted to LLCs. At the same time, numerous S corporations still exist in the sport industry and in all other industry segments.

C CORPORATIONS

Corporations are entities whose formation complies with specific state laws. Thus, corporations are "fictitious" legal entities that exist only through the rights given to them by specific statutory law. Corporations are often referred to as C corporations to distinguish them from S corporations. Corporations need to develop bylaws and articles of incorporation that specify how they will conduct business. The articles of incorporation typically contain the corporate name, the number of shares the corporation will issue, the corporation's initial address, and the name and address of each of the initial incorporators (Cheeseman, 2001).

A corporation can be formed in any state as long as it complies with specific rules. Rules may relate to activities such as conducting annual meetings, keeping minutes from each meeting, and electing boards of directors. Delaware is the "friendliest" corporation state, with laws that assist a company in fending off a takeover attempt. The Delaware business laws are very favorable to corporations and contain numerous advantages compared with laws in other states (as highlighted in the sidebar below.

Corporations have several major advantages and disadvantages. The primary advantage sought by those seeking to incorporate is the liability protection available to the owners (shareholders). The primary disadvantages of incorporating are double taxation, the costs involved in forming the corporation, and the complexities associated with complying with all pertinent government regulations. The various advantages and disadvantages associated with incorporating are highlighted here.

Advantages

- Unlimited life of the corporation
- Liability of the corporation limited to the extent of corporate assets
- Creditors not permitted to go after individual investors for payment over and beyond their equity investment
- Ownership interest easily transferable in the form of shares
- Ability to hire a broad base of talented managers
- Tax benefit: dividends paid to corporation are 70% tax free
- Greater bargaining position with vendors who are more willing to provide credit to a corporation versus a single owner
- Ability to issue publicly traded debt and equity

Disadvantages

- Complex formation process
- Need to answer to shareholders who might have ulterior motives

Advantages of Forming a Corporation in Delaware

The following advantages are available for corporations domiciled in Delaware:

- Delaware has a court of chancery, which is a business court that hears only business cases, without a jury and with appointed judges.
- Fees are low; corporate formation charges can be as little as $90, and franchise taxes can be as low as $200 a year.
- Shares of stock are not subject to Delaware taxes if the owner lives outside the state.
- Delaware-based corporations do not have to pay taxes on income earned outside the state as long as no income is earned in the state (Delaware InterCorp, 2000).

Favorable laws have helped develop Delaware as the premiere state for incorporating businesses; more than half of the publicly incorporated companies in the United States were formed there (Lipin, 2000). These favorable laws include a dedicated judge that handles only business-related cases; such cases are not heard by a jury. Due in part to these legal advantages afforded to businesses incorporated in Delaware, a research study indicated that Delaware-based businesses from 1991 to 1996 were worth 5% more than corporations formed in other states (Lipin, 2000). Nevada has also become a frequently cited state for new corporations because it has adopted similar business-friendly laws.

- Sometimes onerous government regulations
- Double taxation

The paperwork associated with incorporating can be voluminous, including initial filings, annual reports, Securities and Exchange Commission filings (for public corporations only), and so on. The expenses associated with documentation make up only one cost and do not include the costs associated with state filing fees (which can be thousands of dollars), hiring entities to represent the corporation in each state where the corporation conducts business (called an agent for service of process), preparing audited financial statements, and a host of additional fees. The other major financial drain for any corporation is the prospect of double taxation.

If the Smiths earned a $100,000 profit as a sole proprietorship or partnership, they might pay $30,000 in taxes and take home or reinvest $70,000 (this assumes that the tax rate is 30%). However, if Bob and Cheryl formed a corporation that returned the same profit, they would take home much less. Assume that the corporation's and the Smiths' personal tax rates were 30%. After the corporation paid $30,000 in taxes, the corporation could distribute up to $70,000 to its shareholders in dividends. If the Smiths received the entire $70,000 as a dividend, they would owe 30% of that amount in taxes. Thus, the after-tax amount that the incorporated Smiths would take home would be only $49,000. But, although Bob and Cheryl would lose $21,000 in take-home pay by incorporating, they might gain much more valuable benefits in that they would not face liability on personal assets, and their odds of obtaining external funding would increase dramatically.

Another concern is the potential for shareholders to rebel and demand a managerial change. If the shareholders are dissatisfied with the corporate strategy or management team, they can vote to change the corporate direction or management. Most major companies have departments that work exclusively with shareholders to address their concerns and to help produce **shareholders' reports**.

SMC is a publicly traded company. It started out as a sole proprietorship, with the founder making specialized golf clubs in her garage. In the 1980s the founder received an order for 10,000 rackets. She took the order and down payment to the bank to borrow money and rent a space. Her attorney suggested at that time that she incorporate the business so she could obtain funds from other investors rather than borrow money from the bank. Three years later she was the CEO of a publicly traded company. Although she had a nice title and salary, she had to give away a large part of her company. At one point she owned 100% of the company, but now she owns only 10%. Although her share of the company has decreased, the value has increased significantly. Her 100% share was worth around $10,000 before her big order; now several years later her 10% stake is worth millions.

LIMITED LIABILITY CORPORATIONS AND PARTNERSHIPS

Forming a traditional corporation can be complex, expensive, and time consuming. Adding the further burden of going public can encourage entities to form a limited liability corporation in place of a traditional corporation. LLCs and LLPs are quickly gaining favor in the United States because of their simplicity. The primary benefit for LLCs and LLPs is their classification as a partnership for federal income tax purposes (Revenue Ruling 88-76, 1988). Besides the tax benefit, LLCs and LLPs obtain the liability protection afforded to corporations.

In contrast to an S corporation, which cannot be owned by either a corporation or a partnership, an LLC or LLP can be owned by another corporation or partnership. Thus, Sport Manufacturing Company can purchase another business that is an LLC and keep that unit separate as an LLC. The major disadvantage of LLCs is their newness. There is no national standard, and each state has unique rules and regulations that will take several years to work their way through the legal systems. However, once all the legalities are settled, LLCs and LLPs will become a primary business structure for new businesses (Cheeseman, 2001).

An LLC or LLP is created through the filing of articles of partnership in the state where the business

Who Wants to Own the NHL?

In 2006, the NHL had 30 teams with 30 different owners who participate in jointly managing the league. However, a work stoppage that cancelled the 2004-2005 season brought forth interest from others to possibly buy the league. Before the work stoppage, the NHL was reportedly worth $4.9 billion according to *Forbes* magazine, with the Detroit Red Wings being the most valuable team at an estimated $266 million. One bid came from two LLCs based in Boston who offered $3.5 billion to purchase all 30 NHL clubs and operate them as independent teams within a large corporate structure ("Two Firms Make Bid," 2005). Another bid came several days later from the National Hockey Group (NHG). The NHG proposed a fan-owned and -operated league, with a proposed board made up of players, managers, and fans (Shank, 2005).

The concept of merging a league into a single entity is not new. Some leagues have started out as a single entity for legal reasons. For example, Major League Soccer (MLS), the WNBA, a women's professional soccer league, and the former XFL were all started as single-entity organizations. The intent of such a business structure is to consolidate operational functions and avoid antitrust law concerns. In fact the MLS structure was brought to court by several players who claimed the league violated antitrust laws. The court concluded that MLS did not violate the provision in the antitrust laws relating to two or more entities conspiring to restrain trade since the MLS was an LLC with owner investors rather than individual team owners. The court concluded that the MLS owned the teams and all intellectual property related to the teams, and the league exercises supervisory authority over most team and league activity (Conrad, 2000).

will be organized. Although the SEC typically does not regulate LLCs and LLPs, it can regulate some of their activities, such as issuing publicly traded debt. The Boston Celtics are an example of a partnership that had to file reports with the SEC because of having publicly traded securities. Now that the team is privately owned it does not need to file any reports with the SEC. The lack of SEC oversight can save a significant amount of money, especially if the LLC or LLP does not need to pay for audited financial statements and other related expenses.

 The Stars were started as an LLC in Delaware. Although the team never played a game in Delaware, that did not prevent the Stars from incorporating there. After several years, investors came forward who wanted to purchase a controlling interest in the basketball league and take it public. As part of the effort to take the league public, the investors wanted each team to be publicly traded as well. Thus, the Stars completed all their government paperwork, audited their books, and sold 1 million shares of class B stock to the public. The original owners were issued 10 million class A shares, and these shares controlled 98% of the voting rights to the team. Thus, the original owners did not lose their managerial power to control the corporation but they also raised needed capital.

CONCLUSION

This chapter covers the various business forms that exist and some of the positive and negative aspects of each. Although the form of a business is typically a legal issue, it also involves important financial considerations. A sole proprietorship can never issue stock, so its capital acquisition options are very limited. In contrast, a corporation can go public, but such an action raises numerous financial reporting requirements. Thus, it is imperative to consider the business structure before you examine what financing options are available or what industry ratios might serve as appropriate frames of reference for comparing one business with another. As highlighted throughout the rest of this book, industry benchmarking standards might exist, but they are irrelevant if you are comparing two different types of business structures.

CLASS DISCUSSION TOPICS

1. If you were the Smiths, what type of business structure would you try to establish?

2. The NFL currently does not allow any team other than the Green Bay Packers to have any shareholders. Should the NFL change this rule?

3. Give the pros and cons of public ownership of a sports franchise. Should more teams be publicly owned so fans can be owners?

4. With all the money the NCAA generates, should it still be considered a nonprofit organization?

5. Would you ever want to start your own business? If so, what do you think you would need in order to be financially successful?

6. Do you think the LLC type of structure gives too much flexibility to business owners, who can hide their assets and avoid financial judgments by claiming the LLC has no money and is just a shell?

7. Do you agree with the concept of double taxation for corporations?

8. Should a business be able to choose what business structure it wants to adopt, or should the government decide?

PART II

PRINCIPLES
OF FINANCIAL ANALYSIS

Now that you know the basics of finance, you can start to analyze a business' strengths and weaknesses. Part II will give you the tools to do that analysis.

Chapter 5, Financial Statements, Forecasts, and Planning, introduces you to the types of financial statements produced in the financial decision-making process. The chapter then outlines the different financial ratios that can be used to compare one company with others in that industry. The process for preparing financial forecasts and budgets is then described. Through forecasts and budgets, a company can plan for the future based on sound financial reasoning. The chapter concludes with break-even analysis, which helps a company determine if its financial planning was realistic.

Chapter 6, Time Value of Money, highlights a simple concept integral to all financial planning: Money loses value over time, and a dollar today is worth more than a dollar tomorrow. Because of the risk associated with the changing value of money, it is important for a company to plan for the future (budget) based on realistic assumptions covered in this chapter.

To properly plan, a company needs to gather and interpret data. As chapter 7, Approaches to Financial Planning, shows you, the key is starting with accurate data. It is impossible to plan based on hunches, so companies need to develop or gather appropriate information. This information will help with the planning process and is highlighted in this chapter. The planning process examines issues such as how to develop a budget and how to incorporate the financial plan into a business plan.

5

FINANCIAL STATEMENTS, FORECASTS, AND PLANNING

CHAPTER OBJECTIVES

After studying this chapter, you should be able to do the following:

- Identify the elements of the balance sheet.
- Identify the elements of the income statement.
- Discuss the cash flow statement and relate it to the income statement and the balance sheet.
- Define common financial ratios that can be used to assess an organization's liquidity, activity, financial leverage, profitability, and inventory as well as the firm's collection cycle.
- Understand the information that needs to be gathered before beginning forecasting.
- Forecast sales as well as profit and loss.
- Understand what drives the need for capital.
- Forecast the balance sheet.
- Relate the projected profit and loss and balance sheet to industry norms as a reasonableness check.
- Discuss how to use break-even analysis as a planning tool.

To achieve success in their ventures, sports administrators and managers must know how to analyze financial statements and must develop skills in financial forecasting and planning. In this chapter, we discuss the "nuts and bolts" of financial statements as well as show how cash flow is derived from these basic financial documents. We also introduce you to the steps involved in financial forecasting and planning. In addition, we describe the basic accounting statements that businesses use for reporting purposes. The techniques we discuss are critical for starting new businesses, investing in new equipment, and making appropriate operating decisions. The chapter addresses the following key concepts underlying financial analysis:

- Types of financial statements
- Interpreting financial statements
- Preparing financial forecasts and budgets
- Break-even analysis

TYPES OF FINANCIAL STATEMENTS

Financial statements are compiled from a firm's accounting records. These financial statements include the balance sheet, the income statement, and the statement of cash flows. Financial statements are intended to provide information about a business in a consistent manner as a result of efforts by accountants to follow generally

accepted accounting principles (GAAP). Two private organizations, the American Institute of Certified Public Accountants and the Financial Accounting Standards Board, as well as the Securities and Exchange Commission, an agency of the federal government, are the authoritative bodies that determine GAAP. For example, the GAAP set forth policies concerning how to categorize depreciation or properly record losses. However, although GAAP are considered appropriate standards, they have come under attack because of loopholes that allowed the accounting scandals in 2001 and 2002 to occur, involving such companies as Enron, WorldCom, and Tyco. In reaction to these scandals, the Sarbanes-Oxley Act was passed by Congress in 2002 as an attempt to make the financial operations of public companies more transparent to the investing public.

The **balance sheet** displays the financial condition of a business at a single point in time, offering information about assets, liabilities, and owners' equity. The **income statement** describes a business' profit or loss over a given length of time, such as a month, quarter, or year. It provides information about a business' operating performance over that period of time. The **statement of cash flows** indicates how the cash position of a business has changed over a given period of time. For example, the firm may see its cash position depleted through the purchasing of machinery or supplies. The firm's cash position can also be diminished through the paying down of debt or the paying of dividends to stockholders. It is possible for the income statement to show that a business had a profitable year, yet the

© Vittoriano Rastelli/CORBIS

Financial statements, including a company's balance sheets, income statements, and statements of cash flow, are intended to provide information about the business in a systematic, consistent manner.

company's cash holdings declined. The statement of cash flows can be used to determine what happened to the business' cash.

BALANCE SHEET

The balance sheet is used by accountants to give a picture of the business at a single point in time, as if the business were standing still. Here is the basic definition that all balance sheets follow:

assets = liabilities + capital provided by owners

Since this basic definition must always hold, capital provided by investors is always equal to the assets of the firm minus the liabilities of the firm.

In a balance sheet, the assets of the firm are listed according to the length of time it takes to convert them to cash. The asset side is normally determined by the nature of the business, the industry it operates in, and financing and operational decisions made by management. In many businesses, management has to decide whether sales are cash or credit transactions, whether equipment should be purchased or leased, and whether cash balances should remain as cash or be invested in short-term securities that can earn a return.

Liquidity refers to the degree of ease and quickness of converting assets to cash. The entries shown under **current assets** are the most liquid since they are expected to be converted to cash in one year or less. Examples of current assets that appear on balance sheets are cash and short-term financial assets. In addition, current assets include accounts receivable, which consist of the dollar amounts not yet collected from customers for goods and services sold to them (after adjustments for bad debts). Inventory consists of raw materials that are used for manufacturing, for work in process, or for finishing goods. Current assets are discussed in more detail in Chapter 12. **Fixed assets** are the assets on the balance sheet with the least liquidity. These assets include real estate, plants, and equipment. Unlike current assets, fixed assets normally are not converted to cash for such day-to-day activities as meeting payroll or paying vendors.

The Stars of David's balance sheet is shown in figure 5.1. Most of the current assets consist of cash and cash equivalents. An additional major category of current assets is accounts receivable. The team also reports prepaid expenses, which are combined with other current assets. Since the Stars are not a manufacturer or retailer, the balance sheet does not include inventory as a current asset. The Stars report equipment and property as fixed assets. Other fixed assets include the value of the franchise itself.

In the liabilities section of the balance sheet, liabilities are listed in the order of when they must be paid. Current liabilities consist of obligations that must be paid down in one year or less, while long-term liabilities consist of items that will not be paid down completely for more than one year. The liabilities and stockholders' equity (capital provided by investors) portions of the balance sheet typically reflect decisions about the sources of financing for the business. For example, decisions concerning the mix of financing provided by debt versus stockholders' equity, as well as short-term versus long-term debt financing, are reflected in the entries shown in the liabilities and stockholders' equity section of the balance sheet.

 The Stars of David's primary current liability is accounts payable, which comprises bills to vendors that have not yet been paid. In addition, the Stars of David, like other professional sports teams, are locked into long-term compensation arrangements with many of their players. Moneys owed for player salaries can be broken down into two categories: long-term liabilities and current liabilities. When a player signs a 10-year contract, only a portion will be immediately due, so the entire contract should not be considered a current liability to the business even though the entire debt will be owed at a later date. The compensation that is due to players, coaches, and management within a year or less is included in the current portion of deferred compensation. This makes sense for financial and practical reasons because the future liability can be very speculative. If a player is injured, retires, or is traded, for example, then the Stars may no longer owe that obligation.

The Stars list the noncurrent portion of deferred compensation under long-term liabilities because this includes compensation to players, coaches, and management under employment contracts that will be payable beyond one year into the future. Most of the team's long-term liabilities are in the form of bank financing.

For the Stars of David, the investment in the business by its owners is denoted by the term *stockholders' equity*.

The net working capital, or working capital, of any business is current assets less current liabilities. When net working capital is positive, this means the firm expects that the cash paid out over the next year will be less than

Assets ($)	As of December 31,		
	2004	2005	2006
Current assets:			
Cash and equivalents	3,109,000	13,622,680	20,351,240
Accounts receivable	1,400,000	5,800,000	3,200,000
Prepaid expenses and other current assets	521,000	637,000	602,000
Total current assets	5,030,000	20,059,680	24,153,240
Fixed assets:			
Property and equipment, net	1,340,000	1,145,000	1,200,000
League franchise, net of amortization	3,700,000	3,550,000	3,400,000
Other assets	4,000,000	5,000,000	4,000,000
Total fixed assets	9,040,000	9,695,000	8,600,000
Total assets	**$14,070,000**	**$29,754,680**	**$32,753,240**

Liabilities (debt) and stockholders' equity ($)	As of December 31,		
	2004	2005	2006
Current liabilities:			
Accounts payable	24,500,000	33,500,000	30,000,000
Deferred compensation, current portion	1,300,000	1,300,000	1,230,000
Total current liabilities	25,800,000	34,800,000	31,230,000
Long-term liabilities:			
Notes payable to bank	50,000,000	50,000,000	50,000,000
Deferred compensation, noncurrent portion	7,600,000	6,360,000	5,200,000
Other noncurrent liabilities	670,000	708,000	690,000
Total long-term liabilities	58,270,000	57,068,000	55,890,000
Stockholders' equity (deficit)	(70,000,000)	(62,113,320)	(54,366,760)
Total liabilities plus stockholders' equity ($)	**$14,070,000**	**$29,754,680**	**$32,753,240**

Figure 5.1   Stars of David's balance sheet.

the cash that will become available over the next year. The Stars have had negative net working capital, which means the team's short-term obligations have exceeded the team's short-term assets. As reported by the Stars of David, their net working capital equaled –$20,770,000 ($5,030,000 – $25,800,000) on December 31, 2004; –$14,740,320 ($20,059,680 – $34,800,000) on December 31, 2005; and –$7,076,760 ($24,153,240 – $31,230,000) on December 31, 2006.

The term *investment in working capital* refers to an increase in net working capital between points in time on the balance sheet. See the following case study example.

Between December 31, 2004, and December 31, 2005, the Stars of David's negative net working capital decreased from –$20,770,000 to –$14,740,320, which represents an increase of $6,029,680 in net working capital. Although this was an improvement in the short-term cash position, expected cash outflows were still exceeding expected cash inflows as of December 31, 2006.

INCOME STATEMENT

The income statement measures a business' profitability over a specific period of time, such as a year or a quarter. Income is defined as follows:

$$income = revenue - expenses$$

Whereas the balance sheet provides us with a snapshot at a single point in time, the income statement can be viewed as a film that portrays how the organization performed between the single snapshots depicted on the balance sheet. The Stars of David's income statement is shown in figure 5.2.

The income statement typically consists of three sections. The first section includes the revenues and expenses from the company's operations. Second, a nonoperating section of the income statement includes financing costs and any income earned by financial investments. For the Stars of David, the interest expense represents financing costs and interest income represents income from investments. Typically the nonoperating section of the income statement includes all taxes

that are paid by the enterprise. The third section of the income statement is the net income of the business.

Under GAAP, revenue is generated when an exchange of goods or services occurs. In addition, revenues and expenses are reported when they occur, even though cash inflows or outflows may or may not have occurred. For example, when goods and services are sold for credit, associated sales and profits are reported even if payment has not yet been received. This is known as accrual basis accounting as opposed to cash basis accounting (discussed in chapter 2), in which revenues and expenses are not recognized until there are actual cash inflows and outflows.

The value of a firm's assets is linked to the future incremental cash flows they will generate, but cash flows do not show up on the income statement. As a result, some expenses that appear on the income statement are not actual cash outlays. One such expense is depreciation. **Depreciation** represents an estimate by the firm's accountants of the cost of equipment and property that are used up by the organization in the process of producing and distributing goods and services.

	Year ending December 31,		
	2004	**2005**	**2006**
Revenues ($):			
Basketball regular season:			
Ticket sales	23,300,000	39,400,000	35,800,000
Fees for television and radio broadcast rights	14,600,000	34,200,000	38,450,000
Promotional advertising	6,000,000	7,600,000	8,900,000
Total revenues	43,900,000	81,200,000	83,150,000
Operating Expenses:			
Team and games expenses	31,600,000	59,333,000	61,630,000
Selling and promotional expenses	4,300,000	4,400,000	4,930,000
General and administrative expenses	5,000,000	5,120,000	4,700,000
Depreciation	272,000	347,000	350,000
Nonoperating Expenses:			
Amortization of league franchise	150,000	150,000	150,000
Earnings before interest and taxes	2,578,000	11,850,000	11,390,000
Interest expense	(3,600,000)	(3,400,000)	(3,300,000)
Interest income	628,000	545,000	427,000
Earnings before taxes	(394,000)	8,995,000	8,517,000
Taxes	0	2,752,320	2,725,440
Net income (net loss)	(394,000)	6,242,680	5,791,560

Figure 5.2 Stars of David's income statement.

 The Stars of David also have a noncash expense that is related to the amortization of their league franchise, which is an intangible asset. Intangible assets are nonphysical fixed assets of the business that provide value, such as goodwill, patents, licenses, trademarks, and copyrights. Owning a league franchise represents an intangible asset because there is value in being the only organization allowed to function as a league franchise in the Greater Hartford Area and to collect all available broadcast royalties and other league-related revenues. Unless one is ready to assume that an intangible asset has unlimited life for accounting purposes, it is necessary to claim amortization over a reporting period, as a result of either obsolescence or the "wearing out" of the intangible asset. As with depreciation, this amortization of intangible assets does not result in a cash outflow for the Stars of David.

Companies report as the cost of goods sold those expenses that are directly related to the production and distribution of goods and services. Such costs include raw materials, direct labor, and manufacturing overhead. Other costs are allocated by the accountants preparing the financial statements to the time period covered by the income statement. Such costs are reported separately as selling costs and as general and administrative costs.

 The Stars of David separately report general and administrative costs and selling and promotional costs but report no cost of goods sold. The Stars do not report cost of goods sold because the team is engaged in the business of entertaining their fans with home games and then appearing on the road for additional games. As a result, the Stars of David report costs and expenses associated with playing over the regular season, which can be viewed as a team-sport franchise's productive activity.

STATEMENT OF CASH FLOWS

From the perspective of financial analysis, the importance of financial statements lies in their ability to provide information about an organization's cash flows. Firms have value when they generate cash flows for investors. By cash flows, we are referring directly to cash flowing into the business as well as cash flowing out of the business. To see this distinction between cash flows and accounting measures of income, recall that income statements include noncash expenses such as depreciation. The amount of depreciation reported on a business' income statement has no impact whatsoever on the cash generated by the business. The reason is that when the business reports depreciation, the dollar amount reported as depreciation is not directly paid to any vendors or employees, as would be the case with other operating expense categories. The statement of cash flows is a financial statement that reports changes in a company's cash holdings over a particular period. The Stars of David's statement of cash flows is shown in figure 5.3.

The Stars of David have three primary sources of cash flows as a result of business activities. These include cash flows from (used in) operating activities, cash flows from (used in) investing activities, and cash flows from (used in) financing activities.

Cash flow refers to the difference between what a company brings in and what it pays out. Thus, cash flow from (used in) operating activities refers to both positive and negative cash flows that result from the firm's basic operating activities. These include operating revenues less all operating expenses other than noncash operating expenses, such as depreciation. When a firm earns revenue, there are positive cash flows, whereas cash expenses are associated with **negative cash flows**. In addition, operating cash flows include the positive cash flows resulting from increasing current liabilities (other than short-term debt) and the negative cash flows associated with increases in current assets (other than cash).

The Stars of David reported positive cash flows from operating activities for the years ending December 31, 2005, and December 31, 2006. The cash flows from investing activities are associated with the business' making additions to fixed assets. Purchases of current and fixed assets lead to negative cash flow resulting from the use of cash to purchase these assets. When current and fixed assets are reduced (i.e., sold or disposed of) during the year, this can be viewed as a positive cash flow because of the cash generated by the sale of the assets. In addition, when current liabilities are increased, there is a positive cash flow from investing activities because of the postponement of the use of cash.

| | Year ending December 31, | |
	2005	2006
Operating activities ($)		
Net income	6,242,680	5,791,560
Depreciation and amortization	497,000	500,000
Changes in current assets and liabilities		
Accounts receivable	(4,400,000)	2,600,000
Prepaid expenses and other current assets	(116,000)	35,000
Accounts payable	9,000,000	(3,500,000)
Deferred compensation, current portion	0	(70,000)
Total cash flow from operating activities	**$11,223,680**	**$5,356,560**
Investing activities ($)		
Sale (acquisition) of fixed assets	1,492,000	1,550,000
Deferred compensation, noncurrent portion	(1,240,000)	(1,160,000)
Other assets	(1,000,000)	1,000,000
Other liabilities	38,000	(18,000)
Total cash flow from investing activities	**($710,000)**	**$1,372,000**
Financing activities ($)		
Change in notes payable	0	0
Dividends	0	0
Total cash flow from financing activities	**$0**	**$0**
Change in cash (on the balance sheet)	**$10,513,680**	**$6,728,560**

Figure 5.3 Stars of David's statement of cash flows.

The cash flows associated with financing activities are cash flows to and from creditors and owners. Such cash flows include changes in the firm's debt and equity. When the firm increases its borrowings, the cash that is created is a positive cash flow. By comparison, paying off a loan results in negative cash flow. When dividends are paid out to stockholders, there is negative cash flow, whereas proceeds from stock issues (i.e., new owners purchasing stock) result in positive cash flow.

TYPES OF FINANCIAL RATIOS

Information from financial statements can be used to compute financial ratios that provide insight into the condition of a business. Specifically, we define commonly used financial ratios that focus on the following areas:

- Liquidity
- Activity
- Financial leverage
- Profitability
- The value of the firm

LIQUIDITY

The liquidity ratios measure the ability of a business to meet short-term financial obligations. Liquidity ratios are associated with the firm's net working capital. A common liquidity ratio is the **current ratio (CR)**, which is computed by dividing current assets by current liabilities.

current ratio =
total current assets /
total current liabilities

The current ratio for the Stars of David as of December 31, 2005, is 0.58.

current ratio =
$20,059,680 / $34,800,000
= 0.58

The team's current ratio is below 1, which indicates that current assets cannot cover current liabilities. If this continues, the Stars may be unable to pay their bills on time without borrowing more money or receiving more cash from the owners.

A second measure of liquidity is the **acid test ratio**, or **quick ratio**, which is obtained by subtracting inventories from current assets and dividing the resulting difference by current liabilities. Since inventories are the least liquid of any current assets, the quick ratio allows one to examine whether a firm can pay its current liabilities without relying on the sale of inventories.

acid test ratio, or quick ratio =
(total current assets – inventories) /
current liabilities

Since there are no inventories to deduct from current liabilities, the quick ratio for the Stars of David is identical to its current ratio.

Two other liquidity measures are the solvency ratio and net working capital. The **solvency ratio** determines how strong the business is in terms of being able to cover its liabilities. The solvency ratio is calculated by dividing net worth by total assets.

solvency ratio = net worth / total assets

Net working capital is not a ratio, but it helps highlight the available current assets after all the current liabilities are paid. Net working capital shows how much cash or other liquid assets might be available if the business had to repay all the liabilities that are due in the next several months. Net working capital is calculated as follows:

net working capital =
current assets – current liabilities

ACTIVITY

Activity ratios measure how effectively a firm manages its assets. The **total asset turnover ratio** is computed by dividing total revenues for a particular accounting period by the average total assets for that period.

total asset turnover ratio = revenues / total assets (average)

For the year ending December 31, 2005, the total asset turnover ratio for the Stars of David is 3.71. The average level of assets is obtained from Star of David's balance sheet shown in Figure 5.1. We need to compute the average of Star of David's assets ending December 31, 2005, and ending December 31, 2004, to obtain the average level of assets during 2005. The average level of assets is equal to ($14,070,000 + $29,754,680)/2 = $21,912,340.

total asset turnover ratio =
$81,200,000 / $21,912,340
= 3.71

The asset turnover ratio gives an indication of how effectively a firm uses its assets to generate sales. If the asset turnover ratio is relatively high, the firm is efficiently using its assets to generate sales. If the ratio is relatively low, the firm is not using its assets as effectively and may wish to consider selling off assets if sales are not increased.

The **inventory turnover ratio** is equal to the cost of goods sold over a particular period divided by the average inventory level during that same period.

inventory turnover ratio =
cost of goods sold / inventory (average)

The inventory turnover ratio tells us how many times during the year the inventory is purchased and sold. A relatively high turnover ratio is usually preferable, although the appropriate ratio is industry specific. For a manufacturing company, the inventory turnover ratio can be easily affected by the technologies used to produce the goods that it sells, as well as by distribution techniques. Inventory management is covered in more detail in chapter 13.

To calculate the **receivables turnover ratio**, we divide revenues by average receivables during the collection period. The ratio of receivables can then be used to derive the **average collection period**, which equals the number of days in the period divided by the receivables turnover ratio. The values of these ratios are highly dependent on a firm's credit sales policies. A firm with generous credit terms will have a higher amount of receivables.

receivables turnover ratio =
total revenues / average receivables

average collection period =
number of days in the period /
receivables turnover ratio

 The Stars of David's receivables turnover and average collection period for the year ending December 31, 2005, are 22.56 and 16.18 days, respectively. The average level of receivables is obtained from Star of David's balance sheet shown in Figure 5.1. We need to compute the average of Star of David's receivables ending December 31, 2005, and ending December 31, 2004, to obtain the average level of receivables during 2005. The average level of receivables is equal to ($1,400,000 + $5,800,000)/2 = $3,600,000.

receivables turnover ratio =
$81,200,000 / $3,600,000
= 22.56

average collection period =
365 days / 22.56 =
16.18 days

The Stars of David do not rely heavily on credit sales, which is reflected in a high receivables ratio. The average collection period for the Stars is also low, relative to that for a manufacturing firm, because most of the team's sales (primarily from ticket sales and broadcast rights) do not involve the granting of credit through extended payment terms.

FINANCIAL LEVERAGE

Financial leverage ratios provide information about the extent to which a business relies on debt (loans) rather than equity (stocks) for financing. Firms with high financial leverage ratios relative to other firms in their industry have a greater likelihood of financial distress and bankruptcy. One measure of financial leverage is the debt ratio, which equals total liabilities divided by total assets.

debt ratio = total liabilities / total assets

 The December 31, 2005, debt ratio for the Stars of David is 3.09.

debt ratio =
$91,868,000 / $29,754,680
= 3.09

The Stars are highly leveraged because their debt is more than three times higher than their assets. The term *leveraged* refers to the extent to which a company relies on borrowing to finance its operations. Since the Stars are highly leveraged, they are paying higher interest costs relative to the value of their assets. Most businesses cannot survive with such a high debt ratio. However, because of the inherent value of a basketball team, the Stars of David can have significant debt, with their players as their only significant asset. Thus, a high debt ratio does not mean they are in financial trouble. The team can still earn significant returns on their minimal assets as reflected in their high profit margin, highlighted in the next section.

An alternative to the debt ratio is to instead measure the extent to which a company is leveraged by calculating the ratio of long-term debt to net worth. The difference between the debt ratio and the ratio of long-term debt to net worth is that the ratio of long-term debt to net worth excludes current liabilities. Similar to the debt ratio is the **debt–equity ratio**, which also analyzes a business' leverage but from the standpoint of the owners' equity rather than all the assets. The debt–equity ratio is calculated as follows:

debt–equity ratio =
total debt / total shareholders' equity

This ratio highlights how much of the debt is financed by shareholders. The higher the ratio, the greater the reliance on shareholder support. A low ratio might indicate that the debt is being purchased through retained earnings or internal sources rather than through shareholders.

An additional financial leverage measurement is the **interest coverage** ratio. To calculate the ratio of interest coverage, we divide **earnings before interest and taxes (EBIT)** by interest. This ratio provides insight into whether a firm has sufficient earnings to cover its interest expense.

interest coverage ratio =
earnings before interest and taxes /
interest expense

The interest coverage ratio is also commonly referred to as the times interest earned ratio.

The Stars of David's interest coverage ratio for the year ending December 31, 2005, is 3.49.

interest coverage ratio =
$11,850,000 / $3,400,000
= 3.49

PROFITABILITY

One of the most critical figures for examining a company's success is **corporate earnings**. The bottom line for companies is their ability to generate sufficient earnings to continue growth and reward shareholders. Earnings are calculated by subtracting total costs from total sales or revenue. The earnings or the corporate losses if costs exceed sales are the key point of analysis for future progress, dividend payments, bankruptcy, and any other potential corporate decisions.

In the year ending December 31, 2005, the Stars of David had a profit, as measured by net income, equal to $6,242,680.

There are numerous commonly used measures of profitability. These include profit margin (gross and net profit margin), return on assets, return on equity, and return on investment. Profit margins are calculated by dividing profits by revenues. **Net profit margin** is computed using net income (earnings after interest and taxes) as a proxy for profits; **gross profit margin** uses earnings before interest and taxes to represent profits.

net profit margin = net income / revenues

gross profit margin =
earnings before interest and taxes / revenues

The Stars of David's profit margins for the year ending December 31, 2005, follow:

net profit margin = $6,242,680 / $81,200,000 = 7.69%

gross profit margin =
$11,850,000 / $81,200,000
= 14.59%

When a firm's net profit margin is high relative to that of other firms in its industry, this is an indication that the firm is able to provide its products at either a low cost or a high price.

The Stars of David have a 7.69% net profit margin, but another team has only a 4.50% net profit margin. There could be very specific reasons for the difference; it could be attributable to better local television rights contracts, a better arena revenue-sharing deal, payroll differences, or simply that some markets can command higher ticket prices for any number of reasons.

Stockholders are primarily concerned about the return on their investment; thus the dividend per share is an important calculation. If the stock price increases, stockholders can realize a gain only if they sell the stock. In contrast, if the corporate board of directors decides to issue a dividend, then stockholders can earn an immediate return on their investment without having to sell.

Other measures of profit do a better job than profit margins in reflecting the investment in capital by the firm or its shareholders. One such measure of profitability is **return on assets (ROA)**, which is defined as profits divided by average assets for the reporting period in question. The average assets can be found on the balance sheet.

return on assets =
net income / average total assets

For the year ending December 31, 2005, the return on assets for the Stars of David is as follows:

return on assets =
$6,242,680 / $21,912,340
= 28.49%

Return on assets (often referred to as ROA) is also known as return on investment because it reflects the amount of profits earned on the investment in all assets of the firm. Any new asset purchased by the firm should be able to generate increased returns over and beyond what could have been earned if the funds had been placed in an equally risky financial investment.

A profitability measure related to ROA is the **return on equity (ROE)**, which is net income divided by average stockholders' equity. Return on equity measures profitability in terms of profits earned on investment in the firm's assets by stockholders only—as opposed to ROA, which measures profitability earned on investments in a firm by all providers of funds, such as lenders, creditors, and stockholders.

return on equity =
net income / average stockholders' equity

 The ROE is not computed for the Stars of David because stockholders' equity is negative since liabilities substantially exceed assets. Consequently, ROE is not a meaningful measure for the team.

DETERMINING THE COMPANY'S VALUE

As we have seen so far, financial statements give information about the basic condition of the firm, but they do not tell us anything about the firm's market value. Market value is based on what stock buyers and sellers establish when they buy and sell shares in the business. For a publicly traded company, the **market value** is simply the price per share of common stock, based on reported prices of shares traded on stock exchanges, multiplied by the number of shares of common stock outstanding.

market value =
price per share of common stock
× average number of outstanding shares

On December 31, 2005, the Stars of David traded at $1.50 per share, Since there were 10 million outstanding shares of common stock on December 31, 2005, the market value of the team, as of December 31, 2005, can be expressed as

market value = $1.50 × 10 million outstanding shares
= $15 million

Whereas market value tells an investor what the investing public thinks a company is worth, a company's book value presents a different version of the company's worth. **Book value** is based on historic

cost of assets minus accumulated depreciation. Although book value represents the value of assets on paper, it does not necessarily represent the true value because an asset might have a replacement cost that is higher than its book value. Thus, an asset might cost $1 million to replace, but the book value could be only $500,000 ($2 million purchase price – $1.5 million in accumulated depreciation). Book value is calculated by subtracting total liabilities from total assets.

book value = total assets – total liabilities

For the Stars of David, the book value on December 31, 2005, equaled –$62,113,320. The reason for the large negative value is that the team has liabilities far exceeding assets on its balance sheet.

The book value for a company is also called the owners' equity because it represents the value the owners have in the business. Owners' equity is also calculated by adding retained earnings and the value of common stocks. Since this is a measure of a company's value, it is also called the **net worth**.

The **book value per share** is another measure of a company's value based on the owners' equity obtained from the balance sheet.

book value per share =
owners' equity / total outstanding shares

The calculation for the Stars of David on December 31, 2005, follows.

book value per share =
–$62,113,320 / 10 million
= –$6.21

As mentioned already, Stars of David shares were selling for $1.50 per share on December 31, 2005. Since the book value was negative, there were expectations of substantial future growth for the Stars in the stock market.

TECHNIQUES TO DETERMINE AN INVESTMENT'S VALUE

Besides all the calculations a corporation can make concerning its value, earnings, liquidity, and so on, investors can use several different techniques to determine whether it was profitable to invest in the company. These techniques include annual return, holding period return, simple rate of return, and dividend payout ratio.

The annual return per share and the annual rate of return for an investment analyze whether there was any increase or decrease in a stock's value and whether any dividends were distributed to stockholders. Assume that an investor purchased a stock on January 1, 2006, and sold it on December 31, 2006. The stock was purchased at $8 per share and sold for $10 per share. During the year the company paid dividends of $0.04 per share. The annual return per share and annual rate of return would be calculated as follows:

$$\text{annual return per share} =$$
$$\text{increase or decrease in value} + \text{dividends}$$
$$= (\$10 - \$8) + \$0.04$$
$$= \$2.04$$

$$\text{annual rate of return} =$$
$$\text{annual return} / \text{initial investment}$$
$$= \$2.04 / \$8.00$$
$$= 25.5\%$$

The 25.5% return helps highlight how good an investment the stock purchase was that year. However, this analysis is effective only for a quick snapshot in time and if the stock was actually sold. If the stock went down the next day, then the annual return would still be an accurate reflection of the value the prior year, but not the investment's true value. This is often referred to as **paper profit** (since this profit is only shown on paper). That is, the stock might have produced a great annual return, but if the stock is not sold the profit could vanish in an instant if the stock price declines.

In contrast to annual return, the holding period return takes into consideration the fact that the stock was possibly not sold. For the stock being analyzed, the **holding period return** indicates what happened to the investment, independent of what might happen in the future. Since the return on the investment during the one-year holding period was 25.5%, then that is the holding period return rate. The **dividend payout ratio** examines the dividends per share relative to how much the company earned per share. The formula is as follows:

$$\text{dividend payout ratio} =$$
$$\text{dividends per share} / \text{earnings per share}$$

If dividends per share are $0.50 and earnings per share equal $3.00, then the dividend payout ratio is 16.67 ($0.50 / $3.00). This means that 16.67% of earnings were repaid to the stockowners as dividends.

To get a sense of how the stock market is valuing a company, one can compute the **price–earnings ratio (PE ratio)**. The PE ratio is equal to the price per share of common stock divided by the earnings per share of common stock. **Earnings per share (EPS)** is calculated as follows:

$$\text{earnings per share} =$$
$$\text{net income} / \text{average number}$$
$$\text{of shares outstanding}$$

If SMC and a competitor reported earnings per share equal to $5, but SMC's shares sell for $15 and its competitor's shares sell for $20 each, then the PE ratio for SMC is 3.

$$\text{price–earnings ratio} = \text{price per share} /$$
$$\text{earnings per share}$$
$$= \$15 / \$5$$
$$= 3$$

By contrast, the PE ratio for SMC's competitor is 4.

$$\text{price–earnings ratio} = \$20 / \$5$$
$$= 4$$

Note that the stock market is valuing SMC's competitor's shares at a higher multiple of earnings than it is valuing SMC's shares. This disparity in PE ratios is usually related to differences in how the financial markets view the quality of earnings, past profitability, or expected future earnings growth, or a combination of two or more of these factors.

Financial statements provide important information about the condition of a firm. By using numbers in financial statements, we can get key information that allows us to summarize an organization's liquidity, activity, financial leverage, and profitability. These ratios also allow a firm to critically examine its operations and ratios in comparison with publicly traded firms in the same industry. However, when appropriate information is available, market values of the firm should be used as a supplement to these accounting-based ratios. Market value is the true street value for a business (i.e., what someone would pay for a business today). However, such a value is based on investor perceptions and the quality of available information about the company.

Before the middle of 2001, Enron had a high market value based on deliberately misstated accounting information that was made available to the public. Ultimately, Enron was not really worth its exaggerated street value.

PREPARING FINANCIAL FORECASTS AND BUDGETS

Now that we have introduced the basics of financial scorekeeping as it relates to income statements, balance sheets, statements of cash flows, and financial ratios, in this section we apply the tools of basic financial measurement to track financial results and prepare financial forecasts. The basic financial statements are probably the most important source of numbers for managing any organization. It is extremely critical for any organization, regardless of size and complexity, to develop a solid accounting and financial information system and to compile up-to-date information. An accounting and financial information system generates detailed financial reports, including income statements, balance sheets, and statements of cash flows. An accountant must be available to help interpret the data provided by the accounting and financial information systems.

Although it may sound like a daunting task for small organizations to develop accounting and financial information systems, in part because of the elaborate record-keeping and report-generating activities required, there are many widely distributed bookkeeping and accounting packages for businesses that can be operated on personal computers. Thus even sole proprietors can generate monthly income statements and current balance sheets with a minimum of effort. These systems also offer a convenient way to archive past records. Having a historical record of income statements and balance sheets is important in order for a business to prepare budgets and projections of future financial results.

As we continue through the remainder of this chapter, we introduce financial forecasting and budget preparation as a tool for planning purposes. We also demonstrate the relationship between sales growth and a business' capital requirements. To prepare financial forecasts and budgets, a business needs to follow a sequential process. The sequence of steps consists of the following:

1. Gathering information
2. Forecasting sales
3. Projecting profits and losses
4. Comparing to industry norms
5. Determining capital needs

All forecasts are based on assumptions, educated guesses, and hunches. The assumptions and hunches included in a forecast should not come out of the blue, however, but rather from experience in combination with the gathering of extensive information. Since forecasts involve an unknown future, it is impossible to be 100% correct. For a business owner, attaining 80% accuracy is very good. Thus, even though a forecast is not absolute, it is better for an organization to use a forecast with an 80% level of accuracy than to use none at all. Proceeding blindly without any forecasts or budgets for the future increases the odds of poor future financial results and ultimately insolvency.

In the sequence just outlined, sales forecasts are prepared before any profit and loss or cash flow forecasts are made. As discussed next, it is reasonable to assume that at least some expenses will have some relationship to sales. Thus, it is fruitless to forecast

No financial forecast will be 100% accurate, but careful planning will allow a business to come closer to its financial target.

expenses (and resulting profit and loss or cash flow) without using sales forecasts as a foundation.

GATHERING INFORMATION

To prepare financial forecasts, it is first necessary to have information on hand about the basic factors that contribute to the success or failure of the business. See the following case study example.

 **Sport Manufacturing Company**

Manufacturers such as Sport Manufacturing Company (SMC) follow trends involving bookings of business, billings, and backlog that signal whether the business will be profitable. If SMC does not book new business, then its customer billings will be down and manufacturing backlog will be reduced. This can spell trouble in the form of less profitable production. Since SMC produces an item that for many consumers is a discretionary purchase, the company needs to be aware of the first signs of a slowing economy because in this type of environment, consumers at the retail level will presumably reduce their purchases of products made by SMC and other sporting goods manufacturers.

Similar to the case study example, as witnessed in the early 2000s, a down economy reduced ticket sales, which reduced the revenue for most professional teams and resulted in the first major economic downturn since the major facility construction boom of the 1990s. Teams that saw the downturn coming renegotiated luxury box contracts and locked in the holders to long-term contracts before the downturn took place. Those that did not gather and analyze appropriate economic data were in trouble when businesses stopped signing contracts because of reduced funds.

As part of the information-gathering process, it is imperative to define the business' target markets. Key questions that must be answered include the following:

- How big are the target markets?
- What is the business' penetration of these markets?
- What is the potential that is remaining for the business to exploit in these markets?
- Who are the competitors, what are their market shares, and what is their pricing strategy?

Answers to these questions are important in order to generate more accurate revenue forecasts.

As the business projects its revenues, it is important to include a "reality check." In particular, is the future projected sales growth truly sustainable? High growth will consume substantial sums of cash and capital, as well as any capital provided by lenders and investors. It is critical to determine whether the firm has sufficient resources to sustain the level of growth built into revenue forecasts.

Information also needs to be obtained about the extent to which expenses vary directly with revenues. If most of the expenses are variable, this means they are tied to the volume of sales. If the expenses of the firm are primarily variable, it may be possible to look at ways of reducing the costs per unit produced in order to improve profitability. When expenses are fixed, this means they are not tied to the volume of sales. See the following case study examples.

 **Sport Manufacturing Company**

Examples of variable costs for SMC include costs of labor and material. If the company finds that it is selling fewer golf clubs, it will reduce production. As production is reduced, SMC can reduce the number of people employed in production as well as the purchase of materials used to manufacture the golf clubs.

As for fixed expenses, it would be reasonable to assume that SMC has extensive machinery and equipment in its manufacturing facilities. The machinery and equipment, along with the manufacturing premises, are long-term capital assets whose costs are considered fixed over any particular time period. If the machinery and equipment are used in a facility that fabricates golf clubs, the annual expense is incurred even if no golf clubs are produced and sold to customers. When expenses are mostly fixed, higher profitability will be associated with higher sales because the cost per unit sold will automatically fall as sales increase. If we assume that most of SMC's expenses are the fixed costs associated with its machinery and equipment, the company needs to maximize golf club sales in order to boost profitability through lowering the cost per golf club sold when sales increase.

In the short run, a major constraint in SMC's attempts to maximize profitability through increased golf club sales is the maximum production capacity of the manufacturing facility. A production constraint is also a sales constraint. If SMC can produce only 800,000 golf clubs in a given year, it will be unable to sell more than 800,000 golf clubs annually. Even if there is demand for one million golf clubs per year, SMC will still be unable to sell that many golf clubs unless it can find some way to increase production.

For a sports team such as the Stars of David, the salaries of players and coaches are the major source of operating expenses. However, salaries are fixed costs. No matter how much revenue is derived from attendance at games, the Stars will be paying the same salaries.

To obtain key information that is needed to prepare financial forecasts and budgets, executives can look to publications issued by trade and professional organizations. Trade and professional organizations have also begun to post information on the Internet. Small business institutes at colleges and universities, which are funded and sponsored by the federal government's Small Business Administration, are excellent sources of information for small business owners. SCORE, an organization that consists of retired business executives who volunteer their time, provides free consulting and information to start-ups. In addition, trade shows can be a way to gain insight through networking and attending seminars. Consultants, vendors, customers, and the company's own sales force can also be useful information sources. More detail on obtaining information of this type is provided in appendix C.

It is also important to obtain benchmark data, either for other firms in the industry or for the industry as a whole. Benchmark data include information on revenues, expenses, profits, net worth, and assets for other firms, making it possible to get a financial profile of the average, or typical, firm in the industry. These data can be used to construct benchmark ratios, such as profitability ratios for the average firm, that serve as a reasonableness check (comparing the results of a forecast for a particular business with the financials of the typical firm) on forecasts of sales and profits (Pratt & Niculita, 2007).

Sport Manufacturing Company
SMC could conceivably find it useful to collect financial information about other manufacturing firms. In addition, as the Smiths begin their efforts to operate a fitness center, they should obtain financial information

The Smiths
for other representative firms or for the industry as a whole in such sectors as

- health clubs,
- retail establishments, and
- service establishments.

Without such benchmarking information, the Smiths and SMC would have no idea if the breakdown of expenses versus revenues and profitability ratios as implied by their financial forecasts is realistic.

The Smiths could rely on fitness industry data from the health club area. From this data Bob and Cheryl might learn, for example, that the average fitness-only club earns about $778 per member each year, which translates to $56 per square foot of facility space (based on 14 square feet per member). On the basis of such data, the Smiths could calculate that if they have a 4,000-square-foot facility and their dues are similar to those of other clubs in the industry, they should be able to generate $224,000 ($56 per square foot × 4,000 square feet) in annual revenue.

Detailed composite financial information is available from *RMA Annual Statement Studies*, available on the Internet, on CD-ROM, and in printed format. These studies give detailed information on revenues, expenses, and profitability as reported by businesses on commercial loan applications. The *RMA Annual Statement Studies* data are broken down by detailed industry category and size of business (as measured by total assets), and they include historical information that allows one to analyze historic growth in sales. Additional detailed composite financial information is available from the Internal Revenue Service. The Internal Revenue Service's company financial statistics are published by disaggregated industry categories in the following annual publications: *Corporation Source Book*, *Partnership Source Book*, and *Sole Proprietorship Source Book*.

For sports teams, such as the Stars of David, published player salary information is useful as a benchmarking tool. Comparing published player salaries helps prevent understating of expenses because of the lack of a reality check. Generalized industry data are also available from *U.S. Industry & Trade Outlook*, which is produced annually by the U.S. Department of Commerce. *Standard*

& Poor's Industry Surveys provides information on 52 basic industry groups and includes discussions of the industry's market structure, trends in the industry, the future outlook of the industry, and financials for publicly traded firms in the industry. Specifically, *Standard & Poor's Industry Surveys* provides coverage of the entertainment industry, which can serve as a reasonable proxy for many types of sport businesses.

Additional relevant information can be obtained via a thorough online search. Given the rapidly changing nature of the Internet, it is impossible to give a comprehensive guide to online sources in a textbook, but such sources can be located by using appropriate keywords in Internet search engines such as Google and Yahoo! An example of an online site that provides useful information is Hoover's Online (www.hoovers. com). Hoover's Online is an Internet-based subscription service that provides financial information, major news, and background for major industry groupings as well as for specific companies within an industry grouping. Industry groupings on Hoover's Online include Professional Sports Teams & Organizations, Sporting Goods Retailing, Sporting Goods (manufacturing), and Professional Sports Gear & Apparel.

Knowledge of an industry's SIC code (Standard Industrial Classification code) or its NAICS code (North American Industry Classification System code) can also enhance research. Both the SIC and NAICS systems are government classification systems for industries. There are several sport-related SICs in the 7900 category range, including 7997, which represents health clubs. The corresponding NAICS code is 71394. Knowing these codes could help the Smiths gain additional information from various government and nongovernment sources. As always, though, people need to remember that the data they obtain are only as good as the source.

FORECASTING SALES

To generate sales forecasts for an established business, the starting point is the most recent full year's sales. It is useful to list sales separately by product line, by sales distribution method (e.g., direct sales, retail sales, online sales), or by geographic market.

Sport Manufacturing Company

As an example, SMC sold four million units in 2006. Assuming that SMC charged $15 per unit sold, its 2006 total revenues equaled $60 million. In table 5.1, SMC's 2006 revenues of $60 million are broken down by sales distribution channel (i.e., by the method for distributing the products to the final customers). As table 5.1 shows, SMC relies heavily on sales to retail chains, with 60% of sales through that distribution channel. There are also significant sales to independent stores and abroad. Sport Manufacturing Company has also invested in distribution on the Internet, although online sales in 2006 were still only 6% of total sales.

After sales force and marketing executives analyze potential sales from various projections, historic sales are examined in order to project future sales. At a minimum, three to five years of the most recent historic sales should be reviewed. This allows one to examine recent trends that are useful in forecasting future sales growth.

The research process, specifically an examination of historic sales data, has shown that over the last 20 years SMC has maintained its position as a sporting goods manufacturer with seasonal sales patterns, and those sales have grown an average of 8% per year. In individual years, sales have been dependent on the strength of the U.S. economy. The forecasts for year 2007 sales will be based on the historical information, supplemented by the experience and research of SMC's analysts.

In table 5.2, three scenarios are presented for forecasting purposes. These include a best-case scenario, a worst-case scenario, and a most likely scenario. The most likely scenario is based on pulling together the best and worst cases. The two extreme cases give the analyst a way to better understand opportunities as well as potential barriers to success (Koller, Goedhart, & Wessels, 2005).

The worst-case scenario assumes that most of SMC's sales are stable and that as a result, 90% of 2006 sales is a reasonable assumption for the worst-case scenario. The 90% range is designed as a

Table 5.1 SMC's 2006 Sales

Distribution channel	2006 sales ($)	Percentage of total
Chain stores	36,000,000	60%
Independent stores	12,525,000	21%
Individual (direct)	375,000	1%
Internet	3,750,000	6%
Foreign	6,000,000	10%
Other	1,350,000	2%
Total	**$60,000,000**	**100%**

Table 5.2　SMC's Sales Forecast for 2007

Distribution channel	2006 sales ($)	Worst case sales ($)	Most likely sales ($)	Best case sales ($)	Decrease
Chain stores	36,000,000	32,400,000	38,880,000	43,200,000	8%
Independent stores	12,525,000	11,272,500	13,527,000	15,030,000	8%
Individual (direct)	375,000	375,000	375,000	375,000	0%
Internet	3,750,000	2,250,000	6,525,000	9,375,000	74%
Foreign	6,000,000	5,400,000	6,480,000	7,200,000	8%
Other	1,350,000	1,350,000	1,350,000	1,350,000	0%
Total	**$60,000,000**	**$53,047,500**	**$67,137,000**	**$76,530,000**	**12%**

cushion in case sales are lower in a subsequent year. If SMC's historic sales had fluctuated substantially from year to year, a worst-case scenario could involve sales of even less than 90% of 2006 sales. In the case of sales over the Internet, that distribution channel is still in its infancy and is subject to greater risk, particularly if other manufacturers decide to use the Internet as a distribution medium. Thus in a worst-case scenario, sales over the Internet are shown as a 40% decline. Sales to individuals are expected to remain the same, even in a worst-case scenario, because SMC does not place any marketing effort into individual sales, and annual sales to individuals have stayed relatively constant over the last decade.

Note that historic sales were used to determine the worst-case scenario. In the event of a new trend that is not reflected in the historic sales information, it is very easy to underestimate the potential sales decline under the worst-case scenario. For example, if a new movement toward consolidation took place in the retail sporting goods sector and certain retail chains that had been SMC customers went out of business, SMC's sales might be subject to unforeseen declines. Furthermore, if SMC made nothing but snow skis and the winter snowfall was poor, or if it missed the snowboarding trend, then sales could plummet.

The best-case scenario assumes that with properly focused marketing efforts, the chain store, independent store, and foreign sales can increase by 20% under extremely favorable conditions. By contrast, since Internet sales are in their infancy, a best-case scenario includes Internet sales growing by a multiple of 2.5 in the event that SMC's efforts to enter this market segment begin to bear immediate fruit. The 2.5 times increase is just an estimate based on either an educated hunch or market expectations.

The most likely scenario represents a composite of the worst-case and best-case scenarios. The best- and worst-case scenarios do not have to be weighted evenly. Instead, the weight applied to each should represent subjective judgment about the relative likelihood that each of these scenarios will occur. In terms of a reasonableness check, note that SMC's sales in its traditional chain store, independent store, and foreign distribution channels are expected to grow at rates that match recent historic growth rates for the business as a whole. Since the Internet is an entirely new distribution channel with a lot of upside potential for growth, Internet sales are projected to grow 74% in 2007 under a most likely scenario. The Internet sales growth causes overall projected sales growth to be 10% for the year 2007, which will surpass the 8% historic norm.

So far, we have developed a sales forecast based on a bottom-up approach. In effect, we have separately forecast each component of sales and then summed up the total sales across components (or distribution channels in our example) to determine total sales.

GENERATING A LONGER-TERM FORECAST

Now that we have prepared a one-year sales forecast, based on a most likely scenario, it is necessary to generate a longer-term forecast. Typically, lenders and investors require at least a three-year projection, shown in table 5.3.

Sport Manufacturing Company

In the case of SMC, we assume that in the chain store, independent store, and foreign distribution channels, sales will continue to grow at their historic 8% average annual

Table 5.3 SMC's Three-Year Sales Forecast

Distribution channel	2006 actual sales ($)	2007 most likely sales ($)	2008 sales ($)	2009 sales ($)
Chain stores	36,000,000	38,880,000	41,990,400	45,349,632
Independent stores	12,525,000	13,527,000	14,609,160	15,777,893
Individual (direct)	375,000	375,000	375,000	375,000
Internet	3,750,000	6,525,000	9,135,000	10,962,000
Foreign	6,000,000	6,480,000	6,998,400	7,558,272
Other	1,350,000	1,350,000	1,350,000	1,350,000
Total	**$60,000,000**	**$67,137,000**	**$74,457,960**	**$81,372,797**

growth rate. In the case of the Internet, we assume that growth will decline from 74% in 2007 to 40% in 2008 and 20% in 2009. This is perfectly consistent with the notion that a new business line will demonstrate extremely high sales growth that declines over time (Ross, Westerfield, & Jaffe, 2005). We also continue to assume that sales to individuals and other sales will remain constant over time.

SPECIAL SITUATIONS

There are special situations that we have not considered in our discussion of preparing sales forecasts. These situations include

- start-ups,
- ownership changes, and
- fast growth.

START-UPS

Sales forecasts for start-ups are particularly difficult because there is no established track record for the business. In addition, trade group and industry data comprise sales figures for ongoing and successful businesses, which are not necessarily relevant for a new business. New businesses tend to have sales that are lower than the sales of an established business with the same level of expenses. In addition, new businesses tend to be strapped for the capital that is necessary to generate sales sufficient to translate into profitable financial results. As a result, pro forma balance sheets and income statements for new businesses are very speculative.

A way of performing a reasonableness check on any sales forecast is to find data on the ratio of sales to net worth for other businesses in the same industry. These ratios are available from the previ-

ously mentioned *RMA Annual Statement Studies*. The amount of capital invested in the business or borrowed can be multiplied by a ratio of sales to net worth to derive an attainable sales level. If other manufacturers comparable to SMC, an established sporting goods manufacturer with stable earnings, have sales-to-net-worth ratios equal to 8%, then the $67,137,000 in forecast sales for 2007 would imply net worth equal to $839,212,500 ($67,137,000 / 0.08). If SMC follows industry norms as represented by the benchmark sales-to-net-worth ratio, and its forecast net worth is substantially less than $839,212,500, it is questionable whether SMC has sufficient investment capital to generate the projected sales.

The use of benchmarking ratios to examine a start-up is more difficult than for an established firm. For example, assume that the top 25% of firms in the industry have a sales-to-net-worth ratio of 15%, the bottom 25% have a sales-to-net-worth ratio of 8%, and the start-up has borrowed $4,000,000 in initial capital. This implies that if the start-up matched the performance of the top 25% of firms in the industry, its sales would equal 0.15 × $4,000,000, or $600,000. If its sales matched the bottom 25% of the industry, then projected sales would be 0.08 × $4,000,000, or $320,000. This provides a range to work with in forecasting sales.

OWNERSHIP CHANGES

If there is an ownership change, the operating history of the business may not be a useful guide for developing future sales forecasts. If the ownership change resulted from poor business performance, new ownership is probably going to institute changes in management. This means the business must halt its negative momentum and engineer a turnaround before sales growth can occur. In addition, ownership changes can result in the loss of customers or key employees, especially in smaller, closely held businesses in which the company's success is tied to the efforts of a key person. Under these circumstances, businesses tend to need to reexamine their product lines and markets.

The Smiths might be able to sell a successful fitness facility, but memberships could plummet immediately after the sale. Perhaps members are no longer joining because the Smiths are no longer associated with the fitness facility, or perhaps the Smiths have chosen to open another facility several miles away.

This example indicates why buyers of existing small businesses often insist that the sales agreement include a noncompete clause. Noncompete clauses prevent the sellers from competing in the same line of business from a location within the same geographic region for a specified number of years. Another way around this problem is for the buyer of the business to retain the seller of the business as a consultant for a specified length of time after the sale is completed.

FAST GROWTH

In the case of businesses that are characterized by fast-growing sales, it is a mistake to assume that this fast growth will continue forever into the future. For example, if corporate sales in the economy have been growing annually at a rate of 6% per year over the past five years and a particular business has been growing at a rate of 20% per year, it is unreasonable to assume that this divergence will continue. Typically, successful start-ups have extremely high growth rates that slow down as the business matures. Businesses that seize new market niches or enter new and growing markets are typically the ones associated with abnormally high growth, and these are the types of businesses that are at risk as other entrants, having witnessed the explosion in growth, try to steal market share (Pratt & Niculita, 2007).

PROJECTING PROFITS AND LOSSES

Thus far, we have generated sales forecasts. Although sales forecasts are useful for planning purposes, we are really interested in profit-and-loss projections and cash flow projections. As we discuss further on, sales can be viewed as a key driver of the expenses shown on an income statement and can ultimately drive the statement of cash flows.

Sport Manufacturing Company

On the basis of the figures shown for SMC in the Introduction to the Case Studies (p. xvi) as well as the sales figures in table 5.3 (p. 84), we have produced an income statement for SMC for 2006 that is shown in figure 5.4. To generate figure 5.4, we have assumed that the $15 million in fixed costs for SMC, as reported in the Introduction to the Case Studies, is split between depreciation ($10 million) and interest expense ($5 million). Depreciation is an accounting-based expense that represents an allowance for wear and tear on plant and equipment. Depreciation is a fixed cost to the business because it does not change with the volume of sales. Interest expense, which represents interest on money borrowed by the business, is also a fixed cost because the firm would have to repay interest expense even if it shut down production facilities. To calculate net income, which is income after corporate taxes are paid, in figure 5.4 we have assumed that the combined federal and state corporate tax rate is 40%.

In figure 5.4, the gross margin was calculated by subtracting cost of goods sold (which includes the variable costs of production) from sales. Cost of goods sold in figure 5.4 was obtained by multiplying the $7 per unit produced by the four million units sold. The $32 million gross margin shown in figure 5.4 indicates that SMC is earning $32 million in profits after deducting direct costs of production from sales but before factoring in other costs of doing business. It is important to examine gross margins because if a business has trouble covering its direct costs of production, even a restructuring and substantial reduction of administrative and overhead costs will not restore the business to profitability.

Normally, operating expenses include all other expenses, other than cost of goods sold, which represents the cost of doing business. In our example, to keep things simple we have included only administrative and selling costs and depreciation as operating expenses. The administrative and selling costs are obtained by multiplying the $1.25 cost per unit sold by the four million units sold. The $10 million annual depreciation expense shown in figure 5.4 represents an estimate by SMC's accountants of the cost of equipment and property that are used up by the organization in the process of producing and distributing goods and services. As noted in the discussion of financial statements earlier in this chapter, depreciation expense is not an actual cash outlay.

Net sales	$60,000,000
Cost of goods sold	$28,000,000
Gross margin	**$32,000,000**
Selling and administrative expenses	$5,000,000
Depreciation	$10,000,000
Earnings before interest and taxes	**$17,000,000**
Interest expense	$5,000,000
Earnings before taxes	**$12,000,000**
Taxes at 40%	$4,800,000
Net income	**$7,200,000**

Figure 5.4 SMC's income statement for the year ending December 31, 2006.

As shown in figure 5.4, SMC's EBIT equal $17 million. The EBIT are equal to sales less cost of goods sold less operating expenses. The EBIT measure the level of profits that are available to all investors and to pay the firm's corporate income tax liabilities.

As reported in figure 5.4, SMC also incurs $5 million in annual interest expense. **Pretax earnings**, or earnings before taxes (EBT), are equal to EBIT less interest expense. In figure 5.4, SMC's EBT equal $12 million, which means that after payment of interest to lenders, the company has $12 million available for distribution to stockholders (owners) and to pay tax liabilities. Net income is equal to EBT minus corporate taxes. In the case of SMC, net income is $7.2 million, which equals the $12 million EBT minus $4.8 million in corporate income taxes. The company's net income represents the profits available to stockholders after accounting for cost of goods sold, operating expenses, interest expense, and corporate income taxes.

Table 5.4 consists of projections of profits over the period from 2006 through 2008, with our sales forecasts from table 5.3 (p. 84) serving as the driver of expenses and ultimately the profits shown in figure 5.4 (Koller et al., 2005). In table 5.4, we have assumed that interest expense and depreciation expense are unchanged, since they are fixed costs. Since cost of goods sold and selling and administrative expenses are variable costs, these expense items must grow as sales grow over the forecast period. To forecast the variable expenses, we use as an illustration the **percent of sales method**, which directly ties variable costs to sales based on assumptions about each variable expense as a percentage of sales. In 2006, cost of goods sold was 47% of sales, while selling and administrative expense was 8% of sales. In our example, we assume that these percentages correspond to historic averages, and we assume that cost of goods sold and selling and administrative expenses as a percentage of sales will remain at their 2006 percentages over the forecasting period. Forecasts of profit and loss are shown in table 5.4 as seen in the net income row.

The percent of sales approach used to develop the three-year forecast is accurate only if financial statement ratios remain constant over time. There are times when these ratios may not be constant (e.g., when there are economies of scale, which are discussed in greater detail in chapter 15). When economies of scale exist, the average cost per unit of sales declines as sales increase, which implies changing ratios of expense items to sales over time. Economies of scale are particularly prevalent when a firm has fixed costs that represent a substantial portion of total costs.

As an example, if a firm has $10 million in fixed costs associated with operating factories, the fixed cost per unit sold is $20 if the firm sells 500,000 units but $10 if the firm sells one million units. The fixed cost per unit sold is calculated by dividing the total fixed cost by the total number of units sold (i.e., $10,000,000 / 500,000). If the variable cost per unit sold is $2, then total cost per unit sold (variable cost per unit sold plus fixed cost per unit sold) equals $22 per unit sold when the firm's annual sales equal 500,000 units and $12 per unit sold when sales equal one million units. Clearly, cost per unit sold declines as sales increase. When expenses are not expected to be a constant percentage of sales, it may be necessary to employ sophisticated statistical techniques that are beyond the scope of this text, such as regression analysis, to forecast the variable expense items. Such economies of scale may actually exist for a manufacturer such as SMC.

Table 5.4 SMC's Profit Forecasts for 2007-2009

	2007 ($)	2008 ($)	2009 ($)
Net sales	67,137,000	74,457,960	81,372,797
Cost of goods sold	31,554,390	34,995,241	38,245,214
Gross margin	**35,582,610**	**39,462,719**	**43,127,583**
Selling and administrative expenses	5,370,960	5,956,637	6,509,824
Depreciation	10,000,000	10,000,000	10,000,000
Earnings before interest and taxes	**20,211,650**	**23,506,082**	**26,617,759**
Interest expense	5,000,000	5,000,000	5,000,000
Earnings before taxes	**15,211,650**	**18,506,082**	**21,617,759**
Taxes at 40%	6,084,660	7,402,433	8,647,104
Net income	**$9,126,990**	**$11,103,649**	**$12,970,655**

COMPARING TO INDUSTRY NORMS

Once profit-and-loss projections have been computed, it is worth referring to industry norms as a reasonableness check. Using the information sources discussed earlier, it is possible to obtain various income entries as percentages of sales for the average firm in an industry. In the case of *RMA Annual Statement Studies*, such data are also available for firms that are the top 25% and bottom 25% performers. These figures provide reasonableness checks for the expense forecasts derived from sales forecasts. Data on industry norms for ratios such as net income to net worth (return on equity) are available as well for assessing the reasonableness of financial projections.

Sport Manufacturing Company

Assume that SMC's net worth is projected to equal $76 million in 2007. On the basis of SMC's projected $9,126,990 net income for 2007 (see table 5.4), the company's return on equity is equal to $9,126,990 / $76,000,000, or 12%. If the average ROE for firms comparable to SMC is 13%, then the profit projections certainly are reasonable. If, on the other hand, comparable firms are earning 8% rates of ROE, then it might be advisable to revisit SMC's profit-and-loss projections, unless there is something unique about SMC that differentiates it from other firms in the same market or industry.

DETERMINING CAPITAL NEEDS

Once sales and profit forecasts are complete, it is necessary to see whether the forecast sales and

profits can be accomplished with the firm's current assets. If the forecast sales and profits grow at too high a rate in the future, it may be necessary for a company to obtain additional capital or assets in the form of inventory and fixed assets. These assets can be acquired only with money obtained through either increased borrowing or the issuance of stock. If the company cannot raise the money to obtain the capital, it can face a crisis caused by the inability to finance the high growth.

To determine capital needs, sustainable growth rate analysis is used. If the annual sales growth rate exceeds the sustainable annual growth rate, then external capital is needed to finance the necessary growth. The sustainable growth rate is calculated as follows:

$$g^* = [P(1 - D)(1 + L)] / [T - P(1 - D)(1 + L)]$$

g^* = sustainable growth

P = net income / sales

D = target level of dividends paid out to stock holders / net income

L = total liabilities / net worth

T = total assets / net worth

Sport Manufacturing Company

From our example in figure 5.4 (p. 86), SMC's net sales in 2006 equaled $60 million, and net income equaled $7.2 million. Thus P equaled 12%. Assume that SMC's board sets D at 50% and that the calculations for L and T are 50% and 80%, respectively. Note that L and T are hypothetical numbers to make the example read better.

$g^* = [0.12(1 - 0.50)(1 + 0.50)] /$
$\qquad [0.80 - 0.12(1 - 0.50)(1 + 0.50)]$
$\qquad = 0.09 / 0.71$
$\qquad = 0.1268,$ or 12.68%

Based on the formula, the sustainable growth rate is 12.7%. Note that this is just above the 12% rate used to project future annual profits for SMC in table 5.4 (p. 87). Consequently, no external capital requirements are needed to fund SMC's projected sales growth.

On the basis of this projected 12% sales growth rate, SMC will barely miss needing a capital infusion to fund growth. Assume that SMC's actual annual growth in sales ended up averaging 14% per year over the next several years, instead of the forecast 12% per year. The company's growth would exceed the 12.7% sustainable growth rate, and SMC would require additional capital to fund its growth. The company's options for obtaining new capital would be to issue new common stock, reduce dividend payouts to current stockholders, or increase borrowing (see chapters 8 through 10). The sustainable growth rate formula also implies that SMC can reduce its assets-to-sales ratio by renting and leasing, as opposed to owning fixed assets, since this will reduce the need for capital. In addition, if SMC is a closely held business, reducing compensation to owners is an option.

Note that our discussion of capital and cash needs did not focus on variations of capital needs during the course of a year when businesses face seasonal sales patterns. For example, SMC is characterized by lower sales in December and January relative to the rest of the year. Even though it might appear that the company does not have to finance sales growth through a capital infusion, SMC still needs to have cash available to meet operating expenses in December and January when cash inflows are relatively lower. One way businesses handle such seasonal patterns in demand is through bank lines of credit, which are drawn down during slow periods of demand and then repaid when sales improve.

Sustainable growth rate analysis suggests that when planning for high rates of sales growth, businesses need to factor in the likelihood of further capital infusions. High sales growth uses up cash and capital.

BREAK-EVEN ANALYSIS

So far this chapter has covered various financial calculations to determine strengths and weaknesses and has examined forecasting and planning. A key concept that embodies all three elements is break-even analysis. Because of its relevance to inventory and production management in addition to its usefulness for guidance in financial forecasting and planning, break-even analysis is also covered in chapter 13.

Break-even analysis is used to determine the level of unit sales required in order for the business to just cover its expenses. In other words, break-even analysis provides the base sales level that is needed to ensure profitability. The **break-even point** occurs when EBIT equal zero (i.e., when pretax operating profits, independent of financing considerations, are zero). The break-even point can be expressed in the following way:

$$\text{EBIT} = \text{revenues} - \text{variable costs} - \text{fixed costs of production} = 0$$

The preceding equation can also be expressed as follows:

$$\text{EBIT} = PQ - VQ - F = 0$$

EBIT = earnings before interest and taxes
P = the selling price per unit sold
Q = unit sales
V = the variable cost per unit sold
F = the fixed costs of production

The break-even point of unit sales (QBE) follows:

$$\text{QBE} = F / (P - V)$$

QBE = break-even point of unit sales
F = the fixed costs of production
P = the selling price per unit sold
V = the variable cost per unit sold

The break-even formula states that the break-even point of unit sales will be higher if fixed costs are higher. The difference between unit price and unit variable cost (P − V) can be viewed as the gross profit per unit sold. The higher the level of gross profit per unit sold, the lower the number of units that need to be sold to break even.

 **Sport Manufacturing Company**

The break-even formula can be demonstrated using the assumptions about SMC's 2006 financials from earlier in the chapter. The company's per unit price (P) is $15. The per unit variable cost (V) is $8.25, which is the sum of the direct manufacturing costs ($7 per unit) and the selling and administrative costs ($1.25 per unit). The fixed cost of production is $15 million, which is the sum of the $10 million depreciation expense and the $5 million interest expense. Plugging these values into the break-even formula, we get the following:

$$QBE = \$15,000,000 \, / \, (\$15 - \$8.25)$$
$$= 2,222,222 \text{ units}$$

As our analysis shows, the four million units that are driving the 2006 financial results for SMC are substantially above the number of units required to just break even. On the basis of the break-even formula, SMC's annual fixed costs would have to increase to $27 million per year in order for the company to just be breaking even at four million units.

Note also that SMC's per unit gross profit margin on each sale is equal to $15 – $8.25, or $6.75 per unit sold. If fixed costs remain at $15 million per year, the per unit gross profit margin would have to be reduced to $3.75 in order for SMC to be breaking even at four million units. This indicates that SMC is in good shape because any reductions in per unit profits could only come about through severe price reductions, significantly reduced sales, or substantial increases in variable costs.

CONCLUSION

In this chapter we discuss the rudiments of financial statement analysis as well as financial forecasting and planning. Specifically, we provide an introduction to financial statements. We discuss the elements of the balance sheet, which summarizes the firm's financial condition at a particular point in time, and the contents of the income statement, which is used to measure a business' profitability over a period of time. The balance sheet and the income statement provide a lead-in to explain changes in the cash position of a firm over a given period. Specifically, we describe changes in cash flows that result from operations, investing activity, and financing. The elements of the balance sheet and income statement are used to compute financial ratios that summarize the firm's liquidity, activity, financial leverage, profitability, and market value.

The need to understand the information contained in financial statements is critical in order to project future profits. When we forecast future sales and profits, we make various assumptions that require extensive analysis of company financial statements, as well as knowledge of typical financials in the industry that the company is part of. This is especially critical since sales and profit forecasts are used in the planning process to determine capital needs and break-even sales.

CLASS DISCUSSION TOPICS

1. Discuss the pros and cons of using the various measures of profitability to examine a company's performance.

2. Discuss the pros and cons of using measures of leverage to assess whether a company faces financial distress.

3. How would you finance the high growth of a business such as Nike if you were not willing to borrow or raise additional capital?

4. How do you reconcile unique characteristics about your business with the information gained through use of industry averages to forecast sales and profit and loss?

5. What are some of the difficulties that can be encountered when trying to project the future profitability of a team-sport franchise?

6. Why is it advisable to use multiple scenarios to project the future financial profitability of a business?

6

TIME VALUE OF MONEY

CHAPTER OBJECTIVES

After studying this chapter, you should be able to do the following:

- Understand the concept of future value, including its calculation for a single amount of cash received today.

- Understand the concept of present value, including calculation of the present value of a single payment at a particular time in the future.

- Calculate the present value of multiple payments received in the future, including perpetuities and annuities.

- Describe basic concepts of risk and return and their relationship to computing the present value of future payments.

- Use risk statistics to define risk, including relating the performance of financial assets to risk.

The book to this point has highlighted the importance of finance in making business decisions and the issues associated with determining value based on various ratios or industry benchmarking standards. However, any analysis cannot be complete without examining the time value of money. It is impossible to examine a $1 investment today versus one from 50 years ago without realizing that $1 from 50 years ago might be worth $50 in today's dollars. This chapter highlights why money is sensitive to time and how to calculate changes in value based on time constraints.

HOW MUCH
IS MONEY WORTH?

In chapter 5 we discuss how to analyze sales and costs, evaluate cash flows, measure profitability, and prepare financial forecasts. A key issue in valuing these flows is their timing. A dollar received today is worth more than a dollar received in the future. **Time value of money** represents the concept that money in today's dollars decreases in value the further out into the future it is expected to be received. With this concept in mind, any investor or business needs to examine the time in which investment decisions will be made and critically examine how that time frame will ultimately affect the invested amount and projected payout.

Sport Manufacturing Company

Assume that Sport Manufacturing Company has a parcel of real estate it wishes to sell, and it has lined up two prospective buyers. One buyer, Speedy Enterprises, is willing to enter into a contract to pay $100,000 immediately for the parcel of land. A second buyer, Acme Limited, has offered to pay $102,500 for the land, but with actual payment to be made in one year's time. At first glance, it may appear that SMC should take the Acme Limited offer, since Acme is willing to pay more for the land—but looks can be deceiving!

The way to evaluate which offer SMC should accept is to note that if SMC accepted the offer from Speedy Enterprises, it could hypothetically deposit the funds in a one-year certificate of deposit (CD) that earns 5% interest per year. Sport Manufacturing Company would start out with $100,000 in the bank (principal) and would earn interest equal to $0.05 \times \$100,000$. As a result, SMC would have the following on deposit in one year:

$$\$100,000 + 0.05 \times \$100,000 = \$105,000$$
or
$$\$100,000 \times 1.05 = \$105,000$$

In other words, SMC would have on deposit its initial $100,000 principal plus $5,000 in interest, which equals $105,000. Factoring in the interest earned during the year, the initial principal is multiplied by 1.05 (i.e., 1 plus the interest rate) to obtain the $105,000 on deposit at the end of the year.

By contrast, if SMC accepted the Acme offer, it would have only $102,500 available in one year, compared with the $105,000 it would have on hand in one year if it accepted the Speedy Enterprises offer. By taking the offer from Acme, SMC would have $2,500 less than if it had invested the initial $100,000 in the one-year CD. Clearly, SMC is better off taking the offer from Speedy Enterprises.

In working through this example we made use of the concept of future value. **Future value (FV)** is the value of an initial lump sum of money after it is invested over one or more periods of time. The future value in one year's time of the $100,000 received from Speedy Enterprises is $105,000. Note that the future value of any given sum reflects the interest earned on that investment.

Another way of looking at this example is to examine how much money SMC must deposit in a one-year CD that earns 5% in order to have $102,500 in one year. The amount of money that would yield $102,500 if invested today at a 5% interest rate is the **present value (PV)** of $102,500 received in one year. We can solve for PV as follows:

$$PV \times 1.05 = \$102,500$$

Solving for PV gives us the following:

$$PV = \$102,500 / 1.05 = \$97,619$$

So, if SMC has $97,619 today, this lump sum can grow to $102,500 in one year as a result of earning interest.

In general, the formula for the present value can be written as shown in the following:

$$PV = C_1 / (1 + r)$$

PV = present value

C_1 = cash flow received at the end of one year

r = appropriate interest rate

The variable r, the interest rate or percentage return that can be earned on an initial amount of money, is also known as the **discount rate**. In our example, the 5% annual return that SMC earns on its financial investment (i.e., a one-year CD) is used as the discount rate in order to value the $102,500 received in one year.

Our analysis of present value indicates that a payment of $102,500 received in one year from Acme has a present value of $97,619 today. In other words, at a 5% interest rate, SMC would find receiving $97,619 today from Acme or $102,500 in one year equally acceptable alternatives. Given $97,619 today, the company can deposit the funds in a one-year CD that will allow it to receive $102,500 in one year.

Since Speedy Enterprises offered to pay $100,000 today, this offer has a present value of $100,000. Thus, our present value analysis suggests that SMC should take the Speedy Enterprises offer.

FUTURE VALUE MORE THAN ONE PERIOD INTO THE FUTURE

So far, we have looked at the concept of present value and future value in the context of cash flows over a single period of time. We will now show how this can be generalized over more than one period. This process is critical because most business deals do not start and end in one year, but rather last several years.

Sport Manufacturing Company

Assume that Adrian Jones owns shares of SMC common stock, and the return on the stock is 8%. To keep things simple, let us also assume that Jones paid $1 per share for SMC's common stock. At the end of one year, she will have $1 plus the return on that dollar at r% for each share. Since r% equals 8%, she will have $1.08 at the end of one year.

$$\$1 + \$1r = \$1 \times (1 + r) = \$1 \times 1.08$$
$$= \$1.08$$

r = expected rate of return

At the end of the year, Jones has two choices. She can cash out her stock and take the $1.08 per share or hold the stock for a second year. The process of holding the stock and accruing a further return over the second year is referred to as **compounding**.

If Jones decides to hold the stock for another year, then at the end of two years she will have the following:

$$\$1 \times (1 + r) \times (1 + r) = \$1 \times (1 + r)^2$$
$$= \$1 \times (1.08)^2$$
$$= \$1.1664$$

At the end of two years, she will have transformed $1.00 into $1.1664. Notice that at the end of two years, she will generate $0.1664 in **compound interest** or return. That is, each payment of interest or return that is reinvested earns a return also.

This process can be generalized over many periods of time (**t**) with the following formula for the future value (FV) of an investment:

$$FV = C_0 \times (1 + r)^t$$

FV = future value

C_0 = the initial amount of cash that is invested today

r = the interest rate or rate of return

t = the number of years over which the cash is invested

We can do this calculation by hand or with the help of a table. Table A.1 in appendix A (pp. 318-319) presents future values of $1 at the end of t periods, which means a variable number of time periods into the future over which the $1 is earning interest. Traditionally, t periods on a future value chart range from 1 year to 20 or 30 years. To use the table, locate the appropriate interest rate or return on the horizontal axis and the appropriate number of periods on the vertical axis. For example, you could find that the future value of $1 that is received two years into the future is $1.1664. This figure is reached if you assume an 8% rate of return. If you started out with $500 and earned an 8% annual return over two years, then the future value at the end of two years would be $583.20.

$$FV = 500 \times 1.1664 = \$583.20$$

As another example, suppose an investor buys a $1,000 bond issued by SMC. The bond pays 10% interest and is redeemable in 20 years. Going to table

A.1 (pp. 318-319), you can find 20 years as the t period and then move across to the column labeled 10% interest. The number on the chart is 6.7275. Thus, FV = $1,000 × 6.7275, which yields a future value for the $1,000 investment after 20 years of $6,728. Through compounding interest, the bond increases more than sixfold if kept for the entire 20 years. This example highlights how the federal government can sell U.S. bonds for $50 now and guarantee payment of $100 in 10 years: Through compounding, the $50 investment can produce a four to five times greater return in 10 years while still allowing the government to pay the investor double his money.

PRESENT VALUE OVER MORE THAN ONE PERIOD INTO THE FUTURE

Assume that Swish James, the best shooter for the Stars of David, has signed a contract including $2 million in deferred compensation that will be paid at the end of two years. Assume that if he were to receive compensation today, he could invest that money in a financial vehicle (such as a CD) that earns a 4% annual return. We would like to know how much money received today would be worth $2 million after earning a 4% annual return for two years. This can be written as follows:

$$PV \times (1 + r)^t = FV$$

PV = present value
r = annual rate of return
t = number of years
FV = future value

$$PV \times (1.04)^2 = \$2,000,000$$

In this equation, PV stands for present value, the amount of money that would need to be invested today in order to grow to $2 million in two years. Solving for PV gives us the following:

$$PV = \$2,000,000 / (1.04)^2$$

$$= \$2,000,000 / 1.0816$$

$$= \$1,849,200$$

This equation indicates that if Swish received $1,849,200 today, invested it, and earned a 4% annual

return, he would have $2 million at the end of two years. This process of obtaining a present value is known as **discounting**. The $2 million is discounted by a **discount factor**, or **present value factor**, which equals $1 / (1.04)^2$, or 0.9246, in this example. Using this discount factor, we can calculate the present value as $2,000,000 × 0.9246, or $1,849,200.

An alternative way to calculate the results obtained from this equation is to use table A.2 in appendix A (pp. 320-321) to obtain a present value factor. This table shows the present value of $1 to be received after t periods. To use the table, locate the appropriate number of periods on the vertical axis and the interest rate on the horizontal axis. In our example, the number of periods is 2 and the interest rate is 4%. Thus the present value factor is 0.9246. If we multiply $2 million by the present value factor, we find that the present value of $2 million received in two years is $1,849,200.

In general, the present value of a sum of money received t periods in the future can be written as follows:

$$PV = C_t / (1 + r)^t = C_t \times PVF_{r,t}$$

PV = present value
C_t = the cash flow received at the end of t periods
r = annual return of interest
$PVF_{r,t}$ = the appropriate present value factor for $1 received t periods into the future

We can extend this example to finding the present value of multiple payments. Assume that Carrie Brown, a player in the Women's National Basketball Association, has signed a contract that will pay her $100,000 immediately, $110,000 at the end of one year, and $115,000 at the end of two years. Assume that she can earn a 4% annual return investing the money. The present value of the cash flows is shown in table 6.1.

The present value of the cash flows under this contract equals $312,094. In other words, the payment structure under this contract is equivalent to paying Brown $312,094 in one lump sum today.

PERPETUITIES AND ANNUITIES

For certain types of finance problems, there are shortcuts for calculating present values. In particular, we discuss shortcut methods for two types of cash flow streams:

Table 6.1 Present Value of Carrie Brown's Cash Flows Over Several Years

Year	Cash flow ($)	Present value factor	Present value ($)
0	100,000	1.0000	100,000
1	110,000	0.9615	105,765
2	115,000	0.9246	106,329
Total			**$312,094**

1. Perpetuities
2. Annuities

PERPETUITIES

A **perpetuity** consists of a single cash flow per year forever into the future. Although perpetuities may not seem to have any real-world relevance, certain financial instruments are in effect perpetuities. These instruments are called consols, which are bonds issued by the British government. The holder of a consol receives yearly interest from the British government forever into the future. As a hypothetical sport example, imagine a solid company such as SMC agreeing to give the founder and her family, for an unlimited number of generations, a $1 million per year payment for eternity. The concept of a perpetuity comes into play when valuing preferred stock since the price of a preferred share is equal to the present value of expected constant dividends that will be paid each year forever into the future. The present value of a perpetuity is equal to the following:

$$PV = C / (1 + r) + C / (1 + r)^2 + C / (1 + r)^3 + \ldots$$

PV = present value

C = a constant annual cash flow

r = the interest rate or rate of return

The dots at the end of the formula indicate that an infinite number of terms complete the formula. The equation is an example of what math texts call an infinite series. Based on mathematical formulas used to solve infinite series, the equation can be simplified:

$$PV = C / r$$

In other words, the present value of a perpetuity is simply the annual cash flow divided by its discount rate (Brigham & Ehrhardt, 2005). Assuming that the perpetuity pays $100 per year at an interest rate of 8%, the present value of the perpetuity is as follows:

$$PV = \$100 / 0.08$$

$$= \$1,250$$

If interest rates fell to 6%, the present value of the perpetuity would rise.

$$PV = \$100 / 0.06$$

$$= \$1,666.67$$

Note that formulas 6.11 and 6.12 indicate that the value of the perpetuity rises as the interest rate declines and falls as the interest rate increases. This is an illustration of a general principle: The present value of any stream of cash flows (whether or not it is in the form of a perpetuity) is inversely related to the discount rate. At higher interest rates, the present value of any future cash flows declines because one can start out with a smaller initial lump sum; as this sum earns a return, it will grow to equal the future cash flow.

ANNUITIES

An **annuity** is a constant stream of payments that is received for a fixed number of periods. Annuities are common in the real world. Home mortgages, leases, student loans, and pensions paid at retirement are all examples of annuities. When evaluating annuities, we utilize the following formula:

$$PV = C / (1 + r) + C / (1 + r)^2 + C / (1 + r)^3 + \cdots + C / (1 + r)^t$$

PV = present value

C = a constant cash flow per period

r = the annual rate of return

t = the number of periods during which the cash flow will be received

This equation is cumbersome, but fortunately it can be simplified to yield the following formula for an annuity that is paid over t periods (Brigham & Ehrhardt, 2005):

$$PV = C\{1 - [1 / (1 + r)^n]\} / r$$

PV = present value

C = a constant cash flow per period

r = the annual rate of return

n = the number of periods during which the cash flow will be received

See the sidebar for an example calculation.

RISK

When we calculated the present value of future cash flows, we did not discuss how to choose a discount rate. As we explain here, the choice of discount rates is tied to the risk of the future cash flows. By risk, we are referring to uncertainty about the future cash flows.

Whenever we compute the present value of a stream of future cash flows, we do not know with 100% certainty that those cash flows will be received. In the sidebar below, we calculated the present value of Eric Mangini's five-year contract, signed January 17, 2006, as the New York Jets' head football coach. In that example, we calculated the cash flows without making any allowances for future uncertainty about whether Mangini would actually receive all of that compensation. As it happens, the job security of head coaches in the National Football League is tenuous at best.

A common way to adjust for uncertainty is to use a discount rate that reflects the riskiness of the cash flows. As we will show, the higher the level of risk of a financial instrument, the higher its rate of return. This implies that we need to use higher discount rates when there is greater riskiness associated with the cash flows being valued.

RETURNS

To measure risk, we need to examine the behavior of returns on different types of financial assets. Thus, before we go any further, it is necessary to focus on what we mean by the term *return*. As a first step, we wish to distinguish between dollar returns and rates of return.

Calculating Eric Mangini's Compensation Package

An example of an annuity is the compensation package received by Eric Mangini, the head football coach of the New York Jets. On January 17, 2006, Mangini signed a contract that would pay $2,500,000 in salary for five years (Crouse, 2006). For our purposes, this is treated as a five-year annuity, effective January 17, 2006. If the appropriate discount rate is 7%, then by plugging these values into the equation we obtain the following:

$$PV = \$2,500,000 \times \{1 - [1 / (1.07)^5]\} / 0.07$$
$$= \text{periodic payment} \times \text{annuity factor}$$
$$= \$2,500,000 \times 4.1002$$
$$= \$10,250,500$$

The present value of Mangini's contract, as of January 17, 2006, when he signed it (and assuming a 7% discount rate), equaled $10,250,000. The numbers in braces in the equation are the present value factor for an annuity. In this example involving the value of Mangini's salary, the present value factor for the annuity equals 4.1002. Table A.3 in appendix A (pp. 322-323) is titled Present Value of $1 per Period for t Periods. Again, interest rates are shown on the horizontal axis, and number of periods is shown on the vertical axis. Consulting the table, you will see that for an interest rate of 7% and an annuity that is

received for five periods, the present value factor is 4.1002, which we obtained in the calculation.

In calculating the value of Eric Mangini's contract at the time it was signed, we have not factored in any potential uncertainty about his receiving the salary in the future. This uncertainty can be viewed as risk, which is our next topic.

Sport Manufacturing Company

Assume that you bought 100 shares of stock in SMC at $10 per share. Your initial investment would equal $1,000.

100 shares × $10 = $1,000

Suppose that SMC paid an annual dividend to all shareholders equal to $0.50 per share. During the year, you would receive the following dividend income:

100 shares × $0.50 = $50

In addition, assume that the price of SMC's stock increased over the year to $11 per share. Since the stock increased in price, you would have a capital gain equal to the change in the stock price over the year multiplied by the number of shares held:

capital gain = (current price − initial price) × number of shares

= ($11 − $10) × 100 shares = $100

The capital gain is equal to the dollar increase in the value of the SMC stock.

Conversely, if the stock declined in price to $9 per share, there would be a capital loss (the negative change in price over the year):

capital loss = ($9 − $10) × 100 shares

= −$100

Since the stock declined in value over the year, the capital loss is equal to the dollar decline in the value of the stock.

In general, **capital gain** is defined as the dollar amount by which a financial instrument (e.g., shares of stock) increases in value over a given time period. The term **capital loss** is used when the value of the financial instrument declines.

The capital gain or loss, like the dividend income, is part of the total return earned by stockholders. In general, the total dollar return on a security is calculated as follows:

total dollar return = capital gain or loss + dividend income

In our first example, where the stock price increased, the total dollar return is positive.

total dollar return = $100 + $50 = $150

In our second example, where the stock price decreased, the total dollar return is negative.

total dollar return = −$100 + $50 = −$50

Rates of return allow us to measure gains and losses in percentage terms. In particular, they provide us with a means of standardizing the measurement of the performance of a financial asset, regardless of the dollar amount invested, which is useful for comparing the performance of different financial assets. Going back to our earlier example, assume that the initial price of the stock (P_0) is $10, that at the end of one year the price of the stock (P_1) is $11, and that the dividend paid per share (D_{t+1}) is $0.50. The return represented by dividends paid to the stockholders of the company, called the dividend yield, is equal to the dividend divided by the initial price of the stock:

dividend yield = D_{t+1} / P_0

D_{t+1} = dividend paid per share in a given year
P_0 = price when the stock was initially purchased

In this example, the dividend yield is $0.50 / $10 = 0.05 = 5\%$.

The rate of return resulting from the capital gain is equal to the change in the price of the stock over the year divided by the initial price.

rate of return = $(P_1 − P_0) / P_0$

P_1 = stock price at the end of year 1
P_0 = price when the stock was initially purchased

If the stock price increases to $11 per share, then the rate of return resulting from the capital gain is equal to 10%.

rate of return = ($11 − $10) / $10
= $1 / $10
= 0.10, or 10%

We now combine our results to obtain the total return, from both the dividend payout and the capital gain, as follows:

total return = dividend return +
return resulting from the capital gain

= 5% + 10%

= 15%

RISK STATISTICS

Now that we have discussed how to measure returns, we need to define what we mean by risk. In a nutshell, the risk of any financial asset can be measured by examining the extent to which the returns on that asset fluctuate over time. In particular, we want to measure the performance of the asset with reference to the extent to which the returns fluctuate relative to their average value. This requires us to develop some statistical measures of performance and risk.

The stock returns shown in table 6.2 are for the portfolio of stocks that make up Standard & Poor's (S&P) 500 Composite Index. With data such as those shown in table 6.2, we can calculate the average, or mean. To compute

the mean, we add up all the annual returns and divide by 47 because we have 47 years of data. If R_t is the rate of return in year t, then the formula for the average rate of return $\bar{R}$ over t years is as follows:

$$\bar{R} = (R_1 + R_2 + \ldots + R_t) / t$$

$\bar{R}$ = average rate of return
R_1 = rate of return in year 1
R_2 = rate of return in year 2
R_t = rate of return in year t
t = number of years

The mean of the returns from 1960 through 2006, shown in table 6.2, is 7.66%. The mean tells us the average of the annual returns for a particular time period. In other words, in our example, annual returns on average tended to be 7.66%. But an examination of table 6.2 reveals that in any given year, the return can be either above or below the average. For example, even though the average return tended to be 7.66% over the 47-year period

Table 6.2 S&P 500 Composite Index Returns From 1960 Through 2006

Year	Annual percent return	Year	Annual percent return
1960	−2.67	1983	34.00
1961	18.66	1984	0.03
1962	−5.87	1985	16.44
1963	12.01	1986	26.49
1964	16.46	1987	21.36
1965	8.36	1988	−7.34
1966	−3.30	1989	21.46
1967	7.82	1990	3.64
1968	7.36	1991	12.43
1969	−0.87	1992	10.52
1970	−14.94	1993	8.58
1971	18.11	1994	2.00
1972	11.10	1995	17.66
1973	−1.62	1996	23.77
1974	−22.88	1997	30.27
1975	4.00	1998	24.28
1976	18.40	1999	22.28
1977	−3.73	2000	7.53
1978	−2.22	2001	−16.33
1979	7.28	2002	−16.77
1980	15.31	2003	−2.89
1981	7.80	2004	17.14
1982	−6.51	2005	6.77
		2006	8.55
Average			**7.66%**
Standard deviation			**12.83%**

from 1960 through 2006, in 14 of those years the return was actually negative.

Since returns in any year of a historic period can differ from the average, we want to measure the extent to which this occurs for a sample of returns. The most common measures of dispersion or variability are the **variance** and its square root, the standard deviation. The variance (s^2) of a sample of annual returns over t years is calculated as follows:

$$s^2 = [1 / (t - 1)] \ [(R_1 - \bar{R})^2 + (R_2 - \bar{R})^2 + (R_3 - \bar{R})^2 + \ldots + (R_t - \bar{R})^2]$$

To calculate the variance, it is necessary to take each of the individual annual returns, subtract the average return $\bar{R}$, square the result, and add all the years together. We then divide the result by the number of years minus one. The standard deviation (**s**) is the square root of the variance:

$$S = \sqrt{s^2}$$

Sport Manufacturing Company

To see the calculation of these statistics as used to analyze the performance of financial securities, assume that SMC issues common stock and that its returns from 2002 through 2005 equal 0.1170, 0.1236, 0.3896, and −0.0965, respectively. The average return for SMC from 2002 through 2005 is calculated as follows:

$$\bar{R} = (R_1 + R_2 + R_3 + R_4) / 4$$
$$= [0.1170 + 0.1236 + 0.3896 + (-0.0965)] / 4$$
$$= 0.5337 / 4$$
$$= 0.1334$$

The variance in SMC's returns over this four-year period is calculated as follows:

$$s^2 = [1 / (4 - 1)] \ [(R_1 - \bar{R})^2 + (R_2 - \bar{R})^2 + (R_3 - \bar{R})^2 + (R_4 - \bar{R})^2]$$
$$= [1 / 3][(0.1170 - 0.1334)^2 + (0.1236 - 0.1334)^2 + (0.3896 - 0.1334)^2 + (-0.0965 - 0.1334)^2]$$
$$= (1 / 3) \ (0.1189)$$
$$= 0.0396$$

The standard deviation, which is the square root of the variance, is 0.1990.

$$s = \sqrt{0.0396} = 0.1990$$

The standard deviation is a measure of the spread, or dispersion, of a sample. The significance of the standard deviation is that unlike the variance, it is measured in the same units as the returns in our sample. Statistical theory suggests a probability of approximately two-thirds that the observations in a sample are in a range between the mean less the standard deviation and the mean plus the standard deviation.[1] Going back to our example, there is a probability of approximately two-thirds that the returns lie between (0.1334 − 0.1990) and (0.1334 + 0.1990) (i.e., between −0.0656 and 0.3324).

As shown in table 6.2, the standard deviation of the annual returns in the S&P 500 Composite Index equals 12.83% from 1960 through 2006. This means that for the years 1960 through 2006, there is approximately a two-thirds probability that the annual returns for the S&P 500 Composite Index lie between (7.66% − 12.83%) and (7.66% + 12.83%), or between −5.17% and 20.49%.

AVERAGE RETURNS AND RISK

Table 6.3 shows summary statistics of annual returns for the portfolio of stocks that make up the S&P 500 Composite Index. In addition, the table includes summary statistics for three-month U.S. Treasury bills. What stands out in table 6.3 is that the standard deviation of the returns on three-month U.S. Treasury bills is very

---

[1] We have assumed that the population (theoretical distribution) of returns for SMC (i.e., all possible outcomes over all possible years) follows the normal distribution, which is the bell-shaped curve that many students are familiar with. Since we are working with a sample that is drawn from a population, there is no guarantee that the annual returns will cleanly fit on the bell-shaped normal distribution. Statistical theory does suggest that as one analyzes larger samples of annual returns (i.e., covering more years), the actual historic data will begin to resemble the theoretical distribution. If we look at SMC's stock returns over a long period of time, we know that there may be some sampling error in our individual sample of returns; but this error is small relative to that for a sample consisting of four years of data. Students interested in going beyond the thumbnail sketch in this footnote should consult a business statistics text, such as Siegal's *Practical Business Statistics* (2000).

small relative to that for common stock. Treasury bills, which are sold once per week by the federal government at an auction, typically mature in less than a year. Since the federal government can use its taxing power to pay its debt obligations, this debt has very little likelihood of default. As a result, we can think of the return on Treasury bills as **risk-free return**.

The lower standard deviation is a reflection of the virtual nonexistence of risk for Treasury bills. Since the annual returns on Treasury bills have a very low standard deviation, they do not fluctuate substantially from their average value. This means there is much more certainty that an individual investor will receive the return on an investment in Treasury bills.

By contrast, the standard deviation of the annual returns on common stock equals 12.83%, which is substantially higher than the 2.68% standard deviation of the annual returns on Treasury bills. This results from the greater year-to-year fluctuation in the annual returns of common stock, which means the annual returns on common stock can deviate substantially from the long-term average in any given year. Although the average return on common stock was 7.66% from 1960 through 2006, there is a greater potential in any given year of a large negative return compared with that for Treasury bills. The larger standard deviation or variance in annual returns is an indicator of greater risk.

Table 6.3 indicates that Treasury bills have less risk than common stock but that common stock on average outperform Treasury bills, as shown by a comparison of the average annual returns of the S&P 500 Composite Index with the average yields on three-month Treasury bills. From 1960 through 2006, an investor on average could have earned 7.66% per year by holding common stock but would have earned only 5.57% per year holding Treasury bills. In other words, an investor in the portfolio of stocks included in the S&P 500 Composite Index earned an excess return of 2.09%, based on the difference between the average returns on stock and the yields on Treasury bills. This excess return can be viewed as a **risk premium** (i.e., the additional annual return that the holders of common stock earned relative to that for a risk-free asset, Treasury bills).

The data in table 6.3 show that investors in the stock market are rewarded with much higher returns than investors in relatively risk-free Treasury bills. This is

The old adage of "With great risk comes great reward" can often be applied to financial risk as well; riskier assets are rewarded with higher average returns.

not to suggest that an individual should not invest in Treasury bills. Instead, the information in table 6.3 suggests that investors in riskier assets are rewarded with higher average returns. By contrast, investors in Treasury bills receive lower returns because the investment is virtually without risk.

A way to understand the choice of risk undertaken by an individual investor is from the standpoint of the length of time the money is to be invested. If the investor plans to use the proceeds of the investment to buy a house in one year, it would be prudent to purchase Treasury bills, since a riskier investment has a higher likelihood of resulting in a capital loss over the year. By contrast, for an investor who is saving

Table 6.3 Means and Standard Deviations for U.S. Treasury Bills and Common Stocks From 1960 Through 2006

	Annual yield on newly issued 3-month Treasury bills	Return on the S&P 500 Composite Index
Mean	5.57%	7.66%
Standard deviation	2.68%	12.83%

for retirement but who will not retire for another 30 years, the greater risk of investing in a stock portfolio may be acceptable because of the potential for higher expected returns over a longer time horizon.

RISK AND THE CHOICE OF A DISCOUNT RATE

Up to this point, we have discussed the concept of risk and the ways investors are compensated for taking on more risk in the financial markets. This brings us full circle, to the issue of putting a value on cash flows that will be received in the future when the cash flows have an element of uncertainty, or risk. As we discuss next, risk is dealt with by choosing a discount rate that factors in risk. We consider this issue under two assumptions:

1. Risk is the same as that for the overall stock market.
2. Risk is different from that for the overall stock market.

RISK IS THE SAME AS THAT FOR THE OVERALL STOCK MARKET

For argument's sake, assume that at the time Mangini signed his long-term contract to serve as the head coach of the New York Jets, he viewed the riskiness of the cash flows as equivalent to that of the overall stock market. In that case, Mangini would have used the current expected return for an index of stock market performance, such as the S&P 500 Composite Index. The expected return on the market index (S&P 500 Composite Index) can be expressed as follows:

$$\text{expected return on the market index} =$$
$$\text{risk-free rate} + \text{expected risk premium}$$

We can look at the return on the S&P 500 Composite Index as the sum of the risk-free rate of return plus a premium for taking on the risk of investing in a stock portfolio. The risk premium is what investors must receive in the financial markets in order to be induced to take on the additional risk associated with holding a diversified stock portfolio such as the S&P 500 Composite Index.

The estimation of the expected return on the market portfolio is straightforward. Assume that the current three-month Treasury bill rate is 4.50%. We can then use 4.50% as our estimate of the risk-free rate. Table 6.3 shows that from 1960 through 2006, the average Treasury bill rate was 5.57%, while the average annual return on the S&P 500 Composite Index

was 7.66%. Thus the historic risk premium from 1960 through 2006 is 2.09% (7.66% − 5.57%). The historic risk premium is a common estimate of the expected risk premium in the future (Brigham & Ehrhardt, 2005). Adding the historic risk premium of 2.09% to the estimated 4.50% risk-free rate, we end up with an estimated expected return on the S&P 500 Composite Index equal to 6.59%. The estimated 6.59% return on a portfolio of stocks contained in the S&P 500 Composite Index can then be used as the discount rate for these cash flows.

RISK IS DIFFERENT FROM THAT FOR THE OVERALL STOCK MARKET

So far we have assumed that the risk of the future cash flows being valued is equal to the overall risk of the stock market, as represented by returns on the S&P 500 Composite Index. If the risk of the cash flows differs from that for the overall stock market, then we cannot use the expected return on the S&P 500 Composite Index as the discount rate. To decide which discount rate to use, we look at the risk that matters to individual investors.

The S&P 500 Composite Index is a highly diversified stock portfolio that contains 500 common stocks. The standard deviations of the returns of individual stocks tend to be considerably higher than the standard deviations of the returns of the S&P 500 Composite Index.[2] The reason for the difference is **diversification**. With diversification, individual stocks can be combined into portfolios. As long as the stocks in the portfolio do not completely move together over time, stocks in the portfolio that earn poor returns are offset by other stocks that earn higher returns. As a result, returns on the portfolio fluctuate less than the returns on individual stocks. Since people have the ability to diversify their portfolios, we can argue that when analyzing the risk of an individual security, we are really concerned about the impact of an individual security on the overall risk of a well-diversified portfolio such as the S&P 500 Composite Index. Specifically, when we measure the risk of an individual security, we are interested in how the risk of a well-diversified portfolio is affected by adding that security to the portfolio.

Under the assumption that investors hold well-diversified portfolios, the capital asset pricing

---

[2]This is confirmed by estimates of standard deviations in the individual returns of Verizon, Ford Motor Company, Walt Disney Company, General Electric, IBM, McDonald's, Sears, Toys "R" Us, and Amazon.com for a recent 10-year period, which were all higher than the standard deviation for the returns on the S&P 500 Composite Index, as reported by Ross, Westerfield, and Jaffe (2005).

model (CAPM) shows that the risk of an individual security can be represented by its beta coefficient.[3] Beta tells us the extent to which the return on the individual security moves with the overall market (the S&P 500 Composite Index). The S&P 500 Composite Index itself has a beta of 1. The beta of a stock that is less risky than the overall market is less than 1. A stock that is more risky than the overall market has a beta exceeding 1.

Under the CAPM, the expected return on an individual security is as follows:

expected return on an individual security =
current risk-free return +
(beta of the individual security × market risk premium)

Sport Manufacturing Company

Assume that SMC has a beta equal to 1.20, that the current risk-free rate is 4.50%, and that the historic market risk premium is 2.09%.

SMC's expected return = 4.50% + (1.20 × 2.09%)
= 7.01%

If SMC is valuing the cash flows of an individual project funded entirely by common stock, then 7.01%

is an appropriate discount rate. The CAPM and the choice of an appropriate discount rate when firms obtain funding via issuance of bonds, loans, internally generated cash, or new equity issues is discussed further in chapter 11.

CONCLUSION

In this chapter, we cover principles of financial analysis that we will use throughout the rest of this textbook. In particular, we use the time value of money to place values on future expected cash flows. This is particularly important for companies that must look at valuing a future stream of lease payments to make decisions about whether to own or lease an asset. The proper analysis of risk is important since a faulty analysis can yield bad estimates of the discount rate used to estimate present value. As a result, in our example of choosing whether to lease or buy an asset, mismeasurement of risk can result in incorrect valuation and ultimately faulty decisions about the course of action to pursue. As a result, understanding the time value of money, as well as risk, will be shown to be important to financial decision making throughout the rest of this book.

[3]In formal statistical terms, beta is equal to the covariance of the return of an individual security with the overall market portfolio divided by the variance of the market portfolio. See Ross et al. (2005) for a more detailed discussion of the assumptions and derivation of the capital asset pricing model.

CLASS DISCUSSION TOPICS

1. Evaluate the following statement: "Since a well-diversified portfolio of stocks tends to outperform U.S. Treasury bills, there is no reason to invest in Treasury bills."

2. There has been increased criticism of corporate executives for being too short-term oriented and not focused enough on the long-run performance of their companies. Should companies place an emphasis on maximizing long-term profits?

3. What happens to the present value of an annuity if the discount rate is increased? What happens to the future value if the discount rate is increased?

4. Assume two athletes sign ten year contracts that pay out a total of $100 million over the life of the contracts. One contract will pay the $100 million in equal installments over the ten years. The other contract will pay the $100 million in installments, but the installments increase 5% per year. Which athlete received the better deal?

5. Jammin Slammin Bailey, the center for the Stars of David, has a nonguaranteed (meaning he receives no salary if cut from the team or injured) contract that pays him $5 million per year for the next five years. Jammin has been severely injured in an automobile accident and will no longer be able to work, let alone play for the Stars of David. When Jammin sues the driver of the other vehicle in court, the jury awards him $25 million to cover the loss of earnings over the next five seasons. Given what we have learned in this chapter, was the jury correct?

6. The returns in table 6.3 have not been adjusted for inflation. What would happen to the expected return if we adjusted the annual returns for inflation?

7. Table 6.3 demonstrated that stocks outperform Treasury bills over long periods of time. If that is the case, why do some people avoid the stock market and invest only in Treasury bills over long periods of time?

8. What kind of asset would have a beta of zero?

7

APPROACHES TO FINANCIAL PLANNING

CHAPTER OBJECTIVES

After studying this chapter, you should be able to do the following:

- Define financial planning.
- Describe how to acquire financial data from internal and external sources.
- Understand how to utilize financial data to help make business decisions.
- Distinguish between long-term and short-term financial planning and understand how to minimize risk.
- Understand how to use pro forma budgets and business plans.

Financial planning entails examining future income and expenses to help steer a company in a given direction. Chapter 6 emphasizes how critical foresight is for financial planning. Pro forma projections provide guidance for making decisions and represent a basic instrument in the financial planning process. Every business decision requires planning. Strategic planning has gained popularity as a way of critically analyzing given business scenarios to generate appropriate solutions. This same strategic planning perspective applies to financial planning. Every monetary issue needs to be examined for fiscal soundness. Every dollar needs to be planned for in order to maximize that dollar's impact. Planning for most typical contingencies can help a business operate smoothly and save money.

This chapter highlights the various components necessary to plan effectively for the future. The first step is to obtain the necessary internal and external data on which to base decisions. The next step is to make use of the data for both short-term and long-term planning. The last section of this chapter deals with the final step: how to develop a pro forma budget as a key to writing an effective business plan.

IMPORTANCE OF FINANCIAL PLANNING

Financial planning can help provide appropriate solutions for the types of problems businesses face every day, such as the need to

- develop new products,
- spend more money on research and development,
- retire a given product line,
- borrow funds for future expansion,
- issue commercial paper,
- issue more stock,
- issue more bonds,
- sell existing assets,
- purchase new assets,
- move the business to another location,
- acquire a competing company, or
- file for bankruptcy protection.

As the list suggests, every future action a business might undertake entails financial planning.

 **Stars of David**

The Stars of David might examine the energy costs for their arena. By computing the energy costs associated with any given luxury box, the Stars could determine how much of a luxury box's budget should be allocated to energy. This amount could be billed to the luxury box owner as a pass-through expense. A pass-through expense is any item that can be calculated separately and added to a client's bill. On the other hand, if the Stars saw the potential for monetary savings in relation to energy use, they might develop an energy management policy in order to achieve the savings. A box that remains vacant during an event does not require the same amount of energy as when it is filled. The Stars could decide to give a refund to any luxury box renter who gives 24-hour notice that the box will remain vacant for an event. If the Stars were charging $50 a night as a pass-through energy expense, the team might offer the renter a $25 refund in return for providing the appropriate notice. The Stars would lose $25, but they would also reduce energy costs in an amount closer to $50. Thus, the team would in fact come out ahead because of appropriate financial planning. Such an analytical approach to developing policies and procedures is an example of how financial planning can help squeeze every penny possible in a tight budget or help develop larger profits.

Another example of financial planning comes from the Texas Rangers. In December 2000, the Texas Rangers made history by signing free agent Alex Rodriguez to a 10-year $252 million contract. Considered by many to be the best player in the league, Rodriguez was now also the highest paid. Shortly after the Rangers signed Rodriguez, they announced an increase in ticket prices. Individual tickets were going to cost $2 more, making the average ticket price $22.08. Club seats increased from $25 to $40, and upper reserved seats and bleacher seats went from $10 to $12 ("Pay-Rod," 2001). Out of all the major league teams, only the New York Yankees and Boston Red Sox averaged higher ticket prices.

But why did the Rangers raise their prices? Would the increased revenue cover Rodriguez's contract? Was the team just savvy in thinking people would pay to see the best ballplayer in baseball? Table 7.1 shows the average attendance at Ameriquest Field before, during, and after Rodriguez played for the Rangers (he was traded to the New York Yankees in February 2004). Attendance did fluctuate throughout his career with the team, but his presence did not produce significant attendance growth.

Table 7.1 Average Attendance at Ameriquest Field

Year	Average attendance
1999	34,253
2000	31,956
2001	34,592
2002	29,043
2003	25,856
2004	31,818

Data from baseball-almanac.com. Available:
www.baseballalmanac.com/teams/rangatte.shtml.

The higher ticket prices or the club's inability to win could also have affected attendance totals.

The same year the Rangers signed Alex Rodriguez, they signed a 10-year $250 million broadcast contract with Fox. This would cover Rodriguez's contract, leaving other revenue such as ticket sales and souvenirs to cover other payroll obligations.

A comparison of Alex Rodriguez's contract with those of other well-known superstars during the same time highlights the fact that his deal was about $100 million more than the next closest long-term contract deal (8 year $160 million contract for Manny Ramirez). However, as highlighted in Table 7.2, when salaries are examined on a yearly basis, versus a long-term contract, two athletes earned more than A-Rod in the 2006-7 season (see table 7.2).

The only contract that comes close to Rodriguez's is Manny Ramirez's deal with the Boston Red Sox. Before the Sox signed Ramirez, they announced an increase in ticket prices for the 2001 season.

These examples highlight the importance of planning and the potential impact if only several hundred dollars or as much as several million dollars are either saved through facility-related policies or raised by adapting marketing strategies. The Rangers thought Alex Rodriguez would be their winning and financial savior, but after several years the reality unfolded that they miscalculated both expectations.

Sound financial planning is also necessary when a company undertakes an advertising campaign; the company needs to develop an advertising budget incorporating forecasts of future advertising expenditures. Table 7.3 in the following case study is an example of an advertising budget worksheet that could help a company establish priorities for future advertising campaigns. These are critical for financial planning because sales forecasts are based on the anticipated advertising campaign and the anticipated resulting sales. If a new product is launched and only a small marketing budget has been provided, the anticipated sales could be severely compromised. At the same time, a large marketing budget that is misspent on the wrong advertising medium can be counterproductive.

Sport Manufacturing Company

If Sport Manufacturing Company decides to switch from advertising primarily in magazines to using athletes as endorsers, this planning decision will be shown on a completed form that lets management know how the strategy will be implemented (see table 7.3).

The marketing budget reflects the new emphasis on endorsing athletes, along with a dramatic cut in the magazine advertisement budget. Note that some

Table 7.2 Top Salaries for Major Professional Sports, 2006-2007

Athlete	Team	Salary in millions ($)
Jason Giambi	New York Yankees	23,428,571
Michael Vick	Atlanta Falcons	23,102,750
Alex Rodriguez	New York Yankees	22,708,525
Derek Jeter	New York Yankees	21,600,000
Kevin Garnett	Minnesota Timberwolves	21,600,000
Shaquille O'Neal	Miami Heat	20,000,000
Matt Hasselbeck	Seattle Seahawks	19,005,280
Jalen Rose	Phoenix Suns	18,441,500
Jason Kidd	New Jersey Nets	18,084,000
Jermaine O'Neal	Indiana Pacers	18,084,000
Orlando Pace	St. Louis Rams	18,000,000
Walter Jones	Seattle Seahawks	17,701,320
Manny Ramirez	Boston Red Sox	17,016,381
Todd Helton	Colorado Rockies	16,600,000
Tom Brady	New England Patriots	15,654,180

Data from the USA Today Salary Database.

Table 7.3 2006 Advertising Budget Categories

Category	Priority	# of insertions	2005 budget ($)	2006 budget ($)	% difference
Magazines	2	200	8,000,000	5,500,000	−31.25
Newspaper advertisements	7	40	1,000,000	1,000,000	0.00
Newspaper supplements	5	26	2,000,000	2,300,000	15.00
Radio	11	900	1,300,000	850,000	−34.60
Television	8	150	2,500,000	2,000,000	−20.00
Endorsements	1	10	1,000,000	8,500,000	750.00
Posters	4	50,000	60,000	140,000	133.00
Special media	3	100	800,000	1,000,000	25.00
Agency fees	16	N/A	1,200,000	1,000,000	−16.66
Trade media	6	60	700,000	750,000	7.14
Consumer incentives	9	100,000	500,000	500,000	0.00
Sales conferences	10	12	230,000	250,000	8.69
Merchandising material	12	400	130,000	150,000	15.38
Trade allowances	13	N/A	100,000	100,000	0.00
Trade free goods	14	2,000	1,000,000	1,050,000	5.00
Sundries	15	N/A	120,000	130,000	8.33
Totals	**N/A**	**$153,898**	**$20,640,000**	**$25,220,000**	**22.19%**

high-priority areas may have a lower budget than certain lower-priority items. For example, posters have one of the lowest allocations in the budget, but they are a high priority. Since the new campaign emphasizes endorsing athletes, giving away posters of the athletes may be a major initiative, but it still does not represent a major expenditure. Other items might have higher budgeted amounts but have a lower priority. For example, the company might purchase certain ads even though they are not a major part of the marketing effort because of a long-standing relationship with the advertising medium or in order to avoid an image backlash. The major declines in the marketing budget are in radio (−34.6%), magazine (−31.25%), and television advertisements (−20%).

Advertising variables may not be as clear to upper management if different segments of the business submit different marketing budgets. A large business may have several different segments, each with its own budget; if these budgets are not consolidated into a final marketing budget, upper management will not have a correct picture of the marketing goals and associated costs. For example, the Stars of David might have different marketing budgets for ticket sales and for the team's Web page or souvenir store. If the various budgets are not consolidated into a simple-to-read document, management will make decisions without all the relevant facts. The planning process cannot be accomplished without this information, and the information paves the way for the overall corporate budget. Although it might appear that examining individual budgets might be easier for some executives, the inability to completely compare and contrast each budget in a synthesized manner can reduce the effectiveness of various techniques such as zero-based budgeting (see p. 109). Thus, some executives like to examine the budgets for individual units but insist on examining a consolidated budget to see what impact any changes in one budget will have on other units.

Management can examine the chart shown in table 7.3 to determine where the marketing emphasis will be in the coming year and what areas represent the greatest spending growth and decline. This information can be correlated with sales forecasts to help management understand why a certain advertising strategy is being suggested. For example, if sales stemming from magazine advertisements increased 20% in the past year, it would make sense for the advertising campaign to show an increase in magazine ads to help spur additional sales from that outlet. However, if the sales force informed management that utilizing athletes as endorsers was expected to produce the greatest surge in exposure, management could understand why magazine advertising was actually declining even though one could expect additional magazine advertisements to increase sales. Thus, the marketing budget chart serves as a tool that management can use to make a logical plan for the future.

DATA GATHERING

Companies and organizations cannot plan without appropriate data. Planning data should be compared against internal projections and external projections such as industry standards. The information from which spending and revenue sources can be identified includes internal data and external data. Internal data are often referred to as primary data since this information is generated by the business itself. External data, or data obtained from other sources, have already been developed and published and so are often referred to as secondary data.

INTERNAL DATA

As the sidebar example below highlights, forecasting cannot be accomplished without reliable internal data. An economic impact study could have significant value, but if it is not accurate, then any reliance on the data would be erroneous. It is critical to have reliable internal as well as external data in order to make decisions. Internal data can include past balance sheets and income statements, audited financial records, annual reports, research and development reports, and countless other documents generated by employees or consultants. Paper trails should not be used to the exclusion of other data. For example,

e-mails may contain valuable data that researchers may miss if they examine printed material only.

Internal data can come from various other sources. Information can be derived from personal observation or through conversation around the water cooler. Numerous additional sources may include surveys conducted by the business to analyze customer concerns. Many sports teams conduct fan surveys to determine why people attend games and how to provide more valuable services. Information about how much and what types of soft drinks or beer are sold can be useful. By analyzing the sales figures in the grandstands and at concession stands, a team can plan its strategy for increasing beverage sales. Similarly, by breaking its operation down into its basic elements, the team can develop a more appropriate budget. This process is often seen in zero-based budgeting.

Many companies utilize zero-based budgeting as a technique to justify future expenditures. In **zero-based budgeting (ZBB)**, every expenditure is justified in comparison with other potential projects. If a team will have $1 million for its marketing budget, every department that wishes to receive some of that money needs to indicate how much money it is requesting and provide justification for the request. If a department has been successful in a particular campaign, those numbers can be used as a justification for receiving a given amount of the funds. Each unit, division, or department might be required to produce formal documentation to justify requested expenditures.

Objective documentation is the key. If the existence of a department could be under review, there may be a temptation to manipulate data to ensure continued employment. For example, if the National Aeronautics and Space Administration (NASA) operated under ZBB

Data Collection at the University of Florida

In a 1995 economic impact study, the University of Florida reported that visitors to the campus spent more than $19 million a year for sports, cultural events, and commencement events (Mercer, 1996). Such a study to develop primary data could be used to show the state legislature the value of investing in University of Florida sports or facilities. Providing empirical, objective data would make it difficult for any opponents to attack proposed funding requests.

Every school is going to be different. For example, Adams State College in Colorado is a small school, but it is the largest employer in the San Luis Valley. A study was conducted in 2005 to evaluate the school's economic impact on the region. The final number was a $70 million economic impact based on more than $40 million in direct economic impact and a multiplier of 1.7. The multiplier means that every $1.00 spent by students or the college community stimulated an additional $0.70 of expenditure. Of the money generated by the school, $1.8 million a year was attributed to visitors attending athletic and cultural events at the college ("New Study," 2005). Although this impact is much less than that of the University of Florida, such a contribution in a small community would possibly have a much more significant effect.

principles, its entire Mars program might be under review after several major disasters costing millions of dollars. Individuals in an affected program might try to paint a picture that is better than what really occurred. However, objective data can help eliminate potential bias or distortion. An excellent way to uncover objective information is to go to external sources.

EXTERNAL DATA

The preceding sidebar highlights the importance of internal data for decision making. By knowing how successful internal operations are, a business can more appropriately plan for the future. External data can serve the same purpose. External data and docu-

Financial Numbers From a Minor League Baseball Team

The following are excerpts from an interview with Chris Canetti, the general manager of a minor league baseball team at the time of the interview several years ago. The information reflects the importance of internal data and how the internal data can generate strategies for future growth.

I receive a lot of resumes where someone says in the cover letter that they love sports, and that's great. You have to love baseball to work in baseball, and you have to love sports to work in sports, but the bottom line is that it is a business. When I have to hire someone I could care less if they played Little League baseball; I want to know what positives they can bring to my business and me and how they can benefit the bottom line. This might encourage or discourage you, but when I went to college I was a communications major. I never took an accounting, marketing, or finance course. For a bachelor's degree in my school the only thing I needed was Economics 101. I wish differently now that I had taken those courses, but a few years ago before I became general manager, the former GM came to me one day and said, "I want you to do the budget." A minor league baseball team makes millions a year in revenue, and I have to make a budget. You can't tell your boss no, so you have to figure it out. I wish I had a course like this [sport finance], it would have made my life a lot easier.

A budget is a model that is set by the team to try to forecast the goals they want to meet for the coming year. . . . If you look at some budgets, they might show a cash-positive year. However, if the team has debt service that is amortized out over the course of time, it will show up as an expense, even though it is not a hard cash expense. With the debt service expense included in the budget, the budget could show a loss. I use a piece-by-piece approach to developing the numbers in this budget. The primary source for these numbers is from historical data. History describes what occurred last year and serves as the base for predicting what might happen in the coming year. For example, if we look at fictitious numbers for last year [pp. 111], we see that the team had $1.4 million in [game-day] concession sales. Assume 200,000 fans attended games last season. By dividing the $1.4 million by the 200,000 fans, we can calculate that an average fan

spends $7 each game on concessions. If we anticipate a 10% increase in attendance, then our budget should also reflect that 10% increase. Our ticket sales would increase 10% and our concession sales would also increase. If fans once again spend on average $7 each, then we can multiply $7 by 220,000 fans (200,000 fans plus the 10% increase in fans), resulting in a budgeted $1.54 million for concession revenue for next season.

A team's stadium lease will always be a major factor in determining an organization's financial picture. The lease is a key consideration when going through the budgeting process. The lease outlines how the parties involved will split the responsibility and control of major expense and revenue categories. These elements often include things such as concession revenue, suite revenue, parking revenue, ticket taxes, stadium maintenance, and utilities. The factors within a lease are unique in almost every team's case. In some instances, a team's lease is written so that a percentage of annual revenues are used to pay debts incurred from stadium construction or renovation. Such cases will affect the team's annual financial statement.

When asked about profit centers, Canetti responded:

Concessions represent one of the greatest profit centers for a team. While a minor league team makes a significant amount on ticket revenue and does not pay players'/coaches' salaries, which are paid by the parent club, concessions are still the best profit center. A team can generate between 50% and 60% profit on concession sales. A team could possibly outsource concessions to another company but then would only receive 35%. This significant potential decline in concession revenue has encouraged us to keep taking care of concessions ourselves to maximize the revenue and flexibility.

Hypothetical Minor League Baseball Team Budget for the 2000 Season

Category	($000)
Revenue	6,140
Direct costs	1,758
Gross profit	**4,382**
Park and game expenses (schedule 1)	992
Team expenses (schedule 2)	196
General/Admin. expenses (schedule 3)	2,422
Debt service (schedule 4)	840
Total expenses	**4,450**
Operating income	**–116**
Sources of revenue:	
Ticket revenue	2,000
Direct ticket costs:	
Facility fee	200
Payment to MLB	60
Ticket production	14
Total costs	**274**
Gross profit	**1,726**
Advertising revenue	1,400
Direct costs:	
Paint/Material	–
Printing	–
Radio	10
Promotional spots	200
Total costs	**210**
Gross profit	**1,190**
Game day concessions	1,400
Group concessions	600
Total concessions revenue	**2,000**
Direct costs:	
Food	380
Soft drinks	70
Beer	80
Supplies/Uniforms	60
Equipment leasing	8
Payroll	240
Payroll taxes	30
Total costs	**868**
Gross profit	**1,132**
Merchandise revenue	340
Direct costs:	
Beginning inventory	70
Purchases	130
Payroll	14
Total costs	**214**
Ending inventory	48
Final costs	**166**
Gross profit	**174**
Other revenue:	
Parking	40
Programs	40
Other	320
Total other revenue	**400**
Direct costs:	
Program	80
Other	160
Total costs	**240**
Gross profit	**160**
Total gross profit	4,382

Departmental gross profit margin	
Ticket department	1,726
Advertising department	1,190
Concessions department	1,132
Merchandise department	174
Other departments	160
Total gross profit	**4,382**
Gross profit margin	**71.37%**

Schedule 1—Park and Game Expenses

Stadium rent	150
Real estate taxes (waived)	0
Utilities	130
Maintenance—grounds	280
Security	110
Umpires	70
Game day payroll	190
Game day payroll taxes	18
Equipment rental	16
Miscellaneous	28
Total park and game expenses	**992**

Schedule 2—Team Expenses

Transportation	80
Lodging	96
Laundry/Clubhouse	10
Uniforms	10
Total team expenses	**196**

Schedule 3—General and Administrative expenses

Salaries	800
Payroll taxes	74
Office operations	4
Dues and fees	60
Promotion and advertising	550
Other (Schedule 5)	984
Total general and admin.	**2,422**

Schedule 4—Debt Service Plus Other Expenses

Interest	180
Depreciation	260
Amortization of contracts	400
Total expenses	**4,450**

Schedule 5—Other Expenses

Amortization	370
Auto expenses	18
Bad debt expenses	10
Bank service charge	40
Contributions	2
Entertainment	10
Insurance	160
Professional fees	60
Miscellaneous	2
Outside services	16
Postage	40
Rent	2
Repairs	16
Supplies	32
Taxes—others	60
Telephone	80
Travel	16
Total other expenses	**934**
Total debt service plus other expenses	**840**

mentation are critical for successful planning. External data can be used to help shape various decisions to properly reflect the true business environment. For example, the data in the sidebar table show the extent to which marketing efforts are succeeding. If the team were facing financial trouble, it could examine prior expenditures to see what efforts were and were not successful (e.g., was the $550,000 spent on promotion and advertising profitable, or is a different campaign needed based on customer response to the prior campaign?). In addition, if the stadium landlords were having trouble with the local officials, as evidenced by news stories and city hearings, the team could attempt to renegotiate the lease to both save money and project a positive public image for the landlords. These are only two examples of the use of external data to help shape sport business decisions.

External data can help shape decisions in many other ways as well. The following are examples of gathering external data:

- Monitoring international terrorist activities to determine if an event needs to be canceled
- Analyzing industry trends to develop appropriate pricing for concession items
- Tracking culinary advances to determine the most effective means of packaging and selling food items
- Reading current articles in trade publications to stay abreast of industry changes
- Attending conferences to hear what other executives are saying about the industry
- Reviewing government census reports to understand demographic changes in the possible fan base

Publications such as *Barron's, Forbes, Business Week*, and the *Wall Street Journal* provide significant general information. More specific information can be obtained from such sources as *Dun & Bradstreet's Key Business Ratios*, which analyzes 14 key ratios for various industries. Both state and federal governments produce significant useful data such as statistical abstracts. Industry trade groups can also produce valuable data to assist with financial planning. Appendix C is a resource section with information on these publications and how to access them.

Among the best information sources for the sport industry are industry publications such as *Athletic Business, Athletic Management, Fitness Management, NCAA News*, and a host of other specialized publications. Each one has unique special features, reports, and surveys that can provide invaluable assistance. One of the premiere publications in the industry is *Street & Smith's*

Sports Business Journal. This weekly publication has special sections devoted to attendance numbers, a stock market index for sport-related companies, and information on sponsorship deals, among other features.

Regular newspapers often list the payrolls for every professional team in leagues such as the NFL, MLB, and the NBA. Such data can help a team compare itself with others, which is called **benchmarking**. Benchmarking allows a business to see if it is paying more for similar work or results. For example the Stars of David can compare their salary range with other teams in the league or can examine specific statistical variables such as the cost per rebound or assist for each player.

Organizations regularly research specific industry benchmarks that can help establish criteria for success or failure. Although the data are only as good as the techniques used to retrieve them, the information can help shape many financial decisions. Numerous managers focus on the bottom line, and the bottom line can be examined by looking at what others in the same industry do to determine if a facility is operating effectively compared with similarly situated facilities. The numbers in table 7.4 represent averages for the fitness club industry as researched by the International Health, Racquet and Sportsclub Association (IHRSA); this information helps provide guidance for fitness facilities establishing their budgets.

Industry-related data come from a variety of sources and appear in a variety of formats. Small Business Administration (SBA) publishes free business plan formats online to help businesses understand what data they will need and what to do with the data. More specific data are often needed from specific industry groups or associations.

 If the Smiths wanted to build a softball complex, they could turn to the Sportsplex Operators and Developers Association (SODA), which publishes industry-specific data. To determine how much it would cost to build a park, they could possibly obtain the information shown in table 7.5 (p. 114), which is derived from a facility cost comparison published by SODA in the 1990s.

Regardless of the type of external data, the reader of such reports needs to compare apples with apples. Some publications calculate return on equity as **net income** divided by average common equity, while others divide net income by the year-end common equity. Comparing data that have been obtained using different equations will lead to inaccuracies. Referring back to NASA's trouble with its Mars program, one expensive blunder occurred, in part, because of human

Table 7.4   Fitness Club Industry Benchmarks

Category	Industry average
Total revenue from nondues sources	27%
Payroll as a percentage of revenue	42%
Total operating expenses as a percentage of revenue	66%
Total fixed expenses as a percentage of revenue	10.7%
EBITDA	23.2%
Spending to maintain the facility and all equipment	6.2%
Revenue per square foot	$45
Revenue per member	$871

EBITDA = earnings before interest, taxes, depreciation, and amortization. Data from C. Winters, 2000, "Budgeting 101," *Club Industry*: 90-91.

error in which measurements were not converted correctly from the metric to the traditional English system. Such a "simple" mistake led to the crashing of a spaceflight. Similarly, incorrectly analyzing an internal rate of return or price–earnings ratio can destroy an investment decision. Thus, all financial statements should be carefully scrutinized to determine what equations and measurement techniques were used and when the data were collected to ensure proper comparisons.

THE FINANCIAL PLANNING PROCESS

Financial planning requires two major activities: forecasting potential revenues and budgeting for future expenses. Once the appropriate data are collected, it is incumbent on management to act on the data. Management cannot hide behind the numbers and not make a decision. Stockholders and voters demand that a business or government entity make decisions that will maximize their investments. The most common managerial decisions have to do with maximizing revenue sources and minimizing expenses.

Financial planning is often based on behavior learned from previous bad habits or mistakes. Failing to turn over inventory quickly enough or not collecting overdue bills in a timely manner leads to reduced income and higher expenses. Both inventory levels and uncollected accounts can significantly decrease profitability if they are high. If excess inventory and uncollected accounts receivable appear on the balance sheet, then a significant amount of money may be tied up and unusable. Both of these problems can also be easily corrected through the implementation of efficiency control mechanisms such as posting systems (based on the due dates of outstanding accounts receivable) or the establishment of guidelines for inspecting the inventory. Many steps that one might categorize as financial planning are just plain commonsense tactics. For example, the following are simple tactics promoted by American Express Small

Business Services to help manage cash flow ("Steps for Improving," 1998):

- Organize billing schedules so overdue bills can be flagged for quicker follow-up.
- Stretch out repayment of suppliers to the maximum time allowed by contract.
- Try to pay bills earlier if suppliers offer incentives for early repayment.
- If suppliers do not offer an incentive program for early payment, ask for such a program.
- Do not hesitate to raise prices; clients are accustomed to small but regular increases.
- Eliminate any unnecessary inventory, which just wastes money.
- Consider leasing rather than buying to free your credit line and to take advantage of tax write-offs.
- Buy from various suppliers to prevent harm if a supplier faces a problem and to take advantage of special offers that other suppliers might make.

These simple strategies are in fact decisions that can be reached through the planning process. A business can decide to pay bills within 10 days if a discount is offered and reinvest any savings into interest-bearing Treasury bonds. Such a planning process appears simple, but numerous managers live "by the seat of their pants" when making decisions and do not consider the long-term consequences. Planning helps determine potential long-term ramifications.

One of the most important planning issues is determining the capital structure for a business. Chapter 11 explains the importance of determining the capital mix, or target capital structure. The planning process can help determine the most appropriate structure for a given year based on economic variables and countless additional pieces of information acquired in the data-collection process. If Nike is overburdened by bond obligations, it might not be able to generate enough return to interest potential stockholders. However, if Nike's equity

Table 7.5 Comparison of Two Sizes of Complexes

Description	Six-field complex in Arizona		Three-field complex in Florida	
	Actual cost ($)	Avg. per field cost ($)	Actual cost ($)	Avg. per field cost ($)
Engineering and architectural plans	40,000	6,666.67	350,000	116,666.67
Site mobilization	140	23.33	122,938	40,979.33
Site grading and preparation	65,480	10,913.33	166,367	55,455.67
Storm drains	0	0	71,632	23,877.33
Sewers	19,036	3,172.67	14,860	4,953.33
Water system	45,000	7,500.00	14,894	4,964.67
Underground cable	6,000	1,000.00	10,000	3,333.33
Well costs	100,000	16,667.67	5,000	1,666.67
Topsoil	6,000	1,000.00	24,000	8,000.00
Sod and soil	69,000	11,500.00	139,445	46,481.67
Shrubs and trees	23,230	3,871.67	298,000	99,333.33
Paths and walls	66,100	11,016.67	72,000	24,000.00
Warning tracks	5,015	835.83	12,000	4,000.00
Area lighting	21,201	3,533.50	131,000	43,666.67
Sports lighting	185,000	30,833.33	220,000	73,333.33
Parking lot paving	101,450	16,908.33	100,000	33,333.33
Fencing	57,900	9,650.00	65,000	21,666.67
Scoreboards	15,000	2,500.00	22,000	7,333.33
Batting cages	48,890	8,148.33	63,775	21,258.33
Tot lot	27,785	4,630.83	62,542	20,847.33
Volleyball court	20,403	3,400.50	27,551	9,183.67
Basketball courts	0	0	88,223	29,407.67
Picnic area	11,772	1,962.00	5,000	1,666.67
Entryway	4,000	666.67	10,000	3,333.33
Snack bars	290,150	48,358.33	446,150	148,716.67
Trash enclosures	4,700	783.33	4,000	1,333.33
Maintenance shed	14,215	2,369.17	66,500	22,166.67
Administration building	300,000	50,000.00	13,750	4,583.33
BBQ area	25,000	4,166.67	3,000	1,000.00
Fees and permits	103	17.17	8,900	2,966.67
General conditions	10,950	1,825.00	109,000	36,333.33
Maintenance equipment	35,000	5,833.33	22,500	7,500.00
Concessions equipment	65,000	10,833.33	40,000	13,333.33
Park furnishing	3,000	500.00	8,000	2,666.67
Computers	0	0	10,000	3,333.33
Video security and PA	17,000	2,833.33	6,000	2,000.00
Bleachers	10,600	1,766.67	20,000	6,666.67
Signage	2,900	483.33	6,000	2,000.00
Inventory and supplies	22,000	3,666.67	8,000	2,666.67
Preopening expenses	16,000	2,666.67	20,000	6,666.67
Legal and accounting	8,500	1,416.67	30,000	10,000.00
Feasibility study	3,800	633.33	25,000	8,333.33
Development fees	144,600	24,100.00	225,000	75,000.00
Total	**$1,641,920**	**$273,653.33**	**$3,168,027**	**$1,056,009.00**

Data from SODA (Sportsplex Operators and Developers Association), 1993, *Sportspark construction costs* (Racine, WI: Author).

is overdiluted, it may be difficult for the company to buy back its shares. Nike could be in trouble if it has issued too many shares and its equity is primarily composed of shareholders' equity rather than retained earnings. This could be a problem if Nike ever wanted to buy back its stock to go private or buy back some of its shares to reduce the number of shareholders and increase the share value for the remaining shareholders.

Economic conditions are an excellent example of the concerns raised in the planning process. **Inflation** and prosperity typically cause a sharp need for corporate capital so that the company can continue to produce more. However, if bonds and preferred stock are issued too quickly, a company can go bankrupt if the economy changes and the company owes too much in interest, **principal**, and required dividend payments.

Revenue and Expenses in NCAA Division I-A Programs

The following examples highlight how an organization's data can be compared with industry data to determine if revenue and expenses match figures for other similar entities. Although the dollar amounts might differ, a percentage analysis can be very useful and appropriate. The first of the following tables shows where the typical NCAA Division I-A moneys come from.

NCAA Division I-A Revenues

Category	Percentage of income
Home gate receipts	30.9
Cash gifts	13.7
Radio and television	12.6
Postseason compensation	7.1
Auxiliary income	7.0
Institutional support	7.0
Student fees	6.6
Away-game guarantees	5.8
Other income	5.7
Investment income	2.0
State aid	1.5

Data from "Fiscally friendly football," 1996, *Sidelines*: 2.

Expenses for typical NCAA Division I-A programs are expressed as percentages in the table that follows.

NCAA Division I-A Expenses

Category	Percentage of income
Salaries and benefits	28.9
Grants-in-aid	16.5
Other expenses	9.2
Operations and maintenance	6.5
Team travel	6.4
Opponents' payments	6.1
Equipment and supplies	5.5
Contract services	3.9
Debt service	3.9
Capital expenses	3.2
Recruiting	2.3
Publicity	2.2
Fund-raising	1.8
Insurance	1.1
Nonathletic expenses	1.0
Taxes	0.9
Administrative travel	0.6

Data from "Fiscally friendly football," 1996, *Sidelines*: 2.

When people talk about revenue sports, they are talking about men's football and basketball. The greatest percentage of revenue is derived from the categories in the next table.

Revenue Percentages for NCAA Division I-A Programs

Category	Percentage
Football	63.3
Men's basketball	20.2
Student fees, state and institutional aid	15.2
Other men's sports	0.8
Women's sports	0.5

Data from "Fiscally friendly football," 1996, *Sidelines*: 2

Expenses (as a percentage of total expenses) for NCAA Division I-A members of the College Football Association in 1995-1996 are shown in the following table.

Expense Percentages for NCAA Division I-A Programs

Category	Percentage
Football	23.9
Support staff	12.9
Women's sports	11.8
Other expenses	9.2
Other men's sports	8.8
Operations and maintenance	6.5
Men's basketball	6.3
Contract services	4.0
Debt service	3.8
Other	12.8

Data from "Fiscally friendly football," 1996, *Sidelines*: 2.

College sports have been turning a profit in recent years. The average Division I-A program earned $660,000 in 1993; this figure increased to $1.2 million in 1995. However, the black ink was made possible by institutional support. Without institutional support, the average Division I-A program operated at a $237,000 deficit, and only 46% of programs were profitable. In 1993, 51% of programs generated a profit (Naughton, 1996). By the time of the next report three years later in 1998, the average Division I-A program's profit had decreased to $437,000 (in 1997). Excluding the institutional support, the average Division I-A program lost $823,000, resulting in an average of more than a half-million-dollar increase in losses for each institution ("NCAA Study," 1998).

(continued)

The following table shows which sports produce the highest concession sales average per attendee at professional sport facilities, regional arenas, and NCAA stadiums.

Ranking of Sports and Events With Highest Expenditure per Attendee

Sport	Average expenditure per attendee ($)
NFL	6.10
NHL	6.10
NBA	5.40
MLB	5.30
Motor sport	3.50
Concerts	3.40
Minor league hockey	2.90
Family shows	2.50
NCAA men's basketball	2.30
NCAA football	1.60

Data from the 1997 Stadium & Arena Managers' Annual Report, (Tampa, FL: Price Waterhouse Sports Group).

Furthermore, during periods in which interest rates are low, bank borrowing may be more economical than issuing bonds. If a bank loan is obtainable at a relatively low interest rate, the main savings will be the costs associated with issuing bonds (versus the minimal costs associated with obtaining a bank loan). If the long-term bond interest rate is lower than the obtainable bank interest rate, then it may be worthwhile to issue the bond because the issuing cost can be recouped over the long term. The opposite result is seen when interest rates are high, which means a business would have more difficulty issuing long-term bonds. The business would have trouble selling long-term bonds to investors if the interest rate is lower than what an investor might be able to obtain in the short run from other investments. Planning helps prevent making the wrong decision and issuing securities that might not be attractive to investors.

SHORT-TERM PLANNING

Short-term planning dictates how a business should proceed within a short time frame, usually less than two years. Short-term planning cannot be undertaken without examining the potential implication of current decisions on the long-term profitability or success of any business. Long-term planning is more oriented toward the future and allows executives to be more creative since so many options and uncertainties play into such decision making. Short-term planning is based on specific research and requires individuals to meet specific goals.

Regardless of the time frame used for planning, accuracy and the ability to properly interpret internal and external data are the keys to success. For example, if the short-term analysis fails to adequately examine internal debt related issues and the external borrowing environment, a business may not last more than several months before creditors file for involuntary bankruptcy.

The short-term planning process requires close scrutiny of internal variables such as cash flow and debt-related issues. Key aspects of short-term planning include how to effectively understand and make decisions based on working capital, net working capital, current ratio, acid test ratio, and the cash budget. These ratios are discussed in chapter 5.

Deciding whether or not to hire a new basketball coach is normally a long-term planning process. Most coaches are not hired for the short term; they are hired to build a program around their skills and strengths. This does not mean that short-term planning will not influence the decision. Ticket sales and player recruiting still need to be undertaken during the hiring process to ensure continued success or prevent falling further behind rival programs. Thus, the hiring process, similar to almost all planning decisions, entails a blend of short- and long-term planning.

For example, the University of Houston hired a former star basketball player at the university and one of the top 50 players in NBA history, Clyde Drexler, as the head basketball coach. Almost immediately thereafter, the university spent a considerable sum to remove several rows of seats and install luxury boxes. Although the initial demand for the boxes was high based on the prospect that the new coach would develop a winning team, those hopes quickly faded. The team performed unremarkably during Drexler's tenure, and after two years he resigned. This can serve as an example of poor short-term planning and inadequate capital management.

Effective planning would have included a cost–benefit analysis of installing the luxury boxes based on the

Before the St. Louis Cardinals could build their new stadium, they needed to complete a thorough financial planning process, including short- and long-term planning.

potential failure of the coach, rather than just on the expectation that a miracle would occur and the hiring would erase years of debt. In fact, attendance had been abysmal for years before the hiring, and during the two years thereafter it improved. Still, there were no guarantees that attendance numbers would not fall once again if the basketball team did not deliver a high-quality product. Short-term planning might have focused on examining the attendance trends associated with the new coach for at least several years after he came to the University of Houston to see if his hiring would in fact increase the attendance numbers. After collecting some empirical data based on actual ticket sales and revenue for a one- or two-year period after the coach's hiring, the university could have made a more accurate short-term plan for capital expenditure during a deficit.

The University of Houston example highlights how most business decisions entail an element of both short- and long-term planning. Another example of how short-term planning can blend into long-term planning is the futures market. The futures market primarily involves commodities such as metals, meats and other foods, and currencies. Most commodities sales are conducted in the spot market, where an item is bought and sold for cash and the exchange is completed immediately.

But in the futures market, transactions involve delivery and payment at some future date. The Stars of David could pay a significant amount of money for a player, but the player might be delivered at a future date because of other contractual obligations. This future obligation often happens with foreign athletes who might be drafted and signed by North American teams but still have to complete their contracts with their foreign teams. If a player is playing in Europe, the payment amount could be affected by fluctuations in the value of the U.S. dollar against the European currency during the waiting period. If the Stars of David do not take short-term preventive steps such as floating the contract amount on the futures market, the price of the contract might be higher when the Stars finally pay for the player (see case study on p. 118).

Floating means paying a certain amount to buy future dollars or other currencies on the currency markets. Some individuals are betting that the currency values will increase, and others are betting that the values will decrease. A similar type of gamble often occurs when people buy stock with the intent that the shares will either go up or down in value. This process is often called

hedging, which entails purchasing futures contracts in situations in which a price change could positively or negatively affect profits. A business could purchase a long hedge when it anticipates a price increase. With a short hedge, a business sells futures contracts to guard against price declines (Brigham & Gapenski, 1994).

The **short** sale is also used in the stock sale context when someone sells short with the intent of borrowing the stock from a broker and waiting for the price to decline before he actually buys the stock. The difference between the value of the borrowed stock and the final amount he paid for it when the stock price declined is the profit generated by this short sale. However, if the stock increases in value the investor will have to pay the higher price—which could result in significant losses for the investor. Purchasing stocks is covered in greater detail in chapter 9.

 To put this example into numerical terms, assume that the Stars of David are willing to pay $1 million for a player currently playing in the U.K. The team negotiates a contract with a British team and agrees to pay £500,000, which at the date of signing is worth approximately $1 million U.S. The contract is not to be paid for six months, when the British team's season is over. The Stars' financial adviser tells the team that the dollar is going to be weaker against the pound in six months. That means that in six months it might take $1.2 million to pay the £500,000. The Stars of David might buy a futures contract for $1.050 million now to deliver £500,000 in six months. Thus, by entering into a futures contract, the Stars can save $150,000 if the currency market acts as their adviser has predicted. If the market goes the other way, the team loses. Thus, if in six months the value of the pound has dropped, it would have been possible for the Stars to pay $950,000 to complete the transaction if they had not entered into the futures contract. Although this process can be considered a gamble, more often than not financial advisers have a good record of reading market trends based on years of statistical analysis that helps identify trends and patterns.

When purchasing a futures contract, the purchaser does not have to put up the full amount. The purchaser needs to put up only an initial **margin**, which for certain Treasury bonds is only $3,000 for each $100,000 in contracts (Brigham & Gapenski, 1994). Although it might seem that this purchase price is very inexpensive, investors need to maintain a certain value in their margin account, called a maintenance margin. If the contract value declines, the futures owner is required to pay more money to cover the maintenance margin.

A futures contract can be satisfied by the actual delivery of the commodities. A farmer could sell a futures contract for 5,000 bushels of oats for a September delivery. A sport nutrition-bar company might buy the contract in March so the company knows how much it will need to pay for ingredients and the farmer knows how much he will be paid for the future delivery of oats. Thus, a futures contract is a definite agreement on the part of a given party to buy something on a specific date and at a specific price. No matter how the price might change, the contract guarantees that the purchaser has locked in a price to protect against such price fluctuations. Futures can be used speculatively or for hedging. People buy speculative futures if it appears that a price might decline or rise, resulting in profits.

By carefully examining financial markets, a business can help increase its profitability and reduce the chances of losing money through inactivity. That is why it is so important to scrutinize short-term strategies related to all facets of a business. Long-term strategies also help guide businesses, as discussed next.

LONG-TERM PLANNING

Long-term goals are often less clear since there are too many variables to allow one to make accurate projections; but even so, obtaining additional research on which to base decisions can result in more accurate projections. Long-term planning focuses on planning for the future with a greater emphasis on external variables, such as industry trends and technological advancements. The Smiths' long-term analysis might focus on developing new exercise techniques or programs that combine some of the hottest fitness trends.

The long-term plan serves as the backbone for developing the proper documentation needed to secure capital support. Potential lenders such as banks or venture capitalists look to the managerial foresight highlighted in the plan. However, no matter how much information the plan contains, a lender will not invest a penny without getting a picture of the business' future profit potential. The profit potential is reflected in the pro forma budget.

As discussed earlier in this chapter, numerous decisions in the sport industry entail both short- and long-term planning. An excellent example involves the XFL. The World Wrestling Federation (WWF) (now known as World Wrestling Entertainment) went public in 2000 and is listed on the New York Stock Exchange. The WWF launched its own football league, called the Extreme Football League (XFL), in 2001. The launch was undertaken with a broadcast partner, NBC, with the intent of capitalizing on the young male audience that dominates in wrestling. The games, scheduled for prime-time Saturday nights, were a complete disaster. The shows had declining ratings each week, and the experiment ended with the WWF taking a $37 million charge to earnings (Grover & Lowry, 2001). A charge to earnings is a fancy term for a loss. Instead of a steady loss from poor sales, a charge represents a one-time loss that the business does not expect to occur again in the future.

Wall Street did not take the news well. Some analysts were skeptical about how the WWF could expand in a saturated market after the XFL collapsed (Grover & Lowry, 2001). The concern was also reflected in a drop in the stock price from $21 per share to around $12 per share after the XFL folded. By November 2001, the company had laid off almost 10% of its employees because lower-than-expected revenues resulted in year-end losses ("WWF Fires COO," 2001).

This example highlights how a long-term plan, such as increasing revenues by launching a new football league to compete with existing leagues, can backfire. With a significant amount of hype and planning, the league had a decent first night because of the novelty of the event. Once advertisers started complaining about the low ratings and the general lack of interest in the new league, a short-term exit planning process had to be undertaken. As the XFL crumbled,

the WWF (later becoming the WWE) had to engage in short-term planning to find other options for continued growth. The WWF started pursuing other projects such as music sales, cookbooks, children's storybooks, and expanding overseas broadcasts, as well as launching a two-hour magazine-style show (Grover & Lowry, 2001). Thus, when the long-term plans failed, the WWF was forced to pursue short-term plans to fill the financial void left after the XFL failed to generate the expected future revenue streams. After a legal battle with the World Wildlife Fund (WWF), the World Wrestling Federation changed its name to World Wrestling Entertainment (WWE) in 2002.

DEVELOPING A PRO FORMA BUDGET

As highlighted in chapter 5, budgets represent the key to financial planning. Financial planning is accomplished through the development of budgets as a road map for a business' financial success. Budgets help establish a means to forecast future performance based on past results and expected external changes such as changes in the market or the economy. The budget also helps

© Reuters/Corbis

Could the demise of the XFL have been prevented? What types of short- and long-term planning would have been necessary to ensure its success?

management establish goals and objectives for the business. Thus, a budget is first and foremost a financial plan for the future. The financial plan highlights what results are anticipated if certain financial actions are taken. For example, if you want to buy a car, you might examine your financial position and determine that you can afford only $100 a month. You can develop a financial plan based on how much of a down payment you can make and your $100 a month available for monthly payments.

A financial plan is often a key component of a pro forma budget and a business plan. A pro forma budget is simply a future budget based on past financial results and expected future financial results. The pro forma budget contains a financial plan for the business, and the two are often combined to help complete the business plan. The business plan is the road map for the business; it contains financial analysis along with other key components such as marketing and production that help an executive or lender determine the potential for future success of the business.

Before considering the pro forma budget as part of the planning process, we should note that there is a significant difference between forecasting and budgeting. A forecast is an estimate of anticipated operations, such as how many hours given machinery will operate. The sales force could be asked what sales they would forecast for the coming quarter. In contrast, a budget is a target agreed on by management as an indicator of success; for example, management might agree that a successful year would entail selling one million tickets. On the basis of this distinction, it is often best to view profit planning and appropriate budgeting from a product or division perspective in which less profitable products or divisions can be isolated for more thorough analysis.

Typical extensive pro forma budgets might incorporate the following:

- A sales budget
- A promotion budget
- A materials, labor, and overhead budget
- A cash budget
- A capital appreciation budget

All the previously listed documents or components are contingent on developing a focused strategic plan. All the numbers in the world are meaningless if there is no direction to the business. Although this text is not a strategic planning text, it is important to note that the hallmark of any business is a concise corporate purpose. This overall mission for the business leads to the development of the corporate scope—a definition of the business' area of concentration. The business' area of concentration is further refined through developing corporate objectives, strategies, and plans that focus on how the business can achieve its corporate purpose. The financial plan is a key document produced after significant foresight has shaped the business' future direction.

The financial plan can be developed in five steps. The first step is to develop a system of projected financial statements, which can help a company analyze how the operating plan will affect the projected profits. The next step requires analysts to determine the funds that will be needed to help fund the long-term plans. The third step entails forecasting what funds will be available over the long term and how much of the funding will be generated internally and externally. The fourth step requires a business to establish and maintain a system of controls governing how funds are allocated and used. The last step requires analysts to examine the results and develop procedures for adjusting the plan if the forecasts are not met (Brigham & Gapenski, 1994).

INCORPORATING THE PRO FORMA BUDGET IN THE BUSINESS PLAN

The hallmark of a successful business involves a detailed business plan that accentuates the pro forma budget. This chapter has focused so far on developing a financial plan, or "road map." Once this plan is developed, it has to be communicated. Some individuals with a strong financial background can examine the pro formas and get a decent picture of a business, but most people need a little more guidance. That guidance comes from a business plan that expands on the financial plan and communicates the business' vision using both words and pro formas. Thus, a business plan blends a financial plan and a business strategy analysis to examine both long- and short-term goals and objectives.

Although there is no one correct way to write a business plan, the following framework provides the most critical elements of a business plan that you might write to submit to a bank or other investors. Within the business plan, the pro forma budget is the concise document used to show that the plan makes financial sense and is viable and accurate. An example of the first page of a pro forma budget is shown in figure 7.1.

The following components (p.122) found in a typical business plan were developed by Florida Atlantic University's Small Business Development Center. There are countless potential variations, however, and software to help with writing business plans is available. Small Business Administration also offers sample forms for writing a business plan at www.sba.gov.

Profit and loss summary ($000)	Year 1	Year 2	Year 3	Year 4	Year 5	Year 6	Year 7	Year 8	Year 9	Year 10
Net revenue:										
Sports core (schedule A)	0	0	6,167	8,543	10,334	11,183	11,252	11,265	11,265	11,265
Leasing (schedule B)	0	0	1,782	2,158	2,214	2,247	2,278	2,310	2,310	2,310
Total net revenue	**0**	**0**	**7,949**	**10,701**	**12,548**	**13,430**	**13,530**	**13,576**	**13,576**	**13,576**
Net margin	0	0	4,210	6,659	8,288	9,013	9,007	8,947	8,947	8,947
Net margin %	**0**	**0**	**53.0%**	**62.2%**	**66.1%**	**67.1%**	**66.6%**	**65.9%**	**65.9%**	**65.9%**
Period costs:										
General and administrative (worksheet 2)	486	709	1,183	1,227	1,245	1,245	1,245	1,245	1,245	1,245
Depreciation (worksheet 2)	51	586	1,139	1,157	1,174	1,192	1,068	937	816	684
Vacancy cost (worksheet 2)	0	0	99	46	42	44	45	47	47	47
Total period costs	**537**	**1,294**	**2,421**	**2,429**	**2,461**	**2,481**	**2,359**	**2,230**	**2,108**	**1,976**
Income from operations	(537)	(1,294)	1,788	4,230	5,827	6,532	6,648	6,717	6,838	6,970
Other income/(expense) (see schedule E)	0	(1,446)	(218)	(834)	(720)	(553)	(371)	(178)	12	209
Charge-out to cap. org. expense (except depreciation)	486	709	0	0	0	0	0	0	0	0
Pretax income	(51)	(2,031)	1,571	3,395	5,106	5,979	6,278	6,539	6,851	7,179
Provision for taxes (N/A due to LLC status)	0	0	0	0	0	0	0	0	0	0
Net income	**(51)**	**(2,031)**	**1,571**	**3,395**	**5,106**	**5,979**	**6,278**	**6,539**	**6,851**	**7,179**
Ratios and valuation (assumes owning land vs. leasing):										
ROE	N/A	N/A	30.0%	46.7%	49.4%	42.9%	35.5%	30.2%	26.6%	23.9%
ROA	N/A	N/A	22.5%	36.8%	40.9%	37.0%	31.5%	27.4%	24.5%	22.3%
Net income/net revenue	N/A	N/A	19.8%	31.7%	40.7%	44.5%	46.4%	48.2%	50.5%	52.9%
Book value	449	3,668	5,238	7,276	10,339	13,927	17,694	21,617	25,727	30,035
Liabilities to net worth	2.28	5.09	0.33	0.27	0.21	0.16	0.13	0.10	0.09	0.07
Interest coverage	N/A	N/A	16.26	38.45	52.97	59.39	60.44	61.06	62.17	63.37
Debt service coverage	N/A	N/A	25.64	42.38	58.10	66.19	67.88	68.97	70.69	72.48

Notes
- Information on this and accompanying pages is confidential. It is being provided to the reader with the understanding that it shall not be shared with others without express permission.
- As of this date, the numbers provided here are preliminary and still undergoing analysis and revision. They are best, current, conservative estimates. We are in the process of refining the financial model and testing the investment, revenue, and expense projections as well as exploring various capitalization strategies.
- Interest expense based on assumption that mortgage principal payments are level over life of notes, with interest payments declining.
- Pro forma assumes organization as an LLC. In future years the company may elect to change to a corporate structure.

Figure 7.1 The first page of a pro forma budget.
Adapted from The Peak Experience, LLC.

- The *plan summary* should be written after all other sections are finished. It describes

  - the purpose of your plan,
  - the product or service that you will sell and why it is unique,
  - second- or third-generation products or services to help maintain sales,
  - the market potential,
  - specific highlights in the marketing plan,
  - the skills provided by the management team,
  - the financial projections for the first several years,
  - your funding needs, and
  - an exit strategy if the business does not succeed.

- The *industry section* should highlight the economics in the industry, industry trends, and potential legal or regulatory concerns, and it should critically analyze the competitive forces you might face. This section requires objective information that can be verified. Most of the information should be documented through secondary data from reliable sources. Sources of secondary data could include government reports, Better Business Bureau reports, reports from national or international trade organizations, research conducted by competitors, or even magazine or newspaper articles. Primary data, as discussed earlier, are data generated by the business itself (e.g., results of a customer satisfaction survey of a competitor's customers to determine if the customers would prefer a different option or service). Any data used to substantiate statements in the industry section should be copied and attached to the business plan as exhibits.

- The *company section* describes the history and background of the business. It can include the mission statement, objectives, goals (long term and short term), and strategies. This section should also list the current principal owner(s) or majority stockholder(s), all members of the board of directors (if applicable), and all key executives. Last, this section should include the business' address; form of organization (sole proprietorship, partnership, limited liability company, or corporation); and any pertinent local, regional, or federal license requirements (such as requirements for handling pool chemicals).

- Any special circumstances concerning the company should be specified in this section, such as what stock purchase options exist if the company goes public or whether key employees have non-compete contracts. Any data an investor would need to make an investment decision should be included. For example, if a company-owned patent is about to expire, meaning that competitors could start manufacturing the previously protected item, the company could face significant hardships. Similarly, if the Smiths had leased a fitness facility and the lease was about to expire, meaning they could be without a facility, such a fact would need to be disclosed. The plan needs to highlight such hardships even if they hurt the prospects for raising capital. The failure to include critical data can lead to allegations of fraud or of negligent or intentional misrepresentation.

- The *analysis of the product or service* is a thorough analysis of the product's or service's unique qualities, which will help distinguish the product or service from those offered by competitors. You want to critically analyze the risks associated with the product or service and the reasons purchasers might not buy your product or service. You will need to critically analyze any market surveys or other research that helps you draw your conclusions about your product or service or that of the competition. Last, this section should identify any ancillary products or services that also might be produced to develop a more significant product or service line. If you were developing an indoor rock-climbing facility, for example, you would examine that facility in relation to

  - any home-based climbing apparatus,
  - any club-based climbing apparatus,
  - options available at health clubs,
  - the uniqueness of the industry,
  - the demand for leisure sports or recreational activities in a given community,
  - the availability of other climbing facilities within a 20-mile radius of the proposed facility,
  - the availability of natural climbing areas nearby and how weather patterns will affect usage,
  - the availability of safety-related products, and
  - the availability of trained instructors to work with patrons.

- The *market section* focuses on the demographic characteristics of the proposed market. Who is the target market? What is its size? Can these people be reached? And do they have the funds necessary to purchase the product or service? You will need to critically examine the market to determine whether the potential customers or clients buy on a regular basis or seasonally, whether they best respond to sales or coupons, and whether there are better locations from which to reach the intended market. Look through a general telephone directory such as the Yellow Pages and identify the competition by name, address, and phone number. Visit the competition to see how big they are, what products or services they offer, whether or not they are busy, and when they are busy. After you analyze the potential market and the competition, you should establish one-year and five-year sales goals.

- The *marketing strategy section* of the business plan applies the product or service characteristics to the customers' demands. This section focuses on how to sell or distribute the product or service to potential buyers. It requires applying the four Ps of marketing—place, product, price, and promotion. Sample brochures, advertisements, announcements, product packaging, product or service guarantees, and related materials should be included. The price for the product or service should be clearly explained and compared with prices charged by competitors. This section should include all relevant information obtained through the marketing research process and used as a basis for the marketing decisions.

- The *operation section* describes how the product will be developed and produced or how the service will be delivered. Here you should discuss critical dates, such as when production will begin, as well as who will produce products, where the inventory will come from, what shipping schedule will be followed, how products will be delivered to clients, and so on. Writing this section requires that you have analyzed the financial and managerial control mechanisms for tracking production, inventory, and shipping, as well as accounting procedures and the like. This section should conclude by specifying the steps that will be taken if the sales goals are not reached (e.g., inventory liquidation) and the revenue such procedures can realize.

- The *management and personnel section* lists all the key individuals necessary for the business to be successful, with brief biographies of past accomplishments and potential references. This section should highlight the key skills required for the business to succeed and indicate how the key individuals fit within the necessary skill areas. In addition to discussing qualifications, you will typically analyze the compensation packages key individuals are receiving or will receive.

- The *financial projections section* addresses when investors can make their money back and what profit they can realize. Anyone who might be interested in investing in your business will probably view this as the most important section of the business plan. Although the product or service, marketing strategy, and personnel are critical areas, investors may be most interested in the return on their money. Projected cash flow needs to be calculated on a month-to-month basis for the first year until a positive cash flow can be realized and then maintained. The cash flow should also be calculated annually for five years. These projections should be augmented with pro forma income statements and balance sheets. From these pro forma statements, the potential investor can start making calculations to determine critical points for business growth and expansion, such as the break-even point or return on investment.

- The *capital needs section* covers what funds will be needed to launch the business and when the funds will be needed. To help establish potential collateral, the plan should highlight what the funds will be used for. Thus, if the funds will be used to purchase a building, a lending institution will probably be more willing to extend the loan knowing that the loan proceeds could be secured by the building. This section also needs to detail how the money will be repaid, over what time period, and what penalties might apply for late payments. Last, this section should cover any ownership potential that might be available. If you are willing to sell a 10% stake in the business to the right investor, you need to explain the potential deal in great detail. Details are required especially if someone else can purchase a controlling interest or can assume liability for financial obligations.

- A *miscellaneous section* can be added that contains relevant pictures, price lists, facility diagrams, a listing of necessary equipment, or a discussion of any unusual risks (Pounds, 1997).

Business plans are written every day, but most never receive any funds. Most business plans fail because of lack of research, preparation, and presentation. The following is a top-10 list of characteristics seen in successful business plans:

1. Clear and realistic financial projections are the most important element.
2. The plan contains detailed and documented objective market research.

3. The plan includes a detailed analysis of all competitors.

4. The plan demonstrates that the management team is more than capable of leading the company.

5. There is a "killer" summary that is only two or three pages long and includes critical projections such as income statements.

6. The plan provides proof of the writer's vision by clearly differentiating the product or service from that of the competition.

7. The document follows a clear plan and, most important, is written in proper English that is clear, precise, and free of grammatical mistakes.

8. The most effective plans are short, rarely exceeding 40 pages. Documents longer than this can become too cumbersome to read.

9. The writer clearly explains the bottom line—why the money is needed and how investors will be repaid.

10. The writer has taken the time to make the plan her own. When people write business plans using their own words, instead of hiring an outside writer or using canned computer software, the reader has a better feel for their sincerity (Elkins, 1996).

CONCLUSION

Vigilance is the key to effective financial planning. Managers must take the time to effectively research all prior actions and potential future actions. Planning cannot focus just on the past; it also requires a critical analysis of the future. By doing their homework, managers can learn a great deal about their businesses. The research required to prepare budgets and develop business plans can provide a significant education about a company. All the individuals in the planning process have valuable information about the business. This insight can be of great help. If chief financial officers meet with individual salespeople, they may uncover reasons why certain products do not sell as well in particular regions and can use this knowledge to help allocate resources more effectively. Thus, the planning process is not designed just to keep employees busy; it is the only technique available to prepare a business for the future. The hurdles and opportunities identified in the planning process lead to finalizing the capital budgeting process covered in chapter 11.

CLASS DISCUSSION TOPICS

1. Discuss a rough budget for your personal finances. What hurdles might you face in preparing the budget and following the budget?

2. Discuss a short-term plan for a perennially losing team, and identify specific steps that could be taken to increase income or generate victories.

3. Discuss a long-term plan for a perennially losing team, and identify specific steps that could be taken to increase income or generate victories.

4. What are some things that can prevent a team from meeting its budget projections?

5. What do you think is the most important primary data for a sport business to develop, and how can the business find this information?

6. What do you think is the most important secondary data for a sport business to develop, and how can the business find this information?

7. Develop a sample survey you believe could be used to obtain critical information on which financial decisions could be made.

8. If you had been in charge of the XFL when it was formed, what might you have done differently to help its chances of surviving?

PART III

CAPITAL STRUCTURING

Without capital, a business cannot successfully operate. Part III explores where the money is and how businesses find the capital they need to successfully operate.

Chapter 8, Obtaining Funding, highlights where the money to start a business comes from. To pay their bills, people starting a business sometimes use their savings, their credit cards, or investment dollars from others. This chapter highlights the various areas where money can come from and how to continue receiving money after a business takes off. Issues such as open markets and other short-term borrowing strategies are compared with various long-term borrowing options. The chapter ends with an analysis of what strategies can be taken to obtain funds from various sources such as the government.

Chapter 9, Capital Stocks, covers the complex world of stocks. Stock certificates represent ownership interest in a company, and a company will sell stocks to raise needed funds. The chapter covers the types of stocks sold, what rights a stockholder has, how to take a company public, and how to increase stock value.

Chapter 10, Bonds, covers the concept of corporate borrowing to raise necessary funds. Besides borrowing from banks or issuing stocks, a corporation with a strong credit rating can issue corporate bonds. When issuing bonds, a corporation needs to consider the cost of issuing the bonds, how it will repay the bonds, and how the bonds fit into the capitalization effort of the business. In addition, the chapter highlights bonds issued by government entities to fund the construction of stadiums and arenas as well as how government entities can help owners fund new facilities through industrial development bonds. The chapter ends with an overview of the capitalization process and how borrowing, stocks, and bonds can work together to develop a comprehensive financing plan.

8

OBTAINING FUNDING

CHAPTER OBJECTIVES

After studying this chapter, you should be able to do the following:

- Describe where money comes from.
- Compare various short-term borrowing strategies.
- Understand how to utilize personal funds and private financing as a source of capital.
- Understand how government-backed borrowing can spur economic growth.
- Understand how to utilize existing resources to leverage a business' financial position.
- Distinguish between leasing and other financial vehicles.

There is no one correct method to fund a sport business. Some individuals acquire a sport business through inheritance and do not need any funds to become owners. This is the case for many professional team owners, such as the Rooney family, who have owned the Pittsburgh Steelers for several generations. Other owners have tapped numerous sources such as their credit cards, relatives, and bank **loans** to keep a business alive. Each business is different and requires its own unique blend of financing. The various funding techniques combine to form the capital structure of a business.

The total number of options and techniques that can be used to obtain funds is all but limitless. Some individuals have made their fortunes through luck, while others have relied on hard work. Arthur Rooney, the famed founder of the Pittsburgh Steelers, bought the franchise for $2,500 in 1933. It is rumored that he obtained the money for the franchise by winning $250,000 at the horse track in 1932 ("Art Rooney," 2007). John Moores, owner of the San Diego Padres, founded BMC Software in 1980. By working hard,

designing innovative products, and making a strong marketing push, he made a fortune ("Company," 2002). With these funds, he purchased the Padres.

A person lucky enough to win the lottery could use his winnings to start a business. Former athletes have taken the money they earned in professional sport and used those funds to help launch or buy a business. Examples include Dave Bing, who started the Bing Group, considered one of the largest black-owned businesses ("Bing Group Capsule," n.d.), and Isiah Thomas, who purchased the entire Continental Basketball Association in 1999 for $9 to $10 million, which included a $5 million down payment and four future payments. Two years later the league was bankrupt, and Thomas' holding company owed at least $5 million to various lenders ("Left for Dead," 2001).

Although this chapter and the subsequent chapters on stocks and bonds (chapters 9 and 10) highlight for-profit businesses, we make some references to funds utilized by government and tax-exempt businesses, primarily in chapter 10. As with for-profit businesses, both government and nonprofit organizations can

© AP Photo

While betting on a horserace like Arthur Rooney (standing far left) did probably isn't the most prudent way to obtain funding, it *is* a unique means to raising capital.

utilize countless techniques to raise funds. One of the major differences between government and nonprofit organizations is the opportunity to receive gifts and the potential tax consequences associated with such funding techniques. Tax issues associated with gifts are covered in chapter 14.

Most fund-raising for sport businesses follows established patterns that have been utilized for years by countless organizations. This chapter highlights the basic approaches to raising funds without necessarily having to incur significant costs or selling owners' equity. Early in the chapter we examine basic funding sources for starting a business, such as personal bank loans, credit cards, or government assistance. The chapter then covers open markets and short-term borrowing options, followed by several long-term borrowing options. The chapter concludes with an analysis of funding options for minority-owned businesses, including advice on how to obtain funding.

UNIQUE FUND-RAISING

Not all funds needed to finance sports events are derived from television rights payments, ticket sales, sponsorship contracts, or similar income-generating techniques. Someone paying money from his or her own wallet can help finance a Special Olympics event or pay a team's payroll. Organizations can put expenses on credit cards; individuals can provide collateral to back a loan; a facility can be used as collateral for obtaining a loan. Obscure revenue-generating techniques can raise significant funds or can be significant failures. Olympic stamps and coins are a good example of these extremes. Canada sold both in its effort to help finance the 1976 Olympic Games.

THE OLYMPIC COIN PROGRAM

The lineage of Olympic coinage is formidable. Anaxilas, a ruler of Sicily, ordered the first recorded minting of a coin struck especially to commemorate a sporting event in about 480 BC. The silver coin honored his victory in a historic chariot race and appropriately depicted the winner bearing a laurel wreath. Since the 1950s, several Olympic host countries have issued a variety of commemorative coins to defray costs of the Games. However, Canada's coin program was considered one of the most successful (*Charlton Standard Catalogue*, 1990).

Basically, the program was aimed at selling collections of 28 specially minted silver $1, $5, and $10 coins. Canada was also the first Olympic host to issue a gold coin in the denomination of $100.

The margin between the cost of production and the face value of coins is known as seigniorage. According to the Canadian legislation authorizing the coins, it was the right of the seignior, or issuing authority, to retain that difference as profit. Profits from sales of the Olympic coins were initially expected to reach between $125 and $500 million. The coins were very successful, but they were issued at the height of an internationally depressed economy. However, through 1977, sales of the coins had reached $386 million. Of the $386 million, $278.7 million represented the face value of all coins delivered and had to be held in reserve by the Canadian government. The expenditures over and above the face value of the coins totaled only $8 million. Thus, the program netted a profit of close to $100 million.

THE OLYMPIC STAMP PROGRAM

The Olympic Stamp Program was yet another unique fund-raising effort designed to help finance the 1976 Olympic Games. Canada Post's fund-raising focused on four areas: Olympic action stamps, commemorative stamps, stamp sculptures, and stamp souvenirs. In 1974 Canada brought out its first set of semipostal issues—postage stamps that carried a surcharge. The purpose of the surcharge was to give the public a convenient opportunity to support the Olympic Games on a voluntary basis. Germany, France, and Japan all have used semipostal stamps when hosting the Games. Additional sets were issued by Canada in 1975 and 1976 (Gandley & Stanley, 1978).

The Olympic action stamps bore two different prices, separated by a plus sign (+). The first price on each stamp indicated the postal value of the stamp, the other the amount of the surcharge; the two amounts combined gave the sale price of the stamp. Thus, a stamp with a 15 + 5 marking included $0.15 of postage and a $0.05 contribution to the Olympic effort. The post office collected $0.20 for each one of these stamps sold. A similar approach was utilized by the U.S. postal service in the 1990s to raise funds for breast cancer research.

To support the Olympic Stamp Program, Canada Post developed a promotional program under the umbrella theme Help It Happen. Advertisements were published in all major Canadian newspapers and magazines and in specialized publications the world over; commercials were aired on television and radio networks. Display stands, posters, and decals were used in post offices to attract the customers' attention. In spite of all the promotion, the stamps did not generate the target figure of $10 million. Purchasers were either opposed to the idea or hesitant to try anything new.

WHERE THE MONEY COMES FROM

Most consumers have faced a financial crisis in which they needed money but found that sources of funds were lacking. Some people can approach their parents and ask for a loan. Money sometimes comes from an inheritance or in the form of a raise. Sometimes increased monetary streams can be expected—such as an annual cost-of-living salary increase to keep a salary at pace with inflation. At other times money might not come in when it is expected. You might anticipate receiving an Internal Revenue Service refund by a certain date and have to change your plans significantly if there is a delay. But what happens when you need a substantial amount of money and your likelihood of receiving a major gift is astronomically small? You need to analyze alternative approaches for raising the needed capital.

Not all capital needs arise from emergencies. Numerous capital structuring changes occur because of anticipated growth—growth that can occur only through the exploration of various capital financing options. This chapter deals with the various capital options available to those seeking to raise needed capital. We give special attention to individual borrowing, SBA loans, commercial lending, and venture capital. Subsequent chapters will cover issuing various types of stocks, issuing bonds, and obtaining capital assistance from the government. There is no one correct method of raising funds, and this chapter presents the diverse techniques available.

 The Smiths are faced with the question of how to raise necessary start-up capital. They do not have a large amount of cash available to support their dreams. What if they want to purchase some expensive exercise equipment for their proposed facility? They do some initial research and discover that there are four primary means of obtaining the equipment: renting, paying cash, obtaining a loan, and leasing (Haynie, 1998).

If the Smiths rent the machines there will be no up-front cash expenditures, except for a possible down payment or security deposit. The Smiths will face lower upkeep and repair costs using this strategy and can return the equipment if they are not satisfied with the quality. However, renting equipment is normally not a good long-term option; renting for several years could cost twice as much as taking out a conventional bank loan or leasing (Haynie, 1998). Note that both rental and lease payments are 100% tax deductible as a business expense.

If the Smiths purchase the equipment with cash, they can avoid **finance charges** and depreciate the equipment. However, even if they had significant cash reserves and they did invest in a machine, they could no longer use those funds to pay for additional growth that might generate a greater return in the future.

A bank loan could be an effective technique for purchasing the equipment. A bank would require background material such as a credit check, tax returns, financial statements, and collateral. On the basis of the need to possibly sell the equipment upon loan default, a bank might provide a loan that covers only a certain percentage of the equipment's actual purchase price. If a new piece of equipment has a purchase price of $10,000 but will be worth only $8,000 by year's end, the bank might limit its exposure by lending only $6,500 toward the purchase.

If the Smiths lease the equipment, they can receive flexible terms and 100% financing. Initial expenses could include 2 to 5% of the purchase price as a down payment plus any applicable taxes and installation, delivery, and related "soft" costs. The key benefit of leasing involves the potential to expense 100% of the payments every month with pretax dollars (Haynie, 1998). Assume that the Smiths finance $36,000 in equipment for $843 per month. If they make $5,000 a month profit, $1,500 of this amount will go to taxes if their tax rate is 30%. But if the Smiths reduce the $5,000 profit by $843, their potential taxes will decline from $1,500 to $1,247 (30% × $4,157). The $253 tax savings when subtracted from the $843 monthly lease obligation results in an actual payment of $590 for the leased equipment. When the $590 cost is multiplied over the actual term of the lease (60 months), the total cost is $35,400, which is less than the purchase price if they had purchased the equipment for $36,000 (Haynie, 1998). One benefit of the **lease option** is that there might not be any initial **capital outlay** to encumber the cash balances. In addition, the Smiths would face less risk if the product broke or became obsolete, and they could obtain a service agreement to keep the machine in working condition.

The same concerns that people face in deciding how to finance items such as equipment or a new business can apply to any decision requiring capital outlays. For example, if an investor wanted to build a golf course, he would need a significant amount of up-front capital to purchase the land and develop the course. It might be several years before the course would be suitable for use, and this would mean several years without any income. Most investors would shy away from a deal that was uncertain and that would not produce revenue for several years.

A 1994 National Golf Foundation report concluded that financing for the average golf course loan requires 40 to 50% equity. This means that to build a $5 million course, developers need to raise approximately $2 to $2.5 million from other sources such as their own money, limited partnerships, corporate investments, syndications, pension funds, or possibly **real estate investment trusts** (REITs) in order to obtain a bank loan (Turley, 1998). Such large equity requirements are based on the competitiveness of the golf course industry, a course's potential resale value, uncertain projected cash flow, uncontrollable factors such as weather conditions, and other variables. Nonetheless, there are experienced golf course lenders who search for opportunities. These lenders can utilize flexibility to design loans that could include (Turley, 1998)

- capitalizing working capital requirements and income shortfalls;
- requiring sufficient cash reserves to cover any possible contingency; or
- offering their own equity participation to help decrease the required borrower's equity, which will help lower the debt interest rate.

Another option is to finance the golf course through the public coffers. Municipal golf courses have been built for years utilizing standard voter-approved bonds or the newer revenue bonds that can be paid back from the course's revenue. Other means to finance a municipal course include general budget allocations (as a line item in a budget), the selling of bonds, and establishing a public development corporation, with the city having a contractor design and construct the course on a turnkey basis (Turley, 1998). In a turnkey operation, the contractor performs all the building construction and design functions for a set price and then turns the building over to the owner when all the work is completed ("Construction Glossary," 2002).

Although multiple funding techniques are available, investors are more cautious than ever about funding golf courses. Lenders are concerned because numerous courses are both being built and going under at the same time. As some analysts claim, it is best to be the second buyer of a golf course; the developer typically pays more to build a course, and if the course fails, the subsequent buyer pays a much lower amount. Thus, lenders are wary of investing millions in a course that might be worth less when

it is completed than it cost to build in the first place (Nemeth-Johannas, 2003).

To investigate the potential value of an investment, a lender might undertake significant research to evaluate how risky the loan will be. Analyzing the golf industry could help a lender decide if he wants to risk loaning money to a potential course developer. When the nation's economy was at its peak from 1998 to 2000, more than 1,100 of the nation's 15,827 golf courses were built (Kaspriske, 2003). Even though golf has been around for more than a century, 7% of all U.S. golf courses were built in that three-year period (Kaspriske, 2003).

However, the recession after the events of September 11, 2001, resulted in a decrease in leisure and business travel, leaving clubs to scramble to keep their members, even with an estimated 26.2 million golfers in the nation (Ripley & Mabe, 2003). A golf course owner was quoted as saying, "Thirty years ago, the average age [of members] was 64; if the average age of your members today isn't 54 [or slightly younger], you're in trouble" (Kaspriske, 2003). First, younger members help ensure long-term success for a country club because they are likely to be members for decades to come. More important, younger members are more inclined than older members to spend money at the club entertaining family, friends, and business associates. Furthermore, when the clubhouse needs updating and the greens need repair, those younger members will usually approve the expenditure (Kaspriske, 2003).

Lenders will also examine the cost of running a business to make sure it is viable. In keeping with the golf example, the average cost percentages for club maintenance are as follows (Thornton, 2005):

Salaries and wages	63%
Chemicals 1	4%
Repairs and maintenance	9%
Other	14%
Total	100%

Thus, a lender considering investing in a new club could examine the projected budget and calculate if the costs are similar to what other clubs in the industry face. By examining projections against benchmarked industry standards, a lender can get a better feel for an investment. The preceding golf course example shows that although there are various ways to fund a project, lenders are going to critically scrutinize any potential deals to minimize their risk. If a lender is going to pursue a riskier loan, he will charge the borrower a higher interest rate to compensate for assuming the higher risk.

What type of research must be done before deciding to invest in golf course construction? Would you be willing to invest your money?

The same options that are possible for building a golf course can be applied to building a professional sports stadium or arena. Because of the hundreds of millions of dollars required to build a stadium or arena, the financing tools utilized by the Smiths or a golf course developer would typically not generate all the necessary funds. The risk of going bankrupt is much lower for a stadium or arena than for the Smiths' fitness center or a golf course. Lenders will still investigate the facility funding plan, but because of the potential involvement of the government, lenders are more inclined to fund these large facilities through a variety of funding strategies. For a privately financed facility, the typical financing tools include loans, bonds, cash contribution, partnerships, equity offerings, and related investment pools. If the project is a public facility, the following financing techniques could be used (Miller, 1998):

- Loans
- General obligation bonds
- Project revenue bonds
- Tax revenue bonds
- Certificates of participation
- Tax incremental financing
- Tax exemptions
- Tax rebates

Loans are simple borrowing agreements in which the borrower agrees to repay the borrowed amount at a set time at a set interest rate. General obligation bonds are bonds issued by a municipality that agrees to utilize any and all tax revenue it obtains to repay the bond. Project revenue bonds are more specific, with revenue generated from the project being dedicated to repay the bond. Tax revenue bonds are backed by general tax revenue collected by the municipality, such as property taxes. With certificates of participation, purchasers buy a share of the lease revenues instead of the bond's being secured by these revenues ("Certificate of Participation," n.d.). These revenues are then usually used to construct a facility.

Tax incremental financing, discussed in greater detail in chapter 14, represents a municipality's decision to forgo taxes from a landowner, such as a stadium owner, to encourage that landowner to build a facility in a given neighborhood. The municipality hopes that bringing the facility into the neighborhood will increase other property values and thus increase the general tax base for the entire municipality. A tax exemption refers to a waiver of tax obligations as an incentive to attract a business or build a new facility. The Texas Motor Speedway received such an exemption, and it was so significant that the school district subsequently sued to recover some of its lost tax revenue (Gibeaut, 1999). A tax rebate is similar to a refund: the municipality returns some or all of the money a business has paid in whichever tax category is being rebated. Thus, a team could receive a rebate of their property taxes but still need to pay sales and utility taxes.

It should be noted that almost every stadium or arena project involves certain government benefits such as tax abatements. The three proposed facilities in New York (Nets, Mets, and Yankees) are receiving an estimated $1.2 billion in public subsidies, including significant tax abatements. Under existing legislation, new commercial developments in certain New York burroughs do not have to pay property tax for the first 15 years. After that the tax is phased in, so full taxes are not paid until the 26th year of the private facility (deMause, 2005).

The Stars of David want to build a new facility. Their arena is very old and does not generate enough revenue opportunities from luxury boxes. The owner is willing to put up $50 million of her own money; the local municipality will put up the land, acquired through eminent domain; and the state will spend $20 million on road and infrastructure improvements to help people get to the arena. That leaves $200 million needed to construct the facility. How can the Stars raise that money? The team can approach local investors and local companies for money, but the most likely source of funding will be the citizens. The Stars will need to develop a unique selling point to garner interest from the voters. Options include an increased sales tax, a users tax, a cigarette tax, or just a bond supported by the taxpayers.

Thus there are numerous techniques available for funding business growth, whether a new gym needs to be built or a team is interested in renovating a stadium. The options are as countless as the number of individuals who have money to invest. Each deal can be structured to meet the needs of the parties involved. As an example of one combination, a deal might include financing from family, friends, corporate partners, and a venture capitalist.

The West Hartford Badminton Club is very active, holding weekly practices and regular tournaments. This nonprofit organization raises money through three primary means: donations, nightly playing fees, and tournament fees. The club has been around for more than 60 years and has a nice following. However, as a nonprofit organization it has had a difficult time raising additional funds and thus has basically just made it every year for the past 5 years. One major disaster such as an increase in rental fees or a poorly attended tournament could spell financial ruin for the club.

After 60 years of tournaments, practices, and matches, WHBC needs to redo its court floors. However, the club is barely making ends meet, and a new floor will cost around $100,000. If the club administrators choose to do nothing, the floor will get worse (and the repair cost will go up), and they run the risk of participants injuring themselves from bumps and cracks on the courts. How can WHBC raise the additional funds needed for repairs?

If the badminton club raises its membership, playing, or tournaments fees, it risks losing members. And since $100,000 is a lot of money, raising fees might not cover the whole expense.

WHBC could attempt to raise the money through tournaments and private donations. Under this scenario, however, it may take a while to collect all the money needed. The club might need to front money in advance to help bring in private donations (e.g., through dinners or dances). Hosting tournaments might damage the floor even further, and participants might get injured because of existing floor damage.

The club could also finance the money through a bank loan. However, interest rates may be as high as 10%, and missed payments could mean foreclosure.

Obviously it would be impossible to describe every means of financing a business in this text; instead we focus on several major sources of funds, including yourself, relatives and friends, banks, nonbank lenders, public stock offerings, bonds, and venture capitalists. Before we discuss each capital acquisition method, it is helpful to identify the three primary categories of sources of capital.

1. *Equity investors.* These investors purchase a portion of the business (e.g., in the form of stock) with the hope of future returns through capital gains or dividend payments. Since equity owners assume significant risk that a business might not succeed, they typically require a higher rate of return to offset the higher risk. This reward is evidenced through either increased stock value or dividend payments to the stock (equity) owner.
2. *Long-term debt obligations,* such as bonds. A bondholder is interested in receiving an appropriate rate of return on the investment with the lowest possible risk. Bondholders do not benefit the way equity investors do if the corporation becomes very successful. However, the risk of losing the investment is greatly reduced because the bonds are secured by collateral.
3. *Short-term loans.* Suppliers of merchandise or raw goods are often the source of loans of this type; they sell goods on the basis that the buyer will pay within 30 days, for example.

Sport Manufacturing Company

SMC wants to build a new manufacturing plant. The company has $1 million in retained earnings to purchase the land and cover site development costs. To raise the additional funds, SMC will sell 100,000 shares of stock for $15 each; sell 1,000 bonds, each with a $1,000 face value; and borrow $2 million from the bank in a short-term loan. The short-term loan will need to be repaid in a year, the bonds will need to be repaid in 15 years, and the stock owners will own a percentage of the company until the stocks are sold or SMC buys them back.

The West Hartford Badminton Club would like to host a league championship tournament. The club holds a meeting with its board members and concludes it will need to raise $500 to cover the referee costs, tables, chairs, trophies, and food to sell at the concession stand. The club could potentially earn revenue from tournament fees, admission fees, and concession sales. The committee decides to take $500

out of the contingency fund (money that is saved for club emergencies). Although this might be risky, especially if the club cannot regenerate the money through sales, the potential for earnings is greater, and WHBC decides to run the tournament.

PERSONAL RESOURCES

Sometimes people accumulate money from a current job with the intention of someday starting their own businesses. Often these sums are wholly inadequate for that purpose. Industry professionals highlight the need to set aside at least two years' worth of living expenses in preparation for starting your own business. This is necessary because most new full-time businesses take at least a year, and sometimes many more years, to earn enough profit to pay the business owner a salary (Pounds, 1997). Proper financial planning can help eliminate numerous hurdles that might arise during a business' formative years. However, the planning process needs to begin long before a business starts up, and sufficient capital reserves are required to sustain the business through cyclical and seasonal downturns.

If you do not have enough cash or investments that could be liquidated to start the business, you might consider a home loan. Home equity financing requires a borrower to utilize his house as collateral when obtaining a loan from a bank or other lending institution. The loan amount is based on the equity the borrower has in the home. Suppose you have a house that is worth $100,000 on the market today. You paid $60,000 for the house 10 years ago, with $10,000 down and a $50,000 mortgage. You paid off $20,000 on the mortgage and still owe $30,000. Thus, if you were to sell the house for $100,000, you would receive $70,000 free and clear of the mortgage ($100,000 – $30,000 remaining on the mortgage). The $70,000 represents the equity you have in the house and is the maximum amount you could borrow from a lending institution.

Home equity loans are traditionally favored over other loans because they carry a lower interest rate. Furthermore, some banks are willing to lend more than 100% of a home's value, depending on what the loan proceeds will be used to purchase. New businesses are highly speculative, and only 20% of new businesses survive (Zikmund & d'Amico, 1996). Therefore, some banks require substantial equity before loaning to a new business; established businesses with significant financial history are more reliable, and owners of these businesses can obtain larger mortgages.

Although most financial advisers do not recommend borrowing on a credit card because of the high interest rates, credit cards can also generate funds from which to start a business. However, anyone using this method of borrowing must be careful to repay the debt as quickly as possible, or the interest charges will negate any potential benefits that could have accrued from not having to approach other lenders such as banks. Furthermore, the high rate of small business failures should serve as a warning that a business owner could be paying off debts for years after a business has failed. With a high interest rate, the repayment obligation could force an individual into bankruptcy (see chapter 17).

The key to utilizing credit cards is to maintain a good **credit rating**. Especially if using personal credit cards, borrowers need to be vigilant in ensuring that purchases and repayments do not hurt their credit rating. A credit rating can plunge if the credit card bills are not paid on time or if payment is always late (see sidebar).

CAN THE GOVERNMENT HELP YOU GET A BANK LOAN?

An individual's credit history might limit her ability to obtain bank financing. However, the government has developed several programs to help small businesses borrow funds, even if the owner does not have the best credit history. The federal government realized the need for helping small businesses in the 1950s. In 1953 it created Small Business Administration (SBA) to "aid, counsel, and protect the interest of the nation's small business community" (SBA, 2002). SBA accomplishes this by working with lending institutions to encourage and promote loans and other financing to small businesses. For example, SBA started the Microloan Program in 1992 with the express purpose of helping individuals realize the American dream of owning their own businesses (Hodges, 1997). The microloans range from $100 to $25,000; the average loan is around $10,000. These loans need to be paid back in four years at 10.8% interest. SBA created more than 100 loan outlets throughout the United States through various nonprofit organizations. The only requirement is that the company requesting funds must prepare a business plan that can meet the loan criteria.

SBA also offers various other programs to encourage investing in small businesses. Its 7(a) Loan Guarantee and Certified Development Company programs provide a guarantee for approved lenders if the borrower defaults on the SBA-backed loan. SBA will not repay the loan; instead, it requires the lender to go after the borrower's collateral and then will supplement any remaining shortfall that might have been guaranteed.

How Credit Card Applicants Are Rated

When determining whom to issue a credit card to, companies often utilize complex computer programs that score an applicant. The scoring technique analyzes distinct credit patterns to determine the likelihood that a borrower will repay any debts. Scores range from 375 to 900, with higher scores indicating lower likelihood of default (Sichelman, 1998). The key factors that can lower a score are late payments, collections, bankruptcies, outstanding debts, a short or nonexistent credit history, credit inquiries, and applications for new credit (Sichelman, 1998). If you are concerned about your potential score, ask a lender to order a report; traditional personal credit reports do not contain a score. Remember to order a credit report every year to see if there are any mistakes. Checking your credit history is also important because of the increased number of identity theft crimes that affect a large number of college students and young adults.

Percentage of Points Given to Help Determine Your Credit Score

Category	Percentage
Payment history	35
Amounts owed	30
Length of credit history	15
New or attempted credit accounts	10
Variety of credit types	10

Data from "Planning for success," 2000, *CampBusiness*: 8-11.

Assume that the Smiths use a 7(a) loan to finance their fitness center. The Smiths enter into a loan with their home as the collateral and 80% of the loan unguaranteed. If they borrow $100,000 from an SBA-approved lending institution, the loan is guaranteed by the SBA for $20,000, but the lending institution first needs to pursue recovery from the Smiths. If their home is sold for $80,000 to pay the debt, the lending institution is still owed $20,000 and would look to SBA to cover the $20,000 balance.

SBA lends money to individuals starting a business if they have (Pounds, 1997)

- excellent credit, including no collection letters in the past 3 years;
- no bankruptcies in the past 10 years;
- a business plan;
- some type of collateral, such as a home; and
- up to one-third of the required capital to put into the business.

Once these criteria have been met, SBA has several lending programs available including the 7(a) and Micro-loan programs, as well as 504 and Certified Development Company, Certified Preferred Lender, and Surety Bond programs. The 7(a) program is the most commonly used. In Hartford, Connecticut, 555 SBA-backed loans were approved in 1999, totaling $124 million. More than 96% of those loans (533) were 7(a) loans, and 50% (279) of all loans were for amounts under $100,000 (SBA, 2002). By 2006 the number had increased to more than 1,500 loans totaling $239 million, including 1,352 loans ($188.1 million) generated under the most widely used 7(a) loan program, which funds general business purposes. The 504 loan program, which is used for fixed-asset financing, accounted for 91 loans totaling $49.1 million. The Microloan Program, which provides smaller loans, produced 44 loans totaling $1.2 million ("SBA Loans," 2006). The market for SBA-guaranteed loans has become so big that a secondary market has been created to sell these loans. Lenders are able to sell the guaranteed portions of the SBA-guaranteed loans to investors and increase their yield on the unguaranteed portions of the SBA loans.

SELF-FUNDING

Funds for a business can also come from the business itself. An established business might utilize deprecia-tion allowances and profits not paid out as dividends as a way of fueling further expansion. For example, if a golf cart purchased for $10,000 has a five-year life, it can be depreciated $2,000 a year. The $2,000 deduction reduces total tax obligations and represents funds that should be set aside to help purchase another golf cart in the future. Most businesses also retain a percentage of their profits, whether at regular or random intervals, for future needs. These retained earnings are for future use and are not intended to pay salaries or other current expenses.

Companies often have extra cash that might be sitting around for one day or several months. Liquid assets can be invested in a bank, in commercial paper, or in Treasury bills for a short period and then withdrawn for any fiscal needs. The interest earned from such investments can be used for future development.

Another example of a self-funding concept is raising prices. If the Stars of David want to hire two new star players, they can anticipate a payroll increase of several million dollars a year. Borrowing funds from a bank or other lending institution can be risky. The Pittsburgh Penguins filed for bankruptcy in 1998, and part of their debt was attributable to players' salaries. Other teams face a similar problem when they attempt to cover their payrolls. A standard industry technique for covering such expenses is to raise ticket prices. If the Stars' ticket prices were raised 10%, the resulting increased income might be enough to fund both players. Although the funds for the new players' salaries come from customers and constitute external funds, they are generated from internal marketing efforts rather than from debt or equity sources.

The University of Milford provides another good example of internally generated capital. Student fees are utilized as a revenue source to help fund the athletic department. If the athletic department needs additional funds, it can petition the students to increase their contribution levels. As with Stars customers, who can avoid purchasing higher-priced tickets, students can reject the higher prices by voting against raising fees. However, if the fees are raised, the athletic department will have a stable source of additional funds to fuel future expansion. The athletic department can also hold fund-raising events such as charity auctions or hoop-a-thons and generate additional revenue without having to tap any debt resources.

The Smiths could also try to raise funds before the fitness center even opens. They could hold a membership drive to sign up prospective members who will be entitled to pay $500 for a two-year membership and $200 a year in subsequent years. If the Smiths sell 200 such memberships, they will have $100,000 to pay for construction costs. However, some states require clubs to keep preopening revenue in escrow until the club is opened (Caro, 2000). Even if they cannot touch these initial funds, the Smiths would have 200 membership contracts that could be used as collateral for a loan. Such collateral is often called contractually obligated revenue or contractually obligated income. Large stadiums and arenas use naming rights and luxury box contracts as collateral to secure loans.

Although it is very difficult for business owners to finance capital growth by themselves, it can be done. Through savings, credit cards, government assistance, or internally generated funds, a business owner can find means to grow. More often than not, though, the business owner will need help from relatives or external investors.

RELATIVES AND FRIENDS

Some people are fortunate enough to have wealthy family members or friends who are willing to invest in a business. But most people do not have a Daddy Warbucks in their circle, and in this case they must go elsewhere for funding. However, if you are able to obtain money from a parent or another relative, there are specific steps you should take to maximize the benefits for you and the other parties. Many people borrow money from friends or relatives on a regular basis, and most of these arrangements are never documented. Most people would not think that their own flesh and blood or best friend could fail to pay a debt. But courtrooms are filled with individuals who have broken such promises.

If the Smiths' parents loaned them money and the venture failed, could the parents claim a bad investment? Under existing IRS regulations, the parents would be able to claim a tax deduction for the lost funds only if they first sued to collect (Marullo, 1998, March). If they sued and were unable to collect, they could claim a nonbusiness bad-debt deduction. The lost amount would be deducted from the parents' long- and short-term capital gains. If the loan loss exceeded the total capital gains, the parents could deduct $3,000 of the nonbusiness bad debt and carry over any remaining amounts to possibly deduct in $3,000 increments in future years (Marullo, 1998, March).

To avoid any improprieties, a business owner should take the following steps when borrowing money from family members or friends who might have to write off a bad debt in the future (Marullo, 1998, March):

- Document the loan with a formal agreement.
- Develop a formal repayment schedule.
- Pledge security, or collateralize the loan.
- Keep accurate records of all repayments.
- Make sure there is proof that the business was solvent when the loan was made.
- Provide the lender with a detailed business plan specifying how the loan will be repaid.

A relative or friend could also play the part of an "angel" who comes to the rescue. An angel is a major investor who can give a small amount or several million (Ambrosini, 2002). One of the most well-known angel investors in the sport industry is Paul Allen, a founder of Microsoft and owner of the Portland Trail Blazers and Seattle Seahawks. Allen operates an angel investment firm that has invested in sport-related entities such as electronic ticketing businesses and Charter Communications, a major cable operator ("Paul Allen," 2002). Unlike venture capitalists, who want the business to go public and who invest only in larger projects, angel investors often come into a project before venture capital investors do or when they anticipate being part of a smaller but still profitable business. No matter who provides the capital, there are always risks associated with accepting money from others. Some concerns are

- whether the lender requires an ownership interest,
- whether the lender will demand a say in management decisions,
- whether there is an exit strategy once the business is sound enough to repay the angel and regain control, and
- whether interest payments will be tax deductible as a business expense.

Friends and acquaintances can also be a good source of funds. People often think they need to approach someone with a fancy car or big house. However, research shows that the average millionaire does not live in such a grand style. In *The Millionaire Next Door*, Albert Hoffman concluded that of the 3.5 million millionaires in the United States in 1996, most owned less expensive cars such as Fords, ran mundane businesses, and lived well below their means (Stehle, 1997). Hoffman suggests that instead of trying to meet potential investors at the polo grounds or the opera house, individuals should go to industry trade shows to meet people who might be willing to invest (Stehle, 1997).

Loyal customers also represent a potential funding source. The Mad River Glen Cooperative is one of the nation's smallest (and oldest) ski resorts, but it is financially sound. Loyal skiers are willing to pay $1,750 a share for stock in the cooperative and $200 a year thereafter. These funds and the dedicated following of loyal skiers help make the single-lift facility successful. The resort's management has critically examined expenses and determined that the resort needs to be open only 90 days a year to make a profit. Since the top customers are also owners, the resort understands its investment options and maintains a lower run price than that of other resorts. The company also does not invest a significant amount in new equipment, such as chairlifts or snow-making machines that could cost $1,000 an hour to operate. Customer loyalty is so strong that when a dividend was paid in 1998 ($16.43 per share), many stockholders suggested that the resort just keep the money (Goo, 2000).

Although family and friends can be a source for capital infusion, many business owners do not want to risk souring a good relationship. What if the initial capital infusion was not enough? What if more funds are needed, but the business owner does not want the initial investor to lose any money? What if the lender needs the money back immediately? Such issues associated with exit strategies are very critical. Individuals who do not want to make enemies of family members or friends might try to find funding through external sources such as the open market.

OPEN MARKETS AND OTHER SHORT-TERM BORROWING

There are several effective techniques for raising funds on either a short- or long-term basis. Long-term equity or capital funding techniques are discussed later in this chapter. Short-term funding techniques include borrowing to purchase inventories, supplies, or other items or to pay expenses in situations in which the repayment period is expected to be less than 90 days. For purchases that require longer funding commitments, midterm, start-up, or long-term funding strategies might be needed.

People often find short-term and long-term funds in the open market. The open market is a free-enterprise environment where anyone who wants to borrow and anyone who wants to lend money can enter into a relationship—somewhat similar to the traditional bazaar in which sellers and customers come together and negotiate on the price of goods. A bank is part of the open market because anyone can enter a bank and, with collateral or a good credit history, borrow money. Likewise, a successful business can be approached by numerous lenders interested in lending it money.

The Stars of David might rely on long-term funding options such as issuing stocks or bonds to purchase a new scoreboard or renovate their arena. They might require short-term funds to pay expenses or salaries if the players are on strike. The Smiths might need to use short-term borrowing to meet current accounts payable but need long-term funding to purchase expensive equipment. Sport Manufacturing Company (SMC) might turn to short-term funds to buy inventories or pay unexpected expenses such as settlement of a lawsuit. The company also might need long-term funds to buy manufacturing equipment or lease a new facility. In other words, every business at times experiences a need for long- or short-term funds.

Short-term funds may be required in order for a business to meet monthly, seasonal, or other temporary financial needs. It does not make sense for a business to obligate itself to several years of interest payments if the money will be available to repay the loan in several months. A major advantage of short-term borrowing is the relative ease of such transactions.

The West Hartford Badminton Club needs to buy some new rackets. The club approaches a local bank, where WHBC has its checking account. A line of credit is available, but it will cost more to draw funds against that line than to borrow money with a short-term loan. WHBC asks a bank official for the terms of a short-term loan. The club would need to pay 6% interest if it repays the $1,000 loan in one year. If the club draws against its line of credit, the interest rate would be 6%, but WHBC would have to maintain a compensating balance of at least $1,000 in its checking account, which does not earn any interest. Another option to consider is borrowing $1,000 from a club member and paying him 5% interest.

Banks and other lending institutions are accustomed to providing short-term loans, whether the money is required for several hours or several months. Many companies maintain a **line of credit** with a lending institution that allows them to borrow short-term funds on a preapproved basis.

Since SMC is such a large and financially strong business, several banks might each provide the company with millions of dollars in lines of credit. For the purpose of this discussion, assume that SMC has a $10 million line of credit. The credit line does not entail any financial obligations (except for a servicing fee) until the money is actually utilized—if SMC never uses the line of credit, the company pays no interest. But if SMC borrows $5 million for several weeks, the company pays interest on the $5 million amount for several weeks and will still have $5 million to borrow if needed in the future.

Even though SMC will pay no interest on any unborrowed amounts, the company will probably pay a fee to keep the line of credit open. The fee is typically a percentage of the credit line. Thus, for a $10 million credit line, the bank might charge 0.5% annually, which would require SMC to pay $50,000 each year to keep the line of credit open.

Another major benefit of short-term borrowing is that this strategy can be used to postpone long-term financing. Sometimes economic conditions or interest rates do not justify issuing bonds or stock. Thus, a "bridge gap" lending option such as short-term borrowing can help cover any financial obligations until conditions are more favorable for obtaining long-term funding. Regardless of the purpose, short-term borrowing is critical for all businesses.

ACCOUNTS PAYABLE

One of the primary techniques for obtaining short-term funding involves accounts payable. Accounts payable represent amounts owed to vendors and suppliers for services that have been rendered or products that have been delivered.

Assume that SMC has a purchasing department that requires a complex invoicing process. The process may be so cumbersome that a given division might run out of supplies before an order can be completely processed. However, the company might have an ongoing relationship with a supply company such that individual departments can purchase up to $100 a month without needing preapproval. All purchases that fall into this category can be calculated at the end of the month, and then SMC can be billed for the total.

This example demonstrates that accounts payable can be more complex than a credit card arrangement. A credit card is another example of an account payable in that the purchaser uses the card to make purchases and is borrowing money from the card issuer until the balance is paid. If the balance is not paid in full at the end of the billing period, the card user is charged interest. Most businesses utilize a blend of short-term borrowing that includes accounts payable and other short-term borrowing options.

Assume that the Smiths need to hire a laundry service to clean gym towels. Instead of paying every week when the laundry is picked up and delivered, Bob and Cheryl may complete an account contract with the laundry service to pay the bill every month. At the end of the first month, they receive a bill for the prior month's service with specific repayment instructions. The laundry service might give a discount if the bill is paid within a week, offer no benefit if the account is paid in full within 30 days, and assess a penalty fee or an interest obligation on the owed amount if the required payment is not made within 30 days. The Smiths are engaging in a type of account payable called a trade credit that one business issues to another. In this example, the trade credit is being offered pursuant to a cash discount option.

A major problem with accounts payable is the often slow turnaround time for repayment. If a business buys season tickets for a team's games but does not pay at the time of purchase, the team may have a problem with this receivable account if it never gets paid or is paid months later. Some suppliers may not mind slow repayment because they can obtain interest payments from the borrower. However, other suppliers may count on repayment to help pay other obligations. In this case the supplier may reduce the total amount owed in order to encourage fast repayment.

The most common technique for encouraging fast repayment is the cash discount. A supplier might provide a business with a cash incentive for paying the obligation within 10 days. Cash discounts are often expressed in the formula 2/10/30. This refers to a 2% discount if the buyer pays in cash within 10 days and full payment is due if payed after the 10th day. If payment is not made within 30 days, the buyer has to pay interest or other penalties as defined by the purchase agreement. Although a 2% discount may not seem large, calculated out for the entire year it represents 36% (Bogen, 1966). To calculate the opportunity you lose by not paying early, divide the 20 days each month that you do not receive a 2% discount into 365 days a year. The resulting 18.25 is then multiplied by the 2% discount that you could have obtained, for an annualized loss of 36.5%. This discount encourages purchasers to pay their bills quickly, which can also reduce collection fees for the supplier. The purchaser also receives a significant benefit in obtaining a 30-day interest-free loan. That is why a cash discount is such a popular short-term funding technique. See chapter 12 for a discussion of cash discounts in the context of accounts receivable.

Sport Manufacturing Company

SMC needs to buy some supplies. After working out an agreement with a local supplier, SMC purchases 10 pieces of material for $50 each, with the sales terms of 10/10/30 (10/10/30 means payment in full is due in 30 days, but the buyer may take a 10% discount if payment is made within 10 days). If payment is made during the discount period, SMC will save $50 ($10 \times 50 \times 0.10$). If payment is not paid within the discounted period, SMC will owe $500.

BANK FINANCING

As discussed in chapter 3, banks are among the cornerstones of the finance system. Banks provide numerous levels of financial assistance, whether through personal banking or comprehensive business banking services. Although accounts payable are a critical tool for commerce, and most businesses utilize accounts payable on a daily basis, bank loans are the most economical and flexible means of short-term financing. Banks provide various services, from savings accounts and business checking accounts to night deposit and automatic bill payment services. They often offer flexible short-term loans ranging from 30 or 60 days to several months. If a 30-day loan comes due, a bank has the flexibility to renew the debt. If the loan is for a longer time period, such as three to five years, it is referred to as a **term loan**. Banks prefer to issue short-term loans in order to get their money back as soon as possible (Spiro, 1996). Unlike short-term loans that come due at the end of the designated time period and are discharged with one payment, term loans often entail regular periodic payments and one **balloon payment**.

If the University of Milford borrowed $5 million from a bank for 5 years, the university might be required to pay $500,000 a year in principal and interest for 4 years, with a large balloon payment approaching $4 million in the fifth year. For a conventional loan, U of M might make the $500,000 payment for 14 years to cover both the principal and interest.

No matter what services are utilized, a bank is more willing to negotiate and customize accounts with businesses that already have an established account. Some banks require businesses with active loans to maintain an average deposit balance equal to 20% of the loaned amount. Such a deposit is often called a compensating balance. This protective balance may not seem significant, but it does represent a cost of borrowing.

 Suppose the Smiths borrow $100,000 from a bank but have to maintain $20,000 in a savings account at the bank throughout the life of the loan. If the Smiths pay 10% on the loan, maintaining the $20,000 in the bank at a low interest rate or with no interest would in essence bring the cost of borrowing to 12.5%, which is calculated as follows:

$$I / (L - B) = \text{cost of borrowing}$$

I = interest paid on loan

L = amount borrowed

B = compensating balance that needs to be maintained

$$\$10,000 / (\$100,000 - \$20,000) = 12.5\%$$

A loan that is contingent on maintaining a minimum balance at the bank is a type of secured loan. Many loans require the use of collateral. Anything of value can be utilized to secure a loan. Some businesses pledge physical property such as land, buildings, inventory, or equipment. Other businesses pledge intangible assets such as accounts receivable or the rights to an invention or patent. Since loans against accounts receivable or inventory are often riskier, some banks do not offer such loans, and businesses need to go to nonbank lenders for these.

Many businesses utilize real estate or machinery as collateral for a loan. However, assets such as inventory, investment assets, or accounts receivable can be pledged if other assets are already being used for collateral. In some instances businesses do not want to encumber an asset because they want to be able to sell it. A company that has pledged a factory as security cannot sell the factory because it does not have a **clear title**—the title is "clouded." Because most debt instruments with any security (especially real property) are recorded by a city or county clerk, potential buyers can determine whether a property has a clouded title. If someone tried to buy the pledged factory, the title could not be passed as free and clear of any encumbrances. After the obligation was paid in full, however, the factory could be sold. This same process operates when individuals buy a house. The mortgage on the house is recorded with a government agency and is discovered when a title search is conducted. The buyer can clear the title by paying the mortgage and having the mortgage company release its claim to the property.

Using current inventories as collateral is a technique that maximizes current value while affording the option to raise additional funds. Asset-based borrowing entails a revolving line of credit secured by accounts receivable, inventories, or both (Hovey, 1998, November). Bally's Total Fitness expanded its business by acquiring debt, and the debt is being secured by accounts receivable (Caro, 2000). Since the chain has numerous members throughout the world, it is guaranteed a certain amount each month from dues. These dues are part of the accounts receivable and are also called contractually obligated revenue or contractually obligated income since they are required by the membership contracts. Bally's can utilize these prospective assets to secure debt obligations, similar to the way a stadium can use the contractually obligated revenue from naming rights contracts as collateral for a bond or other debt instruments.

Standard & Poor's raised its corporate credit rating on Bally Total Fitness to a B– from a CCC+ and removed it from credit watch, after being placed on the list on August 17, 2005 ("Club Hopping," 2004). Bally's obtained limited waivers relating to its 10.5% senior notes due 2011 and 9.875% senior subordinated notes due 2007 ("Club Hopping," 2004). As of September 30, 2004, Bally's debt was $747.7 million. To restore investor creditability, Bally's Total Fitness was to commence a search for a new chief executive officer (CEO) as part of its financial structuring process ("Liberation Investments," 2005). Bally's indenture violations originated from its failure to file with the SEC its financial statements for the quarter end of June 30, 2004, and to deliver the financial statements to the board trustee and lenders ("Liberation Investments," 2005). By 2007 Ballys had been delisted from the NYSE and was flirting with filing for Chapter 11 bankruptcy protection (see chapter 17) (Dow Jones Newswire, 2007).

If the borrower defaults on one of these secured loans, the lender can seize the assets as with any other collateral. On the basis of the potential difficulty a lender might have in collecting receivables or selling inventory, the lender might loan only up to 85% of the

Collateral Values

The following table shows common collateral values that are needed to secure credit from financial institutions. According to these industry standards, if you have accounts receivable of $100,000 and you allow the bank to monitor the receivables, you could possibly obtain an $80,000 loan secured by the receivables.

Value of Factored Assets in Obtaining Loans

Collateral	Percentage loaned
Accounts receivable, monitored	80
Accounts receivable, unmonitored	70
Inventory, monitored	50
Inventory, unmonitored	40
Owned equipment, % of book value	50
New equipment, % purchase price	80
Used equipment, % purchase price	75
Real estate	65-90
U.S. government securities	90
Investment-grade municipal bonds	80
Bonds or preferred stock	75
Stocks below AA grade	50
NYSE, AMEX, NASDAQ shares	65
Cash value of insurance policies	100
Cash	100

Data from "Planning for success," 2000, *CampBusiness*: 8-11.

value in receivables and 55% of the value of the inventories (Hovey, 1998, November). Asset-based loans are normally provided at the prime rate plus 2% for a creditworthy business. Although these loans are not especially hard to obtain, they do require significant paperwork. A borrower typically needs to provide three years' profit-and-loss statements, current and past financial statements, inventory aging reports, personal financial and tax return statements for the past three years, and sales projections for the coming year (Hovey, 1998, November). After receiving a loan, the borrower must comply with additional paperwork requirements such as providing monthly reports on accounts payable and receivable.

Some commonly utilized documents that provide security for an asset-backed loan are bills of lading, trust receipts, and warehouse receipts. A bill of lading pledges commodities or merchandise in transit as collateral for a loan. Goods covered by a trust receipt are held in trust for the lending institution but could be housed in a separate area at the borrower's business. Once those goods are sold, the cash from the sales is first paid to the bank to satisfy the debt. A warehouse receipt performs the same function as a bill of lading, but it applies when the inventory is stored in a bonded warehouse to protect the bank's collateral. Title to the

assets rests with the lender until a release document is provided to the warehouse. The warehouse can then release the specified assets. Although secured loans provide significant protection for the lender, collateral may not be required if a business has a strong credit rating or a good relationship with the lending bank.

Banks have significant flexibility, within federal guidelines, to offer various customized services. Twenty years ago, banks were typically smaller than they are today and often had strong personal relationships with customers. Banks could provide a broader range of services for business owners whom the bank employees knew and had done business with in the past. However, having a "personal banker" is more unusual today. Recent mergers have consolidated numerous smaller banks into more impersonal businesses. But even with larger banks, it is still important for businesses to communicate with bank employees on a regular basis. Loan officers and their supervisors are important contacts. Knowing several bank employees in these positions provides protection if bank personnel move to different locations (Nelton, 1998, November). Developing personal relationships can help if you ever need to apply for a loan—it is to your advantage if you are more than just a name on an application, possibly a friend and someone the bankers would judge as highly credible.

Banks frequently expect the owner of a proposed new business to put some of his own money at risk. The underlying thinking is, why should the bank invest in the project if the owner is not willing to risk his own money? Equity capital represents a firm commitment by the owner to work for the business' best interest. The owner wants to succeed in order to avoid losing his own money, as well as the bank's money. A bank could require equity capital to approach approximately 40% of the amount needed to fund the new business (Horine, 1999). Even if no equity is required to obtain the bank loan, banks traditionally require audited financial statements to help calculate standard ratios, such as debt–equity and acid test ratios, and these figures can help determine the prospect for default. Banks might also require business plans, pro forma budgets, personnel profiles, sample products, and other information that can help them make a lending decision. Most banks require a borrower to complete a formal application, which could include a summary of the business, profiles of the top executives, financial statements, pro forma budgets, and a detailed repayment plan (Griffin, 1991).

Once the loan papers have been approved, an agreement is signed between the parties. This document is called a promissory note. The note specifies the amount borrowed, the interest rate to be charged, any repayment terms, whether or not the loan is collateralized, and any and all other terms and conditions the parties have agreed on. After the note is signed, the borrower receives the loan proceeds.

Whether the loan is backed by a personal guarantee, collateral, or a mortgage, banks offer numerous financial options that make short-term borrowing fairly simple. Lines of credit are more complicated but still represent an effective use of bank resources to cover immediate fiscal needs. A lending institution charges interest only on the amount actually borrowed from the credit line but can also charge a commitment fee

The Five Cs of Credit

Regardless of the requested loan amount, people should not quit their jobs before obtaining a loan. A bank will check to see if an applicant is currently employed in order to help establish her ability to repay or "service" the loan. The potential borrower's employment status is just one variable that banks and other lending institutions might investigate. Banks commonly refer to the **five Cs** of credit when deciding whether or not to loan someone money. The five Cs are character, capacity, collateral, capital, and condition.

1. *Character* refers to the applicant's credit history and the applicant's truthfulness. Did the applicant disclose all outstanding debt? Did she list any prior bankruptcy? Does the applicant have favorable business or professional references? Does it appear that she is willing to repay the loan? The answers to such questions help determine whether or not the lender can trust the applicant.

2. *Capacity* represents the lender's determination as to whether the potential business has the right management team and philosophy to become a profitable enterprise that will earn more than enough money to pay the loan.

3. *Collateral* refers to anything of value that can be pledged to guarantee final repayment of the loan. Collateral can include a home, property, equipment, collectibles, a legal judgment, or even a lottery payoff.

4. *Capital* represents the equity that the applicant will put into her own business. A lending institution will not be very interested in loaning money to help launch a new business if the business owner does not think the business will succeed. If the applicant believes the business will be a success, then she must support her conviction by investing some of her own money. Banks typically require a 30% to 35% equity or cash investment in the business by the loan applicant (Pounds, 1997). Capital also refers to any excess cash that might be available to pay any unexpected expenses.

5. *Condition* is the applicant's primary opportunity to sell the lender on the value of the business. The lender will want to know if the industry is growing, if there are competitors, whether the product has a long life cycle, whether a location or distribution channel is available to sell the product, and so on. By thoroughly researching the proposed business and presenting the lender with a comprehensive business plan that addresses these issues (see chapter 7), the applicant greatly increases the chance of securing a loan.

that could range from 0.05% to 1% (Battersby, 1999). The commitment fee can be waived if the borrower has compensating balances in other accounts. Three types of lines of credit are available:

1. A nonbinding line of credit is an open account for the business to borrow from. If the business experiences hardships and has financial trouble, however, the line of credit can be revoked.

2. A committed line of credit requires the potential borrower to pay a commitment fee to lock the line of credit into place, thus guaranteeing needed funds.

3. A revolving line of credit requires the borrower to undergo an annual review and renewal of the credit line (Battersby, 1999).

A **revolving credit** agreement is similar to a line of credit in allowing a company to borrow a specified sum, but there is a major distinction. A line of credit allows the borrower to access a certain amount of money if needed. However, the bank or the company can withdraw from the agreement at any time. A revolving credit agreement is a contract whereby the borrower agrees to pay an annual commitment fee, a small percentage of the unused amount, to compensate the bank for entering into the commitment (Brigham & Gapenski, 1994). If the company uses only half the available credit, it is charged the commitment fee for the unused amount and is charged the agreed-on interest for the amount borrowed. Since the revolving credit agreement is a contract, both parties need to undertake formal contract cancellation steps to end it.

COMMERCIAL PAPER

Businesses can raise short-term funds from other nonbank businesses by issuing commercial paper (CP). Commercial paper is a promissory note that might mature in one to nine months. Commercial paper is not often seen in the sport industry; however, it is common among some large manufacturers and sales finance companies, such as General Motors Acceptance Corporation (GMAC). Large corporations are also among the largest purchasers of CP, which they acquire with liquid funds to gain some interest. Similar to other short-term lending, if a large corporation needs money to pay bills, it can sell the CP it previously purchased. The business that issues the CP determines the interest rates charged based on what rates would draw the greatest investor interest. Specialized CP dealers quote CP prices on the open market. Rates and prices change as economic conditions change; and as companies need more money, they may offer better rates.

PRIVATE PLACEMENT THROUGH NONBANK LENDERS

Various options are available for obtaining cash from other sources. **Private placement** refers to the process of obtaining funds from private parties such as investors, venture capital investors, or other companies interested in investing in a business. These investments can take the form of debt instruments, equity interest, or a blend of the two.

Nonbank lenders are the most frequent source other than banks for financing smaller businesses. These lenders do not include angel investors, family members, and friends, who can also serve as lenders. Nonbank lenders can be independent businesses or can work in conjunction with the government. Some companies that offer nonbank loans include AT&T Small Business Lending Corporation, Heller First Capital, Business Lenders, Money Store Investment Corporation, and GE Capital Small Business Finance Corporation. Nonbank loans often have a higher interest rate based on risk factors, which might have been what dissuaded a bank from providing the loan in the first place. These loans are also often attached to special purchasing deals offered by suppliers (see discussion of supplier financing on p.146).

The list of potential lending sources is almost limitless. This section covers private companies, private investment group financing, factoring, installment sales, supplier financing, and leasing. These financing methods do not entail selling any equity position in the business. Thus, no ownership interest is given up to obtain the funds.

We discuss mergers and acquisitions in chapter 15, but every business owner has the option of selling a portion of the business or the entire business in order to acquire funds. Several **buyout** funds established for the sport industry in 1999 provide funds to businesses or purchase entire businesses. Chase Manhattan joined with International Management Group to form the IMG/Chase Sports Capital fund. The fund had $170 million to help finance sport businesses and used some of those funds to purchase the Skip Barber Racing School in Connecticut (Tan, 2000). Although selling an entire business entails obtaining funds for the sellers, the process should not be thought of as selling out. The owner may have sold the business, but the potential cash infusion from a financially stronger business might have been what was necessary to finance further expansion. Many businesses would have failed had they not been purchased by a buyer who funded future growth.

PRIVATE COMPANIES

Other nonbank lenders include private companies that are licensed by the U.S. SBA. These small business investment companies (SBICs) can provide either debt financing by issuing long-term loans or equity financing by acquiring an ownership interest in a company (Pryde, 1998). However, SBICs are barred by law from acquiring a controlling interest in a company. SBIC owners are required to contribute $5 million of their own money, which makes them highly selective in picking high-quality investments. The SBICs also prefer to invest close to home and typically invest around $500,000 in each company (Pryde, 1998). Many investments are in specialized companies, which might include minority-owned businesses and socially or economically disadvantaged companies. To qualify for an SBIC loan or equity investment, a company's net worth must be less than $18 million, and the business must have had after-tax earnings of less than $6 million in the two previous years (Pryde, 1998).

Some private-placement investors, such as some venture capitalists, require significant control over managerial decisions. However some "hands-off" private-placement investors do not require any seats on the board of directors or any managerial involvement. These individuals are typically content with a 25% return per year (Reynes, 1998, October). Hands-off private-placement deals are best suited for developed companies that are already publicly traded or that plan on pursuing a public offering in two to three years.

Most cities have local brokers, bankers, or regional brokerage firms that can help coordinate private-placement deals. These individuals typically get paid a percentage of the money they help raise (5%-15%). It is important to be careful when working with anyone trying to help you raise funds. Since deals are contingent on getting funding, numerous scams and incomplete deals can cost a company both money and lost time. If any broker or investment banker asks for money up front, there is no guarantee you will receive anything (Reynes, 1998, October). In contrast, individuals who receive a percentage after a deal has been completed are more likely to engage in more prudent conduct to guarantee payment for themselves and their firms.

Through private placement, an investor might purchase convertible debentures. A convertible debenture pays a certain predetermined interest rate to the investor. After a specified time period, convertible debentures can be converted into stock or maintained as a loan. The opportunity to convert the loan to stock is a choice made by the loan holder, the issuer, or both (Reynes, 1998, October). In one example involving a company that manufactured drug-screening kits, investors had the option to purchase convertible debentures in $5,000 blocks. The company's shares were selling for $0.38 each. After three years, the lenders could choose to get their money back and all interest owed, or they could convert their debenture to stock at $0.75 a share. Converting to stocks would have been the best option for the lenders because the stocks were then selling for $3 to $4 per share (Reynes, 1998, October). Debenture offerings are discussed further in chapter 10.

PRIVATE INVESTMENT GROUP FINANCING

Entrepreneurs can also turn to a private investment group (PIG) for nonbank funding. A PIG can pool money from a variety of sources including individuals, endowments, pension funds, private investors, and institutional investors (Hovey, 1997). Private investment groups traditionally invest in stable companies that have shown continued growth for several years. These investors typically prefer investing in manufacturing- or distribution-based companies rather than retail or service companies (Hovey, 1997).

Private investment groups normally invest more than $1 million in a company and buy stocks and possibly secure loans to raise the necessary capital. However, such investments do not come without a hefty price. Private investment groups typically require a rate of return of 30% to 35% per year (Hovey, 1997). This rate of return may seem high, but venture capital or angel investors who invest in certain industries or products typically invest in riskier young firms and demand a higher **annual return**—*often over 50%* (Hovey, 1997).

A PIG deal might take 6 to 18 months to complete, and a $10 million deal might cost up to $340,000 to finalize. This figure is the sum of $100,000 to $200,000 for the mergers and acquisitions adviser; $30,000 to $100,000 for legal fees; and $25,000 to $40,000 for accounting fees (Hovey, 1997).

FACTORING ACCOUNTS RECEIVABLE

Private parties can also provide short-term funds through factoring. Factoring entails selling assets. The assets sold are either inventories or accounts receivable, and they are purchased by a specialized financing company.

If the Smiths have $10,000 owed to them by members who have yet to pay their bills, Bob and Cheryl could possibly sell the accounts receivable for $7,500 and immediately utilize those funds.

There are several ways to accomplish factoring of receivables. One way is for a company to purchase the receivables, and another is for a company to purchase only the rights without transferal of actual administrative duties. The first technique is called factoring without recourse. A factor (the company that purchases the receivables) purchasing without recourse assumes complete responsibility in debt collection. Customers are instructed to send their payments to the factor. The factor receives a commission on the accounts that are paid and charges interest on the money loaned to the business until the accounts are paid.

 Assume that the Smiths are owed $10,000 and that Acme Factoring purchases the accounts receivable without recourse. Acme might receive 10% of the $10,000, or $1,000, as commission and might loan the Smiths $7,000 on the remaining receivables at 5%. If Acme collects the entire $10,000, Acme profits from the $1,000 commission and from receiving 5% interest on the $7,000 loan. The remaining $3,000 might be returned to the Smiths according to the negotiated contract provisions.

In the second type of factoring—factoring with recourse—the original holder of the receivables is still responsible for obtaining repayment and collects all payments, but sends those payments to a finance company. This technique is also called accounts receivable financing. A finance company might advance money contingent on the borrower's agreeing to collect and actively manage the receivables. The factoring company might advance 70% to 95% of all receivables sold to it and then pay the remaining percentage when the last receivables are collected (Bogen, 1966). Again, the factoring company makes money by charging interest on the money advanced to the company selling the receivables. Regardless of the technique utilized, factoring accounts receivable is more expensive than bank borrowing because the factor charges a higher interest rate based on the potential risk factors.

INSTALLMENT SALES

Installment sales are common in the auto sales industry. An individual makes a down payment and makes monthly payments of principal and interest for a specified number of months or years. These contracts are typically for three or four years. The purchaser's failure to make timely payments gives the installment contract holder the right to repossess the car. Thus, the person holding the installment contract has title and true ownership.

Installment sales contracts can be found in the sporting goods industry (e.g., when someone buys an abdominal workout machine seen in an infomercial for three installments of $19.99 each). The purchaser has obtained the opportunity to receive the product contingent on future payments. Similar deals are made in almost all businesses, by which a party to a contract can make several payments. If the U of M sells their broadcasting rights to a television station, the station might pay 33% when the contract is signed, 33% before the season starts, and 33% when the season ends.

SUPPLIER FINANCING

Businesses can also obtain financial assistance from those who sell them necessary equipment or supplies. Such an arrangement can take a variety of forms, from loaning equipment to reducing purchase prices to extending credit or creating longer repayment terms (Hodges, 1997). Assistance from suppliers represents just one technique in **creative financing**. By casting a wide net, a business can find numerous potential coentrepreneurs interested in possibly joining forces. Arrowhead Pond in Anaheim is a good example of such a deal; Aramark paid a significant amount for the rights to provide food and concession services for the facility. Aramark is hoping to write the building cost off as a tax expense and to generate significant long-term revenue from the exclusive contract. In 2006 the facility's sponsors changed and it became the Honda Center.

 Sport Manufacturing Company could also utilize supplier financing by entering into an agreement with a new company that manufactures pressing machines. The new company could provide the machines at a

discount or offer more attractive financing options compared with other equipment providers and in return request using SMC as a referral for other potential buyers. The agreement could allow other prospective equipment buyers to visit SMC and see the machines in operation.

An established company might also offer financing options, but the terms might not be as favorable as those of a new company or a major competitor that is trying to gain market share. This example can often be seen in consumer car sales, where various manufacturers offer lower-interest loans to win a potential customer away from a different manufacturer.

OPERATING VERSUS CAPITAL LEASES

Leasing, whether from the selling company or from a leasing agent or corporation, can also provide the funds needed to obtain equipment or other assets. By leasing equipment, money can be saved to purchase other assets or equipment.

The Smiths might have to spend a significant amount to purchase new equipment. However, their initial expenditure would be much less if they leased the equipment instead. Fitness equipment leasing evolved in the mid-1990s; and in 1999, between 25% and 40% of all fitness equipment was being leased (Cohen, 1999). The numbers increased through the first part of 2005 because the cost of operating health clubs kept increasing, and leasing freed up additional funds to pay for other expenses. For a facility that leases equipment, the average leased amount is $40,000. This amount is based on the total equipment value, the credit rating, financial conditions, and business experience. Fitness equipment does not depreciate as quickly as other assets, such as a car, and thus often serves as collateral for the lease. However, since the Smiths are still new to their profession, they might need to post a security deposit of 10% to 25% of the equipment's value (Cohen, 1999).

The Smiths could obtain either a capital or an operating lease. Under a capital lease, Bob and Cheryl would make their monthly lease payments and at the end of the lease term could pay a specified price,

normally $1, and acquire the ownership rights for the equipment (Cohen, 1999). In contrast, an operating lease allows the lessee to return the equipment at the end of the lease or to buy it for a percentage of the original cost. Operating leases are often called service leases because the contract normally requires both financing and maintenance. Operating leases are not fully amortized, which means the lease payments are insufficient to recover the full cost of the equipment.

A major advantage of the operating lease is a cancellation clause that gives the lessee (the Smiths) or the lessors (the equipment company) the opportunity to terminate the lease within a specified period. The cancellation clause could call for a 30-day written notice. Regardless of the time requirement, the benefit for the Smiths would be that they could, within 30 days, switch to a cheaper equipment supplier or one that provides more advanced equipment.

In contrast to the operating lease, the capital lease has one major advantage: the right to own the equipment when the lease ends. However, a capital lease does not have any maintenance provision, the lease is not cancelable, and the lease payments will equal the equipment's cost. A capital lease is often called a finance lease because of the nature of the lease arrangement.

The Smiths might find a nice piece of equipment sold by XYZ Manufacturing. They could negotiate price and delivery specifications with XYZ. Bob and Cheryl could then apply to have a finance company buy the equipment and lease it back to them. The Smiths would have an amortized lease with an interest percentage built into it. If the equipment cost $10,000 and the interest rate was 10%, the Smiths would have paid $11,000 when all the lease payments had been rendered.

There are several issues to examine when determining whether to purchase or lease new assets. Leasing new assets has the following advantages (Bogen, 1966):

- Funds that would normally be used to purchase assets could be used for working capital and other needs.
- No external financing is required, or the amount of such funds would be minimal.

- The corporation's financial picture is strengthened because investments in fixed assets are reduced and debt service is not increased (however, additional debt obligation to pay for the lease would be required).
- No significant capital outlay is required, since most leases do not entail a significant down payment.
- Corporations can often avoid a large maturity payment such as is involved when a corporation retires a bond issue.
- Unlike the situation with stock sales, there is no increased dilution of the shareholder's equity through leasing.
- The entire lease payment is deducted from **taxable income**, which often produces a significant benefit over asset ownership. Other assets such as buildings and equipment can be depreciated if purchased, but the land is not deductible.
- Technological obsolescence due to the rapid increase in technology can be avoided when one is able to rapidly replace older leased equipment.
- Leasing equipment can eliminate numerous repair and upkeep expenses that could be covered by the lease agreement.

Although there are significant advantages to leasing assets, such as lower up-front costs, tax deduction, and a positive effect on credit rating, there are also some distinct disadvantages:

- Gross lease costs are traditionally higher than financing costs if extended over the life of the asset.
- After the point at which an asset would have been paid for if purchased, the lessee is still making regular lease payments throughout the lease period rather than the life of the asset.
- Modifying the asset requires the lessor's permission, eliminating the lessee's ability to actually control the asset.
- A lessee loses the benefits associated with inflation, increased values, or increased salvage values because the asset is turned over after the lease period ends, and the lessor gains these benefits.
- A long lease obligation may force a company to keep using older equipment covered by the lease in order to avoid paying any penalties for breaching the lease (Bogen, 1966).

- Because leases entail no significant capital requirements, some companies may lease too much equipment, not realizing that their fixed lease obligations are growing significantly and that the lease obligations would still be owed even if all their sales stopped.
- A lessor can always confiscate the equipment upon default, leaving the company without machinery.

Whichever leasing technique is used, there are specific tax and balance sheet impacts. The big tax benefit of a lease is the ability to deduct lease expenses as a business expense. If the Smiths buy the equipment instead, they will be able to depreciate the equipment cost over five years only as set forth by IRS regulations. The tax benefit is available only under specific circumstances if the lease meets the following conditions (Brigham & Gapenski, 1994):

- The initial lease term cannot exceed 80% of the equipment's estimated useful life, which means that when the lease ends the equipment still should have at least 20% of its useful life remaining.
- The equipment's residual value at the end of the lease must equal at least 20% of its initial value.
- No party can be allowed to purchase the equipment at a predetermined price when the lease ends. This concern can be eliminated by allowing the lessee to purchase the equipment at the equipment's fair market value once the lease ends.
- The lessee cannot make any investments in or improvements to the equipment other than through the lease payments.
- There cannot be any contractual provision limiting the equipment's use until after the lease expires.

An example of the depreciation versus business expense deduction highlights the value of a lease to the bottom line.

If the Smiths bought $2 million in equipment with a three-year class life, they would receive a depreciation allowance of $660,000 in the first year, $900,000 in the second year, $300,000 in the third year, and $140,000 in the fourth year. If the Smiths were taxed at 40% (federal and state taxes combined), the purchase would provide a total tax savings of $800,000. Assuming a discount rate of 6%, the present value of the tax savings would be $671,680. If the Smiths leased double the amount of equipment for one year for a $2 million lease payment, they would likewise have an $800,000 tax savings ($2,000,000 × 40%). However, since the lease option benefits are derived in the first year, there is a $42,559 savings compared with the present value from the purchase option (Brigham & Gapenski, 1994). The problem with this analysis is that the $2 million lease obligation appears very high when the purchase price is also $2 million. The example makes sense only because we are supposing that the Smiths would lease twice as much equipment as they would have purchased. If they were to lease the same amount of equipment, the tax savings as a function of present value would be significantly less. It is obviously important to make proper comparisons between items to be leased or purchased.

Leases also affect financial statements. Leases were called "off-balance-sheet financing" for many years because neither the leased asset nor the lease liability (payment requirements) appeared on a company's balance sheet. Since leased assets and obligations did not appear on the balance sheet, an investor might not know that all the equipment in a business was leased and that the business owed over $1 million annually in lease obligations, for example. These facts would be critical for any investor. On the basis of this concern, the Financial Accounting Standards Board issued a ruling that leased assets need to be reported as fixed assets, and the present value of future lease payments needs to be recorded as a liability (Brigham & Gapenski, 1994). An operating lease is now recorded on the balance sheet. A capital lease is recorded on the books as either an asset or an obligation. An asset is considered part of a capital lease if ownership of the asset is transferred to the lessee when the lease expires, if the lease contains a bargain purchase option, or if the lease term exceeds 75% of the asset's economic life (Spiro, 1996).

LONG-TERM BORROWING

This chapter has covered various financing techniques that are often short-term solutions. Borrowing on a credit card is not a long-term option because of the high interest rates. Furthermore,

factoring is a stopgap solution, and other funding options would need to be pursued in subsequent times of financial need. Other funding options, such as a bank's line of credit, can be either short or long term. Installment contracts can be short term for a car or long term for equipment that might last longer than 10 years.

The most traditional forms of long-term funding are stocks and bonds (discussed in the next two chapters). Whereas these two options are normally available for larger businesses, smaller or new companies often do not have these alternatives. Various long-term funding options, such as mortgages or long-term loans, exist for medium-sized businesses. Mezzanine financing is also available as a bridge loan for businesses that wish to expand but are not yet ready for a public offering. This section covers mezzanine financing and venture capital financing.

MEZZANINE FINANCING

Although raising short-term start-up capital is often very difficult, the scenario for existing companies is different. A company with a successful track record has fewer problems raising money because it should be able to show sustained income. These companies can utilize mezzanine financing, a type of financing available to established companies that show growth potential but that are not yet ready for a capital stock offering (Hovey, 1998, March). Companies can typically utilize mezzanine financing to raise between $1 million and $20 million through a combination of borrowing money from and selling stocks to the same investor (Hovey, 1998, March).

Financing typically works through payment of interest on the borrowed amount for about five years. After that time period, the business can cash out the investor by going public or can **refinance** for a longer period. The investor has the benefit of earning a good rate of interest, typically prime plus 2 to 4 points, or, if the business has increased in value, selling the stock for a capital gain (Hovey, 1998, March). There is no set amount that needs to be raised. So the Smiths, after operating their business for several years, could possibly raise $2 million in unsecured, partially secured, or secured debt financing and perhaps $1 million in equity financing. Such deals typically take between three and five months to complete, and the total fee cost (attorneys, accountants, and investment bankers) can equal 5% of the deal (Hovey, 1998, March).

The rule of thumb for mezzanine lending is that a company can *leverage two to three times its cash flow in senior secured debt. It can raise total debt four to five times cash flow with a mezzanine deal. So if the company is doing $2 million in cash flow, it can probably raise $4 million to $6 million in senior debt and $4 million to $5 million more in mezzanine financing, for a total debt of $10 million or five times cash flow. (Hovey, 1998, March, p. 42)*

Although mezzanine lending can help a company grow before a possible public offering, some businesses need a larger boost to expand more rapidly or to more expediently position themselves for a public offering. Whereas the previously discussed angel investor might stay with an investment for the long term, a venture capital investor normally remains with an investment until the business invested in goes bankrupt, gets purchased by someone else, or goes public.

VENTURE CAPITAL

Venture capital represents an opportunity for individuals with marketable ideas or products to raise funds from private investors willing to take a risk in owning part of the company in exchange for their investment. Venture capital, commonly called VC, is similar to mezzanine financing in that it blends debt-based loans with the potential for equity interest if the borrower goes public. In 1996, capital investments of more than $10.1 billion were made in U.S.-based companies (Reynes, 1997). The numbers were much greater for 1999 because numerous Internet businesses were launched through VC infusions.

 Venture capital investors might invest several million in the Smiths' proposed fitness facility, but at a price to the Smiths. The Smiths might need to surrender a large percentage of the company (possibly over 50% depending on the deal) to the investor. Thus, they might no longer be the primary owners—and then would not be working for themselves. Or Bob and Cheryl might have to give an investor a position on the board of directors and possibly give the investor some managerial control.

VC investors are primarily interested in technology-based industries in which a winning company can pay off many times over, versus a mildly successful company that will show only marginal profits. Ven-ture capitalists like to see gross margins over 50%. A company making a 30% profit a year represents too great a risk and does not attract the strong investor interest that could make an initial public offering (IPO) successful (Evanson, 1998, January).

Venture capital investors have shied away from the sport industry in the past, but sport-related Internet companies are starting to garner VC interest. Not all Internet businesses are drawing VC interest, however. Venture capitalists are attracted to companies that have clear access to a channel of distribution, whether it is the company's own or someone else's (Evanson, 1998, January). The collapse of the dot-com economy in the 1990s ended several years later with the success of Internet companies such as eBay, Google, and Yahoo. By 2005 VC investors were once again pouring money into Internet companies as well as pharmaceutical and biotechnology companies.

Regardless of the method used to obtain initial funding or short-term funding, any successful business will also require long-term financing. VC and mezzanine investors may pay a premium for the ability to transfer their investment from a debt instrument to an equity interest. The equity interest is developed through giving the investor a share of the business. Providing a share of the business is made easier with stock. It is preferable to give a VC investor one million shares of two million outstanding shares instead of a contract stating that she owns 50% of a business. That is, a contract indicating a 50% ownership in a business is often much harder to sell than stocks, especially stocks listed on an organized exchange.

FUNDING FOR SMALL OR MINORITY-OWNED BUSINESSES

This section expands on prior analysis to look more closely at other capital options for smaller or minority-owned businesses and indicates where to go for help if you are having trouble finding funding.

SMALL BUSINESS ASSOCIATION LOANS FOR THE INNER CITY

An additional government source the Smiths could look to is SBA, discussed earlier in the chapter. SBA can offer assistance in obtaining various types of loans, including 7(a), 504, Microlenders, Small Business Lending Company, bank-regulated Certified Development Corporation, and SBIC-related loans or programs. In addition, SBA can provide assistance in conjunction with other capital efforts. For example, Detroit obtained $100 million from the federal government to develop an empowerment zone (Detroit Empowerment Zone Transition Office, n.d.). The empowerment zone is designed to foster revitalization of a community. Businesses moving to such a zone may receive wage credits, **tax-exempt bonds**, section 179 (depreciation) expensing, and assistance in obtaining SBA-backed loans. Property taxes also were to be frozen for those new businesses for five years. In conjunction with this effort, the Detroit Recreation Department put forth an empowerment zone initiative that received more than $10 million in Title XX funding for such projects as Roving Recreation and Recreation Facilities Enhancement Project (Detroit Empowerment Zone Transition Office, n.d.). Blending various government levels and agencies can help develop innovative capital acquisition programs and reduce operating costs. This is especially true in the context of minority-based programs.

A HELPING HAND FOR MINORITY BUSINESS OWNERS

Although the capital sources just mentioned all present some strong opportunities for a new business or established business to obtain funds for growth, other companies might not have the same opportunities. Minorities and women have traditionally faced hardships in acquiring capital for their businesses. Some of these hardships were attributable to minimal or nonexistent credit histories for business owners who had never had credit cards in their own names or who represented too high a risk for traditional capital lenders. To prevent potential continued discrimination—whether disparate impact (unintentional) or disparate treatment (intentional)—numerous support opportunities have been established to help minorities and women obtain funding.

 Although the Smiths are thinking about entering into an equal partnership, Cheryl could possibly become the primary owner or proprietor with a 51% stake in the fitness center. Under such an arrangement, the center would probably be considered a female-owned business and qualify for some special capital opportunities. As a female-owned business, the fitness center could also become eligible for specific government set-aside contracts.

Female-owned companies can utilize the Women's Prequalified Loan Program, guaranteed by the SBA, to borrow up to $250,000. Guarantees are for 80% of loans under $100,000 and 75% for loans over $100,000 (Broome, 1997). To qualify for the SBA-guaranteed loan, the business needs to be a female-owned business (at least 51% of the business needs to be owned, managed, or operated by women), have less than $5 million in sales, and employ fewer than 100 workers (Broome, 1997). If a loan under $100,000 is sought, the process just requires a one-page application. For loans over $100,000 the applicant needs to submit an expanded application, business plan, resumes of the primary officials, recent financial statements or tax returns, and a personal financial statement (Broome, 1997). Loans over $50,000 have an interest obligation at the prime rate. Loans under $50,000 can cost the prime rate plus up to 4% interest (Broome, 1997).

The following paragraphs describe some minority-oriented funding programs.

The National Minority Supplier Development Council (NMSDC) has 42 regional affiliates and works with 3,500 businesses to help minority-owned companies acquire goods and services. Such assistance is not meant to be charity. Rather, the companies involved in NMSDC participate to help generate additional sales. Through the provision of flexible payment options or collateralized sales to minorities who otherwise might not obtain such preferential treatment, new sales and potential clients can be developed. The NMSDC has proceeded one step further to create the Business Consortium Fund, which helps minority business owners obtain financing for raw materials, employee salaries, and other contract-related expenses (Nelton, 1998, June). The Business Consortium Fund limits loans to $500,000 over a maximum of four years and requires the borrower to have a purchase order specifying where the funds will be spent.

Although NMSDC aims to help minority-owned business owners, the definition of a minority has created a controversy. In 2000, NMSDC redefined the minority-owned business as a business with as little as 30% nonwhite ownership. But even if less than one-third of a business needs to be minority owned in order for the business to qualify as a minority business, the rules also require qualified businesses to have 51% of their voting stock held by minorities (Wynter & Thomas, 2000). The rule change was designed to give larger minority-controlled businesses that have a high number of nonminority investors the opportunity to compete more effectively with other businesses.

Apart from the Business Consortium Fund, minority-owned companies may obtain capital from specialized small business investment companies (SSBICs) licensed by SBA. Local chambers of commerce, economic development committees, and various national associations can also help minorities and women find needed capital. Appendix C in this book lists several associations that can help in obtaining capital.

CONCLUSION

This chapter covers the basic elements of capital financing. Numerous options exist for finding necessary funds, but even people with business experience can face rejection. It is not uncommon for a businessperson to approach multiple lenders and be refused by all. This does not mean the individual is a bad businessperson; it may mean the economic environment is not right, the lending market is tight, or there is not enough collateral to secure the obligation, among a host of other things.

No matter what capital source you attempt to tap, you will need several key tools. The primary tools are either audited financial statements or pro forma statements (see chapter 7). You will also need a realistic road map for your business (i.e., a business plan) that will help investors determine what direction you will be taking to guarantee a strong likelihood of success. Although the proper documentation is important, you also need a strong team of professionals helping you through the process. An accountant, attorney, and financial planner or investment banker might be critical for your capital acquisition success.

Selling investors on your project is significantly different from selling potential customers. Customers may be interested in product features, customer service, and warranties. In contrast, investors are interested in margin (profit), market size, a competitive environment, return on investment, product development opportunities, and related financial issues (Evanson, 1997). The financial planning process (discussed in chapter 7) helps identify these issues.

Persistency is the key to successfully securing capital. This chapter focuses more on short-term funding in situations in which quick decisions are necessary and businesses may not have the time to pursue long-term funding options. It is always important to have in place the capital infrastructure, such as a line of credit, in case you might need money and do not have the time to try various options. The next two chapters discuss long-term funding options that often take months or years of planning to be successful.

CLASS DISCUSSION TOPICS

1. If you have ever applied for a credit card, what were you required to show to obtain credit?

2. If you have ever borrowed money to buy a car, what was involved in that process?

3. If you have ever borrowed money for college, what steps were involved in that process?

4. What would you want from a friend (e.g., collateral, a contract) if you loaned the person $1,000?

5. If a friend asked you for a $1,000 loan to start a business, what information would you want to obtain to help you make your decision?

6. Is there value in "sweat equity," or the owner's involvement in a company to help fund a business?

7. Have you ever defaulted on a loan, and what were the ramifications?

8. Considering the high failure rate of new businesses, if you had the money, would you lend money to someone else to help start a business if you knew there was a 75% chance that the business would fail?

9. If you had to develop a strategy to fund building a sports facility based exclusively on borrowing funds, what sources would you pursue? What do you think your chances of success would be? What criteria could help or hurt your chances of obtaining funds?

9

CAPITAL STOCKS

CHAPTER OBJECTIVES

After studying this chapter, you should be able to do the following:

- Compare the different classes of stock available.
- Describe the rights of a stockholder.
- Understand how a company decides whether to go public.
- Describe how a smaller sport business can issue stock.
- Understand how stocks are issued.
- Understand the evolution of sport stocks.
- Compare the various publicly traded sport businesses.

Chapter 8 covers borrowing on the open market as a form of capital acquisition. Another major form of capital acquisition is selling the business to a group of individuals who purchase stock in the company. Stocks, which represent ownership in the business, can be sold on the open market or through very private transactions. Whereas some businesses are owned by thousands of shareholders, others are owned by only one shareholder. Each business is different, and the number and types of shares sold are based on the capital needs of the company when it initially issues stock and future financial needs that might warrant the issuance of additional shares.

Stock certificates represent an investor's ownership right in a business. A stockholder pays a designated amount to acquire an ownership interest in a company. Each share represents an ownership interest. That is why a stockholder is also referred to as a shareholder. If you own 1,000 shares of a company's stock and 100,000 shares were issued, you own 1% of the company.

This chapter covers the types of stocks that can be purchased, the ways shareholders participate in a business, the process of issuing stock (often called "going public"), the reasons for increases in the value of shares, and the types of sport stocks that are available.

COMMON STOCK

As the name implies, the type of stock that is most frequently issued and utilized is **common stock**. Nike, for example, has issued millions of shares of both class A and class B common stock. Phil Knight, the original cofounder, owns 95.5% of the class A shares and 95,652,015 class B shares, which together make up approximately 36.1% of the outstanding shares.

Common stocks represent an equity ownership right in a company. Each share denotes a percentage ownership of the corporation. Since Phil Knight owns more than 95 million shares and Nike has in total 268 million shares outstanding, he owns 35.7% (this number differs from the 36.1% previously mentioned because of the inclusion of the class A shares) of the business. As a partial owner, Knight is entitled to a proportional share of profits earned by the company. If Nike had a $10 million profit and the board of directors decided to pay the entire amount to its common shareholders, then Knight would be entitled to a dividend of $3.57 million.

Knight has certain rights, risks, and obligations as an owner. His rights include the right to help set the direction of the corporation through voting his shares. He also faces risks, such as the possibility of losing his investment and the prospect of any recovery if Nike ever goes bankrupt and there is no money left after the bondholders are repaid. Common stocks are low on the repayment list after secured creditors are repaid and holders of preferred shares are paid. Also, he has obligations to the business, which could include the prohibition of self-dealing or taking a business opportunity for himself.

Shares can be purchased through several means. Online brokers allow investors to purchase stocks themselves over the Internet, usually at a reduced cost. Investors can also purchase shares through an investment adviser or broker. These individuals charge more than a no-frills online service, but an investor can ask questions and possibly pay to acquire detailed research on stocks. Using either technique can expose investors to significant risk if a stock drops in value. Although some people such as day traders might make a fortune, numerous individuals also lose fortunes on a regular basis. Buying stocks is akin to gambling. Someone can have the best information about a horse race, similar to having great information about a company, but that does not guarantee a win. Investors rely on information about new product launches, key executive retirings, large contracts that have been signed, and numerous additional factors. One of the most commonly sought pieces of information is industry ratios, which help highlight if a stock is over- or undervalued or whether a stock is performing well compared with others in the same industry segment.

Because of the potential for significant losses and because investors are often risk averse (not wanting to invest in risky stocks for fear of losing precious money such as a retirement fund), investors try to minimize their risks. One technique that reduces the risk of purchasing stock is to purchase shares in a mutual fund. A mutual fund normally represents millions of dollars from investors who want to spread their risk and opportunity for gain over many stocks. There are specialized mutual funds that can invest in sport stocks, social equity stocks, global stocks, or aggressive growth stocks. A mutual fund might have millions of shares in hundreds of stocks, and professional administrators of each fund analyze each stock and try to pick the best time to buy or sell the fund's shares.

Another technique to reduce the risk of investing in stocks is dollar cost averaging, where an investor purchases shares on a routine basis in the same company regardless of the price. Through this technique, an investor will purchase shares possibly at $4.00 per stock one month, $6.00 another, and maybe $3.00 in yet another month. Over time, this technique is one of the best ways to lower the risks of paying too much for stocks since they are being purchased at the highest prices as well as the lowest prices, which averages out the total investment amount over time.

PREFERRED STOCK

Preferred stock earns its name from the dividend preference it carries in relation to common stock. Although a corporation might not issue a dividend to common stock shareholders, it may be bound to provide dividends to the preferred stock shareholders. The dividend is cumulative in that if it is not paid to holders of preferred stock in a given year, the next year the corporation will owe two years' worth of dividends. The dividend to the preferred shareholders needs to be paid before common stockholders can receive their dividends. The requirement to pay a dividend, if one is issued, makes a preferred stock a blend between a bond with a required interest payment and a stock with its associated equity benefits. The requirement to pay a fixed dividend increases the issuing company's **financial leverage**. In the eyes of lenders, preferred stock represents equity and is shown in the equity section of the balance sheet.

Other benefits that are available for preferred stockholders can include (Bogen, 1966)

- the right to dividend payments before common stock shareholders receive dividend payments;
- preference as to assets in distribution;
- voting power for preferred stock, available under limited circumstances;
- strong redemption provisions;
- subscription privileges to future stock offerings; and
- the right to convert preferred stock to common stock.

Some investors rely on dividend income as their primary return on an equity investment. For these investors, preferred shares would be the most prudent investment because preferred stock shareholders are entitled to a dividend payment before common stock shareholders receive any dividends.

Regarding preference in distribution, some corporations specifically authorize preferred stockholders to receive the first of any return upon liquidation of a corporation's assets. If no such preference is provided for in the corporate bylaws, all classes of stock share equally in any distributions. Preferred stockholders often perceive their investment as riskier than bonds because the preferred shareholders' claims are sub-ordinate to those of the bondholders in the event the company is liquidated. Furthermore, bondholders are more likely than preferred shareholders to continue receiving disbursements during hard times (Brigham & Gapenski, 1994).

The right to vote is given to preferred stockholders in limited situations, such as when the board of directors fails to pay a required dividend over a specified number of quarters. Preferred stockholders can also vote on issues affecting their status when dividends are in **arrears**.

The conversion privilege attached to some preferred stocks can be a very attractive feature. Assume that Sport Manufacturing Company (SMC) issues a preferred stock that can be converted two to one. Such a provision means that one preferred share can be exchanged at a given time for two common shares. Assume that SMC's common stock is selling at $20, but management decides to raise $5 million by selling 100,000 shares of preferred stock at $50 par value. At the $50 price, it would *not* be worthwhile to convert the preferred stock to common stock. However, if the common stock subsequently rises to $30 a share, it would be advantageous to convert the preferred stock to common stock (Bogen, 1966); the shareholder would receive two common shares valued at a combined $60, while his initial investment was only $50 per preferred share. This results in a $10 profit from the conversion.

If the conversion had occurred when the common shares were valued at only $20 per share, the shareholder would have lost $10 in the conversion process. Thus, conversion typically occurs only when the conversion process will increase the investor's return. If preferred shares are not converted to common shares, they can continue to pay the required dividends, or they might be called. Preferred shares could be issued with a **call provision**. The call provision might require that 2% of the shares be retired each year. A **sinking fund** could be established to help pay for buying back the preferred shares. Under a 2% buyback plan, the preferred shares would mature in a maximum of 50 years.

Preferred stock can also pose a risk if certain provisions are attached that might help sell the stock but can also be utilized as a weapon. In one case, a small meatpacking company sold preferred stock with a condition that no bonds could be issued without the approval of 75% of the preferred stockholders (Bogen, 1966). Although the restriction was onerous, management thought it would be a valuable tool to help sell the stock to skeptical buyers. Years later when the company needed funds for expansion, it discovered that a larger competitor had purchased more than 25% of the preferred stock and could block the proposed sale of new bonds. This situation forced the smaller company to merge with the larger company on unfavorable terms.

SHAREHOLDERS' RIGHTS

In the United States, the basic rights and obligations of stockholders are set forth in the laws of the state in which the business is incorporated. Incorporation is the formal process of applying to be registered as a stock-issuing corporation, and each state has different laws. A disproportionately large number of businesses are incorporated in several states, including Delaware and Nevada, as a result of favorable tax or liability laws designed to attract corporations. Besides being spelled out in specific state laws, stockholders' rights can also be found in the corporation's bylaws, charter, or articles of incorporation.

Stockholders have the following legal rights (Bogen, 1966):

- To receive evidence of ownership such as a stock certificate (see figure 9.1)
- To transfer the stock freely, within limited rules
- To exercise the right to vote in person or by proxy as set forth in the corporation's bylaws
- To receive dividends and other disbursements on a pro rata basis according to the number of shares held
- To receive disbursements on a pro rata basis when a partial or complete liquidation of corporate assets occurs
- To bring action on behalf of the corporation against board members who do not act in the corporation's best interest (commonly referred to as stockholders' derivative actions)
- To obtain information from the corporation to help safeguard the stockholders' investment (such as an annual report)
- To subscribe pro rata to new shares of company stocks when authorized by law (commonly referred to as stockholders' preemptive right)

Figure 9.1 Example of a stock certificate.

Reprinted by permission of the United States Basketball League, Inc.

As an owner of the business, a stockholder has the right to participate in profits earned by the company if the board of directors approves such a payment. Whether to issue a dividend is a very important decision for the board. If a dividend is declared, most investors see that decision as a sign that the business is doing well since the business is able to cover its internal fiscal needs and still has extra money available to pay the shareholders. In contrast, some investors and analysts may view paying a dividend as a sign that the business has no good investment prospects in which to reinvest its additional capital.

The board of directors is responsible for making the final determination as to where the extra funds, if any, should be invested; and it is assumed that these decisions are made with the shareholders' interest in mind. The board of directors is elected by the shareholders to run the company on behalf of the shareholders. A successful board does more than just pay dividends to shareholders. A board is judged successful according to whether or not its decisions increase the stock's value.

The **preemptive right** is one of a stockholder's most important rights. Preemptive rights protect a stockholder's power of control and prevent dilution of the stock's value. Suppose investor A owns all 1,000 shares of outstanding stock in the Stars of David, and the shares are valued at $100 each. The market value of the company would be $100,000. If the company sold an additional 1,000 shares at $40 each, the total market value would be $140,000. When the total value is divided by the total shares, the stock value drops to $70 per share. To prevent such a loss for the prior investor and to prevent a windfall for new investors, the preemptive right gives investor A the right to buy the new stock before anyone else.

The right to exercise control over a business is one of the primary purposes of the preemptive right. If you own 10% of the business, you are entitled to purchase 10% of the newly issued shares. This gives you the right to exercise the same amount of control over the business that you did before, even if new shares dilute the total number of outstanding shares. The right to control a corporation is one of the most basic stockholder rights, since if you have an investment in something you want to be able to protect that investment.

There are several ways stockholders can control a corporation's direction. These include voting power, holding companies, and defensive tactics.

VOTING POWER

A major right for corporate owners is the right of certain stockholders to control the corporation through their voting power. Stockholders have the right to elect board members who then hire the company's management team. Smaller companies may have their major shareholders serving as owners, board members, and even managers. Larger businesses have board members who are elected for several-year terms only, to allow the opportunity to elect new board members. Board members are typically elected annually. Each shareholder is entitled to one vote for each share held. Control can be exercised by a large shareholder such as Mr. Jacobs, who controlled 99% of the Cleveland Indians' voting stock when they were publicly traded. Others can also exercise control: a block of family members who own significant shares in a business, a group of unrelated investors (from individuals to banks, corporations, foundations, and pension plans) that own a large voting bloc, a board member who might wield coercive control over fellow board members, or even bankers or financiers who can exercise considerable control.

Regardless of who is in direct control, most larger businesses with traded stocks rely on the proxy process for voting on key matters such as electing new board members or changing the business' bylaws or articles of incorporation. A proxy is basically a power of attorney given by a registered stockholder, who appoints someone else to vote on her behalf. Proxies are regularly mailed to all stockholders before the meeting of the board of directors.

The Securities and Exchange Commission (SEC) has very detailed laws to ensure equality and a democratic voting process for all shareholders of voting stocks. Thus, some regulations cover the process of hearing dissenting opinions or proposals and the requirement that management summarize these proposals in its proxy solicitation statement (Bogen, 1966). Although proxy fights typically do not occur on a regular basis, they can occur for a business in transition or one facing financial peril. A proxy fight can also occur when one company is trying to take over another company. A strong philosophical rift between key members of the management team can also lead to a proxy fight. Stockholders can be contacted by a marketing company that has been hired to try to sway their vote through letters, newspaper advertisements, or, in the case of large shareholders, personal phone calls.

HOLDING COMPANIES

Besides controlling the board of directors, parties can obtain control by investing in a company. A company that has one million outstanding shares can be effectively controlled by anyone who purchases 50.01%

of the voting stock. Thus, a company can purchase 50.01% of another company and then effectively control the purchased company. A company does not even need to use its own money to acquire a controlling interest. In fact, some companies have been leveraged through another company, such as a holding company, that utilizes the financial resources of the company it is trying to control to help issue bonds or nonvoting preferred stock in order to help finance the purchase. Through this technique, a holding company can purchase controlling shares of several different businesses. The Smiths, for example, could purchase a majority share of several fitness clubs to develop their own fitness network without having to purchase each club in its entirety. Thus, the Smiths could grow without spending the money to buy each club they want in their network.

DEFENSIVE TACTICS

Other businesses or individuals often purchase sport businesses. These transactions are often very amiable, as when private parties purchase the shares of a publicly traded company. This was the scenario when Larry Dolan purchased the publicly traded Cleveland Indians, buying the outstanding shares of the team from Jacobs and other shareholders for $323 million (Kurdziel, 2000). But not all purchases or attempts to change a corporation are welcomed. An unwelcome attempt to purchase the shares of a company is called a **hostile takeover**. Hostile takeovers can be vigorously defended against, with significant funds being paid by each side or even several suitors trying to win a bidding war. Other times, a takeover might still be hostile, but if the acquired company does not have the resources to fight, it could be forced to accept the takeover without any recourse. However, most hostile takeovers are fought in court or financial markets if the company was not able to implement any defensive tactics.

If a company cannot change its board or acquire other companies to make itself less attractive as a takeover option, it can utilize other techniques to appear less desirable for a hostile takeover. **Golden parachute** contracts requiring huge payments to executives if they are terminated can make a company less attractive. If a potential suitor discovers it might be necessary to pay an extra $20 million to former executives, a deal can quickly die.

Stock purchase **warrants** can also be utilized as a defensive tool. Warrants that can be exercised at a price not much higher than the current market price can help discourage efforts by outsiders to acquire control. As an outside company attempts to buy shares on the open market, the price of the shares will continue to rise. However, management can buy shares at the fixed warrant price, which will allow them to purchase more shares. The mere fact that management has such an option can dissuade a potential hostile takeover. The potential for a takeover can also be affected if the corporation is in financial trouble and stockholder assistance is necessary in order for it to survive or a suitor is needed to save it from bankruptcy.

Although shareholders can benefit from profits paid out through dividends, shareholders can also face losses that diminish the value of their investment. Stockholders cannot be punished or forced to pay more money if the business faces economic losses, but the share value can decline or the company can go out of business, rendering the stock valueless. Shareholders, much like any other business owner, have responsibilities for business losses. As discussed in chapter 4, shareholders are not personally liable for a corporation's debts, but they can be asked to contribute additional funds to keep the corporation from going bankrupt. Although no shareholder can be forced to purchase additional shares, they sometimes purchase additional shares to see if they can help the business through rough times.

GOING PUBLIC

The first step for any corporation is deciding whether to go public. The decision is not simple; in fact it is very expensive and time consuming. Chapter 4 (and the sidebar on p. 159) outlines the advantages and disadvantages of the corporation as a legal entity.

Besides the advantages and disadvantages of going public, specific advantages and disadvantages are associated with financing through the issuance of common stock (see sidebar on p. 160).

The second step, after a corporation decides to go public, is to determine whether the stock will be publicly traded. Going public is the process of making a company's ownership available to new potential owners and investors. However, just because a company has issued stock and has gone public does not mean the shares will be available to the general public. Whereas most large corporations are publicly owned and traded, small corporations are often owned by only a few shareholders, such as family members. Numerous stocks are privately held, or closely held, with only a few owners. Publicly held stocks are made available to an unlimited number of investors as long as shares are available for purchase.

The company also has to decide whether it wants the shares listed on a major exchange or wants to have unlisted shares traded on the over-the-counter (OTC)

Advantages and Disadvantages of Going Public

Advantages

- Owners are allowed to diversify their investments instead of having all their assets locked into the company.
- A liquid asset is created (a privately held company would be harder to sell).
- Going public helps raise new cash for growth.
- A value for the company is established based on the combined value of outstanding shares.

Disadvantages

- Increased operating costs are associated with all the quarterly and yearly reporting requirements.
- The company is required to disclose sensitive data that a competitor can use against the business.
- Self-dealing and nepotism are not allowed.
- There is a risk that the value of shares will drop if the market for the shares is slow and they are not traded enough, or if the company or its sector falls into disfavor.
- Loss of control of the business is possible if investors acquire enough stock.

Data from Brigham and Gapenski, 1994.

market. Some companies might prefer to avoid some regulations imposed by larger listing exchanges and thus will opt for being unlisted. To be listed, a company has to pay a small fee and meet an exchange's minimum entrance requirements. The company also needs to examine who the potential investors are. Institutional investors, such as pension funds or insurance companies, own about 55% of all common stocks and account for 80% of all stock transactions (Brigham & Gapenski, 1994).

Once a decision is made to sell shares to the general public, the shares will go through three possible phases. The first phase is the **initial public offering (IPO)**, when shares are sold on the new issue market. The first time shares are ever sold is called the **private offering**. The purpose of the IPO is to raise new capital for the business and to put money into the owner's hands. Once shares have been sold during the IPO, the shares move into the second phase, the secondary market. In the secondary market, stocks are bought and sold for all publicly traded businesses after the IPO. The first day SMC's stock was issued, the stock was part of the new issue market. Any subsequent transactions would occur in the secondary market, with one exception. If SMC decided to issue more shares, these shares would move into the third phase. The third phase is the primary market, which exists for companies that have already had an IPO but want to issue more shares to generate additional funds.

New shares can be sold to five possible types of buyers:

- Existing shareholders on a pro rata basis
- Investment bankers, who will then sell the shares to the general public in an IPO
- Several major purchasers in a private placement
- Employees in an employee stock purchase plan
- Buyers in a dividend reinvestment plan

Selling shares to existing shareholders is fairly simple and entails letting shareholders know when the shares will be available and at what price. Shareholders then have the opportunity to indicate whether they will subscribe. This is called **preemption**. Through preemption a shareholder has the first right to buy new shares. Shareholders value this right because it prevents share dilution. For example, if you own 10% of Nike you hold significant power. If Nike were to issue several million more shares to expand (such as to help pay for building a new factory), you could maintain your 10% stake by purchasing 10% of the new stocks. However, if you pass on making this purchase, the new shares will result in share dilution, so your stake in the company might decline to 7% or 8%. This also means you have fewer votes at shareholder meetings.

Investment bankers operate as intermediaries to help facilitate the marketing and transfer of stock ownership. A large investor such as a mutual fund or a pension fund might contact an investment banker to secure a large position in an IPO. These large buyers

Advantages and Disadvantages of Financing Through Stock

Advantages

- There is no fixed cost associated with issuing stock, whereas a company that issues bonds or commercial paper (see chapter 10) will have to allocate a fixed amount in the budget for debt service.
- Common stocks do not carry any fixed maturity date at which they need to be paid.
- Issuing common stock can help raise new capital without affecting the company's bond rating.
- At times, such as when interest rates are low and the demand for bonds is also low, it is easier to sell common stock.

Disadvantages

- Issuing bonds or commercial paper provides a predictable fixed cost for repayment in contrast to stocks, which represent a stake in the company's future profits.
- The costs associated with issuing stocks and all ancillary activities can make issuing common stock more expensive than issuing preferred stock or debt instruments.
- Some investors may see issuing new stock as a negative sign that the company needs to sell more of itself in order to survive.

Data from Brigham and Gapenski, 1994.

often indicate in advance that they are interested in purchasing shares. Thus, the issuing corporation knows in advance that a certain minimum number of shares will be purchased through the investment bankers.

A private-placement transaction occurs when one or more investors purchase most shares in a company. One advantage of such a sale is the lower flotation costs associated with trying to find potential buyers, since one major potential shareholder is already identified. Flotation costs are the costs to sell shares to the general public. If a major purchaser is identified in advance, then less effort and cost need to be expended because a majority of the shares are already sold. Another major advantage is the ability to circumvent the SEC requirements, since shares do not need to go through SEC registration. Although the prospects of gaining a large partner are great, private placements do not comply with SEC requirements, so it is often hard to sell the shares except to another large investor or institutional investor. Private placements are discussed in greater detail later in this chapter.

Employees can obtain an equity interest in their place of employment by buying shares in the company. The process in which employees buy stock in a company is often referred to as an **employee stock ownership plan** (ESOP). In these plans, the company often uses its own profits to buy shares for the employees. Over time, enough shares are purchased

that the employees eventually own the company. Since Congress believes it is an important goal to allow employees the right to buy into their employer, the federal tax code provides specific benefits for companies engaged in ESOPs. Besides being able to deduct the interest on debt used to acquire the stock, a company can deduct some of the principal used to acquire the stock and can also deduct the dividend payments made to the employee stockholders. In addition to the tax benefits, an ESOP can help prevent takeovers by other firms because the employees own a significant number of shares.

Another benefit of an ESOP is that it can replace the employee retirement program. Thus, instead of pouring millions into a pension fund, the company can issue and then buy shares for its employees. The employees obtain a valuable asset that will hopefully increase over time, and the employer obtains a new avenue for selling additional shares. The final benefit associated with an ESOP is the potential for increased employee morale. Employees are more prone to work harder when they know their productivity will benefit themselves fiscally. If employees work harder and generate increased income, the company benefits; and as owners, the employees will also eventually benefit.

Although ESOPs provide significant benefits, they can also have some disadvantages. The biggest disadvantage is the dynamic shift in power within a business as employees become owners.

Initial Public Offerings

A record number of IPOs produced unprecedented results in 1999. In 1975, only 12 IPOs were issued; during the first day of trading, the average return was a net loss of 1.5%. By 1990, there were 111 IPOs, which produced a first day's return of 10.5%. In 1999, 485 IPOs were launched, with a net average return the first day of 69.5%. Eighteen of these IPOs had their shares increase more than 1,000% during their first year. These dramatic increases do not always produce wonderful results for small investors, however. Typically 80% to 90% of the shares in an IPO are sold to institutional investors, so individual investors have not been able to reap these grand returns ("Doors to IPOs," 2000).

In the fourth quarter of 2000, the total number of IPOs was 56, with a total value of $15.1 billion. By the fourth quarter of 2001, the economic downturn significantly affected the marketplace for IPOs, and the number was down to 26, with a total value of $10 billion ("Q4 IPO Scorecard," n.d.). By 2006 the IPO market had heated up again, and there were 198 IPOs raising over $43 billion. Although the numbers were not as significant as those from several years earlier, the value was more significant, and some of the names behind the IPOs were significant, such as Hertz rental car company.

Assembly line workers who are used to being told what to do might now have a say in how the CEO acts. Labor negotiations can become very tricky because management must try to produce a fair labor agreement with union workers; but the union workers might also be shareholders, and the more money paid in salary, the lower the profits for the company. The government (Department of Labor) can also cancel an ESOP if it was designed to fight a takeover and was not properly developed. Another concern arises in relation to retirees and pension holders whose entire **portfolios** might be composed of shares in the company. As long as the company is doing well, everyone will be happy. However, if the stock declines, the result can be devastating. A retiree could see his portfolio decline from $500,000 to $100,000 if the stock loses 80% of its value as a result of a negative industry analysis, for example.

A **dividend reinvestment plan** allows a shareholder to transfer all dividends back into the company to obtain more shares.

Assume, for example, that the Stars offer such an opportunity. Say the team paid a $0.50 dividend in a given quarter, and you had 20 shares and reinvested the dividend to purchase additional shares. If the shares were selling for $10 each at that time, you would receive one additional share rather than a dividend check for $10.

Since the math usually does not involve round numbers such as these, a shareholder normally obtains a percentage of a share. Thus, in a given quarter a shareholder might receive 0.756 of a share through dividend reinvestment. After the next dividend amount is reinvested, she might have built up to one complete share and started working on the next complete share.

PROSPECTUS

Before making a stock offering, the issuer or underwriter needs to develop a **prospectus** describing the company and all the potential risks and benefits associated with purchasing the stock. The prospectus often contains information on key employees and members of the board, information on how the funds will be used and the products that will be sold, audited financial statements, the sales forecast, pro forma budgets, the dividend policy, and related documentation. The audited financial statement, prepared by an independent accounting firm, describes the business and the management structure and explains what the managers are paid, who the principal shareholders are, what the underwriting agreement is, and who is involved in the stock sales syndicate.

The SEC has to approve the prospectus before it can be sent to potential investors. However, the issuer or underwriter has the opportunity to distribute rough drafts of the prospectus prior to SEC approval to help generate investor interest. The preapproved document is called a **red herring**. The red herring, along with company executives, is then shopped around in a marketing blitz by the underwriter through visits with potential major investors such as institutional investors. Significant oral information can be passed on in this process, but no written material other than the prospectus can be given, and no sales can be made at these meetings. Once the SEC obtains all the necessary information, it can approve the prospectus for general distribution.

SELLING SHARES

Stocks have value only if they are purchased. New issues need to be priced at a level that will interest potential investors. If the stock is priced too high, investors may see this as a sign that the stock "is out of their league." Other investors will see a high issue price as a sign of value. In contrast, people may perceive a low price either as an indication of an inferior company or as an attempt to garner ownership from smaller investors. Traditionally, stock prices for new issues are based on the average price of similar stock issues (Spiro, 1996). Issuing new shares for existing stocks is simpler because the current market value for the shares can be utilized as the benchmark price. If investors believe the stock is correctly valued, they can purchase at the offering price or wait to see if investors bid the price up or down.

Current stockholders, institutional investors, investment bankers, potential investors, or even current employees can purchase stocks. Current stockholders might be the first choice for many corporations; some laws require that current shareholders have the first right to buy stocks in order to maintain their pro rata interest in earnings, assets, and voting rights. The process of offering stocks first to existing shareholders is called a "privileged subscription." Shareholders often find this privilege a very important benefit, similar to receiving dividends.

Shareholders are given a right to subscribe to shares before they are offered to the general public. These shares are normally priced a little lower than the price at which the general public could purchase the same shares. The right might allow a shareholder to purchase one share of the new stock for every three shares of existing stock owned by the shareholder. However, shareholders do not need to purchase stocks through the right and can in fact sell their rights on the open market to others who would like to buy new shares at a lower price. No matter who exercises the right, the right becomes valueless after the subscription date expires.

 If the Stars offer current shareholders the right to buy one unit of new stock for every five units they currently own, such a right would normally vest (expire) after a set period such as three months. If the right is not exercised in that time period, the right is extinguished, and any desired new shares would have to be purchased at their market price.

Although subscription rights can help ensure some purchases from dedicated investors, there are no guarantees for the issuer. Issuing stock can be like throwing a party—all the key individuals may be there, but perhaps no one will be there. To ensure that the stock is sold, an issuing company often utilizes the assistance of an investment banker to underwrite the stock offering. An underwriting is similar to an insurance policy. If sales are good and all the shares are bought, then the investment banker will not have to purchase any shares. However, if sales are mediocre, the investment banker may need to purchase a significant number of shares. The investment bankers charge either a commission or a set fee for their services. Investment bankers often attempt to sell stock concurrently with the issuing company to hedge the prospect of their having to buy a large number of shares.

Investment bankers are the primary vehicle for independent sales. The services offered by investment bankers or investment houses include the following (Bogen, 1966):

- Giving advice on the security type to offer and the exact terms of the issue
- Giving assistance in underwriting a security issue
- Purchasing a security issue outright
- Helping a company comply with state and federal requirements
- Distributing new securities to investors
- Helping stabilize the price of a new issue by buying shares in the marketplace to support interest in the issue
- Providing additional advice after a security is issued

PRIVATE PLACEMENT

Private placement can occur in the borrowing market (the bond market, in particular) as a loan is obtained from private parties. Similarly, private placement can occur with the issuing of stocks when stocks are sold by at least one institutional investor. Life insurance companies have been involved in numerous private placements because of their strong **purchasing power.** Companies that issue stocks are often interested in pursuing private-placement sale of their shares because this allows them to avoid some SEC rules and to drastically reduce the marketing costs.

Since the SEC knows that companies would like to avoid stringent rules if possible, it has developed a two-part test for private offerings. The first is a consideration of the potential investor's sophistication. The investor must have enough knowledge to understand the risks and rewards inherent in the offering. The second component is a limitation of potential buyers to a maximum of 35 investors. Private-placement securities have other restrictions such as being restricted from resale to the public market for at least two years. Private placements are covered in greater detail in the next section.

REGULATION D AND SMALL CORPORATE OFFERING REGISTRATION (SCOR) OFFERINGS

Although professional teams or larger conglomerates can issue stock without significant difficulty, smaller companies often think a potential stock offering is unattainable. This misconception can deprive businesses of significant potential capital. Pursuant to federal securities laws, companies that wish to raise under $1 million in any given 12-month period are excused from certain burdensome requirements such as registering the security or submitting an audited financial statement. An audited financial statement can cost up to $100,000 and even more for larger companies needing or wanting to comply with Sarbanes-Oxley and other corporate laws (Evanson, 1998, January). This exemption is found in the Securities Exchange Act, Regulation D, Section 504; sales of such shares are commonly called Regulation D or 504 offerings. Because of the risks associated with these stocks, the company selling them cannot publicly sell or advertise the shares. Although federal laws govern these offerings, the issuing corporation still needs to comply with the incorporating state's laws. Colorado, Florida, and New York have some of the least restrictive laws for such offerings (Evanson, 1998, January). The keys to a 504 offering involve

- contacting the security commission in the issuing state to determine what rules apply,
- analyzing what financing structure can fit within the confines of the applicable laws, and

- hiring competent professionals (accountant, lawyer, or financial consultant) to help with the process (Evanson, 1998, January).

If the Smiths pursue this route to finance their fitness center, they will need to complete a Form D with the SEC, which would qualify them for 504 status. Once they complete the three steps just listed, Bob and Cheryl can contact the NASDAQ Bulletin Board to get their shares quoted and ultimately traded on the OTC Bulletin Board. The Smiths will probably think they are in the big time—their company will now be publicly traded. All investors and potential investors have a more positive feeling when a national market exists for buying and selling shares. It should be noted, however, that bulletin board stocks tend to be less liquid than stocks listed on an organized exchange because of less frequent trading.

The key to issuing any Regulation D, SCOR, or private-placement offering is providing sufficient warning to potential investors about the potential risks inherent in the stocks. The disclosure information shown on pages 164-165 is adapted from a real offering.

The sample disclosure information was targeted to accredited investors. The SEC allows smaller offerings such as private-placement offerings to be conducted with no registration requirements at the federal level as long as the securities are sold only to accredited and nonaccredited investors. An offering can be made to an unlimited number of accredited investors. Accredited investors must fall into one of the following categories (Cheeseman, 2001):

- Anyone with a net worth of at least $1 million
- Anyone with an annual income of at least $200,000 for the previous two years who reasonably expects to earn $200,000 in income during the current year
- Any corporation or partnership with over $5 million in total assets
- Insiders of the issuing company such as directors or officers
- Certain institutional investors such as pension plans or registered investment companies

Nonaccredited investors are persons who do not meet this definition. A private-placement or SCOR

Disclosure information for Smith's Fitness Center (adapted from a template for a real offering)

Smith's Fitness Center

THE SECURITIES OFFERED HEREBY HAVE NOT BEEN REGISTERED UNDER THE SECURITIES ACT OF 1933 (THE ACT) OR THE SECURITIES LAWS OF ANY STATE AND ARE BEING OFFERED AND SOLD IN EXEMPTIONS FROM THE REGISTRATION REQUIREMENTS OF THE ACT AND SUCH LAWS.

THE SECURITIES OFFERED CURRENTLY WILL ONLY BE OFFERED TO "ACCREDITED INVESTORS" AS SUCH TERM IS DEFINED IN RULE 105 OF THE ACT AND THE SECTION HEADED "INVESTORS."

THE SECURITIES OFFERED HEREBY INVOLVE A HIGH DEGREE OF RISK, AND INVESTORS SHOULD NOT INVEST ANY FUNDS IN THIS OFFERING UNLESS THEY CAN AFFORD TO LOSE THEIR ENTIRE INVESTMENT. SEE "RISK FACTORS AND OTHER IMPORTANT CONSIDERATIONS." IN MAKING AN INVESTMENT DECISION, INVESTORS MUST RELY ON THEIR OWN EXAMINATION OF THE ISSUER AND THE TERMS OF THE OFFERING, INCLUDING THE MERITS AND RISKS INVOLVED.

NO PERSON HAS BEEN AUTHORIZED TO GIVE ANY INFORMATION OR MAKE ANY REPRESENTATION NOT CONTAINED IN THIS BUSINESS PLAN, AND ANY INFORMATION OR STATEMENT NOT CONTAINED HEREIN MUST NOT BE RELIED ON AS HAVING BEEN AUTHORIZED BY THE COMPANY. THIS BUSINESS PLAN HAS BEEN PREPARED SOLELY FOR THE BENEFIT OF PERSONS INTERESTED IN THE OFFERING AND MAY NOT BE REPRODUCED OR USED FOR ANY OTHER PURPOSES. THE DELIVERY OF THIS BUSINESS PLAN DOES NOT IMPLY THAT THE INFORMATION CONTAINED HEREIN IS CORRECT AS OF ANY TIME SUBSEQUENT TO ITS DATE.

Summary of Offering

Smith's Fitness Center, Inc. ("the Company") is offering shares of Common Stock $0.001 par value ("Common Stock") pursuant to this offering on the following terms:

- The offering is intended to raise $2,000,000. This offering is not subject to receiving subscriptions for any minimum amount.
- The minimum investment is $50,000.
- The Company intends to accept subscriptions for shares of Common Stock in amounts in excess of $2,000,000 in this offering at its sole discretion. This offering is not subject to a maximum number of shares of Common Stock being sold.

Use of Proceeds

The proceeds from this offering will be used for the following purposes:

- Purchasing existing fitness facilities or renovating warehouse space into new fitness facilities
- Hiring athletic trainers and employees to work in sales and finance
- Purchasing or leasing exercise equipment
- Ongoing working capital requirements

Investors

The shares of Common Stock are being offered only to "accredited investors," as such term is defined in Regulation D promulgated under the Securities Act of 1933. Accredited investors are investors who either

- had individual income in excess of $200,000 in each of 1998 and 1999 or joint income with their spouses in excess of $300,000 in each such year and have a reasonable expectation of reaching the same income level in 1999 or
- have an individual net worth (together with their spouses) in excess of $1,000,000.

These standards represent minimum requirements for investors and do not necessarily mean that these securities are a suitable investment for any investor meeting these requirements. See "Risk Factors and Other Important Considerations." Moreover, the Company reserves the right to reject subscriptions in whole or in part for any reason.

The Company has established a minimum purchase requirement of $50,000. The Company may, however, in its sole discretion, accept a subscription for less than the minimum requirement.

Restrictions on Transfer of Offered Securities

The Common Stock is not registered under the 1933 Act or the securities laws of any State ("State Acts"), and the Common Stock may not be resold unless it is subsequently registered under the 1933 Act and any applicable State Acts, or an exemption from such registration is available. Holders of the Common Stock have no right to require such registration, and the Company has no plans to register its securities. Shareholders may thus be required to retain their investment in the Common Stock for an indefinite period. Each certificate representing shares of Common Stock sold in this offering will bear a legend setting forth certain restrictions on transferability.

In addition, the securities laws of certain states may require that additional restrictions on transferability be imposed on securities sold in such jurisdictions and that additional restrictive legends be placed on the certificates representing the Common Stock.

Foreword

This Business Plan and Financing Memorandum ("the Business Plan") has been prepared by Smith's Fitness Center, Inc. ("SFC" or "the Company") to convey information about the Company and its plans.

The financial and sales projections contained herein are considered by SFC management to be reasonable. Management believes that the statements regarding the uniqueness and value of the Company's strategy are accurate as of the date of the Business Plan. The financial projections and statements contained herein constitute the baseline set of the Company's objectives for the near term but should not be relied on as a promise or representation of future performance.

This Business Plan is being made available to a limited number of accredited investors that are assumed to be familiar with the risks of investing in start-up enterprises, capable of evaluating these risks, and capable of protecting their own interests.

No person other than the officers of the Company has been authorized in connection with this Business Plan to give any information or to make any representation not contained herein. This document is not to be reproduced or distributed without the express written permission of AIM management.

For more information, contact

Bob Smith
President
SFC, Inc.
123 Anystreet
Anytown, CT USA
555-555-5555 phone
555-555-5556 fax

---

offering can have no more than 35 nonaccredited investors. Nonaccredited investors must have a certain level of investing sophistication or be represented by an adviser such as a lawyer or accountant. A company cannot advertise to the general public in order to attract nonaccredited investors.

Although the SEC tries to reduce registration rules for smaller offerings, that does not mean there are no other possible regulations. Under SEC Rule 144, any security sold pursuant to a private-placement or SCOR offering must be held by the buyer for at least one year from the date when the securities were purchased. These regulations are lifted after two years. However, between the first and second years there are additional restrictions on how many shares can be sold at any given time (Cheeseman, 2001). The following securities have no registration requirements and can be sold without significant regulation (Cheeseman, 2001):

- Government-issued securities
- Short-term notes that mature in less than nine months
- Securities offered by nonprofit issuers such as youth sports organizations
- Insurance and annuity contracts issued by insurance companies
- Securities issued through a corporate reorganization in exchange for prior securities

In addition to 504 offerings, the Smiths could utilize a Small Corporate Offering Registration (SCOR) offering. These are available in every state except Alabama, Delaware, Hawaii, and Nebraska (Evanson, 1998, January). A SCOR offering might present a good opportunity for Bob and Cheryl to offer their stocks in several states if they are interested in raising less than $1 million annually. However, the Form U-7 requirements for a SCOR offering are so complex (even though only 50 questions are asked) that the Smiths would be better off filing a full-scale IPO and raising more than $1 million. Although the form is complex, it was designed for business owners to complete rather than an army of attorneys (Reynes, 1998, May). The Smiths could attempt to raise $200,000 to $400,000; but the cost associated with raising that sum, including personnel hours, would be between $30,000 and $120,000 (Reynes, 1998, May). Although this appears to be a large chunk of the money raised, it should be noted that a large **public offering** by a major corporation could cost between 15% and 25% of the amount raised. Besides the personnel hours needed to complete the SCOR forms, a filing fee is required that could range from as low as $200 to a high of $2,500 for registration in California (Reynes, 1998, May).

The SCOR filing process might be complex, but the SCOR marketing options have been simplified, so the Smiths could advertise for investors in the newspaper, by direct mail, or even over the Internet (Reynes, 1998, May). Furthermore, SCOR offerings are more attractive than venture capital infusion; people with venture capital might want to have decision-making powers, impose certain rules, or both.

INITIAL PUBLIC OFFERING

No matter what offering option is chosen, the business needs to hit the primary market with an IPO to launch its stock activities. The IPO can range from informal to very formal, depending on the stock offering. Before an IPO can be undertaken, the business needs to formalize its existence as a corporation. Corporation issues are covered in detail in chapter 4. However, we note here that a business' articles of incorporation specify how many shares can be issued. The corporate bylaws might specify how shares can be transferred and when shareholders can inspect the corporate records, as well as delineate similar rules affecting issuing and selling shares (Cheeseman, 2001).

For a full-scale common stock issue, a company first must file a registration statement with the SEC. The registration documents are very lengthy and require considerable time and expense to complete. The SEC can suspend or prohibit the offering if it finds any statements that are misleading or inaccurate. After filing for registration, the company and its underwriting syndicate of investment bankers distribute a preliminary prospectus. This prospectus could provide as follows:

> *A registration statement relating to these securities has been filed with the SEC but has not become effective. Information contained herein is subject to completion or amendment. These securities may not be sold nor may offers to buy be accepted prior to the time the registration statement becomes effective. This prospectus shall not constitute an offer to sell or the solicitation of an offer to buy, nor shall there be any sale of these securities in any state in which such offer, solicitation, or sale would be unlawful prior to registration or qualification under the securities laws of any such state. ("IPO Basics," 1999)*

After the preliminary prospectus is issued, the company's top officials must go on a road show to promote the stock sale. During this time the SEC reviews the registration and might request additional information. If the SEC approves the registration, the company and its syndicate need to establish a price and the number of shares that will be sold. The final prospectus and any necessary amendments are distributed when the stocks are made available to the public. The IPO closes when the money is received and the stock certificates are delivered. This usually occurs around three days after trading has started. It takes approximately two to three and a half months from the start of the IPO process for the money to be received ("IPO Basics," 1999).

The decision to issue stocks is not something to be taken lightly. The costs are normally very steep. But also, it is not enough just to determine that a stock offering is the proper direction for a company. The company also has to determine what priority will be given to stock. This prioritization can be seen in preferred stock and the various rights given to different classes of shareholders.

FAILED OFFERINGS

Every year, many companies go out of business. Even companies that have issued stock can face financial troubles. Publicly traded companies that flounder can find themselves being delisted by one of the exchanges. In 1998, Golden Bear Golf, a company primarily owned by Jack Nicklaus, faced some hard times, including suits by shareholders claiming the company had underreported 1997 losses by $20 million (Mullen, 1998). Furthermore, the company's assets had decreased so that it no longer met the

NASDAQ capital requirements (at least $4 million in assets), and it was delisted. **Delisting** meant the shares would no longer be traded on NASDAQ; shareholders would have to trade their shares on the less prestigious OTC Bulletin Board or the pink sheets (the least formal trading market for NASDAQ, which handles shares that are very infrequently traded, such as private-placement or Regulation D shares) ("Nicklaus Company's Stock," 1998). When the stock had been initially offered in 1996, the company was able to raise $37 million. Golden Bear sold its string of golf centers in 1998 and then shut down Paragon, the golf course construction subsidiary that had generated the questionable accounting practices. After the restructuring, the company was taken private in 2000, when it was bought by Nicklaus and his family ("Golden Bear," n.d.).

Although the Golden Bear example focuses on a sport-specific stock and no other large publicly traded sport companies were delisted since, 17 publicly traded Internet companies were delisted by 2006. Some sport companies such as the Boston Celtics are no longer traded on exchanges, but that was a voluntary exit from an exchange. Delisting refers to the process of kicking a stock out of an exchange because it failed to meet exchange requirements.

Common or preferred stocks are sold when a company is interested in selling ownership or equity rights to others for needed funds. The primary benefit of such an approach is the elimination of the need to pay a set interest payment even during rough times. However, many companies do not want to dilute their ownership interest and prefer to finance growth through debt instruments. We have already discussed bank loans and various types of nonbank loans. An additional strategy for stronger companies such as the Stars or SMC would be to issue bonds, which we discuss in the next chapter. It should be noted that nonprofit organizations such as the University of Milford, West Hartford Badminton Club, public schools, and public park and recreation departments cannot issue common stocks, but they can issue bonds and obtain additional funding from other sources.

INCREASING STOCK VALUES

After selling shares, a corporation and all the employees are responsible for increasing the stock's value. One of the foremost benefits associated with purchasing stocks is the potential for increased equity value. If the business is doing well financially, it increases in value. A business increases in value through a rise in the value of its shares.

As noted previously, the success of any management team is based on the extent to which it can increase a stock's value and provide dividends to the company's owners. You can examine this success by looking at the company's PE ratio, the ratio of the stock price to the company earnings. A high ratio indicates that a company's stock is selling for much more than the per share earnings. A stock with a high PE ratio reflects strong investor demand, but the company has not produced significant enough revenue to justify the high stock price. Thus, a "hot" stock can have high PE ratios until its earnings meet expectations or the share prices decline. If the earnings of such a company decrease, the value of the stock could plummet, thus greatly affecting the PE ratio.

The rapid rise in the stock market during 2000, propelled by Internet companies, provides such an example. Most prominent stocks in the largest traditional companies were trading at 20 times their earnings in 1999. Similarly, the top NASDAQ shares in 1995 were trading at 20 times their earnings. However, the demand for Internet stocks and the low earnings of Internet companies pushed the PE ratios of the NASDAQ-100 to around 90 times earnings in March 2000 (Browning, 2000). At the same time, the PE ratio for Standard & Poor's 500 was around 25 and for the Dow was around 20. The PE ratio of the World Wrestling Federation (now WWE) in February 2002 was 19.07 (Yahoo! Finance—WWF, 2002).

Price–earnings ratios can show significant fluctuation. Yahoo had a PE ratio of almost –1,000 at the start of 1999 and then had shot up to over 2,000 just one year later (Browning, 2000). By 2002, Yahoo's PE ratio had settled at 236.71 (Yahoo! Finance—YHOO, 2002). Stocks can change quickly over the years. A stock might increase so much in value that the company can split the stocks so they are not as expensive. This happened with some of the Internet stocks that were trading in the several-hundred-dollar days. Although WWE was trading at a PE ratio of 25.29 in 2007 (compared with 19.07 in 2002), Yahoo stocks had undergone significant changes, and their revenue also skyrocketed so that by 2007 the PE ratio was 36.82 (compared with 236.71 in 2002).

Shares can go up in price on the basis of a multitude of factors. One primary category affecting stock prices is external factors. Examples of external factors that can affect the value of professional sports teams include the following:

- Antitrust decisions affecting the league
- Labor disputes and unwillingness of players to cross the picket lines to play
- Environmental regulations affecting the arena

- A change in workplace safety rules that apply to operating the team
- New rules related to employment practices in the workplace, such as the classification of food vendors as employees rather than independent contractors
- The folding of a rival league or the success of another league

Stock prices can also be affected by internal strategic policy decisions. Examples of such decisions include whether to

- trade a star player or hire a new coach,
- increase the number of preseason games,
- borrow money for expansion or issue more stocks,
- declare a dividend, and
- consolidate television and radio broadcasting operations in-house.

Teams that go public sell shares for an attractive price (normally under $25 per share) in odd lots to fans who wish to buy a few shares and frame the certificate as part of a sports memorabilia collection (Much, 1996).

The Cleveland Indians made a splash in the stock market, but they were just as quickly taken off the market. The Tribe's shares were doing well in the 1999 baseball season until the team lost in the division series. The day after the series ended, the stock declined 4.9% ("Go Figure," 1999). Several days later, a deal was announced in which an Ohio attorney (Larry Dolan) agreed to buy the team for $320 million, including assuming $35 million in debt (Walker, 1999). The planned purchase to take the Indians private only two years after they had gone public would mean a significant windfall for shareholders. At a price of over $22 per share if the purchase was approved, shareholders could have earned a 50% return on their investment in less than two years (Walker, 1999). The reward was worth the wait for investors who initially purchased shares for $15 each but then saw the stock drop to $10 per share for several months until the team's primary shareholder, Jacobs, announced his intent to sell.

Publicly traded professional teams are found throughout the world. The country that most recently saw a team open itself to public ownership is Germany. The owners of Germany's 1995 and 1996 champion soccer team, BV Borussia 09 Dortmund, voted to become a corporation and issue stock to the public. Publicly traded soccer teams already exist in England and Holland. In fact England has a "Kick-Index" that tracks 20 soccer stocks in the United Kingdom. The index reached its highest point in 1997, but through 1999 it declined 35%. The only team that has shown financial strength is Manchester United, which was worth about a billion dollars before the 2000 market crash ("German Soccer," 1999). This value was proven in 2005 when American Malcolm Glazer purchased Manchester United for more than $1 billion, including debt, and delisted the team.

Although it is typically financially strong companies that are interested in launching an IPO, some businesses try to take advantage of a strong stock market to offer an IPO that might not be all that strong. For example, a San Diego A-league soccer team, the Flash, filed preliminary documents with the SEC to go public. The announcement came even though the team was losing money (more than $795,000 in the first six months after going public), had attendance of around only 3,000 per game, and had $67,196 in the bank (Palazzo, 1999). By 2002, the shares were trading for $0.17 each ("Stock Quote," 2002). That was the last year of the club in its publicly traded state; it was resurrected a year later as a private group playing in a lower division.

Sport entities besides professional teams also issued stock in the late 1990s to take advantage of the IPO craze. Although numerous Internet-based companies were the primary beneficiaries of such IPOs, traditional businesses were also successful.

Sponsorships Increase Stock Values

Is sponsoring a major professional league worth the investment? A sales increase is one positive indicator, but stock values can also increase. According to a 2005 study, sponsoring a professional league can result in increased stock prices for the sponsors. The study examined 53 publicly traded companies whose stocks gained $257 million in market value ($13.6 billion in economic value) in the first trading week after announcing sponsorship deals with the NBA, the NFL, the NHL, MLB, or the PGA (Howard, 2005). Companies sponsoring the NFL or MLB had slight gains (due to the high costs of such deals) versus larger spikes for sponsoring the other leagues. Smaller companies, those with smaller market shares, and those products with a clear connection to the league being sponsored had larger increases in stock value (Howard, 2005).

The Influence of Internal and External Factors on Publicly Traded Sports Organizations

Internal and external factors have played a part in the success and failure of several publicly traded sports organizations (Much, 1996):

- The Cleveland Cavaliers went public in 1970 for $5 per share, but shares dropped to as low as $0.50 per share in 1982. The team went private in 1984 for $1.25 per share.
- The New England Patriots went public in 1960 for $5 per share and went private in 1976 for $15 per share.
- The Baltimore Orioles went on a roller-coaster ride in the 1970s, with their stock price ranging from $8 to $25.50. In 1979 the team went private, with liquidation value earning shareholders $49.60 per share over a three-year period.
- The Milwaukee Bucks went public in 1968 for $5 per share and went private for $12 per share 11 years later.

WWF (now WWE) raised almost $200 million in a 1999 public offering, fueled by its success in such programs as "Raw is WAR" and "Smack Down" on national television ("Ready to Wrestle," 1999).

Some people purchase shares in publicly traded sport businesses to impress their friends. The Green Bay Packers' shares are an excellent example of such a purchase, since the shares issued in 1997 have very little value on the open market (see next section).

Other stocks have more value, but it might be harder to place a value on these shares other than the actual market value. However, ancillary benefits can be significant. For example, people who own shares in Tribune may have purchased them for their investment value but also in order to be eligible for the annual shareholders games at Wrigley Field for the Tribune-owned Chicago Cubs (Newberry, 2001).

SPORT STOCKS

Stock offerings in professional sport are not new. The Green Bay Packers sold their first 1,000 shares in 1923 for $5 each (Lascari, 1998). However, in 1935 the company went into receivership and was reorganized as a Wisconsin nonprofit stock corporation; it then issued another 3,000 shares at $5 each. In 1950 the Packers had another stock offering that raised $118,000. By 1997 there were 4,627 stockholders, who were given 1,000 shares for every share owned, which resulted in 4,627,000 shares outstanding. After amending their articles of incorporation, the Packers were able to sell an additional 5,373,000 shares. A fourth sale was consummated in 1997, with each new share selling for $200 plus a handling fee of $15 (Lascari, 1998).

Significant restrictions prohibited almost all transfers of the new stock except back to the Packers for $0.025 per share, to family members as gifts, or as a bequest after death. Additional rules prohibit a stockholder from making any profit or even receiving a dividend. Furthermore, to comply with NFL rules, each stockholder had to pledge that he or she had not been involved in any litigation alleging fraud, had not been convicted of a felony, and had not participated

© Getty Images

Purchases of Green Bay Packers stock are mostly for show, as each share has very little value on the open market. But, to die-hard Packers' fans, the value lies in the experience.

in sport gambling. Even with all these restrictions, the Packers sold 120,000 shares and raised over $24 million. Most purchasers bought the stock as a novelty to claim ownership in the Packers.

As noted previously in this chapter and in chapter 1, several teams are attempting to cash in on the interest of sports fans to sell parts or all of their teams to the general public. Some stocks have done very well, while others have not. For example, the Cleveland Indians went public (a limited ownership right with very few voting rights) in 1998 at an initial price of $15 a share, which correlated to a team value of $232 million. However, within seven months the stock had fallen over 50% and was trading at $7.13 a share, which translated to a team value of approximately $113 million (Much & Phillips, 1999). Each of the four million class A common shares was entitled to one vote. However, the 2,281,667 class B shares, all owned by the owner of the team, were each entitled to 10,000 votes (Lascari, 1998). Thus, Jacobs retained 99.98% control of the company and was entitled to elect the entire board of directors.

The Indians were unusually lucky with the timing of their stock offering. The year the Indians went public, they went to the World Series. The prospectus, which showed income through December 31, 1997,

highlighted $140 million in revenue and $22.5 million in net income (see figure 9.2) (Much & Phillips, 1999). These numbers were very much inflated; almost 90% of the income that year came from postseason and nonbaseball activities. If interest income, gains from player transactions, league expansion proceeds, and postseason income are removed from the team's net income, the net income drops to $1.76 million (Much & Phillips, 1999).

The $15 per share IPO, which implied a $232 million franchise value, priced the stock at 131.7 times the adjusted earnings from regular-season revenue (Much & Phillips, 1999). By pricing themselves so high, the Indians provided virtually no opportunity for price appreciation. Thus, when the 1998 revenue numbers were published for the quarter ending September 30, showing a 37% increase in third-quarter operating profit, the stock price barely budged (Much & Phillips, 1999). As previously mentioned, Larry Dolan purchased the team in 1999 for approximately $320 million.

Stocks in professional teams have had a mediocre reception from the investing public. "Pure-play" investments that include only a professional sports team have several major problems, such as seasonal revenue streams, potential labor strife, limited invest-

Evolution of the Celtics

The Boston Celtics went public in 1986 when 40% of the team was sold for $18.50 per share. As of 1998, 5.3 million shares were outstanding and owned by more than 50,000 shareholders (Lascari, 1998). Unlike the Packers' shares, which are not approved by the SEC or covered by any federal or state laws, the Boston Celtics' shares (publicly traded from 1986 to 2002) complied with all federal laws and were openly traded on the New York Stock Exchange. The team's symbol on the NYSE was BOS. (Symbols for companies instead of company names are shown on ticker systems that display the most recent share prices.)

The Celtics have gone through several major changes over the years, including purchasing and selling radio and television stations. In 1998 the stock underwent additional changes forced by legislative requirements. The Revenue Act of 1987 required that a limited partnership (a business structure similar to that of the Celtics when the team was formed) be taxed at the partnership rate. On the basis of a grandfather clause, the Celtics' limited partnership would be taxed at the corporate rate beginning July 1, 1998. In June 1998, the Boston Celtics Limited Partnership reorganized into two separate entities:

1. Boston Celtics Limited Partnership II, which was formed to remain on the NYSE and be taxed as a corporation
2. Castle Creek Partners, which was formed as a nonpublic entity with "pass-through" tax treatment (Much & Phillips, 1999)

Each stockholder had a choice of an interest in either entity. There were 2,703,364 publicly traded units of a master limited partnership that could be traded on the New York Stock Exchange. Unlike common stock, which could entitle the owner to an equity position (ownership) in the team, the units were only claims against the company's cash flow. In September 2002, the Celtics were bought for $360 million and once again became a privately owned team (Frost, 2002).

	($000)
Reported net income	22,570
Interest income, net of interest expense	(2,371)
Gains on player transactions	(2,696)
League expansion proceeds	(9,286)
Playoff game revenue	(5,700)
Pretax income (adjusted to highlight only traditional revenue)	**2,517**
Pro forma income taxes	(755)
Pro forma adjusted net income	**1,762**

Figure 9.2 Cleveland Indians' 1997 adjusted net income.
Data from P. Much and J. Phillips, 1999, *Sports teams and the stock market [Marketing letter]* (Chicago, IL: Houlihan Lokey Howard & Zukin).

ment liquidity, reliance on other business owners to generate a product, and intense media and government scrutiny (Much & Phillips, 1999). A pure play refers to a corporation that participates in only one industry segment. For example, the Celtics and the Indians were exclusively sports teams and thus were a pure play. In contrast, a blended company could encompass a team and other unrelated businesses; an example is the Florida Panthers hockey team and their resort holdings. Other examples include diverse companies such as Disney, Tribune, Comcast, and Time Warner.

Although a **pure-play stock** offering for a team might not be a sound investment option for stockholders other than the primary team owner (because of significant risks), "blends" can produce more significant revenue streams through the addition of other revenue-producing units to a professional team. In the case of the NHL's Florida Panthers, additional units were combined with a pure play, producing a comprehensive business entity capable of utilizing additional revenue to offset potential losses associated with a professional team. In 1996, Florida Panthers Holdings (parent company of the NHL's Florida Panthers—NYSE: PAW) sold 7.3 million shares of class A stock to the public, and team owner H. Wayne Huizenga retained 5.3 million shares (Much & Phillips, 1999). The shares sold for $10 each, which valued the team at $126 million.

Shortly after issuing the stock, the company evolved from just the team to a diversified leisure and recreation company that included six resorts, an arena management company, two ice rinks, and one golf facility. This growth was funded through additional stock sales that increased outstanding shares from 12.6 million in 1996 to 35.1 million in 1998. Compared with the sport segment, the company's leisure and rec-

reation side brought significant economic prosperity to the parent company. Table 9.1 presents the revenue, operating income, depreciation, and cash flow for the company's two divisions in 1997 and 1998.

As highlighted in table 9.1, the $235 million increase in revenue produced by the resorts helped offset the continued losses incurred by the sport side of the company. However, the marriage between the leisure and sport divisions would be short lived; management at the 1998 annual meeting announced the potential to spin off the sport division into a separate public company (Much & Phillips, 1999). A spin-off would indicate that in this particular attempt at blending, the company was not successful. In fact, in 2001, the team portion of the business was sold to concentrate the corporate efforts on the resort and property management side of the business. With the Panthers out of the corporate umbrella, former owner Huizenga concentrated his efforts on the resort side of the business and changed the **stock symbol** (ticker symbol) to RST (Boca Resorts), which is still publicly traded ("Panthers' New Ownership," 2002).

The Panthers are not alone in their inability to fully develop a blended structure. Poor performance has also hounded Ascent Entertainment Group, which owned several businesses including the NHL's Colorado Avalanche and the NBA's Denver Nuggets. On the basis of double-digit losses for years, Ascent's parent company, Comsat Corporation, divested its remaining interest in Ascent in 1996. Ascent suffered operating losses of $42.4 million in 1997 and was facing even larger losses in 1998 (Much & Phillips, 1999).

In 1999 the Colorado Avalanche and Denver Nuggets were tentatively sold, along with their arena, for $400 million, with the buyer assuming some debt associated with the arena ("Two Denver Franchises,"

Table 9.1 Florida Panthers Holdings' Financial Highlights

1997 ($000)			
	Sports	Leisure	Total company
Revenue	36,695	17,567	54,262
Operating income	(10,533)	4,053	(8,379)
Depreciation	4,239	1,459	5,698
Cash flow	(6,294)	5,512	(2,681)
1998 ($000)			
	Sports	Leisure	Total company
Revenue	43,586	252,603	296,189
Operating income	(17,503)	52,769	25,452
Depreciation	5,168	17,950	23,155
Cash flow	(12,335)	70,719	48,607

Data from P. Much and J. Phillips, 1999, *Sports teams and the stock market [Marketing letter]* (Chicago, IL: Houlihan Lokey Howard & Zukin).

1999). The sale did not go unchallenged; a potential suitor sued, saying that Ascent shareholders would make more money from a different offer to buy the team and that a potential conflict of interest had not been made public (Lewis, 1999). After several suits were filed, the teams were resold. The original buyers returned with a $450 million offer, which appeared to be enough to close the deal ("Wal-Mart Heir," 2000). The teams (as well as the Denver Avalanche and the Pepsi Center) were eventually purchased for $450 million by Stanley Kroenke ("Owner," 2002).

In addition to pure-play and blended professional sport-related corporations, another variation has emerged recently—a vertically integrated combination whereby the sports team benefits other corporate units. Some examples of such combinations are Walt Disney (Mighty Ducks of Anaheim), Tribune (Chicago Cubs), and Fox Entertainment Group (Los Angeles Dodgers and a minority interest in the New York Knicks, New York Rangers, Los Angeles Lakers, and Los Angeles Kings) (Much & Phillips, 1999). The Ducks and Dodgers have subsequently been sold. These vertically integrated combinations have proved to be much more effective than pure-play sport businesses because the broadcasting arms of each company can generate significant sport advertising income without having to pay significant fees for broadcasting rights.

The history of sport stocks is reminiscent of a roller coaster. With strong interest in IPOs in the late 1990s, several more teams are considering public offerings. However, investor interest appears to be waning on new sport issues. If a team or other business does not have the ability or interest to pursue a larger public offering, it can still sell stock through a smaller stock offering such

as a Regulation D or SCOR offering, discussed earlier in the chapter.

CONCLUSION

The ability to reach more potential investors is a major advantage for a company issuing stock. Investors who might never express interest in a company might be willing to gamble and invest a small amount in order to be part of the ownership team. Large mutual funds could also purchase a high number of shares. No matter who owns the shares, a publicly traded company has greater access to capital than almost all nonpublicly traded companies.

Teams such as the Boston Celtics, Cleveland Indians, Florida Panthers, and Green Bay Packers have all flirted with issuing stock to the public or are still publicly traded because of the potential for significant capital enhancement. Furthermore, large sport businesses such as Nike, Disney (Anaheim Ducks, ABC, and ESPN), and WWE cannot grow without the capital infusion afforded by issuing stock.

Although shareholders have some obligations and significant rights, a publicly traded company needs to comply with numerous regulations and reporting requirements, which can make the decision to go public unattractive—regardless of how much money could be raised. In fact, because of the often very quick decisions that need to be made in sport, public ownership may not be an attractive option. If the issuance of stock is not available as a capital acquisition tool, a company can entertain the idea of issuing bonds (see chapter 10) or other instruments to borrow funds.

CLASS DISCUSSION TOPICS

1. How many people in your class own stocks?

2. Have you ever purchased stocks yourself or been given stocks? If you purchased them yourself, what factors went into buying those shares?

3. Have you ever thought about buying stocks? Have you ever researched them?

4. Would you ever buy any sport stocks? Why or why not?

5. What sport stocks would you consider purchasing? Why?

6. Would you invest in a mutual fund? Why or why not?

7. Have you ever lost money on an investment? Explain what happened and what you learned from the process.

8. Do you think it is a good investment to buy the publicly available shares in the Green Bay Packers?

9. What key facts about a stock might make you think it would be a good investment idea?

10

BONDS

CHAPTER OBJECTIVES

After studying this chapter, you should be able to do the following:

- Understand how issuing bonds creates a fixed-cost solution to raising funds.
- Describe the types of bonds that are available and how they are secured.
- Understand how a company repays bondholders.
- Understand the dynamics of using government-issued bonds to finance sports facilities.
- Describe capital structuring through various examples.

In chapter 8, we consider short-term funding through bank loans and other capitalization techniques such as venture capital. Chapter 9 covers equity ownership through stocks as a means of raising capital. This chapter focuses on a tool utilized by both the private and the public sectors—bonds. A **bond** is an obligation that needs to be repaid with interest, similar to a loan from a bank. The difference is that bonds are typically issued by larger corporations or government entities with a good repayment history and are sought after by investors because of either favorable interest rates or tax benefits. The high desirability of these bonds creates a market for their purchase and sale that is similar to the stock market. Thus, bonds have the financing characteristics of loans (covered in chapter 8), as well as a market in which they can be bought and sold, like stocks (covered in chapter 9).

This chapter first looks at the types of corporate bonds available, the costs associated with issuing such bonds, and various repayment methods. Next, we consider government bonds utilized to finance stadium and arena construction and related projects; this section highlights the various types of bonds issued by government entities and how they are issued. The last part of the chapter presents an example of a strategy in which various capital acquisition techniques are combined, then examines concerns associated with raising too much or too little capital.

CORPORATE BONDS

Bonds issued by businesses are often referred to as **corporate bonds** because bonds can normally only be issued by the largest corporations. Similar to a mortgage loan, a mortgage bond is a bond backed by specified real estate. If the bond issuer defaults, the **bondholders** can foreclose on the property and sell the property to satisfy the claim.

A bond is similar to a long-term loan in that it is a contract under which a borrower agrees to make specified interest and principal payments on specified dates for a specified time period. Every bond has some restrictions attached. These restrictions (called bond covenants) are similar to typical contract terms that limit both parties. A company issuing bonds might attach restrictions that allow the company to pay a lesser amount if the investor tries to redeem the bond before its maturity date. Similarly, investors might demand restrictions on a company to protect their investment. These restrictions could include limiting the extent of acquisition activity and capital spending, requiring minimum levels of liquidity, restricting a company's right to issue additional equity, and limit-

ing the size of the debt–equity ratio.

In addition to the bonds already discussed, there are convertible bonds (discussed later in this chapter) and warrant bonds (not included in the scope of this book); income bonds that pay interest only when income is earned; indexed bonds whose interest rates increase if inflation rises (the index typically tracks a well-regarded index such as the **consumer price index**); and **zero coupon bonds** or original issue **discount bonds**, which carry no interest rate but are originally sold at a price lower than **par value** and appreciate in value over time (Brigham & Gapenski, 1994).

A type of bond that was popular in the 1970s and 1980s was the **junk bond**. In the late 1970s, Michael Milken of Drexel Burnham Lambert analyzed the often overlooked area of junk bonds and concluded that riskier bonds paid a higher return compared with other bonds. He concluded that junk bonds were a strong investment even though they were associated with significant risk.

On the basis of his analysis, Milken convinced more institutional investors to buy risky bonds, and the market for junk bonds was born. These high-risk, high-yield bonds were often utilized in **leveraged buyouts** in which a company used debt instruments to help buy other companies. Ted Turner offered to buy CBS by offering CBS shareholders junk bonds for their shares. The shareholders balked at the offer, which then fizzled and disappeared. However, numerous savings and loans invested in other junk bonds, which helped usher in the savings and loan collapse. But savings and loans were not the only victims. Drexel Burnham Lambert was also forced into bankruptcy in 1989, and Milken was jailed for his activities (Brigham & Gapenski, 1994).

Milken faced a 98-count federal indictment alleging such acts as bribery, insider trading, and stock manipulation. These all stemmed from Milken's interest in pushing the often riskier junk bonds. He plea-bargained to six counts of minor securities violations, including involvement with a client who failed to make Securities and Exchange Commission (SEC) disclosures. Even though the case was very weak, it appeared that the judge was trying to send the message that bond manipulation would be strictly scrutinized, and Milken was sentenced to 10 years in prison, but released after two years (Wanniski, 1991).

BOND FINANCING

Individuals often do not appreciate how important it is to choose the right funding vehicle for a business. If an owner makes a quick decision and the business has some poor years, the debt obligation could turn a strong investment into a fiscal disaster. But even with the downside associated with a financial obligation that can last more than 30 years, bonds have significant positive attributes (see sidebar).

Other factors that affect a business' decision to issue bonds include the general business environment and the prevailing interest in the specific business that is issuing bonds. If interest rates are generally low, then every business may have difficulty issuing bonds. But if a specific business is facing a potential hardship, it may be impossible for that business to issue bonds. For example, if a labor dispute arises within the players' association, the Stars might face a difficult market in which to issue their bonds even though other businesses may not be having a problem in this regard. One way of avoiding such a problem is to provide some type of pledge to guarantee repayment (e.g., by issuing a secured bond).

SECURED VERSUS UNSECURED BONDS

One disadvantage of **secured bonds** is related to a corporation's ability to control secured assets. If an asset is secured, by the terms of the security agreement the corporation does not have exclusive use of the asset and might need to obtain approval before using the asset for various activities. Unsecured bonds provide the greatest flexibility for the issuing corporation but minimal protection for the bond purchaser. A secured bondholder receives preferential treatment over subsequent bondholders, whether those subsequent bondholders are secured or unsecured.

Various types of secured bonds can be issued. Collateral trust bonds are secured by stock or other bonds. The collateral security is deposited with a trust company, which holds the assets for the bondholders' benefit (Bogen, 1966). An equipment trust obligation is a secured transaction whereby a corporation can acquire equipment under a collateral bill of sale. Title to the equipment does not pass to the corporation until the obligation has been paid, and a trustee retains title to the equipment until the obligation is **discharged**.

In another type of arrangement, a second corporation, in addition to the original issuer, can guarantee a bond; and these guaranteed bonds can be very marketable if the backing corporation has an excellent credit rating, because the bondholder has two guarantees for repayment—the original issuer and the guarantor. Guaranteed bonds are often issued in cases in which a large corporation is helping a small company expand and there is an existing or intended working relationship between the companies. For example, a professional sports team might guarantee the bond issued by a minor league affiliate. In another type of situation, similar to that with guarantees, a larger corporation can purchase a smaller corporation and assume the bond obligations incurred by the smaller corporation.

DEBENTURES

A **debenture** is an unsecured bond, meaning there are no assets to secure the bond (guarantee repayment) if the bond issuer defaults. Normally, because of the lack of protection for debenture bondholders,

Advantages and Disadvantages of Bond Financing

Advantages
- Interest on bonds is tax deductible (versus stock dividends, which are not deductible).
- Bond financing can be reasonably inexpensive for an established company with a good credit rating.
- There is a strong, established market for trading and issuing bonds.

Disadvantages
- Interest is a fixed charge that needs to be paid regardless of whether income was or was not earned.
- The principal loaned amount must be paid in full when the bond matures.
- Issuing bonds can harm a company's credit rating and make it more difficult for the company to borrow money in the future.
- If the bond is secured by collateral, a corporation might not be able to sell or otherwise dispose of the asset without bondholder approval.
- Bondholders have the upper hand whenever a company declares bankruptcy.

only companies with the best credit rating can issue such bonds. Although debenture bonds are generally unsecured, there are several techniques to extend protection to such bondholders. To provide investors with additional security that a debenture will be repaid, some companies issue **subordinate debentures**. These bonds provide some security because assets are pledged to back them. However, claims on these assets are subordinate to senior claims against the assets.

For example, a mortgage bond issue could be secured by SMC's equipment, and any amount of the equipment value that is not securing the mortgage bond issue (senior claim) can be used to secure repayment of the subordinate debentures. Assume that SMC backs a $10 million mortgage bond issue with property valued at $15 million. SMC issues subordinate bonds in the amount of $10 million several years later, after the property has appreciated. However, if SMC were to file for bankruptcy protection, their land and buildings would be worth only $16 million. The mortgage bondholders would recover their $10 million. The subordinate bondholders are still in a better position than unsecured creditors because there is still $6 million from the assets after the mortgage bond is satisfied. The $6 million would go to the subordinate bondholders, who would probably be paid on a pro rata basis ($600 for each $1,000 bond they held).

Debenture bonds can be issued with clauses to protect investors. In a covenant of equal coverage, the debenture bond is treated as equal to a secured mortgage if a mortgage is ever obtained in the future. Thus, both the mortgage and debenture bonds would be secured. Additionally, a debenture can be issued with a specific condition that no dividends will be paid to

An Unusual Way to Secure a Bond

In 1998, in an effort to acquire considerable cash in advance of his actual payday, Chicago White Sox slugger Frank Thomas, working with a New York City investment banking firm, was attempting to raise $20 million. The money would be raised through an offering of bonds in Thomas' name backed by his guaranteed annual salary of $7 million per year through 2006. The bonds would have probably paid a rate of approximately 9%. It was assumed that Thomas could earn more than 9% by reinvesting the $20 million somewhere else. Otherwise, borrowing the money would be no benefit to him ("Thomas Secures," 1998). However, shortly after an attempt was made to launch the bond, the idea was scrapped because there were too many inhibitive conditions in the player's contract, such as a morals clause, that could limit repayment. Furthermore, players can lose their entitlement to compensation if they are injured in a non-team-related event or if players go on strike; and in this case, Thomas would lose his entitlement to compensation if he decided to take the bond money and not play anymore (Kaplan, 1998, November). Since 1998, Thomas has often been injured and performed sporadically at times, which justifies the nervousness of potential investors back in 1998.

However, in 2006 the 38-year-old slugger led the Oakland Athletics with 39 homers and 114 RBIs. Thomas has hit .305 with 487 homers and 1,579 RBIs in 17 major league seasons, 16 with the Chicago White Sox. His success with the Athletics prompted the Toronto Blue Jays to reach a tentative deal with the slugger for the 2007 and 2008 seasons. Under the $18.12 million contract, Thomas receives a $9.12 million signing bonus, a $1 million salary in 2007, and $8 million in 2008. The deal includes a $10 million vesting option for 2009 that would become guaranteed if Thomas makes 1,000 plate appearances in the next two seasons or 525 plate appearances in 2008 ("Blue Jays Sign Thomas," 2006).

In February 2001, William Andrews securitized the remaining $5 million he was owed by the NFL's Atlanta Falcons. Andrews had last played in the NFL in 1996. But, as part of his playing contract, he was owed $200,000 per year over 25 years. Instead of waiting for these annual payments, Andrews decided to take the deferred compensation and sell it in the form of a bond to Hanleigh, a sport insurance company. Hanleigh paid $2 million to Andrews for the right to the future compensation stream. This marked the first sale of a bond securitized by an individual athlete's deferred compensation in the history of professional sport. Although the $2 million is only 40% of the amount Andrews was to be paid over the next 25 years, the securitization gave the athlete immediate access to a large sum of money. He then had the ability to invest and grow that $2 million. The transaction was overseen by NDH Capital, a small Connecticut financing company (Kaplan, 2001).

stockholders unless such moneys are derived from future earnings or unless the corporate assets exceed liabilities by a specified amount (Bogen, 1966).

Regardless of the asset used to secure a debt instrument, the security helps increase the instrument's liquidity, lowers the cost of capital to borrowers, and helps develop greater efficiency through the financial marketplace (Brigham & Gapenski, 1994). Thus, whether the Smiths pledge their home to secure a mortgage or the Stars use contractually obligated revenue from their broadcasting contract, the security helps seal the deal and allows the flow of needed capital.

Whether they are secured or unsecured, bonds are covered by a contract called an indenture. The indenture is issued to a trust company that acts as a trustee for the bondholders. The indenture has to follow specific SEC guidelines related to the trustees and their duties: Trustees must have no conflict of interest and must have financial responsibility, make periodic reports to bondholders, provide appropriate default notice, protect bondholders after default, and fulfill related obligations (Bogen, 1966).

Most bonds are **bearer bonds**, with the bondholder retaining possession of the bond document. Bonds typically have **coupons** attached to them that the bondholder can redeem at her bank on a semiannual basis to receive the specified interest payment. Such bonds are called coupon bonds. Coupon bonds are the easiest to transfer to other potential purchasers because the person in actual physical possession of the bond is entitled to redeem the coupon. In contrast, a registered bond is issued in the name of the bondholder. If such shares are transferred, the registered bondholder needs to endorse the bonds to the new owner, and the new owner has to have his name added to the corporate books. Because of the registration requirement, such bonds are less marketable.

Some corporations have issued income bonds during reorganizations or in exchange for preferred stock. Income bonds pay interest only if the corporation earns income. If no income is earned, no interest is paid. Such a contingency requirement reduces the fixed costs that would normally be allocated for paying the interest on a coupon or registered bond. Thus, if a company is facing rough financial times, it does not need to worry about paying interest to the bondholders. This frees up a significant amount of money to help the business staff in operation. However, when the company starts turning a profit, it is required to start paying interest to the bondholders. An indenture specifies the formula for calculating the required payments under an income bond. One rule typically applied to income bonds is that the interest is cumulative. This means that if interest is not paid in a given year because income is low, it must be paid the next year, when there is more income, along with the interest for that next year.

ISSUE SIZE AND MATURITY

One of the primary concerns associated with bonds is determining the appropriate interest rate to attach to the bonds and determining how many bonds should be issued. When corporations are seeking millions of dollars, they do not resort to guesswork to determine the appropriate interest rate. Long- and short-term forecasting becomes a serious matter—a difference of one-tenth of a percentage point can cost millions in interest or may make an offering so unattractive that no one purchases the issue.

There are several agencies that rate bonds, such as Moody's Investors Service and Standard & Poor's. These entities examine the bond issuer and determine the potential for default based on various factors such as revenue stream to repay the bonds, current economic conditions, interest rates, and past repayment history. After analyzing all the relevant criteria, the rating agency establishes a rating for a bond. The highest rating is typically AAA or Aaa depending on the agency. Bonds with such a rating have the lowest risk for default and do not need to pay as high an interest rate. Bonds that have a low rating are sometimes classified as junk bonds and need to pay a much higher interest rate to attract investors. Even if Moody's and Standard & Poor's give a bond a high rating, the potential for default always exists. Investors would not have considered Enron bonds high risk, but they turned out to be. Thus, the potential for default needs to be considered; the riskier the bond, the higher the interest rate needed to attract potential investors.

To help reduce the potential disasters associated with choosing an inappropriate interest rate, corporations appraise the supply and demand for money, which affect interest rates. Interest rates represent a true example of supply and demand in that if there is a glut of money on the market, whether as a result of government actions or strictly market forces, interest rates are lower than when there is a smaller money supply. However, if the money supply is tight, interest rates are higher because more corporations are fighting to obtain scarcer funds, and the competition bids up the interest rates.

The demand for long-term funds arises from four major sources: mortgage borrowing, corporate bond financing, state and local government bond financing, and long-term U.S. Treasury borrowing (Bogen,

1966). The various entities that have money available and those that need funds are all affected by the Federal Reserve. As discussed in chapter 3, the Federal Reserve can control the supply and demand and affect interest rates through monetary policies. The Federal Reserve tends to relax the money supply during recessionary times and restrict money during prosperous times. Such a strategy is designed to foster stable growth without significant fluctuation (Bogen, 1966).

The suppliers for long-term funds are very diverse; they include (Bogen, 1966),

- life insurance companies,
- savings and loan associations,
- mutual savings banks,
- commercial banks that might acquire bonds,
- insurance companies (fire, property, and casualty),
- corporate pension funds,
- state and local government retirement funds
- union retirement plans, and
- mutual funds that purchase bonds.

COSTS OF ISSUING BONDS

Although bonds can raise substantial funds, they are very expensive to issue. The primary cost associated with issuing bonds is the required interest payments. Such payments are due on a semiannual basis for as long as the bond is outstanding. A 20-year $100 million bond issued with 10% interest would require semiannual payments of $5 million for 20 years.

Another cost associated with issuing bonds is the discount or risk premium at which they are sold. The discount for the $100 million bond issue might be $5 million, which means the issuing or selling entity for the bonds would take $5 million (5%) as a fee to process and help sell the bonds. Every transaction is different, but the typical issuing fee for bonds is around 5%. This cost effectively increases the interest rate because the $10 million annual interest obligation is based on $100 million. So the company would still owe $100 million for the bonds but receive only $95 million after paying the fee. This added cost must be built into the bond's repayment schedule. Thus, the actual interest cost for such a bond would be 10.25%. The $5 million cost for the bond issue can be amortized over the bond's life by putting aside $250,000 a year for 20 years. Thus, the actual cost to the bond issuer is $10.25 million a year. Additional expenses could include legal fees for pre-

paring the indenture, recording the mortgage(s), and general legal advice, as well as marketing expenses.

The following case study is a good illustration of the importance of bond financing and the effect it can have on a company.

 **Sport Manufacturing Company**

Sport Manufacturing Company (SMC) has two million shares of capital stock and has earnings of 20% on sales before taxes (see table 10.1).

Although the company is interested in expanding sales, it realizes it needs to raise $6 million to double sales. Since stock is already outstanding, the company decides to sell $6 million in 5% bonds that would generate $300,000 in annual interest charges. The potential effect on stockholders is shown in table 10.2.

As the example shows, by issuing $6 million in bonds to expand sales, SMC is able to increase earnings 49% in a good year, from $319,000 to $475,000. However, the fixed charge of $300,000 can dramatically reduce earnings in a poor year because the interest expense needs to be paid regardless of business conditions (Bogen, 1966).

As the example highlights, bond financing exagger-

Table 10.1 Sport Manufacturing Company's Financial Highlights ($000)

	Poor year	Normal year	Good year
Sales	1,000	2,000	3,000
Expenses	800	1,600	2,400
Operating profit	**200**	**400**	**600**
Federal taxes	89	185	281
Profit after taxes	**111**	**215**	**319**
Earnings for stock	5.5%	10.7%	15.9%

Table 10.2 Sport Manufacturing Company's Financial Highlights ($000)

	Poor year	Normal year	Good year
Sales	2,000	4,000	6,000
Expenses	1,600	3,200	4,800
Operating profit	**400**	**800**	**1,200**
Interest on bonds	300	300	300
Profit after interest	**100**	**500**	**900**
Federal taxes	41	233	425
Profit after taxes	**59**	**267**	**475**
Earnings for stock	2.9%	13.3%	23.7%

ates the effect of sales fluctuations through the new fixed business expense. If the $6 million had been raised with an additional stock offering, the stockholders' earnings would be lower in good years, but there would be no potential **deficit** in the poor year.

If SMC decided to issue $6 million in shares of common stock rather than $6 million in bonds, the impact would be significant. In a poor year the operating profit would increase to $400,000, similar to what would happen with financing through bonds. However, with only two million shares outstanding, the earnings per share are 10% ($200,000 earnings divided by two million shares). Based on eight million shares and $400,000 in earnings, the earnings per share decrease to 5%.

LOAN REPAYMENT

Up to now we have looked at the types of bonds that can be issued. In this section we turn our attention to repayment and refunding mechanisms. Normally bond repayment occurs when the bond matures and the issuer repays all remaining obligations. Most bonds are redeemable when they mature. At that point the issuing company pays the bondholder the bond's cash value. Some bonds are redeemable at par, at the holder's option. The par value is the arbitrary initial value the bond was issued for and that helps establish its value. These bonds are often sold at a lower interest rate: If the prevailing interest rate for bonds is 10%, the redeemable bonds might pay only 9.5%. The lower interest rate is justified in that the bondholder has the option of redeeming the bond before it matures and is then able to take the proceeds and invest in another bond. If the interest rate increases, then the investor may want to take the proceeds and purchase a bond with a higher rate. However, if the interest rate declines, the investor still has a bond paying 9.5% interest.

Sometimes a company faces hardships that can force it to pay off the bondholders before maturity. If interest rates drop several percentage points, a company may not be able to afford the prior interest rate. Normally, changes in interest rates do not affect the maturity date, and the issuer is stuck with the higher rate. However, if the bond was issued with a call provision, the issuer can exercise the call provision after a specified number of years. The call allows the issuer to

pay the **face value** of the bond plus a fixed payment, such as a year's worth of coupon payments. Once a bond is called and paid, the company can issue new bonds at the lower interest rate. Callable bonds have higher interest rates than noncallable bonds to compensate investors for the risk of the bonds being redeemed by the issuer before they mature.

Repayment can be accomplished through the following techniques:

- Sinking funds
- Serial bonds
- Bond redemption before maturity
- Convertible bonds

SINKING FUNDS

The most common technique for repaying a note is to use a sinking fund in which moneys are set aside, either in preset amounts or on a variable basis. For example, the Stars of David could deposit a preset amount of $1 million a year into a sinking fund account. The amount can grow to well over $20 million in 20 years, and the funds can be used to repay loans, bonds, and notes as they mature. In certain instances, the price of a bond may decline because the associated interest rates are unfavorable. In those instances, the sinking fund account can be used to buy bonds on the open market and retire them at an earlier date (Bogen, 1966). This practice can save significant interest obligations.

Sinking funds can be created through various means. Annual payments of a fixed amount or a percentage of profit can also be utilized. Bonds issued for the purpose of acquiring fixed assets could also be retired through the establishment of a sinking fund using annual depreciation allowances for the asset. That means the tax savings associated with depreciating an asset can be set aside to repay the bond. No matter what approach is used, the key is that a sinking fund is a way to actually set aside funds to repay the bonds in the future—a much better approach than trying to obtain funds at the last minute.

SERIAL BONDS

Serial bonds are a series of bonds issued with maturity dates at predetermined redemption dates. These types of bonds could include $1 million in bonds due in 20 years, and a company can issue such bonds every year for a 10-year period so the bonds would need to be repaid in a series 20 to 30 years later. Serial bonds for a $50 million bond offering could include $5 million of bond obligations that mature in the 15th year, with increased retirement obligations in subsequent years until the final bonds are retired in the 30th year.

Serial bonds are often issued by states and municipalities, which have fairly reliable tax revenue. Since corporate revenue is more difficult to project in the long run, serial bonds are less popular as a way of meeting corporate funding needs. However, some corporations are willing to utilize serial bonds for short-term debt but utilize sinking funds for long-term obligations. Some corporations set equal serial maturities over several years and then provide a large balloon payment at the end. If a 10-year bond issue for $10 million was issued under this format, the corporation might have serial maturity of $400,000 a year for 9 years and make a final balloon payment of $5.5 million in the 10th year (Bogen, 1966).

BOND REDEMPTION BEFORE MATURITY

The sinking fund and serial maturation are just two techniques that companies can use to redeem bonds. Corporations can also issue newer bonds with more favorable interest rates and use the proceeds to buy older bonds on the open market. Numerous corporations issue bonds on a regular basis in an effort to take advantage of favorable interest rates and to avoid the potential impact if interest rates rise. Such bonds often have a call provision to allow the corporation to repurchase the bonds at a moderate premium if interest rates drastically change. Some bonds are **convertibles**, which means they can be redeemed when the bondholder converts the bonds to stocks (see the next section). Other bonds are retired through retained earnings, the selling of assets, or the issuing of more equity. If all these techniques fail, the corporation can ask the bondholders for a voluntary extension of the bond's maturity date.

As just mentioned, a corporation may issue callable bonds that it can repurchase before the maturity date. If a bond is not callable, there are two other means of repurchasing. The company can purchase a bond on the open market or from a bondholder who is willing to exchange it voluntarily. Note that even if a corporation issues callable bonds, the callable provision typically does not take effect on a 20-year bond until at least the 10th year. Until then, the bondholder is protected from an attempt by the corporation to call the bond any time interest rates decline or if the corporation attempts to issue new bonds with a lower interest rate. The protection against having a bond

called can encourage larger investors such as life insurance companies to accept a lower yield, on the express condition that a bond will not be callable.

CONVERTIBLE BONDS

Some corporations issue bonds that can be converted to common stock. These bonds are designed to redeem themselves and retire the debt through converting the debt to equity ownership. This approach increases equity ownership while reducing the total corporate debt. Reducing the corporate debt can dramatically increase the corporate credit rating, which can make it easier for the company to borrow additional funds or issue additional bonds. However, when a bond is converted to stock, it does not bring any new funds into the business but merely redistributes debt obligations to owners' equity.

Convertible bonds have some very strong benefits for both the issuing company and the potential bond buyer. Buyers often prefer convertible bonds because investors can obtain interest payments on their investment but can also choose to switch to the equity ownership option if the corporation starts to experience significant growth. Buyers might also prefer convertibles because they still retain the position of a secured creditor but also have an option to purchase stock. This might not be an important reason to purchase the bond, but if the stock price soars, it can suddenly become a key benefit.

Corporations can also benefit from convertibles. When bonds are converted, the conversion usually occurs at a share price that is higher than it would have been if the shares had been purchased earlier. Thus, if the conversion occurs, the corporation can lower its debt obligation by exchanging that obligation for shares that are valued significantly less on the corporate books. This helps the corporation because it can sell its own shares at a higher rate compared with the bondholder, who might buy stock on the open market that might not directly benefit the corporation. However, this benefit is also one of the primary reasons why some corporations do not want to issue convertible bonds. Some corporations do not want to dilute the stockholders' equity. Furthermore, since it is uncertain whether or when a bondholder might wish to convert bonds to stocks, convertible bonds add a degree of uncertainty to the corporation's capital structure.

Convertible securities are analyzed based on their conversion ratio. The conversion ratio (CR) represents the number of shares a bondholder will receive on conversion. Another important number is the conversion price (CP), which represents how much the company will receive when the bondholder purchases the shares. Assume that SMC issues a $1,000 bond that can be converted to 20 shares of common stock. The CR is 20, since 20 shares will be received. The CP is calculated with the following formula:

The CP can conversely be used to calculate the CR,

$$\frac{\text{par value of bond}}{\text{shares received}} = \text{conversion price}$$

$$\frac{\$1,000}{20} = \$50 \text{ CP per share}$$

as follows (Brigham & Gapenski, 1994):

The issuing price for a convertible security is nor-

$$\frac{\text{par value of bond}}{\text{conversion price (CP)}} = \text{conversion ratio (CR)}$$

$$\frac{\$1,000}{\$50} = 20 \text{ shares}$$

mally set at 10% to 30% above the prevailing market price for shares. Thus, the $50 CP would be appropriate if the shares were currently selling at the $35 to $45 price range. Most convertibles have fixed CPs and CRs for the bond's life. Some convertibles contain "step-up" clauses that allow the CP to increase over time. Thus, a bond could be issued with a $50 CP during the bond's first five years, with the CP able to rise to $55 per share thereafter. The step-up is allowed if the conversion instrument contains specific language authorizing the increased cost for converting the bond to shares.

Almost all convertibles have specific clauses designed to protect the convertible holder from stock splits (discussed later in this chapter) and the sale of common stock below the CP. If the sales price decreases, then the CP must also be lowered. If the CP for a convertible was stated as $50 per share and the stock was selling for $35 per share, there would be no incentive to convert. If the stock price rose, there would be an incentive. Conversely, if the stock value drops significantly and the company has to issue new shares at $25 each, the company will renegotiate the CP and reduce it to keep the bondholders happy. Similarly, if a stock split occurs and bondholders have the right to convert the bond to 40 shares at a CP of $20, they will receive 80 shares at $10 each if they exercise the conversion (Brigham & Gapenski, 1994).

Investors may not want to exercise a conversion, but a company can force a conversion if the bond issue had a call provision. Assume that SMC issues a $1,000 bond with a $50 CP, a 20-share CR, and a share price of $60, and the bond has a call price of $1,050. If SMC wants to exercise the call provision, the bondholder will have to calculate under which scenario he would make the greatest income. If he accepts the call, he will receive $1,050. If he converts the bond, he will receive 20 shares valued at $60 each, or a total of $1,200 (Brigham & Gapenski, 1994). Most investors would rather take the $1,200 even if they did not favor equity ownership, since they could always sell the shares on the market.

GOVERNMENT-ISSUED BONDS

Bonds are documents representing a loan agreement and specifying the agreement's terms. Corporations and government entities are the most frequent issuers of bonds. Thus, the Smiths are too small as a start-up to issue bonds; the badminton club is a nonprofit, and only the largest nonprofits are able to issue bonds. An example of a government entity that has issued a bond is our fictitious University of Milford. Government-issued bonds for building sports facilities have several unique attributes. Special laws, elections, or referendums are often required in order for the bonds to be issued. Once the legal hurdles have been overcome, numerous additional steps need to be taken, from entering into a lease agreement with a professional team to acquiring funds for infrastructure repairs. The following example depicts this complex process.

In a general election, the citizens of Houston, Texas, voted to authorize a sports authority to issue bonds for the construction of a baseball and football stadium. The sports authority had been created after passage of a law by the Texas legislature providing for formation of the authority to raise taxes and issue bonds. The Harris County–Houston Sports Authority agreed to borrow $236.5 million to construct a new downtown baseball stadium (Williams, 1998). The money was to be borrowed in two ways: $34.7 million was to be raised through a zero-interest loan from business leaders, with repayment due starting in 2009. The remaining $201.8 million was raised through **revenue bonds** at an interest rate of 5.61%, with debt service to start at $10.3 million in 1999 and increase to $22.8 million by 2028 (Williams, 1998). The revenue bonds are secured from revenue collected through special hotel and rental car taxes.

Only $180 million of the offering was to go to stadium construction; the remaining $21.8 million was to be used to cover other finance-related costs such as issuing the bonds. The $21.8 million also went to purchase bond insurance, which helped increase the **bond rating** (Aaa from Moody's and AAA from Standard & Poor's). This in turn allowed the bonds to be issued at a lower interest rate (Williams, 1998). The bond underwriters included Salomon Smith Barney; Chase Securities of Texas; Goldman, Sachs & Company; Samuel A. Ramirez & Company; Siebert Brandford Shank & Company; Artemis Capital Group; Estrada Hinojosa & Company; J.P. Morgan & Company; and Paine Webber. Bond issues of this magnitude by government entities often have numerous companies helping to underwrite them, including some minority-owned firms and local firms that are involved for political reasons.

Not all bond deals need to be complex. In 2006 the Hennepin County Board approved a 0.15% increase in sales tax to fund $350 million in bonds. The funds were to be used to help build a baseball stadium for the Minnesota Twins. The County was to pay $350 million of the $522 million construction cost, with the Twins picking up $130 million of the bill. The stadium is supposed to be completed in time for the 2010 season ("Hennepin County," 2006).

TYPES OF GOVERNMENT-ISSUED BONDS

Numerous types of bonds can be issued in the sport industry. Earlier sections of this chapter cover several types of bonds that can help sport corporations. This section centers on bonds issued by various government entities. Bonds represent the most likely funding source for publicly financed projects such as stadiums and arenas.

Although bonds for stadiums and arenas are the type of bonds most typically studied, sports facilities are low on the list of total expenditures for bond proceeds. Other public projects garner a greater amount of bond dollars. The greatest amount of funding is directed to school projects. Other major projects funded by bonds include park and recreation departments, convention centers, and administrative offices. This section focuses on stadiums and arenas financed with bonds. The same principles that relate to securing and repayment of bonds apply to all projects funded with government-issued bonds. The primary types of bonds considered here are general obligation bonds and revenue bonds. Other financing techniques, such as lease-backed financing (lease revenue bonds) and certificates of participation, can be used by the government entity, which then leases the facility to another government entity or sports authority (Greenberg & Gray, 1996).

GENERAL OBLIGATION BONDS

General obligation bonds (GOBs) are among the instruments most commonly used to fund facilities. These bonds are often called **full faith and credit** obligations because the city, county, municipality, state, or other government unit pledges to repay the obligation with existing tax revenues or by levying new taxes (Greenberg & Gray, 1996). General obligation bonds and other bonds are rated by independent companies such as Moody's and Standard & Poor's based on the issuer's ability to repay the loan. General obligation bonds are often highly rated since currently existing and future tax revenue sources can be tapped for repayment. Bond ratings can be influenced by a multitude of factors, including (Greenberg & Gray, 1996)

- the level of coverage (ability to repay the loan with existing revenue streams);
- the strength, breadth, and reliability of the tax base;
- the historical performance of the revenue stream;
- the risk associated with the project;
- the underlying economic strength of the stadium or arena or the community;
- political volatility; and
- whether or not the project is economically viable.

The strength of the tax base is one of the most important criteria for GOBs. A small city with a low tax base might suffer significantly if property values decrease or sales drop significantly. In contrast, a large city with hundreds of thousands of properties can experience downturns in the economy but still have a large enough tax base that the damage could be minimal.

Raters often look at the purpose of the project and the anticipated long-term benefits. Projects such as Camden Yards or Coors Field revolutionized the manner in which stadiums were viewed. These stadiums could be seen as catalysts for change that could revitalize an entire downtown community. If the downtown was revitalized, property values would increase. The increased property values would result in higher tax revenue, which would generate additional funds from which to repay bonds.

REVENUE BONDS

A more specific type of bond is the revenue bond; here the tax revenue to support repayment may come from the project itself. For example, an entrance tax of $1.50 per ticket could be charged, and all revenues from this tax would first be allocated to repaying the revenue bond. These bonds traditionally have a lower credit rating than other bonds because there are significant financial risks associated with limiting repayment requirements to a specific tax source. This concern arose during the 1998 NBA strike. If games were canceled and admission revenue was lost, some bond issuers might not have had any of their anticipated revenue sources to repay revenue bondholders whose bonds were secured by attendance taxes or other revenue sources ("Securitizing Sports," 1998). Since NHL teams are normally not the anchor tenants at most arenas, the threat of defaulting on bonds was not a major concern during the 2004-2005 NHL lockout.

Sometimes a public entity targets a specific tax to finance a bond. Cleveland utilized a sin tax on alcohol and tobacco sales to help finance Jacobs Field and Gund Arena. San Antonio utilized a sales tax–based bond issue to help finance building the Alamodome.

© Getty Images

Whether they realize it or not, fans often help with the repayment of bonds by extra taxes that are applied to their tickets or sin taxes that are applied to alcohol purchases.

Special tax bonds are repayable from a specific pledged source and are not backed by the full faith and credit of the issuing entity. Thus, if the specific revenue source is inadequate, there may not be enough tax revenue to repay the bondholders. Tax and revenue anticipation notes can be issued to fund the project before revenue starts arriving. Similarly, a bond anticipation note or tax-exempt commercial paper can help bridge the gap during construction until revenue is generated to repay the interim note and start repaying special tax bonds (Greenberg & Gray, 1996).

BOND ACQUISITION PROCESS

Bond acquisition is a complex process for sports facilities that can take several years. The first step often entails determining whether or not tax revenue can be raised from alternative sources. For example, the proposal for an arena in Denton County, Texas, included "calling" a half-cent sales tax to raise some of the required funds. This process starts with calling the election, which entails applying for the tax to appear on a future election ballot. Once an election is held and the half-cent tax is approved, the municipality needs to close the bond backed by the half-cent tax. With the prospect for the sales tax bonds, the municipality can then proceed with calling an election for the GOB. The GOB goes through the same process of being put on a future ballot. If the voters approve the GOB, the next step is closing the bond. The voting process alone can take 10 months to complete (*Overview*, 1995).

REPAYMENT SOURCES

Whichever type of bond is issued, repayment will always be the key concern for investors. There are other factors that can be very important to a potential investor, such as whether the bond is tax exempt (see chapter 14 for tax-related factors), whether the government entity purchased bond repayment insurance, and whether contractually obligated revenue (COR) is sufficient to repay the bond. Even with these variables, investors will look toward a stable and adequate repayment source as an additional assurance that the bond will be paid. Significant funding sources include (Greenberg & Gray, 1996)

- utility taxes,
- ticket surcharges,
- car rental taxes,
- real estate taxes,
- specific sales taxes,

- possessory interest taxes,
- tourist development taxes,
- restaurant sales taxes,
- excise or sin taxes,
- lottery and gaming revenue,
- nontax fees such as permits,
- general appropriations, and
- general sales and use taxes.

A utility tax, for example, is a cost added to an electric, water, or gas bill to help pay for the bond's debt service. In the 1990s, the San Francisco Giants were considering a move to San Jose, California. The proposed stadium was to be partially financed by a utility tax. Opponents of the stadium distributed light-switch covers to communicate the idea that every time people turned on the lights, they would be paying for the proposed stadium. The stadium ballot measure was defeated by the strong activists against the tax.

A possessory interest tax designed to tax the primary facility user is charged to whoever possesses control of the facility. Tourist development taxes and car rental taxes are designed primarily to tax out-of-towners who visit the city. This is a popular technique because it is easy to tell a voting population that you are attempting to get out-of-towners to pay for the facility (Howard & Crompton, 2004).

Excise taxes are general taxes added to various products; sin taxes are more specifically geared to be added to the cost of alcohol and tobacco products. Sin taxes were utilized to help finance building the arena and stadium in Cleveland.

Nontax fees are special expenses passed on to particular parties (e.g., raising the permit costs for other developers in the city). Such a tax can stimulate a backlash from citizens who do not want to pay a greater share of the funding for the facility than others are paying. General appropriations are among the most favored funding options. **Appropriations** are funds that are set aside for specific purposes. Through political dealings a municipality might convince the state legislature or federal government to give a "gift" appropriation from the budget to help pay the facility construction expenses or to fund bond repayments. The San Antonio Alamodome was built as a bus stop to help secure a federal appropriation for interstate transportation.

Although these revenue sources can often support significant repayment obligations, CORs can also provide a significant guarantee that a debt will be repaid. Contractually obligated revenues are any contract whereby a party agrees to pay a specific sum for a guaranteed number of years. Typical long-term contracts that form the basis of COR backing include (Greenberg & Gray, 1996)

- premium seat contracts,
- luxury box contracts,
- concession and novelty rights contracts,
- naming rights contracts,
- pouring rights (beer and soft drink) contracts,
- personal seat licenses, and
- parking rights contracts.

Contractually obligated revenues have two primary functions. They can be used as a source of revenue to guarantee repayment of bonds or other loans. They also can be utilized as an independent funding source. If the bonds are all covered through other revenue streams, the team or facility may be able to sell the naming rights and use those funds to enhance its bottom line.

Several examples will suggest how stadium and arena builders can utilize a blend of bonds and CORs to finance a stadium. The Rangers Ballpark in Arlington was opened in 1994 at a cost of $190 million. A majority of the project (71%) was financed through a 30-year 5% sales tax that was projected to raise $11 million yearly. The public sector also contributed 13% to the deal through a $1 per ticket surcharge. The Texas Rangers contributed 16% to the project by selling $30 million in luxury suite contracts (Greenberg & Gray, 1996).

The Gateway project in Cleveland was financed through a tax-exempt county bond offering that raised 45% of the $152 million needed to build the Gund Arena (now the Quicken Loans Arena). Liquor and cigarette taxes (sin taxes) covered another 42%, and private naming rights covered the remaining 13% (Greenberg & Gray, 1996). The bonds were sold to various investors, and the income stream used to repay the bonds came from state capital improvement funds and a countywide sin tax. The sin tax taxed alcohol at $3.00 per gallon of liquor and $0.16 per gallon of beer, and cigarettes were taxed at $0.045 per pack. These taxes were to be in place for 15 years (Greenberg & Gray, 1996). More than $238 million was raised in the 15 years since the sin tax was adopted to help fund Jacobs Field and Gund Arena. Cuyahoga County ended up paying $87 million to help build the facility. In 2005, voters approved a 10-year extension for the sin tax to help pay off the debt for the Cleveland Browns Stadium ("'Sinners' as Saints," 2005).

The Ice Palace in Tampa may be one of the most complex projects in terms of the multitude of funding sources used to cover the $160 million needed to complete the facility in 1996. The Tampa Bay Lightning's parent company issued private-project revenue bonds to cover 30% of the costs. The Tampa Sports Authority issued tax-exempt bonds backed by a state sales tax rebate, estimated at $2 million annually (19% of the costs), and a county tourist tax bond backed by non–ad valorem revenue, which would also generate $2 million annually. Another $750,000 per year (7%) was backed by city parking bonds. The sports authority also issued taxable bonds that included a requirement for a ticket surcharge of $0.50 per ticket, which was projected to generate $1.5 million annually (11%) and backed by a county loan or pledge. Additionally, the city issued a surcharge bond backed by a $0.25 surcharge per ticket, which was expected to generate $250,000 yearly (2%). Last, the city provided 2% of the construction costs through public land acquisition, which was accomplished through use of eminent domain (Greenberg & Gray, 1996).

Eminent domain is the process by which government units can take land from individual landowners. Land or property can be taken if the seized land will be used for the public good. Government units have to pay the fair market value for the land but utilize this process to build roads, new schools, or even new arenas or stadiums. In addition, eminent domain can be used to take more than just land. The city of Baltimore attempted to invoke eminent domain to take the Baltimore Colts, which prompted the team to pack all their belongings into trucks and move to Indianapolis in the middle of the night ("Eminent Domain," 2002).

After it has been determined where potential tax revenue can be found to repay the bonds, a public entity considering issuing bonds needs to examine the potential municipal bond rating. Bond ratings for stadium projects are normally fairly high because of the backing of major cities that presumably will not go bankrupt. However, lenders have become somewhat more leery of these deals in recent years because of the possibility that the oversaturated television market might reduce future broadcast contracts. Lenders can also be concerned when teams and leagues face a multitude of challenges, from fickle fans to legal challenges of league policies. For example, say the University of Milford issues $50 million in bonds to fund new buildings and a new stadium. If bond repayment is tied to student tuition revenue, the university could be in serious trouble if student enrollment significantly decreases. If student tuition drops by 20%, the impact on bonds could be significant, and the lender might speed up the repayment schedule.

GOVERNMENT ASSISTANCE: INDUSTRIAL DEVELOPMENT BONDS

So far, this chapter has focused on debt- and equity-based capital acquisition. The Stars, the University of Milford, or SMC can utilize any one or several of the capital acquisition techniques we have considered. However, the Smiths may not have enough money to start the process to obtain needed capital. Many small businesses, including minority-owned businesses, need some additional help to acquire needed capital while still relying on bonds.

Although most bond offerings are too cost prohibitive for smaller companies to issue, there are other bond-based funding options that such businesses can secure with local government assistance. Government units in each state have the authority, through sport authorities, economic development commissions, and similar divisions, to offer small-issue **industrial development bonds (IDBs)**.

Assume that the Smiths wish to build their fitness center in a run-down part of town that they think will turn around and become a prime location for young professionals. The Smiths can approach city hall with a request for assistance to help revive the area. Working with the city's economic development commission and planning committee, Bob and Cheryl present a deal to city hall that city hall approves. The city issues the IDB, which is really a corporate bond for the Smiths' business but appears to be a tax-free municipal bond issued by the city (Hovey, 1998, July). The proceeds from the bond are used to buy equipment or purchase the building.

Federal law allows a business owner to raise up to $10 million using IDBs. The IDBs carry an interest rate ranging from one-half to three-quarters of the prime interest rate, with a 30-year maturity. The one drawback to IDBs is the transaction costs (ranging from 2% to 5%), which can erase all interest savings and make smaller bonds uneconomical (Hovey, 1998, July). In 1996, over $2.7 billion was raised for businesses through use of this financing method, with these funds used to create new jobs (Hovey, 1998, July). The process requires a significant amount of paperwork, and company owners must compete with other projects (such as public housing and urban renewal) that are trying to secure tax-free bonds. The key to obtaining these bonds is to show that you can generate jobs. A rule of thumb is that every $50,000 in bond funding should create one full-time-equivalent job (Hovey, 1998, July).

Although these tax-free bonds have significant benefits, the Smiths would need to examine some rules and regulations to determine whether or not an IDB would be appropriate for their fitness center. If they used the IDB-generated funds to pay for equipment, the money would go further than if they used the funds for construction. The reason is that many states require people using funds obtained from IDBs to pay union or prevailing wages. Union wages might need to be paid for construction, but wages are not relevant to equipment purchases. Another issue is that borrowers may need to contact a bank to secure a letter of credit guaranteeing repayment of the bond, and the letter of credit could cost around 1% of the borrowed amount (Hovey, 1998, July). Such added costs or restrictions might make IDBs impractical for some borrowers.

CAPITALIZATION PROBLEMS AND ISSUES

As highlighted throughout this chapter and chapters 8 and 9, a company must carefully examine its funding needs. Capital or debt structures are not random acts of choosing numbers. The consequences of issuing too many shares or bonds can have a significant negative impact. Likewise, the failure to issue enough shares or bonds can also be a disaster. This section covers the concerns associated with overcapitalization, undercapitalization, and recapitalization.

Assume that the Smiths have been operating their fitness center for two years and decide to expand. Investors may be interested if the prospective earnings are high enough to meet their investment needs. However, many of the issues raised throughout this chapter come into play in determining exactly how Bob and Cheryl would pursue obtaining the funds. An attorney friend has suggested that they might want to incorporate to take advantage of liability reduction benefits. The Smiths decide not to issue bonds, but to have preferred stock issued to themselves, with a dividend requirement of $50,000 a year. Their business plan shows that future earnings before taxes should be $400,000 a year, but

even in a poor year their COR will produce a minimum of $200,000 in pretax earnings. Therefore, even in a poor year, and even if they received only $100,000 after-tax profit, they still could cover dividend obligations twice over.

Bob and Cheryl therefore decide to issue 20,000 shares of 5% preferred stock at $50 par value. Based on these figures, the yearly dividend will be $2.50 per share. The Smiths did not base their calculations on pie in the sky; they analyzed the worst possible earnings scenario and calculated how much they could withdraw from the business while still maintaining owner equity return. If the company has a strong year with $400,000 in earnings, reduced to $200,000 after taxes, they will have a $50,000 obligation for their preferred stocks and $150,000 for common stocks. The Smiths decide to sell common stock valued at 12.5 times expected earnings ($150,000) or $1,875,000 in potential value. If stocks at that time are selling for 10 times earnings on average, then the stock would be selling on the market for $1,500,000 in total.

The Smiths' next step is to determine a selling price for the stocks. On the basis of the $1,875,000 valuation for the common stocks, they choose to sell the stock for $10 per share. However, if they wanted to price the stock higher, at $50, for example, then they would not issue as many shares. To arrive at the requisite $1,875,000 value, they would issue only 37,500 shares at the $50 price. Using the $10 stock price, the initial capital structure for the business is as follows:

20,000 shares of preferred stock ($50 par value) = $1,000,000

187,500 shares of common stock ($10 per share) = $1,875,000

The fitness center's net assets would total $2,875,000 in this scenario. Bob and Cheryl would have funded their business entirely through stocks.

OVERCAPITALIZATION

A critical concern that needs to be discussed before we move to part IV, Financial Management, is overcapitalization. A company can raise too much money and not have the financial means to pay everything off. The most serious form of overcapitalization entails issuing too much bond-backed capital. Interest payments are due even if excess cash is lying around and not gaining any return. Too many cumulative preferred shares can also represent a significant cash flow problem, especially in periods of depression. Overcapitalization can also occur with stocks when too many shares are on the market, which reduces the earnings per share.

 If the Smiths issued one million shares and earned only a $150,000 profit from which to pay common stockholders' dividends, then the dividend would amount to only $0.15 per share. On the basis of the 12.5 times earnings figure used in the previous analysis, the Smiths' stock would now have a market value of only $1.87 per share (Bogen, 1966). Such a low stock price could scare away many investors who might think the stock was too speculative.

UNDERCAPITALIZATION

Besides having too many financial obligations, a company can issue too few shares or bonds in relation to the expected earnings. If a company becomes valuable and there are only a few shares available, the cost per share might be very high. Individual shares for various companies or partnerships have been worth several thousand dollars. Highly priced shares often scare away potential investors.

 Suppose that the Smiths issued only 10,000 shares of common stock and still had $150,000 in earnings, with the entire amount to be used to pay dividends. Each stock would receive $15 per share in dividends. If the stock sold at 12.5 times earnings, the shares would sell for $187.50 (Bogen, 1966).

Another concern with undercapitalization is that if most of the funds for growth come from internal sources such as retained earnings, the business may have a hard time raising funds externally. Similar to the situation for a consumer, a business needs to borrow through accounts payable and bank loans to develop a credit history. There are consumers who prefer to pay for everything with cash. Although you might think these people are being fiscally respon-

sible, they in fact are hurting themselves by not developing a history of borrowing and paying debts in a timely manner. A business also needs to borrow enough from a variety of lenders to establish a credit history. Undercapitalization hampers the ability of a business to develop a strong credit history.

RECAPITALIZATION

A key technique in capitalization is recapitalization, which can be performed through a **stock split**. If shares are trading at too high a price, the corporation's board of directors may decide to bring down the price by issuing a large number of shares in exchange for outstanding stock. Stock splits can be two for one, or three for one, or any other variation, including fractions. Stocks can be split from common stock into either just common stock or common stock and preferred stock.

 Preferred stocks can also be recapitalized. For example, if SMC had to pay a 5% dividend on preferred stocks and had not paid the dividend in several years, the company might ask the shareholders to return the shares. The shareholders would receive in exchange additional shares that could include a higher dividend rate to make up for the unpaid dividends.

Recapitalization can occur with bonds as well. However, the process for recapitalization of bonds is more elaborate. To recapitalize bonds, a corporation needs to go to the bondholders and ask them for approval before changing interest or principal payments. Any changes that do not affect principal or interest payments can be made by amending the indenture, if the indenture provides for changes. This might seem complex, but it is basically a change in the contractual terms, and contract changes are not that difficult if all the parties agree to the changes.

To help encourage bondholders to extend the principal repayment period, the corporation can offer to raise the interest rate, establish a sinking fund for retirement of the bonds or provide additional security as collateral (or both), or make the bond convertible (Bogen, 1966). If recapitalization does not appear feasible and the interest owed on the bonds is excessive, the corporation can ask bondholders to agree to postponing payments for a given period or have the bonds "stamped," indicating that interest will be paid only when earned (Bogen, 1966).

CONCLUSION

This chapter highlights various capital acquisition techniques. Sport businesses, whether for-profit or nonprofit, need to acquire funds in order to keep operating or to expand. Finding capital is often the most difficult task for new as well as established businesses. There is no one way to acquire capital, nor are there any guaranteed techniques. Issuing bonds is among the most difficult ways to raise funds.

It takes a significant amount of work to issue a bond, and typically only the largest companies do so. Most sport businesses utilize stock or bank financing rather than bonds. However, major privately financed construction projects, such as stadiums or arenas, can be financed through bonds secured by the facilities. Furthermore, stadiums and arenas built with public funds are almost always built using bonds guaranteed by a variety of taxes or revenue streams. Thus, bond financing is often the most visible form of capital acquisition in the sport industry.

CLASS DISCUSSION TOPICS

1. After reading about the various capital acquisition techniques, which one do you think would be the best for the Smiths, the University of Milford, SMC, or the Stars, based on all that you have learned from the case studies to date?

2. Should the general population pay the debt service for bonds issued to pay for a stadium or arena that is used primarily by a privately owned professional team? Debate the topic, citing all the pros and cons associated with the question. What innovative ideas could be used to help repay the bonds?

3. What is the value of bonds versus stocks?

4. What happens when a company defaults on paying a bond?

5. Is a bond a safer investment for an investor than other investing options such as stocks?

6. Should companies be allowed to sell junk bonds?

7. Besides the various backings for bonds highlighted in this chapter, what other resources can be tapped to help repay government-backed bonds to build stadiums and arenas?

8. What do you think the biggest problems are with under- and overcapitalization?

PART IV

FINANCIAL MANAGEMENT

Once a business gains capital, it has to know how to wisely spend that capital. Part IV looks at the various options businesses have to manage their money.

Chapter 11, Capital Budgeting, starts by identifying the goal of capital budgeting and gives a brief overview of capital spending. The chapter then provides an analysis of how much it costs to acquire capital. Once a company knows how much capital costs, it can develop a capital budgeting decision analysis to see which method is most beneficial. No decision is without risk, so risks need to be considered, and the final analysis will produce a realistic cash flow based on the identified assumptions.

Chapter 12, Short-Term Financial Management, highlights various strategies for funding short-term growth. The first step involves a review of current assets and liabilities. Once these variables are understood, a company can examine both cash and credit management to make sure it is maximizing its cash flow while not losing money by granting credit to weak borrowers. Through utilizing a strong collections management program, a company can make sure it receives payment in a timely manner or obtains additional revenue by charging interest on short-term lending to others.

Chapter 13, Inventory and Production Management, highlights how money can be either lost or preserved through effective management of the production and inventory process. The chapter first highlights the cost of doing business and then examines the process of inventory and production management.

CAPITAL BUDGETING

CHAPTER OBJECTIVES

After studying this chapter, you should be able to do the following:

- Define capital budgeting.
- Distinguish between the different techniques of capital budgeting.
- Understand the process of calculating the cost of capital.
- Calculate and use the weighted average cost of capital and the capital asset pricing model formulas.
- Understand how to make capital decisions.
- Distinguish between present value and net present value calculations.
- Understand payback rules such as the internal rate of return.
- Describe cash flow and how it works.

Sports managers have many decisions to make with respect to financial management. One of the most important decisions involves the use of funds for long-term projects such as purchasing equipment, constructing a new facility, or renovating an existing structure. The process of making investments toward these types of fixed assets, both tangible and intangible, is known as capital budgeting. Capital budgeting is a key component of long-term success for a sports organization. **Capital** is the long-term funding that is necessary for the acquisition of fixed assets (Brigham & Ehrhardt, 2005). With respect to the sport industry, the largest area of capital spending is facility construction and renovation. Each year, billions of dollars are spent on facility projects such as stadiums, arenas, fitness facilities, and corporate offices. New income streams are also an important component of capital budgeting. A sports manager must decide if the positive future cash flow from a capital project will be large enough to offset the project's cost.

This chapter focuses on the basics of capital budgeting. We discuss the cost of capital, the methods of making capital budgeting decisions, and ways of projecting future cash flows from capital projects.

GOAL OF CAPITAL BUDGETING

The goal of capital budgeting is to select those investment opportunities that are worth more than they cost. Also, businesses should initially invest in those projects that provide the greatest return for their investment. Given the long-term effects associated with any investment, we can see why capital budgeting is a primary focus for sport businesses or organizations.

A sport business can raise and spend capital funds in countless ways. An integral part of financial management is determining the best capital sources. Efficient capital spending leads to growth and success for a sport business. To grow, a business must invest some of its available capital in fixed assets such as land, equipment, or machinery. For example, the University of Milford cannot improve its recreational offerings without investing in new equipment and facilities. But although a for-profit business should invest in those projects that will result in the largest return on investment, this may not always be true for government or nonprofit organizations.

CAPITAL SPENDING

Before critically analyzing capital budgeting, we must focus on the meaning of capital spending. **Capital spending** is the net spending on fixed assets. Net spending is the total money a business uses to acquire **real assets**, less the sale of previously owned real assets (Brigham & Ehrhardt, 2005). Recently there has been a significant increase in the level of capital spending. With respect to arenas and stadiums, the construction boom has been fostered by several occurrences. On the financial side, team owners believe that capital expenditures for facility amenities such as luxury suites, club seats, concessions, and parking will result in new income streams. Additionally, there was an obvious need for new facilities to replace older structures that required major repairs, such as Veterans Stadium in Philadelphia or Busch Stadium in St. Louis.

Sport businesses spend money to acquire real assets, but they may also sell them. The sale of these real assets must be included when calculating total capital spending.

 **Sport Manufacturing Company** If Sport Manufacturing Company invests $10 million through purchasing fixed assets and also sells $4 million in fixed assets, its net spending on fixed assets is $6 million. Although SMC budgeted $10 million to acquire new fixed assets, it produced income through the sale of existing assets that were part of the previous balance sheet.

Capital budgeting and purchasing capital items are long-term endeavors. When we refer to items as long term, this usually means a time frame greater than one year. Long-term assets such as equipment and facilities have a productive life that is longer than one year. With respect to capital, it is often not possible for a business to allocate the amount of money necessary for purchasing high-priced fixed assets in one single year. Therefore, the business must develop capital budgets that detail how the funds will be raised and allocated over an extended period of time. This is the primary reason for the separation of current, or short-term, items from capital items in financial statements.

The funding mix required for capital expenditures is referred to as the capital structure. In general, the traditional corporate capital structure includes debt (bonds and long-term loans), preferred stock, and common stock (Ross, Westerfield, & Jordan, 2006). These capital vehicles are discussed in part III, but they are referred to again in this chapter within the context of analyzing their budgeting implications. All these capital sources have an accompanying cost. If a sport business wishes to borrow funds from a bank to construct a new facility, it must pay interest on the borrowed amount. The interest that is paid in addition to the principal being borrowed is referred to as the debt's cost. The next section deals with each form of capital and covers methods to measure the accompanying costs.

For nonprofit organizations such as the U of M, additional sources of funding include donations and gifts. Supporters of nonprofit organizations often make financial donations toward new capital projects. For example, a U of M alumnus may donate a significant amount of money toward constructing a new sports facility. Many nonprofit organizations rely on these donations for a portion, or all, of the funds necessary to complete capital projects. These donations are very important to nonprofit organizations because unlike corporations, they cannot raise capital through equity ownership.

COST OF CAPITAL

Sport businesses can use four traditional forms of capital to fund growth: debt, common stock, preferred stock, and retained earnings. The four traditional forms of capital are known as capital components. They all have one common trait: The persons or institutions that provide the capital expect—or demand—a return on investment (Brigham & Ehrhardt, 2005). A bank or financial institution that loans money to a small business expects to be repaid the loan principal plus interest. A common stockholder or investor expects the firm to invest in capital spending projects that will increase the value of the company and ultimately result in increased stock value. This expected return on the investment means there is a cost to the business in acquiring the capital funds. In the case of a bank loan, the cost of capital is the amount of interest owed to the creditor. This section develops methods to measure the cost of capital for debt and equity. Sport businesses need to understand and appreciate the fact that any capital acquisition technique has a cost, and that end cost will dictate how much capital can be raised.

We must make a quick point about retained earnings before moving forward. **Retained earnings**

© Getty Images

By smartly investing in capital, a company can hope to strengthen and increase the value of their company stock.

are funds that are kept by a business to be used for reinvestment in the company. This reinvestment often takes the form of capital spending. Management believes that the stockholders will benefit more from this reinvestment than from having the money returned through dividend payments. Because the retained earnings can be used by the business to purchase additional stock, the cost of retained earnings is considered to be the cost of common stock. Therefore, we will discuss the cost of retained earnings along with the cost of common stock.

It is important to mention that companies develop strategies for structuring their capital. For example, the Stars may have 50% of their capital in the form of debt, 30% in preferred stock, and 20% in common stock. These proportions, referred to as a target capital structure, may vary greatly across businesses and industries (Ross et al., 2006). Within some professional sports leagues, capital structure is somewhat controlled by the league. For example, the NFL has restrictions on the level of debt that each team can maintain. The NFL set the debt limit as a financial safeguard to ensure that none of its teams have excess debt that will lead to future financial difficulties. The debt limit was increased from $125 million to $150 million in 2005. This increase was made possible by the increases in league revenues from media contracts and team valuations (Fitch, 2005). If a league member is at its debt limit, it must raise capital through other sources, perhaps by attracting new equity investors.

Most sport businesses finance their capital budgets through a combination of debt and equity. Each form of capital has an associated cost. Some businesses may decide to structure their capital budgets such that they rely on one single form of capital, but this is uncommon for large corporations. For government-owned and -operated institutions such as U of M's athletic department, the sources of capital are primarily debt and money raised through gifts and donations. The University of Milford is operated by the state of Connecticut and has no individual private ownership rights. Its income comes from sources such as donations, ticket sales, sponsorships, student fees, and broadcast fees. These funds are used to cover the current expenses involved in operating a collegiate athletic program. The university usually raises money for capital projects from donations or the issuance of debt. The state is ultimately responsible for paying the bondholders if the university defaults.

The Smiths, the Stars of David, and SMC can also raise capital by selling equity ownership rights or borrowing funds. For example, the Stars may raise money by issuing common stock to the public, but they may also borrow from banks or issue bonds. Other professional teams utilize similar capital funding techniques. The city of Milford could have passed a resolution to issue $2 million in city bonds to partially fund a new minor league baseball stadium that could be used by the local team as well as the university. If the university were to build the facility itself, it would have to wait for several more years and raise over $1 million. This creative joint use can benefit multiple parties and reduce overall community spending.

Several factors can influence the decision on capital structuring. For example, a weak stock market may make the issuance of stock less attractive than it might be otherwise. As stock prices fall, a business needs to issue more shares in order to raise the necessary capital funds. Also, there is a cost associated with issuing new stock. Most businesses work with a financial institution to help with a public offering, and there is a cost for these services. The expenses related to issuing new stock are known as flotation costs (Ross et al., 2006). Immoo, Lochhead, Ritter, and Zhao (1996) found that a company that wants to raise $2 to $10 million in capital through a common stock offering will have flotation costs of approximately 13.28% of the total amount of capital being raised. Thus, if a business wants to raise $2 million in capital, it will actually need to raise approximately $2.26 million. The additional $260,000 will be needed to cover the flotation costs.

Immoo et al. (1996) also found that the average flotation cost is significantly less when capital is raised through debt. In the $2 to $10 million debt range, the average flotation cost is 4.39%, one-third the level of common stock flotation costs. Whether debt or equity is used, many of the flotation costs, such as attorneys' fees, are fixed and are not greatly affected by the amount of capital being raised. Therefore, most businesses do not like to raise capital in relatively small quantities. Other businesses also elect to raise capital through one single source, debt or equity, each year in an effort to minimize flotation costs (Ross et al., 2006).

A professional sports team example will illustrate average cost of capital for debt. Assume the Stars decide to go public by issuing stock, and the team raises $300 million in its initial public offering. If the average flotation costs for such an offering are 8%, then $24 million will be paid to float the shares, and $4.5 to $6 million of that amount might represent attorneys' fees that need to be paid even if only $100 million had been raised through the offering.

Selecting one capital source each year has short-term effects on a target capital structure. This strategy makes it difficult to maintain the target structure. A business' target capital structure may also be affected by outside economic forces such as the stock market or interest rates. Interest rates have an effect on the cost of issuing debt. Therefore, a business may want to select debt as its capital source (in order to maintain its capital target), but it may be more cost-effective to issue new stock. This is especially true when stock prices are relatively high.

Thus far, we have discussed the general principles of capital, the forms of capital, and the importance of capital cost. The next step is to develop a method for accurately measuring new capital costs. The most commonly used method to measure the cost of capital is the **weighted average cost of capital** (WACC). The WACC focuses on determining the average cost of each capital component and weights each based on its contribution to the total capital amount. In general, a sport business will maximize its value when it minimizes its WACC (Ross et al., 2006).

To calculate the WACC, we must separate capital into each of the three potential capital sources available for a business: debt, preferred stock, and common stock. As stated earlier, the cost of retaining earnings and the cost of issuing common stock are calculated similarly. In doing the calculation of the WACC as outlined in this chapter, retained earnings are implicitly included in the value of common stock. Whether new shares of stock are issued or whether retained earnings are used to finance a capital project, the cost of funds is identical (ignoring underwriting and flotation costs). The following sections deal with the cost of debt first, followed by the cost of equity and the cost of combining the capital mix in the WACC.

COST OF DEBT

Debt is important because many smaller businesses raise most of their capital through this capital component, usually in the form of bank loans (Brigham & Ehrhardt, 2005).

 Bob and Cheryl Smith have a relatively small business. They may borrow money from a bank or similar financial institution to fund new capital spending. The principal amount they borrow must be repaid over time with interest. The interest is the cost of borrowing the funds. If the Smiths borrow $200,000 at an interest rate of 8%, the cost of debt is, excluding taxes, also 8%. But, the cost of debt is misleading unless the potential tax implications are extracted. Taxes are covered in chapter 14, but it is important to note here that since the debt repayment of 8% is probably tax deductible, the Smiths will not pay 8% per year. The true cost will be $16,000 (8% × $200,000) minus what tax savings can be generated by reducing the Smiths' income by $16,000. Assuming a 40% combined federal and state tax rate for the business, the potential cost could drop from $16,000 to $9,600 ($16,000 − 40%).

Many large corporations also issue debt through bonds and debentures. A bond is a long-term promissory note issued by a business. For most bonds, the business agrees to pay back the amount borrowed at a specified future date (usually 10 to 30 years for long-term bonds) in addition to a coupon payment, which is a percentage of the bond's value. The coupon payment for most corporate coupon bonds is made semiannually (twice per year). For example, a business can sell 25-year bonds with a value of $1,000 and a semiannual coupon payment of 6%. Anyone who purchases a bond will receive semiannual payments of $60 for 25 years. Also, at the end of the 25 years,

the creditor will receive $1,000. In this example, the annual cost of debt for the life of the bond would average around 12%.

As discussed in the previous chapter, a debenture is a long-term bond. However, unlike regular bonds that are secured by corporate assets, a debenture is unsecured. The only protection a debenture holder has to guarantee repayment is the good name of the company that issues the debenture. If the corporation faces financial hardships, the debenture holders are similar to all other unsecured lenders in that they are often the last group to be repaid, if they are paid at all.

From these examples, it initially appears that measuring the rate of return required by debt holders is fairly straightforward. How much will debt holders demand in future payments in order to make the necessary funds available today? For a small business, ascertaining this may be as simple as determining the annual interest rate on a bank loan. However, it can be a bit more complex for a large corporation. Given that the WACC is used in the planning process for the issuance of future debt, a financial manager is making a prediction or estimation of the future cost of debt. It is not always easy to determine the coupon payment that must be offered in order to attract future bond purchasers. If a business issues a new bond at a time when interest rates are on the rise, it will have a hard time selling the bonds without increasing the interest rate paid to purchasers. Therefore, determining the appropriate rate of return is not an exact science. Nevertheless, by using the correct information the analyst can make a credible estimate.

WHAT IS THE CORRECT INFORMATION?

A financial manager can analyze historical data on past debt instruments to make a prediction about the future. Suppose that SMC wants to issue new 25-year bonds to raise capital. Through past experience, the financial manager knows that similar bonds have been issued for each of the past five years. She also knows that the business' financial position has not changed over that time period and that those previous bonds were issued with a 10% coupon rate. Additionally, the financial manager should look at the current yield on a bond with the same maturity and credit rating, as determined by Moody's or Standard and Poor's, as well as the current debt costs for similar businesses. For example, suppose the Stars of David are investigating the issuance of debt to build a new arena. It would be beneficial for the team to gather information on the cost of debt incurred by other teams that have recently financed facility construction.

CALCULATING THE COST OF DEBT

One other important debt feature is crucial to the cost-of-debt calculation. To encourage capital investment in the United States, the federal government and most state governments provide a tax deduction on the interest payments made to debt holders. For most corporations, the federal tax rate for interest deductions is 35%. Most states also give tax allowances for interest deductions, usually at about a 5% rate (Brigham & Ehrhardt, 2005). In total, the average tax rate for interest deductions is approximately 40%. This tax savings reduces the overall cost of debt for a sport business.

Assume we want to calculate the cost of debt for SMC. The cost of debt can be written as a mathematical formula:

$$D = R - (R \times T)$$

D = cost of debt

R = interest rate paid to debt holder

T = marginal tax rate on interest payments

The rate of return required by debt holders is the interest rate, or **R**, that is paid on the debt. The tax saving is the rate of return required by debt holders multiplied by the **marginal tax** rate on interest payments, which we will abbreviate as **T**. We can rewrite the cost of debt this way:

$$D = R \times (1 - T)$$

 **Sport Manufacturing Company**

In our example, we will assume that SMC borrows $1,000,000 at an interest rate of 6% and has a marginal tax rate of 40%. Their actual cost of debt is calculated as follows:

$$D = 6\% \times (1 - 0.4)$$
$$D = 3.6\%$$

Therefore, SMC's cost of debt is 3.6% annually. Multiplying 3.6% by $1,000,000 shows that the cost of debt in dollars is $36,000. The tax deduction associated with making interest payments will save SMC 2.4%, or $24,000, of the original $1,000,000 that was borrowed.

COST OF EQUITY

Capital can also be acquired by selling ownership in the business, also known as the issuance of equity. Equity is separated into two different classifications: preferred stock and common stock.

COST OF PREFERRED STOCK

Preferred stock has a few unique characteristics that are important when calculating its cost. First, dividend payments on preferred stock are not tax deductible for the corporation paying the dividends. Additionally, individual investors must pay tax on the money they receive from being preferred shareholders. Corporations are permitted to claim that 70% of the funds they receive from being preferred shareholders in other corporations are tax deductible (Ross et al., 2006). No tax savings such as we saw with debt are available for firms that issue preferred stock. Also, although firms have no legal requirement to pay yearly dividends on preferred stock, they usually make every attempt to do so. If a company misses a dividend payment, it has to pay the back-owed dividend the next time a dividend payment is declared. The reason is that dividends must be paid on preferred stock before they are paid to common stockholders. Also, in some cases, preferred stockholders have the right to take control of a company if they do not receive dividend payments. To avoid defaulting on required payments, management pays dividends as regularly as possible to keep preferred stockholders happy. Also, the failure to make dividend payments to preferred stockholders is a signal that a firm may be in financial distress. This may eventually lead to difficulty in issuing future capital in either the debt or the equity market (Ross et al., 2006).

As discussed in chapter 10, preferred stocks pay a fixed dividend to an investor, similar to a bond's coupon payment. Dividends can be postponed until future years; the firm's board of directors is responsible for making this decision (Ross et al., 2006). Also, as stated earlier, preferred stock dividends are not tax deductible, so we do not need to include a tax savings component in our cost calculation.

All preferred stock has a predetermined share value, called the par value, and a fixed dividend payment per share. For example, Nike preferred stock has a $1 par value and an annual fixed dividend payment of $0.10 (*Standard & Poor's*, 1999). The cost of preferred stock is the dividend payment, which we abbreviate as **v**, divided by the issuing price, **P**. In our calculations, we also abbreviate the cost of preferred stock as **S**.

As stated earlier, there are flotation costs associated with issuing new stock. The flotation costs decrease the amount of cash the firm actually receives from the sale of new preferred stock. For example, if the Stars issue new preferred stock for $100 per share and the flotation cost is 6%, SMC will receive only $94 per share. Therefore, we should include the flotation cost in the calculation of P and redefine P as the net issuing price. Given the information we have, the cost of preferred stock can be written as follows:

$$\text{cost of preferred stock} = \frac{\text{preferred stock dividend}}{\text{net issuing price}}$$

or

$$S = \frac{v}{P}$$

S = cost of preferred stock

v = preferred stock dividend

P = net issuing price

 Assume that the Stars of David want to issue $20 million of new preferred stock. The new preferred stock will have a $100 par value and pay an annual dividend of $5 per share, and the flotation cost will be 4%. The cost of preferred stock is then calculated as follows:

$$S = \frac{\$5}{\$100 - \$4} = \frac{\$5}{\$96} = 5.208\%$$

The cost of issuing new preferred stock for the Stars is 5.208%. As you can see, flotation costs have an effect on the cost of preferred stock. Without the flotation costs, the cost would be 5%. Although the change of 0.208% may seem small, in this example in which $20 million of preferred stock is issued, the increased cost annually paid by the Stars is $41,600.

COST OF COMMON STOCK

The last capital component to be considered is common stock. With respect to common stock, a firm can raise capital through two methods. First, it can issue new common stock. To attract new common stock shareholders, the firm must sell the stock shares at an attractive price. Prospective stockholders will purchase the stock if they believe the value of the

stock will increase in the future. The annual percentage return (holding period return) associated with annual dividend payments and increases in stock price must exceed the returns on investments of equivalent risk. If it does not, people will invest their money in other opportunities.

The 1990s were a decade in which a number of initial public offerings (IPOs) occurred for sport-related businesses. However, the recession in 2001 and 2002 slowed the growth rate of sport business IPOs considerably. In fact, several public sport businesses such as the Boston Celtics returned to being private entities. As we saw in chapter 9, an initial public offering is the first offering of a stock to the general public. The shares that are made available can be primary offerings (new shares that are sold to raise additional capital) or secondary offerings, which occur when the company ownership sells a portion of their existing shares (Brealey, Myers, & Marcus, 2004).

After being issued, the stock is bought and sold through a public market such as the New York Stock Exchange or the American Stock Exchange. Traditionally, sports teams have been privately owned and operated. But within the past two decades, we have seen organizations such as the Florida Panthers, Orlando Predators, Cleveland Indians, and Boston Celtics go public. Several teams such as the Atlanta Braves, California Angels, and Los Angeles Dodgers have been subsidiaries of larger public corporations such as Time Warner, Disney, and the Fox Corporation.

A sport business can also raise capital through retaining earnings that would otherwise be used to pay common stockholder dividends. By not paying dividends, the firm is retaining funds for use in capital spending. The capital spending goal is to increase the business' value. If the business' value grows as a result of the capital spending, the common stock price should also increase. Most common stockholders will gladly forgo current dividend payments if the retained earnings will lead to an increase in the firm's stock price that is greater than the expected dividend payment.

Dividend policy is an important part of corporate finance. Financial managers continually struggle with the trade-off between dividend payments and retained earnings. They are looking for the appropriate levels of each that will keep the stockholders happy and also allow the firm to grow. It is impossible to make every investor happy, and there are never any guarantees. For example, SMC could pour $100 million into retained earnings and build a new production facility. Investors might be ecstatic with the prospects of future increased value. However, a day after the plant opens a competitor can produce a better model and send the business' stock into a dramatic tailspin. Thus, retained earnings represent a potential risk, but all business decisions contain an element of risk.

Ultimately, the important aspect of common stock is that common stock shareholders require a return on their investment. This expected return on investment is vital for calculating the cost of common stock. In the simplest terms, the cost of common stock is the rate of return demanded by stockholders.

We must include several factors in calculating the cost of common stock. Similar to the situation with preferred stock, flotation costs are incurred when new common stock is issued. Also, issuing new common stock increases the overall supply of common shares available in the market. The increased supply of stock will cause the price of all shares to drop. This often forces the firm to sell the new stock at a lower price and reduce the amount of capital that is raised. All these additional costs discourage some businesses from issuing new common stock. Most older and larger businesses do not regularly offer new common stock on the open market. Instead, they elect to raise capital through retained earnings that would otherwise be paid as dividends or by issuing bonds or commercial paper.

There is an **opportunity cost**, also known as **implicit cost**, to shareholders if a business retains earnings to raise capital. The shareholders are forgoing dividends when earnings are retained. Shareholders could have reinvested those dividend payments in stocks, bonds, and other opportunities that may have resulted in a positive return. Therefore, the retained earnings should result in an increase in a business' value that is greater than the amount a shareholder can expect to earn if the money is paid out as dividends. The difficult task for a financial manager is to calculate this amount in dollars and cents. Similar to the situation with issuing new stock, the amount shareholders could make by investing their dividend payments in the best alternative can also serve to help measure the cost of common stock. Thus, the cost of common stock involves many different factors such as dividend payments, flotation costs, the rate of return of other investment opportunities, and the risk involved in investing in common stock. We now present three different methods for measuring the cost of common stock.

Flotation costs—trying to gauge interest—must be factored in when a sport business considers issuing common stock.

CAPITAL ASSET PRICING MODEL

The first method of measuring the cost of common stock is the **capital asset pricing model (CAPM)**. It is the most commonly used approach for measuring the cost of capital (Brigham & Ehrhardt, 2005). It begins by estimating the rate of return on a risk-free investment such as a U.S. Treasury bond. Within the mathematical formula for the CAPM, we refer to the rate of return on a risk-free investment as **F**. In addition to risk-free investments, the shareholder can also purchase riskier investments such as corporate stocks and bonds. The CAPM also builds this into the calculation of the common stock cost. The most obvious investment decision would be for the shareholder to purchase more shares in the same business. Given this, we want to develop a measure of the expected return on the firm's stock. The return is, in part, based on the risk of the stock.

Risk is an important component of common stocks. Stocks with large price swings are considered more volatile than others and therefore have a higher risk level. Those stocks with a high level of risk must have the potential for a large increase in value. There are several accepted measures of a stock's level of risk. The CAPM incorporates the most commonly used measure, which is known as the beta coefficient. The beta coefficient is a measure of an individual stock's volatility. A stock with volatility similar to that of the overall stock market has a beta coefficient of 1.0. A stock that is half as volatile as the stock market has a beta of 0.5, and a stock that is twice as volatile has a beta of 2.0. The risk of a stock increases as the beta coefficient increases. Information on stocks' beta coefficients is readily available in publications such as *Value Line Investment Survey, Standard & Poor's,* and *Moody's.*

Another key component of CAPM is estimating the expected rate of return for the overall market. We want to develop the overall average return that can be expected from investing in the stock market. Using all this information, we develop an equation that will measure the expected cost of common stock:

$$C = F + \{(M - F) \times B\}$$

C = expected cost of common stock

F = expected rate of return from a risk-free investment

M = expected rate of return for the overall market

B = the company's beta coefficient

This equation attempts to measure the cost of common stock in two ways. First, it estimates the cost of a very safe investment through F, defined as the rate of return on a risk-free investment. In addition, the model builds in an additional measure of cost for the individual corporation being analyzed. This is done by first deducting the rate of return for a risk-free investment, F, from the overall stock market rate of return, M. This amount is then multiplied by the beta coefficient of the individual business' stock. The result is a measure of the additional cost, above that of a risk-free investment, for an individual business' common stock. This amount is then added to F, the cost of a risk-free investment. The sum is the total cost of common stock using the CAPM method. This method is popular because it incorporates several important variables (risk-free investment cost, overall market cost, and the individual stock's level of risk) into the computation of the cost of common stock.

 **Sport Manufacturing Company** Assume that SMC wants to raise capital by forgoing dividend payments to its stockholders. It will retain the earnings and use the funds to build a new distribution center. The company must determine its cost of raising the capital through retained earnings. Under current economic conditions, a risk-free investment will return 5%, SMC estimates the expected rate of return for the overall stock market to be 8%, and the firm's beta coefficient is 1.2. To summarize: F = 5%; M = 8%; and B = 1.2. The CAPM equation is as follows:

$$C = F + \{(M - F) \times B\}$$
$$= 5\% + [(8\% - 5\%)\,1.2]$$
$$= 5\% + 3.6\%$$
$$= 8.6\%$$

The estimated cost of common stock for SMC is 8.6%.

It is important to understand that the CAPM is not a perfect measure. Although it arrives at an exact percentage, there is still some unpredictability in the various components used to help calculate CAPM and in the final CAPM figure. We are making an estimate of the overall stock market performance that may be inaccurate. It is very difficult to predict the future performance of the stock market. In addition, the beta coefficient is a measure of the individual stock's risk, which can change over time. Last, there may be some difficulty in selecting the appropriate risk-free investment. There are many different types of short- and long-term Treasury bonds, many of which have different rates of return. Any change in these variables greatly affects the final result when we are using the CAPM.

BOND YIELD PLUS RISK PREMIUM MODEL

The second method of estimating the cost of common stock is much simpler but also much more subjective. Some financial analysts believe the cost of common stock is closely related to the firm's cost of debt. The cost of common stock will be several percentage points higher than the firm's cost of debt because of the higher level of risk associated with stock. Intuitively this makes sense: Firms with low-risk, low-interest-rate bonds should also have a low cost of common stock. Conversely, firms with high-risk and high-interest-rate debt should have a higher cost for issuing common stock.

On the basis of these concepts, the bond yield plus risk premium model was developed. It measures the cost of common stock as the yield from the firm's bonds plus some risk premium. The risk premium is usually in the 3% to 5% range and is selected by financial analysts (Brigham & Ehrhardt, 2005). One shortcoming of this model is that the risk premium is not an exact measure based on available financial data.

Sport Manufacturing Company

To return to the example of SMC, we may find that the company has outstanding bonds that were issued at 7%. We would add some risk premium to the 7% to arrive at the cost of common stock. If we say that the risk premium is 4%, we will estimate the overall cost of common stock as 11%. As with the CAPM, we cannot state that 11% will definitely be the cost of common stock for SMC. We are making an estimation of the cost.

DIVIDEND GROWTH MODEL

A third method for determining the cost of common stock is the dividend growth model. The price of common stock and its expected rate of return are, in part, related to the expected dividends that will be paid on the stock. Stockholders expect to earn some level of dividends. This is usually the amount paid in past years. But stockholders also expect that the annual dividend payments will increase in the future. Therefore, the cost of common stock is the sum of these two values (Griffin, 1991). We can represent the dividend growth model through the following equation:

$$C = \frac{E}{N} + G$$

C = required rate of return for stockholders (this serves as a measure of the cost of common stock)

E = annual dividend payment (for simplicity, we assume that these payments are fixed at the same level each year)

N = current price per share of the stock

G = annual growth rate of dividends.

The equation captures the notion that investors expect to receive a certain level of return from purchasing a common stock. That return is the **dividend yield**, as measured by the annual dividend payment divided by the current stock price, plus the expected annual dividend growth rate. For a firm to invest capital in projects, capital that would otherwise go to common stock shareholders, it must assure stockholders that the capital investment will result in a higher return than C, the required rate of return for stockholders. Although this method seems fairly straightforward, there are some problems. It can be very difficult to accurately predict the annual growth rate of dividends (G). Security analysts spend countless hours analyzing company financial data to determine future performance and profitability. Despite such efforts, they are often wrong. This is especially true for companies with very abnormal past financial performances.

Overall economic cycles and industry trends can also influence an individual business' future performance. This often occurs in some sport segments that rely on products with short life cycles. For example, very few people had even heard of professional poker or Texas hold 'em before 2003. Despite this, poker events have seen tremendous growth over the past several years. TV networks such as ESPN, Bravo, Fox Sports, and the Travel Channel have all dedicated airtime to poker events, and some players have become celebrities. Although it is unlikely that poker's popularity will continue for years to come, it is often difficult to predict these consumer trends. Who would have predicted five years ago that people would prefer to watch poker over sporting leagues such as the NHL and MLS?

CALCULATION OF THE WEIGHTED AVERAGE COST OF CAPITAL

We now have measures for the three primary components of capital: debt, preferred stock, and common stock. The next step is to combine these measures and develop an overall cost of capital. As stated earlier, the most common method is the WACC. The WACC uses the targeted levels, or proportions, of the three components along with the cost measures developed for each. Most firms have a targeted capital structure. The target is the proportion of debt to preferred stock to common stock that the business believes will be best for its future success. The proportions of target capital are represented by weights that are given to each capital type. When added up, the weights must equal 1. For example, if the debt portion has a weight of 0.1, this means that 10% of the business' targeted capital structure is funded through a debt instrument.

We can use any of the three previously discussed methods to calculate C, the cost of common stock. In the following example the CAPM is used. The equation that follows solves for the WACC.

$$WACC = (W_D \times D) + (W_S \times S) + (W_C \times C)$$

WACC = weighted average cost of capital

W_D = target weight for debt

D = cost of debt

W_S = target weight for preferred stock

S = cost of preferred stock

W_C = target weight for common stock

C = cost of common stock

Also, remember that we have already identified methods to measure D, S, and C, as highlighted by their formulas below.

$$D = R \times (1 - T)$$

$$S = \frac{v}{P}$$

$$C = F + \{(M - F) \times B\}$$

If we were to start from the beginning, we would first develop the costs of debt, preferred stock, and common stock and then weight each component, based on the target capital structure, to determine the WACC.

Sport Manufacturing Company

Assume that SMC has a targeted capital structure in which 20% will be in the form of debt, 55% will be in preferred stock, and 25% will be common stock. In addition, through the use of the measures described earlier, SMC has found that its after-tax cost of debt (D) is 8.5%, its cost of preferred stock (S) is 9.2%, and its cost of common stock (C) is 10.2%. The company needs to raise $10 million in new capital to make major renovations to its administrative offices and production facility. Management wants to know what the average cost of the capital will be if the targeted capital structure is followed. The best way to show this is to solve the formula for WACC.

$$WACC = (W_D \times D) + (W_S \times S) + (W_C \times C)$$
$$= (0.20 \times 8.5\%) + (0.55 \times 9.2\%) + (0.25 \times 10.2\%)$$
$$= 1.70\% + 5.06\% + 2.55\%$$
$$= 9.31\%$$

The WACC for SMC is 9.31%. In addition, for every $1 of new capital that is raised, 20% should be in the form of debt and have an after-tax cost of 8.5%; 55% should be preferred stock and have a cost of 9.2%; and last, 25% should be raised through common stock and have a cost of 10.2%.

Note that the WACC is the cost of new capital only. We are attempting to develop cost measures as part of the capital budgeting process. This estimate should not be used to make statements about the cost of previously issued capital. Previous capital was raised under different economic and financial circumstances, and such circumstances can greatly influence the cost of capital. Last, note that the weights used are based on a targeted capital structure. If the firm actually raises capital in proportions that vary from the targets, this will greatly affect the WACC. Again, WACC is a method to estimate the cost of capital. Any changes in the variables used in the model will change the WACC.

As with any estimations of the future, the WACC will not be accurate in every instance. As stated earlier, outside factors such as interest rates and tax rates play a role in determining WACC. Any changes in these factors would obviously affect the cost of capital. Additionally, a firm may change policies related to dividend payments, investment strategy, or capital structure. Any changes in these areas would greatly influence the WACC. For example, a change in investment assets may markedly affect the risk premium for the company. Ultimately, this may also affect the cost of common stock.

Our discussion of WACC and the cost of capital has primarily focused on publicly held businesses. Numerous businesses in the sport industry are small businesses or privately held companies (or both). Neither of these types of businesses has stocks that are openly bought and sold. This presents some unique problems when determining the cost of capital. The price of preferred and common stock is not easily obtainable because the stocks are not traded on the open market. Overall, the same principles for the cost of capital determination apply for small businesses and privately held companies. It is, however, more dif-

ficult to obtain accurate and usable financial data. In addition, many small firms do not pay any dividends. Earnings are often retained and used to grow the company. This can make it very difficult to calculate accurate costs of preferred and common stock.

In addition, most small businesses do not have publicly traded bonds. The bond yield plus risk premium method for determining the cost of common stock relies on knowing a business' bond yield. It is usually not appropriate to apply this method to small businesses.

We have now developed a method for measuring the cost of capital. The next step is to develop a method for making capital budgeting decisions. Sports managers are continually presented with a number of capital projects. They must decide which projects are worthy of being undertaken and which should be bypassed. The next section develops several different methods for making these capital budgeting decisions.

Trends in Stadium Financing

The past 20 years have seen an explosion in the construction of professional sports stadiums and arenas. New facilities have opened for teams such as the Houston Texans, Cincinnati Reds, Philadelphia Phillies, Arizona Cardinals, Charlotte Bobcats, and St. Louis Cardinals. There are several reasons for this trend in sports facility construction. Because of changes in facility design, a stadium such as FedEx Field in Washington, D.C., can produce substantially more revenue for the Redskins franchise than their previous home, Robert F. Kennedy Stadium. For example, FedEx Field has 208 luxury suites that bring in more than $15 million annually, as well as 15,000 club seats that sell for $1,000 to $2,000 per year.

The new income generated from the facility is critical for the financial success of the Redskins. As operating costs increase, due in part to rising player salaries, teams must find new income streams. Stadium revenues along with ticket sales, national broadcast rights fees, and team merchandise revenues are the main sources of income. However, unlike other revenue sources, most stadium income is not shared equally among all franchises. In the four major professional leagues, teams keep 100% of revenues from parking, concessions, advertising, and stadium naming rights. New facilities are often built to maximize these revenue sources.

Another important aspect of new professional sports facility construction is the source of funding. New facilities can cost between $250 and $500 million. It has been estimated that a new Yankee Stadium in New York could cost over $1 billion. In contrast, the Los Angeles Forum was built in 1967 for $15 million (Howard & Crompton, 2004). Given these high construction costs, the recent trend has been for new facilities to be jointly financed between the team ownership and the public sector. A popular financing method is for local and state governments to issue debt, through municipal bonds, that will be repaid at a later date. The public sector can use financing sources such as state lotteries, sales taxes, and ticket surcharges to raise the funds for debt repayment.

Cities and states have been involved in sports facility construction since the inception of professional sport. However, the end of the 20th century saw a new trend of franchise free agency. Team owners were willing to move to a city that would build a new stadium mostly financed by the public sector. Along with having a new stadium, team owners were allowed to keep a significant share of the stadium revenues. Many cities and states were willing to make such deals because of their strong interest in acquiring a professional franchise. The decade of the 1990s saw this occur several times. Art Modell moved his NFL franchise to Baltimore when the city of Cleveland refused to build a new publicly financed football stadium. Baltimore was willing to build Modell a new stadium as well as allow the team to play rent free. Modell also received all revenues from concessions, parking, and in-stadium advertising. In addition, the city permitted Modell to keep up to $75 million from the sale of permanent seat licenses (PSLs). The money from the sale of PSLs was to be used to cover the costs associated with the team's relocation and the construction of a new practice facility in Maryland. In return, Modell agreed to sign a 30-year lease and cover all operational and maintenance costs associated with the new facility, estimated at $3 to $4 million annually (Stellino, 1995).

A similar deal was signed by Georgia Frontiere, the owner of the St. Louis Rams, when she moved the team from Los Angeles. The city of St. Louis spent $260 million to build a new domed stadium for the team. In addition, the city covered the Rams' operating losses from their last season in Los Angeles and paid off $30 million in debt that the team owed to southern California. St. Louis also paid a $29 million league relocation fee and constructed a $15 million training center for the team. All these benefits allowed the team to quickly remove itself from its financial difficulties and become profitable (Stellino, 1995). This new financial success may have played a major role in the Rams' ability to acquire the necessary talent to win Super Bowl XXXIV in 2000.

However, as the 20th century drew to a close, taxpayers in several cities began to rebel. Legislators in Minnesota and voters in North Carolina rejected stadium projects that would have used public subsidization to build a new baseball facility for the Minnesota Twins. Despite this, we have still seen some teams relocate. For the 2005 season, the Montreal Expos relocated to Washington, D.C. In the NBA, the Vancouver Grizzlies moved to Memphis. One of the reasons for these moves was the promise of new sports facilities.

In most cases, team owners must contribute some funds for constructing the new facilities. In a few cases such as FedEx Field in Washington, D.C., and the Wachovia Center in Philadelphia, the team ownership has contributed a majority of the funds and also retained facility ownership. Usually, the capital necessary for these projects is financed through debt. There have been several new trends in the issuance of private stadium debt. Historically, financial institutions viewed these projects and the accompanying revenue streams as fairly high risk. As a result, the team owners' cost of capital was relatively high. Owners were usually forced to use existing assets as collateral to secure the necessary loans. In some instances, it was difficult for team owners to find financial institutions that would provide the capital. However, as facilities such as Baltimore's Camden Yards, Denver's Coors Field, and the Palace of Auburn Hills have proved to be great sources of revenue, financial institutions have loosened their purse strings. Creditors have begun to issue debt based on the future revenue streams from the facilities. Some owners can now secure loans with the expectation of future revenue streams, as opposed to existing collateral.

Another recent trend has been the refinancing of facility debt. The late 1990s and early 21st century saw some of the lowest interest rates in decades. The interest rates issued in the late 1980s and early 1990s for facility debt were significantly higher. As a result, several sports organizations refinanced their preexisting facility debt and, in some instances, saved millions of dollars. For example, in 1999 the New Jersey Sports and Exposition Authority used a complex financial technique known as a "swaption" to refinance its debt. The authority saved $9.1 million, which was used to help pay for renovation of the New York Giants' practice facility and the Continental Arena (Kaplan, 1999). The United States Tennis Association (USTA) used a similar technique to refinance a 1994 debt issuance that was used for renovations made to the National Tennis Center in Queens, New York. The USTA was able to save $3.25 million as the interest rate of its debt dropped from 6.4% to 5.94% (Kaplan, 1999). In a trend similar to that seen with American homeowners who refinanced their mortgages in the late 1990s, several sports organizations took advantage of low interest rates to save millions of dollars.

Another trend in sports facility financing is giving teams cash payments to stay in older facilities. For example, under the terms of a 10-year $186 million agreement reached in 2001, the New Orleans Saints were being paid millions to stay in the Superdome. The 2005 payment was for almost $13 million, and a large percentage of that sum had to be borrowed by the state ("Louisiana Forks Over," 2005). This arrangement was in danger of coming to an end because of the effects of hurricane Katrina. New Orleans was in no condition to keep making payments to keep the team in town, which was part of the impetus for the Saints to investigate a move to San Antonio. Ultimately, the city, state, Saints' ownership, and NFL were able to reach an agreement to keep the team in the New Orleans Superdome after its post-Katrina renovation.

CAPITAL BUDGETING DECISION METHODS

Sport businesses have a variety of options with respect to spending funds. Capital spending on fixed assets such as equipment, facilities, and new technology is common. This section presents several methods for making decisions on how to allocate capital funds. Before examining decision making, we must consider the importance of time. Then we look at net present value, the payback rule, the discounted payback rule, and the internal rate of return. The first point of analysis needs to be the present value of an income stream as determined through the time value of money.

IMPORTANCE OF TIME

An important element of capital budgeting is time. Capital spending and obtaining the returns from capital projects occur over many years. Therefore, the timing of the costs and revenues is critical. In chapter 6 we discuss the time value of money and the importance of determining the present value of a future stream of income. The following case study example can help explain the importance of understanding time, but feel free to skip it if you think you have a good grasp of the concept. For those wishing a quick review, please read the following example.

 The University of Milford (U of M) is approached by a wealthy philanthropist who would like to make a large donation to the athletic department. The philanthropist offers two options for how the money will be paid:

1. The athletic department can receive a $500,000 check today.
2. The athletic department can receive a $550,000 check in one year.

The decision is based on which option is more valuable. If the present value of $550,000 in one year is greater than the present value of the $500,000 check received today, U of M should select option 2. But how do we determine which option is more valuable? Obviously, $500,000 today is worth more than $500,000 a year from now, but is $500,000 today worth more than $550,000 a year from now? U of M

can invest the $500,000 today in an interest-bearing account and have more than $500,000 in one year. But can it make an additional $50,000 from the investment? Suppose U of M investigates the payoff from the best risk-free investment opportunity, probably a U.S. government security, and learns that the annual interest rate is 7.0%. Therefore, $500,000 invested in a U.S. government security will give U of M $535,000 in one year. Under these circumstances, the university should obviously select option 2 and take the $550,000 in one year.

Another method for making this decision is to calculate the present value of option 2. Using this process, U of M will determine the current dollar value of receiving $550,000 in one year. To make the decision, the university will need to know the expected rate of return. The rate of return is the reward demanded by investors for waiting one year to receive a payment. Assume that U of M would expect no more than a 7.0% return from its best alternative risk-free investment. Therefore, we will use 7.0% as the rate of return. The rate of return is then used

$$\text{discount factor} = \frac{1}{1+r}$$

to develop a discount factor. Mathematically, the discount factor is expressed as follows:

r = the expected return

The discount factor is then used to determine the present value of the $550,000 that will be received in one year. The future payout, in this case $550,000, is represented by FP. The following mathematical formula represents this concept.

$$PV = R \times FP$$

PV = present value
R = discount factor

$$PV = \frac{1}{1.07} \times FP$$
$$PV = \frac{1}{1.07} \times 550,000$$

FP = future payout

Here is the calculation for our example:

$$PV = 0.9346 \times \$550,000$$
$$PV = \$514,030$$

As you can see, $514,030 is the present value of receiving $550,000 in one year. Since this is greater than $500,000, U of M should select option 2. However, if we go through the same process but assume that the expected rate of return is 15%, this would cause the present value of option 2 to become $478,280. In this instance, the university should select option 1. The rate of return is very important in the determination of present value. In general, it represents the reward investors demand for accepting a payment made at a later date. This has obvious ramifications for capital spending, the investment of money today in an effort to receive future cash flows.

Although the calculations in this example help establish which choice will be the most economical, they do not take into account other variables. For example, if U of M does not build a park with the $500,000 this year, inflation and increased building costs might force the university to pay $575,000 next year. Furthermore, the future contains numerous variables that might make budgeting decisions that much more difficult. U of M's athletic department might approve an additional $500,000 for a new field, but those funds might not be available if the athletic department waits a year to receive the $550,000 from the philanthropist.

NET PRESENT VALUE

The calculation of present value leads us to the next important facet of capital budgeting. For all capital investments, a successful sports manager should calculate the present value of the expected future income related to the project. An investment is considered wise if the present value of this future income is greater than the necessary investment. The financial term associated with this process is **net present value (NPV)**. The NPV is the difference between the present value of the future income and the required investment. It can be represented as follows:

$$NPV = PV - RI$$

NPV = net present value

PV = present value of future income

RI = required investment

The following case study example highlights how to apply NPV.

 The University of Milford must decide if it wants to spend $1 million to construct 10 new luxury suites in the basketball arena. Each suite will last for 10 years. At the end of 10 years, we will assume that the suites will need to be replaced and will have no salvage value. For simplicity, we will also assume that each luxury suite can be rented for $30,000 per year and that no other income will be made from the suites. The construction project will take one year. Therefore, the first income from the suites will be earned one year from today. If we think of one year from now as the end of year 1, income will flow into U of M at the ends of years 1 through 10. Even though this example is not completely accurate, it depicts the concept of NPV in a simplified manner.

The University of Milford must calculate the NPV of this investment opportunity before making the decision. So each year, starting next year, U of M will have $300,000 in income for the next 10 years. Overall, the project will generate $3 million in income. However, the present value of the income stream must be calculated. Unlike the situation in the previous example, in which one **payoff** was to be received one year into the future, here there is a stream of future payoffs. Thus, the present value of each future year's payoff must be calculated. The following mathematical formula is used to calculate cash flows in future years (Brigham & Ehrhardt, 2005):

$$PV = \left(\frac{1}{1+r} \times FP_1\right) + \left(\frac{1}{(1+r)^2} \times FP_2\right) +$$
$$\left(\frac{1}{(1+r)^3} \times FP_3\right) + \cdots + \left(\frac{1}{(1+r)^{10}} \times FP_{10}\right)$$

FP_1 = future payoff one year from now

FP_2 = future payoff two years from now and so on

These calculations will continue up to the end of year 10. We will assume that the rate of return for U of M is 8%. We can rewrite the equation as:

$$PV = \left(\frac{1}{1.08} \times \$300,000\right) + \left(\frac{1}{1.08^2} \times \$300,000\right) +$$
$$\left(\frac{1}{1.08^3} \times \$300,000\right) + \cdots +$$
$$\left(\frac{1}{1.08^{10}} \times \$300,000\right)$$
$$= \$2,013,000$$

The present value of $2,013,000 can then be used to calculate the NPV of the capital expenditure. Note that these calculations can be done manually. However, if the rate of return and stream of income are constant throughout a project, an annuity table, such as table A.3 (pp. 322-323), can be used. The table will save a great deal of time and frustration! As stated previously, the initial investment is $1 million, and the present value of the stream of income is $2,013,000. So, we can calculate the NPV as follows:

$$NPV = \$2,013,000 - \$1,000,000$$
$$= \$1,013,000$$

The NPV of the construction of 10 luxury boxes is positive and slightly over $1 million. The project definitely is worth more than it costs the U of M athletic department.

Net present value is an important capital budgeting component. Any project that has a negative NPV should not be undertaken. The reason is that the project's cost is higher than the projected income—financially, it is a losing proposition. However, not all projects that have a positive NPV must be undertaken. We will return to the selection of capital spending projects in a later section.

Next, it is important to note that there are other methods besides NPV for making a capital budgeting decision. All these methods have strengths and weaknesses. The NPV method was presented first because it is the most often used and is regarded as the best. Although it is important to recognize and discuss these other methods, the NPV method is strongly recommended.

THE PAYBACK RULE

A second method of analyzing the value of a capital project is through the use of the payback rule. The payback rule analyzes how long it will take a business to receive its money back after investing in a capital project. The money is paid back through the stream of future income related to the project. The payback rule may be best explained through the following case study example.

Assume that U of M has $1 million that it wants to invest in a capital project. The initial investment will result in a future cash flow into the university. The university has determined it has two possible capital projects costing $1 million each. It must decide which one to select. These are the two choices:

Project A: A new outdoor aquatics facility. The facility will produce $250,000 in revenue in the first year and $300,000 per year for two subsequent years. In the fourth and final year, the cash flow will be $400,000. For simplicity, we will assume that there are no other costs or revenues. The total revenue for the next four years will total $1.25 million.

Project B: A new recreational gymnasium to be used for adult and youth sports leagues. This facility will produce $100,000 in the first year and $450,000 per year for the two subsequent years. However, it is estimated that because of a decrease in future demand, the cash flow for the fourth year will be only $100,000. The total revenue for the next four years will be $1.1 million.

The question is, which capital project should U of M select? The university is going to use the payback rule to make this decision. U of M has decided that all of the initial $1 million investment must be paid back within three years. If this cannot occur, capital funds will not be allocated for the project. Table 11.1 depicts the cash flows over time, the expected **payback periods**, and the NPV for each project.

Examining table 11.1, we see that it will take four years for project A to repay the investment, whereas the investment for project B will be repaid within three years. Given U of M's payback rule of three years, project B is the one to select. The cash flow from this project can repay the $1 million initial investment in three years.

The decision would change dramatically if we utilized the NPV method. To determine NPV, we assume that the opportunity cost of capital is 8%. We find that the NPV of project A is $20,842, and the NPV for project B is –$90,880. Using the NPV method, project B would be rejected and U of M would select project A.

Table 11.1 Time Line of Cash Flows for Projects A and B

Project	P_0	P_1	P_2	P_3	P_4	Payback period	Net present value at 8%
A	–$1 million	$250,000	$300,000	$300,000	$400,000	4 years	$20,842
B	–$1 million	$100,000	$450,000	$450,000	$100,000	3 years	–$90,880

As you can see from the example, which capital budgeting decision method is used can have a major effect on capital budgeting. The reason for the difference is that the payback rule equally weights all cash flows. With use of the payback rule, the importance of time is ignored. This rule centers on which investment option will repay the initial outlay in the shortest amount of time. The NPV method discounts future cash flows based on the opportunity cost of capital. It also looks at the entire cash flow over the life of the project, in this case four years. The university's payback rule of three years means that only the cash flows in the first three years are important; even if project A had a cash flow of $1 billion in the fourth year, it would not be selected. The cash flow in the fourth year is meaningless in this example if we are using the payback rule. This is another obvious weakness of the payback rule; it ignores the cash flows after the arbitrarily selected payback date.

To account for the payback rule's failure to recognize the time value of money, the discounted payback rule has been developed.

DISCOUNTED PAYBACK RULE

The **discounted payback rule** discounts the future cash flows based on the opportunity cost of capital.

To return to our previous example, table 11.2 shows the cash flows when U of M applies the discounted payback rule, incorporating an 8% rate of return.

Using the discounted payback rule, the payback period remains at four years for project A. Project B does not produce enough cash flow in four years to cover the initial investment. Therefore, using the discounted payback rule and a predetermined three-year maximum payback period, both projects are rejected. However, remember that using the NPV method would lead to the selection of project A, and the original payback rule would result in the selection of project B. Again, which capital budgeting decision method is used has a major impact on the disbursement of long-term capital.

INTERNAL RATE OF RETURN METHOD

The last method for making capital budgeting decisions is to use the **internal rate of return** (IRR). As with NPV and the discounted payback rule, IRR relies on the opportunity cost of capital and the time value of money. As stated earlier, the opportunity cost of capital is the return obtained by investing the capital in the next best alternative. For example, if you can place $100,000 in an interest-bearing investment that will result in your having $110,000 at the end of one year, the rate of return is 10%. Therefore, you would invest only in projects that can return more than $110,000. The IRR method emphasizes finding the rate of return for which NPV equals zero. Table 11.3 displays a situation in which a $1,000 capital investment results in a $750 cash flow in one year and a $500 cash flow in two years.

The goal of the IRR method is to find the rate of return for which NPV equals zero. The mathematical model for our example in table 11.3 is as follows:

$$NPV = P_0 + \frac{P_1}{1+r} + \frac{P_2}{1+r^2} = 0$$

P_0 = cash flow at time zero

P_1 = cash flow in first year

r = rate of return

P_2 = cash flow in second year

To complete the formula we need to solve for r, the rate of return. This can be difficult without the proper computer software. If you attempt to solve the formula manually, it will be a matter of trial and error. The trial-and-error process for manual calculation requires you to estimate for r and keep lowering or raising r until the equation equals zero. With a computer you can perform the analysis almost instantaneously. If we input the information from table 11.3, the equation can be rewritten as:

$$NPV = -\$1,000 + \frac{\$750}{1+r} + \frac{\$500}{1+r^2} = 0$$

Table 11.2 Time Line of Discounted Cash Flows for Projects A and B

Project	P_0	P_1	P_2	P_3	P_4	Payback period	Net present value at 8%
A	−$1 million	$231,481	$257,210	$238,150	$294,009	4 years	$20,842
B	−$1 million	$92,593	$385,802	$357,225	$73,502	>4 years	−$90,880

Table 11.3 Time Line of Cash Flows

Time 0 (P_0)	In one year (P_1)	In two years (P_2)
−$1,000	$750	$500

We must now solve for r. Using trial and error, let's start with a 10% rate of return. If we solve the equation when r = 0.10, we find that the NPV equals $95.10. We now know that the IRR for which NPV will equal zero is greater than 0.10. We continue this trial-and-error process until we find the rate of return at which NPV equals zero. In our example, NPV will equal zero when r equals 0.175. A wise sports manager will undertake this capital project if he believes its opportunity cost of capital is less than 17.5%. In other words, he will go ahead with the project if no other investment choices have an expected rate of return greater than 17.5%.

RISK AND CAPITAL BUDGETING

The Smiths

Should the Smiths construct a new $3 million fitness center that will result in an annual increase of $300,000 in profit? Initially, you might answer yes, noting that an additional $300,000 in profit, a 10% return on investment, is fairly high. But what if the Smiths can also take that $3 million and purchase U.S. Treasury bonds that are guaranteed to provide a 9% return each year? Initially, the new fitness center still appears to be the best opportunity. But is the 10% return guaranteed? No. The 9% return from the U.S. Treasury bonds is definitely guaranteed. The expected return on the new fitness center is greater, but there is no guarantee that the return on investment will be 10%. It is an expected return.

This example illustrates the importance of risk and uncertainty. When you are calculating the return on investment for capital expenditures, risk is very important. Different capital projects have different levels of risk. To accept a higher level of risk for a project, the investor must expect the returns to also be higher. In every case, a wise sports manager faced with the choice of selecting one of two capital investment opportunities with equal returns will select the one with the lower risk.

There is some level of risk with all capital projects. Calculations of expected returns on investments and pro forma budgets are forecasts of future costs and revenues. Therefore, when discussing capital investment, we refer to expected payoffs and expected rates of return. Pro forma budgets are discussed in chapter 7.

PROJECTING CASH FLOW

The discussion to this point has centered on capital budgeting from the cost side. The calculation of capital costs is an integral part of capital budgeting, but it is only half the story. The other half deals with income and with developing methods to estimate future income that results from capital investment. The combination of expenses and income is known as the cash flow. The accurate projection of cash flows, both expenses and income, is a key to making wise capital budgeting decisions. Although no projection of future income is going to be totally accurate, it is imperative for a financial manager to make the best and most accurate attempt.

Chapter 5 covers the use of financial tools such as balance sheets and income statements to explain a business' current and past financial positions. Projecting cash flow also relies on financial tools, but the emphasis shifts to pro forma statements, discussed in chapter 7. Pro forma statements are very important to capital budgeting because an organization is investing capital today that will result in future cash flows.

The future cash flows that result from capital investment are dependent on many business factors. For example, if U of M plans to spend $100 million on a new 50,000-seat football stadium, the future cash flow resulting from this spending may be difficult to accurately estimate. The following is a list of factors that may affect future cash flow for such a project:

- Is there demand for 50,000 tickets to U of M football games? Before construction, an in-depth **market analysis** should be undertaken to determine spectator demand.

- How important is ticket price to the spectators? Would an increase in the ticket price affect spectator demand?

- The University of Milford cannot assume it will always put a winning team on the field. How will winning and losing affect spectator attendance?

- If the project succeeds and the 50,000 seats are filled on a regular basis, can the stadium be expanded in the future?

- If the capital is raised, in part, through booster donations, how will this affect fund-raising efforts for other parts of the athletic program and the university? Will other projects or budgets be affected by the stadium project?

- How much additional cash will flow into the athletic department? If the new stadium is built, will it really have an effect on future cash flow as compared with the current cash flow from football games?

- In addition to football games, what other uses would the facility have, and what would the cash flow be from those uses?

- If luxury seating or boxes are included, is there a demand from corporate clients for these seats? What is the fair price for the luxury seating or boxes?

- How much will it cost to maintain and repair the stadium once it is built?

- What will be the cost for the capital required to construct the facility?

All the factors listed are important when projecting the cash flow from a new university sports facility. It is necessary to ask questions related to market demand, sales projections, operating costs, and capital costs when attempting to project future cash flow. Again, remember that projecting future cash flow is not an exact science. A financial manager attempts to make the best possible estimation based on available data and research.

We will define a project's cash flows as the net cash inflows and investment expenditures associated with the project (Brigham & Ehrhardt, 2005). Again, projecting future cash flow is the most difficult facet of capital budgeting.

For a sports organization, many different people and departments should be involved in any major capital projects. For example, when the University of Milford constructs its new stadium, several departments will be involved in this process. The ticketing and marketing departments need to make projections on ticket sales and ticket pricing. The university's construction planners and outside construction firms need to estimate construction costs. Perhaps the university's physical plant department should be consulted to estimate maintenance costs. An event planner or promoter can help determine what revenues will be generated from other events being held in the stadium. The university's advancement or fund-raising office can estimate the effect of stadium fund-raising on other university fund-raising endeavors.

Several capital budgeting methods such as the payback rule, discounted payback rule, NPV, and IRR have already been presented. It is essential to remember that all these sound financial techniques are worthless if poor cash flow projections are made. Poor decisions will result if cash flow estimations are inaccurate.

An organization's financial staff must play a prominent role in projecting the cash flow. It is the job of the financial managers to take all the information obtained from other departments and develop accurate projections. There are several common pitfalls that must be avoided. For a number of reasons such as career advancement, emotional ties, or possible benefits to their department, some individuals in other departments may be strong supporters of specific capital projects. This bias may affect the accuracy of the information they provide to the financial staff. It is the responsibility of the financial staff to ensure that projections are as accurate as possible. Unfortunately, this is not always easy.

All businesses have a limited capital budget and many alternatives for capital spending. Each project must be evaluated on its own financial worth and also needs to be compared with other options. Those investment opportunities that fit within the capital budget and have the highest NPV are the most attractive. In the real world, the process of quantifying the NPV of investment choices is not this easy. Many confounding factors come into play. One capital spending project may affect another, and some may need to happen simultaneously to be successful. It is management's job to decipher all this information.

MEASURING RELEVANT CASH FLOW

The first step in projecting cash flow is to measure the relevant cash flow for a capital project. All existing firms have a cash flow. The key to accurately measuring a single project's cash flow is to include only new cash flow. The new, or incremental, cash flow is the additional future cash flow, either internal or external to the business, that results only from the decision to undertake a project. Any cash flow that occurs regardless of the presence of a new project should not be included in the calculation of relevant cash flow. This is a very important concept that you need to remember throughout this discussion. With respect to measuring incremental cash flows, there are several common errors financial managers make.

The first common error relates to measuring sunk costs. **Sunk costs** are costs that have already occurred and do not change regardless of the decision to undertake a project.

 U of M might pay $20,000 for a feasibility study on the construction of a new student recreation building. If as a result of this report the university decides not to construct the building, it would still have to pay for the feasibility study. The cost is incurred regardless of the outcome. According to our definition of incremental cash flow, the $20,000 is not important in making the capital spending decision. The money has already been spent, and it should not be included as a cost when U of M is projecting cash flow for the capital project.

Another important aspect of projecting relevant cash flow, and the second common error, is opportunity cost. Opportunity cost refers to the most valuable alternative that is forgone if a particular capital project is undertaken.

 Returning to the U of M example, the recreation building must be built on a piece of land. The university has a parcel of land that can be used, but the land could also be used for new playing fields or a swimming pool. Initially, you might think that the cost of land is zero because U of M already owns the land. This is not accurate. There is an opportunity cost associated with using that piece of land; the university is forgoing its next best alternative use of the land. The next best alternative may be to build a swimming pool. The university must estimate the value of the land and include this in its projection of project costs. This is especially true if the university will need to buy a new piece of land in the future to build a pool.

Failure to analyze the impact of any funding decision is a third common error. Most new capital spending projects have an effect on the overall organization.

 If U of M elects to build the new student recreation building, there may be side effects felt by other parts of the university. Perhaps student fees will increase for activities that do not take place in the new recreation center. Visitors to the new facility will learn more about other activities at the university and might pay to attend them. This is an example of a positive side effect, also known as a spillover effect. However, there can also be negative spillover effects. Students may decide to decrease their activities at other university venues or events in order to go to the new facility. This drop in attendance, and most likely income, at other locations is directly related to the new project. These types of spillover effects must be factored into projecting cash flows.

The failure to appreciate the impact of a decision on net working capital is another common error. New projects normally result in an increase in net working capital. Most projects need some cash on hand to pay for short-term expenses that arise.

 U of M may need to purchase a scoreboard for the new facility using net working capital. Additional net working capital must be allotted for any new project. We could expect the increased investment in net working capital to be recouped by the university at the end of the project's life span. If the new facility has a life span of 30 years, at the end of that 30 years the scoreboard will no longer be needed. The scoreboard can possibly be sold for scrap value, and some of the initial investment in net working capital can be recouped. The increase in net working capital should almost be viewed as a loan that will be repaid at the end of the project's life span.

The last common error is including interest payments in the cash flow projections. We are interested only in the cash flows, both income and expense, that result directly from the project's assets. Interest payments and dividends are payments to creditors and shareholders. They are not expenses that result from the assets themselves. But perhaps more important, as already discussed, interest and dividend payments were included in calculating capital costs. If we also include them as cash outflows, we would be double counting these payments. They have already been accounted for in the cost of capital, so they do not need to be included as expenses (Brigham & Ehrhardt, 2005).

As you can see, some aspects of projecting cash flow are complex. The easiest way to explain the projection of cash flow for a capital project is probably through an example.

EXAMPLE OF PROJECTING CASH FLOW: NEW FITNESS FACILITY

Pro forma financial statements must be developed to project cash flow for the Smiths' new fitness facility construction project. Pro formas are the easiest and most convenient method for projecting cash flow. To develop these statements, we need estimates of items such as fixed costs, variable costs, unit sales, and sales price per unit. Information must also be obtained on the change in net working capital and the total required investment. For our example, several numbers will be simplified. We will limit the life span of the facility to four years. A four-year life span is somewhat unrealistic (the facility would probably last much longer than that), but it will make our example of projecting cash flow much easier to understand. The important thing is to understand the concepts of projecting cash flow.

Several assumptions will be made for the new facility. The new facility will be built on land valued at $250,000. The Smiths currently own the property and have already had an offer from another business to purchase the land for this amount. The construction cost of the building will be $400,000. The equipment that will be required, such as fitness machines, weights, and computers, will cost $100,000. The equipment can be fully depreciated over four years. For simplicity we will assume that the new facility can be constructed in one year and will open for business the following year. Therefore, all the land, building, and equipment costs will occur in the same **fiscal year** (2007), and income from the facility will occur from 2008 to 2011. This assumption is also somewhat unrealistic, but it will make the example much easier to understand. Table 11.4 provides an overview of the investment costs for the project.

At the end of the building's four-year life span, the land will still have a value of $250,000 and the building

will be worth $200,000. Therefore, straight-line depreciation will be used to depreciate the $200,000 loss in value over the four years. The value of the equipment will be equal to the cost of removing it from the site; therefore we will state that the overall value of the equipment in four years will be zero.

The Smiths believe that 1,000 memberships can be sold at an average price of $500 per year. Bob and Cheryl estimate that they will incur about $100 per person in variable costs (e.g., staff salaries, benefits, and supplies such as towels). For a membership level of 1,000, fixed costs such as rent, electricity, and water will be approximately $70,000 per year. Again for simplicity, we will assume that there is no inflation and that the level of sales will remain at 1,000 memberships for each of the four years of operation.

Also, to open the new facility, the Smiths must initially increase their net working capital. The net working capital for the entire organization will be increased from its prior level of $65,000 to $75,000. The additional $10,000 in the first year must be included as a cash flow. However, the $10,000 will be retained at the end of the project, and that must also be included in the projections of total cash flow. The new facility will be subject to federal, state, and local taxes. The total cumulative tax rate will be 35%. Last, the WACC for the Smiths is 9.5%, and we will assume an interest rate (r) of 5%.

From all this information, we can construct our pro forma statement of cash flows as shown in table 11.5. As you can see, a pro forma cash flow statement is somewhat complex. But it does capture the expected inflows and outflows of cash for the new facility during its four-year operational life span. There are several important aspects to discuss here. First, notice that depreciation is added back into the calculation of cash flow. Depreciation is an item that is included as part of a business' balance sheet in order to calculate its accounting value. However, it is not a flow of cash into or out of a firm. Therefore, although it is initially deducted in the cash flow statement, depreciation is ultimately added back into the cash flow.

This is very important and is worth reemphasizing—the cash flow statement measures the inflows and outflows of cash for a firm, and depreciation is not a cash flow. The important result from the cash flow statement is that it provides a projection for the amount of cash that will accrue from operating the new facility. The cash flows range from $230,750 in 2008 to $250,750 in 2011. The difference in cash flows occurs because the Smiths must increase their net working capital in 2008 in order to start the operation. However, they will get this $10,000 back in 2011 when the facility closes.

Table 11.4   Investment Outlays for 2007 (Year 1)

Fixed assets	Cost ($)
Land	250,000
Building	400,000
Equipment	100,000
Total initial investment	**$750,000**

Table 11.5 Net Cash Flows

	2008 (year 2)	2009 (year 3)	2010 (year 4)	2011 (year 5)
Unit sales	1,000	1,000	1,000	1,000
Sales price	$500	$500	$500	$500
Net sales	**$500,000**	**$500,000**	**$500,000**	**$500,000**
Variable costs	$100,000	$100,000	$100,000	$100,000
Fixed costs	$70,000	$70,000	$70,000	$70,000
Depreciation (building)	$50,000	$50,000	$50,000	$50,000
Depreciation (equipment)	$25,000	$25,000	$25,000	$25,000
Earnings before taxes	**$255,000**	**$255,000**	**$255,000**	**$255,000**
Taxes (35%)	$89,250	$89,250	$89,250	$89,250
Projected net operating income	**$165,750**	**$165,750**	**$165,750**	**$165,750**
Add back noncash expenses*	$75,000	$75,000	$75,000	$75,000
Cash flow from operations	**$240,750**	**$240,750**	**$240,750**	**$240,750**
Investment in net working capital	($10,000)			$10,000
Total projected cash flow	**$230,750**	**$240,750**	**$240,750**	**$250,750**

*Depreciation is used for tax purposes. However, it is not a cash flow, and therefore the $75,000 is added back into the cash flow statement.

The next step for Bob and Cheryl is to make the decision about undertaking this project. At this point, they have a projection on the cost of construction for the facility and the projected cash flows during the life of the operation. The importance of the time value of money must be mentioned. The Smiths are using capital today to construct a facility that will increase future cash flow. The future cash flow must be discounted to account for the time value of money.

 In the example of the Smiths' project, we will assume that there is no inflation. The time line in table 11.6 captures the cash flow analysis. Additionally, the value of the land must be included in the cost of the project.

Based on the assumptions that have been made and the projected cash flows that are presented in tables 11.5, 11.6, and 11.7 we can calculate the net present value, internal rate of return, and discounted payback period. You should be able to make these calculations on your own.

Table 11.6 Time Line of Net Cash Flows (2007-2011)

Year	Net cash flow ($)
2007	−750,000
2008	230,750
2009	240,750
2010	240,750
2011	250,750

Net Present Value

$$NPV = P_0 + \{P_1 / (1 + r)\} + \{P_2 / (1 + r)^2\} + \{P_3 / (1 + r)^3\} + \{P_4 / (1 + r)^4\}$$

Assume $r = 5\%$.

$$NPV = -\$750,000 + \{\$230,750 / (1 + 0.05)\} + \{\$240,750 / (1 + 0.05)^2\} + \{\$240,750 / (1 + 0.05)^3\} + \{\$250,750 / (1 + 0.05)^4\}$$

$$NPV = -\$750,000 + \{\$230,750 / 1.05\} + \{\$240,750 / 1.1025\} + \{\$240,750 / 1.1576\} + \{\$250,750 / 1.2155\}$$

$$NPV = -\$750,000 + \$219,762 + \$218,367 + \$207,969 + \$206,293 = \$102,391$$

Internal Rate of Return

$$NPV = P_0 + \{P_1 / (1 + r)\} + \{P_2 / (1 + r)^2\} + \{P_3 / (1 + r)^3\} + \{P_4 / (1 + r)^4\} = 0$$

$$NPV = -\$750,000 + \{\$230,750 / (1 + r)\} + \{\$240,750 / (1 + r)^2\} + \{\$240,750 / (1 + r)^3\} + \{\$250,750 / (1 + r)^4\} = 0$$

Through trial and error, we find that for NPV to equal 0 in the previous equation, r must equal 0.1066, or 10.66%.

Table 11.7 presents the calculations for determining the discounted payback period. For each time

Table 11.7 Discounted Payback Period (5% interest rate)

	2007	2008	2009	2010	2011	Discounted payback period
Cash flow	−$750,000	$230,750	$240,750	$240,750	$250,750	
Discounted cash flow	−$750,000	$219,762	$218,367	$207,969	$206,293	
Aggregate discounted cash flow		−$530,238	−$311,871	−$103,902	$102,391	Approximately 3.5 years

period, the discounted cash flow values, which were calculated when determining the NPV, are deducted from the initial investment. The discounted paypack period is the estimated length of time it will take to repay the investment after discounting the value of the cash flows due to the passage of time. In this case, it will take approximately 3.5 years to generate the cash flows necessary to repay the initial $750,000 investment.

As the calculations show, the NPV of this project is $102,391. Because the NPV is positive, it appears that this is a capital project that could be undertaken. Additionally, the IRR is higher than the weighted average cost of capital (WACC), 10.7% versus 9.5%. Therefore, a manager who uses IRR as a basis for capital budgeting decisions would also accept this project. Finally, through use of the discounted payback method, it would take approximately 3.5 years to pay back the initial capital outlay of $750,000. Thus, someone basing his decision on the discounted payback method may elect to pass on this project and search for other business opportunities. As stated earlier, the Smiths want to recoup their investment within 4 years. As this example clearly shows, there can be discrepancies across capital budgeting decision techniques.

All these measures including IRR, NPV, and the discounted payback method can be used by a financial manager in making the capital budgeting decision for this project.

You should note that a project should not be undertaken solely because it has a positive NPV or an IRR that is higher than the WACC. Capital budgeting is one part of a sports organization's overall financial management strategy. The capital project must fit into the organization's long-term objectives. A sporting goods company may have an opportunity to invest in a capital project involving athlete representation that will result in a positive NPV. However, if this project does not fit into the overall organizational objective, it should not be undertaken.

CONCLUSION

Capital spending is an integral part of financial management. Ultimately, it ensures the long-term success of the organization. Sport businesses must develop capital budgets that will increase the stock value. The primary sources of capital for private or public sport businesses and organizations are debt and equity. Equity can take the form of preferred stock, common stock, and retained earnings. Government-owned and nonprofit sports organizations do not have ownership rights and therefore cannot raise capital through the sale of equity ownership interests. However, these organizations can raise money through donations and gifts. Many college athletic departments rely on donations as a major source of capital for spending in areas such as facility construction and equipment.

The cost of capital is a primary concern for all sport businesses. A capital project should be undertaken only if the projected revenue is greater than the projected cost. Otherwise, the funds can be more efficiently used in other ways (e.g., redistributed to shareholders or owners). There are several ways to calculate the costs of the various capital components. The CAPM, bond yield plus risk premium model, and dividend growth model can all be used to calculate the cost of common stock. Once the cost of each capital component has been determined, the WACC method is most commonly used to calculate the overall cost of capital.

The cost of capital is only one piece of capital budgeting. Managers must also determine the additional revenue that will be generated from a capital project. Only new or marginal revenue should be considered when making this projection. Because of risk and uncertainty, it is best to establish a range of expected revenues. Best-case, worst-case, and most likely (also called middle-of-the-road) estimates of future revenues are recommended.

The next step is to use the cost and revenue estimates to project cash flow statements. These pro forma statements are critical for making a final capital budgeting decision. They allow a financial manager to organize and analyze a wealth of data related to a capital project.

A wise financial manager must analyze the validity of the projections that are included in calculating cash flows. If poor or inaccurate projections are used, the results are worthless. Accurate financial data are critical for the success of capital budgeting decisions. Businesses often develop several measures for projecting cash flows. For example, they might make several projections based on different economic conditions. Perhaps a business develops worst-case, best-case, and most likely projections. The worst-case projection would capture a situation in which sales are low, economic conditions are poor, and costs are larger than expected. Calculations of the WACC, NPV, and IRR would provide the financial manager with the absolutely worst result. This is valuable information to have when making a capital budgeting decision. Similarly, it is beneficial to know what the best-case scenario is. This projection provides a measure of the projected return when all variables are at their best. As you can probably guess, the most likely scenario would be the most realistic based on the available information. But although the most likely scenario is the most realistic, it is valuable to have projections for the range of other possible outcomes.

The final step is to make a decision on the capital project. The capital budgeting decision will affect the future direction of the sports organization. For example, constructing a new facility, signing a professional athlete to a long-term contract, or purchasing new technology has major effects on a sport business' future value. Three models used in capital budgeting are NPV, the discounted payback rule, and IRR. Each has inherent strengths and weaknesses. Financial managers should use the method or methods that they believe are most appropriate for their organizations.

CLASS DISCUSSION TOPICS

1. Why is a business' capital structure important?
2. What would happen if a business had too much in bonds or stocks as part of its capital structure?
3. Which funding option would be the most economical to issue if you were trying to raise $100 million?
4. What does flotation cost mean?
5. Why is the time value of money important?
6. Why is the payback rule important when analyzing financial issues?
7. What does the IRR mean?
8. If you were to make a capital budgeting decision based on project cash flows, would you prefer to use NPV, the IRR method, the payback rule, or the discounted payback rule? Why would you use the method that you have selected? What is the advantage of using multiple methods?
9. There are several methods for determining the cost of common stock. Which method do you think is the best, and why?
10. What is the present value of receiving $5 million in 10 years assuming that the discount factor is 5%?

12

SHORT-TERM FINANCIAL MANAGEMENT

CHAPTER OBJECTIVES

After studying this chapter, you should be able to do the following:

- Understand the definition of net working capital and see how net working capital is calculated.

- Discuss cash management by sport businesses, including how much cash to hold.

- Understand what is involved in the efficient collection and disbursement of cash.

- Describe how firms manage the granting of credit and how they set credit terms.

- Identify issues that arise as businesses engage in collections management, the conversion of accounts receivable to cash.

In chapters 8 and 11, we focus on long-range financing, particularly capital budgeting. In this chapter, our focus is the management of working capital (i.e., the current assets and liabilities of a business).

Working capital management can be viewed as short-term financial management because it centers on current assets and liabilities that generate inflows or outflows of cash to or from a business within a year or less. For example, short-term financial management is occurring if SMC buys raw materials, pays for them in cash, and then uses the raw materials to produce and sell golf clubs within one year for cash. By contrast, capital budgeting is not considered short-term financial management because it tends to focus on projects of several years' duration. For example, if SMC buys machinery to assemble tennis rackets, the machine may be used for several years until it either becomes obsolete or wears out. The analysis of the decision to buy the machinery relies on the tools of capital budgeting that were introduced in chapter 11.

In this chapter, we focus on several key areas of short-term financial management. These areas include cash management, credit management, and collections management. But first we briefly review current assets and liabilities.

REVIEW OF CURRENT ASSETS AND LIABILITIES

Figure 12.1 provides a breakdown of current assets and current liabilities for all manufacturing corporations in the United States in the second quarter of 2006. Current assets include cash and other assets expected to be converted to cash within one year. Current assets total $1,979.2 billion, while current liabilities total $1,466.7 billion. Net working capital (current assets minus current liabilities) equal $512.5 billion.

As shown in figure 12.1, accounts receivable are an extremely important current asset based on their value relative to other current assets. Accounts receiv-

able consist of unpaid bills for goods and services that have been sold to customers.

To operate their fitness center, the Smiths bill their patrons for membership dues. When the patrons are initially billed, accounts receivable increase. As membership dues are paid, the **account balance** in accounts receivable declines, and the balance in cash increases.

Inventories consist of raw materials, work in progress, and finished goods awaiting shipment to customers. Inventories are discussed in more detail in chapter 13. Cash consists of currency, funds in checking accounts, and funds in savings accounts. Marketable securities include commercial paper, short-term unsecured debt that is sold by other firms, U.S. Treasury bills, and state and local government-issued debt.

Other current assets include prepaid expenses (such as rent, utilities, and insurance) that have been purchased for use within one year. Prepaid expenses are items of value that have future usefulness in business operations. For example, all businesses purchase various types of insurance policies for protection against burglary, fire, personal injury, business interruption, and injury and death to employees (e.g., workers' compensation policies). Insurance premiums (i.e., the cost of insurance) are typically paid in advance. The unexpired portion of the already paid insurance policy is a current asset.

One of the key issues for financial managers in any business is choosing how much cash to hold. This choice involves various trade-offs. On the one hand, holding large amounts of cash reduces the likelihood that the business will run out of cash and need to raise funds on short notice. On the other hand, there is a cost in the form of lost investment income as a result of hold-

Current assets ($billions)		Current liabilities ($)	
Cash	265.5	Short-term debt	138.3
Marketable securities	198.8	Accounts payable	436.4
Accounts receivable	633.9	Accrued income taxes	65.1
Inventories	569.7	Current payments due on long-term debt	103.7
Other current assets	311.3	Other current liabilities	723.2
Total	**$1,979.2**	**Total**	**$1,466.7**

Figure 12.1 Current assets and liabilities for all U.S. manufacturing corporations in Second Quarter of 2006. All numbers are in billions.

From U.S. Department of Commerce, Bureau of the Census, *Quarterly Financial Report for Manufacturing, Mining and Trade Corporations: 2006: Quarter 2.*

ing cash balances rather than investing those proceeds in marketable securities that can earn a return.

From a balance sheet perspective, one business' assets are another business' liabilities. As an example, assume a wholesale supplier bills SMC for a shipment. Until SMC pays the bill, the balance owed by SMC is part of the wholesale supplier's accounts receivable, a short-term asset. At the same time, the unpaid bill is a short-term liability for SMC. This is the reason accounts payable are a major short-term liability for firms. Accounts payable are outstanding payments owed to other companies.

To finance investments in current assets, a company must rely on various types of short-term debt (i.e., loans). Commercial banks are the most common source of short-term loans (Ross, Westerfield, & Jaffe, 2005). Issuing commercial paper is another technique large corporations use to borrow needed funds. Although many short-term loans are unsecured, companies may offer inventories or receivables as security or may sell inventories or accounts receivable to financial institutions at a discount. Short-term loans, including bank lending, commercial paper, secured loans, and inventories or receivables sold at a discount to financial institutions are discussed in chapter 8.

When businesses either issue long-term debt or take out a loan that is paid down over more than one year, all payments due within the next year or sooner are classified as current payments on long-term debt. Current payments on long-term debt are viewed as a current liability.

Another current liability is accrued income taxes. This category results from differences in the way revenues and expenses are reported for income tax purposes and the way they are accounted for in order to prepare an income statement. These differences in reporting income for tax purposes and for the objective of preparing financial statements are particularly prevalent in large publicly traded companies. For larger companies, it is not unusual to try to claim all available expenses that reduce tax liabilities while showing stockholders the largest amount of reported income possible under generally accepted accounting principles (GAAP; see chapter 5) (Fraser & Ormiston, 2001).[1] As a result of the differences in reporting income for tax purposes, as opposed to GAAP, it is perfectly legal that a company's net income on an income statement differs from what is reported to the IRS.

---

[1]See Fraser and Ormiston (2001, p. 65) for a more extensive discussion of differences between taxable and reported income.

Other current liabilities include accrued liabilities and unearned or deferred credits. Accrued liabilities result from the recording of expenses at the time they are incurred but before the time they will actually be paid. Thus they are liabilities because there will be an eventual outflow of cash to satisfy particular obligations.

 As an example of an accrued liability, the Stars might report deferred compensation owed to players as a current liability. Any player salaries that would be paid within a one-year period would be a current liability.

Numerous companies record advance payments for services or products as a liability when the cash is received. When advance payments are recorded this way, they are recognized as unearned, or deferred, credits.

CASH MANAGEMENT

In December 2005, individuals and corporations in the United States held roughly $1.34 trillion in cash, consisting of $731 billion in currency and traveler's checks and $638 billion in checking deposits (Federal Reserve System, 2006). Cash does not earn interest, yet individuals and corporations hold large amounts of it anyway. The reason for holding cash is the need for liquidity—having an asset on hand for immediate transactions.

As a part of cash management, financial managers face decisions about how much liquidity their business should retain. If the business decides to keep excessive amounts of cash in the bank, then it loses interest that it could have earned through investing that cash in marketable securities. If the business keeps too little cash in the bank, it will be forced to make repeated sales of securities in order to pay its bills. These repeated sales of securities will also saddle the business with excessive brokerage and other costs associated with each transaction. Too little cash can also lead to frequent trips to banks to obtain loans or utilize lines of credit.

In addition to dealing with trade-offs between holding cash and holding marketable securities, a second facet of cash management involves the efficient collection and disbursement of cash. This aspect of

How a business deals with excessive amounts of cash is one aspect of cash management.

cash management requires an understanding of the relationship between businesses and their banks.

LIQUIDITY

A simple way of looking at the trade-offs between holding cash and holding marketable securities was developed by Baumol (1952). In Baumol's framework, a firm has to choose between holding cash and holding U.S. Treasury bills. Baumol viewed cash as something that is steadily depleted to pay bills. When the business runs out of cash, it replenishes its cash supplies by selling Treasury bills that it holds. For each additional dollar of cash held, there is lost interest that could have been obtained through holding Treasury bills. If too little cash is held, there is a brokerage expense associated with selling Treasury bills to replenish cash.

In the Baumol model, the cash management problem is shaped in terms of the optimum amount of Treasury bills sold each time the cash balance has to be replenished. The optimum amount of Treasury bills sold, **Q**, is equal to the following:

$$Q = (2 \times a \times c / i)^{0.5}$$

Q = the optimum amount of Treasury bills sold

a = annual disbursements

c = cost per sale of Treasury bills

i = interest rate

Assume that the interest rate on Treasury bills is 5%, the cost per sale is $30, and the business pays out $1 million per year in cash. The optimum Q is then $34,641.

$$Q = (2 \times 1,000,000 \times 30 / 0.05)^{0.5}$$
$$= \$34,641$$

The firm will sell $34,641 of Treasury bills approximately 29 times per year ($1,000,000 / $34,461), or slightly more often than once every two weeks. The average cash balance held is equal to half the amount of Treasury bills sold. In our example, the average cash balance equals $17,321.

$$\$34,641 / 2 = \$17,321$$

Note that in the Baumol formula the optimum amount of Treasury bills sold decreases as the interest rate rises. In other words, it pays to hold lower cash balances as interest rates increase. On the other hand, as the brokerage cost per sale of Treasury bills increases, the Baumol model implies that the business should hold higher cash balances to avoid the cost of selling Treasury bills, which would be greater than the interest earned.

Sport Manufacturing Company

Assume that Sport Manufacturing Company (SMC) is finding that its outgoing cash is currently exceeding incoming cash by $500,000 per week. The company's financial managers need to determine the appropriate amount of cash for SMC to have on hand. If SMC begins the current week with $1 million in cash, its cash balance will drop to zero in exactly two weeks because $500,000 of the firm's initial cash will be consumed each week. Sport Manufacturing Company's average cash balance will then equal $1,000,000 / 2 = $500,000.

By contrast, if SMC started with $3 million in cash, cash would last exactly six weeks as a result of SMC's consuming $500,000 per week in cash. The average cash balance over the six-week period would be $3,000,000 / 2 = $1,500,000. What this illustrates is that if SMC sets the initial cash balance at a higher level, it will not have to replenish cash as frequently. As a result, SMC's brokerage expenses will be reduced. The trade-off is that by maintaining higher cash balances, SMC sacrifices interest income that could have been earned on marketable securities.

To use the Baumol model to determine the optimum cash balance, assume that the cost per sale of Treasury bills equals $1,000 and the interest rate on Treasury bills equals 3%. Annual disbursements equal $500,000 × 52 weeks = $26,000,000. Using the Baumol model, Q equals the following:

$$Q = (2 \times \$26,000,000 \times \$1,000 / 0.03)^{0.5}$$

$$= \$1,316,561$$

SMC, based on this calculation, will liquidate Treasury bills approximately 20 times per year ($26,000,000 / $1,316,561).

Although the Baumol model demonstrates the analytical issues involved when we consider trade-offs between holding cash and marketable securities, it is simplistic relative to real-world business decisions. Unlike the situation described in the Baumol model, businesses do not deplete their cash reserves on a steady basis. Firms may find that over a one-month period there is a net inflow of cash as customers pay bills, whereas in the next month there is a net outflow of cash as suppliers are paid. There are more complicated models that allow for more unpredictable outflows and inflows (see Ross et al., 2005).

Another limitation of the Baumol model is its assumption that the only option other than holding cash is to invest in Treasury bills. In the real world, it is possible to invest in other assets such as stocks. As discussed in detail in the section "Marketable Securities" in chapter 3 (p. 36), stocks are risky relative to Treasury bills.

In our discussion of cash management, we have ignored another possibility for cash replenishment, which is borrowing rather than selling marketable securities. Numerous businesses draw on bank lines of credit when cash reserves are low. With borrowing, the analysis becomes more complicated since the interest rate paid to the bank is likely to be higher than the rate earned on marketable securities. If you were the financial manager of SMC, you would face a trade-off between the interest that would be sacrificed on sold-off marketable securities and the interest rate that would have to be paid on borrowings. If the interest charged on borrowed funds is substantially above the rate earned on marketable securities, selling off marketable securities as a means of raising cash would be preferable to borrowing additional amounts.

As a matter of practice, businesses that have idle cash will invest in marketable securities with maturities of one year or less (i.e., money market instruments). Businesses may put their cash into **money market mutual funds**, which invest in short-term securities for a management fee. One of the benefits is the diversification provided by the fund manager's investment in many different short-term instruments. In addition, banks offer "sweep accounts" for corporate customers. The bank takes all available funds in a sweep account at the end of each business day and invests them for the corporate customer. Thus, the rate of return is higher than in other traditional bank accounts.

The reason that businesses invest idle cash balances in money market instruments is that for any given change in interest rates, the values of longer maturity debt securities change more than those of shorter-maturity debt securities. Thus investors holding instruments with longer-term maturities face greater risk due to greater fluctuations in value associated with interest rate swings. This risk is known as interest rate risk. Given that the invested excess cash balances of the business may be needed at a moment's notice for large disbursements, businesses invest in money market instruments so that they are less subject to interest rate risk. As discussed in chapter 6, the expected returns on the instruments with shorter maturities are also lower because of the reduction in risk.

COLLECTION AND DISBURSEMENT OF CASH

When businesses pay bills or receive payment for debts, they have the possibility of earning additional revenue or of losing the opportunity to earn additional revenue. Because of the time delays associated with writing, depositing, and cashing checks, some money can be lost. Checks that are written by the firm but not yet cleared represent payment **float**. Checks received by the firm and deposited but not yet cleared represent availability float. Net float represents the net effect of checks in the process of collection and is equal to the difference between payment float and availability float. With the increased use of electronic transfers, especially

Web-based transactions, float can be reduced. The next example illustrates net float.

Sport Manufacturing Company

Although we have discussed a business' liquidity, it is necessary to be more precise about how cash enters and exits the corporation and how the available cash balance is computed. Assume that SMC has $1 million on deposit in a bank checking account. Suppose also that SMC writes a $300,000 check to a supplier of graphite for its tennis rackets and mails the payment to a supplier. Immediately, SMC will adjust its ledgers to show a cash balance of $700,000. The company's bank will not learn anything about this check until the supplier has received the check, the supplier has deposited the check at the supplier's bank, and that bank has presented the check to SMC's bank. While waiting for the check to clear, SMC's bank continues to show in its ledger that the company has $1 million in its account. Thus SMC gains the benefit of an extra $300,000 in the bank while the check is still clearing. This extra $300,000 is the payment float.

Although the float sounds like something SMC can take advantage of, it is really a two-way street. Assume that at the same time SMC writes the $300,000 check, the company receives a $100,000 check from the purchasing department of Sports Authority, which keeps SMC's golf clubs in stock in its national chain of sporting goods stores. Sport Manufacturing Company deposits the $100,000 check, and both the company and bank ledger balances are increased by $100,000. Unfortunately for SMC, it does not have access to the $100,000 immediately; SMC's bank does not actually have the $100,000 until it has sent the check to and received the payment from Sports Authority's bank. While SMC's bank is waiting for the check, it makes SMC wait to have access to the $100,000 payment. Under current Federal Reserve regulations, this wait can be anywhere from one to five business days for most checks. While the bank waits for payment, the bank will show that SMC has an available balance of $1 million and an availability float equal to $100,000.

In effect, SMC gains from the payment float of $300,000 but loses as a result of the $100,000 availability float. The difference between payment float and availability float is the net float. In our example, the net float is $300,000 − $100,000 = $200,000. This can be important because if the net

float exists for five days and the bank pays interest of 5% on the account, SMC will gain approximately $140 in interest during the five-day period. Although this may seem insignificant, if SMC is able to maintain an average of $200,000 per day in float because of the timing of all of its transactions, the interest earned per year would be $10,000.[2]

Both SMC and Sports Authority can reduce availability float by encouraging vendors to make electronic payments. For example, if either firm has a Web site that includes online ordering and payment collection capabilities that are convenient and easy for a potential customer to use, this can eliminate a substantial portion of availability float. Electronic funds transfers are available for use as soon as the funds are transferred to the vendor's bank from the customer's bank.

If you are a financial manager for SMC, your true concern is the available balance rather than the balance recorded on the bank ledger. If you know there may be a one- or two-week delay before some of the checks written to suppliers are presented for payment, then you may be able to get by on a smaller cash balance. This is what is known as playing the float.

In effect, you can increase your available cash balance by increasing your net float. This means that checks received from customers should be cleared rapidly, while checks to suppliers are cleared more slowly. Net float can be increased even more by encouraging instantaneous electronic funds transfers. Although managing float may not seem like a significant activity for a business, for a large company it can be very significant. Assume that a company averages $100 million per day in sales. If it can increase collections by one day, the business frees up $100 million, which is then available to the shareholders or for capital projects.

There are several techniques for accelerating collections. One technique that many large companies use is concentration banking. Customers make payments at a local office as opposed to corporate headquarters, and the local branch office then deposits the checks into a local bank branch. Surplus funds from the local bank account are then periodically transferred to a concentration account at one of the

---

[2]This analysis does not include the additional interest earned because of compounding.

company's main banks. These transfers can be made electronically, which allows for next-day availability of the funds at corporate headquarters.

Concentration banking reduces float for two reasons. First, because the branch office is closer to the customer, mailing time is reduced. Second, since the customer's check is more likely to be drawn on a local bank, the time it takes for the check to clear is lessened.

Concentration banking can also be combined with a lockbox system. In a lockbox system, the company pays a local bank to handle the administrative chores, so it is not necessary to establish a branch office to handle receipt of payments. A company with a national market will establish regions as collection points. Within each region, the company rents a locked post office box. All customers within a region are then required to send payments to the locked post office box in that region. The local bank, on behalf of the company, empties the box regularly and deposits the checks in the company's local bank account. Surplus funds are transferred periodically to one of the company's principal banks. The number of collection points, or regions, that are required depends on how quickly the mail is delivered.

 **Sport Manufacturing Company**
Assume that SMC decides to work with a West Coast bank in setting up a lockbox in Sacramento, California, for handling payments from customers in the western half of the United States. Suppose that the average number of daily payments to the lockbox is 500, the average payment size is $1,000, the rate of interest per day that can be earned on funds invested in marketable securities is 0.02%, the savings in mailing time is 1.4 days, and the savings in processing time is 0.5 day. The lockbox would result in SMC's increasing its collected balance by 500 items per day $\times$ $1,000 per item $\times$ (1.4 + 0.5) days saved = $950,000. The $950,000 invested at a return of 0.02% per day equals $950,000 $\times$ 0.0002 = $190 per day. Typically, the bank's charge for providing the lockbox service will be on a per check basis. Suppose the bank charges $0.30 per check. This results in a daily charge that equals $0.30 $\times$ 500 = $150 per day. Thus, SMC gains $190 – $150 = $40 per day, which does not include additional savings that result from SMC's not processing its own checks.

Slowing down disbursements is another technique for increasing net float. In extreme cases, businesses maintain disbursement accounts in several locations around the country. These businesses then use computer algorithms that look up each supplier's zip code so that a check is drawn on the most distant disbursement account.

 **Sport Manufacturing Company**
Assume that SMC's corporate headquarters is located in Connecticut. If SMC pays its suppliers with checks drawn on a New York bank account, it may find that when the check is deposited by the supplier, it is only another one to two days before the check is presented to SMC's bank for payment. SMC can set up disbursement checking accounts in different parts of the United States (e.g., by arranging to write checks drawn on banks in such remote locations as Helena, Montana; Pierre, South Dakota; or Abilene, Texas). In these cases, it may be three to four days before each check is presented for payment. This allows SMC the opportunity to gain additional float days.

Historically, collection and disbursement activity involved movement of paper checks. There is currently a movement toward more electronic collection and disbursement. In the past, the main hindrance to paperless activities was that many smaller businesses and consumers were unable to operate electronically. This has changed as the Internal Revenue Service and state and local tax authorities have implemented electronic transmission of payroll, income, and sales tax payments. As businesses and individuals increasingly use electronic funds transfers to pay bills, there will be faster collections and reduced availability float. Businesses are establishing Web sites that allow customers to authorize immediate electronic payments via transfers from customer bank accounts. This is particularly true with credit cards and utility bills.

CREDIT MANAGEMENT

The amount of accounts receivable held by the business is determined by the extent to which that business sells on credit, as opposed to cash. In addition, the terms of credit become important in determining the amount of accounts receivable appearing on the balance sheet. For example, if SMC offers its customers the terms of net 30 days, the customers have 30 days from the date of purchase to pay the amount owed. Under these circumstances, most of SMC's customers will pay near the end of the 30 days. To encourage its customers to pay earlier, SMC may offer terms of 1/10/30 (1%/10, net 30), which means that customers have 30 days to pay the balance owed, and they receive a 1% discount if payment occurs within 10 days of purchase. Another formula for credit terms is 2/10/30, which means the discount is 2% if payment occurs within 10 days.

In the case of 1/10/30, the customer who pays SMC after 10 days is in effect receiving 20 days of credit at interest equal to the 1% forgone discount. Since there are roughly 18 such periods in the year (360 days a year / 20 days each period), the annual interest equals 18 × 1%, or 18%. If SMC changed the terms to 2/10/60, the cost of credit for 60 days minus the cost for 10 days (for paying early) would equal the cost for 50 days, which is 2% in lost discounts. This is equivalent to 360 / 50 = 7.2 such periods per year, or 7.2 × 2% = 14.4% interest per year.

To summarize thus far, the terms of a sale define what the cash customer pays for the merchandise. In addition, the terms of sale set the interest rate charged for credit. If SMC increases the discount from 1/10/30 to 2/10/30, the price for the cash customer has been reduced, but there has been an increase in the interest rate charged to the credit buyer.

If a customer has a poor credit record, SMC may insist that the buyer pay either COD (cash on delivery) or CBD (cash before delivery). There are various ways to assess the creditworthiness of a customer. One way is to have a credit agency perform a credit check. The most prominent of the credit agencies is Dun & Bradstreet. Credit agencies typically report the experience that other firms have had in collecting payments from the customer. Credit bureaus also provide this kind of information. Similar information is available over the Internet through sites such as www.businesscreditusa.com, which provides some basic credit information.

The business' own bank can do a credit check by contacting the customer's bank, which will provide information on the customer's average bank balance, access to bank credit, and reputation.

If the customer is a publicly traded firm, there are inexpensive ways of collecting information about how this customer is assessed in the financial markets.

Although a precipitous drop in a company's stock price does not imply that the firm is going into bankruptcy, it indicates that the company's future prospects are no longer as bright as they were previously.

SMC may be supplying its tennis rackets and golf equipment to a publicly traded chain of sporting goods stores and can easily look up the chain's Moody's or Standard & Poor's rating. Moody's and Standard & Poor's rate the outstanding bonds of publicly traded companies in terms of the likelihood of default. Given the availability of stock price data on the Internet through such sites as Yahoo! Finance, SMC can look at the recent behavior of the customer's stock price.

COLLECTIONS MANAGEMENT

In addition to managing credit, it is important for businesses to manage collections. Collections management focuses on converting receivables to cash and refers to efforts made to obtain payment of past due accounts. In addition, the credit manager needs to have records of the collections experience of the company in dealing with customers who currently have credit terms. This information is relevant for determining whether credit should continue to be extended in the future.

A business' general collections experience also needs to be monitored, since this will determine whether the firm's terms are appropriate. One reporting tool involves the average **days sales outstanding**, or days in receivables. Our example involving SMC can illustrate the use of this tool.

Assume that the terms on all SMC sales to customers are 1/10/30. Assume that 65% of the customers take the 1% discount and pay on day 10, while the remaining 35% pay on day 30. The average days sales outstanding equals 0.65 × 10 days + 0.35 × 30 days = 17 days.

Since payments to a business tend to arrive more sporadically than in our example, it is necessary to first calculate average daily sales. As noted in the

The Benefits of Electronic Funds Transfers

One of the most important developments in collections management over the past 20 years has been electronic funds transfers (EFTs). EFTs are now utilized by 80% to 90% of all health clubs in the United States. The EFT systems withdraw funds automatically from a customer's bank account. Because the withdrawals are done electronically and at set times, such as the fifth day of each month, the process streamlines the collection and accounting process (Ernest, 2002). This process can save a significant amount of time and lost cash due to payment delays. A third party, which can also provide additional support such as membership retention and marketing assistance, often administers the process. The Smiths could also utilize EFTs to establish an accurate flow of revenue on which a bank loan or other borrowing could be secured.

Another benefit of such a payment system is the time lag for terminating the service. If someone wants to cancel the service, she has to give advance notice; otherwise she would have to make an additional payment, which represents additional cash the Smiths might not otherwise have received from that customer. Furthermore, if a customer breaches the contract, the Smiths could keep collecting the disputed amount until the matter is resolved without incurring a significant collection problem.

Introduction to the Case Studies (pp. xv-xviii), SMC's annual sales are $4 million. Therefore, its average daily sales = $4,000,000 / 365 days = $10,959 per day. Once the average daily sales is calculated, that figure is divided into the existing accounts receivable to obtain the average daily sales outstanding. If accounts receivable equal $186,300, then average daily sales outstanding equals $186,300 / $10,959 = 17 days. This means that when making a purchase, the average SMC customer pays in 17 days.

If SMC analyzes daily or weekly data on sales and accounts receivable and finds that average daily sales outstanding stays at 17 days over a one-month period, then some customers are paying later. In addition, some accounts may be overdue. With sales outstanding staying at 17 days, a significant number of SMC customers are not paying their bills immediately or taking advantage of early payment discounts. Although some customers might pay early, it appears that more customers are waiting longer than the discount period. Keep in mind that for a company such as SMC that has seasonal sales patterns, the calculated average daily sales outstanding will fluctuate during the year. The reason is that for these businesses, receivables are low before the major selling season and high afterward. As a result, average daily sales outstanding on a particular date may need to be compared with past averages for the same date.

An aging report, which tabulates receivables by the accounts' ages, can provide more detailed information. Table 12.1 (p.226) presents an example. Note that a significant number of customers are past due (40% of accounts are outstanding more than 30 days). Any company that displays a report like the one shown in

table 12.1 has serious collections problems and should be reviewing its collections policies.

The usual procedure for collecting overdue accounts is to send out an invoice. If the invoice does not result in payment, then follow-up letters are sent to the customer about the delinquency of the account. In addition, several telephone calls can be made to the customer. There is a very fine line here that any company needs to appreciate. If a company is too aggressive, it could lose a customer who might be facing some temporary hard times. On the other hand, if the company is too passive, it could face repeated abuses by customers who do not pay their debts as they come due. If all these efforts by the company are not fruitful, then the company may turn to a collections agency. Typically, collections agencies charge anywhere from 15% to 50% of the amount collected. An additional option is to retain an attorney in order to file suit against the customer. Yet another option is to write off the debt as a bad debt. However, to be able to deduct these losses from income for tax purposes, the company must show that it made "reasonable" efforts to collect the debt.[3]

---

[3]The rules governing the deduction of bad-debt losses are complicated. Whether a company has to go to court to obtain a judgment against the debtor depends on the particular situation. For example, if the company can show that the court would return a judgment of uncollectible, then going to court is unnecessary. Bankruptcy is generally considered evidence by the IRS that at least a portion of the debt can be viewed as bad. The deduction of bad-debt losses is summarized in IRS Publication 535, *Business Expenses* (2007).

Table 12.1 Sample Aging Report

Age of account	Percent of total accounts receivable
0 to 30 days	60
31 to 60 days	15
61 to 90 days	15
90 to 120 days	6
121 days plus	4
Total	**100%**

For smaller businesses, it may be too expensive to employ someone in credit management and collections. Under these circumstances, the business may sell its accounts receivable directly to a financial institution, called a factor. The factor buys the receivables of the firm at a discount, which is typically 1% (Brealey & Myers, 2004). The company and the factor agree on credit terms for each customer. The customer sends payments to the factor, which bears the risk that the customer will not pay. Factors are discussed in chapter 8.

CONCLUSION

This chapter outlines the various types of current assets and liabilities, known as working capital on a company's balance sheet, including cash, marketable securities, accounts receivable, inventories, short-term loans, accounts payable, accrued income taxes, and current payments due on long-term debt. Net working capital refers to current assets minus current liabilities, as highlighted in chapter 5.

Financial managers face trade-offs between holding cash and holding interest-bearing securities. If interest rates are high, it is desirable to hold relatively less cash. Borrowing serves as an alternative to liquidating securities to replenish cash in the event of a deficiency. The cash that appears in company ledgers is not the same as the available balance in the company's bank account. The difference is net float. We discuss how companies can play the float so as to reduce their required cash holdings, as well as how companies can manage the float by speeding up collections and slowing down payments.

The chapter also deals with the intricacies of credit management, specifically establishing the length of the payment period and the size of any cash discounts. We discuss sources of information that can be used to assess a customer's creditworthiness, as well as collection measures and procedures. All these steps help create a plan of action to most effectively utilize a business' cash reserves for reinvestment or to pay expenses such as manufacturing and inventory costs, which are discussed in the next chapter.

CLASS DISCUSSION TOPICS

1. How does the emergence of lower-cost brokerage services over the Internet affect the cash balances that a firm must maintain?

2. How should a business monitor collections activity?

3. How has the advent of greater volumes of electronic funds transfers affected the accumulation of float by a business?

4. Businesses can increase cash flow by stretching out payments to venders by an additional fifteen days. If this is so obvious, why is it that companies do not necessarily do this?

5. If a company has excess amounts of cash available, should that cash be used to pay its venders in a quicker fashion?

6. Is it better business practice to make all customers pay before receiving a product, as opposed to having receivables?

13

INVENTORY AND PRODUCTION MANAGEMENT

CHAPTER OBJECTIVES

After studying this chapter, you should be able to do the following:

- Distinguish between variable and fixed costs.
- Understand how to determine product costs and prices and how to reduce costs.
- Understand inventory management.
- Understand how to forecast inventory needs.
- Understand the costs associated with managing inventory.
- Calculate the optimum economic ordering quantity.
- Describe inventory turnover and inventory obsolescence.
- Calculate manufacturing costs, including labor costs.

This chapter focuses on inventory and production management, which are critical components of the manufacturing analysis process. All companies that manufacture products need to carefully examine how they use their inventory to ensure they are not wasting any money. Similarly, companies need to examine how they produce products to maximize efficiency and minimize waste. Although we mostly use SMC as an example throughout this chapter, the principles illustrated also apply to other sport-related businesses. The Smiths might have exercise equipment stored in inventory. They might also need to stock produce for the juice bar, and the produce would be subject to spoilage if not used soon enough. Similarly, the Stars of David and the University of Milford need to purchase souvenir goods for their concession shops. A change in team logo would make this inventory obsolete. Thus, inventory management issues are critical for all sport businesses.

Although finance is not all about expenses, managing and controlling expenses are primary financial disciplines. Controlling expenses is one of the most important elements in inventory and production management. If inventory is not utilized, money is wasted and expenses for storage costs increase. If a machine sits idle, the business loses money from the lack of production, and expenses increase for machine downtime. This chapter deals first with business costs and then with the entire inventory management process, including forecasting demand, purchasing optimum quantities, storing inventory, auditing inventory, and utilizing inventory. We then discuss production analysis, with a primary focus on manufacturing costs, break-even analysis, variance analysis, and labor cost concerns.

BUSINESS COSTS

As highlighted in chapter 7, a business needs to plan for various expenses. Expenses can include office supplies, raw inventory, facility costs (from mortgages to electrical bills), corporate perks such as season tickets, and an endless number of other expenses. It is difficult to categorize every dollar spent by a business because some expenses are grouped into a generic category called general expenses instead of being recorded separately. General expenses for a sport-related business can be highly diverse, as seen in the following example using the Stars of David.

 The Stars have significant expenses over and beyond those related to the players and coaches. The following are some of the possible operating expenses for the team's home arena.

- Utilities, which can include lights, sewage, electricity, gas or propane, air conditioning, heating systems, and telephones
- Cleaning the facility after a game, which can include playing areas, seating areas, locker rooms, bathrooms, team offices, pressrooms, and concession areas
- Game-day personnel, which can include ticket takers; ushers; security officers; and traffic control, police, fire, EMT, and related personnel (either directly hired or outsourced to an outside vendor)
- Insurance-related expenses, which could entail the following insurance policies: general liability, property damage, comprehensive, business interruption, air casualty, key person, and employee practices liability insurance, as well as other related policies
- Ordinary repair and maintenance costs for everything from computers and photocopiers to athletic trainers' equipment and the scoreboard
- Miscellaneous expenses, which can include the following:
  - Scoreboard operations
  - Court maintenance costs
  - All office equipment and supplies
  - All employee benefits, whether health insurance or retirement accounts
  - Parking lot maintenance including lighting, repainting, and so on

These expenses can be diagrammed in the same way as the expenses faced by any sport business. An expense map is similar to a road map and identifies what areas of the business are incurring expenses and where possible cost savings can come from. A typical partial expense map could resemble the following:

Expenses

Personnel	Storage
Maintenance	Coaches
Player salaries	Marketing

Scouts	Media
Advertising	Insurance
Administrative	Media food table
Graphics	Facility
Legal	Media guides
Travel	Utilities
Accountant	Modem lines

As discussed in chapter 7, if the Texas Rangers pay $252 million for Alex Rodriguez, how will such a salary affect ticket prices? Player salaries are a fixed expense—at the start of the season, the team knows what its total salary obligation will be except for possible bonuses and reductions in salaries if players are injured, cut, or traded. Knowing how much its payroll is, the team can determine all other expenses. Similarly, the team can determine the potential revenue from broadcast rights, luxury seating, and sponsorship income. On the basis of these potential income areas, the team can examine how much it might need to charge ticket holders to ensure that it can cover its costs. Thus, expenses have a direct impact on prices of various items, from tickets to concessions.

We all know basic costs such as the price of going to McDonald's and spending $5 for a meal. When you do this, the cost to you is $5. If you earn $10 per hour, you can calculate your cost as 50% of your hourly wage. On the basis of an eight-hour day, you could calculate your $5 meal as 6.25% of your daily wage. In essence, cost analysis is similar for a sport business.

TYPES OF BUSINESS COSTS

There are several types of costs that any business might face. An example of a variable cost for a sport business might be salaries for the ushers, which could change from one game to the next according to the number of expected fans. An example of a fixed cost, on the other hand, is a team's lease payment to a city, which needs to be made no matter how many games are played. The following sections deal with the various types of costs that accrue in businesses.

VARIABLE COSTS

Variable costs vary with each unit produced as seen in the following SMC case study example.

Sport Manufacturing Company

If SMC acquired $2 million in steel in 2005, the company bought raw materials that would be classified as variable costs. The company might need to purchase more steel or might have too much. If SMC sees an increase in orders and needs to make 1,000 more golf clubs than it had previously planned to make, the variable costs would increase. However, even if SMC needs to purchase more steel, the variable cost per golf club could actually decrease because the company might be able to buy the greater quantity of steel at a discount, and the variable cost per club would then decline.

SEMIVARIABLE COSTS

Costs can also be classified as semivariable. These costs vary with the amount of activity, but they are not directly proportional to the amount of the activity. A good example of semivariable costs is maintenance. There is normally some uniformity with regard to the cost of regularly maintaining a piece of machinery. However, if SMC's club-making machine is running three hours more than usual each day, maintenance will probably need to be conducted more frequently. The costs of health care premiums paid by an employer could also be semivariable. The cost of a premium may be constant, but the total amount paid by the employer may vary with the number of employees covered by the plan.

FIXED COSTS

Fixed costs are the last major cost category. Fixed costs stay the same no matter what changes occur in usage or sales. Property taxes and depreciation expenses are just two examples of fixed costs. The West Hartford Badminton Club has a fixed cost associated with using its gym. No matter if 10 or 50 people show up for a practice, the operating and maintenance costs still need to be paid. One of the biggest fixed costs for a sport business is salaries. Athletes need to be paid regardless of the number of people who attend a game.

OTHER WAYS OF CLASSIFYING COSTS

Through cost accounting, which is the method used to ferret out the true costs associated with any given activity, costs could be identified or classified according to additional levels other than variable, semivariable, and fixed. Some of these additional categories include material, manufacturing, labor, factory overhead, and general and administrative costs. Material costs are the costs of the material used to make a given product.

For SMC, the steel—identified earlier as a variable cost—can also be classified as a manufacturing cost. The company needs the steel to make its clubs.

Labor costs are the costs needed to transform the material into the finished product. Factory overhead is the cost associated with all the equipment and buildings used as the material is converted to a finished product. Factory overhead traditionally includes rent or mortgage, machine costs, depreciation, electricity, and so on. The last major category is general and administrative costs. These costs typically include salaries for employees in the sales or other nonmanufacturing departments, marketing expenses, research and development, and related expenses not associated with manufacturing.

Before we discuss costs further, it is important to note that many businesses use terms such as *overhead* or *indirect costs*. Overhead refers to all the additional costs (over and beyond all the combined manufacturing costs) associated with getting a product to market, such as administrative, legal, marketing, and related costs. An indirect cost is a cost associated with—but not necessarily part of the process of—converting raw materials to the finished product. A good sport example of an indirect cost is scouts for a pro team. The scouts do not coach the athletes to become better or in any way enhance the value of a player; but without scouts, a team would not be able to put the best product on the field. Businesses should not use the terms *overhead* and *indirect* because they are misleading; all expenses, whether variable or fixed, add a cost component to the product. For example, we should not use the term *indirect labor* because either the labor is productive and needs to be accounted for or is unnecessary and needs to be eliminated. Nonetheless, because executives frequently use the terms *overhead* and *indirect expenses*, we briefly discuss them here.

Even though indirect expenses are not the most accurate measure for analyzing costs, people most frequently refer to direct and indirect labor costs when discussing the manufacturing expenses of a given product or service. Examples of **direct costs** are such items as raw materials for SMC's golf clubs and player salaries for the Stars. **Indirect costs** could include employee salaries and benefits associated with office personnel who do not design, manufacture, or distribute the golf clubs (e.g., secretaries). Traditionally, indirect costs are added directly to the cost of a manufactured item, even if these costs are wholly unrelated to the manufacturing process.

HIDDEN COSTS

Some costs are "hidden" and thus hard to appreciate when making financial decisions. Building a new facility involves numerous costs that are not obvious. These hidden costs can significantly affect such issues as building change orders or potential price increases based on the material used and any price increases that might pass through under the contract. For example, U of M is considering building a new stadium with a $100,000 budget. A construction company starts the building process, and then a local homeowner sues everyone for diminishing the value of his property. The suit will cost money but will not add any value to the facility or help pay for its construction. Thus, it was hidden in the initial budget because it was not anticipated.

Additionally, there could be hidden costs related to unexpected environmental issues. An environmental impact analysis as part of the due diligence process is a standard expense. Due diligence entails a thorough investigation of a proposed business deal to determine whether there are any potential legal or financial problems. The environmental impact analysis is designed to determine whether the land is contaminated or whether any environmental remediation might be required. Issues other than contamination (e.g., endangered species issues) may also arise. These issues can undercut an entire project.

Local laws may require development of wetlands to replace areas converted by construction. It might be impossible to create or maintain wetlands if a stadium needs space for parking lots; thus a facility may not be able to comply with the law. Nevertheless, government entities still require compliance. To address this conflict, some companies have developed wetland mitigation banks from which a business can buy its share of acreage without having to retain wetlands at the construction site. For example, U of M might be required to leave two acres as wetlands. Instead of losing all the possible parking spaces, the stadium can go to the mitigation bank and purchase two acres that might be located around a city park. The bank owners then assume the responsibility of keeping the wetlands in good shape and allowing wildlife to utilize the space. The cost of buying the space is offset by the high cost that would be involved in developing and maintaining the wetlands at the stadium site. Such a project was built outside Houston on 580 acres. The government granted credits for the acres, and the owners sold the credits to private companies that did not want to develop wetlands or wanted to avoid time delays associated with building a wetland project (Breyer, 1998).

ANALYZING COSTS

Regardless of how costs are classified, it is impossible to fully appreciate an item's cost without developing a cost summary sheet. The cost summary sheet breaks down all the costs incurred during manufacture of an item. One can also price services in this manner by calculating the labor cost for each activity that is part of the service.

SMC's cost sheet shows the various categories of costs over and above the raw materials used to create a putter, such as taxes, depreciation, profits, and related expenses. Numerous pro forma budgets fail investor scrutiny because the pro forma does not identify these cost categories. A cost sheet makes it more difficult to overlook any cost category.

 **Sport Manufacturing Company**

Using the Super Putter cost sheet here would help SMC determine optimum pricing strategies and allow management to identify where cost reductions can be made.

The cost sheet establishes several key variables that help SMC determine its profitability and related standards:

- SMC's profit is $12, which is built into the cost analysis.
- Profit as a percentage of sales price is 8% ($96.25 target price / $12 profit).
- Gross margin is net sales price ($104) minus the material costs ($25) = $79.
- Value added is the net sales price ($104) minus total purchases ($27.50) = $76.50.
- Cash flow is after-tax profits ($12) plus depreciation ($10) = $22.
- Contribution margin is the net sales price ($104) minus total variable cost ($57.75) = $46.25.

The value-added component is the key point for a specialized company such as SMC or the Stars. Sport Manufacturing Company has unique skills as evidenced by its ability to manufacture a putter that is highly regarded by golf professionals. On the basis of this uniqueness, the company is able to charge more than other golf club manufacturers. The uniqueness adds value to the product, in the same way winning a championship would add value to the Stars. After winning a championship, the Stars would be able to charge a higher ticket price because people would be willing to pay more to see them.

Super Putter Cost Sheet

Description	Cost per packaged unit ($)
Part A	10.00
Part B	6.00
Part C	4.00
Part D	1.00
Primer	0.75
Paint	1.25
Packaging	2.00
Material costs	**$25.00**
Supplies and repairs	1.50
Utilities	1.00
Total purchases	**$27.50**
Cost at step 1	14.00
Cost at step 2	5.00
Cost at step 3	1.50
Quality-related losses	4.00
Sales and distribution costs	5.00
Short-term interest	0.75
Total variable costs	**$57.75**
Manufacturing	7.25
Distribution	3.50
Research and development	2.50
Administrative	2.00
Long-term interest	1.25
Total manufacturing cost less depreciation	**$74.25**
Depreciation	10.00
Total cost	**$84.25**
Net profit	12.00
Target price after tax	**$96.25**
Provisions for taxes	7.75
Net target selling price	**$104.00**
Discount and terms	6.00
Total target price	**$110.00**

REDUCING COSTS

Besides analyzing costs, it is important to examine techniques to reduce costs. Systematic cost reduction can be accomplished through various techniques, such as engineered standards and cost control reports. These techniques can help identify waste and appropriate remedial measures. For example, instead of having a secretary for each executive, the Stars could centralize the secretarial staff so that there are three secretaries for five executives—saving two salaries while still accommodating the executives' needs. Other cost reduction techniques are discussed elsewhere in this text, such as reissuing bonds at a lower interest rate (see "Loan Repayment," p. 181).

Companies use capital cost reduction techniques to reduce the cost of issuing stocks or bonds. A company can issue more stock than it actually releases to the public in order to reduce future issuing expense. If and when the company needs to release the additional shares, the capital costs have already been covered, so most of the proceeds from sales of the additional shares go directly to the corporation.

Although capital cost reduction produces significant benefits, cost reduction can also occur in other areas, such as inventory and the manufacturing process. First we discuss ways to reduce costs in the manufacturing process; then in the next section we consider inventory management, through which a company examines the length of time that inventory just sits in storage and wastes the company's money. Examining such costs gives a business an opportunity to identify where costs might be excessive and to reduce these costs.

The simplest means to meet a production and sales budget is to increase selling price. However, this strategy may lead to lost sales and lost goodwill. Reducing internal costs can also help make the budget. Cost reduction can result from various strategies, such as reducing labor costs or streamlining the manufacturing process. As an example, various cost reduction strategies can be undertaken to reduce utility expenses. Businesses can change the wattage of light bulbs or reduce the amount of water used to flush a toilet. The electricity and water usage can be plotted, and the benefits associated with conservation efforts can also be tracked.

Numerous cost reduction strategies also apply to running machinery. Machinery can be very expensive to operate, and businesses that utilize machinery can identify ways to save in this area by doing the following (Feiner, 1977):

- Analyzing costs based on machine centers (a group of similar machines working together) or groups versus product runs or other evaluation methods
- Establishing preventive maintenance programs that can prolong machine life and reduce costly repairs
- Evaluating utility conservation programs to determine if machines are using energy as effectively as possible
- Ensuring that employees are not misusing the machines
- Analyzing true equipment requirements to reduce the need for certain equipment or reallocate floor space for more effective income generation
- Setting aside money (e.g., in a sinking fund) to help purchase new or refurbished equipment to replace outdated equipment

INVENTORY MANAGEMENT

Most college, semiprofessional, and amateur sports facilities have similar costs. For example, each facility has maintenance, personnel, electricity, construction, and related costs. Similarly, each facility tries to minimize the operating costs while still providing the best services. No matter where expenses might arise, financial managers need to carefully track expenses to ensure that money is not being misspent.

Inventory management is an effective tool for managing variable and semivariable costs. If excess inventory sits in a storage facility, the company not only loses the use of the money tied up in the inventory (and might even need to pay financing charges if the inventory was purchased with borrowed funds) but also has to pay inventory storage expenses. On the other hand, if there is not enough inventory available, customers may not receive items they have purchased; this can result in lower sales and the loss of consumer goodwill. To avoid these problems, managers utilize techniques such as order forecasting to determine when they might have to purchase inventories or when certain expenses will arise.

KEY COMPONENTS OF AN INVENTORY MANAGEMENT SYSTEM

The key components of any inventory management system are forecasting, purchasing, storing, auditing,

© Human Kinetics

Any sport business has to manage and control its expenses—whether they are variable expenses that will change over time, semivariable expenses that change only to some extent over time, or fixed expenses. What types of expenses do you see here?

and utilizing inventory. These five components are discussed in the sections that follow.

FORECASTING INVENTORY

Here we briefly examine forecasting in general and then focus on one of the most critical forecasting areas, inventory forecasting. For example, we can develop a thorough forecast by analyzing what activities occur to generate a sale. A 35-point cost-of-sales questionnaire designed to solicit the information needed to develop a comprehensive forecast is shown on page 234. The questionnaire identifies some of the dynamic issues associated with determining the potential costs of manufacturing an item. Some people think that manufacturing expenses can be reduced simply by cutting costs. However, how can you reduce costs? The questionnaire poses questions that any manager needs to ask and answer to identify variables that can affect pricing and that might represent a potential area for cost savings.

Forecasting involves a little of both science and art to effectively set the stage for determining optimum sales, inventory, production levels, and manufacturing costs. Forecasts for some variables are simple, such as yearly property tax or insurance obligations; in these cases the business knows what the expenses will

be and when they must be paid. On the other hand, whereas the Smiths may be sure of certain expenses such as rent, they cannot know when a sound system will break or whether they will suffer any theft. Unpredictable variables that can either positively or negatively affect projections will always come into play. However, by developing a competently researched forecast, managers can either avoid or account for variability. Inventory forecasting helps establish what inventory purchases will need to be made throughout the year and the most effective techniques for reordering additional inventory.

PURCHASING INVENTORY

Purchasing needed materials might appear to be a relatively easy process for most businesses. However, if you examine your own individual buying patterns, you may discover inefficiencies that cost you significantly. If you wait too long to buy gas on a highway, you may be stuck paying several more cents a gallon than you would otherwise. If you have a headache and buy a pain reliever at a convenience store, you will pay much more than if you had purchased it at a discount drugstore. Similarly, the failure of a business to effectively manage purchases and material costs can cost a company millions of dollars.

35-Point Cost-of-Sales Questionnaire

Material Costs

1. What percentage of sales are direct materials?
2. How is the standard cost for materials established?
3. How often are these costs reviewed and by what procedure?
4. Are "free stock" items included as a direct or indirect cost?
5. How effectively and accurately are purchase parts invoiced and material (stores) requisitions processed?
6. Is a part-numbering system maintained?
7. Does cost accounting's purchase price agree with purchasing's current record and if not, what corrective action is required?

Direct Labor Costs

8. What percentage of sales is direct labor?
9. What percentage of total salary and wages is direct labor?
10. Which departments (cost centers) are being measured by performance reports, and are line managers making effective use of these reports?
11. Are standard labor hours based on historical actuals or industrial engineering standards?
12. How current are these standards?
13. How accurate are the standard dollar labor rates, and do they reflect shift differentials?
14. How is cost accounting notified of changes in the labor rate or in the standard hours?

Overhead Costs

15. What percentage of sales is overhead?
16. What percentage of overhead is classified as indirect labor, and is it all truly indirect?
17. What percentage of the overhead represents variable, semivariable, and fixed costs?
18. How is overhead applied, and is there more than one rate?
19. Is any of the overhead pool applied to materials, and is the rate sufficient to fully absorb actual expenses?
20. Do overhead expenses exist by department?

Variances

21. How are variances reported—by job, standard production runs, or on an exception basis?
22. Are material variances segregated from labor variances?
23. Are labor variances segregated by rate and efficiency factors?
24. Are material variances segregated by price and usage?
25. Are variance results oriented so that causes can be quickly identified and corrected?
26. How effective are variance reports? Who receives, reviews, and analyzes these reports?
27. Are sufficient data provided so all jobs can be adequately reviewed?
28. Who determines which jobs or production runs will be reviewed?
29. Is cost estimating plugged into your variance reporting?
30. Can any of these variances be honestly billed to the customer to reflect changes?

Inventory Related

31. Are book to physical adjustments recorded as discovered?
32. Are inventory cycles conducted, and how often?
33. How are production losses and shrinkages controlled, reported, and booked?

Other

34. Are gross profit margin analyses performed on a regular basis?
35. Are product line profit-and-loss statements prepared and shared with those who can make a definite contribution toward improving future results?

Reprinted, by permission, from R.R. Feiner, 1977, *Operational financial analysis: A practical handbook with forms* (Englewood Cliffs, NJ: Prentice Hall), 45-46.

Some of the commonplace inefficiencies that a company might face are (Feiner, 1977)

- intermittent, ineffective, or short production runs (a production run is a manufactured amount that has been predetermined, such as when SMC has a production run of 1,000 clubs planned for February);
- double handling of materials because some materials were not available when needed;
- inadequate development of proper tooling methods because the production runs are too short;
- failure to realize quantity discounts;
- failure to define economical order quantities; and
- downtime of machines that are waiting for parts but still incur all fixed operating costs.

If the Smiths are charged $20 for each office supply delivery, they should forecast their potential needs for an extended period of time so they can order all the supplies possibly needed during that period; this will reduce delivery charges. Sound planning can help them consolidate orders.

INVENTORY TURNOVER RATIO

The problems identified in the preceding section are just some of the concerns associated with poor management of the raw goods required to manufacture the final product. It is fairly easy to identify a machine that is not in use, and it is obvious when you have to pay an extra premium for a small order. However, it is often difficult or even impossible to notice when raw materials are just sitting in storage for extended periods and out of a manager's view. Inventory **turnover** is a method used to determine if in fact inventory is just sitting around. The inventory turnover ratio also helps identify whether management is adequately managing resources.

An inventory turnover ratio can be applied to both finished goods and raw goods. The calculation for finished goods turnover is as follows:

finished goods turnover ratio =
cost of goods sold /
average finished goods inventory

Assuming that the cost of goods sold is $385,000 and the average finished goods inventory is $65,000, the turnover ratio will be $385,000 / $65,000 = 5.92. This number can also be expressed in working days: 42.7 days of unsold finished goods sitting in inventory. To calculate the number of working days, divide the number of working days in the year (253) by the turnover ratio (5.92) (Feiner, 1977). The number of working days (253) is constant for any company that is closed on weekends and federal holidays. There is no correct ratio for inventory turnover. However, the faster the inventory is turned over, the more money will be made. Some sport businesses are likely to have a high inventory turnover rate (e.g., concession items are typically bought and sold very frequently). On the other hand, a yacht sales company might sell only a few boats each year, but the profit margin on each boat can sustain the business.

We can do the same calculation for raw materials using the following formula:

raw materials turnover ratio =
raw materials consumed /
average raw materials inventory

Using the preceding formula, if a company spends $135,000 on raw materials and maintains an average inventory of $17,000 in raw goods, the company's turnover ratio would be the following:

raw materials turnover ratio = $135,000 / $17,000
= 7.94

The 7.94 ratio translates to 31.9 days that raw materials are generally in inventory before they are consumed. The more quickly raw materials are consumed, the lower the inventory handling costs. This number is important because it serves as a benchmark to help identify potential waste, and management must vigilantly monitor whether this number increases or decreases. Knowing about any decreases will help the manager identify what is being done correctly in order to maintain the success. Any increases represent a trouble sign that raw materials are sitting around incurring unnecessary expenses.

Assume that SMC has incurred costs of $400,000 for the rackets it produces and $125,000 for the raw materials consumed. Also assume that the average finished goods inventory is $50,000 and that the average raw materials inventory is $15,000. Based on these numbers, the inventory turnover ratios would be as follows:

$$\text{finished goods} = \$400{,}000 / \$50{,}000$$
$$= \text{a turnover ratio of } 8$$
$$\text{raw materials} = \$125{,}000 / \$15{,}000$$
$$= \text{a turnover ratio of } 8.33$$

Thus, in our example, the number of working days required to turn over the inventory is 31.6 days for finished goods (253 / 8) and 30.4 days for raw materials (253 / 8.33). The data obtained through this calculation can be compared with ratios from similar companies to determine whether SMC is storing and selling its inventory effectively. Comparison data can be obtained from banks and trade associations (Feiner, 1977).

PURCHASING CONCERNS

Purchasing concerns arise when inventory is not ordered in a timely manner, ordered too quickly, or ordered in too small or too large an amount. Centralized purchasing is one technique for reducing these potential problems. Centralized purchasing moves the decision making and execution away from individual departments. Centralizing the purchasing function provides benefits such as the following (Feiner, 1977):

- Managers can focus on their specialties rather than on administrative issues surrounding purchasing.
- Responsibility is given to a single person rather than numerous individual managers.
- Clerical effort and inventory control problems can be reduced.
- Problems of potential shortages can be identified early.
- Price negotiation can be improved because of the ability to buy bigger lots and redistribute the materials throughout an organization.

Purchasing is only the second step in the inventory management process. Inventories are typically not purchased on an as-needed basis because the costs for ordering small amounts would be prohibitive. Thus a business places larger orders, and excess inventory needs to be stored for future use.

STORING INVENTORY

As you have already seen, inventory-related costs can be significant over and beyond the cost for the storage facility itself. Inventories can be classified as raw materials, work-in-process, and finished goods. At each level, the inventory needs to be stored, moved, modified, shipped, packaged, and sent through related processes; and all these steps cost money. Some of these expenses can be reduced through joint warehousing with other businesses or through the development of automated systems to more effectively move the right parts at the right time.

Raw materials can pose unique storage concerns when in liquid or bulk form. If SMC has purchased a large amount of steel for forging clubs, the metal might take up significant space or may need to be stored in special areas. Work-in-process is a term for refined raw materials that have not yet reached the finished product stage. These materials need to be stored in a location from which they can easily be moved to the finishing area. In a typical manufacturing plant that produces millions of products each year, the amount of goods classified as work-in-process can be significant. This is especially true if the manufacturing process takes more than a week and products are manufactured in a cycle in which new runs are started each or every other week. If the product takes three weeks to manufacture and a new production run is launched every other week, a significant amount of work-in-process is being stored at various stages of completion.

INVENTORY STORAGE COSTS

Inventory management is the process of lowering the total costs associated with all the inventories required to sustain efficient operations (Brigham & Gapenski, 1994). In other words, by effectively tracking inventory costs, a company can reduce costs while continuing to operate efficiently. Costs can be broken down into four main areas: carrying costs, ordering costs, shipping and receiving costs, and costs associated with running out of inventory. The carrying, or storing, costs are the most expensive component of the inventory costs. These costs generally rise in direct proportion to the average amount of inventories carried. Thus the more inventory being stored, the greater the carrying costs, as the following example shows.

Sport Manufacturing Company Assume that SMC sells S units of rackets each year, and the company has to place equal-sized orders N times a year for the raw materials needed to build the rackets. The ratio of S to N (S / N) will indicate how many units are purchased with each order. The average inventory

Inventory Concerns in the NFL

The NFL racks up $3.2 billion in retail sales, which makes it the largest sports brand and the seventh-largest brand in the world behind the likes of Coca-Cola. Approximately 31% of sports fans over age 12 own some type of NFL product.

Although some teams are popular sellers, what happens to those products that are not sold? Manufacturers need to produce enough goods from each team to cover fan needs, especially in case a team does very well. No retailer wants to be without a team's merchandise if the team is having a great season. Manufacturers need to play a guessing game, and if a team is doing well they must ramp up production and shipment—even though the team might tank later in the season. In fact, all championship events have T-shirts produced with the winning team's name on them. How can they be available so quickly that they are worn within a minute of the game's ending? The manufacturer prints two versions of the shirts, one for each team. The winning team receives their shirts, and the other team's shirts are destroyed or given away to charity organizations.

level (A) can be expressed with the following formula (Brigham & Gapenski, 1994):

$$A = \text{units per order} / 2$$
$$= (S / N) / 2$$

A = average inventory level

S = units of rackets sold in a year

N = number of orders of raw materials in a year

The number of units purchased per order is divided by 2 to obtain the "average" number of units to be ordered. If SMC sold 120,000 rackets and placed four orders a year for raw materials, the formula would be completed as follows:

$$A = (120,000 / 4) / 2$$
$$= 30,000 / 2$$
$$= 15,000 \text{ units}$$

Thus, SMC carries an average inventory of 15,000 units. The company orders 30,000 units at a time, so when a shipment is received, the inventory level should be close to 0 units; after the order is received, the inventory level will be slightly over 30,000 units. By knowing the average inventory level, we can calculate carrying costs.

If SMC pays $2 per unit, then the average inventory value is $2 × 15,000 units, or $30,000. Most businesses have a cost of capital based on having to borrow money to purchase inventory. If SMC has a cost of capital of 10%, then there will be $3,000 in inventory carrying costs for one year. This cost needs to be added to the storage costs, which include space, utilities, security, taxes, and so on. These annual costs come to $2,000 a year. In addition, the following annual costs also need to be added to the total carrying costs: $500 for insurance and $1,000 for inventory losses. SMC's total carrying costs for carrying the $30,000 average inventory are $3,000 + $2,000 + $500 + $1,000 = $6,500 (Brigham & Gapenski, 1994). We can calculate the $6,500 cost as a percentage (C) by dividing it by the $30,000 average inventory: $6,500 / $30,000 = 0.217, or 21.7%. The annual percentage cost can be used in subsequent forecasts to determine potential carrying costs.

$$TCC = (C)(P)(A)$$

TCC = total carrying costs

C = carrying costs divided by value of average inventory

P = product price

A = average inventory

If SMC increased its average inventory value to $40,000—which would change A to 20,000—and the price (P) remained at $2, the carrying costs would be calculated as follows:

$$TCC = (0.217)(\$2)(20,000)$$
$$= \$8,680$$

The TCC of $8,680 is a $2,180 increase over the previous cost of $6,500. This example highlights how the carrying costs increase when larger inventories are ordered. The increase would be reduced if the turnover rate was much greater. Thus, if 240,000 units were sold each year, the 100% increase in sales coupled with larger inventory purchases could reduce some of the carrying costs, which could result in increased profits or having funds to pay the capital costs earlier.

As noted previously, there are four types of costs associated with inventory. Carrying costs are the largest; but ordering costs, shipping and receiving costs, and the cost of running out of inventory are also important. These costs are often fixed and include such items as the cost of research on purchase options, interoffice memos, phone calls, taking delivery, and moving raw materials. The fixed costs associated with inventory ordering are represented by F. To calculate the total ordering cost we multiply F by N, with N representing the number of orders per year. The equation is often written as follows:

$$TOC = (F)(N)$$

TOC = total ordering costs

F = fixed cost of inventory ordering

N = number of orders per year, which is calculated as follows:

$$N = (S / 2A)$$

S = total units sold in a year

A = the average inventory

Thus TOC can also be written as (F)(S / 2A). This equation can be applied to our SMC example.

Sport Manufacturing Company

Using SMC's previous number of 120,000 units sold and average inventory of 15,000 units, the total ordering costs would be calculated as follows if SMC incurred $100 in expenses to place an order:

$$TOC = \$100 \times 120,000 / 30,000$$
$$= \$400$$

Thus, the total ordering cost is $400 a year based on the four orders. Through knowing TOC and TCC, we can calculate the total inventory costs. In this case, SMC's total inventory cost is $400 + $6,500 = $6,900.

The numbers in the examples presented do not include certain other costs such as lost sales, loss of consumer goodwill, and the disruption of production schedules associated with not having enough inventory in storage (Brigham & Gapenski, 1994).

INVENTORY VALUATION

Purchase costs, **replacement costs**, and the proper accounting technique to measure true revenue are components necessary for determining the effects of storing inventory over extended periods. This process is often called the cost-of-goods-sold method, which analyzes the replacement cost for sold inventory. Two basic techniques can be used to value inventory: LIFO and FIFO. LIFO, which stands for **last in**, **first out**, values inventory based on the current price of replacing an item. FIFO, which stands for **first in**, **first out**, reports valuation based on the price paid earlier for an item. Corporations prefer to use LIFO because any increase in inventory prices results in less income and a corresponding lower tax obligation. Shareholders prefer FIFO because the increased price generates additional revenue and possibly larger dividends.

Stars of David

Assume that the Stars buy souvenir gold cups for their future championship celebrations. They pay $30 per cup in 2002 and buy a supply that can last five years. However, by the year 2007 when the Stars use the last of the gold cups, the cups are valued at $500 each. The income statement for the mythical Stars Souvenir Store, which sells nothing but the cups, might be as shown here for the LIFO and the FIFO methods.

Stars Souvenir Store Income Statement

LIFO	
Sales (100 units at $1,000 each)	$100,000
COGS (100 units at replacement value $500)	50,000
Gross profit	**$50,000**
Selling expense	20,000
Net profit before taxes	**$30,000**
FIFO	
Sales (100 units at $1,000 each)	$100,000
COGS (100 units at replacement value $30)	3,000
Gross profit	**$97,000**
Selling expense	20,000
Net profit before taxes	**$77,000**

COGS = cost of goods sold.

Sport Manufacturing Company

Another example should help highlight the difference between LIFO and FIFO. Assume that SMC has one item valued at $5, one valued at $6, and one valued at $7; the selling price of all three items is $8. Two items are sold for a combined $16 ($8 each). Under the FIFO method, the items that had cost $5 and $6 would be sold first. This would result in a $5 profit ($16 – $11) and leave $7 in the closing inventory T-account. In contrast, under the LIFO method, the two items sold would be the $6 and $7 items. Under this scenario SMC would generate only $3 profit ($16 – $13), and the closing inventory would be the $5 item.

Most accountants would want to recognize the loss associated with decreased inventory values in the current accounting period. Two valuation techniques can be utilized to do this: cost valuation and market valuation. The following example shows how the two values can be compared to help determine a decrease in inventory value. Assume that an item costs $5, the replacement cost is $3.50, the selling price is $6, the disposition cost is $2, and the normal profit is $1.

The disposition cost is the cost to dispose of an item in inventory. Some items cannot just be thrown into the garbage. Items that are large or heavy, for example, may need to be hauled to a dump, and the cost of hauling them is their disposition cost. The replacement cost ($3.50) is lower than the net realizable value (NRV), which is $6 – $2 = $4. Since the replacement cost is lower than the NRV, the $3.50 amount is used. Since the initial cost was $5.00 and since the lower number (between cost and market) is $3.50, the loss that would be reported is $1.50 ($5 – $3.50). If the company buys another item at the $3.50 cost, the new item will generate a $0.50 profit. We calculate this profit by subtracting the replacement cost ($3.50) and the disposition cost ($2) from the $6 selling price. Thus, the higher-cost item would result in an initial loss, but the lower replacement cost will generate a profit in the long term.

Stars of David

The Stars would earn a much higher rate of return if the FIFO method was used to calculate the store's pretax profit. However, the potential tax liability is also significantly higher. In the LIFO example, the income would be lower and taxes would be lower, but a more realistic estimate of the pretax profit is shown because any new cups would need to be purchased at the $500 price. Either technique is valid, and both conform to generally accepted accounting practices. A company has to decide which treatment of a given transaction is most appropriate for its needs. The FIFO method may be more appropriate if the Stars want to show a higher rate of return for investors. Such financial maneuvering is not dishonest, since the team's annual report will indicate that the FIFO method was used to calculate the inventory's value.

LOST INVENTORY

One of the consequences of storing inventory is the possibility of losing it. Inventory can be lost for various reasons, from simple misplacement to theft, spoilage, or obsolescence. Inventory is an asset. As with any other asset, if care is not taken it can be lost. For example, if the Stars do not properly track beer, they could lose beer as a consequence of misreported sales or even theft (e.g., by the cleaning crew). Employee honesty can be greatly enhanced when the employees know that inventory management practices are in place.

Besides losing money by paying to store inventory, inventory obsolescence can greatly increase inventory costs. A store that carries Shaquille O'Neal jerseys from the Orlando Magic will definitely find them a tough sell compared with Miami Heat jerseys. Although some consumers might be interested in buying an Orlando jersey as a collector's item, the costs associated with carrying the jersey for a possible sale once every six months might not justify keeping the jerseys. Factors that come into play when you are analyzing whether to carry an obsolete product include

- the potential activity or lack of activity in relation to the item,
- the amount of storage space required,
- the amount of physical activity required to move the item,
- the item's replacement cost if a replacement were ever required,
- whether replacement parts could ever be found and their potential cost, and
- how critical the item is for the overall business operation.

If these considerations indicate that the item is expendable, then the cost analysis should determine whether the company is wasting money by keeping it. Assume that the item would cost $100 a year to keep in inventory based on the cost per square foot for storage, utilities, human resources, and so on. If the replacement cost is $500 and there is a 50% chance the item could be used or sold in the next 10 years, then disposing of the item would be a low-risk choice.

If inventory becomes obsolete (e.g., a professional sports team relocates, such as when the Houston Oilers became the Tennessee Titans), the inventory can be given away to charity or sold at a significant markdown. If your company is a subchapter S corporation, you can usually take a tax deduction for your cost of producing the goods. However, if you are a C corporation, you can deduct the cost of the inventory plus half the difference between the cost and the fair market value of the goods—which cannot exceed twice the cost of inventory (Marullo, 1997, December). S and C corporations are discussed in chapter 4.

AUDITING INVENTORY

A key component of any inventory management system is taking a physical inventory. Whether you are counting production parts or supplies, physical inventory taking is a critical step in controlling inaccurate inventory purchasing behavior or determining a business' true value. Often people just count physical units, which is not the most effective way to take inventory. You may see this in supermarkets—for example, an inventory taker counts the number of potato chip bags on the shelf. In other settings, some people use a "line" system, drawing a line on a box and placing another order when items in the box dip below the line. Others use a two-bin system. They have two bins of parts, for example, and when one bin is emptied, they place an order, using the items in the second bin while waiting for the order to arrive.

As an alternative to just counting units, an inventory-taking protocol can help accurately determine the value of inventory units that might otherwise be difficult to track. An effective inventory-taking protocol could require the following steps (Feiner, 1977):

- Analyzing the degree of obsolescence in the inventory
- Identifying fast- and slow-moving items
- Properly classifying the inventory based on need, value, or other variables
- Identifying the cause of lost or stolen inventory items
- Identifying techniques to help move slow inventory

Numerous inventory management systems exist to help reduce carrying costs and optimize the production process.

POINT OF SALE

One key inventory management technique is the point-of-sale inventory management system. These systems are used at stores such as supermarkets, drugstores, and sporting goods stores. The system uses bar codes on packages. The bar code is scanned when an item enters a store and when it is sold. Computers track the item's movement, and sophisticated systems can identify when the items are selling, at what price they are sold, how often to reorder, and related information.

JUST IN TIME

Just-in-time (JIT) inventory systems are often found in the manufacturing industry when numerous suppliers are required to provide multiple and flexible inventory options for a manufacturer. Japanese manufacturers developed the JIT system so that needed components

What options does a business have when its inventory becomes obsolete?

© AP PHOTO/La Presse, Andr Pichette

could be delivered at the exact moment they would be needed to complete the production process. By utilizing such a strategy, businesses thought they could avoid having a buffer, or safety inventory, and all the associated costs.

The JIT system is timing based. Everything has to be calculated to within minutes so that an entire assembly line is not shut down because of one missing screw. The JIT system was designed on the basis of highly predictable requirements, real-time communications between all parties, and coordinated suppliers (Spiro, 1996). Just-in-time systems can save money, but if they are not perfectly coordinated, the process does not work. For example, the manufacturer must have strong faith that each supplier's deliveries will be at least 98% defect free. A shipment with too many defects would unduly hinder the entire process because the manufacturer would not have the benefit of possibly testing every component while in storage.

Another concern relating to JIT systems is the impact of sudden emergencies on the system. In the wake of the September 11, 2001, tragedies, according to a major study conducted by the trucking industry, 39% of companies surveyed experienced major disruptions in their supply chain as a result of the attacks ("Managers Rethinking," 2001). Similar major disruptions occurred after the horrible hurricane season in 2005. As a result of these disruptions, many companies started developing a new mind-set and looking toward just in-case (JIC) systems. These systems are designed to maintain a safety stock so that the company can eliminate as much inefficiency as possible. Thus, JIT should not be taken as a directive to remove every item in inventory. Rather, a safety stock should be kept to guard against a major disaster or other concerns, while at the same time efforts are made to monitor and reduce inefficiencies.

ECONOMIC ORDER QUANTITY

One of the most important elements in the inventory auditing process is tracking how much to order. Determining the optimum order quantity is important for reducing storage and ordering costs.

Since the JIT system is not right for every manufacturer, other techniques need to be adopted to help reduce inventory costs while maintaining adequate reserves. One such technique is a mathematical model called the economic order quantity (EOQ) model. The EOQ model attempts to determine the optimum number of units to be ordered whenever an order is placed. Large inventories mean increased warehousing costs, interest expenses, insurance costs, and larger amounts of obsolete inventory. At the same time, the larger the order, the less often the orders need to be placed, which reduces ordering costs. By knowing the optimum numbers of components to order, a manager can reduce the number of orders that need to be placed and the number of extra units kept in inventory. The equation for the EOQ model is as follows:

$$EOQ = \sqrt{\frac{2(F)(U)}{C}}$$

In the model, F stands for the costs associated with placing an order, such as paperwork or personnel time to place an order or write a check, which are activities independent of the order size. U stands for the sales in units per year of the item that will be placed in inventory. C represents the costs per year associated with carrying the units in inventory, including storage rental costs, insurance, and handling charges. The model works only in cases in which the inventory and sales numbers behave in a predictable manner. The formula shown is based on the assumption that, on average, half of each shipment is carried in inventory. If the fixed cost per order (F) is $5, the number of units sold each year (U) is 5,000, and the carrying cost per unit per year (C) is $0.80, the formula would be completed as follows:

$$\sqrt{\frac{2 \times \$5 \times 5,000}{\$0.80}} = 250 \text{ units}$$

If the managers of this hypothetical company utilized good inventory management practices, they would place orders in lots of 250 units at a time (Spiro, 1996).

Some companies have a hard time identifying the exact cost of carrying an item, and it is easier for them to calculate the EOQ based on industry norms. Here is the formula for calculating EOQ based on industry norms or internally generated percentage of a product's selling price:

$$EOQ = \sqrt{[2(F)(S)]/(C)(P)}$$

Under this version of the formula,

F = fixed cost of placing and receiving orders,

S = units sold annually,

C = annual carrying costs expressed as a percentage, and

P = purchase price of the inventory.

 Assume that the Stars order 26,000 shirts each year. The team calculates that the carrying costs are 25% of the inventory. The shirts are sold for $9 each, but the inventory cost is only $4.92 each. The fixed cost per order is $1,000. Plugging these numbers into the EOQ formula produces the following results (Brigham & Gapenski, 1994):

$$EOQ = \sqrt{[2(\$1,000)(26,000)]/(0.25)(\$4.92)}$$
$$= \sqrt{42,276,423}$$
$$= 6,500 \text{ units}$$

Dividing the 26,000 annual inventory by the EOQ of 6,500 units gives a total of four orders annually. Dividing 26,000 by 52 weeks gives a weekly usage rate of 500 shirts. Thus, after an order of 6,500 is received, 500 units will be subtracted from the inventory each week. Based on these numbers, the average inventory level will be 3,250 shirts at a cost of $4.92 each, which produces an inventory value of about $16,000. Economies of scale could be achieved if the Stars sold 52,000 shirts, which would be a 100% increase in sales. Economies of scale represent the most beneficial purchasing or ordering quantity to receive a price reduction. Thus, through more efficient ordering or by ordering larger quantities, a business can reduce the per unit cost significantly. Economies of scale can also be accomplished when companies join together to buy products when individually they might not be able to order a large enough quantity to obtain a break, but collectively they can place such an order. The EOQ would increase from 6,500 to 9,195—a 41% increase.

Although these ordering points provide an exact number to order, the world is not exact. The Stars will not sell 500 shirts each week. Some weeks they might sell several thousand shirts and other weeks no shirts at all. This reality forces us to set an order point with flexibility. For example, a lag period needs to be built in since it might take several weeks to receive an order. Thus, a several-week supply needs to be reached before a reorder is placed. In addition, a safety stock should be maintained. A safety stock might be necessary to avoid delays in receiving orders or when sales suddenly increase. This concern is highlighted in the following Stars example.

 Even though the preceding example showed an EOQ of 6,500 shirts, the Stars might order 7,500 shirts to help maintain a 1,000-shirt safety stock. The team might also place an order when there are still 1,000 shirts in inventory to maintain the EOQ and the necessary safety stock (Brigham & Gapenski, 1994). Note that any safety stock will increase the total carrying cost. If an additional 1,000 shirts are ordered, the additional carrying cost is calculated as follows:

additional carrying cost =
(safety stock)(P)(C)

P = the purchase price for the inventory

C = the annual carrying costs expressed as a percentage

Using the definitions and numbers already given, the additional carrying cost for the Stars is $1,230.

additional carrying cost $= 1,000(\$4.92)(0.25)$
$$= \$1,230$$

The 1,000 additional shirts will increase the Stars' carrying costs from $4,000, as we will see, to $5,230 (Brigham & Gapenski, 1994).

The information we have can be plugged into the TOC and TCC formulas to calculate the total inventory costs (TIC). Remember, TOC = (F)(S / Q) and TCC = (C)(P)(Q / 2). Thus, the equations would be calculated as follows (Brigham & Gapenski, 1994):

$$TIC = TOC + TCC$$
$$= [(\$1,000)(26,000 / 6,500)] +$$
$$[(0.25)(\$4.92)(6,500 / 2)]$$
$$= \$4,000 + \$4,000$$
$$= \$8,000$$

This example shows that the total inventory costs, excluding the cost of the shirts, is $8,000.

QUANTITY DISCOUNTS

Another wrinkle can be added to the Stars example. The EOQ is fine if no discounts are offered for larger orders. However, most suppliers are forced to provide larger purchasers with a discount to attract their business. Any discount can change the optimal ordering quantity since the discount can provide a tangible savings over and above any additional storage costs that might be incurred from having to store the extra inventory. The question then becomes, what would be the optimum ordering quantity if the supplier provided a discount for larger orders?

 Assume that the Stars' supplier offered a 2% discount for orders equal to or greater than 10,000 shirts. Based on an order of 6,500 shirts in the previous example, the TIC was calculated at $8,000. We can rewrite the TIC equation using the 10,000-shirt order size and decreasing the price from $4.92 per shirt to $4.82 based on the 2% discount (Brigham & Gapenski, 1994).

$$TIC = [(\$1,000)(26,000 / 10,000)] + [(0.25)(\$4.82)(10,000 / 2)]$$
$$= \$2,600 + \$6,025$$
$$= \$8,625$$

The carrying cost increases because the average inventory is larger, but the ordering cost declines since fewer orders are placed. Based on these numbers it would seem that adding 4,000 more shirts to the inventory increases inventory costs by only $625 per year. However, this analysis fails to take into consideration the savings of approximately $0.10 per shirt. The total yearly savings based on the 2% discount is $2,558. Thus, even after reducing the savings in shirt prices by the added inventory carrying cost ($625), the Stars would generate a net savings of $1,933 each year by taking advantage of the larger-order discount (Brigham & Gapenski, 1994).

INVENTORY CONVERSION PERIOD

Another calculation, one that is similar to the finished goods or raw materials turnover ratio, is the inventory conversion period (ICP) (Feiner, 1977). The ICP is the average length of time required to convert the raw materials to finished inventory and then sell the goods. We calculate the ICP by dividing inventory by the sales per day.

 If we estimate that SMC has $5 million in inventory and will have $20 million in sales in the coming year, the calculation is as follows:

$$ICP = inventory / sales per day$$
$$= \$5,000,000 / (\$20,000,000 / 360 days)$$
$$= 90 days$$

The equation indicates that it is 90 days from the time raw materials are received until the rackets or clubs are manufactured and then sold.

The shorter the ICP, the more money the business will make if it makes a small profit on each item. For expensive items, the ICP may not be as relevant, since building one stadium might generate $20 million in profits for a builder but take three years to complete.

Regardless of the technique used to monitor inventory levels, a purchasing plan needs to be developed to optimize expenditures and carrying costs. This chapter provides several suggestions that will help with this decision. One of the best techniques to optimize purchasing and inventory control is centralized purchasing. Imagine what would happen if a collegiate athletic department allowed each team to buy its own office supplies. Each team might have several hundred pens sitting in a drawer unused. In contrast, if the entire department bought several boxes of pens at a time, it could reduce total purchases. Centralized purchasing is designed to facilitate more effective purchasing, but it also allows a business to utilize inventories more effectively. The other benefits associated with centralized purchasing were addressed earlier in this chapter.

UTILIZING INVENTORY

Businesses need to answer numerous questions in order to determine whether raw materials are being effectively utilized. The following are some of the key questions.

- How effective has management been in increasing the inventory turnover rate?
- How is purchasing controlled to make sure purchases are in economical quantities that do not unduly increase inventory carrying costs?
- Are any components of the manufacturing process sent to external sources for finishing, and can any such steps be completed internally?
- What is the relationship between direct and indirect labor costs?
- What steps are taken to reduce the need for overtime labor?

- Are the labor and materials costs clearly defined to allow accurate tracking?
- Are accurate records kept concerning equipment maintenance and repair costs?
- Who contracts for equipment rental or leasing, and how is that process supervised?
- What control mechanisms are in place to reduce pilferage and deterioration of supplies?

These are just some of the questions that are raised when a business starts putting the forecasting and inventory systems together with production and manufacturing. Before the manufacturing process can begin, SMC needs to develop a production budget.

PRODUCTION ANALYSIS

The production budget combines the desired inventory levels with forecast sales projections. The total production run that will be manufactured can be calculated by means of the following formula (Griffin, 1991):

total production =
sales in units + desired ending inventory –
projected beginning inventory

This formula can help a company determine if it needs to reduce the number of units produced if sales are low or if the inventory level is too high. The formula can be applied to calculate SMC's total production needs.

Sport Manufacturing Company

Assume that SMC had forecast an ending inventory of 1,000 golf clubs in 2006. The beginning inventory for 2006 was 500 clubs, which means that after the 2005 sales year was completed, there were 500 clubs left in inventory. The company sold 10,000 clubs in 2006. The formula can be calculated as follows:

$$\text{total production} = 10{,}000 + 1{,}000 - 500$$

$$= 10{,}500 \text{ clubs}$$

Thus, SMC needed to produce 10,500 clubs in order to serve all sales and to maintain an inventory of 1,000 clubs.

Another key component related to utilization is determining if a business is properly utilizing the workforce. Employers can calculate whether or not employees are performing their jobs efficiently. Time–motion studies undertaken by Frank Gilbreth (1868-1924) were conducted by industrialists to determine how long it would take for an assembly line worker to perform a given task (Bridges & Roquemore, 1996). Similarly, SMC could ascertain that an average golf club takes 4 hours to manufacture. Thus, in a 40-hour work week, an employee should manufacture 10 clubs. Employees who do not reach that goal are not utilizing their skills

Amazon Floats

Amazon.com uses a different inventory management system, which is referred to as a minimal inventory system utilizing a negative operating cycle. People also call the system a float, as highlighted in chapter 12. The key to the system is that inventory is available through other suppliers so that the vendor does not really carry an inventory. The Internet bookseller Amazon carries only a small fraction of books in its inventory. Most book titles are not ordered until a customer places an order with Amazon. The result is that Amazon turns over the inventory 26 times a year compared with other booksellers such as Barnes & Noble, which has an inventory turnover of 10 (Mayer, 1998).

The negative operating cycles are what really separates Amazon from other booksellers and general retailers. Most companies need to buy a product, stock it, and move it to a different sales location before they can sell it. Amazon charges a customer's credit card account when the order is placed. The book distributor or publisher sends the book directly to the purchaser within days after it has been ordered. The credit card company pays Amazon within a day. Amazon then takes on average 46 days to pay its suppliers, the book distributors. Thus, instead of having to pay to finance sales (through borrowing money to purchase the books it sells—its inventory), Amazon makes even more money by having the customer's money for 45 days to reinvest and earn interest on (Mayer, 1998).

effectively. Management can track employee performance and engage in retraining or other steps to work with employees who are not effectively using their time.

The two steps outlined represent just two types of measurement techniques to help management identify costs associated with the production process. However, the manufacturing process entails unique components and costs that are necessary to transform the inventory, utilizing the standards set forth in the production budget. Production management is the topic we turn to next.

PRODUCTION MANAGEMENT

This chapter focuses primarily on financing inventory and the costs associated with holding and liquidating inventory. However, most businesses do not maintain inventory in the same condition in which it was purchased unless they are in the wholesale business. Most companies utilize the inventory to develop some other marketable item. A professional team would have a useless inventory of players unless they actually competed. A golf club manufacturer must transform metal into a club in order to generate revenues. This transformation process costs money. Conversion costs entail direct materials, direct labor, and factory overhead. Direct materials are all the raw goods that will be used to make the product. For a golf club, the direct materials might include the metal as well as rubber for the grip. Direct labor entails the personnel time required to actually turn the metal and rubber into the club. The factory overhead involves the proportional costs of machinery and energy that are utilized to transform the metal and rubber into the club. Conversion costs do not include any nonmanufacturing costs such as administrative, advertising, and selling-related expenses.

The conversion costs associated with any manufacturing process are fairly simple to calculate. We can calculate direct material by dividing the cost of all the materials by the number of units that can be manufactured. If SMC paid $300,000 for metal and rubber and can produce 100,000 clubs with the materials, then the direct material cost is $3 per unit. Direct labor can be calculated in a similar manner.

Sport Manufacturing Company

If SMC employees can manufacture one club in 4 hours, the calculation to determine labor costs is very basic. The biggest mistake people make in determining labor costs is failing to include benefits in the calculation. If an SMC production line worker earns $10 per hour, the direct labor amount might not be $40 per club. If we assume that the employee's benefits amount to 40% of wages, the actual cost is $56 per club.

The last component necessary for calculating conversion costs is factory overhead (FO). To determine factory overhead, a manufacturer calculates all the costs associated with the production process that do not include direct material or direct labor. Typical factory overhead costs could include lease expenses on equipment, interest payments owed for financed equipment, depreciation of factory equipment, utilities, insurance, maintenance, taxes, and any other expense that can be directly linked to the manufacturing process.

Sport Manufacturing Company

Assume that SMC pays $20,000 annually for factory overhead costs. Furthermore, assume that the factory operates for 4,000 hours to produce a run of golf clubs. By dividing the $20,000 by the 4,000 hours, we can determine that the factory overhead cost per hour is $5. Since it takes 4 hours to make a club, the FO is $20 per club, assuming customized production of the clubs. By adding the direct materials, labor, and FO, we can calculate the manufacturing conversion costs for producing one golf club.

Direct material	$3
Direct labor	$56
Factory overhead	$20
Total	$79

The $79 conversion cost is critical because SMC needs this number to determine the lowest price it can charge a distributor for the clubs. Nonmanufacturing costs need to be added to the $79 to determine the break-even point. If the total nonmanufacturing costs are $8 per unit, the club's break-even point is $87.

BREAK-EVEN ANALYSIS

The manufacturing process involves several key financial issues. One of the most important entails calculating an appropriate production run to maximize profits. To achieve the lowest production cost per unit, companies normally need to undertake large manufacturing runs. The setup cost per unit is the measurement tool used to determine if the manufacturing process is economical. Break-even analysis can also be used to calculate the number of additional items necessary to make a certain profit. Break-even analysis is discussed in chapter 5, but there the context is the financial statement rather than manufacturing. Although the concepts are similar, break-even analysis associated with manufacturing focuses on specific manufactured items versus the business overall.

Instead of conversion costs, the following break-even analysis utilizes fixed costs. Fixed costs are the costs incurred no matter how many units are manufactured, whereas variable costs change with the quantity being produced. The formula to calculate the break-even point follows:

$$\text{sale price} \times N = F + (\text{variable costs} \times N)$$

N = quantity

F = fixed costs

Quantity, often referred to as N as in this formula, denotes the units that need to be sold to break even. The break-even point is calculated in the next example.

 **Sport Manufacturing Company**

Assume that SMC has $100,000 in fixed costs for making tennis rackets. The variable cost per racket is $5. If these special-discount rackets sell for $10 each, we can calculate how many units need to be sold to break even. Applying the numbers, the equation is as follows:

$$\$10 \times N = \$100,000 + (\$5 \times N)$$

$$\$5N = \$100,000$$

$$N = 20,000$$

Thus, SMC needs to sell 20,000 of these rackets to break even. But what if SMC needs to make $40,000 from the rackets in order to undertake manufacturing them for an acceptable profit? The equation is as follows:

$$\$10 \times N = \$140,000 + (\$5 \times N)$$

$$\$5N = \$140,000$$

$$N = 28,000$$

The company would need to manufacture and sell 28,000 units to make the profit margin desired from this product line. Since the fixed costs are covered after 20,000 units have been manufactured, each unit over 20,000 has a $5 profit based on the $10 sales price minus the $5 variable costs.

Planning and pro forma budgets, discussed in chapter 7, also apply to manufacturing break-even analysis. We cannot perform a break-even analysis without referring to projected budgets for such items as sales and production runs. These data are critical for identifying how many units may be sold and how many units must be produced to meet the sales demand. A company can manufacture enough units to meet the break-even point; but if the units are not being sold, the company will not break even and will in fact be losing money as a consequence of having inventory sit on shelves.

All the factors addressed throughout this chapter help establish the numbers needed to create a realistic sales budget. The sales budget represents the number of units that the company anticipates should be sold in an upcoming time period. A sales budget is based on a multitude of factors or techniques. The unit costs, anticipated demand, the competition, consumer interest, and a host of additional variables help create the sales budget. In addition, salespeople can be asked what they anticipate future sales might be, and customers can be asked how much they might order in the future. A company can also estimate a specific percentage growth over the sales volume in the prior period. A sample sales budget was presented in the Introduction to the Case Studies (see p. xvi).

VARIANCE ANALYSIS

It is relatively simple to calculate the break-even point or the optimum manufacturing run for making a specific profit, but these numbers are meaningless if the actual production runs are not monitored to ensure that the costs conform to the projections. Variance analysis is the process of establishing performance standards. Once the standards are established, a business needs to determine if it is reaching the standards. Are the actual fixed costs higher than projected? Why are they higher? For example, are energy prices higher than anticipated? Are variable costs above expectations? These costs could be higher because of an unanticipated increase in the price of iron if iron is one of the metals the business needs. If the costs are below expectations, the business will generate a greater profit than expected. If any cost is too high, the business must lower costs to meet the production budget. Cost reduction strategies might need to target a specific cost area or the entire production process. If costs are increasing across the board, a business may consider reducing some costs by taking drastic steps such as terminating employees or taking one day off from production each week.

LABOR COSTS

One of the greatest expenses associated with the manufacturing process is personnel cost. Although most people do not consider people to be machines, they in fact are a part of the manufacturing process. Similar to a cutting machine that might help make a racket, a person can help make a sports product. To produce the product of a baseball game, you need to have players who can produce the game. Depending on the product's quality, the human machines that produce the games can be either very expensive or cheap. Thus, baseball players in the major leagues might get paid a significant amount for the product they produce, whereas players in the minor leagues might get paid very little for their product; even though both sets of players are producing the same product, they are producing at different quality levels. Whether for players or administrative personnel, expenses can be significant; and businesses need to carefully track labor costs. Salaries are among the primary components of labor costs, and these costs can be higher in the sport industry compared with other labor markets.

Salaries for some positions may be straightforward (e.g., minimum wage positions paying $5.85 an hour). This is the current federal minimum wage rate, but some states have higher rates. New York's minimum wage mirrors the federal rate, but California's rate is $6.75 per hour ($8.50 in some circumstances in San Francisco) and Connecticut's rate is $7.10 per hour. However, salaries in sport can be very complicated. Professional athletes have numerous clauses in their contracts that call for benefits several times over and beyond the base salaries. It is not only athletes who have complicated salaries, though. Coaches can have complicated salary packages, too.

The costs associated with labor can be immense. The biggest budget item for most businesses is salaries and benefits. Many companies attempt to boost their bottom line by reducing salaries through terminations. Businesses are also reducing benefits

and requiring employees to pay a greater share for health insurance to help decrease employee-related costs. Since labor is so expensive, businesses often need to determine if they are paying too much for their employees. This question can be answered through examination of a company's earnings per hour (Feiner, 1977). A way to calculate earnings per hour is to divide total sales by the expected total number of hours worked. The earnings per hour ratio helps management determine how effectively a plant is running. The next example involves this ratio.

Sport Manufacturing Company

Assume that SMC forecasts sales to total $200,000 and that direct and indirect labor will entail 13,000 hours. By dividing the total sales by the expected total hours, we can develop the earnings per hour. Here, the earnings per hour are $200,000 / 13,000, which is $15.38 per hour. If the labor costs are less than $15.38 per hour, SMC will be able to cover its labor costs. Note that this analysis does not include raw materials and other fixed costs that are over and above the labor costs.

Labor costs are such a significant component of the manufacturing process that the costs need to be compared with those for other companies in the same industry. Management can use such a benchmark as a negotiation tool if the competitors have a lower labor cost. If the competition pays more, a business can use its creativity to make up any difference. Through innovation, a company can reduce labor costs and increase its profitability. In the hot Internet market of the late 1990s, many companies were moving away from traditional salary-based motivation and toward stock options and other incentives that did not require a significant capital outlay. Although stock options can be a strong benefit, some observers thought that such deals helped lead executives to push for increasing their share value over true growth. This was seen in the WorldCom and Enron scandals.

Employers have often attempted to reduce employee-related costs. Employers need to reduce labor costs to maximize profit, one reason why employers fight so hard against unionization. Unionization might mean sharing power; but more important, when employees can negotiate as one,

Salary Packages

In 1998, University of Wisconsin football coach Barry Alvarez had a highly complex salary package totaling more than $600,000, including $210,000 for his TV show, $140,000 for a Reebok consulting contract, $71,000 from radio shows, $15,033 for two bowl game bonuses, and $864 in complimentary tickets. The coach also received $8,288 from camps and clinics ("UW Athletic Department," 1998). The income derived from the TV show, radio shows, and shoe endorsements was paid by external companies rather than the university, but it still represents part of the overall employment package. The women's basketball coach also received a sizable package. Besides a base salary of more than $100,000 a year, Jane Albright-Dieterle received $43,500 from camps and clinics, $20,000 from Reebok, a $10,000 country club membership, and $5,200 from the Badger Store as part of her $186,700 total package ("UW Athletic Department," 1998).

Several years later the benefits are similar, but the numbers are significantly higher. Under his five-year contract expiring in 2008, Coach Alvarez receives $500,000 a year in base salary, along with a golf club membership, housing, and two cars. He also is entitled to bonuses, such as a potential yearly bonus for exceptional achievement of $1.2 million (increasing each year by $100,000). If he is fired without cause, the university must pay him the remainder of his contract; if he leaves early, he will have to pay his salary and $50,000 to terminate the contract. Numerous other football coaches have similar packages worth more than $1 million a year.

they normally can generate a higher per employee salary and larger group benefits. To combat rising employee-related expenses, employers are resorting to various tactics that they hope can lower costs.

Several universities, most notably the University of Pennsylvania, Stanford University, and Tufts, have outsourced facility workers such as custodians (Nicklin, 1997). Outsourcing can allow the universities to concentrate more fully on their primary strengths (education and research), but it also can reduce benefit costs. A university employee who earns $30,000 per year and receives significant benefits, including tuition reimbursement, can cost the university well over $50,000. However, if the custodian is terminated and then signs with a janitorial service that has an exclusive contract with the university, the cost for the same worker could decrease to under $40,000. The $10,000 savings can be magnified by economies of scale; the janitorial service can hire more people for less money and still make its profit. According to the principle of economies of scale, the larger the number of individuals involved, the greater the savings. Thus, although a $10,000 savings may not seem significant in itself, if the university requires the services of 100 janitors, the savings could be over $1 million. Outsourcing is just one technique organizations consider when attempting to reduce labor costs. Through lowering these costs, overall

manufacturing costs can also be reduced. Thus, if inventory or manufacturing costs are too high, a business can consider reducing costs by controlling other expense areas such as labor costs.

CONCLUSION

Some of the material in this chapter, such as the information on manufacturing-related costs, does not apply to all businesses. However, all businesses need to manage their resources, and that is inventory management. Even an entity such as the University of Milford has inventory. It manages land, facilities, chemicals, equipment, and other assets. These assets need to be tracked, maintained, repurchased, and sold. Carrying and ordering costs need to be included in any budget.

Even businesses that do not traditionally manufacture products do manufacture value. The Stars do not manufacture any products such as widgets. They manufacture basketball-related entertainment products. Thus, even the Stars need to analyze manufacturing-related costs and determine whether or not the players are working together cohesively. If the players are not working well together, the manufacturing process will not work as effectively, and the "machinery" for producing a winning season will need to be overhauled.

CLASS DISCUSSION TOPICS

1. What do you think is the most effective way to manage inventory?

2. What forecasting strategies would you utilize if you were managing a ski resort that had to deal with uncontrollable weather factors?

3. What strategies do you think might be useful in reducing employee theft if you ran a team's gift shop? Would your strategies change if you were managing a concession stand, and employees took food or beverages?

4. What cost reduction strategies could be used by SMC or the University of Milford?

5. Should coaches receive large contractual perks, and if so, what are some means to deal with Title IX or Equal Pay Act concerns? Should coaches get paid more than teachers?

6. If you overproduced T-shirts for a given team and could not resell the remaining shirts, what would you do with them?

7. Develop a list of all the fixed costs you could imagine for a professional basketball team.

8. Develop a list of all the variable costs you could imagine for a nonprofit sports event such as a 5K road race.

9. How should professional sports teams handle their high labor costs, especially when fans are upset that they have to pay so much to attend games?

PART V

PROFITS

If a business successfully manages its money, it should be able to make a profit through its investments. Part V takes a closer look at how businesses can grow their profits.

Chapter 14, Taxation and Legal Issues, covers the legal ramifications of success—taxes. If a company loses money, taxes might be minimal; but if a company does well, it might need to pay significant taxes depending on the type of legal status the company has. Taxes can have an impact on athletes as well as teams and leagues, so this chapter analyzes some of the complexities of the American taxation system. The chapter ends with an analysis of financial risk management to reduce losing money.

Chapter 15, Spending Earnings, explores how once a company has paid its taxes it can reinvest its earnings or pay its owners. If the company wants to reward its owners, it can pay them a dividend of cash or additional ownership shares. Profits can also be reinvested (e.g., by building new factories) to make the company more valuable, or they can be used to buy or merge with other companies to hopefully increase future profits. The chapter offers specific sport industry examples of successes and failures involving mergers and acquisitions.

14

TAXATION AND LEGAL ISSUES

CHAPTER OBJECTIVES

After studying this chapter, you should be able to do the following:

- Understand some of the tax concerns affecting the sport industry.
- Understand the issues associated with minority ownership of a sport business.
- Describe the importance of tax planning in sport.
- Calculate the marginal tax rate.
- Understand how tax law is applied to athletes.
- Understand the basics of financial risk management.

Legal issues abound in the finance field. Securities and Exchange Commission regulations are voluminous. Legal issues can apply to the wording of the prospectus and to footnotes added to financial statements to provide details on transactions. Legal issues involve not only federal law but also numerous state laws. For example, blue-sky laws in almost all states regulate securities dealers or the selling of securities in the state. In this chapter, we start by focusing on the legal and tax ramifications of a sport business' structure and then expand on the discussion of corporations and partnerships from chapter 4. The chapter then deals with various tax-related concerns such as tax planning, taxes in sport, and taxes affecting teams and athletes. The topics of the final section are financial risk management and insurance as a financial parachute.

BENEFITS OF CORPORATE STATUS

Chapter 4 highlights some of the benefits afforded to corporations and partnerships. Corporations have several distinct advantages that can aid sport businesses, and professional sports teams have benefited from these opportunities for many years. Corporations and some partnerships can use losses to offset tax liabilities that occur in other business enterprises. Former San Francisco 49ers owner Edward DeBartolo Jr. transferred ownership in the team to his father's real estate company to create additional tax losses (Euchner, 1993). The New York Yankees reorganized in 1991, and the structural changes allowed limited partners to claim losses on their personal income taxes (Euchner, 1993).

In 2004, Congress passed a new law that could boost teams' values by about 5%, which equals millions of dollars. The new corporate tax law lets teams deduct the entire franchise value (including concession, player, and broadcast contracts) over a 15-year period; under the prior law, only player contracts could be written off, and only up to half the franchise's value ("Provision Could Boost," 2004). Thus, having corporate status offers specific and valuable advantages over other ownership forms.

Proper business and financial structuring can save millions of dollars. The **estates** of NFL team owners George Halas and Paul Brown were both assessed at more than $100 million in back taxes by the IRS. However, on the basis of shrewd business reorganization efforts, the estates in fact received an aggregate IRS refund of $2.5 million (Much, 1997, September 9). The tax benefit was established through the cre-

ation of minority ownership rights in the teams and the resultant lower value attributable to the minority interests. An example will clarify how this worked. Let's suppose that a company has 100 shares of stock. If numerous people own the shares, anyone interested in buying the company needs to buy a majority of the shares, but she will not have complete control unless she buys all 100 shares. If someone owns 49 shares, that person's shares represent 49% of the business. The reason for the lower value is that not as many people would be interested in buying a minority interest since they would not be the primary owner and could never sell the entire business. As explained further on, by giving away shares to various relatives or colleagues, a team owner can dramatically reduce the book values of all shares.

In the case involving the estate of the late Paul Brown, former owner of the Cincinnati Bengals, the IRS sought over $40 million in estate taxes. The controversy that brought the dispute before U.S. Tax Court judge John O. Colvin entailed a 1983 stock option transaction that the government claimed was a scam. In that transaction, Brown had transferred 117 of his shares in the team to John Sawyer (another stockholder) for $30,000 per share. The sales contract allowed Brown to keep one share and still maintain complete control over the team. Another contract required Sawyer to sell, if Brown's sons exercised an option to buy, 329 of the now 330 shares Sawyer had for $25,000 each in 1993. The IRS unsuccessfully argued that the stock shares were sold significantly below the shares' true market value. The court ruled against the IRS based on the fact that even though the contract allowed the sons an option to buy back the team at a lower price, there was potential risk that the team would be worth less in 1993 than in 1983 (Much, 1997, September 9). If there had been no possibility of the value going down, and the sons could have bought back the team at a lower price than what had been paid for the team, then the IRS would have prevailed.

Another key component in the Bengals' deal involved the minority ownership interest. A minority owner traditionally does not have significant pull in any business; a minority share does, however, have the ability to drastically decrease the value of the team, as previously mentioned. Suppose you own 99% of a house, and your parents own the remaining 1%. If the house is worth $100,000, no one would ever pay $100,000 for it because that individual would never be the complete owner. Someone might pay $70,000 for the house with the intent to buy the remaining 1% from your parents. There is no requirement that your parents in fact sell their percentage share of the house, so the buyer would be taking a risk. This risk element reduces the value of the majority share.

The same concept applies to a professional sports team and other sport businesses. Although more people are willing to take a risk in buying a professional team, minority shares can still reduce the value of the majority shares. This reduced value can drastically decrease taxes that might be owed either on capital gains or on an inheritance, since the minority interests reduce all other values.

Although team values have significantly increased over the past decade, this does not necessarily increase value for some teams' minority owners. Anyone interested in purchasing a business would attempt to pay a higher amount for the largest share and then pay a lower amount for smaller shares. A potential purchaser might be willing to pay more for a larger share, after which he could assume managerial control and make life miserable for minority owners.

In contrast, if a minority owner is a holdout, the majority shares can decrease in value. Assume that the developer of a stadium wants to buy 10 houses that are located on the land where the playing field will be. Nine homeowners are willing to sell, but the 10th owner refuses. The other owners will receive either reduced offers for their houses or a revocation of the offer, since the missing house reduces the value of the deal. The developer will not want to build the stadium if there will be a house on the 50-yard line. Thus, not owning all 10 houses reduces the value of all the houses. Similarly, not owning an entire team can reduce the team's value and save on taxes.

Although the Bengals' deal held up in court, not every attempt to avoid estate taxes is successful. The Robbie family faced a $47 million tax bill after the death of former Miami Dolphins owner Joe Robbie. The family did not have the money and were forced to sell the team to Wayne Huizenga (Much, 1997, September 9). On the basis of these tax issues, the NFL has been considering changing the amount a general partner needs to own, with the aim of helping families reduce estate tax concerns. In 2000, a general partner in an NFL team was required to own at least 30% of a team. The new rule would apply to someone who has been an owner of a team for at least 10 years and would allow him to remain a general partner while owning only 10% of the team as long as he maintained his decision-making power. The rule would allow an owner to transfer ownership to children in an effort to avoid the 55% estate tax ("NFL Looking," 2000).

TAXES

No matter what organizational structure is chosen for a business, every manager needs to know some tax basics. The value of any financial asset or instrument is contingent on the cash flow produced by the investment. This cash flow is subject to taxation when disbursed and when received. If the tax rate on a given investment cash stream is too high, the investor will opt for a different investment that may have a lower return but also lower taxes. For example, cautious investors often purchase tax-free bonds rather than stock or other types of investment vehicles. Although the interest rate is lower, tax-free bonds may be more practical than investments that pay a higher interest rate because taxes on a taxable investment may cancel out any benefit derived from the higher interest rate.

An example will help show why this is so. If Milford starts building a stadium (for U of M) and issues a $1,000 tax-free bond that pays 5% interest each year, the investor will "take home" $50 each year. In contrast, if the investor buys a $1,000 face-value bond issued by SMC that pays 7%, her $70 per year interest will be subject to taxation. If her tax rate is 30%, then instead of taking home $70, she will take home only $49 after taxes. Although the difference is only a dollar, the purchaser of the tax-free bond also has the comfort of a secure investment; most tax-free bonds are issued by government entities and have a low default rate. The difference could be much more significant when riskier bonds, such as junk bonds, are being purchased.

Two formulas can help an investor determine which of two investment options would return the most after taxes. Assume that Jane Doe wants to invest $10,000 in bonds. She is taxed at a rate of 31%. She is considering investing in Milford's municipal tax-free bond (a "muni") with a 10% yield. Munis are attractive investment vehicles because they help communities grow and pay their holders interest that is tax free. Doe wants to determine the **tax-equivalent yield** for a taxable bond that would produce the same rate of return as the muni. The formula is as follows:

$$\text{tax-equivalent yield} = \text{yield on muni} / (1 - \text{marginal tax rate})$$
$$= 10\% / (1 - 0.31)$$
$$= 14.5\%$$

This formula determines the taxable bond yield, but what if we know the taxable bond yield and want to determine the equivalent muni yield? Another formula determines the desired minimum muni yield (Brigham & Gapenski, 1994):

yield on muni = (taxable bond yield) ×

(1 − marginal tax rate)

= 14.5%(1 − 0.31)

= 10.0%

The formulas illustrate the types of calculations an investor or business needs to make in order to do tax planning. Making the wrong choice can cost an investor a significant amount of money. In contrast, through undertaking a simple analytical step, an investor can save a significant amount of money. The difference between the bond returns would entice most investors to choose a taxable bond if the return is over 14.5% and tax-free bonds are paying less than 10% interest. Careful tax planning is not just an exercise in trying to keep the government happy or to avoid an audit; it gives people or businesses information about various investment options to help them maximize revenues.

TAX PLANNING

Almost everyone is familiar with taxes. We pay taxes at the gas pump in the form of gas taxes. We pay sales taxes at the cash register. We may pay a surcharge on a ticket to a game or other event. We also may pay **income tax** at the federal or state level or both. Thus, the average person is often all too familiar with taxes. However, corporations and businesses have unique tax concerns. We might not feel the impact of tax withholdings when our employers pay our taxes and we readjust the amount paid when we complete our tax forms. However, businesses often have to pay sales, employee, transportation, property, income, and possibly numerous additional taxes. If a business does not properly plan for all potential tax liabilities, it can lose significant revenue.

In 1958 the Federal Tax Code had 650 pages. By 1998 the Federal Tax Code had 2,862 pages ("Tax Numbers," 2000). Although it is not clear how many pages are in the latest tax code, some estimates put the number at more than 60,000. The case study example on page 257 highlights how important tax planning is for a business.

Businesses that fail to properly analyze tax implications can overstate anticipated income, which can lead to litigation from shareholders based on the inaccurate information. Numerous taxes can apply, including sales, property, and ad valorem taxes. Although some taxes are direct pass-through taxes to the ultimate consumer, other taxes are borne by the company manufacturing the product. If a golf club manufacturing company is based in Europe, the host country may impose a value-added tax, which is a tax applied to the value added at every stage of the manufacturing process. When the raw aluminum is transformed into a shaft, a tax may be imposed. This type of tax may be charged at all phases of the manufacturing process and is incorporated into the sales price. However, no separate sales tax is imposed on the clubs when they are sold. Furthermore, many European countries offer travelers a value-added tax refund as they leave the country. This tax example applies only to European companies.

The two key concepts for analyzing taxing structures are marginal and average tax rates. The marginal tax rate is defined as the percentage tax liability imposed on the next dollar of income earned by the company or individual (Spiro, 1996). In contrast, the average tax rate is the total tax liability imposed on all taxable income. Suppose a tax structure calls for a tax of 20% on all income under $100,000 and a 25%

Taxing Visiting Athletes

To help finance new sports facilities in Pittsburgh, the city's taxing authority (Department of Finance) decided to tax out-of-town athletes for games they played in Pittsburgh. The city estimated it would receive $1 million a year. The tax is based on a "duty day," which is calculated by determining what percentage of the athlete's income was earned in Pittsburgh during a given year. If an athlete played in Pittsburgh on only 5 of the 200 days on which he played or practiced his sport over the year, then the taxable income would be based on 5 days. For a player who earned $200,000 a year to play on 200 days, the tax would be only $50 a year. However, as of 2000 the city had obtained only a small portion ($26,000) of the expected $1 million, and only 35 of the 47 teams playing in the city had registered to pay the tax ("Athlete's Tax Fails," 2000). The tax on athletes is not unique; the same tax applies to any nonresident earning money in a given state or jurisdiction. Thus, the athletes are not being targeted, but it is easier to enforce the law on this group since everyone knows when athletes are in the state or jurisdiction and basically how much they are earning there.

The Cleveland Indians Before the Supreme Court

A case involving the Cleveland Indians wound up on the United States Supreme Court docket. Major League Baseball owners violated the players' free agency rights from 1986 through 1988. Pursuant to an agreement reached after a negative arbitration award, the owners agreed to pay $280 million to the players who had been harmed. A dispute arose over the percentage of the back pay that would be subject to Social Security taxes. The Indians were supposed to pay a total of $2.1 million to 22 players. The issue before the court was whether the team should have paid taxes at the 1994 rate when the arbitration award was finalized or at the lower 1986 rate when the disputed wages were earned. The team paid the higher rate and asked for a refund, and the trial court and appellate court each agreed that the lower rate should have been paid; but the IRS appealed the case to the highest court in the land (Greenberger, 2000). The Supreme Court ruled that the tax rate for 1994, when the payment was to be made, was the applicable tax year, not the year the money was initially earned ("Back Pay," 2001).

tax on income between $100,001 and $200,000. If the Smiths earned $140,000 in income, their taxes would be $30,000 ([0.20 × $100,000 = $20,000] + [0.25 × $40,000 = $10,000]). The marginal tax rate is 25% for all income over $140,000 (i.e., the next dollar of income earned). To calculate the average tax rate, we divide the $30,000 total tax burden by the $140,000 income, which produces an average tax rate of 21.4%. The average tax rate is important for historical purposes (e.g., if you want to know how much of your income has been paid in taxes over the past five years).

However, the more critical point of analysis for financial managers is the marginal tax rate, the rate on the next dollar earned. If a company knows that the next $100,000 earned will be taxed at a very high rate, it might decide not to earn that extra money because the resulting tax obligation would negate any added value from raising the next $100,000 in income. However, if additional income adds to the corporation's bottom line, then the corporation should attempt to earn that additional income even if a large percentage will go to taxes. The only exception is the situation in which a corporation earns just a few more dollars that send it into a higher tax bracket. In this case the additional income could in fact cost the business money because it has earned only a few more dollars but is now subject to a tax rate that might be 5% to 10% higher.

TAXING SPORT

It is beyond the scope of this text to critically analyze all tax-related issues. However, in this section we overview some significant tax issues that affect the sport industry.

Various tax implications are associated with purchasing a professional sports team. For example, a major legal battle arose in connection with a 1997 tax

court decision about whether or not stadium leases could be amortized when a professional team with a very good facility lease is purchased ("Portions of New Orleans," 1998). The case involved the New Orleans Saints, sold in 1985. When a team is sold, the primary assets are the players' contracts, franchise rights, and possibly a favorable lease. A business' goodwill is a Section 197 amortizable asset that can be amortized over 15 years. However, Section 197(e)(6) specifically excludes a sports franchise from such **amortization**. Thus, the team, or more specifically the expenditure directly attributable to the sports franchise rights, is not amortizable.

However, if the team has switched some of the value away from the team franchise and allocated that sum to the lease, the lease value can be amortized over the time remaining on the lease. The cost of acquiring a leasehold is a capital expenditure recoverable through amortization. Such a benefit can be taken only if someone is willing to pay for the lease, which would occur only if the fair value exceeds the rent obligation established under the terms of the lease agreement. For example, if the team has been paying $100,000 a year to lease a facility and the fair market value for leasing the facility under a new lease would be $200,000, then the $100,000 value could be amortized over the remainder of the lease term.

The Saints were purchased for more than $70 million. The team and the IRS took different approaches in establishing whether or not the lease was amortizable, but they agreed that if it was, the value would be $16 million. The court concluded that the lease agreement, modified in 1975, was a premium lease and as such was amortizable. However, the court also held that if new lease terms are negotiated at the time the team is purchased, such new lease terms cannot be amortized ("Portions of New Orleans," 1998).

Besides potential tax implications associated with lease values, tax issues can arise as they relate to benefits generated for team owners through public tax dollars. This concern can arise when a team negotiates a favorable contract that might be "too good." For example, Charlotte Hornets owner George Shinn was sued by a community activist for $4.1 million ("Shinn Faces Suit," 1998). The suit concerned the revenue Shinn had received from the Charlotte Coliseum based on parking and concession profits. Originally the lease between the Coliseum and Shinn had given the Coliseum 100% of parking and concession profits during Hornets games. This arrangement was changed in 1995 to give Shinn 50% of the profits, which over three seasons had totaled $4.1 million.

The suit claimed that the lease agreement was unconstitutional because it conferred "privileges upon private parties without public benefit" ("Shinn Faces Suit," 1998, p. 5B). The activist was in essence claiming that in getting a change in the contract terms without public input, approval, or benefit, Shinn was receiving an unconstitutional benefit and that the benefits of the contractual change should revert back to Charlotte citizens. Thus, tax implications can benefit team owners or can raise the specter of public coffers being raided by the wealthy, creating a legal backlash.

Potential legal backlashes associated with favorable stadium financing deals were addressed by Congress in the 1986 Tax Act. Before passage of the act, municipalities were able to issue tax-exempt bonds for sports facilities. Tax-exempt bonds are more attractive for investors and might carry a better rate than taxable bonds. The interest coupons are tax-exempt, but any capital gains from the bonds are taxable. The benefit associated with tax-exempt bonds became problematic when the main tenant of the public building was a professional sports franchise. The government viewed such facilities, even if they were run by the local government, as private-purpose facilities and therefore not qualified for the tax-exempt status (Greenberg & Gray, 1996).

One loophole in the legislation allows bonds to retain their tax-exempt status. Under the private-activity test, a bond is not tax exempt if 10% of the facility's use is controlled by a private business or if 10% of revenues to repay the bonds are derived from the private use. This loophole has been utilized by numerous stadium and arena projects, with deals structured in such a way that a primary facility user will be charged less than 10% of the required principal and interest repayment amounts (Greenberg & Gray, 1996). Thus, many lease agreements limit the payment from the primary user to minimal amounts such as parking revenue, which normally would not come close to covering 10% of the annual debt service.

Additional attempts to prevent the raiding of public coffers or to deny a major advantage to a sports team can be seen in legislation proposed by Illinois congressman William O. Lipinski titled the Taxpayer's Right to View Act of 1992 (H.R. 4736, 1992). The bill, which was not passed, was based on the premise that most sports facilities are funded by taxpayers, and it is unfair for taxpayers to pay for a facility but not be able to enjoy watching events broadcast from there if the events are aired on pay TV instead of "free" TV. The legislation

A sport business must analyze the tax implications of all its activities.

also focused on nonprofit educational institutions that receive significant tax incentives and then try to broadcast events to taxpayers on a pay-per-view basis. The legislation called for taxpayers to have free access to events that are sponsored by nonprofit organizations and held in taxpayer-financed facilities. The bill also would have prohibited cable operators from charging or collecting a fee for pay-per-view broadcasts of an event held in a facility built, renovated, or maintained with taxpayers' financial support.

Although the Taxpayer's Right to View Act of 1992 was not successful, the IRS has been able to develop some equity by forcing nonprofit educational institutions such as schools involved in bowl games and some athletic departments to pay taxes if they are in fact engaged in a business enterprise. Two college football bowl games faced this issue in 1991 when the IRS ruled that Mobil's contribution to the Cotton Bowl ($1.5 million) and John Hancock Mutual Life Insurance Company's $1 million payment to its bowl constituted unrelated business income (Lederman, 1991). The primary mission of the bowl games is educational, but the IRS concluded that the sponsorship payments were made in essence for advertisements whose benefit is not educational. Thus, since the advertisements were not "substantially related" to the primary mission of education, the revenue was taxable at about 34% (Lederman, 1991).

NOTHING IS FREE

So far we have considered just a few tax-related issues, but the IRS has developed so many complex rules that it is almost impossible to engage in any

revenue-generating project without raising a potential tax-related concern.

If the West Hartford Badminton Club wants to raise some money through a fund-raising campaign, most people would think that as a nonprofit organization it should not face significant tax hurdles. However, there is a complex set of tax requirements for treating gifts, even to a nonprofit organization. Suppose the WHBC is trying to raise $10,000 for resurfacing the gym floor. The club members decide to have a walk-a-thon and a raffle for a new car. They will also just ask people for donations and give donors gifts based on the size of the donation.

The IRS rules are fairly clear for the walk-a-thon; because there is no expected return to the donor, the donor can deduct the entire donation. Those who have lost money on the raffle can claim a donation for charitable purposes. The winner of the car will need to claim the gift on his tax return. However, the complexity arises with the last fund-raising option. As of 1998, the IRS requires individuals to reduce their donation amount by any premiums (gifts) they receive if the premiums are valued at more than 2% of the donation or $71, whichever is less (McAllister, 1998). Thus if a person gives $100 and receives a $10 gift, the total donation is only $90 (since $10 is greater than 2%, it cannot be disregarded). If a donor gives $4,000 and receives a plaque, the plaque can be disregarded if it is worth less than $71 (since $71 is less than 2%, which is $80 in this example) (McAllister, 1998).

How Free Is "Free" TV?

Who pays for games to be aired on free TV? Pursuant to the eight-year $17.6 billion contract to broadcast NFL games on ABC/ESPN, CBS, and Fox, CBS has asked its affiliates to ante up between $30 million and $50 million per year to help defray the costs. These costs would have to be passed on to advertisers, who would be obliged to increase prices to help cover their increased costs. ESPN has also asked affiliates for a 20% hike in cable fees that would probably be passed on to consumers (McGraw, 1998). Thus, it would be the consumer who would pay even more to watch games on either free TV or cable as a consequence of the increased price of consumer products advertised during the broadcast.

The NFL Network was launched in 2003 as a vehicle to broadcast films, clips, and thousands of hours of footage owned by the NFL. In 2006 the NFL Network began airing eight exclusive games made available only through the network, which forced cable providers to purchase the network so they could air the extra games. The NFL Network charged a fee that some cable operators claimed was too high. Congress held hearings in 2006 on the broadcast games and whether the NFL was violating the spirit of the law of an antitrust exemption given to the league when the AFL and NFL merged. The NFL Network was able to blunt some of this criticism by broadcasting a number of college bowl games late in 2006.

These rules are further complicated by additional rules that provide for disregarding low-cost logo premiums if the donation is over $35.50 and the total cost for the premium is under $7.10. The amounts applied to logo premiums are adjusted annually for inflation. Clarity becomes the key to helping donors understand their gifts, and the IRS requires charitable organizations to give donors a breakdown of deductions that may be claimed whenever they contribute more than $75 and receive something of value (Blum, 1993). In 2002, the IRS ruled that the 2% rule was no longer being followed, so premiums need to be reported only if they are valued at $71 or more.

CHARITABLE PLANNING

Various techniques can be utilized to raise funds for nonprofit organizations. The issue just discussed is only one tax-related concern associated with giving money. A more important concern relates to large donations and the various tax ramifications associated with such charitable gifts. All nonprofits try to attract large donations. Although small gifts are nice, it is usually impossible to run larger programs without some large gifts. The manner in which these gifts are given significantly affects how much the recipient can receive and the total benefit the donor receives.

 Assume that the University of Milford has an alumna who wishes to give $500,000 to the university. However, she does not want to just hand the money over because she bought the asset for $100,000 and would have to pay capital gains taxes on the $400,000 increase in value. The university could suggest using a charitable remainder trust to provide a benefit to the university and give the donor the option of reducing her tax liability. A charitable remainder trust (CRT) allows donors to give gifts at a future date but retain during their lifetimes the interest income from the asset. The donor receives a current tax deduction, whereas if the gift was transferred after the individual's death, it would be the estate that would receive the deduction. The assets deposited in the trust can appreciate without the donor's having to pay tax on the income from the trust, and the donor does not need to pay capital gains taxes if the trust increases in value.

Using the $500,000 figure, assume that the donor currently receives a 3% return on the asset ($15,000 a year), that her tax bracket is 30%, and that the estate tax bracket is 55%. From the CRT the donor wishes to receive a 7% return, or $35,000 a year, over the course of her life. The table shows the analysis for the options available to the donor if she deposits the asset in the CRT, keeps the asset, or sells the asset.

The table shows that the lifetime net spendable income increases 181% when the CRT is compared with selling the asset and increases 256% when compared with keeping the asset (Fagan, 1999). If the donor kept the asset, she would have a lower income level but would be able to pass more money on to her heirs. If she sold the asset, she would receive the greatest up-front return, but her heirs would get a smaller amount with this option because of the high estate tax rate. If the donor's goal was to raise the highest amount of after-tax income over the life of the gift, then the CRT would be her best option. The example shows that proper tax planning can help educate donors about opportunities that can maximize their potential gifts.

	Charitable remainder trust	Keep	Sell
Market value ($)	500,000	500,000	500,000
Capital gains ($)	0	0	112,000
Charitable tax deduction ($)	162,295	0	0
Income for donor ($)	576,122	225,000	407,400
After-tax income ($)	403,285	157,500	299,180
Value to heirs ($)	0	225,000	174,600

ATHLETES AND TAXES

Although nonprofit organizations and their donors need to be concerned about tax implications of donations, professional sports teams can face the same challenges. For instance, in 1988 the Philadelphia Phillies gave Mike Schmidt a $2,150,000 contract that included a $100,000 charitable donation made in Schmidt's name but with the tax deduction to go to the club ("1988 Baseball Salaries," 1988). Under this arrangement, Schmidt would have to include the $100,000 in his income even if he did not receive the money and if the club took the deduction pursuant to Federal Regulation 1.61-2(c). Teams regularly provide such bonuses to players as a means of increasing the player's take-home pay without increasing the player's salary. The additional amount usually is not counted against any salary cap constraints if it is an earnable bonus. Players appreciate the bonus because it can help their marketing and public relations effort, even if they have to pay taxes on the amount.

Numerous additional tax-related concerns can also arise for an athlete, such as how to categorize income. For example, a professional athlete's salary is subject to income tax withholdings, but signing bonuses are not considered remuneration for services and generally are not subject to the employer's withholding taxes. However, the tax law clearly indicates that bonuses paid to baseball players that are predicated on continued employment are subject to withholding (Revenue Ruling, 1958). Numerous other revenue rulings issued by federal tax courts have also addressed bonuses and whether or not a player can give part of a bonus to a parent and claim the payment to the parent as a business expense. In one case a player gave $40,000 of his $70,000 bonus to his mother, but the tax court did not allow the expense deduction (*Allen v. Commissioner*, 1968). However, in another case, the tax court allowed the expense. In this case the player had paid his father a portion of the bonus, in part for his father's shrewd handling of the contract negotiation process and the years his father had spent coaching and training him (*Hundley v. Commissioner*, 1967).

Business expenses for a professional athlete can be highly diverse. The following are some of the expenditures that are classified as business expenses for athletes (*Robinson v. Commissioner*, 1965):

- Game tickets for individuals who train with the athlete to help improve the athlete's skills
- Expenses for operating a training camp or for off-season conditioning
- Dues for a players' association
- Expenses for tax planning and investment advising
- Agent fees
- Fines imposed by a league or team for misconduct

Even though the case involving fines is more than 35 years old, it is still the law of the land, and all the items listed are still considered valid expenses to reduce an athlete's tax obligations.

As the list suggests, careful planning by an athlete can reduce potential tax obligations. A professional athlete can run a summer camp and his own off-season training regime at the same facility using the same personnel. Through legal but creative accounting techniques, the expenses can be covered either under the athlete's personal business expenses or on the camp's tax return to help minimize tax obligations. It is important to recognize and appreciate that the failure to properly plan can destroy an athlete as easily as it can destroy a business. Former Dallas Cowboy great Tony Dorsett became so involved in ill-advised tax shelters that by 1985 the IRS had taken his paychecks and put liens on his homes to satisfy a $414,274 tax obligation (Rosenblatt, 1989).

The same tax issues associated with bonuses and business expenses also affect various other monetary matters, such as

- deferred income and nonqualified deferred income plans for player salaries,
- local and city taxes charged to players who earn money by playing in a given area or city such as Pittsburgh, and
- the creation of nonprofit charities by players that are designed to give family members jobs and to give the players a qualified tax deduction.

TAXING THE TEAMS

Tax planning requires analyzing a company's or institution's long-term plans to determine the most appropriate path toward minimizing tax obligations. For example, a company expecting significant future profits may want to wait until the next tax year to purchase expensive equipment in order to maximize potential tax savings. The long-term plan can also help determine whether buying or leasing represents the greater tax benefit. In addition, long-term planning can help a business develop an appropriate strategy for categorizing income and expenses.

DEPRECIATION OF ASSETS

The way costs are categorized can help determine the total allowed tax benefits. Teams can incur current expenses and capital asset expenses, and they can purchase nondepreciable assets. Current expenses can be written off the year they are incurred. Thus, if the Stars spend $10,000 on office supplies, those expenses can be utilized to decrease income earned that year and ultimately reduce the tax burden.

Capital assets are expensive assets that have a longer life. Machinery is a good example of a capital asset; a machine used to form Sport Manufacturing Company's tennis rackets may be very expensive and may last more than five years. The government allows companies to reduce their tax burden to help save money to repurchase another machine in the future. If a machine lasts about five years and costs $1 million, SMC can depreciate it by $200,000 a year for five years. If the machine is sold after five years to another business for $500,000, the new owners can keep depreciating the machine. These owners will be able to depreciate $100,000 a year for five years.

Capital assets typically exclude salaries, which are normally classified as current expenses. This holds true for all industries except the sport industry. The salaries of athletes involved in professional sports are the only type of salaries that are depreciable (Euchner, 1993). The owner of a professional franchise can claim depreciation for five years after purchasing a franchise. In 1976, Congress passed the Tax Reform Act, which limited 50% of the franchise purchase price to players' salaries. Before that, a team buyer could claim 90% of the purchase price toward depreciable player salaries.

In 1986, Doubleday sold the New York Mets to two major stockholders, Nelson Doubleday Jr. and Fred Wilpon (Euchner, 1993). The new owners did not change the management structure, but technically there was a new ownership group. When the transfer took place, exactly six years after Doubleday had bought the team, the company had just exhausted the player depreciation benefits. The new owners were then able to start the five-year depreciation clock over again.

Players are not the only assets that can be depreciated by a professional team. Other capital assets that can be depreciated include (Euchner, 1993)

- the franchise itself,
- lease contracts,
- concession contracts,
- broadcast contracts, and
- customer lists.

All these contracts and marketing assets, as well as the goodwill inherent in the team, are assets that have value. The revenue stream available from luxury box lease contracts, concession contracts, and broadcast contracts can diminish over time; and although these are income-earning assets, they can be depreciated, as with all other major capital assets. In 2004 Congress passed a law allowing teams to deduct the entire franchise value over 15 years.

As previously indicated, the methods by which assets, expenses, and income are categorized in the planning process significantly affect all tax decisions. Income taxes can be markedly reduced on the basis of how income is classified. Active income is classified as **earned income**. Passive income is income derived from transactions such as renting that do not involve regular work activities.

Suppose the Smiths earn $100,000 a year but rent out a portion of their facility for a gymnastics tutor and as a result lose $20,000. The reason for the loss could be wear and tear or extra utility expenses. Even though this is a loss, it will not reduce the Smiths' tax obligation because active and passive income are separate activities for the purposes of taxation. However, if Bob and Cheryl increase their business rental income by $20,000 and reduce their salaries by the same amount, they will have the same total income but will reduce their taxable income by $20,000 (Goldhirsh, 1996).

This example suggests how income can be manipulated to reduce tax obligations. Although such moves are legal, they can raise concerns with IRS auditors. A business owner or manager should undertake such a strategy only after careful consultation with trained tax advisers.

Tax-related issues can be highly diverse and can cover every possible facet of a business. Even when money is paid to others, tax issues arise. An employee's withholding and Social Security taxes are just two of the many taxes an employer needs to consider. Pension plans also involve significant tax-related issues. Contributions to an approved pension plan are tax deductible for the employer. Thus, an expensive employee relations technique can be less costly when tax advantages are analyzed. We cannot consider every conceivable tax benefit or cost in this text. Instead the aim is to indicate the broad range of tax and legal constraints affecting sport businesses.

FINANCIAL RISK MANAGEMENT

Risk management is the process designed to identify problems and produce solutions for various risks ranging from tax concerns to litigation-based issues. One solution that any risk management plan must include is insurance, which can save a business a tremendous amount of money. Insurance protection represents an attempt to shift the risks associated with a financial loss.

Some people prefer to run a business without insurance. Their thinking may be based on the calculation that if they do experience a loss, the cost of the loss will be lower than the premium payments that would have been required if they had purchased insurance. Others might base their gamble on the implementation of a significant risk management program that might reduce future claims. Although some managers are willing to take such risks or do not have the capital needed to purchase insurance, most are much more risk averse and prefer to ensure predictable outcomes through insurance or other risk reduction tools (Williams, Smith, & Young, 1995).

Risk management is designed to help reduce or eliminate potential hazards. A hazard is a condition that increases the likelihood of a loss. An example of a physical hazard is a defective gym floor; a moral hazard involves an effect on a person's behavior (Williams et al., 1995). A moral hazard is present, for example, if the owner or manager of a gym might not know whether a closet has been properly locked and thus does not know whether a student could enter the closet, remove a trampoline, and get injured. Having an insurance policy to cover such an accident decreases the concern the person might have.

Insurance represents a finance technique termed risk transfer. The risk of a financial loss is transferred to another party. If a sport business does not have any insurance coverage, it is retaining the risk of any potential loss. Risk financing is a passive activity compared with risk management. Risk management is designed for **loss prevention**. Risk financing is designed to help settle a financial dispute after a loss has occurred—it establishes who will pay. Regardless, though, of whether the financial risk is transferred or retained, a business needs to allocate money for both risk financing and risk management.

For example, the Smiths might think that all they need to budget for is an insurance premium of $1,800 a year. However, they also need to calculate other expenses such as potential legal fees. Some of these, such as quarterly retainers for an attorney, may be easy to budget for; but the Smiths would not be able to easily budget for a new building in case a fire destroys the fitness center. Risk transfer would allow Bob and Cheryl to budget the insurance costs and then know that the insurance company would cover any significant losses in the future. The Smiths could also allocate $500 or more a month to pay for any future losses. Until these funds are used, they can be deposited into an interest-earning account. Bob and Cheryl would hope that they could save several thousand dollars and not have to pay any insurance premiums if they engage in self-insurance.

If there are no losses for several years, the Smiths' reserves could be substantial; and if any loss did occur they might have enough in reserve to pay for it. If they faced a loss that the reserves could not cover, they would be forced to borrow funds.

In contrast, the Stars might have a much more sophisticated self-insurance program. Because the team has more money, and possibly more money to set aside, the Stars could establish specific accounts to handle claims or could even own their own insurance company, which is referred to as a captive insurer (Williams et al., 1995). The team could also join with other teams in the league to pool their resources and create an insurance fund to pay any loss incurred by any member of the group.

LOST INCOME

The risks that a sport business or organization can face could include various categories of decreased revenues (Williams et al., 1995):

- Lost rent if a subtenant does not pay the rent on time
- Interruption in business services through theft or vandalism of company property
- Interruption in the delivery of supplies (e.g., when a power outage occurs)
- A reduced amount recovered from accounts receivable when debtors do not pay their accounts on time

Other sources of lost income could include competition, environmental restrictions, legal changes, and numerous other internal and external variables. A risk management program can help identify all these potential ways in which income can be lost. Organizations can then develop proactive strategies to help reduce the potential impact of any given loss.

LEGAL CHALLENGES

One risk management concern that any financial analysis must cover relates to potential future legal ramifications from any decision. For example,

While some circumstances are unavoidable, sound financial risk management for a sport business can help identify potential losses of income, understand potential legal ramifications of any decision, and determine whether the business is in financial trouble.

government entities can develop unique financing schemes to help build a facility. However, the fact that the government is involved does not guarantee that a legal challenge cannot invalidate provisions that might have made the deal financially beneficial. For example, a 1,500-acre cow pasture was converted into the 150,000-plus-seat Texas Motor Speedway. The developer and city entered into an agreement that the privately owned track would not have to pay any property taxes. A local school district sued the city to terminate what it called a "sweetheart deal" that deprived the school district of badly needed tax revenue.

The deal was founded on tax incremental financing (TIF). As noted earlier in the text, TIF is a financing vehicle whereby taxes for a facility such as a stadium are deferred. The municipality is gambling that with the new development, property around the stadium will increase in value, thus increasing the tax base. When the tax base increases, the municipality will receive higher taxes, which presumably will offset the tax savings given to encourage the stadium owners

to build in a neighborhood with depressed property values. Tax incremental financing represents a potential win–win for all parties; the stadium owner receives a tax break, local citizens see increases in property values, and the municipality earns more tax revenue.

However, in the case of the Texas Motor Speedway, the school district claimed that the TIF led to unfair competition—it allowed developers to receive undeserved government charity, which would eventually hurt homeowners. Homeowners would be forced to pay higher property taxes because of losses in the city's tax income resulting from the deal. The Texas Motor Speedway cost approximately $204.5 million. Tax money covered $9 million in road improvements, $20 million for land acquisition, and $100 million in waived property taxes (Gibeaut, 1999). The developer was required to make only $2.2 million in total lease payments and after 30 years could buy the facility from the city (Fort Worth) for $500,000. In comparison with tax abatements that allow reduced future taxes, the Speedway was built with a TIF that provided the up-front money. The TIF is supposed to generate increased tax revenue from other adjoining properties or businesses that are anticipated to grow because of the presence of the new facility.

FINANCIAL RISK ANALYSIS

So far we have focused on business structure concerns affecting the bottom line, tax considerations, government regulations affecting sport financing, and risk financing. In addition, risk management can rely directly on financial ratios. For example, leverage ratios help measure the extent to which an organization is in debt. The more a business borrows, the higher the leverage ratio becomes. A highly leveraged business is more vulnerable to changes in business environments. A business facing significant leverage may be forced by a debt holder to buy insurance to help protect pledged assets. Two specific techniques that can help identify leverage-related financial risk are the long-term debt to net worth ratio and the times interest earned ratio discussed in chapter 5 (Williams et al., 1995).

Liquidity ratios measure the ability of a company to raise cash in the short run. If a company does not have the ability to raise cash for emergencies, it is not on strong footing to deal with fiscal risks. Several ratios that can be used to evaluate a business' ability to cover short-term obligations are the net working capital to assets ratio, the current ratio, and the acid test ratio (Williams et al., 1995). These ratios are also covered in chapter 5.

Risk managers in sport also examine ratios to determine whether a team is in financial trouble. According to Fitch IBCA, an international rating agency, several measures can help determine the soundness of a professional sports team. Using collateral coverage, Fitch IBCA expects collateral to cover team debt at least two times over ("Changing Game," 1999). The analysts also think that team debt to contractually obligated revenue should not exceed two times. Last, they recommend as a general guideline a minimum ratio of operating income to annual debt service of 1.5 times for investment-grade franchises in 1999 ("Changing Game," 1999).

Another financial measure for risks associated with a business is based on how stockholders view the business and whether they perceive the business as facing significant risks. Market valuation ratios such as the price–earnings (PE) ratio can provide a barometer of confidence. A high PE ratio is a strong sign that investors expect the organization's earnings to grow at a high rate. Another ratio is Tobin's q ratio, which analyzes how efficiently a business has invested its assets. Tobin's q is calculated by dividing the business' market value by the replacement value for the business' assets. A ratio above 1.0 implies that assets are worth more within the firm than if they were invested elsewhere. This number can be critical in risk management analysis when a buyer acquires a business and has to determine whether to liquidate the business' assets. If Tobin's q ratio is under 1.0, then an acquiring business might decide not to replace broken machinery because the added investment would not generate enough revenue to increase the business' value (Williams et al., 1995).

CONCLUSION

Legal issues are normally not the primary concern associated with financial management. However, every business decision has both financial and legal ramifications. If the financial statements do not comply with Securities and Exchange Commission reporting requirements, legal flags will wave. If a corporation engages in investments contrary to its bylaws, additional legal concerns can arise. The list of potential legal concerns goes on and on. The breadth of legal challenges facing a sport finance manager is equally significant. As seen in the business structure, taxation, and risk management sections in this chapter, a finance manager faces countless potential legal hurdles that are either self-imposed or imposed by external entities. Luckily, similar to hiring accountants and financial advisors, a company can hire skilled lawyers to help navigate the potentially confusing legal maze.

CLASS DISCUSSION TOPICS

1. Should professional team owners be allowed to depreciate players' salaries? Take the pro or con side of this question.

2. Should the Mobil Cotton Bowl and Ohio State University have been subject to taxes for unrelated business income even though funds from the advertising efforts were utilized for educational activities?

3. Should athletes have to pay tax in states they play in but do not live in?

4. Should the heirs of team owners have to pay taxes if they inherit a team? If so, should they pay taxes on the value of the team when originally purchased or at the appreciated value?

5. What are the tax benefits, if any, of having a corporate status?

6. What is financial risk management, and how can it be used by a sport business?

7. Do you have insurance to protect against losses and if not, why not?

8. What risk management strategies do you take on a daily basis to protect your finances (everything from insurance to preventing identity theft)?

15

SPENDING EARNINGS

CHAPTER OBJECTIVES

After studying this chapter, you should be able to do the following:

- Describe different types of dividend policies and how they are used.
- Outline the dividend payment process.
- Describe how a business utilizes retained earnings.
- Understand how mergers and acquisitions are a way for a sport business to expand.
- Describe the legal concerns associated with mergers and acquisitions.
- Calculate the value of a consolidated business after a merger.

In earlier chapters, we focus on learning the fundamentals of sport finance and understanding the sources of revenues and expenses. If all goes well, a business will have the **ability to pay** all its costs from income. If income equals costs, the business will break even. However, the goal for a profit-driven business is not only to cover costs but also to maximize profits. If a business generates positive earnings, it then must decide how best to distribute the excess earnings. The earnings distribution process is a major decision for a sport business. It has significant short- and long-term ramifications.

The options a sports manager has with respect to distributing earnings differ depending on the business. Among our five case studies, Sport Manufacturing Company and the Stars of David are publicly traded with shareholders, while the other three cases either are not yet publicly traded or based on their structure cannot be publicly traded. Given that this chapter centers on how earnings are distributed and used to increase the value of a firm, we focus primarily on for-profit corporations similar to SMC and the Stars of David.

Before discussing the earnings of for-profit organizations, we should note that nonprofit sports organizations, such as collegiate athletic departments, charitable foundations, and the YMCA, might also have revenues that exceed costs. These organizations have several options for their earnings. They may elect to reinvest these funds back into the organization. For example, the University of Milford may elect to add new sports, increase funding for athletic scholarships, or improve sports facilities. Some major college athletic departments with excess funds have established scholarships for students who are not athletes. A local YMCA may decide to increase the size of its staff or add new activities. In some cases, nonprofit sports organizations elect to save these excess funds to protect against future financial difficulty. Although nonprofit organizations have a variety of options, what they cannot do is show an accounting profit for the fiscal year.

In general, for-profit sport businesses have three choices for using earnings:

1. Pay dividends to shareholders, if it is a share-issuing business.
2. Retain earnings for reinvestment in the business
3. Reinvest in other firms by purchasing a percentage or acquiring other firms outright

Retained earnings are used primarily for long-term financial planning and capital budgeting. Retained earnings are discussed briefly in this chapter, but the major focus is the payment of dividends and mergers with and acquisitions of other firms.

The key to making the right decision about earnings distributions is to select the option that will produce the greatest value to the ownership or, in the case of a publicly held company, the shareholders. Although shareholders directly benefit from receiving a dividend payment, they may derive the greatest long-term value from forgoing dividend payments and allowing the earnings to be reinvested back into the firm. The reinvestment may be used to research and design a new product line, purchase new equipment, or hire additional human resources. Management may also attempt to increase the business' value by using the earnings to acquire another firm. It is management's responsibility to make these critical decisions. At all times, management must base the decision on which option is best for the shareholders or ownership. See the following case study example.

 The Stars of David may decrease dividend payments to their shareholders and use the funds to construct a new practice facility. Although the reinvestment for capital improvements decreases the dividends received by shareholders, the Stars' management believes the end result will be an increase in the stock value.

DIVIDEND PAYMENTS

A dividend is a payment made out of earnings, in the form of either cash or stock, to a business' owners or shareholders (Brigham & Ehrhardt, 2005). Dividends are paid to reward stockholders for staying with the corporation. Some stocks steadily appreciate in value, and that capital appreciation is the reward stockholders need in order to justify their investment. Other corporations may have a steady stock price but reward stockholders by paying a regular dividend payment. Thus, while the Stars of David have not had a significant increase in their stock value over the years, they have paid steady dividends that sometimes amounted to about $0.50 per share. However, for the 2005 and 2006 fiscal years, no dividends were paid to unit holders.

Paying dividends is one method of distributing profits. For many corporations, it is a major cash expenditure. Large companies such as IBM and Microsoft spend millions of dollars in making dividend payments to their shareholders. However, numerous companies also elect to make no dividend payments. A firm's board of directors determines the amounts of dividend payments and makes all other dividend decisions not otherwise specified in the corporate bylaws or on the stock certificates.

Initially, you would think that a firm would want to give as much money back to its shareholders as possible. But it also makes financial sense for the firm to take the money and invest it for the shareholders. Deciding which option to select can be both difficult and controversial for financial managers. Shareholders and financial analysts can be critical if they believe management is pursuing a poor dividend policy. Such negative feelings can affect a stock's performance.

A business may also make distributions to its ownership. A distribution is similar to a dividend, but it is paid out of sources other than current or accumulated retained earnings. For simplicity, we refer to any payment by a firm to its shareholders as a dividend. Typically, dividends are most commonly paid by large corporations. Smaller corporations often need to reinvest the money in order to grow. For example, in the late 1990s Speedway Motorsports was a growing company involved in the motor sport industry. It owned and operated several racetracks across the United States. In its 1998 annual report, the company stated that it would not pay dividends for the foreseeable future in order to reinvest money for company growth. However, by 2003 Speedway Motorsports had enough cash on hand to feel comfortable in paying dividends to its shareholders. The company paid out dividends of $0.31, $0.32, and $0.33 respectively for the years 2004 through 2006 (Speedway, 2005; Speedway, 2006) In contrast, Nike paid a $0.37 quarterly **dividend per share** in December of 2006 (Nike, 2006).

Dividend policies can be somewhat confusing. There are many good reasons for a corporation to pay high dividends, but there are as many good reasons to pay relatively low dividends. This section covers the ways dividends are paid, the various types of dividends, and reasons for the payment of high and low dividends.

DIVIDEND PAYMENT PROCESS

The process of paying dividends is well defined. The following case study example, adapted from an example in another industry (Ross, Westerfield, & Jaffe, 2005), shows how the process works.

Sport Manufacturing Company

- On June 1, Sport Manufacturing Company passes a resolution to pay a dividend of a specified amount, let's say $2 per share. The date of the announcement, June 1, is referred to as the declaration date. Sport Manufacturing Company's board of directors also announces that the dividend will be paid on June 30 to all shareholders of record as of June 18.

- An important date in the process comes up four business days before June 18. June 14 is the ex-dividend date and is used to determine those shareholders who are eligible to receive dividends so that the dividend checks are distributed to the appropriate shareholders. Before June 14, the stock is traded "with dividend," meaning that shareholders are eligible for a dividend payment. After June 14, the stock trades as **ex-dividend**, meaning that the purchaser will not receive a dividend payment. This date is important for ensuring there is no confusion as to who is to receive the dividend payment.

- June 18 is the record date, the date on which all shareholders of record are designated to receive their payment. The firm will prepare a list, based on the ex-dividend date, of those individuals who are believed to be shareholders. These persons are the **holders of record** and will receive dividend checks. Errors do sometimes occur, and dividend checks get mailed to the wrong persons. However, the ex-dividend date helps minimize such errors.

- June 30 is the payment date. All dividend checks are mailed to the people who are believed to be the shareholders of record.

CASH DIVIDENDS

The most common type of dividend is a regular cash dividend. Some publicly traded companies typically pay cash dividends on a quarterly basis as a regular business practice. In addition to the regular cash dividend paid annually, semiannually, or quarterly, a business may also make special one-time payments. These special or additional dividend payments are called extra cash dividends or special dividends. For the most part, the extra payments differ from the regular dividends in name only. As the name implies, these dividends might not be repeated in the future. Last, a liquidating dividend is a payment made to shareholders as a result of some part of the business being liquidated, or sold off. All or part of the cash from the sale is distributed to the shareholders. Regardless of the name, a cash dividend payment reduces the firm's cash and retained earnings (Ross et al., 2005).

As discussed later, not all corporations pay dividends; and even if a dividend is paid one year, this does not mean the board of directors will authorize a dividend the next year. However, any interruption in the payment cycle can have a chilling effect on analysts and shareholders, who may view the suspension of dividends as a sign of economic hardship.

STOCK DIVIDENDS

Corporations have other alternatives to a cash dividend if they wish to distribute earnings back to their shareholders. A firm may elect to buy back stock or issue new stock to existing shareholders. The payment of a dividend in stock can have a dilutive effect on share price, which is not the case with cash dividends. There are also some differences between cash dividends and **stock dividends** in regard to tax policies. Dividend payments are taxed as income for shareholders, whereas the money earned from the sale of stock is taxed as capital gains.

In recent U.S. history, the tax rates for income have been higher than the tax rate for capital gains, but the 1986 Tax Reform Act reduced the gap. As of January 2006, the capital gains tax rate was 15% for stocks owned for more than one year and 28% for stocks owned for less than one year. For tax purposes, the tax is recognized the year in which the stock is sold. With respect to the payment of taxes on dividends, which are treated by the U.S. Internal Revenue Service as income, table 15.1 provides details on the taxes paid based on a person's or family's level of income. As you can see, although the gap has decreased since before 1986, there is still a gap between the capital gains and income tax rates for most individuals. Thus, it would appear that on the basis of taxation policy, many stockholders would prefer the repurchase of stock over dividend payments (Brealey, Myers, & Marcus, 2004).

The decision to buy back shares is made by the corporation's board of directors, but the board considers market conditions and the impact on the shareholders. Typically a board with extra cash might buy back stocks when the value is depressed to help increase the stock value. When the company buys back stock, the number of shares outstanding decreases, and the book value per share can increase.

Distribution of earnings is not the only reason for a company to repurchase stock. A business may also repurchase stock when it wants to change its capital structure. A business may borrow money, in other words go into debt, in order to repurchase stock from shareholders and lower equity. This action will have the final effect of changing the firm's capital structure (WACC). The WACC was discussed in chapter 11 as a tool to measure the effectiveness of a corporation's capital structure.

DETERMINING THE APPROPRIATE DIVIDEND LEVEL

Another important aspect of dividend policy is arriving at the appropriate dividend level. According to Brealey, Myers, and Marcus (2004), there are three traditional views with respect to paying dividends. The groups of people who hold these views are the rightists, the leftists, and the middle-of-the-roaders.

The rightists believe that a business should pay the highest possible dividends. This group notes that the perceived business value increases as the level of dividend payments increases. Financial analysts believe that the perception of a business becomes more positive as higher dividends are paid, and this in turn increases the business' stock value. In addition, dividends are cash in hand, whereas a capital gain is risky. There is always uncertainty surrounding the reinvestment of earnings, and the investments

Table 15.1 Taxes Paid Based on a Person's or Family's Level of Income

Single filer	Married, filing jointly	Married, filing separately	Tax rate
Up to $7,550	Up to $15,100	Up to $7,550	10%
$7,551-$30,650	$15,101-$61,300	$7,551-$30,650	15%
$30,651-$74,200	$61,301-$123,700	$30,651-$61,850	25%
$74,201-$154,800	$123,701-$188,450	$61,851-$94,225	28%
$154,801-$336,550	$188,451-$336,550	$94,226-$168,275	33%
$336,551 or more	$336,551 or more	$168,276 or more	35%

Adapted from tax table found at: http://finance.yahoo.com/how-to-guide/taxes/16214.

selected may not increase the business' value. This uncertainty and risk are eliminated if the excess cash is directly paid to the shareholders in the form of dividends.

Like all investors, financial analysts or researchers can fall anywhere on the spectrum, but some may be rightists because they believe an efficient and free capital market does not exist. That is, these researchers do not think it matters if high or low dividends are paid. In contrast, the leftists believe the capital markets are imperfect and do not perform efficiently. Dividend policy is therefore important. This analysis is important for investors because boards of directors that follow the leftist ideology would be more inclined to pay dividends to ensure that shareholders are happy. We should note that some investors use their stock portfolios as a source of cash income. The quarterly dividend payments allow them to receive this cash. Without the dividends, these investors would need to periodically sell some of their stock and also incur the transaction costs associated with these sales. Also, these investors are more susceptible to the ups and downs of the stock market because they are selling pieces of their portfolios at different times.

Shareholders often demand that management make high dividend payments. The rightists have explained and justified this in several ways. The best justification may simply be that many shareholders do not trust management to spend the earnings properly. The shareholders may not believe that management has their best interests at heart and would prefer that the earnings be paid out through dividends. This gives shareholders the power to control the money, but it limits the business' investment decisions.

The leftists hold the opposite view of dividend policy. They strongly believe that dividend payments should be low. The focus of their argument is based on a single issue: taxes. As stated earlier, dividends are taxed as income, not capital gains. Therefore, the leftists believe that whenever income tax rates are higher than capital gains tax rates, the only option is to pay low dividends. The excess cash can be used in one of two ways.

First, the cash can be used for investment opportunities that will allow the business' value to grow. The company can engage in capital projects that will increase the business' value and ultimately its stock price. If a shareholder wants cash, he can sell his stock at the higher price and pay the capital gains tax, which is lower than the income tax. Second, the firm can use the excess cash to repurchase stock. The shareholders will receive cash for the shares they sell and will be taxed at the lower capital gains tax rate.

With respect to dividend policy, middle-of-the-roaders believe there is a middle ground between the two sides where the smart dividend policy lies. This group believes that the value of a company is not affected by dividend policy. Proponents of this approach claim that if either raising or lowering dividend payments could increase the business' value, companies would already be using such strategies to affect their stock price. In fact, some businesses do use this strategy in an attempt to influence their share price. Most middle-of-the-road managers do not believe that stock prices could be manipulated simply through changes in the dividend policy. Each company arrives at some level of dividends that is appropriate for most of the shareholders. This middle-ground dividend payment satisfies the greatest number of shareholders and has no effect on business value. According to this view, smart managers would adjust the dividend policy if they believed the change would positively affect business value.

The dividend policy is an important issue for public companies. It is closely related to several other financial management decisions such as borrowing, capital structuring, and investment decisions. For example, if a business decides to use its excess cash to pay dividends, it must rely on more borrowing for investment opportunities. This will greatly affect its capital structure and long-term planning. Dividends can be very controversial. As we have discussed, there are several different views on their importance to the business and the appropriate dividend policy for a company to follow.

REINVESTMENT

As stated earlier, an alternative to distributing earnings to shareholders through dividends is to reinvest the funds back into the business. **Reinvestment** is a key component in financial management. A company must continually reinvest if it hopes to thrive and grow. One method of reinvesting funds is through retaining earnings. The business forgoes payment to stockholders and keeps the earnings for capital investment. The board of directors decides whether to cancel dividends and often sends out a press release when it files the quarterly report on the company's earnings. The suspension or canceling of a dividend is also reported in the corporation's annual report. As stated in chapter 11, the expected return from capital projects must be greater than the return stockholders receive from investing the dividend payments. If it is not, then the funds should be paid out as dividends.

The level of earnings that should be retained for capital investment is closely tied to a business' capital structure, capital budgeting decisions, and dividend

By reinvesting their earnings back into their company, this fitness facility guarantees it has the most up-to-date equipment for its clients.

policy. Obviously, businesses that prefer to pay relatively high dividends retain a smaller percentage of earnings. It is important to note that there are legal restrictions on the amount of dividends that can be paid. On a business' balance sheet, dividend payments cannot exceed retained earnings. This policy, known as the impairment of capital rule, was established to protect creditors. It prohibits a business that is in financial distress from liquidating its assets through dividend payments. In the absence of this legal stipulation, a business could distribute all its capital assets, and creditors would have nothing to reclaim (Brigham & Ehrhardt, 2005).

The business' size also plays a role in the amount of funds that should be used for reinvestment. For smaller businesses, other capital sources such as debt or the issuance of new common stock may be relatively expensive. Thus, a smaller business would most likely elect to finance capital spending through retained earnings. Larger businesses can issue finance capital, such as stocks and bonds, at a much lower cost compared with small businesses. Therefore, they are more likely to pay higher dividends and retain a smaller percentage of earnings than are smaller businesses.

As discussed in chapter 11, businesses also have a target capital structure. The target is the proportion of debt to equity that is believed to be best for increasing shareholder value. The level of reinvestment in the company is often a product of this capital structure. A business may lower retained earnings if it wants to repurchase stock. The result will be an alteration in the capital structure and level of reinvestment.

Last, managerial control may also affect the level of retained earnings. Some businesses with the need for additional capital are hesitant to issue new stock. In issuing new stock, management always faces the possibility of relinquishing control. To avoid this situation, management can take the alternative option of retaining a higher level of earnings. The earnings are then used to reinvest in the business.

MERGERS AND ACQUISITIONS

In a **merger**, one business blends its business with the acquired business. Thus, company A can merge with company B, and the new entity could be called company C. In contrast, in an **acquisition** the acquiring company maintains control of the acquired company and serves in a dominant position over the acquired company. Thus, in an acquisition, company A can acquire company B and still be company A. A merger can be part of an acquisition, such as the merger of accounting departments from two different companies.

A merger is an investment, made under uncertainty, in which the acquiring business' goal is to increase its value or shareholders' wealth. As with other investment opportunities, a business should acquire another business only if it believes that a positive gain in net present value will occur. Unfortunately, given the level of uncertainty, it is very difficult to calculate the net present value of an acquisition candidate (Ross et al., 2005). Unlike the situation when a company decides to invest in long-term capital, it is difficult to place a value on the additional expenses and income associated with a merger.

The Smiths may eventually turn their small fitness center into a highly successful operation. However, the growth potential for their single location is limited. If they wish to increase their business size, they may look to expanding into new locations. One method of expansion may be to acquire and operate other centers. After acquiring other centers, the Smiths would have the ability to increase income and grow their company.

The number of mergers in the sport industry has increased greatly over the past decade. Several sport and entertainment companies such as Disney, News Corporation, and SFX Entertainment have acquired smaller companies to increase the scope of their operations. These acquisitions have been somewhat controversial and may have a large impact on the future financial landscape within the sport industry. A listing of sport holdings for some of the major corporate entities in the sport industry is shown below.

Aside from the major acquisitions, hundreds of smaller mergers and acquisitions occur each year within the sport industry. In 1995 alone, 9,030 mergers and acquisitions totaling more than $500 billion were reported (Crow, Phillips, & Gillentine, 2000). The number of mergers skyrocketed between 1995 and 2000. In the first three quarters of 1998, a total of 10,104 mergers were reported to the Department of Justice, with a combined value of $1.3 trillion (Crow et al., 2000). Merger mania did subside in the early 21st century because of an economic slowdown in the United States. In 2002, the value of all U.S. mergers dropped to $500 billion. The number rebounded by 2004, with more than $750 billion in mergers occurring in that year (Rosenbuh, 2004). Not all these were sport mergers, but they indicate a trend. Several sport mergers are discussed throughout this chapter.

Company acquisition for the sole sake of diversification is normally not a wise financial strategy. Companies normally should merge only if there is a belief that the new company will result in some additional value that is not possible if separate enterprises are maintained. If no additional value is earned through a merger or acquisition, it may not be in the best financial interests of either side. However,

Selected Sport Holdings for Major Sport-Related Corporations

Corporation	Selected sport holdings
News Corp.	New York Knicks (40%), New York Rangers (40%), Madison Square Garden (40%), Fox Broadcasting Co., Fox Sports Net, Fox Sports regional networks, FX Network, British Sky Broadcasting (40%), FUEL network, SPEED network, DirecTV (40%)
Walt Disney	ESPN, ESPN2, ESPN Classic, ESPNU, ESPN International, ESPN.com, ESPN News, ESPN Zone restaurants, ABC Sports, ESPN the Magazine, Walt Disney Wide World of Sports Complex
Comcast	The Golf Channel; Outdoor Life Network; ownership interest in Comcast-Spectacor, which operates the following: Philadelphia Flyers, Philadelphia 76ers, Philadelphia Phantoms, Wachovia Center, Wachovia Spectrum, Comcast SportsNet, Flyers Skate Zone, New Era Tickets, Global Spectrum, Ovations Catering

Probably the best source for this would be the annual report for each of the three companies. News Corporation Annual Report, Disney Corporation Annual Report, and Comcast Incorporated Annual Report. The dates for each report are 2006. There is no single source that lists the current corporate holdings for each company.

not all mergers are for financial growth. Some companies want to eliminate or reduce competition by purchasing a competitor and then shutting it down. Other companies may buy a competitor for leverage with unions so that the unions cannot use the other business as an example of concessions they want. Still other businesses may merge to avoid a takeover by another company.

We need to remember also that many mergers are unwelcome. Although the purchase of a small corporation by a large corporation may make the owners of the small company wealthy, some owners do not want to sell. This can lead to a hostile takeover. Hostile takeovers can also occur when one corporation is trying to buy another one and a third corporation arrives on the scene, offering more money. In December 2001, Monster.com offered to pay $355 million for HotJobs.com, and the companies worked on a merger for six months. However, at the last minute, Yahoo! upped the ante by $81 million, offering $436 million for HotJobs. Within three weeks, HotJobs agreed to Yahoo!'s hostile bid (Thornton, 2002). This is just one example of a hostile takeover. Other examples have occurred in all the fields.

Similarly, large hedge funds have purchased entire companies, such as Kmart's owner purchasing Sears.

In fact, with the stock market down, hostile bids were on the increase from $40 billion in 2000 to $94 billion in 2001. The surge was also prompted by changes in accounting practices. Recent rule changes do not require a company to reduce its earnings by the amortized value of the goodwill from the acquired firm (Thornton, 2002). **Goodwill** is the difference between what an acquiring company pays for a business and what the acquired business' assets were valued at on its balance sheet. The potential goodwill for sport businesses such as professional teams is very high. The fact that an acquiring company can now capitalize goodwill rather than amortizing it increases the balance sheet assets for the acquiring firm and makes it look stronger.

Not all hostile takeovers are successful, though, since companies can undertake various steps to protect themselves (see below). Among these steps are issuing new shares to dilute the market, selling key assets, and approaching a "white knight" to make a counteroffer (Cheeseman, 2001). Other approaches include adopting "poison pills" that require the would-be buyer to possibly pay executives a large fee if it purchases the company or require the would-be buyer to pay more for the shares. In fact, poison pills have increased the value of the companies that have

Schwinn Splits Up

One of the larger sport mergers in the past 10 years involved the bankruptcy and splitting of Schwinn/GT Corporation. Schwinn was one of the largest bicycle manufacturers in the world. Unfortunately, the company faced hard financial times in 2000 and had to seek bankruptcy protection. Huffy Corporation placed an offer to the bankruptcy judge to pay $68.3 million for Schwinn. Two individual companies, Pacific Cycles and Direct Focus, combined to make another offer (Brennan, 2001). Pacific Cycles and Direct Focus posted a $1.5 million deposit to challenge the "stalking-horse" sale agreement between Schwinn and Huffy. Pacific Cycles and Direct Focus were required to surpass Huffy's offer by $5 million or lose its deposit. (A stalking-horse sale agreement, entered into when a company knows there may be other suitors, allows another suitor to top the existing offer and purchase the company. A company enters into this type of agreement when it knows that bidding will be spirited or thinks the sale price is too low and hopes that someone will come along and raise the offer. In other words, if company A is being sought by several companies, it can enter into an agreement with company X to sell the business to company X. However, the agreement could provide that if another company, such as company Z, comes along and offers more money, company A can terminate its agreement with company X and sell to company Z.)

Schwinn, which had started operations in 1895, had 25% of the domestic bicycle market but had applied for bankruptcy in 1992 and again in 2001. Two divisions were going on sale, a bicycle division and a fitness division. The winner of the bicycle unit was Pacific Cycles and Direct Focus, which were later sold in 2004 to Dorel Industries. The Wisconsin-based global consumer products company is now the owner of the Schwinn line of mountain, road, and hybrid bicycles ("About Schwinn," 2007). The fitness unit was purchased by Direct Focus, which is the parent company of Bowflex and Nautilus. Direct Focus was interested in using its purchase of Schwinn's fitness unit to launch a major push in indoor biking to take advantage of the popularity of stationary cycling classes (Janda, 2001).

adopted them by 35.9% versus only a 31.9% premium for companies that did not have them (Thornton, 2002).

A successful sports manager must be highly attentive to the possibility of acquiring other companies or possibly becoming the target of an acquisition attempt. The discussion in the remainder of this section focuses on the types of mergers, justifications for mergers, the legal forms of acquisition that occur within sport, and other forms of acquisition.

TYPES OF MERGERS

Ross, Westerfield, and Jaffe (2005) separate mergers into three categories: horizontal, vertical, and conglomerate.

HORIZONTAL MERGERS

A **horizontal merger** takes place when two companies in the same line of business are joined. The sports shoe industry has seen two recent mergers that have dramatically changed the business landscape. In 2003, Nike spent $350 million to acquire one of their competitors, Converse. This merger brought together two traditional shoe manufacturers. In a much bigger deal, adidas-Salomon spent $3.8 billion to acquire Reebok in January of 2006. Reebok and adidas together will have about a 20% market share in the sports shoe industry. These two mergers could have significant long-term ramifications on the industry. In deals such as these, management believes the new merged company will have a higher value than the two separate businesses. Other examples of horizontal mergers in the sport industry include Aramark's acquisition of both Volume Service America in 1999 and Ogden Corporation's entertainment division for $236 million in 2000. SMG, another facility management company, which is partially owned by Aramark, merged with Leisure Management International in 2000 ("Aramark Acquires," 2000).

VERTICAL MERGERS

In a **vertical merger**, a buyer expands operations forward toward the final consumer or backward in the direction of the source of raw materials. Livingstone (1997) refers to these different market levels as upstream and downstream. A downstream market is further along in the production process, while an upstream market is closer to the original raw materials. In either situation, a business expands by acquiring other companies that are part of the production process. In 1998, Intrawest, the operator of several mountain resorts in North America, acquired

two companies, Breeze and Max Snowboards. Both companies rented ski and snowboard equipment. By acquiring these two businesses, Intrawest was able to extend its operations upstream because rental equipment is a necessity for many consumers who want to ski. Intrawest not only has control of the ski mountains and the corresponding income streams but also rents the equipment needed to ski on its mountains ("For the Record," 1998, September).

CONGLOMERATE MERGERS

A **conglomerate merger** occurs when companies in unrelated lines of business come together. The merged companies can be involved in businesses that have no business link. SFX Entertainment had traditionally been in the entertainment industry through the ownership of amphitheaters and concert halls, as well as through participation in the music promotion business. With its acquisitions of the Marquee Group, Integrated Sports International, and FAME, SFX expanded into sport marketing, sports event production, and athlete representation. It appeared with these deals that SFX was attempting to become the largest integrated sport and entertainment conglomerate in the world. However, in 2000, SFX was bought by an even larger entertainment company, Clear Channel. That purchase is discussed later in this chapter. Another conglomerate merger occurred in 2005 when Quicksilver, a famous surfboard manufacturing company, bought Rossignol, a ski company, for $320 million. Although the deal involved different sports, they are both outdoor sports, and both companies had various lines of equipment and apparel (Grant, 2005).

CREDIBLE JUSTIFICATIONS FOR MERGERS

There must be credible justification for a merger to occur. As stated earlier, if no additional value is generated through a merger, then it is probably wisest to maintain the status quo and keep the companies independent. Perhaps the best justification for a merger, especially in the case of a horizontal merger, is **economies of scale**. A company achieves economies of scale by increasing its size. The adage "bigger is better" is a good way to sum up the idea of economies of scale. Two companies that duplicate activities may be more profitable if they merge operations. If the Smiths acquire another fitness center, economies of scale may result. Corporate responsibilities such as accounting, staff development, and office management for the two facilities could be combined, with the potential for substantial cost savings. Although the consolidation of these operations should have little effect on revenues, it may lead to a decrease in expenses. Ultimately, this will increase earnings and the value of the merged company.

Another credible justification for a merger in the sport industry is the prospect that a company can save on costs not related to economies of scale. For example, Cablevision, the New York–based broadcasting company, had paid over $40 million annually for the local television broadcast rights of the New York Yankees. The 12-year $486 million broadcasting deal between the Yankees and Cablevision ended in the year 2000. In the fall of 1998, Cablevision made a reported bid of $525 million to purchase 70% of the Yankees (King & Brockington, 1998). Part of the rationale for the acquisition was that it would allow Cablevision to save $40 million per year. Instead of annually paying local broadcast fees to the Yankees, Cablevision could purchase part ownership of the team and use the ownership rights to reduce or eliminate the broadcasting payments. Cablevision would have owned both the television outlet and the team. Ultimately, the two sides were unable to agree on some details within the acquisition, such as team control, and the deal was abandoned. Ironically, the New York Yankees then decided to begin their own regional sports network, the YES Network. So Cablevision not only was unable to acquire ownership interest in the Yankees, they also lost the television rights to broadcast Yankees games.

A merger or acquisition is also a wise financial endeavor if the merged entity can generate revenues that are not possible if the firms remain separate. Two firms may have complementary resources or products that when combined will result in substantial revenues. As a consequence of the merger, there may be a very successful future for the combined company. For example, Action Sports Media is a sport marketing agency that works with colleges and universities on sponsorship and signage sales. In May 1999, the firm filed a **letter of intent** to buy StadiaNet Sports. StadiaNet Sports installs and programs large-screen video displays and scoreboards, primarily for college sports facilities ("For the Record," 1999). The acquisi-

tion allows Action Sports Media to be involved in not only the sales of signage and advertising for video displays but also the installation and programming of the scoreboards. In theory, a college or university can work with Action Sports Media on the total process of installing and financing its video displays and scoreboards. This was not possible before Action Sports Media acquired StadiaNet Sports.

A corporate acquisition may also be a wise maneuver if a business believes the targeted company is poorly managed. A business may view the other company as underperforming because of poor management and believe it can transform the targeted company into a financially successful business. Through acquisition, the business believes it can improve its own value by instituting more effective management in the underperforming company.

Last, a merger can be the most effective way to invest surplus funds. As mentioned earlier, a successful business with a substantial amount of net income has several options. It can distribute the income to shareholders by increasing dividend payments, or the company may repurchase its stock. A third option is for the business to invest its surplus cash by purchasing the stock of other companies. Often, businesses with surplus cash and a lack of good alternative investment choices redirect their capital toward purchasing other companies. The strategy may be very wise in that a business that fails to redirect its cash may itself become a target for takeover. Businesses with significant excess cash face the possibility of acquisition because other companies may believe they can acquire the business and redirect the cash in a profitable manner.

MERGERS AND ANTITRUST LAW

Within the legal system, mergers and acquisitions are regulated by antitrust law. There are three primary statutes that come into play. The first statute, passed in 1890, is the Sherman Antitrust Act, which decrees that "every contract, combination . . . or conspiracy, in restraint of trade," is illegal (Sherman Antitrust Act, 1890). It was enacted in response to the monopolies that developed in the middle to late 1800s in industries

A Fitness Merger

In December 2001, Bally Total Fitness merged with Crunch Fitness. The total purchase price was estimated at $90 million for the 19 Crunch Fitness clubs in five states. The merged company increased Bally's size to approximately 420 clubs throughout North America, serving more than four million members ("Bally," 2001). Several years later, when Bally was facing financial hardship, it sold its Crunch Fitness interest.

such as steel, iron, and the railroads. The goal was to protect consumers from large corporations that controlled entire industries. However, the wording of the statute was vague, and thus the law was difficult to enforce.

The Federal Trade Commission Act of 1914 was a step toward tightening the restrictions on monopolies and collusive behavior. It prohibited unfair methods of competition as well as unfair or deceptive acts or practices (Blair & Kaserman, 1985). The act also established an agency, the Federal Trade Commission, that was given the responsibility of enforcing the antitrust laws. The third and most enforceable of these statutes was the Clayton Act of 1914. Section 7 of the Clayton Act addressed mergers and acquisitions. It prohibited the acquisition of another firm's stock in cases in which the result would be to lessen competition and create a monopoly (Blair & Kaserman, 1985). However, the Clayton Act had one obvious loophole. It did not prohibit the acquisition of another firm's assets. The loophole was used extensively until 1950, when it was closed with the passage of the Cellar-Kefauver Act. Section 7 of the Clayton Act was amended to the following:

> No corporation engaged in commerce shall acquire, directly or indirectly, the whole or any part of the stock or other share capital and no corporation subject to the jurisdiction of the Federal Trade Commission shall acquire the whole or any part of the assets of another corporation engaged also in commerce, where in any line of commerce in any section of the country, the effect of such acquisition may be substantially to lessen competition, or to tend to create a monopoly. (Blair & Kaserman, 1985, p. 226)

The improved Clayton Act not only forbade mergers that constrained trade or greatly lessened market competition but also prohibited any merger that potentially restrained trade. Thus, the Clayton Act has been the primary statute used to stop mergers that could have created a monopoly within an industry.

Antitrust law is enforced by two federal government agencies: the Federal Trade Commission (FTC) and the U.S. Department of Justice. The Department of Justice has the power to file a civil suit to block any merger, and the FTC can initiate an official proceeding to analyze the effect of a merger on competition within an industry. Ultimately, either department can attempt to legally stop two firms from merging if it believes the result will decrease competition and harm consumers.

Since the passage of the Hart-Scott-Rodino Act of 1976, all firms are required by law to inform the government of any acquisitions of stock that exceed a certain dollar amount. Originally, that dollar amount was $15 million. However, over the years that number has been increased. As of January 2005, the amount is $53.1 million. The government must also be informed if greater than 15% of the targeted firm's stock is purchased (Woodworth & Sher, 2005).

Very few mergers are contested by the Department of Justice or the FTC. Within the American sport industry, no major antitrust cases have arisen from a corporate merger. As the industry continues to develop and more mergers occur, it is likely that some acquisitions will be closely scrutinized by federal agencies such as the FTC.

Although there have not been any significant challenges to sport mergers, the government has become involved in several transactions. For example, when the NFL merged with the American Football League (AFL), Congress reviewed the proposed merger to assess its impact on broadcast football games. In response to the inquiry, the legislature passed the 1968 Sports Broadcasting Act, which allowed the merger to proceed as long as professional football did not air games on Saturdays during the college football season. Thus, even today, no NFL games are played on Saturday during the college football season. After the regular college football season ends, the NFL once again starts airing games on Saturdays. This legislation was developed to prevent professional football from overrunning college football.

VARIOUS FORMS OF ACQUISITION

An acquisition can take many forms. Numerous issues play into how a company acquires another company. For example, is the acquisition friendly or will it be strongly

The NFL–AFL Merger

The NFL–AFL merger was not the first merger for the NFL. In 1949 the NFL merged with three teams from the rival All-America Football Conference, bringing Cleveland, San Francisco, and Baltimore into the NFL (Crow et al., 2000). The NFL–AFL merger was originally inked in 1966, but there were four years of political wrangling before Congress approved the deal and the merger was completed (Crow et al., 2000).

contested? The merger between Hewlett-Packard and Compaq is an example of a merger that became contentious. Millions of dollars were spent to convince people that the merger was right or wrong for the shareholders. This section examines some acquisition concerns, such as whether it is better to purchase another business' stock or just their assets.

There are three methods of legally acquiring another business. The first of these methods is the merger of two companies; the other two methods are purchasing voting stock and purchasing assets.

MERGING TWO COMPANIES

A merger occurs when one company is completely absorbed by another. For example, in 1999, Easton Sports, the aluminum baseball bat manufacturer, acquired Stix Baseball, a wooden bat producer. The merged company would operate under the Easton Sports name and produce bats with both the Easton and Stix brand names (Byrd, 1999). The advantage for Easton was that the company would have a presence in the wooden and aluminum bat markets. This presence was important in view of debates in collegiate sport about abandoning aluminum bats. If the NCAA approved the new rules, Easton would lose a significant market. However, by acquiring a wooden bat manufacturer, the company was anticipating being able to fill a need for wooden bats if the new rules were approved. There was no need to invest in new machinery or production sites. Easton simply purchased another company that already had those resources.

The advantages of mergers are that they are legally simple and relatively inexpensive. There is no title transfer of property or assets. One disadvantage is that a merger must be approved by a stockholder vote within each company. The management team of the business being sold must cooperate and approve the deal. This is sometimes problematic because the merger may result in the termination of some high-level managers. These managers may make a concerted effort to block the merger. Because of this concern, some deals include clauses that guarantee management positions in the new company or provide for golden parachutes. A golden parachute is a large monetary payoff to a top-level manager in exchange for her support of a merger.

PURCHASING VOTING STOCK

In a second form of acquisition, a company purchases the voting stock in another company in exchange for cash, stock in the existing company, or both. This is achieved through a tender offer, or a public offer by one company to directly buy the stock of another. An advantage of this acquisition method is that shareholders' meetings do not have to take place and management can be bypassed. The buyer can go directly to the shareholders for their approval. If a majority of the shareholders agree to sell, the purchaser will have control of the company. In March 1999, Marquee Group stockholders approved a merger with SFX Entertainment. As part of the deal, Marquee common stockholders received 0.0815 shares of SFX class A common stock for every share of Marquee stock. Approximately 1.4 million shares of SFX stock were exchanged for the Marquee stock (SFX Entertainment, 1999). In 2007 French luxury good maker, PPR

What's in a Name?

Sports executives in a merger might overlook the merger's impact on naming rights. If bank A has its name on a stadium under a 20-year contract, will that name change if bank A is purchased by bank B? The answer is yes. However, the potential costs of making such a changeover can be significant. It may cost a naming-rights company millions of dollars to change the corporate images on the signage in a sports facility. Areas of change may include advertising stickers on walls, seats, cup holders, stairs, concession products, and building exteriors. Philadelphia's CoreStates Center was renamed First Union Center after CoreStates Financial was purchased by First Union in 1999. In 2001 First Union then merged with Wachovia Banks. The facility in Philadelphia is now named the Wachovia Center. Likewise, the new Boston Garden was supposed to open as the Shawmut Center. However, Shawmut National Group was purchased by Fleet Financial Group, which renamed the facility the FleetCenter. Fleet Bank was eventually bought out by Banknorth, and the facility is now named Banknorth Garden.

Not all name changes go well after a merger. The name can be changed only if the contract provides for such a change. A dispute arose concerning Buffalo's Marine Midland Arena when Marine Midland was acquired by HSBC Holdings. The Buffalo Sabres initially did not want to change the facility's name since they argued that the contract with Marine Midland did not allow the name to be transferred ("Business Bulletin," 2000).

SA (owner of Gucci and Yves Saint Laurent) bought 27.1% in Puma AG, the third largest sporting goods maker in the world. The initial purchase was the start of an offer to buy all the shares at a price of 330 euros per share ($441.11), which placed a value on Puma of $7.1 billion (Moulson, 2007).

Management sometimes fights the stock acquisition, and this can lead to conflict. The process has the potential to be much longer and more expensive if management attempts to block the acquisition. Shareholders may also hold out in an effort to increase the stock's acquisition price. If current shareholders can force up the sale price of the stock, they will receive more money when they ultimately sell the stock. As highlighted in chapter 9, several shareholder groups sued Ascent over the proposed sale of the Denver Nuggets, based on the shareholders' opinion that the bid was too low and that higher bids had been rejected. The higher bids would have earned the shareholders a greater return. Any conflict typically raises the acquisition price for the purchasing firm. Note that many stock acquisitions ultimately become mergers. Management from both sides negotiate for a merger, usually protecting the self-interests of both.

At other times management might lead the charge to purchase a company. The growth of investment bankers and private equity in the sport industry grew significantly in the first couple years of the 21st century. Once such purchase involved the CEO of Aramark, Joseph Neubauer, and other investors taking the public company private through a leveraged buyout (LBO; see chapter 10). Aramark was sold for $6.24 billion, but its debt increased under the deal from $1.76 to $6.2 billion, which meant the company's interest payments increased from $139.9 million to $590.9 million annually. Due to this increased debt, Aramark's corporate credit rating was decreased into junk bond status by Standard & Poor's (Simon and Yao, 2007).

PURCHASING ASSETS

The last acquisition method to consider is the purchase of one company's assets by another business. This method requires voter approval by the acquired company and is the least common of the three forms. The benefit of purchasing assets is that the acquiring company can increase its inventory or capital assets without acquiring potential liability, debt, or other concerns from the seller. The legal process of acquiring assets such as real estate, production sites, and machinery can be very costly.

MERGER ACCOUNTING

With respect to accounting issues, mergers and acquisitions can be highly complex. Using generally accepted accounting principles (GAAP), mergers are handled as either a purchase of assets or a pooling of interests. The two methods have very little effect on the real value of the merged firm; however, there are some differences between the two that we discuss here. The results of a pooling of interests are shown in figure 15.1, a through c. With the pooling of interests method, the two companies are merged, and their balance sheets are simply added together to form

Figure 15.1 *(a)* Company A's balance sheet, *(b)* company B's balance sheet, *(c)* and their combined balance sheet.

the balance sheet for the new company. The new company is jointly owned by all the stockholders in the previously separate companies. The pooling of assets method is very simple, and the total assets are unchanged by the merger.

The purchase of assets method is somewhat more complex. This method requires applying the fair market value to the acquired company's assets. In addition, an asset category called goodwill is created for accounting purposes. Goodwill is the difference between the acquisition price and the fair value of the acquired business' assets. Figure 15.2, a through c, provides an example of the purchase of assets method. The balance sheets used in figure 15.1, a and b, are again displayed. Assume that company A is going to acquire company B for $15 million in cash. The money is raised through borrowing from a financial institution. On its balance sheet, company B has reported $6 million in fixed assets. However, at the time of acquisition, company B is appraised at $10 million. Since company B also has $2 million in working capital, the balance sheet assets are $12 million. Therefore, company A is paying $3 million in excess of the estimated market value of company B's total net assets. The difference is represented on the combined balance sheet as goodwill. Figure 15.2c shows the new firm's balance sheet after acquisition.

To recap, the total assets of the combined companies are $28 million, $7 million more than when the two company balance sheets were separate. Of that $7 million, $4 million is from the revaluation of company B's fixed assets, and $3 million is from goodwill. The goodwill is the amount paid in excess of the fair market value of company B. A buyer may pay an additional amount such as this because there are a number of intangible assets that are not included on the balance sheet—assets such as employee talent and future growth opportunities. The additional $3 million pays for such assets.

Which of the two methods is best? As you can see, the major difference between them is goodwill. Goodwill has several important tax ramifications. Goodwill must be amortized over a period of years, not to exceed 40 years. The goodwill amortization expense is then deducted from reported income. However, unlike depreciation, goodwill is not tax deductible. Given the goodwill expense, the purchase of assets method usually results in lower reported income than the pooling of assets method. Also, since the fixed assets are revalued using the purchase of assets method, often the overall value of the merged company increases. The combined larger book value and lower reported income can have a negative effect on company performance measures such as return on equity (ROE) and return on assets (ROA). The resulting lower measures may paint a picture that is not as strong as when the pooling of assets method is used (Brealey et al., 2004).

Note that the choice of accounting methods used for acquisitions has no effect on tax-deductible expenses or cash flows. Therefore, the net present value of the merged firm is not affected by the selection of merger accounting methods. Also, no evidence exists to suggest that more value is created

a

ASSETS		LIABILITIES & SHAREHOLDERS' EQUITY	
(in millions)		*(in millions)*	
Working capital	$3	Equity	$13
Fixed assets	10		
Total	**$13**	**Total**	**$13**

b

ASSETS		LIABILITIES & SHAREHOLDERS' EQUITY	
(in millions)		*(in millions)*	
Working capital	$2	Equity	$8
Fixed assets	6		
Total	**$8**	**Total**	**$8**

c

ASSETS		LIABILITIES & SHAREHOLDERS' EQUITY	
(in millions)		*(in millions)*	
Working capital	$5	Equity	$15
Fixed assets	20	Debt	13
Goodwill	3		
Total	**$28**	**Total**	**$28**

Figure 15.2 *(a)* Company A's balance sheet, *(b)* company B's balance sheet, and *(c)* their combined balance sheet.

for the acquiring business under one method or the other (Ross et al., 2005). The differences are in the accounting methods only.

CURRENT SPORT INDUSTRY EXAMPLE

We have already discussed several merger and acquisition examples. However, a sport-specific example will illustrate the concerns that these types of transactions have raised in the sport industry and how these concerns were overcome.

An excellent example of a company's acquiring another business in an attempt to increase its own value is News Corporation, owned by Rupert Murdoch. News Corporation operates television networks such as the Fox Network, Fox Sports, and BSkyB. As part of an overall business strategy, News Corporation acquired the Los Angeles Dodgers for $311 million in 1998 (Chass, 1998). One reason for the purchase was to provide broadcast content for the company's television networks. Therefore, although the Dodgers may not have been a company that provided large profits, Murdoch's goal was to use them to help his other business ventures such as television and radio broadcasting.

Murdoch has used this strategy successfully in North America, Europe, and Australia, where he is involved in professional sports such as baseball, soccer, and rugby. In 1998, he also made a $1 billion bid for Manchester United, the English Premier League soccer club. Murdoch wanted to use the ownership right of the league's most popular team to improve his negotiating position with the English Premier League (Kaplan, 1998, September). The merger was blocked by antitrust regulators in Great Britain. News Corporation already owned BSkyB, the television outlet that has exclusive rights to broadcast all Premier League games. British regulators believed that cross-ownership of a team and the exclusive television broadcaster could lead to anticompetitive behavior (Rofe, 1999). In addition, Murdoch was eyeing the possibility of starting a European "super league," which would also be broadcast on his network. Ultimately, because of antitrust concerns, the British government did not permit News Corporation's purchase of Manchester United. No European "super league" has emerged, with the exception of the UEFA Champions League, which is not controlled by Murdoch and News Corporation.

Interestingly, Murdoch's goal of using the Los Angeles Dodgers to generate profits for his other holdings in broadcasting failed to materialize. In 2004, Murdoch sold the Dodgers to real estate mogul Frank McCourt for $430 million (Frew, 2004). In 2005, Manchester United was sold to Tampa Bay Buccaneers owner Malcolm Glazer for $1.4 billion ("Man Utd," 2005).

Murdoch has attempted to use acquisition in the past to compete in the sports broadcasting industry. In April 1999, he purchased half of Liberty Media's interests in regional cable networks. The price tag for the acquisition was $1.4 billion. The buyout gave

By acquiring other businesses, Rupert Murdoch has increased the value of his company to $56.6512 billion (http://money.cnn.com/magazines/fortune/fortune500/snapshots/1381.html; accessed 5/3/07).

© AP Photo/Bryan Charlton

Murdoch control over additional cable outlets, along with the rights to several sports programs. News Corporation reportedly made the acquisition as part of an overall business strategy to build a network of regional cable outlets that would compete with ESPN for sports programming (Brockington & Rofe, 1999). To expand his American TV holdings even more, Murdoch purchased a 34% stake in DirecTV in 2003. That purchase came at a cost of $6.6 billion (News Corporation, 2004)

CONCLUSION

Successful sport businesses must determine how to use their positive earnings. There are three primary ways in which companies use these funds: paying dividends to stockholders, acquiring other firms, and reinvesting in themselves. Paying dividends is often a popular choice with stockholders, but this may not be in the best long-term interests of the stockholders or the firm. There are three views on dividend payments. The rightists believe that the highest possible level of dividends should be paid to stockholders. The leftists think that dividend payments should be relatively small. The middle-of-the-roaders believe that dividend payments should be at a level that satisfies the greatest number of stockholders. Paying dividends involves a somewhat complex process. The process has been established to ensure that the proper parties receive dividend payments in a fair and timely manner.

Another option for using earnings is to reinvest in the business. This reinvestment usually takes the form of spending on capital projects such as purchasing new equipment, investing in talent, or constructing new facilities. Sport is somewhat unique in that capital spending can take the form of hiring coaches and players. For example, the Texas Rangers signed Alex Rodriguez to a 10-year $252 million contract in 2000. This is definitely a form of capital spending. In other industries, very few long-term employment contracts make up such a large portion of a business' expenses. Reinvestment allows for growth and future financial success. It is an integral part of capital budgeting and long-term financial planning.

Last, earnings can be used to acquire other businesses. Acquisitions can entail horizontal mergers, vertical mergers, or conglomerates. For a merger to be successful, the value of the merged companies must be greater than the value of the two businesses if they were to remain as separate entities. Recently, there has been an increase in mergers and acquisitions in the sport industry. Entertainment companies such as Rupert Murdoch's News Corporation, Nike, and Comcast-Spectacor have acquired other businesses in an attempt to expand their presence in the sport and entertainment industries. Using business earnings is an important aspect of financial management that plays a major role in determining long-term business success.

CLASS DISCUSSION TOPICS

1. Is consolidation in the sport industry good?
2. Do you think it would be worthwhile to create another football league similar to the United States Football League or the XFL? Would another baseball, hockey, or basketball league be a better investment?
3. If you could make 10% from a government bond or 10% from investing in a professional sports team, which one would you invest in and why?
4. Why should a business set a record date when issuing a dividend?
5. If you had this responsibility within a corporation, under what circumstances would you make a decision to reinvest versus issuing a dividend?
6. Which group (rightist, leftist, or middle-of-the-roader) has views that you believe make the most sense?
7. Explain the fundamental accounting difference between using the pooling of interests method versus the purchase of assets methods when dealing with the merger of two sport organizations.
8. What are the primary components of the Sherman Antitrust Act of 1890 and the Clayton Act of 1914? What is their significance to the management of the sport industry?
9. Explain the differences between horizontal, vertical, and conglomerate mergers.

PART VI

FINANCIAL TROUBLESHOOTING

Every business needs to be prepared for times of financial trouble. Part VI takes a look at the auditing process as well as what happens when a business needs to close.

Chapter 16, Auditing, covers the important process of ensuring accuracy of a company's financial numbers. The chapter begins by outlining why auditing is undertaken and describing the types of audits. The chapter then moves on to cover types of internal controls that can help prevent financial fraud. Through independent audits a company can show external investors, lenders, and others its true financial state. By understanding the auditing process, readers receive a better grasp of the information auditors analyze and how they can find fraud.

Every investor at some point needs to exit the investment by selling or writing off the investment as a loss. Chapter 17, Exit Strategy, first covers how to detect red flags indicating financial distress. If a company is in trouble, it can try to reorganize informally or sell its assets through the liquidation process. A company can also seek bankruptcy protection from the courts to allow it to pay its bills or to avoid paying obligations already owed. Some companies also sell their assets to pay bills since they might not have any other valuable items to sell. A company can also try to sell itself and find a new owner with deeper pockets to pay for future growth.

16

AUDITING

CHAPTER OBJECTIVES

After studying this chapter, you should be able to do the following:

- Define the purposes of auditing.
- Understand the problems associated with poor auditing.
- Describe the types of audits.
- Understand the importance of selecting competent and unbiased auditors.
- Understand how the auditing process works.
- Understand how sport fraud can occur through sloppy financial analysis.

Auditing is one of the most important areas within the field of accounting. Although the focus of this textbook is on financial management, it is also beneficial for a sports manager to be knowledgeable in the basics of auditing. The importance of knowing how income or expenses can be excluded from financial statements was made abundantly clear in the early 21st century with numerous corporate scandals. Well-known companies such as Enron, Adelphia, Tyco, and WorldCom made news with their accounting scandals. These scandals led to criminal charges against some prominent corporate executives such as Dennis Kozlowski, John Rigas, and Kenneth Lay. Although such scandals are not common in sport businesses, they are possible.

The goal of this chapter is to provide you with an introduction to auditing. If you wish to find out more about the field, you should consult a textbook devoted to auditing. This chapter deals primarily with the principles of auditing and their applicability to the sport industry.

PURPOSES OF AUDITING

Auditing has two fundamental roles. First, auditing ensures that all financial statements accurately portray a firm's financial position. Second, audits allow managers to analyze their operation's efficiency.

ENSURING ACCURACY OF FINANCIAL INFORMATION

The primary role of auditing is to ensure the accuracy of financial information. The purpose of auditing is to investigate and determine if the financial statements produced by the sport business have been prepared in accordance with appropriate financial reporting practices (Holmes & Burns, 1979). This may seem like a relatively simple matter, but it can be very complex.

In this text we discuss numerous financial measures that are predicated on accurate financial data. The ratios are only as good as the numbers used to calculate them. Auditing is not limited to simply analyzing financial statements, however. To ensure that the financial statements are accurate, an auditor must study the entire business. This often involves analyzing a business' internal processes to see whether they successfully control the flow of financial information. For example, an auditor must examine the processes involved in functional areas such as employee payroll, the purchase of goods and services, and inventory control to determine if the financial statements

accurately represent the auditee. Additionally, an auditor must have knowledge of the industry being examined. One benefit of auditing is discouraging and detecting fraudulent activities or mistakes (see "Detecting Fraud" on pp. 299-301). It is important to note that all businesses and organizations, regardless of size, scope, and mission, must undergo some type of periodic audit.

The West Hartford Badminton Club collects $5.00 a night from members and $8.00 a night from nonmembers during peak playing times. These funds need to be recorded in a meaningful manner so that someone can ensure that everyone has paid to play. The club's vice president checks the totals every day to determine if any errors have been made. If there are 15 players and there is $90, then she can do the math and determine that there are 10 members and 5 nonmembers playing. If the player records indicate that 7 nonmembers and 9 members are playing that day, then she knows that $11 is missing. This example highlights how auditing is similar to the investigation process.

There is a need for honest and candid public disclosure of financial information by businesses and organizations, both public and private. It is just as important for publicly operated sports organizations, such as university athletic departments, to have accurate financial records as it is for private companies, such as professional sports franchises and sporting goods manufacturers. Auditing is designed to identify problems and to ensure investor confidence in a company's financial statements. However, if the independent auditors help manipulate the numbers, as is alleged to have occurred in the Enron scandal, the entire rationale for independent auditing is lost.

Although it might be difficult for a sport business to engage in the same illegal activities as WorldCom, SMC could face the same problem. If SMC's chief financial officer did not pay certain bills and wrote checks to himself, then the company could think it was paying the accounts payable when in fact its obligations were increasing every month. If SMC failed to properly audit its finances, such a scheme could go undetected for months until lawsuits are filed or accounts closed.

ANALYZING OPERATIONAL EFFICIENCY

Audits may detect areas in which a sport business could operate more efficiently, which could lead to an increase in profits (Arens & Loebbecke, 2006). For nonprofit organizations, this increased efficiency may allow the organization to do more with its available resources. For example, the athletic director at the University of Milford is given a fixed yearly budget. Efficient use of these funds will allow that athletic director to maximize the number of opportunities for the coaches and student-athletes. Therefore, it is as important for an athletic director to audit the organization to increase efficiency as it is for the manager of a multibillion-dollar private corporation.

CATEGORIES OF AUDITS

Audits can be separated into two general categories: internal and independent. Internal audits are completed by staff members within a business. Most large businesses have a financial department that oversees internal audits. An internal auditor serves several different functions. Usually the internal auditor is involved in preparing an organization's financial statements to ensure their accuracy. The auditor is also involved in the establishment of internal controls for the organization. An auditor may develop an internal control system to track the purchase, receipt, and distribution of inventory for a retail sales company such as Modell's or Dick's Sporting Goods. Without a system that tracks the use and physical location of equipment, it may be easy for an employee to steal business property. As another example of establishing internal controls, an internal auditor for the University of Milford may develop a bar code system to track

the use and physical location of office equipment such as computers, fax machines, and telephones. A phone tracking system for the U of M might require a telephone user to enter a special code to make a long-distance call. The system can then track all calls to show if an employee is using the phone excessively or for personal purposes.

Independent audits, as the name implies, involve an external review of the finances by individuals who are not directly involved with the documents being reviewed. Thus, an independent audit can be performed by someone from another division in the company who has not been involved in generating the document in question. Likewise, an independent audit can also be performed by external entities, such as public accounting firms, that can verify the truthfulness of the documents being reviewed. The latter is the type of audit most commonly seen in corporate finance. Independent audits are discussed in greater detail later in this chapter.

There is a third general category of audit that is outside the scope of this textbook. The IRS can request an audit of any business. Usually, the IRS audits a business to determine whether or not the correct amount of federal taxes has been paid. Businesses that fail to pay or that underpay taxes can face substantial monetary fines and penalties. In this chapter we focus on independent audits because they are the most common, and this type of audit most directly affects sport finance managers.

INTERNAL CONTROLS

As stated earlier, auditing involves more than verifying a business' financial statements. An auditor must also examine a business' system of internal controls. Internal controls are the processes and mechanisms used in the management of a business (Meigs, Whittington, & Meigs, 1982). For example, all businesses have employees who are compensated for their labor. There are many steps in paying employees. All five of our sports organization cases must develop a system to calculate the number

WorldCom

Although it might be hard to replicate the complex schemes Enron used to cover its financial problems, WorldCom engaged in outright fraud that auditors should have checked. The WorldCom downfall was based on classifying debt as capital expenditures. This change resulted in a capitalization of expenses rather than having the expenses deducted as they were incurred and paid. This led to higher reported profits because approximately $3.8 billion in expenses were improperly classified ("WorldCom Charged," 2002).

of hours worked by each employee and the wage rate at which each will be compensated. In addition, deductions must be made for expenses such as income taxes, health benefits, and retirement plan payments. Last, paychecks must be processed and distributed to all employees. It is important that an efficient, consistent, and accurate system be developed for this process. An inferior system will mean a lack of internal control, increasing the probability of financial errors. These errors could mean that an employee is not paid or is paid an inaccurate amount.

A strong internal control system is a means to avoid many financial errors. Therefore, those developing procedures for managing financial matters should stress internal control. A good example is the Stars' parking lot attendants. Their facility has a large parking lot, and two employees help process people through the gates. The Stars use two attendants because parking revenue is split between the team and the municipal entity that owns the facility. To guarantee accuracy, the team employs a person to take the money, and the municipality employs a person who has a counter to register how many cars have entered the parking lot. The number of cars clicked can be reconciled with the amount of money collected to make sure both sides have the correct number. A system of strong internal controls also makes it easier for managers to prepare for financial audits because they will have the materials needed by the auditor.

Poor internal controls may also increase the likelihood of fraud. For example, if one person oversees the entire payroll system for a small sports organization, say 20 employees, committing a fraud would be rather easy for that employee. Such a scenario could easily happen to the Smiths. If they hire a bookkeeper to process all their revenue and expenses, they need to install policies and procedures to make sure the bookkeeper does not embezzle money. A procedure must exist for ensuring the accuracy of this person's work; without oversight, a fraudulent act can easily occur. Perhaps the bookkeeper could overpay employees or place people on the payroll who are not actually working for the Smiths.

INDEPENDENT AUDITS

Independent auditors are not associated with the business being audited. Although they are hired by the business, their responsibility is to provide assurance that the business' financial information is reliable and accurate. The issue of independence is very important. The audited business may not be pleased with the findings of an independent auditor, but the auditor has an ethical duty to honestly report his findings (Whittington & Pany, 2006) For public corporations, auditors must complete an auditor's report that summarizes their findings. As in the general field of accounting, auditors use standard procedures to analyze and report their findings. There are also several professional associations that oversee the auditing field, some of which are shown in the next list (p.289):

Legal but Not Necessarily Honest

Many companies "play games" with financial statements to present an interpretation of the data that shows the company in the best light. It is the role of the auditor to make sure these tricks are properly recorded and communicated to all interested parties. Some of the legal – but not necessarily honest – tricks include the following:

- Companies might promote their earnings by publicizing a pro forma figure that excludes many normal expense items such as interest and marketing expenses.

- If the earnings are low or negative, a company might list instead EBITDA—earnings before interest, taxes, depreciation, and amortization.

- Companies might not report the potential impact of stock-options grants on their earnings.

- Especially in the late 1990s, some businesses reported large earnings acquired through selling their investments in start-ups. Although these are real earnings, they are the earnings of an offshoot rather than of the core business, and there is no guarantee that any future similar earnings might ever be realized (Scherreik, 2000).

Abbreviation	Name
AAA	American Accounting Association
AICPA	American Institute of Certified Public Accountants
ASB	Auditing Standards Board
FAF	Financial Accounting Foundation
FEI	Financial Executives Institute
IIA	Institute of Internal Auditors-
NAA	National Association of Accountants
PCAOB	Public Company Accounting Oversight Board
SSCPA	State Societies of Certified Public Accountants

The accuracy of an auditor's report is very important. Under U.S. common law and securities law, third parties such as investors, creditors, and government agencies can sue independent auditors. Monetary damages may have to be paid if it is determined that the independent auditor is guilty of a crime (Whittington & Pany, 2006). In March 2002, the accounting firm of Arthur Andersen was indicted in a federal court for its involvement in the Enron scandal. The U.S. Department of Justice claimed that Andersen obstructed justice by allegedly aiding Enron in the destruction of key financial documents. Deputy Attorney General Larry Thompson stated in *USA Today* that "Andersen personnel engaged in the wholesale destruction of tons of paperwork and attempted to purge huge volumes of electronic data or information. . . . At the time, Andersen knew full well that these documents were relevant to the inquiries into Enron's collapse" (Farrell, 2002). In June 2002, Andersen was found guilty in a

U.S. Federal Court of obstructing justice by shredding Enron documents. As a result of the conviction, the Securities and Exchange Commission forced the firm to surrender its accounting licenses. Andersen's business quickly disappeared, and the company reduced the number of employees from a high of 85,000 to about 200. In May 2005 the court decision against Andersen was overturned by a U.S. appeals court. However, the decision was much too late to help Andersen, which had lost almost all its clients.

In response to the accounting scandals of the early 21st century, the U.S. Congress moved quickly to enact new legislation that addresses the ethics and behavior of accounting and auditing firms. In the summer of 2002, the Sarbanes-Oxley Act was passed by Congress and quickly signed into law by President Bush. Sarbanes-Oxley includes a series of reforms restricting the types of consulting that certified public accountants may perform for audit clients. In addition, the Public Company Accounting Oversight Board (PCAOB) was established. The PCAOB tightened federal regulation of accounting practices and has developed stricter rules for the auditing process (Whittington & Pany, 2006).

TYPES OF INDEPENDENT AUDITS

There are four distinct types of audits. The first, the audit of financial statements, is the most common, and this type of audit receives the bulk of attention in this chapter. The three other types of audits, operational audits, compliance audits, and integrated audits are usually referred to as audit activities (Whittington & Pany, 2006). Although attestation and assurance are provided through these audits, as discussed later in the chapter, the central theme is to analyze a business' efficiency and regulatory compliance. What follows is a brief description of each of the four types of audits, which are also characterized in table 16.1.

Table 16.1 Types of Audits

Type of audit	Role of audit	Audit tasks
Financial statement audit	Ensure the accuracy of financial statements	Review documents, records, and other sources of financial evidence
Operational audit	Evaluate the efficiency and effectiveness of organizational activities	Interview employees; analyze processes and written reports
Compliance audit	Determine if specific rules, procedures, or regulations set by higher authorities are being met	Analyze written materials, stated regulations and standards, and methods for meeting these regulations and standards
Integrated audit	Assure both the effectiveness of internal financial reporting and the accuracy of completed financial statements	Document both the accuracy of the financial statements and the management's effectiveness in internally controlling the accounting processes

1. *Financial statements audit.* This type of audit is done to determine if a business' financial statements meet generally accepted accounting principles. Most often, these financial statements include income statements, statements of cash flows, and the statement of financial position (i.e., balance sheets).
2. *Operational audit.* An operational audit reviews some part of a business' operating methods and procedures. The goal is to determine if the business is operating at its maximum efficiency and effectiveness. Usually, an operational audit assesses efficiency and also yields recommendations for improved effectiveness. For example, SMC may undergo an operational audit to analyze the efficiency and effectiveness of its product distribution system. The result may be that the business uses the auditor's recommendations to develop new methods for transporting products from the production site to retailers.
3. *Compliance audit.* The goal of the compliance audit is to determine if the auditee is following the specific rules, regulations, and procedures set by some higher authority. Within collegiate athletics, the NCAA periodically visits member institutions to audit their operations. For example, the association may analyze the system a college or university uses to ensure student-athlete eligibility. The NCAA has specific rules and regulations with respect to eligibility. Failure to follow these guidelines may lead to rules violations and probation. In an attempt to minimize these violations, the NCAA works with member institutions to develop effective mechanisms for following rules and regulations. In addition, the NCAA has instituted five-year self-studies and peer reviews for collegiate athletic programs as a method of instituting compliance audits.

 The University of Milford starts gathering data for its audit in the third or fourth year. The last year is spent compiling the data and completing a report that addresses both the positive and negative concerns raised by the self-study. If the university uncovers any potential academic or financial abuse, the audit allows U of M to highlight such concerns. The process also shows that the university's own internal investigation system can uncover such problems and that the university can institute its own reforms or punishment.

4. *Integrated audit.* As a result of the Sarbanes-Oxley Act, all publicly traded companies are required to complete an integrated audit. This type of audit includes assurance of both the effectiveness of internal financial reporting and the completed financial statements. The independent auditor must report on both the accuracy of the financial statements and the management's effectiveness in internally controlling the accounting processes. As a public company, SMC must undergo an annual integrated audit.

MATERIALITY AND MEANINGFULNESS

One of the most important concepts within auditing is materiality. **Materiality** concerns the levels of misstatement that are allowable in financial information. Since no financial system is perfect, misstatements do occur. The auditor must determine the level of misstatement that will affect the fairness of the information. For example, a large sport manufacturing company such as SMC may have millions of dollars in revenues and expenses. For such an organization, a financial misstatement of $10,000 may be considered immaterial with respect to the overall financial position of the business. However, a $10,000 misstatement for a small sport business such as WHBC would probably be considered material. In each situation, the auditor must determine where to draw the line.

In general, a misstatement can be considered material if knowledge of the misstatement affects a decision made by a reasonable user of the statements (Arens & Loebbecke, 2006). A misstatement that is relatively small or one that does not affect the overall fairness of the financial statements is considered immaterial. If misstatements are relatively large or pervasively affect an organization's financial documents, an auditor may not be comfortable in issuing an unqualified auditor's report (see "Receiving the Auditor's Report" on pp.297-298). In this case, the auditor may issue a qualified opinion or an adverse opinion about the documents. Obviously, an auditee wants to avoid this result. Such a finding may dramatically decrease the confidence that investors and creditors have in the company's financial statements.

ROLE OF TECHNOLOGY

Technology has drastically changed how businesses acquire, process, and manage financial information. As a result, auditors have changed the manner in which they organize and analyze information. Here we examine two technological advances that have greatly affected auditing.

ELECTRONIC DATA PROCESSING SYSTEMS

Electronic data processing (EDP) systems allow businesses to simplify operations such as accounts payable, payroll, and inventory control. This technology has increased efficiency and accuracy in the reporting of financial information. At the same time, businesses must take steps to make sure that information produced through use of an EDP system is accurate. First, they must ensure that the EDP systems themselves do not have errors. A poor EDP system can result in more misstatements than the old system of human recording and calculating. Second, as always, an EDP system is only as good as the data inputted. Errors in the inputting of data can be very costly.

The increased efficiency gained through EDP may, in some cases, result in a loss of internal control. Too often, managers assume that financial information is accurate because it has been generated through an EDP system; this assumption can be costly. For example, WHBC may use an EDP system to produce a monthly statement of the revenues generated through membership fees. This would appear to be a simple procedure, but problems may occur if the payment amounts are inaccurately entered by employees or are not entered in a timely fashion. If membership fees received on the last day of the month are not processed for several days, the monthly statement will not be accurate. An EDP system cannot recognize a discrepancy such as this, yet it is still an obvious accounting error. As the saying goes, "Garbage in, garbage out."

EDP can offer a significant benefit, but if technological hurdles arise, the systems can also quickly become worthless. The Y2K scare of the late 1990s is a great example of the possibility of errors due to technology. Many businesses invested substantial resources toward Y2K compliance in areas such as payroll and finance. As we all know, the investment was wise. January 1, 2000, came and went with very few problems attributable to computers and technology. However, without the precautions and safeguards, many businesses could have had substantial technological problems.

Today, more than ever before, businesses rely on computer technology and the Internet. When EDP was first developed, its cost made it attractive to only the largest businesses. Now it is cost-effective for even the smallest businesses. For a relatively low investment in software, any business can have an EDP system that is both powerful and user-friendly. These systems have revolutionized the means by which businesses collect, process, and analyze financial information.

Because of the threat of computer viruses and breakdowns, all EDP systems must be backed up.

Managers should be able to feel confident that if their primary EDP systems become inoperable, a backup system is in place. Auditors can help with this process. First, through their work with the financial statements, auditors can analyze a client's EDP and make recommendations for ensuring the safety and accuracy of financial information. In addition, businesses should undergo periodic operational audits in order to ensure the efficiency and effectiveness of their EDP.

INTERNET AND ELECTRONIC MAIL

Other technological advances that have changed organizational finances and audits are the Internet and electronic mail. Organizations with multiple locations can now communicate much more efficiently. A sporting goods retailer with multiple stores can utilize technological advances to have the sales from each store automatically sent to a central location so management can track revenue. If sales are lower on one day as compared with other days, management can investigate what caused the decline to prevent its occurrence in the future. Transactions such as multiple electronic funds transfers from numerous bank accounts now occur without the use of paper and without human contact. Although this increases efficiency, it also leads to new types of problems. Computer fraud is a new concern, and new internal controls have been developed to ensure the accuracy of transactions and processes.

Technology has also had a significant influence on how sports products are bought and sold. Organizations such as professional sports teams, collegiate athletic programs, and sporting goods manufacturers sell their products over the Internet, place orders online, and market their products via Web sites. Electronic commerce has dramatically changed the sport industry. With the increase in ticket sales via the Web, the threat of counterfeit tickets also arises. One recent innovation in ticket sales is the use of bar-coded tickets. Most large sports facilities today use handheld bar-code scanning devices to permit entry. This system helps minimize counterfeiting and has also reduced costs for sports organizations by permitting customers to print their own tickets. Sports managers must ensure that their systems can track these sales effectively. Auditors must be able to attest to the accuracy of these transactions and the financial statements that result from them.

In addition to the problems caused by viruses, computer-related crime is increasing at a rapid pace. Several major computer-related extortion cases have occurred in the last decade when hackers broke into retail Web sites and stole credit card numbers, threatening to publish the numbers if they were not paid a specified amount. Customers will purchase with confidence only if a Web site protects financial transactions.

Technology has greatly changed the landscape of auditing and will continue to do so. A successful sports manager must be prepared to use new technologies not only to make money but also to effectively track these funds.

BENEFITS OF INDEPENDENT AUDITS

Companies derive several significant benefits from undergoing periodic independent audits, including societal benefits. Poor decisions that businesses make based on inaccurate financial information can have a negative effect on a society at large. Resources may be mistakenly allotted to inefficient or unworthy projects, thereby decreasing overall economic productivity. Additionally, individual and institutional investors may make poor decisions in selecting investment options. In most instances, investors use corporate financial statements in their investment decision-making processes. Although the positive effect of independent audits on individual businesses is obvious, the societal benefit of audits must not be overlooked. Accurate financial information about businesses is vital for maintaining an efficient economy. Holmes and Burns (1979) separated the benefits from accurate independent auditing into three categories based on who derives the benefit:

1. Benefits primarily for auditees

- Independent audits provide credibility and reliability to financial statements.
- Audits dissuade management and employees from committing acts of fraud.
- Audited financial statements lessen the likelihood of government audits by ensuring that the basis for the preparation of tax returns and other financial documents is accurate.
- Audited financial statements increase investor or creditor confidence and broaden the sources of outside financing.
- Independent audits uncover errors in the auditee's financial records, which may lead to the recovery of lost revenue or may decrease costs.
- Independent audits ensure that the business is consistently following stated policies and procedures.

2. Benefits primarily for other members of the business community

- Audited financial statements give vendors and other creditors a credible basis for making decisions about extending credit.
- Audited statements are a credible basis on which potential and current investors can evaluate investment and management performance.
- Audited statements provide insurance companies a credible and accurate basis for settling claims for insurance-covered losses.
- Audited statements provide labor unions and the auditee an objective basis on which to settle disputes over wages and fringe benefits.
- Audited statements provide the buyer and seller a basis for negotiating the terms for the sale or merger of business entities.

3. Benefits primarily for government entities and the legal community

- Government agencies gain additional assurance concerning the dependability and accuracy of tax returns and financial reports.
- Independent audits of financial statements from public interest organizations such as banks and public utilities provide government agencies with an independent means to focus their special examination resources.
- Audited financial statements give the legal community an independent basis for settling bankruptcy actions.

AUDITING PROCESS

This section of the chapter covers the process of conducting an audit. The first step is to select the appropriate auditor. After describing the selection process, we discuss how a business should prepare for an audit, the various types of audits that can be undertaken, and the auditor's report.

SELECTING THE AUDITOR

As stated earlier, an independent auditor plays a vital role in managing a sport business' finances. Despite any temptation to do so, the auditee should not influence the independent character of the audit. The auditor's report attests to the accuracy of financial statements. Creditors and stockholders have more

Profits and Losses for Pro Sports Teams

Are the revenues and expenses of professional sports teams accurate? To obtain concessions from municipalities or labor unions, numerous teams and leagues are claiming they are losing money. The accuracy of these numbers was called into question a number of times in the early 21st century in both baseball and hockey. Before the 2004-2005 NHL lockout, the league owners claimed they had lost $224 million the previous year. *Forbes* magazine, however, analyzed NHL finances and concluded that the league lost only $96 million. When former Securities and Exchange Commission chairman Arthur Levitt Jr. audited the financial records for the 2002-2003 season, he concluded that the league lost $273 million. Thus, the question must be asked: Who is correct? It should be noted that the NHL owners did not cooperate with *Forbes* in their research, and therefore unofficial financial records were used to determine that the NHL lost only $96 million. The players' union, relying on the *Forbes* number, concluded that the league was not negotiating in good faith and that the NHL was not as financially distressed as the league owners claimed. The problem with this stance is that even if one uses the Forbes numbers, the league was still losing almost $100 million a year.

Major League Baseball faced similar auditing-related concerns when Nelson Doubleday accused Bud Selig of allegedly conspiring with a former Andersen consultant to manufacture "phantom losses" for the New York Mets. Doubleday claimed that MLB wanted to devalue his ownership share because another co-owner was trying to buy him out. If the shares could be devalued, the co-owner may have been able to buy out Doubleday at a reduced price. Before that situation, MLB had another financial controversy when 14 former limited partners of the Montreal Expos sued Commissioner Selig, claiming he conspired to dilute their investment in the team ("Doubleday," 2002).

confidence in organizations that have audits completed by credible auditing firms. Therefore, the selection of an auditor is very important. A business should seek out an auditor who has experience in the industry in question. Although audits can be expensive, with typical audits for medium-sized firms costing more than $100,000, a specialized auditor in the sport industry is well worth the investment. The top accounting firms such as PricewaterhouseCoopers, Deloitte, KPMG, and other larger accounting firms have departments that specialize in the sport industry.

Each industry has its own unique characteristics that a specialized auditor can understand without needing to do as much research as other auditors would. For example, professional sports teams have several unique financial traits. Under federal tax laws, new team owners are permitted to depreciate the value of player contracts over five years. The players are treated as a capital investment similar to plants and equipment. Also, the pay structure for players can be complex because of signing bonuses, performance incentives, and deferred payments that are not seen in other industries. A professional team should seek out an auditor with experience in analyzing these types of financial documents. It would be easy for an inexperienced auditor to make an error that would call into question the accuracy of the team's financial statements.

© Bongarts/Getty Images

By analyzing the process and offering unbiased feedback, the independant auditor makes sure businesses are playing by the rules.

Public companies need to meet certain requirements as they select their auditing firms. The New York Stock Exchange requires its member corporations to establish a committee to select their auditing firms (Holmes & Burns, 1979). This committee must consist of nonemployees of the corporation. Most firms elect to have their boards of directors choose their independent auditors. The goal of not having management select the auditing firm is to ensure objectivity from the audit. The possibility of fraud within the auditing process would be increased if management selected the auditing firm.

PREPARING FOR THE AUDITOR

After selecting the auditing firm, a business must prepare for the audit. An auditor needs specific types of information in order to do her job. The following are some of the organizational materials that should be collected in preparation for the auditor.

- *Internally prepared documents.* These include operating documents such as sales invoices, purchase orders, general ledgers, payroll records, receiving forms, and other standard accounting worksheets.
- *Externally prepared documents.* These include documents such as bank statements, loan documents, and vendor statements.
- *Nonfinancial records.* Auditors often need corporate information that is not financial. Documents in this category include articles of incorporation, minutes of organizational meetings, past internal or independent auditors' reports, organizational charts, and job descriptions.

Additionally, independent auditors may need to physically verify assets. For example, they may need to see direct evidence of assets such as inventory, equipment, computers, and office furniture. The auditor may walk through an office to verify that the organization has items such as chairs, desks, and computers that it claims as assets in financial statements.

An auditor may also wish to obtain oral testimony from management, employees, or customers to ensure that the organizational information is accurate. Arrangements should be made so that these people are available to the independent auditor. In general, there are no problems with oral testimony unless there are misstatements—accidental or fraudulent.

The audit examines various business segments. We now focus on the areas of operation that are most important for a sports organization when it is undergoing an internal or independent audit.

CASH AUDITING

For many sport businesses, cash is the most important current asset. For example, WHBC may bring in a high level of cash on a daily basis through collecting user fees. Businesses or organizations such as the University of Milford that produce a sports event also have a high level of cash transactions. Items such as game tickets, team merchandise, and concessions are largely sold through cash transactions. Although customers are using credit cards at a higher rate than in the past, sports organizations such as college athletic departments, professional teams, and sports facilities must develop systems to control cash.

Unfortunately, cash is also the asset most susceptible to theft and fraud. It is easily transferable, liquid, and difficult to trace. Countless cases of fraud involving cash occur each year. In one example, a small business with two store locations had an employee who was responsible for both reconciling the organization's bank accounts and making the daily deposits. Each location would submit its daily cash amounts to the employee along with a completed bank deposit slip. The employee was then responsible for depositing the cash at the bank. This might appear to be an efficient and logical system. However, it also made cash fraud quite easy. The employee simply kept a portion of the daily cash receipts, completed a new deposit slip for the decreased amount, and deposited that amount. Since the employee did the **account reconciliation**, no one noticed that not all of the cash made it into the company bank account. On paper, everything seemed to be in order. In reality, the employee was keeping thousands of dollars in company revenue. The person was eventually caught when another employee found an old deposit slip in the garbage. That employee notified the owner of the business, and the fraud was uncovered (Colbert & Bolton, 1998).

The role of the auditor is to ensure that cash assets are not overstated and that financial statements accurately represent the cash level. The usual method is to make sure that cash that should have been collected has been both collected and accurately recorded. For example, an audit of SMC involves matching the daily sales receipts from the cash registers with the cash deposit slips. All cash that is received through sales should be deposited into the business' bank account. Only the level of cash necessary for daily operations should be left in the cash register. Meigs et al. (1982) make the following suggestions for handling daily cash receipts:

- No single employee should be responsible for handling cash transactions from beginning to end. For example, the person who operates the cash register should not also oversee the daily cash deposits to the bank.

- Cash handling should be separated from cash recording and deposit. This can be accomplished by having one person open all letters and process all checks. Another person could be responsible for depositing the checks. Thus, each party can independently examine the cash or checks to be deposited to verify the amounts.

- Cash receipts should be centralized. For example, a sports facility may have several different locations where game tickets are sold. A system should be developed to track the cash activities at each location, and the cash should ultimately be collected in one location. A lack of cash centralization increases the number of people handling the cash and the likelihood of theft.

- Cash receipts should be deposited on a daily basis. Cash should not be left in the place of business for more than one day. The only exception may be a small amount of **petty cash** that is necessary for emergency or relatively small purchases.

- When possible, make all payments by check, credit card, or debit card. Checks, credit cards, and debit cards are easier to track and minimize the likelihood of theft.

Another important responsibility for the auditor is to examine the auditee's management of cash balances to ensure operational efficiency. In some instances, a business may have too much cash on hand. An auditor may recommend that the organization reinvest the cash back into the business or invest in other opportunities. Conversely, the auditor may find that the organization has relatively low cash balances. It can be troublesome if the business does not have enough cash on hand to meet short-term debt obligations such as accounts payable to vendors or suppliers.

INVENTORY AUDITING

Another large asset for most sport businesses is inventory. Chapter 13 covers inventory- and production-related issues. Apart from its conventional meaning, inventory can also be defined as products and materials that have a life of less than one year. For some sport businesses, inventories are not their greatest asset. For professional teams, whose primary assets are the players, inventory exists, but it is not as valuable as the players. Minor league players might be considered inventory, but they have little value until they make it to the highest professional ranks. The value of a minor league team stems from its goodwill. Recall that goodwill is any value over the team's book value that others might pay in order to purchase the team. If the team's assets are worth $1 million but someone is willing to pay $2 million to purchase it, then the team has $1 million in goodwill. The goodwill is value inherent in the minor league team, which might be based on the fact that there are only a limited number of minor league teams, that the team has a good relationship with a major league team, or that the facility the team plays in is brand new and has numerous amenities.

Although it is very difficult to calculate goodwill, auditing items such as inventory and other assets can help establish a potential value range for goodwill. For example, through auditing the inventory a team might discover boxes of old uniforms that might have limited monetary value, but when used as a promotional item in an old-timers game, they can generate significant value based on the goodwill associated with the team's history. Inventory auditing will not determine a team's goodwill, but it can be used in conjunction with other valuation techniques to develop a more accurate value.

Inventory auditing is the process of determining exactly what inventory exists and the inventory's value. Tracking entails the process of identifying where inventory might be located and the inventory's value. Inventory counting, on the other hand, refers to the process of identifying exactly how many units of a given item exist in inventory.

Running Away With the Kids' Money

The former treasurer of the Southern Connecticut Youth Hockey League was accused of embezzling $21,462 from the league over a six-month period. She allegedly took checks for the league and deposited them in her own account. She left her position and was responsible for training the next treasurer. However, she allegedly delayed giving him the records, and when they were finally turned over, there were many accounts that were delinquent and for which registration checks had been issued but never deposited (Leo, 2000).

Internal control is a key to successfully managing inventory. A sports manager must develop a system that tracks all inventory from the time it is purchased to the time it is distributed to consumers or users. Inventory must be purchased, received, recorded, stored, and distributed. Management is responsible for developing internal systems to efficiently perform all these operations (Whittington & Pany, 2006). At any point in this process an item might get lost, broken, stolen, or become obsolete, and only through auditing can a company truly know the status of most of their assets.

An accurate inventory count, whether of retail goods or materials used for production, leads to increased efficiency. Technology has been a key in improving systems of internal control. Computerized systems allow managers to track inventory quickly. This is especially helpful to businesses such as SMC that are involved in the production of sport-related goods. Inventory is a large component of their total assets.

Two strategies in particular can be used to improve inventory control and also make the process of auditing, both internal and independent, much simpler. The first strategy is to have one centralized location where inventory is received and distributed (Holmes & Burns, 1979). For example, a concessionaire may be responsible for overseeing a dozen or more sales locations in a major sports facility. The concessionaire must ensure that each location has the products that will be prepared and sold. Inventory tracking is more accurate if all products are distributed from one central area. This allows management greater control over all products.

A second strategy is to develop a computer scanning system to track inventory (see chapter 13). Sporting goods stores are an example of a business that typically uses a computer scanning system. In most sporting goods stores, the products are bar coded. The computerized bar codes, usually placed on products by the manufacturer, are used to track material, determine its availability, and facilitate the sale. This type of integrated system allows management to determine exact inventory levels. When stock level is depleted, management has the information and can order more inventories from suppliers. Bar codes are another example of internal controls.

Major manufacturing plants also use computer tracking systems. Intermediate goods are maintained in some type of storage facility until they are required for the manufacturing process. Most often, computer systems are used to track when these intermediate goods are received, stored, and distributed to the production line.

With respect to auditing, technology and computerization have made it much easier to ensure that financial statements report inventory accurately. Computer programs can quickly produce reports on the types, amounts, and condition of inventory. Another important aspect of inventory auditing is the determination of fair value. An auditor must base the value of inventory on its quantity, quality, and condition. In addition to examining computer-generated inventory reports, the auditor may also physically locate inventory within the organization. Last, operational audits may lead to recommendations that will improve the efficiency of inventory control systems.

PLANT, PROPERTY, AND EQUIPMENT AUDITING

Plant, property, and equipment are similar to inventory in that they are physical assets. The difference is that plant, property, and equipment are physical assets that have a productive life greater than one year. Examples of plant, property, and equipment for a collegiate athletic program such as the University of Milford are computers; facilities; and equipment such as goalposts, motor vehicles, and playing fields.

In the process of auditing, the auditor ascertains that all plant, property, and equipment that are listed as assets actually exist. This is usually not difficult for assets such as land, buildings, and heavy machinery. Often the difficult task is determining a fair value for these assets, especially with assets such as land that may fluctuate in value over time. Also, depreciation must be factored into the determination of fair value for plant, property, and equipment.

Similar to the situation with inventory, bar codes are often used to track equipment such as computers, copiers, and office furniture. Bar codes are usually placed on these items to clearly identify the owners. Specialized bar-coded stickers that are nonremovable reduce the ability of a potential thief to hide the item's true ownership. An auditor may periodically visit various organizational locations to ensure that items such as computers are actually where they are supposed to be located.

PAYROLL AUDITING

All sport businesses, regardless of size, scope, and mission, have one thing in common. They all have employees who are paid a wage in return for their labor. The ultimate result of a payroll system is that each employee receives a paycheck. The process of arriving at this final result can be complex. First, a system must be established to track the correct amount to be paid. For employees paid on an hourly basis, a system must be developed to accurately determine the number of hours worked. Employees may be required to fill out weekly time cards or use computerized time card machines. Payroll auditing is the process of tracking employee compensation to ensure accuracy. It determines if employees are working too much overtime or whether personnel costs are in line with budgetary projections.

Computerized hand scanners are a new technology that has made auditing employee activity simpler and that can improve the accuracy and reliability of the payroll process. The system requires making a handprint of all employees. A machine is then installed that identifies the handprint of each employee as she arrives for and departs from work. The computerized system can then calculate the total number of hours each employee works. Although such systems may be expensive to install, they can dramatically decrease the probability of payroll fraud. It is impossible for employees to fraudulently have other people clock in for them or fill out false time cards. The system also ensures that employees receive an accurate amount of pay. Other technology also exists to accomplish accurate tracking, such as swipe cards, retina scanners, and computerized punch systems that can track personnel activity.

In addition to determining the amount of gross pay, payroll preparation involves calculating income tax deductions; Social Security payments; and deductions for benefits such as retirement, union dues, and health insurance. An efficient and accurate system must be used for determining these payments. Failure to make payments for items such as federal or state income taxes will quickly lead to government audits.

When possible, the various payroll duties should be handled by different people. For example, within SMC's payroll department one person should not be responsible for the timekeeping system and the determination of employee wages. It would be very easy for this person to fraudulently overpay employees.

With respect to distributing paychecks, a system must be in place to ensure that employees receive their own proper paychecks. One central location should be used to distribute all paychecks. Also, employees should be required to sign a document verifying that they have received their checks. In large organizations, employees should be required to show proper identification. Additionally, unclaimed paychecks should not be left in the business' offices for an extended period of time. They are subject to possible theft if left in the office. The paychecks should be deposited in a special bank account for unclaimed wages. To reconcile the firm's accounts, efforts should be made to distribute the unclaimed checks to the people to whom they were issued.

Most large sports organizations now require employees to have a checking or savings account with a bank or other financial institution. The employees' pay is electronically wired to these accounts on payday. This system limits the likelihood of any type of fraud since no physical paycheck is produced. Employees are then issued paper receipts of their pay and deductions, or these records are accessible through a secure online computerized system.

Last, at no time should employees be paid with cash. It is very difficult to track cash. An employee may claim that he did not receive his pay and request additional money. Also, there is little documentation associated with cash distributions. This makes it very difficult to accurately audit a payroll department. Checks are much easier to track because the employer receives the canceled checks and the withdrawals appear on the business' bank statements.

RECEIVING THE AUDITOR'S REPORT

For public corporations, the auditor is required to submit an independent auditor's report that is totally unbiased. Auditors usually provide a report when completing an audit for private corporations, non-profit organizations, and government agencies. Of the several types of auditing reports, the standard unqualified auditor's report is the most common (see p. 298) (Arens & Loebbecke, 2006). The report is unqualified if no information is lacking and nothing that differs from the standard accounting practices set forth by the Auditing Standards Board is found. The standard unqualified auditor's report has seven parts:

1. *Report title.* Auditing standards require that a report have a title that includes the word *independent.*

2. *Audit report address.* The report is usually addressed to the auditee, its board of directors, or stockholders.

3. *Introductory paragraph.* This paragraph explains management's role and responsibilities as they apply to the auditor (i.e., that management helped provide documentation or access to facilities). It also lists all the financial statements that were audited and the time periods of those statements.

4. *Scope paragraph.* This paragraph describes the nature of the audit and what the auditor did in the audit. It also outlines the business areas examined by the auditor.

5. *Opinion paragraph.* This last paragraph states the auditor's opinion. Within this section, the auditor attests to the accuracy of the financial information provided by the auditee.

6. *Name of the certified public accountant's firm.*

7. *Audit report date.*

The other possible audit opinions are as follows:

- Qualified opinion
- Adverse opinion
- Disclaimer of opinion

Although the use of qualified reports is common, these reports are being examined more carefully in the wake of the recent accounting scandals involving Enron, Tyco, and WorldCom. A report is qualified because information is lacking or because other problems prevented the auditor from giving a more complete report. In a qualified opinion, the auditor will state that the company has departures from standard practices or perhaps that the company did not give him full access to necessary documents. Companies, auditors, and the government are all thinking about how to develop appropriate reports that contain as much additional information as possible to move the final report from qualified to unqualified status.

Example of a Standard Unqualified Independent Auditor's Report for a Sport Organization

Can you identify each of the seven parts of an auditor's report?

Brady, Kelsey, Adams, Delong, and Crimmins, PC
Certified Public Accountants
Box 324
Noelle Trunfio Park Central
Philadelphia, PA 18360
312-555-4433

Independent Auditor's Report

To the Stockholders
Sport Manufacturing Company Diversified Sports Unlimited

We have audited the balance sheets of Sport Manufacturing Company Diversified Sports Unlimited as of July 31, 2007 and 2006, and the related statements of retained earnings, income, and cash flows for the years then ended. These financial statements are the responsibility of Sport Manufacturing Company Diversified Sports Unlimited's management. Our responsibility is to express an opinion on these financial statements based on our audits.

We conducted our audits in accordance with generally accepted auditing standards. Those standards require that we perform the audit to obtain assurance about whether the financial statements are free of material misstatement. An audit includes examining, on a test basis, evidence supporting the amounts and disclosures in the financial statements. An audit also includes assessing the accounting principles used and significant estimates made by management, as well as evaluating the overall financial statement presentation. We believe that our audits provide a reasonable basis for our opinion.

In our opinion, the financial statements referred to above present fairly, in all material respects, the financial position of Sport Manufacturing Company Diversified Sports Unlimited as of July 31, 2007 and 2006, and the results of its operations and its cash flows for the years then ended in conformity with generally accepted accounting principles.

Brady, Kelsey, Adams, Delong, and Crimmins, PC, CPAs
December 10, 2008

DETECTING FRAUD

Financial fraud can be a major problem for a sport business. Fraud can take many different forms. It can be as simple as theft of merchandise by a clerk in a sporting goods store or the filing of false time cards by employees in a sporting goods manufacturing plant. Inventory and payroll auditing are two of the types of auditing overviewed in this chapter that can help detect these types of fraud.

Fraud can also involve complex schemes to embezzle millions of dollars from a sport business. Later in the chapter, we look at the case of John Spano. Spano committed bank fraud in an attempt to acquire a professional hockey franchise. In part because of poor auditing of financial records submitted by Spano, several banks and the NHL were led to believe that Spano was a highly successful businessman. Ultimately, this was found to be incorrect. But Spano came very close to committing one of the largest frauds in sport history.

Fraud does not always mean theft. Managers may also prepare inaccurate financial statements in an effort to misrepresent the financial position of an organization. In 1997, management of Paragon Construction International, a subsidiary of Golden Bear Golf, underrepresented its losses by more than $20 million. Management allegedly hid expenses and falsified records to conceal poor financial performance (Mullen, 1998). Shareholders and bondholders were injured when they made financial decisions about Golden Bear based on these fraudulent financial statements. The fraudulent acts were eventually uncovered, and Golden Bear refiled its financial statements. The new statements showed that the company had lost eight times the amount earlier reported. Stock in the company was eventually delisted from the NASDAQ stock exchange, and a class action lawsuit was filed on behalf of investors and creditors. In December 1999, Golden Bear settled the lawsuit and paid investors $0.75 for each of the 2.7 million shares of outstanding stock. The money was paid by Golden Bear Golf, its insurance provider, and its auditor ("Golden Bear," 1999).

Fraud can be a serious financial problem for a small sport business with limited resources, such as WHBC. It is not easy for these businesses to recover from fraud. One incident of fraud could lead to bankruptcy, dissolution, or both. Additionally, small businesses are susceptible to fraud because employees usually have multiple duties, and internal control is difficult. Often there are many employees who have access to assets such as cash, inventory, and office equipment. However, steps can be taken to minimize

the likelihood of fraud. Colbert and Bolton (1998) make the following recommendations for small businesses:

- *Segregation of duties.* Duties such as depositing cash and reconciling bank accounts should be given to different staff members. Also, different employees should complete duties such as preparing and signing checks. This will allow for a system of checks and balances so that no single person has total unfettered control.

- *Inventory of assets.* To prevent stolen assets such as plant, property, and equipment, a business should undergo periodic inventory checks. Each item listed in the financial statements as plant, property, and equipment should be physically located. In addition, the financial statements should be cross-checked to ensure that every listed asset is physically present.

- *Mandated vacations.* Each employee should use at least a portion of her allotted vacation time each year. It is also suggested that vacation days be taken as a block. This is an effective way to detect fraud. Some fraud cases, especially with cash, occur on a recurring or daily basis. It is much easier to detect the fraud if the employee is away from the business for an extended period of time.

- *Analytical procedures.* Simple analytical procedures such as tracking the daily deposits, weekly sales, and monthly sales totals may be enough to uncover some fraud.

- *Practical considerations.* For a small business, the first four recommendations may be difficult to implement. Employees may not want to take their vacations in a block, or there may not be enough employees to allow segregation of all duties. In addition to these recommendations, smaller companies can take some practical steps to minimize fraud. A small business owner may request that his bank send the business' bank statements to his home address instead of to the business. This allows the owner the opportunity to review deposit slips, bank statements, and canceled checks before other employees have access to them. This procedure not only may allow the owner to uncover fraud but also may deter employees from committing fraud.

One of the most infamous cases of fraud in the sport industry occurred in 1997. John Spano, a 33-year-old Dallas businessman, purchased the New York Islanders professional hockey team. He agreed to pay John Pickett, the previous team owner, $165 million. At the time, Spano claimed to have $55 million in available assets and a net worth of more than $230 million. Spano stated that he had a $107 million trust fund, $52 million in Treasury bills, and $40 million in a money market account. He also claimed to have made millions of dollars in the South African stock market (Ranalli, 1997).

To finance the deal, Spano obtained an $80 million loan from Boston's Fleet Financial Group. One of the largest lenders in the sport industry, Fleet had financed deals for teams such as the Baltimore Ravens, Washington Redskins, Phoenix Coyotes, and Los Angeles Lakers (Munroe, 1997). Unfortunately, Fleet was so enthusiastic about lending funds to Spano that it failed to correctly confirm Spano's net worth. As Fleet would later learn, Spano's actual net worth was less than $2 million.

Spano began by lying about his personal wealth and falsifying financial documents in order to obtain approval for a bank loan from the Fleet Financial Group. As part of the team purchase, on April 7, 1997, Spano was required to make a $24.4 million payment that was to cover the down payment for the team acquisition as well as interest prepayments on the bank loan. Spano did not make this payment, but he did give the bank a wire-transfer number as proof that the funds were available. However, the wire-transfer number was a fake (Ranalli, 1997).

Shortly after the missed payment, the NHL, John Pickett, and Fleet Financial Group started to question Spano's actual net worth. Federal investigators quickly uncovered Spano's scheme. Spano had begun by allegedly misrepresenting his financial wealth to Joseph Lynch, an executive for Detroit-based Comerica Bank. On the basis of financial statements supplied by Spano, Lynch attested to Spano's claimed net worth of over $230 million. However, Lynch did not obtain independent verification of the financial documents supplied by Spano. Spano then used the support from Comerica Bank to secure the $80 million loan from Fleet Financial Group ("Rumblings," 1997).

Spano's trouble began in earnest on April 7, 1997, when he was to make the $24.4 million payment to Fleet and Pickett. Obviously, he did not have the necessary funds. It was at that time that he provided the fake wire-transfer number to Fleet. In addition, Fleet Bank received a fax letter from Lynch verifying Spano's ability to make the $24.4 million payment. Federal investigators learned that the letter was a forgery. Spano had written the letter and reprogrammed his fax machine to make it appear that the letter had originated from Lynch's office. Investigators knew it was a forgery because it bore marks that were identical to those on a fax machine in one of Spano's companies ("Rumblings," 1997).

In July 1997, federal authorities pressed bank fraud charges against Spano. At the time, a Long Island newspaper reported that Spano was living in the Cayman Islands. However, Spano eventually surrendered to federal authorities and was charged with six counts of fraud in three different states—Texas, Massachusetts, and New York. If he had been convicted of all charges, Spano would have faced up to 60 years in prison ("Business Briefcase," 1997). After considerable negotiations between the federal government and defense attorneys, Spano agreed to a plea bargain. He pleaded guilty to six counts of fraud, two each in Texas, Massachusetts, and New York. In January 1998, Spano was sentenced to all six counts in New York and faced up to 63 months in prison. At the time, there were still several ongoing federal investigations related to alleged mail and wire fraud committed by Spano in New York and Massachusetts (Chase, 1998).

The fallout from Spano's attempt to financially misrepresent himself was considerable. On July 20, 1997, David Splaine resigned his position as senior vice president for Fleet Financial Group. Splaine was the loan officer who had approved the $80 million loan to Spano. Splaine had failed to accurately confirm Spano's real net worth (Vennochi, 1997). In addition, investigators for Comerica Bank learned that Joseph Lynch had been a guest of Spano's at a four-star hotel on Long Island at a cost of over $2,000. The bank had clear policies stating that employees were not permitted to receive gifts, fees, or vacations from clients. In January 1998, Lynch resigned from his position with Comerica Bank ("Briefly," 1998).

As federal authorities further investigated Spano's business dealings, they uncovered several other acts of fraud. In one bizarre business deal, Spano formed a partnership with Lenco Holdings, a South African company. The partnership was formed to sell kitchen pots and pans. Spano informed Lenco that he had secured an order for the cookware from the Nordstrom department store chain. Spano then allegedly sent a fraudulent Nordstrom invoice to Lenco, and Lenco in turn sent Spano the cookware to deliver it to Nordstrom. However, Spano failed to pay the $1.9 million due to Lenco for the cookware. The location of the now infamous cookware is still unknown (Bedell, 1997).

Spano also owed more than $250,000 to a Dallas law firm that worked for him during his attempt to acquire the New York Islanders. In addition, Spano owed more than $2.4 million to two different Dallas investment companies for loans they had made to him (Bedell, 1997).

The case of John Spano is unique in the sport industry, in which there have been very few cases of financial fraud. However, as the professional sport industry becomes more profitable, the likelihood of financial fraud increases. The John Spano case served as a wake-up call for all professional sports leagues. As a result, the NHL and other leagues have placed a greater emphasis on verifying the financial position of prospective owners. Similar steps are now taken by MLB after a scandal involving the first owner of the Colorado Rockies. Owner Michael Monus, who was also chairman of Phar-Mor pharmacies, improperly used corporate assets to acquire sports teams. He funneled $10 million from Phar-Mor into a then fledgling and now defunct basketball league, World Basketball League (Schroeder & Schiller, 1992). Monus was convicted of a 109-count indictment, including charges of mail, wire, and bank fraud.

CONCLUSION

Financial statement auditing is the objective examination of financial statements that are prepared by an organization. An auditor examines these statements to determine if they have been prepared according to generally accepted accounting standards. Financial audits are important because they ensure the accuracy of financial statements and deter management and employees from committing theft and fraud. Audits also lend credibility to financial statements,

which can increase confidence on the part of other companies and investors. This makes it easier for businesses to work with investors and creditors. Last, accurate financial statements should lessen the possibility of government audits.

Two other types of audits are operational audits and compliance audits. Operational audits examine a business' policies and procedures to determine if they are appropriate and efficient. These audits can result in organizational changes that can affect a business' long-term efficiency and productivity. Compliance audits are undertaken to ensure that a business is adhering to rules and regulations established by an outside group such as a government agency. For example, any large employer in the United States must meet workplace regulations that have been developed by the Occupational Safety and Health Administration.

Technology has had a significant effect on auditing and financial operations in the sport industry over the past two decades. It allows businesses to quickly and efficiently process financial data and generate financial reports. Also, technology has been used to improve operational systems in areas such as payroll, inventory control, and accounting, which are critical to auditing. Last, technology has helped minimize fraud and theft.

CLASS DISCUSSION TOPICS

1. What are the two fundamental roles of auditing?

2. Provide three specific examples of how the operational efficiency of an organization may be improved through the use of internal audits.

3. How would you go about auditing the Smiths, Sport Manufacturing Company, the University of Milford, or the Stars of David?

4. How can you balance the need for making sure accounts are accurate and the need to allow individuals to work without the fear that someone is watching their every move?

5. Why is accuracy so important?

6. What are the primary benefits for an organization of using an independent auditor?

7. What are the advantages of using an independent auditor versus using an internal auditor?

8. Is it ethically correct to "permanently borrow" office supplies?

9. How would you approach someone if you thought that person had engaged in fraud?

10. Provide two examples of where advances made in technology have changed the manner in which audits occur.

17

EXIT STRATEGY

CHAPTER OBJECTIVES

After studying this chapter, you should be able to do the following:

- Describe the techniques that can help spot financial trouble.
- Understand how to reorganize a troubled business.
- Compare the types of bankruptcies available.
- Describe the process of selling a business.
- Calculate the value of a sport business.

At various times during a business' life cycle, the going may get tough. Bills may go unpaid, debtors may not pay accounts receivable on time, shipments may be late or get canceled, distributors may stop extending credit, or a host of other problems can force a business owner to think about various options. Such options are as diverse as the owners themselves. Some owners may just decide to transfer the business to a family member or a current business partner. Others may consider selling the company or just selling the assets. Still others may simply close shop or, worse, be *forced* to close shop. No matter what strategy or technique the owner ultimately applies, each has particular legal and financial ramifications that the individual needs to consider to avoid increasing financial obligations or to reduce potential costs.

When management is stretched to the point of no return, there is often a tendency to try to resolve immediate difficulties rather than examine long-term financial problems. Such short-term thinking can result in lost concessions, reduced bargaining power with creditors, or other long-term ramifications.

This chapter explains what to do at the point of no return. We start by examining red flags that might signal financial trouble. Next we discuss various options for dealing with financial problems, such as informal reorganization; informal liquidation; Chapter 7, 11, and 13 **bankruptcy**; involuntary bankruptcy; and removal of business assets. The chapter ends with an analysis of what is required to sell a business and how to determine the value of a business that is being sold.

RED FLAGS

Before deciding to terminate operations, a business needs to know when it is in trouble. Most businesses cannot just decide to close their doors; there are usually existing financial obligations such as accounts payable, long-term labor contracts, long-term lease obligations, repayment to equity investors, and debts. The decision to close is not an easy one, nor is it made without significant managerial forethought. Most executives take pride in their managerial skills and would not want to be remembered as the person who lost a business.

Luckily, a number of indicators can help signal financial trouble and provide adequate warning to an executive. For example, if orders start declining significantly, a business can examine the reasons and take corrective action to avoid losing market share. If a new competitor comes into the market with a more advanced and cheaper product, then the business needs to make adjustments to stay competitive. Key factors associated with business failures include economic weakness, industry downturns, poor location, too much debt, too little capital, and countless others. These concerns can lead to temporary cash flow problems that can often be worked out. However, sometimes the concerns indicate a permanent problem.

One sign of trouble is a lender's request for early repayment of a loan. A bank or other lender may call the loan under certain conditions; the primary reason is poor financial performance. If a sport business has been losing money steadily for several years, banks may feel uncomfortable with their loans and demand immediate repayment. The following are other conditions under which a bank might call a loan or not renew a line of credit (Broni, 1999):

- Loan covenants have been repeatedly violated.
- The bank is losing money on the relationship.
- New bank managers favor a different loan mix or institute new policies.
- The bank does not understand or is uncomfortable with the industry segment.
- The bank's credit exposure in the industry segment is too great.
- A loan guarantor's financial condition has deteriorated.
- The bank has lost faith in the business' management team.

If a bank or lending institution "pulls the plug," the business needs to establish a policy to deal with the lost cash. The first step is often to negotiate a short-term extension to try to resolve any problems or secure new funding. If the business is on strong financial ground, it might be easy to approach another bank. If a problem caused the bank to pull the funds, it might be worthwhile to ask the bank what the problem was. If the problem is one that can be fixed, such as untimely reporting, then the business owner can explain this to another potential lender and take measures to correct the problem.

If the business has assets, the assets could help secure needed funds. Asset-based loans, as the name implies, can be obtained on the basis of the existing inventory or accounts receivable. If the business owns a valuable asset such as buildings or land, these could be pledged as collateral to secure more funds. However, if these options are not available, the business might need to approach a commercial finance company that specializes in "unbankable" loans. Since these loans are riskier, they entail a higher interest rate. The business may also need to frequently report earnings in order to keep the lender abreast of financial conditions. However, once the business can show sustained success

Prolonged decreased attendance could be a sign that a sport business is failing.

and compliance with loan terms for one to two years, then usually the owner can apply again for conventional bank loans.

Losing a bank loan is just one sign that a business is in trouble. If the business cannot pull itself through the hard financial times, it may be necessary to resort to informal or formal attempts to satisfy debt holders. Debt holders can be satisfied through informal reorganization or liquidation, bankruptcy, removal of assets, or selling of the business.

INFORMAL REORGANIZATION

Informal reorganization allows a business to recover and reestablish itself after facing a temporary financial crisis. These voluntary plans in which all parties try to come to an agreement are often called "workouts." Workouts are successful only if the debtor is a good moral risk, if the debtor can show the ability to recover, and if the general business conditions are favorable for recovery (Brigham & Gapenski, 1994).

The informal reorganization process comprises extensions and composition. Extensions are extensions of the time allowed for repaying a debt. If a debt is owed and due in one year, an extension could be worked out for the borrower to repay the debt in two years instead. Composition is the process of asking to repay a lower amount. A debt holder would rather receive $900 from the company versus only $500 in bankruptcy proceedings from a $1,000 debt. Most often a workout involves a combination of these two methods.

Sport Manufacturing Company

If SMC owes several lenders $10 million, it might be possible to develop a workout in which the company pays 25% of the debt immediately and 20% a year for the next three years. Thus, in four years SMC will have repaid 85% of the original debt, and the debt will be discharged.

© Getty Images

Bouncing Dividend Checks

A common concern of companies facing bankruptcy is the elimination of existing credit lines. Lenders are hesitant to increase the amount the company owes since there is no guarantee they will get their money back. On the other hand, there is also the possibility that the additional funds will in fact save the business and allow for continued long-term profits for the creditor. Cutting off the credit line can cause significant hardships even if a company is not in bankruptcy.

In 1999 a major publicity blunder occurred when the paying agent for the nation's largest bicycle manufacturer, Huffy Corporation, announced that it would not honor the company's dividend checks. The company's lenders, including Bank One and BankAmerica, cut off funding on the unsecured lines of credit after Huffy defaulted on its credit agreement. Unfortunately, however, Huffy had already sent out dividend payments of $850,000, or about $0.085 for each of the 10 million outstanding shares, and the checks bounced ("Huffy Checks," 1999). Thus, when banks start cutting off funding, a red flag should go off about the business' financial stability.

Huffy's problem did not end there; the company filed for bankruptcy protection shortly thereafter. The company was delisted in August 2004, with several major problems such as the failure to manufacture their bikes overseas to reduce costs, poor acquisitions that stunted growth, and the inability to shed their image as a low-end bicycle manufacturer (Krantz, 2004). It should be noted that numerous smaller sport businesses write bad checks on a regular basis. Although some businesspeople do this on purpose to defraud, others are just trying to keep their businesses going and are hoping that a check is in the mail to cover the funds.

Even though lenders might not receive the entire amount they are owed, most lenders would be happy to recover 85% of the original loaned amount versus possibly nothing, or a much smaller amount, if the borrower goes bankrupt. Not all banks are willing to engage in workouts, but most understand the value of negotiating the best deal they can in order to receive the largest possible share of their initial loan. The lenders might demand interest payments during the payback period to help cover the extension and might also demand additional security, such as personal pledges or asset-backed pledges.

INFORMAL LIQUIDATION

Informal reorganization is effective if the company can turn around, but some companies cannot fix their problems. If the company's debt is larger than its net worth, the company will probably need to go through bankruptcy protection. However, if the company has more assets than debt, it is "worth more dead than alive." **Assignment** is the term used for the informal liquidation process. Lenders normally obtain a greater return through assignment than through bankruptcy. That is why lenders should focus on encouraging informal reorganization or liquidation rather than trying to force a company into bankruptcy.

BANKRUPTCY PROTECTION

Bankruptcy is the primary technique used by business owners when they are facing mounting obligations and do not have the resources to finance continued operations. The U.S. bankruptcy laws were first passed in 1898. The laws were developed to prevent a creditor from racing to the courthouse against debtors. Before the bankruptcy laws, creditors would make a mad dash to the courthouse in an effort to be the first to file so that they could establish a higher repayment priority over subsequent filers. The bankruptcy laws are designed to give all creditors with equal standing (secured and unsecured creditors) the right to be put into a common pool, with each creditor having the same rights. All secured creditors are entitled to have their obligations repaid first with the sale of the secured assets. The unsecured creditors would then together receive proportional repayments of their loans based on what moneys remain after the secured creditors are paid.

Bankruptcy petitions hit a new high in 1988 at 1.44 million. That number declined 8.5% to 1.3 million petitions in 1999. Personal filings, which account for most bankruptcy petitions, declined 8.3%, while business filings declined 14.6% between 1998 and 1999 (Dreazen, 2000). The numbers rose sharply in 2005 before the new laws that make bankruptcy filing more difficult took effect. An all-time high of 1.78 million petitions were filed in 2005, but the numbers dropped

37.6% to 1.1 million in 2006. A majority of the cases filed were no-business cases, with 34,222 business filings in 2005 and 27,333 business filings in 2006. Most of the filings are Chapter 7 (personal liquidation) cases, with 833,147 in 2006. That was followed by Chapter 13 (personal debt reorganization) filings totaling 272,937; Chapter 11 (business) at 6,003; and Chapter 12 (family farmers), with only 376 cases in 2006 ("Bankruptcy Filings Decline," 2006).

There are 291 bankruptcy courts serving 90 judicial districts throughout the United States (Brigham & Gapenski, 1994). Although the newspapers do not typically report smaller bankruptcies, several major sport-related bankruptcies occurred in the past several years. Some of the highly publicized petitions include those of Starter Corporation, Just For Feet, and the Pittsburgh Penguins.

In 1999, Starter faced a major creditor that felt uncomfortable with the company's debt and called the debt as a result. Starter, which had been the premiere licensed apparel company for many years, was unable to secure additional funds and was forced to seek bankruptcy protection. The company's assets were liquidated, and the bank was able to obtain approximately 90% of its funds. However, Starter pursued litigation because the bank pulled its debt right before the peak sales season. Starter had paid for inventory early in the year, and the debt would have been paid after the primary sales period in the fourth quarter (Sack & Nadim, 2002). The case was later settled without any admission of guilt or wrongdoing.

Just For Feet developed a unique bankruptcy plan to try to survive. The company faced bankruptcy protection after expanding too quickly through acquisitions. In the second quarter of 1999, the company posted $25.9 million in losses compared with net income of $8 million the previous year. The financial hardships were forcing the shoe retailer to close 85

of its 362 stores. Just For Feet had $200 million of 11% senior subordinate notes due in 2009 and other unsecured creditors. A senior **subordinate debt** is a loan secured by a general claim on a company's assets and is repaid after all secured debts have been paid. These holders were to receive 100% of the common stocks in a newly reorganized company emerging from the shell of the former Just For Feet. The former shareholders would lose their shares and in exchange receive warrants allowing them to purchase up to 10% of the new company's shares ("Just For Feet," 1999). In 2000, Footstar purchased Just For Feet's major assets, including its name.

The Bankruptcy Reform Act of 1978 produced the bankruptcy system utilized through 2005. Major reforms went into effect on October 17, 2005, with regard to who can file for Chapter 7 (personal debt liquidation) or Chapter 13 (personal debt reorganization) bankruptcy. The new laws make filing for bankruptcy harder and more time consuming. Under the new law, all debtors need to get credit counseling before they can file a bankruptcy case ("New Bankruptcy Law," 2005). All potential filers must complete their counseling with an agency approved by the U.S. Trustee's office. Unlike in previous years, some filers with higher incomes will not be allowed to use Chapter 7 (which extinguished almost all debts owed), but will instead have to repay at least some of their debt under Chapter 13.

Filers will have to measure their current monthly income against the median income for families of comparable size in their home states. Under the previous law, monthly income was income at the time of the claim. The new law focuses on a filer's average income over the six months before the application for bankruptcy. If the filer's income is less than or equal to the median income, he can file for Chapter 7. If it is more than the median the filer must pass "the means

Players With Financial Problems

Sammy Sosa may be hitting home runs, but his charity is not. The Sammy Sosa Charitable Foundation in the Dominican Republic was pushed to the brink of bankruptcy through mismanagement. Sosa's major contribution was an office building. The charity was established to benefit victims of hurricane George in 1998, but only $82,842 was allocated to relief supplies. An article in *Fortune* magazine highlighted various improprieties including failure of tenants to pay rent, the use of funds to buy Sosa's brother a sports car, and expenses of $2,000 a month for storing relief supplies in a Miami warehouse ("Sosa's Charity," 2000).

Numerous athletes have faced financial problems, from agents squandering money to simply spending too much. Athletes who have filed for bankruptcy protection include Mike Tyson in 2003, Riddick Bowe in 2005, and former Detroit Red Wing Darren McCarty in 2006. These are only some of the athletes who have found themselves in financial trouble and needed help.

test," another requirement of the new law, in order to file for Chapter 7.

Some filers sell their possessions to pay off their debts. Under the new laws, filers must value their property at the replacement cost if purchased from a retail vendor, taking into account the property's age and condition. Under the old bankruptcy law, what property debtors were allowed to keep was determined by the laws of the state where they lived (as long as they lived there for at least three months). Under the new law, filers must live in a state for at least two years before filing in order to use that state's exemption laws. This law prevents forum shopping, with potential filers moving to an area just to protect their assets from legitimate debt obligations. Even if someone qualifies for bankruptcy, finding a lawyer to represent her might be difficult. The new law puts more responsibility on the lawyer, including vouching for the accuracy of all the information their clients provide them. More time is needed, which will lead to higher legal fees ("New Bankruptcy Law," 2005).

The bankruptcy code contains nine chapters, but the chapters are not numbered consecutively. Chapters 1, 3, and 5 contain general provisions; Chapter 9 applies to municipalities declaring bankruptcy; Chapter 12 deals with family-owned farms; and Chapter 15 establishes a system of trusts to administer bankruptcy proceedings. Three primary bankruptcy options are available to debtors to obtain court protection from creditors, depending on the existing circumstances; these are provided for in Chapters 7, 11, and 13.

CHAPTER 7 BANKRUPTCY

Chapter 7 bankruptcies entail a procedure for the orderly liquidation of the debtor's assets to repay creditors based on a priority established by statute. A trustee is appointed to gather and liquidate assets and then distribute the proceeds to creditors.

One of the many benefits associated with having a trustee to administer the bankruptcy estate is the power the trustee can wield. A trustee can invalidate a transaction made by the debtor if the trustee believes the transaction was preferential or fraudulent. Thus, if the owner of the Stars of David pays her son-in-law $50,000 for some consulting work two weeks before the team declares bankruptcy, the trustee could invalidate the payment if the son-in-law in fact did not do anything.

Chapter 7 is designed to make sure the debtor does not engage in fraud, provide for an equitable distribution of the debtor's assets among the creditors, and allow the debtor to clean the debts and start from scratch. Distribution of the assets is based on preference. Preference is allocated from the most- to the least-secured creditors such that assets are distributed in the following order (Brigham & Gapenski, 1994):

1. Proceeds of sold items pledged for a lien or mortgage to which secured creditors are entitled
2. Trustee-incurred costs associated with administering the bankrupt business
3. Expenses that were incurred after an involuntary case had been filed but before a trustee was appointed
4. Wages due to workers earned within three months before filing for bankruptcy
5. Claims related to unpaid contributions to employee benefits plans that should have been paid in the previous six months
6. Any unsecured claims for customer deposits
7. Any taxes due at the federal, state, or local level
8. Liabilities associated with unfunded pension plans
9. Payments to general or unsecured creditors
10. Preferred stock
11. Common stock

CHAPTER 11 BANKRUPTCY

Chapter 11 bankruptcy provides an outline for a formal business reorganization supervised by the court. When a business owner files a voluntary Chapter 11 petition, he becomes a debtor in possession of the business, and the business becomes a property of the bankruptcy estate (Kupetz, 1998). The debtor is authorized to keep running the business and make all necessary business decisions until otherwise ordered by the bankruptcy court. The reason the debtor is allowed to continue running the business is that Chapter 11 bankruptcies are designed to rehabilitate the debtor, make sure all creditors are treated equally, and maximize the business' value to help pay as much of the debt as possible (Kupetz, 1998). A debtor can be issued debtor-in-possession financing for short-term liquidity purposes; these loans are given preference for repayment because they are made with the knowledge that the borrower is in bankruptcy and with the hope that the funds may help him out of bankruptcy.

Specific protections are afforded a debtor in Chapter 11 proceedings, including an automatic stay that prohibits the commencement or continuation of any legal action against the business (Cheeseman, 2001). Creditors can obtain relief from the stay, but courts traditionally attempt to assist the debtor as much as possible, including limiting the distractions caused by creditors pursuing litigation, through vigorously enforcing the stay.

Although the debtor is authorized to sell assets and enter into transactions in the ordinary course of business that benefit the company, creditors can petition the court to appoint a trustee. A trustee can be appointed if the creditors can show that some improprieties are evident. Such improprieties can include debtor fraud, dishonesty, incompetence, or gross mismanagement (Kupetz, 1998).

The debtor has the obligation in Chapter 11 proceedings to file a reorganization plan within 120 days after filing for bankruptcy protection. Such a plan gives a debtor the opportunity to try to turn the business around in four months. The debtor can stop making interest and principal payments until the plan is approved. Each creditor must be addressed in the plan, and the creditors have a final vote on whether they wish to accept the reorganization plan. Creditors have the right to vote against the plan, but this right is severely limited if the plan provides the creditors with at least as much as they might have obtained if the debtor had filed under Chapter 7. Such a reorganization effort involves all creditors regardless of the amount each creditor is owed. This differs from the situation with a workout, which normally entails only the largest creditors. Workouts are more informal and, as discussed earlier, are generally voluntary actions taken by a creditor to reduce its losses or costs or to help create a future business opportunity with the same debtor at a different time.

Creditors can also be coerced into accepting an extension agreement, which does not reduce the obligation but delays repayment for a specified period of time. A standstill, or moratorium, agreement allows the debtor to delay repayment for a given time period without facing interest charges or penalties.

CHAPTER 13 BANKRUPTCY

Chapter 13 bankruptcy is designed only for consumers, so we will just touch on it. A debtor needs to voluntarily file a petition indicating that she is insolvent or unable to pay her debts as they come due. The trustee who administers the plan is paid 10% of the debts paid under the plan (Cheeseman, 2001).

If the Smiths' fitness center is operated as a sole proprietorship, the business cannot file for bankruptcy under Chapter 13; but the Smiths can file for Chapter 13 personally if they are still earning money, have unsecured debts of less than $100,000, and have secured debts of less than $350,000. Bob and Cheryl would have to make a plan to repay the creditors and start making payments within 30 days after filing the plan.

INVOLUNTARY BANKRUPTCY

A business owner may think he can turn the business around, but creditors can force his hand if they think otherwise. An involuntary bankruptcy occurs when three or more unsecured creditors who hold bona fide debts of at least a combined $10,000 file a petition against the debtor. If there are fewer than 12 creditors in all, only one needs to file a petition for involuntary bankruptcy against the debtor. When a petition for involuntary bankruptcy is filed, a summons is issued to the debtor requiring the debtor to respond to the claims within 20 days. If the debtor does not respond in a timely manner, the court can enter an order for relief against the debtor. The order for relief might entail a creditor's being allowed to seize some of the debtor's property. If the debtor responds, the court will grant relief only if the debtor does not pay his obligations as they become due. In most instances, the debtor is allowed to keep operating the business. However, if the creditors who petitioned for involuntary bankruptcy are concerned about the debtor's actions, under certain circumstances they can ask the court to appoint a trustee to take possession of the business (Kupetz, 1998).

Bankruptcy issues often arise in the health club industry as a result of mismanagement. However, bankruptcy actions can also take place in the professional sport arena. The American Basketball League, the first women's professional basketball league to show strong box office success, folded in its third year after competition arose from the Women's National Basketball Association. In 1998 the Pittsburgh Penguins filed for bankruptcy protection. The Penguins had filed for Chapter 11 protection in 1975 when they owed $6.5 million. However, the 1998 Penguins owed more than $35 million just to one former player, Mario Lemieux (Hoffman, 1998). To keep the team alive and in Pittsburgh, U.S. Bankruptcy Court judge Bernard Markovitz approved Lemieux as the team's new owner ("Bankruptcy Judge," 1999).

Banks and other lenders are not the only options available when times become rough. When financial concerns arise, a business can sometimes look inside itself to find an answer. One such answer lies in liquidating assets such as stocks or other liquid assets. If no such assets exist, the business might have to sell other assets such as property.

REMOVAL OF BUSINESS ASSETS

A business owner might decide to condense a business by removing assets. Selling assets can reduce business costs or raise cash. Such transactions are often highlighted on annual reports as a footnote indicating a one-time write-off. Otherwise, the transactions would appear to boost the company's income when there is no possibility of ever generating these levels of funds again. Selling assets, or downsizing, occurs frequently. The Boston Celtics used to own their own television and radio stations but sold them because these assets did not fit into the team's business plans.

Owners can use several techniques to downsize a business and remove assets so that the new business will be smaller. The primary reason a company would wish to downsize is reduced income. Instead of closing the business, a business owner might wish to downsize and hope that at a later date it could once again grow. The first technique is taking out profits as dividends.

Dividends could be paid to the owner rather than reinvested into the business. Dividends can be paid at any time, but they cannot be paid if such payments would make the company insolvent (Nicholas, 1990). When a business is paying dividends, it is essential to check government regulations, articles of incorporation, and bylaws to make sure all dividend restrictions are followed. Individual shareholders can sue and recover damages for illegally paid dividends.

Other ways in which owners can remove assets from a business include increasing their own salaries, paying themselves bonuses, and funding benefits of various kinds. If a business owner wishes to increase her salary and the business is incorporated, the board of directors, shareholders, or both might have to approve the new salary. Owners of smaller businesses such as the Smiths may be able to take out as much as they want in salaries, especially if they do not have any debts. Business owners who have outstanding debt can still pay themselves a larger salary as long as the salary is reasonable. A salary could be considered unreasonable if it leaves the company insolvent or if the IRS views it as a way to give the business a tax deduction instead of paying nondeductible dividends (Nicholas, 1990). A salary is considered reasonable if it is justified based on such variables as extra work, more duties, or exceptional service.

Business owners can also compensate themselves for independent projects in the same way an independent contractor is paid. Owners can pay themselves commissions on sales in order to remove additional dollars from the business. In bankruptcy proceedings it would be difficult for debtors to contest a commission payment if it was a payment for a legitimate service. If, on the other hand, the owner did not in fact do any work to earn the extra money, then a debtor could challenge such payments and demand that they be returned to the bankruptcy estate.

Money can also be removed through paying bonuses. The IRS might try to fight a bonus as a disguised dividend. However, the businesses can tie the bonus to the compensation package to protect its reasonableness. Similarly, a business owner can receive significant fringe benefits in the form of game tickets, company cars, and travel to business conferences. Owners who are considered employees could also receive employee benefits such as insurance, pensions, financial counseling, employee stock purchase plans, and any other benefit afforded to employees.

A business owner can loan himself money from the business. The risk of being rejected for the loan is eliminated, and leisurely repayment plans can be developed. The loan could also be interest free, and the owner might not have to pay taxes on the loaned amount. However, any time there exists self-dealing, the potential for abuse can arise and lead to disas-

---

Horses Heading off Track

Bankruptcy can provide an opportunity to grow again. In 2004, Fair Grounds horse racing track was in bankruptcy after it failed to pay Louisiana horsemen $90 million, from underpaying video poker proceeds to racing purses. The New Orleans track initially entered into an agreement to sell 86% of the track to a horse owner for $40 million, but it received an offer of $47 million from Churchill Downs ("Churchill Downs," 2004). Thus, although the ownership changed, the city did not lose the horse track as a valuable community asset.

trous results. The Rigas family, founders of cable television giant Adelphia, was under investigation in 2002 for off-balance-sheet loans to, among other things, help support the Buffalo Sabres to the tune of $76.5 million. The Sabres were owned at the time of the loans by the Rigas family (Grover & Lowry, 2002). Issuing inappropriate loans can cause an incorporated business owner to lose her liability shield if a debtor pierces the corporate veil. Thus, even if you are loaning yourself money, you need to adequately document the transaction.

Finally, a business owner can sell or lease property to the business (Nicholas, 1990). If the Smiths owned a vacant lot, they could sell the lot to the fitness center for a price slightly above the market value and then build a new facility on the lot. Since the Smiths own the fitness center, they would be the primary beneficiaries of the sale. However, if the land was in their name and the fitness center was incorporated, then any debts owed by the fitness center could not be repaid with proceeds from selling the land, since the lot belongs to the Smiths as individuals and not to the fitness center.

Despite the many options for withdrawing assets from a business, most business owners would rather just sell the business in its entirety and obtain the funds immediately, rather than in a piecemeal fashion.

SELLING A BUSINESS

Any business goes through ups and downs, but sometimes owners are not willing to accept the stress associated with such cyclical patterns. Business owners may decide to sell their businesses for a number of reasons, including the following:

- Wishing to retire
- Wanting to make a profit
- Wanting to change careers
- Wanting to get out while they can
- Finding the level of competition unacceptable

One trend that is helping to foster business sales is the fact that many baby boomers who own businesses are entering their 50s, 60s, and 70s and want to retire, travel, or manage their pensions or investments.

The first step in selling any business is to gather together all relevant financial information. If an independent auditor has reviewed the company's financial condition, the audited statements are the best tool to use in selling a successful business. Having several years' worth of audited financial statements helps shorten the buyer's due diligence investigation time

and can accelerate the process of acquiring financing to buy the business.

A key component of any purchase decision is exactly what will be purchased. As discussed earlier in this chapter, Footstar purchased some assets of Just For Feet for $66.8 million in 2000. Footstar purchased 79 Just For Feet superstores, 23 specialty stores, the Just For Feet name, and its Internet business ("Footstar," 2000). Footstar made a business decision by choosing to purchase specific assets rather than the entire company. This decision might have been based on a number of factors, such as Just For Feet's debt obligations from lease agreements or numerous other debt and liability concerns.

Four options exist for selling a business: a taxable sale of company stock, a tax-free sale of company stock, a taxable sale of company assets, and a tax-free sale of company assets (Lee, 1999). Each option involves different concerns. A cash purchase takes less time than a stock deal because there are fewer compliance issues. A sale can raise concerns for the buying company. For example, if a company issues more stock to buy another company, will the new shares give rise to preemptive rights to current shareholders? A sale can also raise concerns that are normally not considered when making a typical asset purchase such as a car, where the only issue might be determining if there exists a clear title.

 **Sport Manufacturing Company**

If SMC bought another golf club manufacturer, would it also acquire the employees? What if the employees had a pension plan? Who would be liable if the pension plan from the purchased business was underfunded? SMC would be dealing with employees who anticipated having a certain amount of money in their pension fund, and the money is not there. If this issue was not resolved in the contract negotiations, SMC would be responsible for making up the deficit.

ASSET VERSUS EQUITY PURCHASE

As already noted, one issue in selling a business is whether or not to sell stock, if the company is incorporated, or the company's assets. A person or another company interested in buying the business would prefer to buy assets rather than stock for various reasons. The primary reason is to reduce the purchasing company's liability—stocks convey ownership and liability for all past obligations. Thus, if the purchased business manufactured lawn dart games, and kids were being injured and parents were suing the company, the new owners would be liable for all possible damages. On the other hand, if only the manufacturer's assets had been purchased, the company itself and all associated liabilities would have been dissolved.

There are also significant tax considerations for the seller and the purchaser of assets as opposed to stock. If you sell assets, the money you receive is taxed as ordinary income up to your basis (cost minus depreciation) in the asset. Any amount in excess of your basis is taxed as capital gains. Stock sales are taxed as long- or short-term capital gains. Ordinary income can be taxed up to 39.6% versus capital gains taxes for individuals, which are at most 20%. Thus, owners of a business would rather sell the stock; the difference between the buying and the selling price could be taxed at about half the rate of assets (Marullo, 1998, August). On the basis of the unfavorable tax treatment a seller faces when selling assets, sellers can normally obtain a higher price for assets than for stock (Marullo, 1998, August).

Another significant benefit attached to selling assets involves the "step-down" basis for depreciable assets (Marullo, 1998, August) as illustrated in the following example.

 Assume that the Stars purchased $100,000 worth of depreciable cameras for their broadcast booth. The cameras might have a depreciable life of five years, which means the Stars could depreciate $20,000 a year for five years. Assume that after five years the team had depreciated the entire amount allowed, $100,000, but the cameras still had a fair market value of $50,000. If the Stars sold the cameras for $50,000, the purchaser would be entitled to the step-down, which means the purchaser could depreciate the cameras once again for five years. Thus, the new owner would be able to depreciate the $50,000 purchase price by $10,000 a year over five years. If the new owner sold the cameras, the third owner would be able to depreciate the cameras from their purchase price. This process can continue for as long as the cameras still have value.

The step-down provision is particularly important in the professional sport industry in that players' contracts are considered depreciable assets. Buyers prefer to purchase assets if they can use the step-down basis to acquire added depreciation without assuming any liability. The step-down basis approach is covered in more detail in chapter 14 (see pp. 261-262).

If the Smiths wish to sell their now successful business, they face a major challenge—determining how much the business is worth. Owners put so much sweat equity into a business that they typically think it is worth much more than it actually is. Owners may have a misconception based on transactions associated with large publicly traded companies, which can sell for up to 20 times their earnings (Livingston, 1998). However, sales of smaller, closely held companies rarely reach such multiples of earnings. Larger corporations have a strong track record and can maintain consistent sales for extended periods, as well as significant goodwill associated with their product or service. An NFL franchise is valuable even with a losing record on the basis of the inherent value of an NFL team. The strong value of NFL teams is based on the strong broadcast agreement and shared revenue. In contrast, a small mom-and-pop gym has a less stable product, and customer loyalty might not transfer over in the same manner as with a large company. Some gym members might have bought memberships just because they were friends of the owner. Fans of the Dallas Cowboys or any other NFL team would still be fans even if their franchise changed ownership several times over a decade.

CALCULATING BUSINESS VALUE

Several techniques can be used to calculate a business' value. The most common are asset-based valuation methods, the market-based approach, and income-based approaches. Next we briefly consider each of these.

The techniques presented here in no way represent a definite science. There is no one correct way to measure a business' value. Someone who loves golf might be willing to pay a premium to buy SMC just so she can own a golf club manufacturing business. This emotional element makes it almost impossible to create a foolproof valuation. Similarly, given the difficulty in valuing goodwill, there must always be a subjective element to valuing a business.

ASSET-BASED VALUATION METHODS

In asset-based approaches to valuation, the business' value is determined based on the value of tangible and intangible assets, net of liabilities. In essence, the net worth is computed based on factoring in assets that appear on the balance sheet along with assets that might not be recorded. Intangible assets, such as goodwill, might not appear on a balance sheet because of the difficulty in determining an accurate value, but nevertheless they do add value to the business. Asset-based approaches (in particular the asset accumulation approach discussed next) are most relevant for valuing an established sport business or in cases in which the valuation is being done in response to the sale of an ownership stake that exceeds 50%.

There are two generally accepted asset-based approaches for valuing sport businesses: the asset accumulation approach and the excess earnings method.

ASSET ACCUMULATION APPROACH

The asset accumulation approach is simply the identification and summation of the current economic values of all assets, tangible and intangible, that are controlled by the sport business as of the date of the valuation. Because the objective of the valuation is to determine the current net worth, or equity value, of the business, it is necessary to deduct all liabilities existing at the date of the valuation from the estimated value of the business' assets.

EXCESS EARNINGS METHOD

In the excess earnings approach, the value of net tangible assets is estimated on the basis of the return that these assets can earn. As a separate process, intangible assets are valued based on the value of excess earnings that can be attributed to the intangible assets. The steps in the excess earnings approach can be summarized as follows:

1. Estimate the value of the tangible assets of the sport business, net of liabilities.

2. Estimate the normal level of earnings for the sport business after a historical review of the business' financial results and subject to forecast of future results. To measure normalized earnings, the compensation of all equity owners, including salary, bonus, and profit sharing, is adjusted to reflect what the cost would be to hire a manager with nonownership status to perform the same tasks as owners.

3. Estimate the annual income that an owner would require to be interested in investing in the net tangible assets of the sport business.

4. Deduct the annual income computed in step 3 from the normal earnings estimated in step 2. This remainder can be viewed as the "excess earnings" that are attributable to the business' intangible assets.

5. This remainder is converted to an economic value by applying a **capitalization rate** that reflects the inherent riskiness in relation to the business' ability to generate the excess earnings over the long run. Capitalization refers to the conversion of a single value of economic income to a current economic value by dividing the measure of economic income by a capitalization rate that is expressed as a percentage. As an example, if the excess earnings generated by the intangible assets equal $400,000 per year and the appropriate capitalization rate is 20%, then the value of the excess earnings equals the following:

$$\frac{\$400,000}{0.20} = \$2,000,000$$

6. The value of the tangible assets and the value of the excess earnings are added together to produce the sport business' value.

MARKET-BASED APPROACH

The market-based approach gives the value of the sport business based on a multiple of operating results, such as profits or revenues. The multiples are based on market transactions involving similar sport businesses. The inherent appeal of this approach is that the value of the business based on market-derived multiples reflects informed decisions negotiated between parties in transactions. When transactions are identified, notions of risk and return are incorporated into the multiples. Thus, the multiplier would vary within the same industry if one business has significant competition while a second business has no competition and is in a great location; the second business should have a higher multiplier.

For many types of closely held businesses, market multiples are derived based on multiples of earnings and revenues that are obtained either from analysis of publicly traded companies similar to the business or from data on actual transactions involving acquired or merging public and private companies. When market values of publicly traded companies are used to establish the value of a closely held business, it is necessary to apply a discount for lack of marketability to the value of the publicly traded companies. The lack-of-marketability discount results from a privately held company's being less valuable than a comparable public company because it is not as quick and easy to convert a business ownership position to cash (i.e., a private company is less liquid). The appropriate lack-of-marketability discount should be between 40% and 63% based on a recent survey of empirical studies (Pratt, Reilly, & Schweihs, 2000). For valuation analysis, there is limited information on transactions that involve sport businesses, and there are very few publicly traded sport businesses in existence.

Many people believe that simple rules of thumb concerning the market multiple should be applied. This would mean applying an arbitrary multiple based on anecdotal information to current annual revenues, rather than actual analysis of empirical data. Such rules do not adjust multiples to reflect differences in operating characteristics and should not be used for any purpose other than as a reasonableness check on the values obtained from the use of other methodologies.

INCOME-BASED APPROACHES

In income-based approaches, a business' value is estimated based on the present value of all earnings and cash flow that the company provides to the owners during the time it is owned. The appeal of this approach for valuing a sport business is that such a business is an operating entity that generates cash flow and earnings for the owners. The value resulting from the revenue- and profit-generating ability of the business is more relevant than the value that can be obtained from selling the business' assets, because many sport businesses are not capital intensive.

One income-based approach, called the **discounted net cash flow** approach, estimates the present value of future economic income that is expected to result from the operations of the business. It is also common to use the net cash flow to equity formula, which requires the following steps:

1. Determine net income after taxes.
2. Add noncash charges (e.g., depreciation).
3. Subtract net capital expenditures necessary to support business operations.
4. Subtract changes in net working capital necessary to support business operations.
5. Add net changes in long-term debt necessary to support business operations.

Net cash flow is used because conceptually it represents all income that an investor can hypothetically take out of the business. Generally, annual net cash flows are projected over a 5- to 10-year period into the future. At the end of the projection period, a terminal value is estimated on the basis of the cash flows that are expected to be earned after the projection period.

The business' value is then computed as the sum of the present value of the annual net cash flows over the forecast period plus the present value of the terminal value (Shapiro, 1999). The present value of any single annual cash flow received in the future is computed by discounting the future cash flows. The concept of discounting recognizes that money received in the future is worth less than it would be today because money invested today can accrue interest over time. Under the assumption that the investor can earn an interest rate of i, the present value of net cash flow (CF) received n years (CF_n) in the future is as follows:

$$\frac{CF_n}{(1+i)^n}$$

For example, if the interest rate (i) is 10%, the present value of $1 million received five years from now is $620,921.

$$\frac{\$1,000,000}{1.10^5} = \$620,921$$

ADDITIONAL CONSIDERATIONS WHEN SELLING A BUSINESS

In addition to determining the business' value, if you are selling a business you should keep the following guidelines in mind:

- Do not let employees know too early that you might be selling; this can affect employee morale.
- Do not let competitors know too early about an impending sale; they might try to steal customers or hinder the sales process.
- Do not accept a purchase agreement calling for the seller to receive cash and a note; the note could be worthless if the new owner runs into financial hardships.
- Do not accept a significant bonus based on future financial success; you will remain tied to the business and its potential success or failure.
- Do not get so involved in the sales process that the business suffers and becomes even more difficult to sell (Livingston, 1998).
- Do not specifically exclude certain assets from the final sale, such as cash, past-due accounts receivable, deposits, refunds, and

other valuable assets such as business records (Parrish & Maloney, 1999). Although it might be hard to part with these valuable assets, their value should be reflected in the business' sale price.

Despite potential problems associated with special purchasing options, if a business has a strong financial future, the potential downside might be minimal, and the seller might want to negotiate a contract attached to the company's future success. As with all contracts, the seller can negotiate a relatively risk-free deal by having the contract maximize success but minimize any losses. For example, the sales contract could specify that the seller is entitled to 10% of the company's profit for the first five years after the sale, but if the company does not have any profits, the seller will be entitled to a preferred collateral position on company assets. A preferred collateral position is a contractual agreement by which lenders can enhance their collateral positions. Thus, unsecured creditors can enter into agreements that provide them with a better position as long as such position does not harm any secured creditors or violate any bankruptcy estate.

SELLING A BUSINESS TO EMPLOYEES

Employee stock ownership plans give employees the opportunity to buy the business. These plans normally funnel pension or retirement funds into company stock, and at a certain point the employees can own a large percentage of the stock

Assume that the Smiths' employees decide they want to buy all the centers in the Smiths' fitness empire. Bob and Cheryl could negotiate an outright purchase of the centers or can undertake various strategies such as giving equity interest in lieu of some retirement benefits. The Smiths could also give the employees the opportunity to purchase the centers using the lease-to-own option, in which the employees pay a lease amount for several years and then buy the centers at a set price.

EXTERNAL SALES ASSISTANCE

If you hire a business broker or investment banker, this individual can help focus your sales search by shopping the company only to those with interest in buying the business and the ability to do so. Many people would love to own a company but do not have the proper experience or the financial knowledge needed to complete the deal. External consultants can help provide an objective arm's-length opinion about a purchaser. Professionals can prequalify potential candidates to make sure they have the necessary resources. If would-be buyers are not prequalified, another John Spano incident could occur (see chapter 16).

Business liquidators are experts in helping to establish a company's value and finding potential buyers for the entire business or just some key assets. Liquidators research businesses to find out what the best assets are and then come in, buy a business, sell all the valuables, and exit with a nice profit.

CONCLUSION

People do not want to think that their businesses will ever go under. However, hard times do occur, and a business owner or manager needs to understand the signs of trouble. If the problem is caught soon enough, it may be possible to save the business. Losses can also result from events that an owner has no way to plan for. If the Stars' star player suffers a career-ending injury, ticket sales could plummet and ratings for game broadcasts could drop. Such a significant loss cannot be planned for. Nonetheless, a business does need to have some contingency plans. A nonprofit organization also can face closure for nonpayment of debt.

By keeping meticulous records, managers can know how much their businesses are worth. They can be aware of impacts that economic changes or competition might have on the business. They can put themselves in a position to see the writing on the wall and determine the best time to sell a business. They can tell what is happening with the competition and how their businesses might be affected. They can plan for the future and stay one step ahead of the external factors.

CLASS DISCUSSION TOPICS

1. What is the best technique for determining a business' value?

2. If you were facing hard financial times, would you be willing to file for bankruptcy? What are the advantages and disadvantages you should consider?

3. Could the Smiths just shut their doors and not pay anything or sell anything?

4. Is it better to buy an entire business or just its assets?

5. Is there a difference in determining the value of a large business such as a professional sports team versus a smaller business such as a health club?

6. Do you think it would be a good idea for a team owner to sell a team to the players?

7. If you were selling a sport business, what strategies would you use to try to find some potential buyers?

APPENDIX A

TIME VALUE OF MONEY

Table A.1 Future Value of $1 at the End of t Periods

Interest rate

Period	1%	2%	3%	4%	5%	6%	7%	8%	9%	10%	11%
1	1.0100	1.0200	1.0300	1.0400	1.0500	1.0600	1.0700	1.0800	1.0900	1.1000	1.1100
2	1.0201	1.0404	1.0609	1.0816	1.1025	1.1236	1.1449	1.1664	1.1881	1.2100	1.2321
3	1.0303	1.0612	1.0927	1.1249	1.1576	1.1910	1.2250	1.2597	1.2950	1.3310	1.3676
4	1.0406	1.0824	1.1255	1.1699	1.2155	1.2625	1.3108	1.3605	1.4116	1.4641	1.5181
5	1.0510	1.1041	1.1593	1.2167	1.2763	1.3382	1.4026	1.4693	1.5386	1.6105	1.6851
6	1.0615	1.1262	1.1941	1.2653	1.3401	1.4185	1.5007	1.5869	1.6771	1.7716	1.8704
7	1.0721	1.1487	1.2299	1.3159	1.4071	1.5036	1.6058	1.7138	1.8280	1.9487	2.0762
8	1.0829	1.1717	1.2668	1.3686	1.4775	1.5938	1.7182	1.8509	1.9926	2.1436	2.3045
9	1.0937	1.1951	1.3048	1.4233	1.5513	1.6895	1.8385	1.9990	2.1719	2.3579	2.5580
10	1.1046	1.2190	1.3439	1.4802	1.6289	1.7908	1.9672	2.1589	2.3674	2.5937	2.8394
11	1.1157	1.2434	1.3842	1.5395	1.7103	1.8983	2.1049	2.3316	2.5804	2.8531	3.1518
12	1.1268	1.2682	1.4258	1.6010	1.7959	2.0122	2.2522	2.5182	2.8127	3.1384	3.4985
13	1.1381	1.2936	1.4685	1.6651	1.8856	2.1329	2.4098	2.7196	3.0658	3.4523	3.8833
14	1.1495	1.3195	1.5126	1.7317	1.9799	2.2609	2.5785	2.9372	3.3417	3.7975	4.3104
15	1.1610	1.3459	1.5580	1.8009	2.0789	2.3966	2.7590	3.1722	3.6425	4.1772	4.7846
16	1.1726	1.3728	1.6047	1.8730	2.1829	2.5404	2.9522	3.4259	3.9703	4.5950	5.3109
17	1.1843	1.4002	1.6528	1.9479	2.2920	2.6928	3.1588	3.7000	4.3276	5.0545	5.8951
18	1.1961	1.4282	1.7024	2.0258	2.4066	2.8543	3.3799	3.9960	4.7171	5.5599	6.5436
19	1.2081	1.4568	1.7535	2.1068	2.5270	3.0256	3.6165	4.3157	5.1417	6.1159	7.2633
20	1.2202	1.4859	1.8061	2.1911	2.6533	3.2071	3.8697	4.6610	5.6044	6.7275	8.0623
21	1.2324	1.5157	1.8603	2.2788	2.7860	3.3996	4.1406	5.0338	6.1088	7.4002	8.9492
22	1.2447	1.5460	1.9161	2.3699	2.9253	3.6035	4.4304	5.4365	6.6586	8.1403	9.9336
23	1.2572	1.5769	1.9736	2.4647	3.0715	3.8197	4.7405	5.8715	7.2579	8.9543	11.0263
24	1.2697	1.6084	2.0328	2.5633	3.2251	4.0489	5.0724	6.3412	7.9111	9.8497	12.2392
25	1.2824	1.6406	2.0938	2.6658	3.3864	4.2919	5.4274	6.8485	8.6231	10.8347	13.5855
30	1.3478	1.8114	2.4273	3.2434	4.3219	5.7435	7.6123	10.0627	13.2677	17.4494	22.8923
40	1.4889	2.2080	3.2620	4.8010	7.0400	10.2857	14.9745	21.7245	31.4094	45.2593	65.0009
50	1.6446	2.6916	4.3839	7.1067	11.4674	18.4202	29.4570	46.9016	74.3575	117.3909	184.5648
60	1.8167	3.2810	5.8916	10.5196	18.6792	32.9877	57.9464	101.2571	176.0313	304.4816	524.0572

*Future value interest factor exceeds 99,999.

12%	14%	15%	16%	18%	20%	24%	28%	32%	36%
1.1200	1.1400	1.1500	1.1600	1.1800	1.2000	1.2400	1.2800	1.3200	1.3600
1.2544	1.2996	1.3225	1.3456	1.3924	1.4400	1.5376	1.6384	1.7424	1.8496
1.4049	1.4815	1.5209	1.5609	1.6430	1.7280	1.9066	2.0972	2.3000	2.5155
1.5735	1.6890	1.7490	1.8106	1.9388	2.0736	2.3642	2.6844	3.0360	3.4210
1.7623	1.9254	2.0114	2.1003	2.2878	2.4883	2.9316	3.4360	4.0075	4.6526
1.9738	2.1950	2.3131	2.4364	2.6996	2.9860	3.6352	4.3980	5.2899	6.3275
2.2107	2.5023	2.6600	2.8262	3.1855	3.5832	4.5077	5.6295	6.9826	8.6054
2.4760	2.8526	3.0590	3.2784	3.7589	4.2998	5.5895	7.2058	9.2170	11.7034
2.7731	3.2519	3.5179	3.8030	4.4355	5.1598	6.9310	9.2234	12.1665	15.9166
3.1058	3.7072	4.0456	4.4114	5.2338	6.1917	8.5944	11.8059	16.0598	21.6466
3.4785	4.2262	4.6524	5.1173	6.1759	7.4301	10.6571	15.1116	21.1989	29.4393
3.8960	4.8179	5.3503	5.9360	7.2876	8.9161	13.2148	19.3428	27.9825	40.0375
4.3635	5.4924	6.1528	6.8858	8.5994	10.6993	16.3863	24.7588	36.9370	54.4510
4.8871	6.2613	7.0757	7.9875	10.1472	12.8392	20.3191	31.6913	48.7568	74.0534
5.4736	7.1379	8.1371	9.2655	11.9737	15.4070	25.1956	40.5648	64.3590	100.7126
6.1304	8.1372	9.3576	10.7480	14.1290	18.4884	31.2426	51.9230	84.9538	136.9691
6.8660	9.2765	10.7613	12.4677	16.6722	22.1861	38.7408	66.4614	112.1390	186.2779
7.6900	10.5752	12.3755	14.4625	19.6733	26.6233	48.0386	85.0706	148.0235	253.3380
8.6128	12.0557	14.2318	16.7765	23.2144	31.9480	59.5679	108.8904	195.3911	344.5397
9.6463	13.7435	16.3665	19.4608	27.3930	38.3376	73.8641	139.3797	257.9162	468.5740
10.8038	15.6676	18.8215	22.5745	32.3238	46.0051	91.5915	178.4060	340.4494	637.2606
12.1003	17.8610	21.6447	26.1864	38.1421	55.2061	113.5735	228.3596	449.3932	866.6744
13.5523	20.3616	24.8915	30.3762	45.0076	66.2474	140.8312	292.3003	593.1990	1,178.6772
15.1786	23.2122	28.6252	35.2364	53.1090	79.4968	174.6306	374.1444	783.0227	1,603.0010
17.0001	26.4619	32.9190	40.8742	62.6686	95.3962	216.5420	478.9049	1,033.5900	2,180.0814
29.9599	50.9502	66.2118	85.8499	143.3706	237.3763	634.8199	1,645.5046	4,142.0748	10,143.0193
93.0510	188.8835	267.8635	378.7212	750.3783	1,469.7716	5,455.9126	19,426.6889	66,520.7670	*
289.0022	700.2330	1,083.6574	1,670.7038	3,927.3569	9,100.4382	46,890.4346	229,349.8616	*	*
897.5969	2,595.9187	4,383.9987	7,370.2014	20,555.1400	56,347.5144	*	*	*	*

Table A.2 Present Value of $1 Received at the End of t Periods

Period	1%	2%	3%	4%	5%	Interest rate 6%	7%	8%	9%	10%	11%
1	0.9901	0.9804	0.9709	0.9615	0.9524	0.9434	0.9346	0.9259	0.9174	0.9091	0.9009
2	0.9803	0.9612	0.9426	0.9246	0.9070	0.8900	0.8734	0.8573	0.8417	0.8264	0.8116
3	0.9706	0.9423	0.9151	0.8890	0.8638	0.8396	0.8163	0.7938	0.7722	0.7513	0.7312
4	0.9610	0.9238	0.8885	0.8548	0.8227	0.7921	0.7629	0.7350	0.7084	0.6830	0.6587
5	0.9515	0.9057	0.8626	0.8219	0.7835	0.7473	0.7130	0.6806	0.6499	0.6209	0.5935
6	0.9420	0.8880	0.8375	0.7903	0.7462	0.7050	0.6663	0.6302	0.5963	0.5645	0.5346
7	0.9327	0.8706	0.8131	0.7599	0.7107	0.6651	0.6227	0.5835	0.5470	0.5132	0.4817
8	0.9235	0.8535	0.7894	0.7307	0.6768	0.6274	0.5820	0.5403	0.5019	0.4665	0.4339
9	0.9143	0.8368	0.7664	0.7026	0.6446	0.5919	0.5439	0.5002	0.4604	0.4241	0.3909
10	0.9053	0.8203	0.7441	0.6756	0.6139	0.5584	0.5083	0.4632	0.4224	0.3855	0.3522
11	0.8963	0.8043	0.7224	0.6496	0.5847	0.5268	0.4751	0.4289	0.3875	0.3505	0.3173
12	0.8874	0.7885	0.7014	0.6246	0.5568	0.4970	0.4440	0.3971	0.3555	0.3186	0.2858
13	0.8787	0.7730	0.6810	0.6006	0.5303	0.4688	0.4150	0.3677	0.3262	0.2897	0.2575
14	0.8700	0.7579	0.6611	0.5775	0.5051	0.4423	0.3878	0.3405	0.2992	0.2633	0.2320
15	0.8613	0.7430	0.6419	0.5553	0.4810	0.4173	0.3624	0.3152	0.2745	0.2394	0.2090
16	0.8528	0.7284	0.6232	0.5339	0.4581	0.3936	0.3387	0.2919	0.2519	0.2176	0.1883
17	0.8444	0.7142	0.6050	0.5134	0.4363	0.3714	0.3166	0.2703	0.2311	0.1978	0.1696
18	0.8360	0.7002	0.5874	0.4936	0.4155	0.3503	0.2959	0.2502	0.2120	0.1799	0.1528
19	0.8277	0.6864	0.5703	0.4746	0.3957	0.3305	0.2765	0.2317	0.1945	0.1635	0.1377
20	0.8195	0.6730	0.5537	0.4564	0.3769	0.3118	0.2584	0.2145	0.1784	0.1486	0.1240
21	0.8114	0.6598	0.5375	0.4388	0.3589	0.2942	0.2415	0.1987	0.1637	0.1351	0.1117
22	0.8034	0.6468	0.5219	0.4220	0.3418	0.2775	0.2257	0.1839	0.1502	0.1228	0.1007
23	0.7954	0.6342	0.5067	0.4057	0.3256	0.2618	0.2109	0.1703	0.1378	0.1117	0.0907
24	0.7876	0.6217	0.4919	0.3901	0.3101	0.2470	0.1971	0.1577	0.1264	0.1015	0.0817
25	0.7798	0.6095	0.4776	0.3751	0.2953	0.2330	0.1842	0.1460	0.1160	0.0923	0.0736
30	0.7419	0.5521	0.4120	0.3083	0.2314	0.1741	0.1314	0.0994	0.0754	0.0573	0.0437
40	0.6717	0.4529	0.3066	0.2083	0.1420	0.0972	0.0668	0.0460	0.0318	0.0221	0.0154
50	0.6080	0.3715	0.2281	0.1407	0.0872	0.0543	0.0339	0.0213	0.0134	0.0085	0.0054
60	0.5504	0.3048	0.1697	0.0951	0.0535	0.0303	0.0173	0.0099	0.0057	0.0033	0.0019

* The present value factor is zero rounded to four decimal places.

12%	14%	15%	16%	18%	20%	24%	28%	32%	36%
0.8929	0.8772	0.8696	0.8621	0.8475	0.8333	0.8065	0.7813	0.7576	0.7353
0.7972	0.7695	0.7561	0.7432	0.7182	0.6944	0.6504	0.6104	0.5739	0.5407
0.7118	0.6750	0.6575	0.6407	0.6086	0.5787	0.5245	0.4768	0.4348	0.3975
0.6355	0.5921	0.5718	0.5523	0.5158	0.4823	0.4230	0.3725	0.3294	0.2923
0.5674	0.5194	0.4972	0.4761	0.4371	0.4019	0.3411	0.2910	0.2495	0.2149
0.5066	0.4556	0.4323	0.4104	0.3704	0.3349	0.2751	0.2274	0.1890	0.1580
0.4523	0.3996	0.3759	0.3538	0.3139	0.2791	0.2218	0.1776	0.1432	0.1162
0.4039	0.3506	0.3269	0.3050	0.2660	0.2326	0.1789	0.1388	0.1085	0.0854
0.3606	0.3075	0.2843	0.2630	0.2255	0.1938	0.1443	0.1084	0.0822	0.0628
0.3220	0.2697	0.2472	0.2267	0.1911	0.1615	0.1164	0.0847	0.0623	0.0462
0.2875	0.2366	0.2149	0.1954	0.1619	0.1346	0.0938	0.0662	0.0472	0.0340
0.2567	0.2076	0.1869	0.1685	0.1372	0.1122	0.0757	0.0517	0.0357	0.0250
0.2292	0.1821	0.1625	0.1452	0.1163	0.0935	0.0610	0.0404	0.0271	0.0184
0.2046	0.1597	0.1413	0.1252	0.0985	0.0779	0.0492	0.0316	0.0205	0.0135
0.1827	0.1401	0.1229	0.1079	0.0835	0.0649	0.0397	0.0247	0.0155	0.0099
0.1631	0.1229	0.1069	0.0930	0.0708	0.0541	0.0320	0.0193	0.0118	0.0073
0.1456	0.1078	0.0929	0.0802	0.0600	0.0451	0.0258	0.0150	0.0089	0.0054
0.1300	0.0946	0.0808	0.0691	0.0508	0.0376	0.0208	0.0118	0.0068	0.0039
0.1161	0.0829	0.0703	0.0596	0.0431	0.0313	0.0168	0.0092	0.0051	0.0029
0.1037	0.0728	0.0611	0.0514	0.0365	0.0261	0.0135	0.0072	0.0039	0.0021
0.0926	0.0638	0.0531	0.0443	0.0309	0.0217	0.0109	0.0056	0.0029	0.0016
0.0826	0.0560	0.0462	0.0382	0.0262	0.0181	0.0088	0.0044	0.0022	0.0012
0.0738	0.0491	0.0402	0.0329	0.0222	0.0151	0.0071	0.0034	0.0017	0.0008
0.0659	0.0431	0.0349	0.0284	0.0188	0.0126	0.0057	0.0027	0.0013	0.0006
0.0588	0.0378	0.0304	0.0245	0.0160	0.0105	0.0046	0.0021	0.0010	0.0005
0.0334	0.0196	0.0151	0.0116	0.0070	0.0042	0.0016	0.0006	0.0002	0.0001
0.0107	0.0053	0.0037	0.0026	0.0013	0.0007	0.0002	0.0001	*	*
0.0035	0.0014	0.0009	0.0006	0.0003	*	*	*	*	*
0.0011	0.0004	0.0002	0.0001	*	*	*	*	*	*

Table A.3 Present Value of $1 per Period for t Periods

Period	1%	2%	3%	4%	5%	6%	7%	8%	9%	10%	11%
1	0.9901	0.9804	0.9709	0.9615	0.9524	0.9434	0.9346	0.9259	0.9174	0.9091	0.9009
2	1.9704	1.9416	1.9135	1.8861	1.8594	1.8334	1.8080	1.7833	1.7591	1.7355	1.7125
3	2.9410	2.8839	2.8286	2.7751	2.7232	2.6730	2.6243	2.5771	2.5313	2.4869	2.4437
4	3.9020	3.8077	3.7171	3.6299	3.5460	3.4651	3.3872	3.3121	3.2397	3.1699	3.1024
5	4.8534	4.7135	4.5797	4.4518	4.3295	4.2124	4.1002	3.9927	3.8897	3.7908	3.6959
6	5.7955	5.6014	5.4172	5.2421	5.0757	4.9173	4.7665	4.6229	4.4859	4.3553	4.2305
7	6.7282	6.4720	6.2303	6.0021	5.7864	5.5824	5.3893	5.2064	5.0330	4.8684	4.7122
8	7.6517	7.3255	7.0197	6.7327	6.4632	6.2098	5.9713	5.7466	5.5348	5.3349	5.1461
9	8.5660	8.1622	7.7861	7.4353	7.1078	6.8017	6.5152	6.2469	5.9952	5.7590	5.5370
10	9.4713	8.9826	8.5302	8.1109	7.7217	7.3601	7.0236	6.7101	6.4177	6.1446	5.8892
11	10.3676	9.7868	9.2526	8.7605	8.3064	7.8869	7.4987	7.1390	6.8052	6.4951	6.2065
12	11.2551	10.5753	9.9540	9.3851	8.8633	8.3838	7.9427	7.5361	7.1607	6.8137	6.4924
13	12.1337	11.3484	10.6350	9.9856	9.3936	8.8527	8.3577	7.9038	7.4869	7.1034	6.7499
14	13.0037	12.1062	11.2961	10.5631	9.8986	9.2950	8.7455	8.2442	7.7862	7.3667	6.9819
15	13.8651	12.8493	11.9379	11.1184	10.3797	9.7122	9.1079	8.5595	8.0607	7.6061	7.1909
16	14.7179	13.5777	12.5611	11.6523	10.8378	10.1059	9.4466	8.8514	8.3126	7.8237	7.3792
17	15.5623	14.2919	13.1661	12.1657	11.2741	10.4773	9.7632	9.1216	8.5436	8.0216	7.5488
18	16.3983	14.9920	13.7535	12.6593	11.6896	10.8276	10.0591	9.3719	8.7556	8.2014	7.7016
19	17.2260	15.6785	14.3238	13.1339	12.0853	11.1581	10.3356	9.6036	8.9501	8.3649	7.8393
20	18.0456	16.3514	14.8775	13.5903	12.4622	11.4699	10.5940	9.8181	9.1285	8.5136	7.9633
21	18.8570	17.0112	15.4150	14.0292	12.8212	11.7641	10.8355	10.0168	9.2922	8.6487	8.0751
22	19.6604	17.6580	15.9369	14.4511	13.1630	12.0416	11.0612	10.2007	9.4424	8.7715	8.1757
23	20.4558	18.2922	16.4436	14.8568	13.4886	12.3034	11.2722	10.3711	9.5802	8.8832	8.2664
24	21.2434	18.9139	16.9355	15.2470	13.7986	12.5504	11.4693	10.5288	9.7066	8.9847	8.3481
25	22.0232	19.5235	17.4131	15.6221	14.0939	12.7834	11.6536	10.6748	9.8226	9.0770	8.4217
30	25.8077	22.3965	19.6004	17.2920	15.3725	13.7648	12.4090	11.2578	10.2737	9.4269	8.6938
40	32.8347	27.3555	23.1148	19.7928	17.1591	15.0463	13.3317	11.9246	10.7574	9.7791	8.9511
50	39.1961	31.4236	25.7298	21.4822	18.2559	15.7619	13.8007	12.2335	10.9617	9.9148	9.0417
60	44.9550	34.7609	27.6756	22.6235	18.9293	16.1614	14.0392	12.3766	11.0480	9.9672	9.0736

Interest rate

12%	14%	15%	16%	18%	20%	24%	28%	32%	36%
0.8929	0.8772	0.8696	0.8621	0.8475	0.8333	0.8065	0.7813	0.7576	0.7353
1.6901	1.6467	1.6257	1.6052	1.5656	1.5278	1.4568	1.3916	1.3315	1.2760
2.4018	2.3216	2.2832	2.2459	2.1743	2.1065	1.9813	1.8684	1.7663	1.6735
3.0373	2.9137	2.8550	2.7982	2.6901	2.5887	2.4043	2.2410	2.0957	1.9658
3.6048	3.4331	3.3522	3.2743	3.1272	2.9906	2.7454	2.5320	2.3452	2.1807
4.1114	3.8887	3.7845	3.6847	3.4976	3.3255	3.0205	2.7594	2.5342	2.3388
4.5638	4.2883	4.1604	4.0386	3.8115	3.6046	3.2423	2.9370	2.6775	2.4550
4.9676	4.6389	4.4873	4.3436	4.0776	3.8372	3.4212	3.0758	2.7860	2.5404
5.3282	4.9464	4.7716	4.6065	4.3030	4.0310	3.5655	3.1842	2.8681	2.6033
5.6502	5.2161	5.0188	4.8332	4.4941	4.1925	3.6819	3.2689	2.9304	2.6495
5.9377	5.4527	5.2337	5.0286	4.6560	4.3271	3.7757	3.3351	2.9776	2.6834
6.1944	5.6603	5.4206	5.1971	4.7932	4.4392	3.8514	3.3868	3.0133	2.7084
6.4235	5.8424	5.5831	5.3423	4.9095	4.5327	3.9124	3.4272	3.0404	2.7268
6.6282	6.0021	5.7245	5.4675	5.0081	4.6106	3.9616	3.4587	3.0609	2.7403
6.8109	6.1422	5.8474	5.5755	5.0916	4.6755	4.0013	3.4834	3.0764	2.7502
6.9740	6.2651	5.9542	5.6685	5.1624	4.7296	4.0333	3.5026	3.0882	2.7575
7.1196	6.3729	6.0472	5.7487	5.2223	4.7746	4.0591	3.5177	3.0971	2.7629
7.2497	6.4674	6.1280	5.8178	5.2732	4.8122	4.0799	3.5294	3.1039	2.7668
7.3658	6.5504	6.1982	5.8775	5.3162	4.8435	4.0967	3.5386	3.1090	2.7697
7.4694	6.6231	6.2593	5.9288	5.3527	4.8696	4.1103	3.5458	3.1129	2.7718
7.5620	6.6870	6.3125	5.9731	5.3837	4.8913	4.1212	3.5514	3.1158	2.7734
7.6446	6.7429	6.3587	6.0113	5.4099	4.9094	4.1300	3.5558	3.1180	2.7746
7.7184	6.7921	6.3988	6.0442	5.4321	4.9245	4.1371	3.5592	3.1197	2.7754
7.7843	6.8351	6.4338	6.0726	5.4509	4.9371	4.1428	3.5619	3.1210	2.7760
7.8431	6.8729	6.4641	6.0971	5.4669	4.9476	4.1474	3.5640	3.1220	2.7765
8.0552	7.0027	6.5660	6.1772	5.5168	4.9789	4.1601	3.5693	3.1242	2.7775
8.2438	7.1050	6.6418	6.2335	5.5482	4.9966	4.1659	3.5712	3.1250	2.7778
8.3045	7.1327	6.6605	6.2463	5.5541	4.9995	4.1666	3.5714	3.1250	2.7778
8.3240	7.1401	6.6651	6.2492	5.5553	4.9999	4.1667	3.5714	3.1250	2.7778

FORMULAS

The following balance sheet and income statement are interpreted through the financial analysis formulas and industry ratios in this appendix. Most of these formulas and ratios are discussed in chapter 5.

Additional facts include SMC's having one million outstanding shares currently selling for $10 a share.

The stock was selling for $8 per share at the start of the year. SMC also has $10 million in outstanding bonds. The bonds are $1,000 face-value bonds redeemable in 20 years, paying 10% interest and currently selling for $1,100 each.

Balance Sheet

ASSETS	($000)	LIABILITIES AND NET WORTH	($000)
Cash	100	Note payable	0
Accounts receivable	60	Accounts payable	150
Inventory	300	Taxes payable	40
Total current assets	**460**	Other accruals	30
Plant and equipment	500	**Total current liabilities**	**220**
Less depreciation	100	Mortgage payable	150
Net	400	Common stock	250
Total assets	**860**	Retained earnings	240
		Total liabilities and net worth	**860**

Income Statement

	($000)
Sales	500
Less: Material and labor	300
Manufacturing costs	30
Cost of goods sold	**330**
Gross profit	**170**
Depreciation	20
Selling expense	20
Profit before interest and taxes	**130**
Interest payments	10
Taxes	40
Profit after taxes	**80**
Dividends	40
Retained earnings	**40**

Profit

profit margin = profit after taxes / sales
(i.e., $80,000 / $500,000 = 0.16, or 16%)

corporate earnings = sales – costs
(i.e., $500,000 – $330,000 = $170,000)

earnings per share = earnings / total shares
(i.e., $170,000 / 1,000,000 = $0.17)

PE ratio = price per share / earnings per share
(i.e., $10.00 / $0.17 = 59 times earnings)

Liquidity

acid test ratio = liquid assets /
current liabilities from cash
and accounts receivable
(i.e., $160,000 / $220,000 = 0.73)

current ratio =
current assets / current liabilities
(i.e., $460,000 / $220,000 = 2.09)

solvency ratio = net worth / total assets
(i.e., $490,000 / $860,000 = 0.57)

working capital =
current assets – current liabilities
(i.e., $460,000 – $220,000 = $240,000)

Company Value

book value = total assets – total liabilities from
total current liabilities plus mortgage payable
(i.e., $860,000 – $370,000 = $490,000)

owners' equity =
common stock + retained earnings
(i.e., $250,000 + $240,000 = $490,000)

book value per share =
owners' equity / outstanding shares
(i.e., $490,000 / 1,000,000 = $0.49)

dividend payout ratio =
dividend per share / earnings per share
(i.e., $0.04 / $0.17 = 0.235, or 23.5%)

net worth = common stock + retained earnings
(i.e., $250,000 + $240,000 = $490,000)

turnover = sales / assets
(i.e., $500,000 / $860,000 = 0.58)

Indebtedness

debt–equity ratio =
total liabilities / shareholders' equity
(i.e., $370,000 / $490,000 = 0.76)

interest coverage (IC) =
(pretax income + interest expense) /
interest expense
(i.e., [$130,000 + $10,000] / $10,000 = 14 times)

Return on Investment

return on assets (ROA) =
net income / total assets
(i.e., $80,000 / $860,000 = 0.09, or 9%)

return on equity (ROE) =
net income / owners' equity
(i.e., $80,000 / $490,000 = 0.16, or 16%)

return on investment capital (ROIV) =
net income / long-term debt + owners' equity
(i.e., $80,000 / [$150,000 + $490,000] = 0.125, or
12.5%)

bond yield = 10%

Investor Information

annual return (per share) =
increase or decrease in value + any dividend
(i.e., $2.00 + $0.04 = $2.04 per share).
On a percentage basis, the annual return
would be divided by the initial investment
(i.e., $2.04 / $8.00 = 0.255, or 25.5%).

current yield =
annual interest payment / current market value
(i.e., $100* / $1,100 = 0.0909, or 9.09%)

Annual interest payment =
bond face value × bond interest rate
(i.e., $1,000 × 10%).

dividend per share =
dividends / outstanding shares
(i.e., $40,000 / 1,000,000 = $0.04 a share)

holding period return (HPR) =
(current income + capital gains) / purchase price
(i.e., $0.04 + $2.00) / $8.00 = 0.255, or 25.5%)

simple rate of return (SRR) =
investment's annual income / initial investment
(i.e., $0.04 / $8.00 = 0.005, or 0.5%)

SUGGESTED RESOURCES

Stocks

North American Securities Administrators Association

750 First Street NE, Suite 1140, Washington, DC 20002

202-737-0900

U-7 registration forms and manuals can be obtained free of charge from the Web page at www.nasaa.org.

Small Business United of Texas

Offers for sale a Small Company Offering Registration (SCOR) kit for companies considering a SCOR offering. Local SCOR offices can be found throughout the United States.

www.score.org

U.S. Securities and Exchange Commission

SEC Headquarters, 100 F Street NE, Washington, DC 20549

202-942-8088

www.sec.gov

U.S. Securities and Exchange Commission EDGAR Database of filings by public companies

www.10kwizard.com

Yahoo! Finance

http://finance.yahoo.com

Minority Business Lenders or Suppliers

Business Consortium Fund

212-243-7360

Certified Development Company (CDC)

Call 800-972-2504 for the nearest CDC office.

National Association of Investment Companies

1300 Pennsylvania Avenue NW, Suite 700, Washington, DC 20004

Phone: 202-204-3001

Fax: 202-204-3022

www.naicvc.com

National Association of Small Business Investment Companies

666 11th Street NW, Suite 750, Washington, DC 20001

Phone: 202-628-5055

Fax: 202-628-5080

www.nasbic.org

National Association of Women Business Owners (NAWBO)

8405 Greensboro Drive, Suite 800, McLean, VA 22102

800-55-NAWBO

www.nawbo.org

National Minority Business Council

120 Broadway, 19th Floor, New York, NY 10271

Phone: 212-693-5050

Fax: 212-693-5048

www.nmbc.org

National Minority Supplier Development Council (NMSDC)

1040 Avenue of the Americas, 2nd Floor, New York, NY 10018

Phone: 212-944-2430

Fax: 212-719-9611

www.nmsdc.org

Service Corps of Retired Executives (SCORE) Association

409 3rd Street SW, 6th Floor, Washington, DC 20024

800-634-0245

www.score.org

Women Incorporated

310-277-1989

Women's Growth Capital Fund of Washington, DC

1029 31st Street NW, Washington, DC 20007

202-342-1431

www.womensgrowthcapital.com

Nonbank Lenders

AT&T Small Business Lending Corporation
800-221-7252

Business Lenders
Corporate Office, 50 State House Square, Hartford, CT 06103
860-244-9202
www.businesslenders.com

Commercial Finance Association
225 West 34th Street, Suite 1815, New York, NY 10122
Phone: 212-594-3490
Fax: 212-564-6053
www.cfa.com

Commercial Finance Group
www.cfgo.net

GE Capital Small Business Finance Corporation
800-447-2025

Heller First Capital Corporation
800-347-6430

Money Store Investment Corporation
800-722-3066

National Venture Capital Association
1655 North Fort Myer Drive, Suite 850, Arlington, VA 22209
Phone: 703-524-2549
Fax: 703-524-3940
www.nvca.org

Mid-Atlantic Venture Funds
Headquarters Office, Ben Franklin Technology Center, Lehigh University
125 Goodman Drive, Bethlehem, PA 18015
Phone: 610-865-6550
Fax: 610-865-6427
www.mavf.com

Venture Capital OnLine
www.vcfodder.com

Factoring Lenders

There are several large factoring lenders, including the businesses that follow. However, smaller businesses often need to go to smaller factoring lenders. A bank or loan broker might have some leads for smaller businesses.

CIT Group of Livingston, NJ
1 CIT Drive, Livingston, NJ 07039
973-740-5000
www.cit.com

Finova Group of Scottsdale, AZ
www.finova.com

GE Capital
www.gecapital.com

Quantum Corporate Funding of New York
1140 Avenue of the Americas, New York, NY 10036
Phone: 800-352-2535 or 212-768-1200
Fax: 212-944-8216
www.quantumfunding.com

Vendor Financing

AT&T Capital Corporation
201-397-3000

Canon Financial Services
800-220-0200
www.cfs.canon.com

GE Capital
www.gecommercialfinance.com

Hewlett-Packard
www.hp.com

IBM Credit Corporation
800-678-6900
www.financing.ibm.com

IKON Capital
www.ikon.com

Oracle Credit Corporation
www.oracle.com

Additional fund-raising information can be found at www.fundraisers.com.

Government Assistance

Federal Reserve Board
www.federalreserve.gov

National Association of Investment Companies (NAIC)
1300 Pennsylvania Avenue NW, Suite 700, Washington, DC 20004
Phone: 202-201-3001
Fax: 202-204-3022
www.naicvc.com

National Association of Small Business Investment Companies (NASBIC)

666 11th Street NW, Suite 750, Washington, DC 20001

Phone: 202-628-5055

Fax: 202-628-5080

www.nasbic.org

United States Small Business Administration

www.sbaonline.sba.gov

Print Resources

Abrams, R.M. (1993). *The successful business plan: Secrets & strategies.* Grants Pass, OR: Oasis Press.

Athletic Business: www.athleticbusiness.com

Athletic Management: 2488 North Triphammer Road, Ithaca, NY 14850; phone: 607-257-6970; fax: 607-257-7328; www.momentummedia.com

Barron's: www.barrons.com

Business Week: P.O. Box 8418, Red Oak, IA 51591; www.businessweek.com

Dun & Bradstreet: www.dnb.com

Fitness Management: 4130 Lien Road, Madison, WI 53704; 800-722-8764; www.fitnessmanagement.com

Forbes: 60 5th Avenue, New York, NY 10011; 800-295-0893; www.forbes.com

Fulks, D.L. (2000). *Revenues and expenses of divisions I and II intercollegiate athletic programs: Financial trends and relationships—1999.* Indianapolis: National Collegiate Athletic Association.

Gabriel, C. (1998). *How to sell your business—and get what you want! A pragmatic guide with revealing tips from 57 sellers.* Westport, CT: Gwent Press.

Hagstrom, R.G. (1998). *The NASCAR way: The business that drives the sport.* New York: Wiley.

Helyar, J. (1994). *Lords of the realm: The real history of baseball.* New York: Ballantine.

Leeds, M., & von Allmen, P. (2002). *The economics of sports.* New York: Addison-Wesley.

Livingstone, J.L. (1997). *The portable MBA in finance and accounting*, 2nd ed. New York: Wiley.

NCAA News: www.ncaa.org

Noll, R.G., & Zimbalist, A., eds. (1997). *Sports, jobs, and taxes: The economic impact of sports teams and stadiums.* Washington, DC: Brookings Institution Press.

Quirk, J., & Fort, R. (1992). *Pay dirt: The business of professional team sports.* Princeton, NJ: Princeton University Press.

Quirk, J., & Fort, R. (1999). *Hard ball: The abuse of power in pro team sports.* Princeton, NJ: Princeton University Press.

Sports Business Daily: 120 West Morehead Street, Suite 220, Charlotte, NC 28202; phone: 704-973-1500; fax: 704-973-1501; www.sportsbusinessdaily.com

Staudohar, P.D. (1996). *Playing for dollars: Labor relations and the sports business.* Ithaca, NY: Cornell University Press.

Street & Smith's SportsBusiness Journal: 120 West Morehead Street, Suite 310, Charlotte, NC 28202; phone: 704-973-1410; fax: 704-973-1401; www.sportsbusinessjournal.com

Wall Street Journal: www.wsj.com

Zimbalist, A. (1999). *Unpaid professionals: Commercialism and conflict in big-time college sports.* Princeton, NJ: Princeton University Press.

ability to pay—The ability to pay refers to a business' or customer's ability to make payment to a vendor. Thus, if you are trying to sell someone concession items, you should examine that individual's ability to purchase the items with either cash or credit.

acceleration clause—Such a clause is often included in a contract to force one party to pay the entire amount owed if another party misses a payment.

account—Accounts represent a record of a relationship between parties. A typical example is a line of credit with a bank or a simple checking account.

account balance—An account balance represents the current account status at the end of a given time period. Thus, at the end of each month a bank might send customers a checking account balance to help them identify how much money they have available for future purchases.

accounting—Accounting is the art of tabulating financial numbers to determine how much money someone earned and spent during a given period.

account reconciliation—If you have ever balanced your own checkbook, you have performed account reconciliation. Account reconciliation entails adjusting the difference between various accountings to ensure that all totals agree.

accounts payable (A/P)—Accounts payable represent outstanding obligations that are owed by a business to vendors, lenders, or anyone else from whom credit was received and goods were purchased on such credit.

accounts receivable (A/R)—Accounts receivable represent moneys that are owed to a business from customers who purchased merchandise or services on credit. Many customers do not have sufficient funds to make cash purchases and thus need credit in order to purchase necessary products or supplies. A/R are not bad; they represent significant sales and can be used as collateral to borrow money. However, A/R can become a burden if they are not repaid in a timely manner.

accrual—Accrual is an accounting term that defines anticipated future expenses and revenues. For example, in some accounting systems (accrual accounting), expenditures and revenues are recorded at the time of the transaction, regardless of when the money is actually disbursed or received. In contrast, in the **cash basis budgeting** (or accounting) system, expenditures and revenues are recorded at the time they are actually disbursed or received.

accrued dividend—Sometimes a company decides to pay a dividend to shareholders, but the company's board of directors does not make a formal declaration. Without a formal declaration, an accrued dividend does not represent a legal obligation, but it is still an obligation that should be paid to shareholders barring any unforeseen needs for such funds.

accrued interest—Similar to accrued dividends (dividends that have been earned but not yet paid), accrued interest is interest that is owed but not yet paid.

acid test ratio (quick ratio)—The acid test is an analysis of the ability of a company to liquidate current assets (excluding harder-to-sell items such as inventory) to pay off current liabilities. Cash is added to marketable securities and accounts receivable, and these liquid assets are divided by current liabilities. If the resulting number is less than 1, then the company does not have enough liquid assets to pay current liabilities. If the ratio is greater than 1, then the company has more than enough liquid assets to pay off current liabilities. If a company has $100 in cash, no marketable securities, $200 in accounts receivable, and $400 in current liabilities, the acid test ratio is ($100 + $200) / $400 = 0.75. Since the ratio is lower than 1, the company cannot cover all its current liabilities.

acquisition—Acquiring control of a corporation through stock purchase or exchange.

activity—Activity refers to the number of transactions occurring in a given account during a given accounting time period.

actual value—Actual value refers to the **book value** of an asset. To determine book value, take an item's original purchase cost and subtract all accumulated depreciation. If you bought a computer with a five-year life for $5,000 and used straight-line depreciation, after one year the actual, or book, value would be $5,000 minus $1,000 (one year's worth of depreciation) = $4,000.

actuaries—Actuaries are expert mathematicians who analyze the risks and premiums for insurance coverage based on probability estimates. Probability estimates help determine the risk that a given event will occur and the potential loss that could be incurred from such an event.

adjustable basis—This term is typically used to describe a tax situation in which the value of an asset is increased through capital expenditures or reduced by depreciation. The adjustable basis for your house changes when you incur such capital expenditures as installing a new roof. Any increase in the house's value when you try to resell the house needs to be adjusted by the cost of the new roof; this reduces your tax liability for any profits from the sale.

adjustable rate mortgage (ARM)—ARMs, also referred to as variable- or flexible-rate mortgages, are a type of mortgage for which the interest rate can change over the loan's lifetime. It is common for ARMs to be low cost for the first several years of the loan and for the interest rate to increase over time. In contrast, the interest rate for fixed-rate mortgages remains stable throughout the loan's lifetime.

adjusted balance method (ABM)—The ABM is one of several financing techniques (see also **average daily balance method** and **past-due balance method**) used to determine interest owed. As an example of how ABM is calculated, if you have a credit card that has an 18% annual interest rate, you will be paying 1.5% interest a month on your adjusted balance. If you used your credit card to buy sporting goods worth $400 in February and paid only $300 in March, you would owe 1.5% interest multiplied by the adjusted $100 balance ($400 – $300). If you made no more purchases in March, you would owe $101.50, representing the $100 balance and $1.50 in interest (Siegel, Shim, & Hartman, 1992).

adjusted gross income (AGI)—AGI is a tax term representing your total gross income minus allowed adjustments for such items as health care costs or mortgage interest.

ad valorem tax—An ad valorem tax is a levy imposed on business property (both real and possibly personal), based primarily on a percentage of the property's value.

after-tax cash flow (ATCF)—ATCF represents all income minus any taxes paid.

aggregate amount—An aggregate amount is the total, or gross, amount of a given item. For example, the aggregate income of the nation is the gross national product.

allowance—In finance terms, an allowance is a credit that a creditor allows a debtor to take for any of a number of reasons. For example, assume you bought 1,000 foam #1 fingers to sell, and 200 of them are defective. Instead of your owing $1,000 for the lot, the seller might give you a $200 allowance or reduce the amount owed to compensate you for the defective products.

amortization—Amortization refers to repaying a loan in installments. As such payments are made, typically on a property mortgage, the debtor's equity in the property increases because each installment comprises both interest and principal. Goodwill can also be amortized over several years instead of just the first year after a business has been purchased.

annual percentage rate (APR)—APR is the ratio of the finance charge to the average amount of credit in use during the lifetime of a loan (Siegel, Shim, & Hartman, 1992). Under the Truth in Lending Act, banks must disclose the APR (in percentage form) and the actual finance charge in dollars.

annual report—At the end of their fiscal years, companies produce an annual report to inform shareholders about the company's financial position. Annual reports are carefully scrutinized by more than just shareholders; potential investors, creditors, lenders, and other interested parties rely on the audited information to help make investment decisions.

annual return—The annual return is the return from a given investment over the course of a year. Assume you purchased a stock on January 1 for $1,000 and sold the stock on the following December 31 for $1,500. During the year, the stock paid a dividend of $50. Your total annual return is calculated as follows:

increased value ($1,500 – $1,000) = $500
dividend income + 50
total return $550

The percentage annual return calculation is:

percentage annual return = total annual return / initial investment

= $550 / $1,000

= 55%

Thus, the annual return on this investment is $550, or 55%. However, not all investments are this successful. If the stock decreased to $800, the annual return would be calculated as follows:

$1,000 decreased to $800 = –$200

+$50 dividend

= –$150 total revenue

percentage annual return = total return / initial investment

= –$150 / $1,000

= –15%

annuity—An annuity is typically a savings account or a retirement account with an insurance company or other investment placement company into which the investor can deposit a lump sum or scheduled deposits. When a particular event occurs, such as retirement, the investor receives regular repayments such as monthly distributions until the entire invested amount is repaid. Annuities have several significant benefits: The government does not tax the interest earned until the funds are distributed; compounding interest quickly increases the investment value; and unlike pensions and individual retirement accounts, annuities normally do not have any limitations on the amount an investor can contribute. One drawback, among several, is that investors normally cannot recover their funds until they reach the age of 59 1/2 without incurring significant penalties (Siegel, Shim, & Hartman, 1992).

appreciation—Appreciation is the increase in an item's value. If you bought 100 shares of a stock for $1,000 and sell them for $2,000, the investment has appreciated $1,000.

appropriation—An appropriation is an amount of money set aside in a budget to cover a particular expense such as inventory or expected wages.

arrears—Being in arrears means being in default of an obligation. You are in arrears if you owe someone $10 to be paid on Friday but do not pay on Friday. Arrearage also refers to the situation in which cumulative preferred stock dividends have been declared but not paid.

ask price—The ask price is the price a seller would like to receive for the item he wishes to sell.

assessed valuation—Government entities require landowners to pay property taxes based on the assessed value of the property. The assessed value is not always the market value; it is often a percentage of the market value of the home and land.

asset—An asset is any resource or goods that might offer future benefits to a business and have value. Examples of assets are buildings, machinery, land, inventory, business goodwill, and related resources. "Hard assets" include such items as inventory and equipment that are tangible (can be touched). Intangible assets such as a company's goodwill, which has value but is hard to quantify, are called "soft assets."

assignment—Assignment refers to the transfer of property (real or personal) from one party to another. By assigning the property, the assignor gives the property to another (the assignee) with the assurance that there are no claims against the property and that the assignor has the right to transfer the property.

assumption—If you cannot pay your bills, someone can assume your debt and then become responsible for repaying the debt.

audit—An audit is an inspection by an independent external entity of all a company's accounting records and business operations. The primary purpose of a company audit by a certified public accountant (CPA) is to validate all financial statements for accuracy so that the government, lenders, shareholders, and others can obtain an accurate view of the company.

average collection period—The average collection period is the average amount of time it takes a business to collect outstanding accounts receivable. The longer the average, the more money is lost because of the inability to use such outstanding funds for investment or other growth opportunities. Furthermore, if the average is long, that means there is a greater likelihood that some accounts receivables might be difficult to collect.

average daily balance method (ADBM)—The ADBM is a method used by banks and credit card companies to calculate interest earned or owed. Using this method, a bank examines your average daily balance throughout the month and divides that amount by the number of days in the month. Assume that on the first day of the month you had $500 in the bank and on the 15th had only $100 in the bank. Also assume that your account earns 10% interest annually, or 0.83% a month. Your average daily balance is calculated as follows:

Number of days		Balance		Weighted balance
15	×	$500	=	$7,500
15	×	$100	=	$1,500
			Total	**$9,000**

The $9,000 weighted balance is divided by 30 days, equaling an average daily balance of $300, which if multiplied by the monthly interest rate produces an interest payment of $2.49.

backup withholding—Sometimes banks, investment companies, or other businesses cannot determine the Social Security number of someone to whom they are required to pay dividends, interest, or other payments. Instead of paying the full amount and possibly depriving the IRS of potential taxes, the entity withholds 20% of the payment and sends it to the IRS.

balance—For strict accounting purposes, balance is calculated by totaling all credits and subtracting all debt. However, in the context of **balance sheets**, balance refers to equality between all assets on the one hand and all liabilities plus owners' equity on the other hand, as shown in the equation assets = liabilities + owners' equity.

balance sheet—A balance sheet is a statement of financial condition prepared at the end of a set time period that lists a company's assets, liabilities, and owners' equity. The balance sheet is balanced when assets equal all liabilities plus the owners' equity. See the following balance sheet of Sport Manufacturing Company for the year ending October 31, 1999.

balloon payment—Some term loans (called balloon loans) require that only interest payments are made until the loan is due; then the entire principal and remaining interest are paid in a balloon payment.

bankruptcy—A business can face bankruptcy when its debt exceeds its assets' fair market value. If a company owes $1 million and its assets are worth only $500,000, the company can voluntarily pursue bankruptcy protection from creditors or can be forced by courts into bankruptcy to help protect any remaining value that the creditors might try to salvage. Three categories of bankruptcy are available: Chapters 7, 11, and 13. Chapter 7 allows an individual's or business' property to be sold and the proceeds to be divided among creditors. Some specifically excluded items, such as a primary home and one auto, are not sold so that the debtor can still survive. Any debts that are not covered by the sale proceeds are discharged. More than one million Chapter 7 bankruptcies were filed in 1997 (Cheeseman, 2001). Chapter 11 allows a company to reorganize and maintain control over its assets and operations while it attempts to resolve repayment schedules and amounts with debtors. Once the courts confirm a reorganization plan, all debts not included in the plan are discharged (Cheeseman, 2001). Chapter 13, which is sometimes called the wage-earner plan, allows a debtor to repay debts over a three-year period. Debts are consolidated based on a court-coordinated and -approved schedule that allows for installment payments (Cheeseman, 2001).

bear and **bear market**—A bear is an individual who believes the stock market will drop (typically more than 20%), and so he sells stocks, "goes **short**," or buys a **put**. A bear market is a prolonged period during which stock prices continue to decline. Bear markets can be caused by poor economic conditions, political collapses, rising interest rates, or a host of other factors that foster pessimism among investors. See **bull** and **bull market**.

bearer bonds—Bearer bonds, or coupon bonds, do not require owners to register their names with the

Balance Sheet

ASSETS		LIABILITIES AND NET WORTH	
	($000)		($000)
Cash	100	Note payable	0
Accounts receivable	60	Accounts payable	150
Inventory	300	Taxes payable	40
Total current assets	**460**	Other accruals	30
Plant and equipment	500	**Total current liabilities**	**220**
Less depreciation	100	Mortgage payable	150
Net	400	Common stock	250
Total assets	**860**	Retained earnings	240
		Total liabilities and net worth	**860**

issuing company or government unit. The person who bears the bond can clip a coupon when it becomes due and cash it in.

benchmarking—Benchmarking is the process of analyzing statistical data to compare companies against one another or against industry standards.

Best's ratings—A.M. Best performs an annual audit of insurance companies to determine their financial stability, which is a valuable tool for those seeking to buy insurance from a solid company or those interested in investing in insurance company stocks. The highest rating is A+.

bid price—A bid price is the highest price a buyer is willing to pay for a security. The asking price is the price proposed by the seller of the security.

bill—There are several different types of bills, but in general, a bill is a written statement describing the terms and conditions of a particular sales transaction.

billing cycle—Companies traditionally bill their clients on a regular basis, typically monthly, bimonthly, quarterly, semiannually, or annually. These billing periods are referred to as billing cycles (they cycle through on a regular basis).

bill of sale—A bill of sale is formal documentation that represents the transfer of title to goods.

bills payable—Bills payable are bills or promissory notes that a company owes, representing a debt. See also **accounts payable**.

bills receivable—Bills receivable refers to notes, checks, drafts, or other contractually obligated instruments representing money or obligations owed to a person or entity. See also **accounts receivable**.

binder—A binder is a temporary payment representing a good-faith deposit between contracting parties to go forward with a contract. The binder binds the parties to the agreement but can be returned if the contract is not finalized. This distinguishes a binder from a deposit, which is normally not returned if the contract is not finalized.

blank endorsement—If you receive a check and sign the back, then you or anyone else who comes into possession of the check can cash it. To prevent others from cashing the check without your permission, you should sign the check and also write "For deposit only to the account of Jane Doe," or a similar phrase, on the check. The check no longer has a blank endorsement but now has a specified endorsement.

blind pool—Investors can join together as limited partners and each contribute a specific amount toward an investment. The combined money can then be invested by a general partner in investments such as stocks, bonds, or real estate. The pool is called a blind pool because the limited partners contribute without knowing exactly where the general partner might invest the money.

blind trust—In the traditional blind trust, one person or several individuals give their assets to a third party who will manage the funds in total independence. For example, President Bush owned part of the Texas Rangers before becoming the governor of Texas, and to avoid any potential conflict of interest, he transferred his ownership interest to a blind trust ("Bush Admits," 2000).

blue-chip stocks—Blue-chip stocks are stocks issued by the strongest companies—those that have a strong reputation for success, offer quality products or services, and are financially secure. Some blue-chip companies are McDonald's, General Electric, IBM, Shell, AT&T, and Bank of America.

bond—A bond is a legal instrument through which a company or government entity promises to repay the bond purchaser both the principal and a specified interest rate; in return the bondholder receives a pledge of assets or can rely on the **full faith and credit** of the issuer. Thus, if IBM wants to expand and issues $50 million in bonds, some investors may rely on IBM's past history of not defaulting on bonds and purchase the bond backed by their faith in the company. The full faith and credit of a company can back bonds not backed by assets. If the company collapses, there will be no collateral from which to repay the investment.

bond discount—Sometimes after a bond is issued the interest rate changes, making the bond less desirable than it was previously. A company's instability can also reduce the value of a bond. A bond is at a discount when the bond's **face value**, or **par value** (what the bond is worth when it is issued), is greater than the **market value**. Market value is what the bond would be worth if sold on a bond market. If the market value exceeds the face value, then the bond is being traded at a premium.

bondholder—A bondholder is anyone who holds legal title to a bond.

bond rating—Two companies, Moody's and Standard & Poor's, issue bond ratings that range from C or D to Aaa or AAA, respectively. An AAA- or

Aaa-rated bond is the highest-quality bond, while ratings at the other extreme (C or D) indicate a lower chance that bondholders will be able to recover their investment. Blue-chip companies or strong government entities (financially strong cities, municipalities, or states) typically have AAA or similar ratings.

bond valuation—Bond valuation is the complex mathematical process used to determine how much an investor should pay for a bond. The equation includes such criteria as present value, interest rate, investor-required rate of return, the bond's maturity date, and the degree of risk.

bond yield—The yield obtained from a bond represents its effective rate of return. One means to measure the yield is the current yield method, which is calculated by dividing the annual interest payment by the bond's current market value. Thus, if you have a bond with a 10% coupon rate and a $1,000 par value that is selling for $975, the **current yield** is (10% × $1,000) / $975 = 10.26%. This method shows that you are earning a little more than the stated interest rate, but it does not take into consideration the bond's maturity date, which can affect the attractiveness of the investment. Two other more complex formulas, **yield to call** and **yield to maturity**, can help provide a more detailed analysis if the bond is held for a set time period or held until it matures.

book value—Book value is calculated by subtracting total liabilities from total assets. See also **actual value**.

book value per share (BVPS)—BVPS represents the value of each share of stock based on its cost when the stock was originally issued. We can calculate BVPS by dividing total stockholders' equity by the number of outstanding shares. If a company's total shareholders' equity is $40 million and there are one million outstanding shares, then the BVPS is $40.

break-even point—The break-even point is the level of revenue generation at which total revenue exactly matches total costs. The break-even analysis is used to help determine when profit could be made on a given product. Assume that you manufacture baseballs and that the variable costs (string, rubber, hourly wages, and so on) are $0.50 per ball. Assume also that fixed costs such as rent are $10,000 per month. If you manufactured and sold 5,000 balls per month, your total costs would be $2,500 (variable) + $10,000 (fixed) = $12,500. To break even, you would need to sell all 5,000 balls at an average price of $2.50 each. If

you made 10,000 balls in a given month and kept the price of $2.50 per ball, then you would have $15,000 in costs and $25,000 in sales, which would generate a $10,000 profit.

break point—Sellers often indicate that if you buy 1 to 100 of an item, the price will be $1 each, for example. If you buy 101 to 500, the price will be reduced to $0.75 each. The break point for the discount is 101 units. A seller might have multiple break points at which the price continues to decline as the order quantity increases.

bridge loan—Sometimes a company needs a short-term loan while it is negotiating a long-term loan. A bridge loan is the solution, but it might cost more than traditional bank loans. A bridge loan might be needed by a buyer who wants to put a deposit down on some property before closing and securing a long-term mortgage.

budget—A budget is a road map or plan expressed in monetary terms that highlights all anticipated assets, debt, expenses, revenue, and net worth.

bull and **bull market**—A bull is an investor who has a favorable outlook on the economy and is willing to invest in stock, bonds, and other securities. A bull market is when there are prolonged market advances over a significant time period. See also **bear** and **bear market**.

business cycle—All businesses go through cyclical conditions in which they may have significant growth and then at a later time experience contraction. The entire economy can also go through cycles that include recovery and recession.

buying power—Buying power can be equated to liquid assets, which represent cash and marketable securities that could be quickly sold to make various purchases. If you do not have liquid assets, you do not have any buying power.

buy order—If you call your stockbroker and indicate that you want to purchase certain securities, you have just placed a buy order.

buyout—In a buyout, one investor, multiple investors, or a business can acquire a controlling interest in a company through buying a majority of that company's stock. Various professional sports teams have gone public and issued stock, and some of these teams were subsequently bought out by an individual investor or investment group and became privately owned teams.

call provision—Companies that issue bonds or preferred stock can pay an investor an amount over the face value of the security and redeem the security before it reaches maturity. A company might undertake this strategy if it wants to reduce amounts owed to bondholders or reduce the number of outstanding stock shares.

capital—Capital is wealth used to produce additional wealth.

capital asset pricing model (CAPM)—The CAPM is a method of measuring the cost of common stock.

capital assets—The term *capital assets* commonly refers to fixed assets such as buildings, fields, stadiums, equipment, and other assets that can be depreciated.

capital gains and **capital losses**—Capital gains are the total gains in value of an investment, excluding dividends. However, dividends can be included in the capital gains if the dividends are reinvested in additional shares of the same stock. Capital losses are all realized losses from an investment. There are both long-term and short-term capital gains and losses. Long-term capital gains or losses are investments that have matured for more than one year and result in capital gains or losses that must be reported to the IRS. Short-term capital gains or losses apply to investments held for less than one year.

capitalization rate (cap rate)—The cap rate is used to determine the rate of return received from a real estate investment. To determine the cap rate, we divide the net operating income (NOI) from the investment's first year by the total investment cost. The higher the cap rate, the lower the perceived value of the investment. If you obtain $10,000 in NOI from a property and the property cost $200,000, then the cap rate is $10,000 / $200,000 = 5%. If banks are paying 8% interest, then the return on the real estate investment would be poor unless the real estate markedly increased in value.

capital markets—There are a number of capital markets in which long-term debt and securities are bought and sold. The most famous capital market is the New York Stock Exchange. Additional markets include the American Stock Exchange, the over-the-counter market (NASDAQ), and numerous regional and foreign exchanges.

capital outlay—A capital outlay is any expenditure for property or equipment for permanent use.

capital spending—Capital spending is the net spending on fixed assets.

cash—There are many terms for cash, including legal tender and numerous slang terms. In the business world, cash includes money, coins, checks, bearer bonds, bank accounts, negotiable instruments, and related liquid assets.

cash basis budgeting—This budgeting process recognizes income and expenses when cash is actually received or paid and does not recognize accounts receivable or accounts payable.

cash discount—Manufacturers or wholesalers often offer discounts for those who purchase items with cash. A cash discount may be expressed by the formula 2/10/30. This formula means that the buyer has 30 days to pay the net amount. However, a buyer who pays the bill within 10 days will receive a 2% discount. Sellers can use multiple discounts in addition to cash discounts, such as seasonal or volume discounts, to offer even greater savings.

cash flow—Cash flow refers to the difference between what a company brings in and what it pays out. Companies can keep track of cash payments and receipts with a cash flow statement.

cash system of accounting—The cash system of accounting calculates expenditures and income only when cash is actually paid or received. This system does not consider accounts receivable or accounts payable.

cats and dogs—A derogatory term referring to stocks that represent a poor investment choice because of their highly speculative nature.

certificate of deposit (CD)—CDs are a type of savings account that pays more than traditional passbook or other savings accounts. They earn higher interest because the depositor has to keep the money in the CD for a longer maturity period than for other types of accounts.

clear title—When real or personal property is sold, the buyer normally wants the property to have a clear title, which means that no liens or other claims exist against the property. If the property is subject to a court-ordered lien, it can still be resold, but with a clouded title.

collateral—Collateral is either real or personal property pledged as security for repaying a loan.

commercial paper (CP)—Large, stable corporations issue commercial paper, or unsecured promissory notes from the corporation for amounts exceeding $25,000. Commercial paper typically carries a higher interest rate than bank accounts or CDs and typically matures in 30, 60, or 90 days.

common stock—Common stocks are shares in either privately held or public companies, representing an equity interest in those companies. Although common stock shareholders own an equity share in the company, if a company goes bankrupt, they are paid only after bondholders and preferred stock shareholders are paid. Stockholders have specific rights, including the right to elect the board of directors and the right of preemption, which entitles them to buy any new stocks from the company before other investors can. Preemption helps the stockholder maintain a proportional share in the company.

compensating balance—Some banks allow a depositor to borrow money but demand that the borrower maintain a specified balance in the bank. Thus, the bank might loan you $10,000 but insist that you maintain a 10% compensating balance to help hedge against the possibility of your defaulting on the loan. The borrower normally does not earn interest on the compensating balance, which effectively increases the interest on the loan. For example, assume that the $10,000 loan has a required interest payment of 8%. Since the $1,000 compensating balance does not earn interest, the true interest rate for the loan is $800 / ($10,000 – $1,000), which equals 8.89%.

compounding—Compounding entails retaining an investment's return from subsequent years after the initial investment, which results in accruing more revenue than if the investment's return was withdrawn immediately upon receipt. Thus, compounding can significantly increase an investment's total return.

compound interest—With many loans, interest is added to the principal loaned amount over the loan's life. If you borrowed $100 at 10% interest compounded annually, you would owe $110 after the first year, $121 for the second year ($110 × 110%), $133 for the third year ($121 × 110%), and so on throughout the life of the loan.

conglomerate merger—This form of merger occurs when companies in unrelated lines of business come together.

consumer credit—Consumer credit includes all nonbusiness debt (personal debt) excluding mortgages. Credit card debt represents part of the overall consumer credit.

Consumer Credit Protection Act (CCPA), also called the **Truth in Lending Act**—The CCPA requires a lender to clearly disclose the loan terms, interest rate, total payments, and total interest amount.

consumer finance companies—Sometimes a consumer has a poor credit history, and banks are unwilling to loan the individual any money. A consumer finance company can also loan the consumer money, through either a secured or an unsecured loan, for a short term and at a higher interest rate. The interest rate is higher because the loan is riskier.

consumer price index (CPI)—The Bureau of Labor Statistics publishes a monthly CPI number, which represents an average of the prices of various goods and services that consumers typically purchase in various urban areas. The CPI provides insight into the purchasing power of the U.S. dollar.

contingency fund—A contingency fund is a reserve account that an individual or entity has put money into to help pay unforeseen bills or cover emergency monetary needs.

controller—A controller is someone who controls or organizes the finances of a company or organization.

conventional mortgage—Typically, mortgages are obtained after a buyer has provided a sizable down payment on real property and offers fixed monthly payments at a set interest rate over a 15- or 30-year term.

convertibles—Convertibles is the term used to describe bonds, debentures, or preferred stocks that can be converted to common stock or other securities. An investor might convert the bonds or preferred stock to obtain an ownership interest or to benefit from dividends or continued growth. Convertible preferred stock can be converted according to a preset conversion price formula at a specified date. Debentures can also be converted to stocks if they are convertible debentures.

corporate bond—A company can issue a debt security (bond) with semiannual interest payments that is traded on the major exchanges. These bonds typically have a $1,000 face value. Bonds are backed by either collateral or the full faith and credit of the corporation.

corporate earnings—Corporate earnings are calculated by subtracting costs from sales. If earnings increase, stock prices should increase; and if earnings decrease, stock prices should decrease. This happened in late 1998, when corporate earnings slid, causing the Dow Jones Industrial Average to drop almost 2,000 points.

cosign—Lending institutions may be reluctant to loan an individual or company money because of a poor credit history. However, if a cosigner agrees to repay the loan if it goes into default, the lending institution will be much more likely to make the loan. The cosigner becomes liable for the entire loan if the borrower defaults.

coupon—When interest is due on a bond, the bondholder can clip the coupon from the bond and present it to a designated institution such as a bank to obtain payment.

creative financing—Sometimes a borrower cannot obtain a mortgage and may pursue creative financing to obtain money from a third party. Creative financing could entail a balloon payment, assumption of a prior mortgage on a property, or an adjustable rate mortgage.

credit—Credit refers to any purchase made on account, which means it is paid at a later date. In accounting terms, a credit represents an increase in funds and is usually listed on the right side in the T-account system. See also **debit**.

creditor—Anyone who is owed money is a creditor.

credit rating—Lenders use credit ratings to determine the risks associated with any given loan or extension of credit. Factors such as job history, housing, income, assets, and credit history help determine an individual's credit rating. Credit rating is a process that tracks an individual's or company's ability to repay borrowed money. Lenders use credit ratings to determine if any new moneys might be advanced.

current assets— Assets that are expected to be converted to cash in one year or less. Examples of current assets that appear on balance sheets are cash and short-term financial assets.

current ratio (CR)—Current ratio expresses a company's ability to cover current liabilities with current assets. To calculate CR, we divide current assets by current liabilities. If a company has $400 million in current assets and $100 million in current liabilities, the CR is four to one, which means the current assets can cover current liabilities four times over.

current yield—The current yield is an investment's return in relation to its current value. For a bond, the annual interest payments are divided by the bond's current market value. If you have a $1,000 bond paying 10% interest, and the bond has a par value of $950, then your current yield is $100 / $950 = 10.5%.

custodial account—A parent or guardian can establish a custodial account for a minor. The account belongs to the minor, but the minor is allowed to make transactions only with the custodian's approval.

days sales outstanding (DSO)—DSO is also referred to as the average collection period (ACP), which represents the length of time it is taking customers to repay debt owed to the company. A high DSO means that a company is not effectively collecting its accounts receivable or that credit is being extended to inappropriate customers.

debenture—Debentures are long-term bonds that are not secured by any collateral. Because these bonds are backed by a company's good name and credit history, companies need good credit ratings to issue debentures.

debit—A debit represents any decrease in revenue or net worth. It is documented by being listed on the left side of a T-account. See also **credit**.

debt—Debt is any money, goods, or services owed to someone else on the basis of a prior contractual agreement.

debt–equity ratio—The debt-equity ratio is one of the ratios obtained from analysis of financial statements and is used to determine how much protection creditors have. To calculate the ratio, divide total liabilities by total shareholders' equity. If a company has long-term debt of $200 million and shareholders' equity of $400 million, the debt–equity ratio is 0.5 to 1. If the debt-equity ratio is higher than 1, the company is not as good an investment as others because the company is paying significant interest costs relative to its assets. If a company is highly leveraged, it is not as good a credit risk compared with companies with low debt–equity ratios.

debtor—A debtor is anyone who has a legal or moral obligation to pay a debt to a creditor.

debt securities—A debt security is any security such as a bond, note, or contract that proves the existence of a debt obligation. Stocks are not a debt security but rather an **equity** security.

debt service—Debt service refers to the repayment of an obligation. The debt service on some new stadiums will be about $20 million per year for approximately 30 years.

deduction—The IRS allows specific deductions such as state and local taxes, employee expenses, and charitable contributions to reduce a taxpayer's **adjusted gross income (AGI)**.

deep-discount bond—Bonds can fall out of favor with investors for various reasons (e.g., when the coupon rate is lower than current yield rates available from newer bonds). When a bond declines more than 25% below its face value, it is called a deep-discount bond.

deferred annuity—A deferred annuity is an **annuity** that begins paying out after a specified period of time. The payout could begin either on a specific date or on the date of a particular event, such as a person's retirement.

deferred profit-sharing plan—If a company has a good year, it can share a portion of the profit through an employee trust to give employees a percentage of their salary as a bonus. The primary benefit of such plans for the company is that they are deductible as a business expense if they meet IRS requirements.

deficit—A deficit represents any excess of expenses over income. In order to overcome the income–expense disparity, a company or individual needs to either reduce savings to cover losses or borrow money.

deflation—Deflation, which is the opposite of **inflation**, refers to conditions in which prices decline over a given period. The reduced prices are normally the result of fewer dollars in the economy.

delisting—If a company fails to follow specified stock exchange rules or regulations such as maintaining a minimum net worth, the company can be delisted from its exchange. Delisting can also occur when a company closes or merges with another company, in which case shareholders with stock in the company are issued different stocks.

demand deposit account—A checking account is an example of a demand deposit account. Funds can be withdrawn on demand through the writing or cashing of a check.

deposit insurance—Federal agencies such as the Federal Deposit Insurance Corporation can insure bank accounts to foster a sense of safety on the part of depositors.

depreciation—Every item deteriorates over time, and a business must replace items as they deteriorate. A business can better afford to purchase new equipment if it takes a charge against earnings (reduces earnings) to write off the costs of a depreciating asset based on a specified formula. The formula is derived from the depreciation base. Assume you buy a computer for $6,000 that has an estimated life of five years. After five years you could sell the computer for its salvage value of $1,000. The depreciation base is the initial cost minus the salvage value, or $5,000 in this case. The depreciation base is divided by the asset's life (five years) to produce a yearly depreciation of $1,000.

direct costs—Direct costs are directly associated with a given program. The direct costs for team promotion might include all costs associated with advertising and personnel.

discharge—The completion of the debt process through repayment of a financial obligation is called discharging the debt. A discharge in bankruptcy is a final court order whereby the debtor is relieved of all further debt obligations.

disclaimer—Accountants or auditors who have not had enough time or received enough information to make a conclusive decision about a company's financial statement can prepare a report with a disclaimer. The disclaimer can indicate that some uncertainties exist (e.g., a pending IRS audit or a lawsuit that can significantly jeopardize the company's financial position).

disclosure—All financial statements, including a company's annual report, must fully disclose all relevant facts such as contractual terms, debt issues, and equity adjustments. Under **Securities and Exchange Commission** regulations, a publicly traded company has to fully disclose to stockholders any disastrous event that could affect the company's financial condition, such as the death of a key executive or major research and development failures.

discount bond—A discount bond is sold in the marketplace below its **face value**.

discount broker—A discount broker is a stockbroker who does not give investment advice but performs trades for clients at a reduced price.

discounted net cash flow—This is a means to determine an investment's value by examining after-tax cash flows and return on an investment. By examining income streams and reducing them to represent the present value of money, an investor can critically examine how much should be paid for a given investment in order to generate a given rate of return.

discounted payback rule—This rule analyzes how long it will take a business to get its money back after investing in a capital project while also factoring in the opportunity cost of capital by discounting the future cash flows.

discount factor, or **present value factor**—The discount factor is an arithmetic calculation that is used to help calculate the **present value** of a given investment.

discounting—Discounting is the formula used to determine the present value of a sum of money to be received in the future. Comprehensive tables allow individuals to easily determine the **present value** of given sums assuming various interest rates.

discount rate—The discount rate is the interest rate or percent return that can be earned from an investment. The discount rate is used when determining the **present value** of an investment option.

discretionary funds—Discretionary funds are moneys set aside for incidental expenses. Typically an executive is given significant latitude in spending discretionary funds.

disposable income—Disposable income is the amount of money available to individuals after they have had taxes, contributions to benefits, union dues, and related deductions taken from their paychecks.

diversification—To reduce investment-related risks, investors often diversify their investments so that if one fails, the overall loss will not be as significant as it would with a single investment. Mutual funds are a classic example of diversification in that the funds traditionally purchase numerous stocks, which helps reduce investor risks.

dividend—A company's board of directors can set aside a portion of the company's net income to benefit the shareholders. Cash dividends can be given, but once received by the shareholder they are taxable. This double taxation (company pays taxes on income, then taxpayers get taxed on their dividends) is one of the key drawbacks of the corporation structure of business. **Stock dividends** consisting of additional shares of stock can also be allocated by the board of directors and are not taxed upon receipt by the shareholder. When additional stocks are given as a dividend, the stockholder pays taxes only when selling them.

dividend payout ratio—Dividend payments can be expressed as a percentage of net earnings: Dividends per share are divided by earnings per share. Assume that a company has $1 million in earnings and that the board has approved a $50,000 dividend payout to the company's 25,000 outstanding shares. The **dividend per share** is $50,000 / 25,000 shares, or $2. The **earnings per share** are $1,000,000 / 25,000, or $40. The dividend payout ratio is $2 / $40, or 5%.

dividend per share (DPS)—If a $1 million dividend is declared and there are one million shares outstanding, the DPS is $1.

dividend reinvestment plan—Stockholders use a dividend reinvestment plan to plow their dividend payments back into purchasing more shares. This approach saves money because the stockholder does not need to pay any stockbroker commissions.

dividend yield—This ratio helps determine what the percentage return is for a stock that pays a dividend. To calculate the dividend yield ratio, divide the dividends per share by the stock's market price per share. A stock that is selling for $10 per share and receiving a $0.50 dividend per share has a 5% dividend yield ($0.50 / $10).

dollar-cost averaging—An investor can reduce the risks associated with stock volatility by investing a given amount of money in a stock on a regular basis no matter what the stock price is. Using this technique, an individual could put aside $100 a month to invest in a given company. Whether the price is $10 or $75 per share, the same $100 is always invested, and over the long haul the investor using this approach is normally very successful.

double entry bookkeeping—Double entry booking is a technique in which all transactions are recorded both as a credit and a debit. This results in a balanced ledger account for both debits and credits. See also **T-system**.

Dow Jones Industrial Average (Dow)—This average tracks the price of 30 blue-chip stocks actively traded on the New York Stock Exchange to serve as a guide to how the stock market is performing. The price-weighted average takes the stocks' closing prices and adjusts the prices to reflect stock splits and dividends.

downside risk analysis—The downside risk analysis approach is a worst-case scenario process in which an investor examines the total potential loss from an investment to help determine whether to enter into an investment or whether to sell an investment.

dowry—A dowry is the total value of property, money, and other assets a prospective wife brings to a marriage.

draft—A draft is a note, such as a check, indicating the transfer of funds from one party to another. The person to whom the check is written is called the payee. The person writing the check is the drawer, and the institution being instructed to pay the payee is the drawee. See also **demand deposit account**.

early-withdrawal penalty—Investors who have money deposited in certain investments such as individual retirement accounts or CDs may have to pay a penalty if they withdraw the investment before the investment's actual maturity date. Thus, you would have to pay a penalty if you had a six-month CD and cashed it in after only four months.

earned income—Earned income is any income obtained through performing labor. Earned income contrasts with passive income, which is income generated from sources, such as stocks or bonds, that do not require any labor.

earnest money—Earnest money is the sum of money given by a buyer to a seller for the purpose of holding a contract open to the buyer for a certain time period. Thus, if you wanted to buy a used car but wanted to check the car out for a day, you could put down an earnest-money deposit. If the car proved acceptable, you would complete the contractual process with the seller. The earnest-money deposit can serve as an earnest-money credit toward the purchase price.

earnings before interest and taxes (EBIT)—EBIT represent a company's earned income, not taking into consideration any owed interest or taxes.

earnings per share (EPS)—Earnings per share helps highlight how much each share of stock is earning in dollar terms and represents one of the most important tools to measure a company's success. To calculate EPS, the company's net income is divided by the total number of outstanding shares. If the company's income is $1 million and there are one million outstanding shares, the EPS is $1.

earnings yield—Earnings yield is the opposite of the price–earnings ratio. This ratio measures the yield obtained from a stock. The higher the yield, the better. For example, if a company's earnings per share is $5 and the market price is $20, then the earnings yield is 25%.

economic indicators—The government, investors, and businesses analyze various economic indicators to help determine market conditions. Examples of leading economic indicators include the **gross national product**, the **consumer price index**, money supply indicators, and the **Dow Jones Industrial Average**.

economics—Economics blends art and science to help explain and chart the most effective and efficient use of scarce resources. Microeconomics analyzes individual markets such as baseball, football, or basketball. Macroeconomics analyzes the big picture, such as the national economy or global economy.

economies of scale—A reduction in cost per unit resulting from increased production, realized through operational efficiencies.

effective annual rate (EAR)—The EAR represents the real annual rate of return for an investment.

effective interest rate—The effective interest rate represents the real rate of interest paid on a loan. To calculate the effective interest rate, the nominal interest rate is divided by the loan amount.

employee stock ownership plan (ESOP)—An ESOP is a plan designed to give employees an ownership interest in the company through distributing company stocks to employees. ESOPs typically vest (allow for collection) when an employee leaves or retires. This allows the stocks to increase in value without the employees having to pay taxes until they are at a lower income level, thus reducing their final tax obligations.

Equal Credit Opportunity Act (ECOA)—The ECOA is a federal law that makes it illegal to discriminate against a loan applicant based on race, age, religion, or gender. The law requires all lenders to respond within 30 days to any applicant and to identify the specific reason an applicant was denied.

equity—Equity refers to an individual's net worth or a company's stock ownership value.

equity investment—An equity investment is an investment in a company through the purchase of company stock.

estate—All real and personal property owned by an individual at the time of the person's death belongs to that person's estate. If a person dies with a will, the will specifies how the estate should be distributed. The U.S. federal government charges an estate tax based on the estate's value; the first

$600,000 (scheduled to increase to $1.2 million in 2007) is tax free.

even lot—Even lots are standard blocks of stocks. An even-lot block on the New York Stock Exchange contains 100 shares.

excise taxes—Numerous taxes exist for various consumed goods. These taxes are generally lumped under the designation excise taxes and are sometimes added to the purchase price of such items as gas, alcohol, and tobacco.

ex-dividend (XD)—Before the date on which a company records a stock dividend is a four-day freeze that allows the stock to trade, but without the right to obtain the dividend. The waiting period is based on the fact that stock transactions typically take five days to settle. Stocks subject to the XD provision normally trade at a reduced price that reflects the market price minus the expected dividend payment.

exempt income—Exempt income is income that is exempt from taxation, such as income from tax-exempt municipal bonds used to finance some stadiums or arenas.

expendable outlays—Expendable outlays are payments for items that are relatively low in cost and are frequently purchased, such as office supplies.

expenditure—An expenditure is any payment made to satisfy a financial obligation or to purchase assets.

expenses—Expenses are any payments, any reduction in value (such as depreciation), or any new legal obligations (such as entering into a binding contract).

experience rating—Insurance companies use a statistical method to determine insurance premiums based on past claims and projections for future claims. Experience ratings allow an insurance company to properly determine the potential payout for a given policy, which helps set the premium price for the policy.

F—The letter *F*, as used in financial calculations, represents a company's fixed operating costs or expected rate of return from a risk-free investment.

face value—The face value, or face amount, is the stated value for a bond or other security. Most bonds, for example, have a $1,000 face value but can be sold for an amount higher or lower than the indicated value. In addition to a face value, a security has a face interest rate, which is the interest rate guaranteed for the security when the security was issued.

Fair Credit Billing Act (FCBA)—The FCBA is a U.S. federal law that is designed to correct problems in credit billing and complaints and that establishes time limits under which bills need to be sent and complaints filed. A similar law, the Fair Credit Reporting Act, establishes specific requirements for the use of and access to personal credit information.

Federal Deposit Insurance Corporation (FDIC)—The FDIC is a U.S. federal agency that insures bank accounts up to $100,000 per each depositor at the bank. All national banks and most commercial banks obtain FDIC insurance to reduce the risk for potential depositors. Before the savings and loan fallout in the 1980s, the federal government ran the Federal Savings and Loan Insurance Corporation, whose duties were assumed by the FDIC after the savings and loan disaster.

Federal Reserve System (Fed)—The Fed was established by Congress in 1913 and comprises 12 Federal Reserve district banks, branches, and all national and state banks (more than 5,800). The system operates to manage the nation's money supply by raising or lowering the reserve amount that banks need to keep on hand, by changing the discount rate charged to commercial banks for borrowing money, and by purchasing and selling government securities (Siegel, Shim, & Hartman, 1992). The system operates similarly to a bank in that member banks can deposit funds in and borrow funds from the Fed in order to run more effectively.

finance charge—Nothing is free, and finance charges are a vehicle that assists in the transfer of money. The two types of finance charges are interest rates and points. Points can be charged when individuals apply for or are given a loan; each point charged represents 1% of the loan amount. Thus, if you were to refinance your home mortgage with a lower interest rate, the lending institution might charge you 1 or 2 points to process the loan, which for a $50,000 loan could be $500 or $1,000, just to obtain the loan.

financial assets—Financial assets are items of value that are intangible but that represent the ownership interest in a business or the investments that are funding the business. Financial assets include bonds, common stock, preferred stock, **money market certificates**, Treasury bills, and related instruments.

financial exigency—A financial exigency is an urgent financial situation (e.g., an athletic department loses a Title IX suit and has to add several new women's teams when it is already losing money).

financial leverage—Financial leverage represents the portion of a company's assets that are financed with debt rather than equity. It is normally beneficial to reinvest your own money (equity) rather than borrow funds; but if you can reinvest borrowed funds and obtain a rate of return greater than your interest and principal payments on the borrowed funds, then leveraging is a potential strong option for growth.

financial leverage ratios—These are various ratios that help identify how a company is financed and whether it has undertaken too much debt to grow. These ratios include the acid test ratio, current ratio, debt ratio, and debt–equity ratio.

financial statements—Corporations report their financial condition in annual, semiannual, and quarterly reports that contain numerous financial statements such as balance sheets, income statements, and cash flow statements.

first in, first out (FIFO)—FIFO has different meanings in banking and inventory management. Using the FIFO method, a bank withdraws any debt from the earliest deposits in an account. Under this method, depositors lose interest—because earlier deposits are reduced by withdrawals—and this makes saving less beneficial. For example, if you deposited $1,000 in June and $1,000 in July but wrote a check for $500 in July, you would earn interest on only $500 in June ($1,000 – $500) but would earn interest on $1,000 for July. The same principle applies to inventory management application of FIFO.

fiscal year—A company's fiscal year is a one-year period used as a basis for analyzing the company's financial performance and creating new budgets for the coming year. Many companies have August 31 as the first date of the fiscal year and the following August 30 as the last day of the fiscal year.

five Cs—Lenders often use five Cs when reviewing a loan application. The five Cs are (1) the *character* of the loan applicant (is the loan applicant a reliable person or company?), (2) the *capacity* of the applicant to earn enough to cover all expenses including the loan costs, (3) the **collateral** that will be used to secure the loan, (4) the **capital** available to the loan applicant (does the appli-

cant have a positive net worth?), and (5) current economic *conditions*, After analyzing the five Cs, a lender normally assigns a loan applicant a **credit rating** that will help determine the default risk for the applicant.

fixed assets—Fixed assets are permanent assets such as buildings or equipment required to run a business. Ice rinks, locker rooms, rental counters, spectator seating, and a Zamboni are all examples of fixed assets.

fixed costs—Fixed costs, or fixed charges, are regular expenses that are incurred regardless of activity, inactivity, or level of activity. Rent is a fixed cost because the same amount is owed regardless of potential business activity. Other examples are taxes, insurance premiums, and fixed salaries.

fixed income—Fixed income does not change over time; a fixed pension plan for former professional athletes, for example, might pay an athlete $2,000 a month for life.

fixed interest rate—A fixed interest rate does not change over time; in contrast, interest on a variable-rate loan, such as on some credit cards that are tied to various federally adjusted interest rates, changes over time.

flat rate—Items that are purchased on a flat rate basis cost the same no matter what quantity is purchased. When the rate can change based on quantity purchased, the price is considered a variable rate.

float—A float exists for money held by a bank or savings institution for checks that have not yet been cashed or deposits that have yet to be credited to a depositor's account.

flow—Flow refers to expenditure or receipt of money between two points in time.

Form 10-Q and **Form 10-K**—The Securities and Exchange Commission requires publicly traded companies to file specific quarterly (10-Q) and annual (10-K) reports featuring comprehensive financial statements.

formula budgeting—Formula budgeting involves establishing predetermined amounts that will be spent on various costs. Thus, if a team earns $1 per hot dog sold, the expenses and revenue can be calculated in the budget by estimating the total number of hot dogs that will be sold by both the purchase and potential sales price.

full faith and credit—See **bond**.

future value (FV)—Future value refers to the value that a given investment or security might have at a given time in the future. An investment's future value can be determined through various means, including the use of a future value table. FV_n is the future value at a specific (n) period. The opposite of future value is **present value**.

garnishment—An individual may lose in a legal proceeding or be required by law to make certain restitutions. Through garnishment, the person's wages, assets, or property can be attached, and any recovery can be used to pay the outstanding obligation. Attachment is the process where a court official or sheriff officially starts the collection process. For example, the sheriff could serve the employer with the court order requiring wage garnishment.

generally accepted accounting principles (GAAP)—The GAAP are industry rules developed to ensure uniformity by accountants. If an accountant follows the GAAP, others will know that there are standards behind how the numbers were calculated and that other accountants would come up with the same results using the same numbers.

general mortgage bonds—These bonds are collateralized by a blanket coverage over all company assets. However, these bonds are subordinate to (have lesser significance than) any bond collateralized by specific property. Thus, a general mortgage bond might cover all office equipment as collateral and be subordinate to another bond or obligation collateralized by photocopier machines.

general obligation bonds (GOBs)—GOBs are municipal bonds issued for such projects as stadiums or arenas, with the interest and principal payments backed by the **full faith and credit** of the municipality that issues the bonds. This means the bonds are backed by all the taxes collected by the municipality even if such taxes are not used for the facility. Under such a bond, a stadium could be constructed from a bond backed by a ticket surcharge. If the host team moves and there are no other tenants, no ticket surcharges would be collected to pay back the bondholders. The bondholders could then proceed against property tax collections or any other taxes for repayment.

golden handcuff—To prevent key employees from leaving, a company can give these employees significant stock options and a pension plan that are designed to penalize them if they leave the company before a given date. Under such a plan, an employee might have 5,000 stock options available after two years, 10,000 after four years, and 25,000 after six years.

golden parachute—Golden parachutes are given to top-level executives, offering these individuals significant money, benefits, or both if the company is purchased and the executives are subsequently terminated. Such an agreement is often created to make a company less attractive for a hostile suitor to purchase.

goodwill—Goodwill is the difference between a company's book value and its market value. The difference is based on the fact that the company has value that is not reflected in its books, or if goodwill is on the books, it is an additional value based on various valuation techniques. The name Coca-Cola, for example, represents a tremendous asset (a name recognized worldwide) that is hard to place a value on. However, some have placed the value on the goodwill of the name at more than $2 billion since that is possibly how much it would cost to develop a similar brand name with worldwide recognition.

gross national product (GNP)—The GNP is a calculation of the total value of products manufactured and services provided in the United States in a given year.

gross national product deflator—The U.S. Department of Commerce publishes a quarterly weighted average of the gross national product to more accurately reflect the price changes for goods and services purchased by consumers, businesses, and the government.

gross profit margin—The gross profit margin is the income of a company before operating expenses, interest, and taxes are paid.

guaranteed dividend—Some stocks pay a regular dividend that is assured by a third party such as the government.

hard asset—A hard asset is any item that has significant value but can be easily bought and sold, such as gold and silver. There are existing markets, so it is easy to sell such assets and convert them to cash or other liquid assets.

hedging—Investors understand that investments by their very nature involve various risks. Thus, investors try to hedge potential losses by undertaking risk-reduction strategies such as diversifying their holdings or purchasing insurance.

high-grade security—Stocks or bonds categorized as high grade have the best investment quality ratings, such as AAA. Independent companies establish the rating after reviewing a company's assets, liabilities, earnings, dividends, management, and related factors.

holder of record—The holder of record is the person whose name is recorded as the purchaser or owner of a given security. Proper recording of ownership is critical for determining who will receive dividends because only the holder of record receives dividends.

holding period return (HPR)—This calculation determines the total return earned when an investment is held for a given period. HPR = (current income + capital gains) / purchase price. If you purchased a stock for $10 and sold it one year later for $12, and during the year received a $1 dividend, then the HPR would be ($1 + $12 – $10) / $10 = 3 / 10, or 30%.

horizontal merger—This type of merger occurs when two companies in the same line of business are joined.

hostile takeover—A hostile takeover occurs against the desires of the target company's management and board of directors.

illiquid—A company is illiquid when it does not have sufficient liquid assets such as stocks and marketable securities to cover short-term debt.

implicit costs—Also called **opportunity costs**, implicit costs represent the cost of the next best alternative forgone. If you build a stadium, you will receive a certain return. However, you also face certain lost income because with the same money you could have built a convention center that might have had a greater impact on a given community.

incentive stock option (ISO)—An ISO is another option for transferring stocks to employees and is considered a benefit such as profit sharing. Compared with other stock-option plans, an ISO receives more favorable tax treatment.

income—Any money received during a given time period by either an individual or a company is considered income. Income can be derived from such sources as salaries, investment returns, asset sales, and many others.

income statement—An income statement tracks a company's revenue and expenses over any given time period. The following is a sample income statement for Sport Manufacturing Company.

income tax—Income tax is a levy imposed by the government on an individual's taxable income. The taxable income is calculated by deducting

Income Statement

	($000)
Sales	500
Less: Material and labor	300
Manufacturing costs	30
Cost of goods sold	**330**
Gross profit	**170**
Depreciation	20
Selling expense	20
Profit before interest and taxes	**130**
Interest payments	10
Taxes	40
Profit after taxes	**80**
Dividends	40
Retained earnings	**40**

all allowable deductions (such as unreimbursed business expenses) from the gross income.

independent audit—These audits involve an external review of the finances by individuals who are not directly involved with the documents that are being reviewed.

index of leading economic indicators—This index consists of several key economic indicators that help shed light on the economy's future direction. The index, published on a monthly basis by the U.S. Department of Commerce, analyzes such data as unemployment claims; stock prices; money supply; new building permits; changes in inventories; new orders for consumer and manufactured goods; vendor delivery delays; and the prices for oil, steel, and other essential materials.

indirect costs—Indirect costs are costs not associated with a specific activity. Administrative overhead and secretarial support are typical indirect costs; these obligations arise even if a given activity does not appear to need such assistance.

industrial development bond (IDB)—Municipalities can issue tax-exempt bonds to fund the building of factories or facilities that are then leased to private industries. Such bonds are usually issued to help attract new businesses to a region.

inflation—Inflation is an increase in the price level of products that could be due to increased demand. The increased demand for products can force prices to increase, which leads to a chain reaction of increasing wages and material costs.

initial public offering (IPO)—An IPO represents a company's first attempt at issuing and hopefully selling stocks to the public.

insider and **insider trading**—An insider is someone who has access to privileged information about a company that can affect the company's stock price. If the insider uses this information to make money on the stock or provides the information to anyone else to help that person make money, then everyone who has relied on such information has engaged in insider trading. Insider trading is a criminal offense if the trading is based on inside information. Insider trading is not always illegal if a company insider decides to purchase or sell company stocks and reports any such trades to the **Securities and Exchange Commission** within a specified time period.

interest (i)—Interest is the amount a lender charges for loaning money to a borrower. **Interest rates** are normally expressed in relation to an annual period. Interest can also mean an equity ownership position with a company. Thus, a professional sports team could own a 10% interest in a broadcasting station, which means it owns 10% of the station.

interest coverage (IC)—IC represents a company's ability to repay a loan by making required interest payments. Interest coverage is calculated by adding pretax income and interest expense and then dividing that sum by the interest expense. Thus, if a company had $90 million in pretax income and $10 million in interest expense, the IC would be ($90 + $10) / $10 = 10 times.

interest rate—The interest rate is the cost of borrowing money expressed in percentage terms over the course of a year. A bank might loan a business a certain sum at an interest rate of 10% a year.

interim financing—Businesses often need some money for a short period between deals or to help finance a quick deal; this borrowing is called interim financing.

internal rate of return (IRR)—This calculation is designed to provide an investor with the effective annual return from a given investment. The initial cash investment is analyzed in comparison with the present value of cash returns.

intrinsic value—Intrinsic value refers to the true value of any property or investment. The true value of a company can be determined through financial analysis, and this value may be different from the company's book value. Such a difference may be attributable to intangible assets, such as a health club's goodwill associated with many years of quality client service.

inventory—An inventory represents goods in stock that have not yet been sold or manufactured.

inventory turnover ratio (ITR)—The ITR shows how frequently a business is able to process and sell inventory. The higher the ITR, the more frequently the business buys inventory and sells finished goods. A high number is usually a good sign; however, if the business is a specialty manufacturer, such as handmade items, the ITR might be very low.

investment club—Single investors may not have the resources to make certain investments. However, people can create investment clubs in which multiple investors combine their money to acquire better investments through greater buying power.

jumbo certificate of deposit—A jumbo certificate of deposit is a CD with a minimum denomination of $100,000. Although jumbos carry a higher interest rate than CDs with lower values, they are not covered by the Federal Deposit Insurance Corporation.

junk bond—A high-yield bond with a low credit rating is called a junk bond. Smaller or new companies without a significant financial track record of sales or earnings often issue these bonds.

last in, first out (LIFO)—The LIFO method is used to calculate both bank interest payments and inventory values. This method does not penalize investors as much as the FIFO method, but it still hurts investors compared with those who receive interest on the actual amount in a given bank account. When we use LIFO to analyze inventories, we calculate ending inventory levels by subtracting the cost of the most recently purchased inventory from the total inventory before we subtract earlier inventories. This formula takes into account the realities of repurchasing subsequent inventories at a higher price.

layering—To garner necessary protection, a baseball team can purchase a $100,000 property liability insurance policy from one broker, a similar policy for $50,000 from another insurer, and an umbrella policy for $1 million. This results in a layering of insurance policies and may be required if certain insurers are not willing to underwrite the entire protection amount required.

lease option—If the owners of a health club wish to rent a warehouse, they might not want to sign a long-term lease that could bind them for significant payments even if the venture was not successful. Instead, with a lease option, they can lease for a specific time period and then have the option of renewing the lease for additional specified periods. The benefit for the tenant is the ability to reduce long-term debt concerns if things go wrong. The landlord benefits in that such a lease option typically results in a higher rent, and the rent normally increases each time the option is exercised.

lender—A lender is any individual or entity that lends money to a borrower for a given interest rate for repayment within a specified time.

letter of credit (LC)—If you own a sporting goods store, you could approach a bank for a letter of credit to help buy more inventory. An LC from the bank to the seller guarantees your credit for a given time period up to a certain amount. Thus, depending on its assessment of your financial strength, the bank could provide a $100,000 LC to be used to help buy inventory. The LC is like a loan from the bank that can be used at any time.

letter of intent—A letter of intent is a document among parties expressing intent to take or to refrain from taking certain actions. Two sporting goods stores could enter into a letter of intent to merge at a future date. Letters of intent are often a precursor to entering a formal contractual agreement, which often takes months; a letter of intent can provide very rough terms and can be completed in several hours.

leveraged buyout (LBO)—You can buy a professional sports franchise using borrowed funds in what is often called a leveraged buyout. The LBO is often completed using the assets of the purchased company as collateral to secure the borrowed funds, and the income or cash flow of the business is used to repay the loan.

leveraging—Leveraging is using borrowed money to make a greater return on investment than what could have been earned if no additional funds were available. Leverage is used only when the expected return on the investment will more than cover the expense of borrowing the funds.

liabilities—The term *liabilities* refers to any legal or financial obligation. Typical examples are long-term debt, retained earnings, shareholders' equity, and taxes owed. Liabilities are the opposite of **assets**.

life cycle costs—These are costs that are generated from the inception through termination of a product. If you own a fitness equipment manufacturing company, your product life cycle costs would include all research, development, prototype, market research, test marketing, full sales, and product withdrawal or cancellation costs. Traditionally, costs are greatest when a product is initially developed.

limited partner—Unlike traditional partners who are wholly liable for a partnership's losses, limited partners can be liable only for their own investment into a partnership. Limited partnerships are attractive in that the investor can maintain an ownership interest while reducing liability exposure. A general partner in a limited partnership invests capital, helps manage the business, and is personally liable for partnership debts.

line-item budget—A line-item budget lists every expense and revenue source on a separate line to help administrators identify every single source of revenue or expenses.

line of credit—A line of credit represents the maximum preapproved amount a company or individual can borrow without having to go to a different lending source.

liquid—Being liquid is a condition in which an individual or company has enough cash or liquid assets that can be sold quickly (CDs, Treasury bonds, high-quality corporate bonds, stocks) to meet current debt obligations. Inventories are traditionally not considered liquid because it can take time to sell inventory. Accounts receivable (A/R) are similar in that it can take time to collect them. Factoring, which entails selling inventories or A/R, is rapidly changing the nature of liquid assets because inventories and A/R can now be sold in a relatively short amount of time.

liquid asset—A liquid asset is a type of asset that can be quickly converted to cash such as stocks and bonds owned by a company.

liquidity—Liquidity can represent the number of stock shares available for investors to trade. Strong liquidity means there is a good supply of stocks available for purchase or trade.

loan—A loan is a transaction between a lender and a borrower in which the borrower contractually agrees to repay the principal amount and interest.

By repaying the loan in a systematic manner, the borrower engages in loan **amortization**.

loan origination fee—In addition to principal, interest, and points, a lender can also impose additional fees on the borrower, including fees for credit checks, auditing of checks, appraisals, title searches, and related expenses required to protect the lender.

loan-to-value ratio (LTV)—The LTV is the ratio of the principal amount borrowed to the collateral's actual value or fair market value (amount borrowed divided by actual value). If you buy a house for $100,000 and take out a mortgage for $60,000, then the LTV is 60%.

loss prevention—Risk management techniques can be used to reduce the chances of being sued. One strategy for reducing financial risk involves purchasing liability, property, casualty, or other insurance policies.

low grade—Investments such as bonds that do not have strong industry ratings are considered low-grade investments and are riskier than high-grade investments.

lump sum distribution—Instead of borrowing money and making monthly payments to satisfy the loan, you could agree to make a lump sum payment at the loan's due date. A retirement pension or other obligation can also be repaid in a lump sum.

managerial accounting—Managerial accounting focuses on the analysis and evaluation of accounting information as part of the managerial process of planning, decision making, and controlling.

margin—If you do not have enough money to purchase stock with cash, you can purchase stock on credit, with the remainder being advanced by the stockbroker. The stocks are kept by the broker as collateral. If you want to buy $10,000 worth of stock, you might need to put down an initial margin requirement of $6,000 while borrowing the remaining $4,000 from the broker. The stock purchaser in essence is borrowing money from the broker and has to pay the broker a given interest rate for using the money. If the price of the security declines and reduces the broker's equity, the broker can issue a margin call that requires the investor to put up more funds to protect the broker. The Federal Reserve Board sets limits on the amount of margins allowed. *Also see* margin (profit).

margin (profit)—A profit margin (sometimes referred to as a net profit margin) represents profits after taxes divided by sales. This calculation shows whether a company made an acceptable percentage of profit based on total sales. A sport manufacturing company with millions in sales and minimal profits is possibly wasting money. In contrast, a company such as a sport services firm may have a lower income level but a higher profit margin. If Sport Manufacturing Company had an after-tax profit of $2 million based on $5 million in sales, then the profit margin would be 40% ($2 million / $5 million). *Also see* margin.

marginal cost—The marginal cost is the change in costs associated with the volume produced. If it costs $1 to produce each of 1,000 baseballs and $0.80 each to produce any additional balls, then the marginal cost of producing additional balls is $0.80.

marginal cost of capital (MCC)—When you are taking out a loan, MCC represents how much more you would need to pay to borrow an additional dollar. If the interest rate declines as the amount of a loan gets larger, the MCC will be lower for each additional dollar. If a bank offers a $1 million loan for 6% and a loan over $1 million for 5.75%, then the cost for borrowing each additional dollar over $1 million is 0.25% less.

marginal tax—The marginal tax is the tax paid on the last dollar earned. Thus, it can be unwise to earn more money after a certain point because the higher earning level results in a higher tax liability.

market—A market is any public location where products or services are bought and sold. There are a number of recognized financial markets, including the New York Stock Exchange, the American Stock Exchange, and the Chicago Mercantile Exchange.

marketable title—A marketable title, one that is free of any problems including financial obligations (called encumbrances), is the most easily transferable property; it is marketable to anyone.

market analysis—A market analysis is any comprehensive analysis of current financial conditions concerning a given company, industry, or the economy.

market indexes, or **market averages**—Various market gauges exist to help investors appreciate market trends. The most famous index is the Dow Jones Industrial Average (Dow), compiled by the *Wall Street Journal* and composed of 30 blue-chip stocks (high-quality stocks) that combined represent approximately 20% of the New York Stock Exchange's total value. In the early 1980s, the Dow was around 1,000, but by 1998 it had reached more than 8,000. Other indexes include Barron's 50-Stock Average, Standard & Poor's 400 industrials, and the Value Line Average.

market-to-book (M/B) ratio—The M/B ratio represents the difference between what a security is listed for on the books and its real market value.

market value—The market value is the true price in a competitive marketplace of a product, service, or investment vehicle. Supply and demand significantly affect the market value, which is why a ticket for the Super Bowl with a face value of $150 may be sold on the street for $2,000. The $2,000 price is the market value.

materiality—This concept refers to the levels of misstatement that are allowable in financial information. Since no financial system is perfect, misstatements do occur. The auditor must determine the level of misstatement that will affect the fairness of the information.

maturity—Maturity is the time when a loan, bond, or other obligation becomes due and payable. Maturity value is the amount owed once the maturity date is reached.

merger—The combining of two or more businesses into one. Mergers are accomplished through a purchase, an acquisition, or a pooling of interests.

money—Any legal tender currency, whether in the form of coins, paper bills, or in some situations other valuable items, is considered money. During Napoleon's reign, soldiers were paid in salt, which was considered a form of money at that time.

money market certificate—Money market certificates are similar to certificates of deposit issued by banks, savings and loans, or credit unions; they usually mature in six months.

money market mutual fund—A money market mutual fund pools investors' money and purchases short-term debt securities such as government securities and commercial paper that will mature in less than one year.

mortgage—A mortgage is a long-term loan (typically 15 or 30 years) secured by real property. If the mortgage loan value is less than the property's market value, the property owner may be able to take out another loan called a second mortgage. Thus, if you buy a house for $100,000 but need a mortgage loan for only $60,000, you might be able to take out a second mortgage loan for around $35,000 to raise money to start a business. A mortgage banker is the individual or company that originates the mortgage loan and can collect payments from the borrower.

multipayment loans—Such loans are often referred to as add-on loans because the interest payments are added on to the principal. Under the actuarial method, interest is computed on unpaid principal at a fixed rate, with each initial payment being applied first to interest and the remainder to principal. The actuarial method is the simplest and most common method used for such consumer loans as mortgages, with the payment amounts often calculated through computer programs.

multiple of gross income rule—Lenders use a rule of thumb called the multiple of gross income rule to determine whether a borrower can afford a given loan. The formula multiplies the person's income by 2.5 to determine the maximum housing price the individual can afford. Thus, if you earn $50,000 per year, you should be approved for a mortgage loan (if there are no other credit problems) for a $125,000 home.

municipal bond insurance—Government-issued municipal bonds are traditionally very secure. However, to help attract investors and increase their security (and reduce the amount of interest that needs to be paid), municipalities can purchase insurance to guarantee repayment of the bond.

municipal bonds—Municipal bonds are issued by government entities and have significant benefits such as the security of a government entity to repay the loan and tax deductibility of income from the bond. However, the interest rates are typically lower than for corporate-issued bonds. Municipal bonds are nicknamed "munis."

mutual funds—Mutual funds provide an opportunity for investors to pool their money and buy a diverse collection of investment securities. These funds are very attractive to investors since they do not require a significant investment, and the risk of loss is lower because the fund invests in numerous companies. Professional managers make the buy and sell decisions.

National Association of Securities Dealers (NASD)—NASD is a self-regulatory organization for stockbrokers who sell **over-the-counter** stocks. The NASD has strong regulatory requirements, including the requirement that disputes with brokers be heard in binding arbitration.

National Association of Securities Dealers Automated Quotations (NASDAQ)—A subsidiary of the NASD, the NASDAQ uses electronic networking to facilitate buying and selling (trading) of the **over-the-counter** market's 5,000 most active stocks.

negative amortization—Negative amortization occurs when someone fails to make outstanding loan payments in a high enough amount to cover the interest owed. The low payment then leads to an increase in the balance owed on the loan.

negative cash flow—Negative cash flow occurs when a business spends more than it makes in a given time period.

negotiable instrument—A negotiable instrument is any document that can easily be converted to cash. A bank draft (check written by a bank) represents a negotiable instrument; any bank will accept and cash such an instrument.

net—Net is the amount left after all expenses or deductions are subtracted.

net asset value (NAV)—NAV refers to a mutual fund's total asset value less any debt, divided by the number of shares outstanding.

net current assets (NCA)—NCA (also called net working capital) refers to the total value of current assets minus current liabilities.

net earnings—Net earnings refers to an individual's take-home pay, which consists of the person's salary minus all tax, insurance, and related deductions.

net income—Net income is calculated by subtracting expenses from revenue.

net present value (NPV)—The NPV is the difference between the **present value** of the future income and the required investment.

net profit margin—The net profit margin is the net income of a company after interest and taxes are paid.

net working capital—Net working capital is the amount of money available to pay bills. It is calculated by subtracting current liabilities from current assets.

net worth—Net worth is the difference between a company's total assets and total liabilities. The resulting number is the owners' or shareholders' equity in the company.

New York Stock Exchange (NYSE)—The NYSE is the largest and most respected securities exchange. Often called the "big board," the NYSE requires that new companies wishing to be listed have, among other characteristics, more than 3,000 shareholders and a market value higher than $18 million. The NYSE had been privately owned, but after merging with Archipelago it became a publicly traded company in 2006. The NYSE works as an auction floor, where members who own seats can trade shares of listed companies on behalf of their clients. Current traders do not use actual seats, but the term has survived over the years. A seat can cost around $2 million and gives the owner the privilege of being able to buy and sell NYSE-listed stocks (Ceron, 2000).

no-load mutual fund—A no-load mutual fund is attractive for many investors in that no commission is charged for buying or selling shares.

nominal interest rate—The nominal interest rate is the stated interest rate on a loan or debt. If you have a $10,000 bond with a nominal interest rate of 5%, you will receive $500 in annual interest income.

note (promissory)—A note is a legally transferable debt instrument wherein the borrower agrees to pay a stated amount at a certain date, and the obligation is good no matter who eventually owns the note. Thus, after you borrow money and sign a note to purchase a car, the note can be sold to several subsequent companies without affecting your obligation to repay.

not-sufficient-funds check (NSF)—If you buy something at a store and your check bounces, the store will receive an NSF notification from your bank.

novation—A novation is a new contract that can be entered into by various parties who take the place of a former party to a legal obligation. If you borrowed money from a bank to help buy a car but want to sell the car, you can have the car's new buyer sign a novation with the bank to assume your original obligation.

obligation—Any indebtedness, such as a student loan or a mortgage loan, that is owed to anyone else is an obligation.

odd lot—Stocks are traditionally sold in blocks, such as 100 shares. An odd lot is any number of shares other than a standard block. An odd lot could consist of one share of stock or even a fraction of one share.

off-board trade—Any purchase of a stock on the over-the-counter exchange or any non-national stock exchange is considered an off-board trade.

offer price—The offer price is the initial price a seller asks for a given item or property. If a professional team owner mentions that he would sell a team for $200 million, then the $200 million price tag becomes the offer price.

open-end credit—A credit card is an example of open-end credit. The cardholder is given a credit limit when the account is opened, but no debt is incurred until the card is used.

opportunity cost—Also called **implicit cost**, opportunity cost is the cost of the next best alternative forgone. If a city invests in a football stadium, then the city will need to forgo building a new convention center that would have been built but for the stadium. This is an additional cost associated with building the stadium, over and beyond the actual construction cost.

option—An option is a contractual right to buy or sell something at a later date. If you wanted to buy a sports team for $1 million but needed to secure necessary financial backing, you could pay the team seller $1,000 for a one-month option. This option would give you the opportunity to try to raise necessary funds during that month. If you do not raise the funds, the team goes back on the market. If you do raise the funds, you can buy the team for $1 million. An option is not a deposit, which is why it does not reduce the purchase price.

overdraft—An overdraft occurs when you write a check without sufficient funds in your account, which can result in a not-sufficient-funds notice to the person cashing the check.

overextended—If you are approaching your credit limit, you might contact your credit card company to ask for an increase in the limit. If the card company increases your limit, even though you do not show the ability to afford the higher limit, the card company has overextended your credit.

over-the-counter (OTC) exchange—Unlike the New York Stock Exchange, which is a formal trading environment, the OTC is not one building or trading floor but a means to trade unlisted securities. Dealers use electronics and telecommunication through the NASDAQ network to make trades.

The New York Stock Exchange requires companies to have significant capitalization, but the OTC does not have the same requirements. There are some major companies, such as Microsoft, whose shares are traded over the counter.

owners' equity—Owners' equity is the value remaining after liabilities are subtracted from assets. Stock and accumulated earnings are added together, then dividends are subtracted to calculate total owners' equity.

P—The letter P has multiple meanings as a symbol, including the price of a stock on a per share basis, the price of a unit of output, and the probability that a given circumstance will occur.

paper profit—Paper profits or losses are unrealized increases or decreases in a security, which are not real profits or losses until the security is sold. This explains how people can lose millions one day and make millions the next without actually doing anything. Such gains and losses are only hypothetical, and real gains or losses occur only when the individual sells.

par value—So that shares can be valued and sold when they are issued, an arbitrary par value is assigned.

passed dividends—A company may have customary dividends, such as biannual dividends, but the board of directors may elect not to pay a dividend. A passed dividend is not a legal obligation owed to shareholders, but it still needs to be paid to individuals who own cumulative preferred stocks.

past-due balance method—If you buy a product on credit and fail to make the necessary payment on time, you owe interest on the amount that is past due. If you pay during the specified time period, then there will be no past-due amount.

payback period—The payback period is the amount of time necessary to recover an initial investment. The payback period can be calculated by dividing the initial investment by the annual cash flow. If you invest $1,000 in a bond that will pay back $100 a year over 20 years, then the payback period is $1,000 / $100, or 10 years.

payment in kind—Payment in kind can be compared to bartering, which involves trading valuable items or services rather than paying money.

payoff—Payoff occurs when a debt is completely satisfied.

penny stocks—Penny stocks is the term used to describe inexpensive, highly speculative stocks traded on the **over-the-counter** market.

pension fund—Pension funds incorporate deposits from employers, with or without employee contributions, into various investment vehicles to develop long-term growth capable of providing employees with money after they retire, quit, or get fired.

percent of monthly gross income rule—The percent of monthly gross income rule is a rule of thumb used by mortgage companies. It states that a person should not purchase a house if the monthly mortgage, insurance, and property taxes exceed 25% of the person's monthly gross income.

percent of sales method—The percent of sales method is a technique that ties variable costs to sales to help calculate expenditures.

performance stock—A performance stock is a stable, solid, growth-oriented stock that has a better investment potential compared with other stocks.

perpetuity—A perpetuity is a single cash flow that lasts forever. If you win a lifetime lottery that pays you $1 million a year for life, that is a perpetuity.

personal property—Personal property includes items such as cars, clothes, and sporting goods that are not attached to the ground.

petty cash—Petty cash is a small amount of funds set aside to cover small purchases that do not meet the requirements for a formal purchase order. The purchase order is a formal document requesting the release of funds to cover an approved expenditure.

point(s)—Mortgage companies add to their loans a processing charge that is expressed in points. A point represents 1% of the face value of a loan. Thus, an $80,000 mortgage with 2 points would result in a processing fee of $1,600.

portfolio—To increase an investor's diversity, the investor might create a portfolio that contains stocks, bonds, CDs, Treasury notes, stamps, Beanie Babies, or any other item that could be considered an investment. Portfolios are created to protect the investor; any one investment vehicle might decline, but such a decline in a well-balanced portfolio would not hurt the investor as much as it would in a concentrated portfolio with few investments.

preemptive right (or preemption)—Allows a shareholder to purchase a percentage of any future shares issued by the company that matches the percentage of shares he currently owns. This allows an investor to maintain the same percentage control of a business before shares are sold to the general public, which can dilute his ownership interest.

preferred stock—A preferred stock has some features similar to those of a stock and some similar to those of a bond. Preferred stocks represent ownership equity and can generate dividend income, but they also have a guaranteed dividend and a superior claim right over other stocks. The superior claim rights allow preferred stock shareholders to sell assets or seize earnings if the company folds.

prepayment fee—Some mortgages or other loans have a provision imposing a prepayment fee or penalty if the note is completely paid before it matures.

present value (PV)—Present value is the current value of a future amount of money. If you win the lottery, you might be able to take several million dollars now or 10 times that amount over a number of years. Such payouts are based on the fact that if you invest a certain sum now, it will be worth more in the future. Individuals can use a present value table to analyze the value of future income streams.

pretax earnings—Pretax earnings are a company's net income before paying taxes.

price–earnings (PE) ratio—The PE ratio is a comparison between a stock's market value and the strength of a company's earnings. The PE ratio can help determine a stock's market price. To calculate this, multiply the estimated earnings per share by the estimated PE ratio. Assume that a sporting goods company expects to have an after-tax profit of $500,000 and has one million outstanding shares. The estimated earnings per share is $0.50. If the estimated PE ratio is 8, then the estimated market price is $0.50 × 8, or $4.00 per share.

price indexes—Various economic indicators (price indexes) help track inflation, the cost of living, and other economic measuring tools. Typical price indexes include the **consumer price index (CPI)**, which measures 400 typical consumer goods and services, and the producer price index (PPI), which tracks the costs of wholesale goods.

primary market—The primary market is the market in which new securities are traded for the first time. The secondary market is the market in which securities are traded after they are initially sold.

prime interest rate—The prime rate is the interest rate that banks charge for loans to their most financially secure customers.

principal—Principal is the amount invested in any given security.

private offering—A private offering is a first-time offering of a given security by a company, traditionally made to current shareholders, executives, institutional buyers, or larger investment institutions before the security is offered to the general public.

private placement—Some securities are initially offered privately rather than in larger financial markets open to the public. A company may issue a bond that is placed solely with current shareholders or larger institutional investors, such as pension funds or insurance companies.

profit—Profit is another term to describe revenue in excess of expenses. See also **margin (profit)**.

program trading—Program trading involves computer-based decision making in which securities are bought and sold according to set parameters. Program trading creates a phenomenon called the triple witching hour, which occurs at 4:15 p.m. EST on the third Friday of March, June, September, and December when numerous securities expire all at once. The triple witching hour at times has produced significant market shifts. However, these shifts are normally corrected the following trading day.

prospectus—A prospectus from a company highlights key financial data about the company and the proposed security but does not discuss when the security will be issued or the exact price.

proxy—A shareholder has a right to vote on company-related business issues. Shareholders who do not attend a shareholders' meeting can sign a proxy allowing a designated person to vote on their behalf.

public debt—A public debt is any debt incurred by a government institution. When a city builds a stadium or arena, it may issue bonds that represent public debt.

public offering—After filing the necessary registration with the **Securities and Exchange Commission**, a company is allowed to offer stock to the general public.

public syndicate—If two businesses wish to join together to buy a professional team, they might create a public syndicate to combine their money and make the purchase. The public syndicate allows the two companies to share costs and expenses on a predetermined basis.

purchasing power—After inflation has been adjusted for, a dollar has less purchasing power than it had in the past. Thus, employees are frequently given raises to maintain their purchasing power or standard of living. Purchasing power also refers to the credit available to someone who wishes to make a large purchase such as a car.

pure-play stock—The stock of a company that has only one line of business (i.e., only the bowling industry) is a pure-play stock. An investor may want to play (invest in) one industry, and the company's exclusive position in that industry makes it a good investment prospect for that investor. Several mutual funds were started in the 1990s to invest in specific sport categories such as auto racing or companies that own or sponsor professional sports teams.

put—A put is an option to sell a commodity or shares of a security at a specified price during a specified time period. This risky investment alternative works as follows. You might pay $100 for an option to sell 100 shares of a given stock. Each put costs you $1 per share and represents an option to sell the 100 shares at $10 each, which is the stock's price when you purchase the put. If after three months (the time specified in the put) the stock decreases to $5 per share, you realize a $500 profit ($5 per share) minus the $100 spent on the put. If the stock increased to $15 per share, you would lose $500 plus the $100 for purchasing the put.

Q—The letter Q in a financial equation represents unit sales for a given product.

quoted price—The quoted price is the last price at which a security was bought and sold.

R—The uppercase letter R is used to represent the appropriate discount factor or interest rate in financial equations.

r—The lowercase letter r represents a correlation coefficient denoting the degree of correlation between given financial variables.

rally—A rally is a sharp upturn in stock prices and trading.

real assets—Real assets are tangible assets such as real estate, gold, and other items you can touch.

Real property consists of land and any buildings or equipment on the land.

real estate investment trust (REIT)—A real estate investment trust provides short-term loans for some construction projects and long-term loans (mortgage REITs) for major projects such as stadiums and arenas.

realized profit or **loss**—After an investment is sold, the investor realizes a profit, a loss, or a **wash**, which means neither losing nor making any money.

realized yield—The realized yield measures the return available if a bond is sold before reaching its maturity. This measure is also called **yield to call**. The calculation involves estimating the potential future value of a bond versus the current value to develop an estimated percentage rate of return on the investment.

receivables turnover ratio (RTR)—The RTR represents how quickly a company is obtaining repayments of accounts receivables. If a company takes too long to collect owed money, it would have a high RTR.

recession—A recession is a downturn in the business cycle in which various economic indicators such as the gross national product, employment rate, consumer spending, and other indicators decline.

red herring—The initial information about a proposed new security is sometimes called a red herring.

refinance—Refinancing involves consolidating or reworking any and possibly all outstanding debts to make repayment easier or to avoid financial hardship such as bankruptcy.

registered security—Some securities such as registered bonds are registered in the owner's name and recorded by the issuing company and the registrar. The registrar is the trustee of a new security's records and is often a bank or similar institution that tracks the registration number of both old and new securities.

reinvestment—Using the dividends, interest, or profits from an investment to buy more of that investment rather than receiving a cash payout.

replacement cost—Replacement costs are the costs you would incur if you needed to replace property. Capital equipment in sport, such as a new Zamboni or a new air-conditioning system, can be very expensive. Thus, companies have to plan for replacement costs either by setting aside money over a long period of time or by ensuring the potential to issue new securities or borrow necessary funds.

retained earnings—Earnings not paid out as dividends but instead reinvested in the core business or used to pay off debt.

return on assets (ROA)—ROA refers to the calculated investment return obtained from assets purchased by a company. Any new assets purchased should be able to generate increased return over and beyond what could have been earned if the money was invested in a CD or other liquid investment option. To calculate ROA, net income is divided by total assets.

return on equity (ROE)—Similar to ROA, ROE relates to whether or not an investment in an ownership position (equity) within a company produced a rate of return greater than what could have been earned if the money had been invested elsewhere. ROE is calculated by dividing net income by shareholders' equity.

return on investment capital (ROIV)—ROIV shows whether or not an investment in a company produced a rate of return greater than what could have been earned if the money had been invested elsewhere. ROIV is calculated by dividing net income by the sum of long-term debt and shareholders' equity.

revenue—Revenue is money coming into a business.

revenue bond—Revenue bonds are government-issued bonds whose interest and principal payments are repaid from specified revenue sources. A baseball stadium could be built using revenue bonds secured by hotel and rental-car tax revenues.

reverse stock split—A company's board of directors can decide to reduce the number of shares outstanding. A reverse stock split reduces the number of shares every investor has but does not reduce the owners' equity percentage. Thus, the number of stock shares outstanding decreases, but the remaining shares increase in value. The opposite of a reverse stock split is a **stock split**, in which the total number of shares is increased and the share values are decreased.

revolving credit—Revolving credit accounts allow a purchaser to obtain a new line of credit as soon as old loans are paid.

risk-free return—A risk-free return is an investment that provides a low return because the investment's risk is so low. To obtain a greater return, an investor needs to invest in a riskier investment. A T-bill or CD is an example of an almost risk-free investment.

risk premium (RP)—RP refers to the fact that if a security is considered risky because of poor repayment history, the security has to pay a premium over other securities to garner investor interest. Thus, an RP could increase the interest on a bond from 4% to 6% on the basis of various risk factors.

roll-up—In a roll-up, an aggressive investment company buys numerous companies in similar industries. For example, a well-funded company could start buying multiple health clubs in a region to gain market dominance.

round lot—A round lot, also called an even lot, is a block of 100 stock shares or a bond with a $1,000 face value.

rule of 69—The rule of 69 helps calculate how long it will take for an investment to double when a certain amount of money is being invested at a certain rate of return expressed as a percentage. The formula is $69 / r(\%) + 0.35$ periods. If you buy a security with a return of 25%, you will double your money in $(69 / 25) + 0.35 = 2.76 + 0.35 = 3.11$ years.

rule of 72—The rule of 72 determines how many years it takes to double an investment. The formula is 72 / the fixed rate of return $(r\%)$. Thus, if you buy land with a fixed rate of return of 25%, it will take you 2.88 years to double your money $(72 / 25 = 2.88)$.

S—The uppercase letter S can represent either a dollar sales volume or the total market value of a company's equity.

s—The lowercase letter s is used to represent the standard deviation.

scheduled payment—Scheduled payments are fixed payments owed on loans or bonds or pursuant to a contract or security.

schedule of estimated income—A schedule of estimated income lists expected revenue sources over a given time period. Such a schedule helps highlight what revenue can be expected so a budget can be developed.

secured bond—A secured bond is a bond secured by a specific item, or collateral, that can be sold if the bond is not repaid.

secured loan—Similar to a secured bond, a secured loan is guaranteed by specified collateral.

securities—Securities are any financial instruments that provide an ownership interest in the issuing company. Typical examples include stocks and bonds.

Securities and Exchange Commission (SEC)—The U.S. federal government established the SEC in the 1930s as an independent regulatory agency to regulate securities markets. To protect investors, the SEC requires full financial disclosure for all securities and regulates issues such as insider trading.

securities exchanges—The Securities and Exchange Commission regulates several privately owned securities exchanges, the most famous of these being the New York Stock Exchange, the American Stock Exchange, and the over-the-counter exchange. Several regional exchanges also exist around the United States and in major foreign cities.

security interest, or **collateral interest**—A security interest gives a lender with a secured loan the right to go to court and take possession of the collateral if the borrower defaults on the loan.

seller's market—A seller's market is a market in which the seller has the advantage because numerous buyers are interested in purchasing the item being sold. This phenomenon is based on supply and demand, when the supply is low and the demand is high. A seller's market exists for professional sports teams because many people would like to buy a team, but only a handful of teams are available in any given year.

sell order—When investors wish to sell a security, they can give their brokers a sell order authorizing the sale. The sell order can be either oral or in writing.

senior debt—A senior debt is a superior obligation (loan) that a borrower has to repay before repaying any other obligations. If a company folds, senior debt would need to be paid before any shareholders could receive money, if any remains. A senior debt obligation can be secured by any, or all, corporate assets.

serial bond—A serial bond matures over regularly scheduled dates, in contrast to a bond that matures on only one given date.

Series E bonds—Series E bonds were issued by the U.S. government from 1941 through 1979, when they were replaced by Series EE and Series HH bonds. These bonds are purchased at 50% of the face amount, and the interest accumulates until the bonds reach their maturity date. These bonds can be redeemed before they mature, but the holder will have to pay a penalty.

shakeout—A shakeout occurs when securities prices tumble with significant trading.

share—A share represents one unit of ownership interest in either a company or a financial vehicle (e.g., a mutual fund).

shareholder—An individual who owns a share in a company.

shareholders' report—Companies that issue stocks report to their owners on a regular basis. These reports highlight a company's current financial condition and other relevant facts. Shareholders' reports are often released annually and provide audited reviews of a company's financial statements by an independent accounting firm to substantiate the claims made by the company.

short—An investor can take a short position by borrowing a security from a broker and then selling the security on the open market. The idea is that the investor is hoping the stock price will decline, at which point the investor will buy the stock at a lower price and will have made a profit. For example, an investor can sell 100 short shares borrowed from the broker for $10 each. Ten days later the stock might have dropped to $5 per share, and at this point the investor buys the stock from the broker and makes a $500 profit. Buying short is very risky—if the stock price increases, you can lose a substantial amount of money because you have to buy the stock at its higher price.

short-term debt—Short-term debts are current liabilities that need to be repaid within one year, such as utility bills, payments for inventory, taxes owed, employee wages owed, and related liabilities.

signature loan—A signature loan is any personal loan secured only by the borrower's signature. No collateral is pledged.

simple interest—Simple interest is computed only on the original loan amount, whereas compound interest is applied to the original principal and all accumulated interest. The simple interest on a $1,000 loan at 10% interest is $100.

simple rate of return (SRR)—The simple rate of return is a method used to calculate the return that can be obtained on a given investment. To calculate SRR, we divide the investment's annual income by the initial investment. If you invest $1,000 and receive an annual return of $75, the SRR is 75 / $1,000 = 7.5%.

simple yield—To calculate the simple yield of a bond, the bond's interest is divided by the face value. If you buy a $1,000 bond paying 5% interest for only $950, then the simple yield is (5% × 1,000) / 950 = 50 / 950 = 5.26%.

single-payment loans—Single-payment loans are paid in full on a given date, with the debtor repaying both the principal and required interest. There are two techniques for determining the appropriate annual percentage rate. Under the **simple interest** method, the amount repaid is computed by adding the original amount and interest, with the interest calculated by means of the following formula: interest = principal × interest rate × time period. Assume you borrow $1,000 for one year at a simple interest rate of 15%. In this situation, you would repay the lender $1,150 at the end of the year. The second method is the discount method; here the initial loan is discounted by the interest that will be owed. Using the same example, instead of receiving $1,000 and paying $1,150, you would borrow $1,000 at 15% but receive only $850, which represents the loan minus your prepayment of the interest you would owe. Unlike the 15% annual percentage rate (APR) under the simple interest method, the APR using the discount method would be 17.64%. The calculation is $150 (interest) / $850 (amount actually received). Thus, the discount method allows a lower payment upon maturity ($850 versus $1,150), but the simple interest method produces a lower APR.

sinking fund—A company can use a sinking fund to set aside money to invest in income-producing securities that are later cashed in to pay off a financial obligation. Without setting aside money in anticipation of repaying a loan, a company may be forced to issue additional securities to raise the necessary cash or may need to borrow the money.

skip-payment privilege—A lender might allow a borrower to skip a payment if the lender is notified in advance that the borrower will miss a payment.

solvency ratio—The solvency ratio is calculated by dividing net worth (assets minus liabilities) by total assets. A company with a high solvency ratio is financially very strong.

special tax bond—A special tax bond is a municipal bond paid for with revenue from excise taxes levied on such items as alcohol or tobacco sales. Such "sin taxes" have been used to fund stadium projects such as Jacobs Field in Cleveland.

speculative bond—A speculative bond is a low-rated bond that might be close to default. An investor might purchase such a bond at a deep discount with the hope that the company can turn around and pay off the bond.

stagflation—Stagflation represents an increase in prices that occurs when businesses are facing a slowdown.

statement of cash flows—A statement of cash flows is an accounting of where revenue is coming from and where it is being spent. These statements must be included in shareholders' annual reports.

stock—Stock refers to wealth people might have, such as cash or other investments.

stock dividend—If a company does not have enough cash to pay a dividend, the company can issue additional stock to shareholders. If a stock dividend is issued, the shares outstanding for the company are increased, and this reduces the per share value of all shares.

stock market, or **stock exchange**—A stock market or exchange is a marketplace where stock and other securities are traded.

stock split—A corporation's board of directors may authorize a stock split if the stock price is too high. Thus, for a share that sells for $200, after a 2-for-1 stock split the investor will have two shares, each worth $100. A stock split can take place for a variety of reasons and according to various formulas (e.g., 3 for 2; 2.3 for 2).

stock symbol—Each company that issues stock on a given stock exchange is given a stock symbol (also called a ticker symbol) that is used to identify the stock.

stock types—Companies can issue various stocks such as common, preferred, and class A or class B stocks. The latter two types of stock give the stockholders different voting rights.

subordinate debenture—A subordinate debenture is an unsecured bond that would be paid only after senior bonds are paid.

subordinate debt—A subordinate debt is a loan secured by just a general claim on a company's assets that would be paid after a secured debt is paid.

sunk costs—Sunk costs are past costs incurred that might affect a subsequent decision. If you bought a gym for $1 million 10 years ago, that cost is a sunk cost. The cost is irrelevant for many decisions, but it would be relevant if you wished to sell and would sell only for a specified rate of return higher than the initial purchase price.

T—The uppercase letter T represents a company's or individual's marginal tax rate on interest payments.

t—The lowercase letter t in a financial formula stands for the time frame for a given investment.

taxable income—Taxable income equals **adjusted gross income (AGI)** minus any allowed deductions or exemptions such as business expenses, capital losses, or charitable giving.

tax basis—The tax basis for an investment is the sum total of all expenses incurred for making a purchase, such as the security's cost, brokerage fee, registration fees, and any others.

tax credit—A tax credit can be created to reduce the total dollars owed to the government and can be associated with specific legislation; such legislation may call for a tax credit for starting a new business in a given neighborhood, for example.

tax-equivalent yield—A formula measures the yield of a tax-free municipal bond against other investments that might require tax payments. The formula is as follows: tax-equivalent yield = tax-exempt yield / (1 – tax rate). If a business has a 28% tax rate and a tax-exempt municipal bond pays 5% interest, the necessary return on a taxable investment would be 5% / (1 – 0.28) = 6.94%. Thus, to maximize your investment return, you should invest in the tax-exempt municipal bond unless you can find another investment that has a return greater than 6.94%.

tax-exempt bonds—Tax-exempt bonds allow investors the opportunity to receive interest income without having to pay taxes on that income. Tax-exempt bonds were essential during the sports facility construction boom in the 1990s; investors were able to buy bonds backed by facility revenue but did not need to pay taxes on the interest income.

tax incremental financing (TIF)—TIF represents tax breaks given to a project with the hope that other businesses will move to the area and increase the property value. The increased property value and resulting greater tax base is supposed to help offset the tax break given to the company that received the TIF.

tax shield—A tax shield refers to any deduction that can ultimately reduce your tax burden. For example if you spend $3,000 a year on mortgage interest and pay tax at the 28% tax rate, you could have a tax shield of ($3,000 × 0.28) = $840.

term loan—A term loan calls for regular periodic payments, usually for three years or more.

time value of money—Money decreases in value over time, and time value of money represents this concept. Because one dollar today is worth more than one dollar next year, investment decisions need to be made with a critical eye toward the future value of a dollar.

tombstone—A tombstone is a formal advertisement by a company or investment bank stating the financial terms of a pending security offering.

total asset turnover ratio—The total asset turnover ratio shows how quickly a company uses its assets to make money. A low ratio means that assets are not being turned over quickly enough to generate additional revenue.

trade—To trade is to exchange or sell a security on either a formal or an informal securities exchange. Those who buy and sell stocks for their own benefit are called traders.

treasurer—A treasurer deals with banks, stockholders, institutional investors, bondholders, and other stakeholders or potential stakeholders to educate them about how a company is doing and what it might need for future growth.

Treasury bill (T-bill)—A T-bill is a short-term government obligation issued in a minimum denomination of $10,000 and scheduled to mature in three months, six months, or a year. T-bills are the safest investment vehicle because they are 100% backed by the U.S. government.

Treasury bond—The U.S. federal government issues bonds in a minimum denomination of $1,000 that mature over 10 years and have semiannual payments of a fixed interest rate.

Treasury notes—Treasury notes are similar to T-bills and Treasury bonds, with similar security and interest rates.

treasury stocks—Treasury stocks are stocks that were once issued by a company and then subsequently repurchased by the company. Such repurchased stocks can be canceled or reissued, but while they are in the company's possession they pay no dividends and have no voting rights. In a similar vein, companies can also have treasury bonds (i.e., bonds repurchased by the issuing company).

trust—A trust is a special account established to benefit a specified individual such as a minor.

T-system—The T-system is used in accounting to post money coming in and going out in an easy-to-read manner.

turnover—Turnover is a means of determining how inventory is managed. A high turnover ratio means a company is quickly replenishing inventory as old inventory is quickly sold. A low turnover ratio reflects that a company has inventory sitting around and is not maximizing its investment. To calculate turnover, sales are divided by assets. Turnover is also calculated for assets to determine how they are being managed.

usury—Usury refers to charging an excessive amount of interest on a loan. Loan sharks often represent a last resort for those who cannot obtain funds from any other source (i.e., their credit rating is bad or they have nothing to borrow against at a pawnshop). However, charging an excessively high interest rate is illegal.

v—The value of dividend payments when calculating the cost of preferred stock.

value (V)—Value is the monetary worth of an item. Value can be expressed as what you could obtain on the market if you had to sell an item. Thus, baseball card price guides might list a card as worth $100, but if you can only find people willing to pay $20 for the card, then the card's value is only $20.

variable costs—Variable costs vary with each unit produced and include items such as raw materials. Semivariable costs vary somewhat with production such as machine maintenance. If a machine is not used maintenance will decrease while if it is used extensively maintenance costs would increase.

variance—Variances represent the difference between the amount budgeted for a given expense and the actual expense incurred.

vertical merger—A buyer expands operations forward toward the final consumer or backward in the direction of the source of raw materials.

voluntary liquidation—As a consequence of severe financial concerns, shareholders may vote to liquidate a company by selling all company assets.

voting rights—Certain stocks carry with them a voting right that allows each shareholder to vote in person or by proxy on such issues as major expenditures, changing board members, or voluntary liquidation.

Wall Street—Wall Street is a street in New York City in the heart of the financial district where the New York Stock Exchange and the American Stock Exchange are located.

warrant—A warrant is an agreement that enables the holder to buy stock at a future date at an advantageous price.

warranty deed—A warranty deed guarantees that a given investment or property has clear title and is free from any encumbrances.

wash—A wash represents no gain or loss when a given investment is sold.

watered stock—A company can exchange capital stock for assets valued at less than the stock's par value. This transaction artificially inflates the value of the exchanged assets.

weighted average cost of capital (WACC)—An average representing the expected return on all of a company's sources of capital. Each source of capital, such as stocks, bonds, and other debt, is weighted in the calculation according to its importance in the company's capital structure.

wholesale banking—Wholesale banking refers to a significant volume of transactions with major corporations or financial institutions.

working capital—Working capital is the amount of money available to pay bills. To calculate working capital, current liabilities are subtracted from current assets. The term *working capital* sometimes refers to current assets only.

year-end dividend—If a company is profitable or if the company's stock requires dividend payments, then the company can pay a dividend at the end of its fiscal year.

year to date (YTD)—The YTD notation on financial statements indicates financial activity from the start of the company's fiscal year to the date specified on the financial statement.

yield (rate of return)—The yield represents the income earned by a given investment.

yield to call (YTC)—YTC represents the yield obtained up to the point that a bond is called by the issuer.

yield to maturity (YTM)—YTM represents the annual yield that holders of a bond would receive if they held on to the bond until it matured. To calculate YTM, we analyze the bond's face value, coupon rate, and market price, taking into consideration the time remaining on the bond until it matures.

zero-based budgeting (ZBB)—The zero-based budget is founded on the concept that organizations and their programs need to justify their existence. The resulting budget would distribute money to the programs that produce the greatest benefits, and the components that produce lower benefits would either be eliminated from the budget or receive fewer funds.

zero coupon bond—A zero coupon bond does not pay interest on a semiannual or annual basis; rather the semiannual interest payments are added to the principal, with the principal and interest being paid at maturity. These bonds are called zero coupon because the bondholder does not need to clip and redeem coupons in order to obtain the interest payments.

z score—The z score is a formula used to measure the probability that a company will go bankrupt; it analyzes a host of financial measures, from retained earnings to total assets.

REFERENCES

1988 baseball salaries. (1988, June). *Sport*, 24.

1997 stadium & arena managers' annual report. (1997). Tampa: Price Waterhouse Sports Group.

About Schwinn. (2007). Available: www.schwinnbike .com/heritage. Retrieved January 4, 2007.

Allen v. Commissioner, 50 T.C. 466. (1968).

Ambrosini, D. (2002, February 10). Bankrolled by an 'Angel.' *Connecticut Post*, p. F1.

Andelman, B. (1993). *Stadium for rent: Tampa Bay's quest for major league baseball.* Jefferson, NC: McFarland.

Aramark acquires Ogden Entertainment. (2000, May-June). *Facility Manager*, 7.

Arens, A.A., & Loebbecke, J.K. (2006). *Auditing: An integrated approach* (11th ed.). Upper Saddle River, NJ: Prentice Hall.

Art Rooney. (2007). Available: www.profootballhof.com/hof/ member.jsp?player_id=183. Retrieved February 17, 2007.

Athlete's tax fails to meet expectations in Pittsburgh. (2000). Available: www.sportslawnews.com/archive/articles/ athletetax.htm. Retrieved February 18, 2007.

Attorney general to check into Red Sox bidding process. (2001, December 23). *Connecticut Post*, p. D3.

Average salary tops $2 million. (2001, December 13). *Connecticut Post*, p. C5.

Baade, R.A. (1994, April 4). *Stadiums, professional sports, and economic development: Assessing the reality.* Heartland Policy Study No. 62. Chicago: Heartland Institute.

Back pay subject to new tax. (2001, April 18). Available: www.acssonline.org/news/20010418- backpaytax.asp. Retrieved February 18, 2002.

Badenhausen, K. (2005, October 4). Wie tees off. *Forbes* [Online]. Available: www.forbes.com/business/2005/10/04/golf-wie-endorse-cz_kb_1005wie .html?partner=yahootix. Retrieved October 18, 2005.

Baim, D. (1994). *The sports stadium as a municipal investment.* Westport, CT: Greenwood Press.

Bally Total Fitness and Crunch to merge. (2001, December). *Fitness Management*, 14.

Bankruptcy filings decline in FY2006. (2006, December 5). Administrative Office of the U.S. Courts. Available: www .uscourts.gov/Press_Releases/bankruptcyfilings120506 .html. Retrieved January 21, 2007.

Bankruptcy judge oks Lemieux's plan to save Penguins. (1999, June 25). *Houston Chronicle*, p. 15B.

Baseball almanac. (2004). Available: www.baseball-almanac.com/teams/rangatte.shtml. Retrieved October 16, 2005.

Battersby, M. (1999, July). Finance options. *Fitness Management*, 36-37.

Baumol, W. (1952, November). Transactions demand for cash: An inventory theoretic approach. *Quarterly Journal of Economics, 66*, 545-556.

Bedell, D. (1997, October 8). Dallas businessman pleads guilty to fraud in failed NHL deal. *Dallas Morning News*, p. 1.

Beltrame, J. (2000, January 24). Canada backs out of pledge to aid hockey teams. *Wall Street Journal*, p. B10.

Bernstein, A. (1998, November 9-15). Sporting goods blues threatening to spread. *Street & Smith's SportsBusiness Journal*, 8.

Big-bucks Redskins top 'Forbes' list. (2005, September 2). *USA Today*, p. 13C.

The Bing Group capsule. (n.d.). Available: www.hoovers .com/uk/co/capsule/3/0,2163,42033,00.html. Retrieved February 6, 2002.

Blair, R.D., & Kaserman, D.L. (1985). *Antitrust economics.* Homewood, IL: Irwin.

Blue Jays sign Thomas for two years, $18.12 million. (2006, November 18). Available: http://sports.espn.go.com/ mlb/news/story?id=2665836. Retrieved January 18, 2007.

Blum, D. (1993, September 22). Booster groups brace for law requiring charities to tell donors how much of a gift is tax-deductible. *Chronicle of Higher Education*, p. A36.

Blum, R. (2006, December 20). Average baseball salaries rise 9 percent. Boston.com. Available: www.boston .com/sports/baseball/articles/2006/12/20/average_ baseball_salary_rises_9_percent/?rss_id=Boston .com+--+Red+Sox+News. Retrieved June 6, 2007.

Bogen, J. (1966). *Corporation finance.* New York: Alexander Hamilton Institute.

Boudette, N. (2001, January 21). Muppet meltdown. *Wall Street Journal*, p. 1A.

Brealey, R.A., Myers, S.C., & Marcus, A.J. (2004). *Fundamentals of corporate finance.* Boston, MA: McGraw Hill-Irwin.

Brennan, T. (2001). Schwinn/GT bidding race begins. Available: www.thedeal.com/cgibin/gx.cg.../View&c=TDDArticle&cid=TDDLYIKOXPC&live=tru. Retrieved August 5, 2001.

Breyer, R. (1998, June 26). Wetlands "bankers" sell credits in land preserves to developers. *Austin American-Statesman*, p. C1.

Bridges, F., & Roquemore, L. (1996). *Management for athletic/sport administration: Theory and practice* (2nd ed.). Decatur, GA: ESM Books.

Briefly. (1998, January 8). *Detroit News*, p. F3.

Briefly. (2000, March 15). *Connecticut Post*, p. D4.

Brigham, E.F., & Ehrhardt, M.C. (2005). *Financial management: Theory and practice* (11th ed.). New York: Dryden Press.

Brigham, E., & Gapenski, L. (1994). *Financial management: Theory and practice* (7th ed.). Fort Worth, TX: Thomson-South-western Press.

Brockington, L., & Rofe, J. (1999, April 5-11). Murdoch grows his sports empire again. *Street & Smith's SportsBusiness Journal, 1*, 1, 47.

Broni, P. (1999, December). Take my loan . . . please. *Inc Magazine*, 163.

Broome, T., Jr. (1997, December). SBA gives women a foot in the door. *Nation's Business*, 44-45.

Brown family eludes IRS tackle. (1997, April 30). *Cincinnati Enquirer*, p. A5.

Browning, E.S. (2000, April 13). Industrials' skid masks strength in old economy. *Wall Street Journal*, p. C1.

Building information & history. (2001). Available: www.united-center.com/history/index.html. Retrieved December 26, 2001.

Bush admits mistake. (2000, January 9). *Connecticut Post*, p. D11.

Business briefcase. (1997, December 17). *Boston Herald*, p. 41.

Business bulletin. (2000, February 10). *Wall Street Journal*, p. A1.

Byrd, A. (1999, May 10-16). Easton adding wooden bats to lineup with Stix purchase. *Street & Smith's SportsBusiness Journal, 2*, 11.

Byrt, F. (2001, January 30). Converse's "Made in USA" ends its long run. *Wall Street Journal*, p. B9.

Calian, S., & Latour, A. (2000, May 15). Stockholm, once a David, is a high-tech Goliath. *Wall Street Journal*, p. C1.

Canada eyes pro team subsidies. (1998, October 10). *Seattle Times*, p. C2.

Caro, R. (2000, January). A financial look at the next millennium. *Fitness Management*, 56.

CBA ceases operations. (2001, February 10). *Connecticut Post*, p. D3.

Ceron, G. (2000, March 13). Prices for a seat on the NYSE fall amid changes. *Wall Street Journal*, p. B19.

Certificate of participation (COP). (n.d.). Available: http://investopedia.com/terms/c/cop.asp. Retrieved February 18, 2002.

Changing game of sports finance [Pamphlet]. (1999, April 28). New York: Fitch IBCA.

The Charlton standard catalogue of Canadian coins (44th ed.). (1990). Toronto: Charlton Press.

Chase, B. (1998, January 12). Hockey team buyer seen admitting $80 million fraud. *American Banker*, p. 1.

Chass, M. (1998, March 18). Turner's plan: Stop Murdoch. *New York Times*, p. C1.

Cheeseman, H. (2001). *Business law* (4th ed.). Upper Saddle River, NJ: Prentice Hall.

Chi, V. (1992, September 30). Coping with the cash crunch. *San Jose Mercury News*, p. 1D.

Chiang, H., & Wilson, Y. (1998, December 24). Appeals court throws out stadium vote challenge. *San Francisco Chronicle*, p. A15.

Churchill Downs to buy troubled track. (2004, September 2). *USA Today*, p. 17C.

Club hopping: Bally Total Fitness off credit watch. (2004, December 13). Available: www.FitnessBusinessPro.com. Retrieved December 13, 2005.

Cohen, A. (1999, July). Fit financing. *Athletic Business*, 11.

Cohen, L., & Holmes, S. (2005, May 30). Can Glazer put this ball in the net? *Business Week*, p. 40.

Coke signs new 4-year NFL deal. (1998, May 23). *Houston Chronicle*, p. 2C.

Colbert, J.L., & Bolton, D.L. (1998, November-December). Accounting: Recommendations for preventing and detecting fraud in a small business. *Forensic Examiner*, 29-31.

Colorado Rockies attendance records. (2007). Available: www.baseball-almanac.com/teams/rockattn.shtml. Retrieved January 12, 2007.

Company. (2002). Available: http://dmotorworks.com/company/bod.shtml. Retrieved February 17, 2002.

Conrad, M. (2000). Court rules MLS a 'single entity' barring antitrust claim. Available: www.sportslawnews.com/archive/Articles%202000/MLSantitrustruling.htm. Retrieved February 24, 2006.

Construction glossary from Home Building Manual. (2002). Available: www.homebuildingmanual.com/glossary.htm. Retrieved February 18, 2007.

Corporate debt may get more play in purchases of sports teams. (2000, March 2). *Wall Street Journal*, p. A1.

Crouse, K. (2006, January 18). Jets break silence for voice of Mangini. *New York Times*, p. C1.

Crow, B., Phillips, D., & Gillentine, M. (Winter, 2000). Corporate partnerships in sports. *International Sports Journal, 4*(1), 27.

Delaware InterCorp. (2000, June 27). Available: www.delawareintercorp.com/why.htm. Retrieved February 18, 2007.

deMause, N. (2005, June 29). NYC stadium subsidies hit $1.2 billion and rising. Available: www.fieldofschemes.com/news/archives/001268.html. Retrieved January 15, 2007.

Detroit Empowerment Zone Transition Office. (n.d.). *Empowerment Zone projects* [Brochure]. Detroit: City of Detroit.

Doors to IPOs open slightly. (2000, March 31). *Connecticut Post*, p. C2.

Doubleday: Baseball manufactures losses. (2002, August 7). *Connecticut Post*, p. D3.

Double play for New York. (2001, December 27). *Connecticut Post*, p. C6.

Douchant, M. (2002, March 25). Shoe wars. Available: www.collegesportingnews.com/article.asp?articleid=16808. Retrieved February 18, 2007.

Dow Jones continues its losing streak. (2002, January 15). *Connecticut Post*, p. C3.

Dow Jones Newswire. (2007, June 1). Ballys Total Fitness to enter bankruptcy; clubs to remain open. AZCentral.com. Available: www.azcentral.com/business/articles/0601biz-bally01-ON.html. Retrieved June 7, 2007.

Dreazen, Y. (2000, March 7). Bankruptcy bills may proceed despite new data. *Wall Street Journal*, p. A4.

Dunphy, S.H. (1998, June 29). Understand the stock market—now. *Houston Chronicle*, pp. 1D, 4D.

Elkins, L. (1996, June). Tips for preparing a business plan. *Nation's Business*, 58.

Eminent domain. (2002). Available: www.sportslawnews.com/archive/jargon/LJEminent.html. Retrieved February 18, 2007.

Ernest, W. (2002, May). Seeing green. *Club Industry*, 41-42.

ESPN to start mobile service. (2005, September 27). Available: http://mobiledia.com/news/37041.html. Retrieved October 1, 2005.

Euchner, C.C. (1993). *Playing the field: Why sports teams move and cities fight to keep them.* Baltimore: Johns Hopkins University Press.

Evanson, D.R. (1997, May). Capital pitches that succeed. *Nation's Business*, 40-41.

Evanson, D.R. (1998, January). Easier avenues to equity capital. *Nation's Business*, 44-46.

Fagan, P. (1999, September). Charitable tax planning. *Jewish Action*, 89.

Farhi, P. (2001, December 30). It's a whole new ballgame. *Washington Post*, p. A01.

Farrell, G. (2002, March 15). Indictment could shred Andersen. *USA Today*, Available: www.usatoday.com/money/energy/enron/2002-03-15-indicted.htm. Retrieved June 5, 2007.

Farrell, G. (2005, July 22). NYSE submits Archipelago merger filing. *USA Today*, p. 2B.

Fatsis, S. (1998, May 8). Michael Jordan's agent scores big in takeover deal. *Wall Street Journal*, p. B6.

Fatsis, S. (1998, May 14). In the NBA, shoe money is no longer a slam-dunk. *Wall Street Journal*, p. B1.

FDIC. (2002). Available: www.fdic.gov/deposit/deposits/insure/index.html. Retrieved February 18, 2007.

Federal Reserve System. (2006). The Federal Reserve Board. Available: www.federalreserve.gov/otherfrb.htm. Retrieved February 20, 2006.

Feiner, R. (1977). *Operational financial analysis: A practical handbook with forms.* Englewood Cliffs, NJ: Prentice Hall.

Fendrich, H. (2001, December 15). Sources: ABC/ESPN near NBA TV deal. Excite News.

Fiscally friendly football. (1996, July-August). *Sidelines* (College Football Association), 2.

Fitch affirms NFL 'A+' rating despite increased allowable club debt levels (2005, August17). Available: www.findarticles.com/p/articles/mi_m0EIN/is_2005_August_17/ai_n14928167. Retrieved September 30, 2006.

Football strike? Who cares? (2001, March 26). *Business Week*, 34.

Footstar completes acquisition. (2000, March 8). *Wall Street Journal*, p. A4.

Form 10-Q. (2006, December 6). Available: http://corporate.wwe.com/documents/2qt200610-q.pdf. Retrieved January 10, 2007.

For the record. (1998, September 21-27). *Street & Smith's SportsBusiness Journal, 1*, 34.

For the record. (1999, May 10-16). *Street & Smith's SportsBusiness Journal, 2*, 38.

Fraser, L., & Ormiston, A. (2001). *Understanding financial statements* (6th ed.). Upper Saddle River, NJ: Prentice Hall.

Freeman, R.J., Shoulders, C.D., & Lynn, E.S. (1988). *Governmental and nonprofit accounting* (3rd ed.). Englewood Cliffs, NJ: Prentice Hall.

Frew, W. (2004, February 1). Murdoch dislodges Dodgers at last. Available: www.theage.com.au/cgi-bin/common/popup-PrintArticle.pl?path=/articles/2004/01/31/1075340897955.html#. Retrieved January 4, 2007.

Fried, G., & Miller, L. (1998). *Employment law*. Greensboro, NC: Carolina Academic Press.

From $50 in 1922 to a half-billion today. (1999, December 26). *Connecticut Post*, p. D3.

From coins to credit cards. (1999, December 19). *Connecticut Post*, p. F4.

Frost, G. (2002). Longtime fans buy Boston Celtics for $360 million. *FindLaw* [Online serial]. Available: http://news.findlaw.com/sports/s/20020927/nbabostoncelticsdc.html. Retrieved September 30, 2002.

Gandley, W., & Stanley, D. (1978). *Canada/B.N.A. postage stamp catalogue* (9th ed.). Paris, ON: Canadian Wholesale Supply.

German soccer team scores unusual goal: Approval to go public. (1999, November 29). *Wall Street Journal*, p. B28.

Gibeaut, J. (1999, March). The money chase. *ABA Journal*, 58.

Gilpin, F. (1998, December 30). Officials cleared in arena probe. *Tampa Tribune*, p. 1.

Glier, R. (1997, July 20). With expectations unfulfilled, Atlantans still searching for legacy from games. *Houston Chronicle*, p. 18B.

Go figure. (1999, October 25). *Sports Illustrated*, 33.

Golden Bear Golf, Inc. (n.d.) Available: http://hoovers.com/print/printh.html. Retrieved February 18, 2002.

Golden Bear Golf Inc. announces settlement. (1999, December 23). Available: www.businesswire.com. Retrieved February 18, 2002.

Goldhirsh, J. (1996, November). There's nothing passive about rental income. *Nation's Business*, 71.

Gomes, L. (2000, February 9). Nike forecasts disappointing sales as outlets for sneakers dwindle. *Wall Street Journal*, p. B10.

Goo, S.K. (2000, January 26). Green Mountain: Loyalty helps VT ski co-op thrive. *Wall Street Journal*, p. NE1.

Grant, L. (2005, March 23). Gnarly: Quicksilver buys ski company. *USA Today*, p. 5B.

Greenberg, M., & Gray, J. (1996). *The stadium game*. Milwaukee, WI. National Sports Law Institute of Marquette University Law School.

Greenberger, R. (2000, October 17). Supreme Court to decide tax case on back pay. *Wall Street Journal*, p. B4.

Griffin, M.P. (1991). *Intermediate finance for nonfinancial managers*. Toronto, ON: Amacom.

Grover, R., & Lowry, T. (2001, September 3). Those smackdowns are taking their toll. *Business Week*, 40.

Grover, R., & Lowry, T. (2002, April 15). A cable clan on thin ice. *Business Week*, 48.

Grover, R., & Lowry, T. (2004, November 22). Rumble in regional sports. *Business Week*, 156-157.

Harper, T. (1999, March 6). He shouts! He scares! *Toronto Star*, p. B1.

Haynie, W.H. (1998, July). Equipment financing. *Fitness Management*, 36-37.

Henderson, J. (1996, September 4). Voters say yes to sales tax. *Tampa Tribune*, p. 1.

Hennepin County approves sales tax for new stadium. (2006, September 8). Available: www.payden.com/pubs/muniBonds/MBCE090806.pdf. Retrieved January 18, 2006.

Hiestand, M. (1992, October). Illinois could eliminate funds for college teams. *USA Today*, p. 10C.

Hiestand, M. (1999, January 12). The B word—billion—no longer out of bounds. *USA Today*, p. 1A.

Hiestand, M. (2004, November 9). NFL again hits TV pay dirt. *USA Today*, p. C1.

High-tech injection. (1999, October 27). *Connecticut Post*, p. C1.

Hodges, S. (1997, February). SBA microloans fuel big ideas. *Nation's Business*, 34-35.

Hoffman, D. (1998, November). Penguins file for bankruptcy. *Stadium & Arena Financing News, 2*(21), 1.

Holmes, A.W., & Burns, D.C. (1979). *Auditing: Standards and procedures* (9th ed.). Homewood, IL: Irwin.

Holmes, S. (2004, September 20). The new Nike. *Business Week*, 78-86.

Horine, L. (1999). *Administration of physical education and sport programs* (4th ed.). Boston: McGraw-Hill.

Hovey, J. (1997, September). A source of funds in search of work. *Nation's Business*, 37-38.

Hovey, J. (1998, March). A little-known pathway to growth. *Nation's Business*, 40-42.

Hovey, J. (1998, July). Cheap funding through bonds. *Nation's Business*, 50-51.

Hovey, J. (1998, November). Using inventory for collateral. *Nation's Business*, 42-43.

Howard, D.R., & Crompton, J.L. (2004). *Financing sport* (2nd ed.). Morgantown, WV: Fitness Information Technology.

Howard, T. (2005, October 14). Investors can capitalize when companies score sport sponsorship. *USA Today*, p. 5B.

H.R. 4736. (1992). Taxpayer's Right to View Act of 1992. 102d Congress, Energy and Commerce Committee.

Hube, K. (2000, January 26). Tax rule crimps small-business deals. *Wall Street Journal*, p. C1.

Huffy checks bounce as lenders cut off credit lines funding. (1999, November 4). *Wall Street Journal*, p. A6.

Hundley v. Commissioner, 48 T.C. 339. (1967).

Immoo, L., Lochhead, S., Ritter, R., & Zhao, Q. (1996). The costs of raising capital. *Journal of Financial Research, 19*, 59-74.

An introduction. (1992). Washington, DC: National Association of Securities Dealers.

Inventory analyst—Easton Sports. (2000, March 3). Available: www.sportlink.com/employment/jobs/jobs2000-016.html. Retrieved February 18, 2002.

Investing's fast track? (1999, February 16). *Houston Chronicle*, p. C1.

Ip, G. (2000, March 10). NASDAQ pumps up to 5000. *Wall Street Journal*, p. C1.

Ip, G. (2000, March 15). Archipelago to set up new stock market. *Wall Street Journal*, p. C1.

IPO basics: A road map. (1999). Available: www.inc.com/articles/details/0,6378,AGD2_ART15744_CNY56_SUB14,00.html. Retrieved June 13, 2003.

Isidore, C. (2002, January 31). Superdome name goes unsold. Available:http://money.cnn.com/2002/01/31/superbowl/superbowl_noname/. Retrieved on September 15, 2006.

Isidore, C. (2004, April 1). AT&T, Kodak, IP out of Dow. Available: www.money.cnn.com/2004/04/04/markets/dow. Retrieved February 20, 2006.

Janda, J. (2001, December). Mad Dogg, Schwinn partnership ends. *Club Industry*, 24.

Jean, S. (2005, January 2). What's your money type? *Hartford Courant*, C1.

Just For Feet sets deal with creditors to seek bankruptcy. (1999, November 3). *Wall Street Journal*, p. B10.

Kaplan, D. (1998, September 14-20). Soccer worth watching. *Street & Smith's SportsBusiness Journal, 1*, 1, 45.

Kaplan, D. (1998, November 9-15). Slugger's bond plan striking out. *Street & Smith's SportsBusiness Journal, 1*, 3.

Kaplan, D. (1999, August 16-22). Lehman gives USTA fasttrack refinance. *Street & Smith's SportsBusiness Journal, 2*, 16.

Kaplan, D. (2001, March 12-18). Securitization era opens for athletes. *Street & Smith's SportsBusiness Journal, 3*, 1, 43.

Kaspriske, R. (2003, November). Buyer's market: A sluggish economy has left many private golf clubs desperate for new members—special report. Available: www.findarticles.com/p/articles/mi_m0HFI/is_11_54/ai_109467586. Retrieved December 1, 2005.

King, B., & Brockington, L. (1998, December 14-20). Forces push both sides in Yanks' deal. *Street & Smith's SportsBusiness Journal 1*, 1, 46.

Klise, E. (1972). *Money and banking* (5th ed.). Cincinnati: South-Western.

Knobler, M. (2004, March 7). The shoe wars: Sneaky pressure—shoe companies' investment in players might also influence their choice of college. Available: http://ajc.com/highschool/content/sports/highschool/0304/07shoeimpact.html. Retrieved October 18, 2005.

Koller, T., Goedhart, M., & Wessels, D. (2005). *Valuation: Measuring and managing the value of companies (*4th ed.). Hoboken: Wiley.

Kowall, S. (2001). The weekly tirade. Available: www.comedyzine.com/tirade154.shtml. Retrieved December 26, 2001.

Kraker, D. (1998). The economics of pro sports: The fans, the owners, and the rules. Available: www.ilsr.org/pubs/pubsrules.html. Retrieved June 18, 2007.

Krantz, M. (2004, October 21). Bike maker Huffy files for Chapter 11. *USA Today*, p. 3B.

Kupetz, D.S. (1998, July). Resolving business financial crises. *California Lawyer*, 66-68.

Kurdziel, K. (2000, April 27). Dolan has one goal for the tribe: Win the World Series. *Sun News*, p. C1.

Lamiell, P. (1999, May 4). Dow index passes 11,000 in record time. *Houston Chronicle*, p. 1C.

Lascari, S. (1998, October-November). Sports facility issues, part two. Stock of sports franchises: A sound investment or scam? *For the Record* (Marquette University Law School), *9*(5), 3.

Lederman, D. (1991, December 11). IRS rules that 2 bowls must pay taxes on money they received from corporate sponsors. *Chronicle of Higher Education*, p. A33.

Lee, C. (1999, July). Managing the process. *ABA Journal*, 62.

Left for dead, CBA breathes new life. (2001). Available: http://lacrossetribune.com/articles/2001/07/30/stories/sports/00lead.txt. Retrieved February 6, 2002.

Leo, A. (2000, December 6). Fund looted from league, woman held. *Connecticut Post*, p. A2.

Lewis, A. (1999, June 8). Suits seek to halt Ascent sale: Prospective buyers wait as shareholders say $400 million bid by Lauries is too low. *Denver Rocky Mountain News*, p. 1B.

Lewis, J. (1936, February 29). Basehits, incorporated. *Liberty*, 48-49.

Liberation investments delivers letter to Bally Total Fitness Holding Corp. (2005, July 19). Available: http://home.businesswire.com/portal/site/google/index.jsp?ndmViewId=news_views&news. Retrieved July 20, 2005.

Lipin, S. (2000, February 28). Firms incorporated in Delaware are valued more by investors. *Wall Street Journal*, p. C21.

Livingston, A. (1998, July). Avoiding pitfalls when selling a business. *Nation's Business*, 25-26.

Livingstone, J.L. (Ed.). (1997). *The portable MBA in finance and accounting* (2nd ed.). New York: Wiley.

Logo Athletic Inc. files for Chapter 11. (2000, November 8). *Connecticut Post*, p. C4.

Louisiana forks over $12.4M to Saints. (2005, July 16). *USA Today*, p. 15C.

Lowry, T., & Grover, R. (2004, November 22). Football's Fear Factor. *Business Week*, 157.

Managers rethinking "just-in-time" inventory management. (2001, December 28). [Trucking Technology Alert]. Available: www.ttnews.com/members/topNews/0008327 .html. Retrieved February 18, 2002.

Man Utd fans vow to fight takeover. (2005, May 13). Available: www.cnn.com/2005/SPORT/football/05/13/united .glazer/index.html. Retrieved January 4, 2007.

Markets consider merger. (2000, March 4). *Connecticut Post*, p. B1.

Martzke, R., & Cherner, R. (2004, August 17). Channeling how to view sports. *USA Today*, pp. 1C-2C.

Marullo, G.G. (1997, February). Easier rules take effect for S corporations. *Nation's Business*, 63.

Marullo, G.G. (1997, December). Tax options for handling obsolete inventories. *Nation's Business*, 25.

Marullo, G.G. (1998, March). Rewards and risks in lending to your child. *Nation's Business*, 27-28.

Marullo, G.G. (1998, August). Selling your business: A preview of the process. *Nation's Business*, 25-26.

Mayer, C. (1998, July 26). Business model hikes Amazon's value. *Houston Chronicle*, p. 5D.

McAllister, P. (1998). Contributions & premiums. *Grantsmanship Center Magazine*, 9.

McGraw, D. (1998, July 13). Big league troubles. *U.S. News and World Report*, 40-46.

Mclean, B. (2000, February). Chase's venture capital elite. *Fortune*, 47.

McMorris, F., Smith, R., & Schroeder, M. (2000, March 15). Insider case involves attempt at two brokers and Web ring. *Wall Street Journal*, p. C1.

Meigs, W.B., Whittington, O.R., & Meigs, R.F. (1982). *Principles of auditing*. Homewood, IL: Irwin.

Mercer, J. (1996, October 11). In dollars and cents, colleges measure what they contribute to their communities. *Chronicle of Higher Education*, p. A47.

Miller, W.S. (1998, August-September). Sport facility issues, part one. The boom in stadium construction & financing new facilities. *For the Record* (Marquette University Law School), *9*(4), 7.

Moffeit, M. (1999, March 28). Off to a fast start. *Houston Chronicle*, p. 8D.

Moore, M. (2005, August 4). adidas-Reebok is hoping to rival Nike: With merger, company will have more clout in market. Available: http://deseretnews.com/ dn/view/0,1249,600153262,00.html. Retrieved October 18, 2005.

Moulson, G. (2007, April 11). Sporting goods maker Puma a takeover target. *The Hartford Courant*, E4.

Much, P. (1996, June 7). *Publicly traded sports team* [Marketing letter]. Chicago: Houlihan Lokey Howard & Zukin.

Much, P. (1997, September 9). *Estate planning for professional sports team owners* [Marketing letter]. Chicago: Houlihan Lokey Howard & Zukin.

Much, P. (1997, December 1). *Sports teams, IPOs, and some baseball nostalgia* [Marketing letter]. Chicago: Houlihan Lokey Howard & Zukin.

Much, P., & Phillips, J. (1999). *Sports teams and the stock market* [Marketing letter]. Chicago: Houlihan Lokey Howard & Zukin.

Mullen, L. (1998, November 30-December 6). Golden Bear Golf hit $14.3 million trap. *Street & Smith's SportsBusiness Journal*, 3.

Munroe, T. (1997, September 5). Fleet shuffles sports group lineup. *Boston Herald*, p. 34.

NASD. (2006). Overview. Available: www.nasd.com. Retrieved February 20, 2006.

National Association for Sport and Physical Education and North American Society for Sport Management. (2000). *Sport management program standards and review protocol*. Reston, VA: Author.

Naughton, J. (1996, November 22). Most intercollegiate athletic programs lost money in 1995, NCAA report says. *Chronicle of Higher Education*, p. A46.

NCAA study shows athletic program costs rising at faster pace than revenues. (1998, October 9). *NCAA News*, p. 1.

Nelton, S. (1998, June). Seeking funding? Get organized. *Nation's Business*, 40-42.

Nelton, S. (1998, November). Sizing up the megabanks. *Nation's Business*, 14-21.

Nemeth-Johannes, C. (2003). Researching your business on the Net. Available: www.abcsmallbiz.com/bizbasics/ gettingstarted/research_biz.html. Retrieved December 3, 2005.

A new ballpark for Missouri. (2007, January 9). Available: http://cardinals.mlb.com/NASApp/mlb/stl/ballpark/ stl_ballpark_newpark_factsheet.jsp. Retrieved January 9, 2007.

The new bankruptcy law. (2005, October). Available: http:// bankruptcy.findlaw.com/new-bankruptcy-law/new-bankruptcy-law-basics/big-changes.html. Retrieved November 20, 2005.

Newberry, J. (2001, August). Free with purchase. *ABA Journal*, 78.

News Corp. in 2004: The DirecTV acquisition and beyond. (2004). Available: www.icmr.icfai.org/casestudies/catalogue/Business%20Strategy3/BSTA099htm. Retrieved January 4, 2007.

New study pegs Adams State economic impact at $70 million. (2005, May 18). Available: www2.adams.edu/news/may0513/may0513.php. Retrieved January 14, 2007.

NFL looking at reducing minimum ownership stake for partners. (2000, June 1). *Sports Business Daily*, p. 8.

The NFL stadium financing landscape. (2001). Available: www.vikings.com/Stadium/Stadiumlandscape.htm. Retrieved December 26, 2001.

NHL Press. (2005, September 12). XM Satellite and NHL announce long-term agreement. Available: www.nhl.com/news/2005/09/234310.html. Retrieved October 17, 2005.

Nicholas, T. (1990). *Cash: How to get it into and out of your corporation*. Wilmington, DE: Enterprise.

Nicklaus company's stock doesn't make NASDAQ cut. (1998, August 14). *Houston Chronicle*, p. 3C.

Nicklin, J. (1997, November 21). Universities seek to cut costs by "outsourcing" more operations. *Chronicle of Higher Education*, p. A35.

Nike increases quarterly dividend 19 percent. (2006, November 17). Available: www.nike.com/nikebiz/news/pressrelease.jhtml;bsessionid=M5LAYTX2NYZMCCQFTBFCF4YKAWMB2IZB?year=2006&month=11&letter=j. Retrieved January 4, 2007.

Nike net rose 17%, revenue fell slightly in fiscal 3rd period. (2000, March 17). *Wall Street Journal*, p. B17.

Noll, R., & Zimbalist, A. (1998). Are new stadiums worth the cost? Available: www.breadnotcircuses.org/brooking.html. Retrieved December 26, 2001.

O'Brian, B., & Tam, P. (1999, October 4). Specialty funds seek piece of pie in growing market. *Wall Street Journal*, p. R25.

Overview of preliminary arena development process. (1995). Denton, TX: Denton County.

Owner. (2002). Available: www.nba.com/nuggets/news/kroenke_bio.html. Retrieved June 23, 2002.

Owners unlikely to OK Redskins sale. (1999, April 7). *Houston Chronicle*, p. 7B.

Palazzo, A. (1999, October 4). Goal of minor league soccer team, the San Diego Flash, is to go public. *Wall Street Journal*, p. B13

Panthers' new ownership group receives NHL approval. (2002). Available: www.flpanthers.com/pressbox/news/ownersapproval.shtml. Retrieved February 18, 2002.

Parrish, A., & Maloney, L. (1999, July). Documenting good intentions. *ABA Journal*, 63.

Parry, T. (2004, April 6). PepsiCo extends NFL sponsorship in $560 million deal. Available: http://promomagazine.com/news/marketing_pepsico_extends_nfl_2/index.html.

Patsuris, P. (2003, October 7). NASCAR pulls into prime time. Available: www.forbes.com/2003/10/07/cx_pp_1007nascar_print.html. Retrieved September 25, 2005.

Paul Allen. (2002). Available: www.thestandard.com/people/profile/0,1923,1302,00.html. Retrieved February 6, 2002.

Pay-Rod: Rangers raise ticket prices for fifth season in row. (2001, January 8). Available: http://sportsillustrated.cnn.com/baseball/mlb/news/2001/01/08/rangers_tickets_ap. Retrieved October 15, 2005.

Penguins file for bankruptcy. (1998, November 2). *Stadium and Arena Financing News*, p. 1.

Pereira, J. (2001, January 23). Converse files for bankruptcy protection, plans to shutter North American plants. *Wall Street Journal*, p. B8.

Planning for success. (2000, November-December). *CampBusiness*, 8-11.

Pope, J. (2004, February 20). Living up to its name, New Balance seeks to broaden its market. Available: www.boston.com/news/education/higher/articles/2004/02/20/living_up_to_its_name_new_balance_seeks_to_broaden_its_market?mode=PF. Retrieved October 18, 2005.

Portions of New Orleans Saints purchase price is allocable to Superdome lease. (1998, Spring/Summer). *Business of Sports*, 2-4.

Pounds, M. (1997, October 27). Finding the money to start up a business and how to write a business plan. *Houston Chronicle*, pp. 1D-2D.

Pratt, P., & Niculita, A. (2007). *Valuing a Business* (5th ed.). New York: McGraw Hill.

Pratt, S., Reilly, R., & Schweihs, R. (2000). *Valuing a business: The analysis and appraisal of closely held companies* (4th ed.). New York: McGraw-Hill.

Pritchard, C. (2001, December 21). Nike shares rise on earnings report [CBS MarketWatch]. www.yahoo&steid=yahoo&dist=yahoo&guid=%7B2C3848A2%2D0AA9%2D420A%2DA268%2D33. Retrieved January 8, 2002.

Profiles of success. (2001). Boston: International Health, Racquet & Sportsclub Association.

Provision could boost teams' values. (2004, August 3). *USA Today*, p. 11C.

Pryde, J. (1998, February). A lending niche helps small

firms. *Nation's Business*, 52-53.

Q4 IPO scorecard (n.d.). Available: http://hoovers.com/ipo/scorecard/0,1334,66,00.html. Retrieved February 18, 2002.

Ranalli, R. (1997, October 8). Islanders' buyer to plead guilty to fraud charges. *Boston Globe*, p. 35.

Ready to wrestle the bulls. (1999, August 4). *Houston Chronicle*, p. 1C.

Reebok and hip-hop violinist Miri Ben-Ari make beautiful music together with first-of-its kind partnership. (2005, August 24). Available: www.reebok.com/useng/news/Miri+Ben+Ari.htm. Retrieved October 18, 2005.

Reports: Thomas agrees to sell CBA, owes $750,000. Available: www.canoe.ca/BasketballCBA/jun28_tho.html. Retrieved February 6, 2002.

Revenue Ruling 58-145, 1955-2 C.B., 25. (1958).

Revenue Ruling 88-76. (1988).

Reynes, R. (1997, November). Venturing out for rapid growth. *Nation's Business*, 54-55.

Reynes, R. (1998, May). Financing for do it yourselfers. *Nation's Business*, 38-40.

Reynes, R. (1998, October). Low-profile money sources. *Nation's Business*, 32-33.

Ripley, J., & Mabe, L.D. (2003, October 24). Changing courses: Foul weather on the fairways, plus a subpar business climate, mean that a dwindling number of golfers are being courted with discounts and coupons. Available: www.sptimes.com/2003/10/24/Northoftampa/Changing_courses.shtml. Retrieved December 1, 2005.

Robinson v. Commissioner, 44 T.C. 20. (1965).

Rodgers, R. (1966). *Banking*. New York: Alexander Hamilton Institute.

Rodriguez's riches: A-Rod concerned about baseball, not business. (2001, January 9). Available: http://sportsil-lustrated.cnn.com/baseball/mlb/news/2001/01/09/arods_riches_ap. Retrieved October 15, 2005.

Rofe, J. (1999, August 23-29). The 800-pound gorilla keeps growing. *Street & Smith's SportsBusiness Journal*, 2, 24.

Rogus, D. (1997, June-July). America's sports stadiums: How much do they really cost you? *Your Money*, 70–79.

Rosenblatt, B. (1989, February 20). Have I got a deal for you, kid. . . . *Sportsinc*, 24.

Rosenbuh, S. (2004, December 27). Mergers: A bit of mania for 2005. *BusinessWeek Online*. Available: www.businessweek.com/bwdaily/dnflash/dec2004/nf20041227_6504_db035.htm. Retrieved January 4, 2007.

Ross, S.A., Westerfield, R.W., & Jaffe, J. (2006). *Funda-mentals of corporate finance* (7th ed.). Boston, MA: McGraw-Hill Irwin.

Rumblings. (1997, August 25). *Crain's Detroit Business*, 34.

Ruxin, R. (1989). *An athlete's guide to agents*. New York: Penguin Books.

Sack, A., & Nadim, A. (2002, January). Strategic choices in a turbulent environment: A case study of Starter Corporation. *Journal of Sport Management 16*(1), 36-53.

Sapsford, J. (2000, March 14). Fed to make banks boost capital to cover venture-investing risk. *Wall Street Journal*, p. A4.

SBA. (2002). Available: http://sbaonline.sba.gov. Retrieved February 6, 2002.

SBA loans top $239 million for the year. (2006, November 13). Available: www.businessnewhaven.com/article_page.lasso?id=40431. Retrieved January 16, 2007.

Scherriek, S. (2000, December 16). What the earnings reports don't tell you. Business Week, 201.

Schreiner, J., & Damsell, K. (1998, November 11). Canucks blame record losses on dollar and taxes. *National Post*, p. C01.

Schroeder, M., & Schiller, Z. (1992, August 24). A scandal waiting to happen. *Business Week*, 32.

Securities regulation in the United States. (1994). Gaithersburg, MD: National Association of Securities Dealers.

Securitizing sports. (1998, November 16). *Stadium and Arena Financing News*, p. 8.

SFX Entertainment and The Marquee Group complete merger. (1999, March 16). Business Wire, Available: http://findarticles.com/p/articles/mi_m0EIN/is_1999_March_16/ai_54113732. Retrieved June 5, 2007.

Shank, A. (2005, March 9). National Hockey Group proposes fan-owned team. *USA Today*, p. 3C.

Shapiro, S. (1999, Winter). Valuation of law practices. *Law Firm Governance 4*(2), 26-33.

Sharecast. (2005, June 15). Manchester United. Available: www.sharecast.com/cgi-bin/sharecast/security.cgi?csi=10245. Retrieved June 15, 2005.

Sheehan, R. (1996). *Keeping score: The economics of big time sports*. South Bend, IN: Diamond Communications.

Shell, A. (2005, August 19). Eight more charged in Reebok case. *USA Today*, p. 5B.

Shinn faces suit over arena profits. (1998, October 24). *Herald Rock Hill*, p. 5B.

Sichelman, L. (1998, August 24). Trumping the credit bureau. *Houston Chronicle*, p. 1D.

Siegal, A. (2000). *Practical business statistics* (4th ed.). New York: McGraw-Hill.

Siegel, J., Shim, J., & Hartman, S. (1992). *Dictionary of personal finance*. New York: Macmillan.

Simon, E., and Yao, D. (2007, February 3). Aramark CEO reaps rich reward in buyout. *The Hartford Courant*, E1.

Singer, T. (1998, May). Baseball's bargains and bandits. *Sport*, 35.

'Sinners' as saints? Seems so in Cleveland. (2005, August 29). *USA Today*, p. 1C.

Sky Media. (2005). Available: http://phx.corporate-ie.net/phoenix.zhtml?c=104016&p=irol-mediaprofile. Retrieved November 1, 2005.

Smith, B. (2001, Fall). If you build it, will they come? *Georgetown Public Policy Review*, *7*(1), 45-60.

Smith, T. (2005, June 15). Yankees reveal new stadium plans. Available: http://mlb.com/NASApp/mlb/content/printer_friendly/mlb/y2005/m06/d15/c1090587.jsp. Retrieved January 15, 2005.

Soccer quotes. (2002). Available: www.soccerinvestor.com. Retrieved June 27, 2002.

SODA (Sportsplex Operators and Developers Association). (1993). *Sportspark construction costs*. Racine, WI: Author.

Sosa's charity mismanaged, on brink of bankruptcy. (2000, April 12). Available: www.sportslawnews.com/current/Sosacharity.htm. Retrieved February 18, 2002.

Speedway Motorsports 10-Q Report. (2006). Available: http://phx.corporate-ir.net/phoenix.zhtml?c=99758&p=irol-sec. Retrieved January 4, 2007.

Speedway Motorsports Annual Report. (2006). Available: http://phx.corporate-ir.net/phoenix.zhtml?c=99758&p=irol-reports. Retrieved January 4, 2007.

Spiro, H. (1996). *Finance for the nonfinancial manager*. New York: Wiley.

Sportsfund. (1996). Fields of opportunity [Promotional brochure]. Portland, ME: Author.

Sports in brief. (2001, January 8). *Seattle Union Record*, p. 1D.

Sports stadiums as "wise investments": An evaluation. (1990, November 26). *The Heartland Institute, Executive Summary*, No. 32.

Standard & Poor's corporate description plus news. (1999). New York: McGraw-Hill.

Starter seeks Chapter 11. (1999, April 20). *Houston Chronicle*, p. 10B.

Stehle, V. (1997, November 27). Rich but not so different. *Chronicle of Philanthropy*, p. 11.

Stellino, V. (1995, November 6). Lease deal for Browns is 30 years. *Baltimore Sun*, p. 1A.

Steps for improving your firm's cash flow. (1998, November). *Nation's Business*, 12.

Stevenson, W. (1982). *Production/operations management*. Homewood, IL: Irwin.

Stock quote. Available: http://finance.yahoo.com/q?s=sds.pk. Retrieved June 12, 2002.

Study: No taxes for stadiums. (2004, March 25). *USA Today*, p. 10C.

Tan, K. (2000, January 31). Interactive technology boosts sports business. *Wall Street Journal*, p. B9.

Tang, F. (2003, June 15). Young talents wooed by shoemakers for endorsements. Available: www.forbes.com/newswire/2003/06/15/rtr1000372.html. Retrieved October 21, 2005.

Tax numbers to know. (2000, January 30). *Connecticut Post*, p. F1.

Tejada, C. (2000, March 1). Clear Channel to acquire SFX for $2.99 billion. *Wall Street Journal*, p. A4.

Thomas secures his future. (1998, July 13). *Sports Illustrated*, *89*(2), 32.

Thornton, E. (2002, January 12). It sure is getting hostile. *Business Week*, 28-30.

Thornton, G. (2005). Golf course restructuring: A business and legal perspective. Available: www.grantthornton.ca/mgt_papers/MIP_template.asp?MIPID=41. Retrieved December 3, 2005.

Top holders of stadium bonds. (1997, September 22). *Stadium and Arena Financing News*, p. 10.

Trip to Super Bowl priceless (and pricey). (2001, January 16). *New Haven Register*, p. A4.

Truex, A. (1999, February 14). Going for broke. *Houston Chronicle*, p. 1B.

Turley, B. (1998, Fall). From tee to green: A primer on golf course development and financing. *Entertainment and Sports Lawyer*, *16*(3), 3-5, 35.

Two Denver franchises sold. (1999, April 27). *Houston Chronicle*, p. 11B.

Two firms make bid to buy entire NHL. (2005, March 4). *Virginian-Pilot*, p. C3.

Undergraduate catalog, 1998-2000. (1998). West Haven, CT: University of New Haven.

Univision, ABC/ESPN pays $425 million for World Cup. (2005, November 2). Available: http://sports.yahoo.com/sow/news?slug=reu-dc&prov=reuters&typ=lgns. Retrieved October 5, 2005.

Up, up and away. (1999, December 30). *Connecticut Post*, p. 1C.

USA Today salaries databases. (2007). Available: http://asp.usatoday.com/sports/baseball/salaries/totalpayroll.aspx?year=2006. Retrieved January 13, 2007.

U.S. standards. (2002). Available: www.nyse/u.s.standards.html. Retrieved January 12, 2002.

UW athletic department personnel incomes. (1998, November 5). *Capital Times*, p. 3C.

Venator net surges, aided by cost-cutting and sales of stores. (2000, March 9). *Wall Street Journal*, p. B14.

Vennochi, J. (1997, July 30). Does the puck stop here? *Boston Globe*, p. E1.

Wahl, G. (2001, December 3). Billions for soccer. *Sports Illustrated*, 34.

Walker, D. (2004, August 27). Shoe companies go toe-to-toe at Olympics. The Milwaukee Journal Sentinel. Available: http://findarticles.com/p/articles/mi_qn4196/is_20040827/ai_n10981599. Retrieved June 1, 2007.

Walker, S. (1999, November 5). Attorney set to buy Cleveland Indians in transaction totaling $320 million. *Wall Street Journal*, p. B2.

Wal-Mart heir buying Denver teams, arena. (2000, April 25). *Connecticut Post*, p. D4.

Wanniski, J. (1991, October 9). Trial by press: James B. Stewart vs. Michael Milken. Available: www.polyeconomics.com/searchbase/10-09-91.html. Retrieved February 18, 2002.

Web billionaire to buy controlling interest in Dallas Mavericks. (2000, January 5). *Wall Street Journal*, p. B16.

Where your tax dollar goes. (2000, January 30). *Connecticut Post*, p. F1.

Whittington, O.R., & Pany, K. (2006). *Principles of auditing* (15th ed.). Boston: McGraw-Hill.

Who is the FDIC? (2006). Available: http://www.fdic.gov/about/learn/symbol/index.html. Retrieved February 20, 2006.

Why Delaware Intercorp, Inc? (2000, June 27). Available: www.delawareintercorp.com/why.htm. Retrieved February 18, 2002.

Williams, C.A., Jr., Smith, M., & Young, P. (1995). *Risk management and insurance* (7th ed.). New York: McGraw-Hill.

Williams, J. (1998, August 14). Stadium financing plan is completed. *Houston Chronicle*, p. 40A.

Winters, C. (2000, November). Budgeting 101. *Club Industry*, 90-91.

Woodworth, R.L., & Sher, S.A. (2005). I need to report that?!?: Hart-Scott-Rodino notification requirements for individuals. *The M&A Lawyer.*, 9(5), Available: www.wsgr.com/PDFSearch/sher_woodworth1005.pdf. Retrieved on June 5, 2007.

Woolworth Corp. agrees to buy Sports Authority for $579.6 million. (1998, May 8). *Wall Street Journal*, p. B9.

World Championship Sports Network. (2005). Available: www.wcsn.com/help/about.jsp. Retrieved November 2, 2005.

WorldCom charged with fraud. (2002, June 27). *Connecticut Post*, p. C1.

WWF fires COO, 39 employees to aid profits. (2001, November 10). *Connecticut Post*, p. B1.

Wynter, L., & Thomas, P. (2000, February 2). New definition of "minority business" splits blacks. *Wall Street Journal*, p. B1.

XFL's hefty losses slam WWF profits. (2001, June 29). *Connecticut Post*, p. B14.

Yahoo! Finance—BOS. (2002). Available: http://?finance.yahoo.com/q?d=t&s-BOS+. Retrieved February 18, 2002.

Yahoo! Finance—WWF. (2002). Available: http://?finance.yahoo.com/q?d=t&s-WWF+. Retrieved February 18, 2002.

Yahoo! Finance—YHOO. (2002). Available: http://?finance.yahoo.com/q?d=t&s-YHOO+. Retrieved February 18, 2002.

Yip, P. (1999, March 30). Changes paved way to 10K. *Houston Chronicle*, p. 1C.

Zikmund, W., & d'Amico, M. (1996). *Basic marketing*. St. Paul, MN: West.

Zimbalist, A. (1999, October 13). The NFL's new math. *Wall Street Journal*, p. A30.

INDEX

Note: The italicized f and t following page numbers indicate figures and tables.

Courtesy of Gil Fried

Gil Fried, JD, is professor and chair of the sport, hospitality, and tourism management department at the University of New Haven. He worked as a financial analyst with Paul Kagan Associates and analyzed numerous broadcasting contracts to determine their value. In addition to writing the first edition of this book, he has written numerous articles, taught graduate and undergraduate courses in sport finance, and lectured on finance topics to various audiences. Besides his teaching, he coordinates the graduate program in management of sports industries at the University of New Haven. Dr. Fried enjoys playing badminton and softball and being involved in his community.

Courtesy of Steven Shapiro

Steven Shapiro, PhD, is a professor in the department of economics and finance at the University of New Haven. Dr. Shapiro worked as a senior economist for the New York Telephone Company and as a research analyst for the Antitrust Division of the U.S. Department of Justice. He has also worked for various management consulting firms as an analyst doing economic and statistical analysis on projects for federal agencies. A coauthor the first edition of this book, he has taught undergraduate and graduate courses in economics and finance for 18 years. He has also written articles on antitrust, litigation economics, and other financial topics. In his leisure time, Dr. Shapiro enjoys hiking and photography.

Courtesy of Timothy DeSchriver

Timothy D. DeSchriver, EdD, is an associate professor in the department of health, nutrition, and exercise sciences at University of Delaware in Newark. Dr. DeSchriver has worked a field economist for the U.S. Department of Labor, and for years he has taught undergraduate and graduate instruction in sport finance and sport economics. He coauthored the book's first edition and has also authored several sport finance–related publications in refereed journals. Dr. DeSchriver participates in road cycling, mountain biking, and hiking in his spare time.